EUROPEAN MARKETING DATA AND STATISTICS 1991

Euromonitor Publications Limited, 87-88 Turnmill Street, London EC1M 5QU

EUROPEAN MARKETING DATA AND STATISTICS 1991
First published 1964
Twenty sixth edition 1991

Researched and published by

EUROMONITOR
87-88 Turnmill Street
London EC1M 5QU
Great Britain

Telephone: (071) 251 8024
Telex: 262433
Fax: (071) 608 3149

European Marketing Data and Statistics 1991

A CIP catalogue record for this book
is available from the British Library

ISBN: 0 86338 395 5

ISSN: 0071-2930

Printed in Great Britain by Bookcraft, Midsomer Norton, Avon, England

Distributed exclusively in North America by
Gale Research Company, Penobscot Building, Detroit, Michigan 48226

CONTENTS

LIST OF CHARTS

FOREWORD

European Marketing Data and Statistics is a compendium of statistical information on the countries of Western and Eastern Europe. Published annually, it provides a wealth of detailed and up-to-date statistical information relevant to international market planning. The information is regularly updated and held on an international database of market information comprising 24 subject areas.

Published annually since the late 1960s, **European Marketing Data and Statistics**, or EMDAS, is now in its 26th edition. Data sections have been thoroughly revised for this new edition, and improved graphics have been included.

The data coverage includes a considerable number of ten- and eleven-year trendings, which permit the analysis of socio-economic trends over a longer time span as a basis for forecasting. The inclusion of figures from the most recent complete year (in this edition 1989) for key parameters ensures that up-to-date information is available for analysis.

In addition to reporting on major European countries, the country coverage also includes smaller European countries and principalities. Although the availability of statistical information on these countries is limited and they are minor markets, it assists in building up a more comprehensive picture of the total European market and will be of interest to academic users.

The data are presented in spreadsheet form and a number of extrapolated tables have been included, together with graphs, marketing maps and diagrams.

Readers requiring guidance on further sources of information are referred to *European Directory of Marketing Information Sources* (Euromonitor 1990) and *European Directory of Non-Official Statistical Sources* (Euromonitor 1988) for more comprehensive listings.

The handbook contains a full alphabetical index, and there is also a guide to sources used in the compilation. The introduction includes an overview of the European market.

A companion volume of marketing data, *International Marketing Data and Statistics* (IMDAS) is also available. Country coverage in IMDAS 1991 provides a comprehensive world-wide context and there are unique regional consolidations (which also bring in comparisons with some European data from this volume).

Several of the databases in **European Marketing Data and Statistics** are still in a formative stage and will be expanded and developed over subsequent editions. User comments are welcomed. Also, whilst we have made every effort to ensure accuracy we cannot accept responsibility for errors which may have occurred.

INTRODUCTION : THE EUROPEAN MARKET - AN OVERVIEW

It has become something of a truism in recent times to observe that the 1990s will be one of the most far-reaching periods of change in the twentieth century. Indeed, within a few years the entire post-war structure of Europe, and the political and economic divisions which emerged in the years after 1945, will have become an irrelevance. In their place, if current predictions are correct, there will emerge a newly formed and significantly united Europe, in which many of the confrontational positions underlying the whole historical division into East and West will be submerged by a prolonged and mutually beneficial drive for growth.

The first element in this process of change, of course, will be the formation of the European Community's Single Market, which is still on schedule for January 1993, and which will both strengthen and unite the twelve countries who now form its membership - although at the cost of some degree of political autonomy for their respective governments. The second, and equally important if rather less predictable, will be the pace of change in the Eastern part of the continent, which has already been such as to overtake many of the most confident predictions of the late 1980s, bringing with it the potential not only for selling to a much larger consumer market but also for manufacturing within that market, with a view to re-exporting to the West.

By the end of 1990 we will already have seen the end of one of the principal statistical tenets used in compiling this volume. The planned reunification of East Germany with its West German counterpart on Oct. 3 marks the fulfilment not only of a long-standing ideal for the peoples of both sides, but indeed of the West German basic law (*Grundgesetz*, or constitution), which has always made specific provision for its extension to cover the territory of the East.

Under the circumstances, the decision to retain the nominal differentiations between East and West Germany, for the purposes of this volume, requires some explanation. Firstly, as noted in the introduction to Section One, the two states remained economically separate during the period which it covers (i.e. up to January 1990), and the agencies which compile statistical information on the two countries could not always be relied upon to use comparable criteria - meaning that it would have been statistically unsound to amalgamate some types of data. Equally to the point, however, is the fact that East Germany, as it was until October 1990, is likely to remain a meaningful concept in marketing terms for some time yet, because of the long period which will elapse before its living standards even start to approach those of the West.

Introduction

1. Opportunities and Risks in Eastern Europe

Eastern Europe's conversion to the once reviled cause of capitalism has been positively breathtaking in recent months. The removal of one-party communist administrations in all but two countries (Bulgaria and the Yugoslavian Federation), and the public abandonment of old-style collectivist and centralist doctrines in all of them, has been accompanied by a convincing growth of private enterprise, most notably in East Germany (now to be incorporated into the Federal Republic), but also in Hungary and Poland. The enactment in September 1990 of the long-overdue privatisation laws in Czechoslovakia, which had permitted no private enterprise whatever until the very end of the 1980s, will open the door to a much wider framework for privatisation.

This is not to say that the region's transition to capitalism will be anything less than painful, and there will be periods of considerable political risk in the next five years whose outcome can by no means be taken for granted by onlookers in the West. It will be primarily the consumers who take the brunt of the social and economic costs of *perestroika*, and there will be times when they would gladly turn the clock back: for example, when they are forced out of thier jobs in factories which now have to deal with a chronic overstaffing problem, or when their savings are swallowed up by rocketing food prices - suddenly inflated by the summary withdrawal of the state subsidies with which East European governments have always sought, until now, to pacify their citizens.

Unhappily, things may have to get worse before they can get better, because of the sheer extent of government indebtedness. Every East European country, except for Romania, is so heavily burdened with public debt that it will remain vulnerable for many years to come to the slightest whim of the international banking community. The increase in international oil prices, which followed Iraq's annexation of Kuwait in August 1990 and which may yet go still higher, is potentially crippling for most of these countries, which are now having to pay the going market rates, in dollars, for the fuel they import from the Soviet Union. Indeed, the prospect of a general rise in world interest rates, which has historically been the world's usual response to a crisis, would be about the worst scenario imaginable for most of them.

Special note should be made in this context of Yugoslavia, where the growth of economic problems, largely connected with the country's external debt, have triggered a burst of political dissent whose main expression has been racial in character. In late 1990 the growing enmity between the ethnically militant Serbs and their counterparts in Croatia or Slovenia has threatened the very bonds which hold the Yugoslavian Federation together. Real standards of living have plummeted since the beginning of 1989, and as 1991 approaches there is little cause for optimism on the consumer front.

2. The Single European Market

The approach of January 1993, and with it the creation of a Single Market for trade and services within the European Community, has had a profound impact on policy alignment in those states which are not EC members. Turkey and Austria have already made formal applications for full membership of the Community - although Turkey seems unlikely to succeed until its relations with Greece improve - and in Sweden, too, the idea of an approach seems increasingly attractive to some.

Cyprus and Malta have been scrambling to tighten up their relations with the Community, via new or revised association agreements, and Scandinavian non-members (Norway, Finland and Sweden) have been forced to align their service industries - mainly banking, insurance and securities markets - with the de facto standards which are emerging in Brussels. Meanwhile, Austria and Switzerland, those two islands of neutrality in the geographical centre of the Community, have come under unprecedented pressure to build new through-routes for transit traffic and generally to conform to the new norms. The issues surrounding Austria's restrictions on truck transport are likely to prove of crucial importance to the development of the Single Market.

About two-thirds of the necessary EC legislation for the Single Market is now in place, although by no means all of it has been incorporated into national legislative systems by member countries. Agreement has been reached on a large proportion of the technical standards which will allow manufacturers in any one member state to sell into any other, providing that their goods meet specified minimum standards. There is also unanimity on the mutual recognition of professional qualifications, one of the main preconditions of job mobility among the professional classes.

There is also substantial agreement on the provisions of the so-called "Social Charter", which relates to employment rights, trade union rights and minimum social welfare entitlements in the Single Market; many of the Charter's key provisions, however, remain optional, and some of the more contentious, including those relating to consultation in the workplace, are unlikely to be implemented by the British Government without a struggle.

There is also a conspicuous lack of agreement on many elements of taxation policy. Attempts to impose uniform corporation taxes, value added taxes, excise duties or capital market duties had met with little success by the autumn of 1990, and it seems possible that the Single Market will have to start without any proper regulation of these potentially distorting factors.

3. Population Development

With a total population of just under 842 million in 1990, including some 284 million Soviet citizens, the continent of Europe represents the world's second largest group of consumers. Practically all of them enjoy above-average standards of living when judged by world standards; most have longer life-spans and lower mortality rates than the global norm; none has to cope with a tropical climate; and in all but a handful of smaller countries there is a significant degree of industrial economy offering the opportunity of rising above the level of agricultural self-sufficiency.

There, however, the similarities end. Beside the relatively prosperous and industrialised countries of the north-west, including most of the European Community and all the member states of the European Free Trade Association, there are substantial populations in the east and the south whose way of life is still very distinct from those of their north-western counterparts, and whose priorities as consumers do not necessarily follow the north-western trend at all.

There are, for instance, at least 60 million Muslims in the non-Soviet part of the continent, mostly in Turkey and Yugoslavia, for whom many of the cultural traditions of the north-west are still relatively unfamiliar. In large areas of Greece, Cyprus or Malta, life for many people goes on without any need for the ubiquitous microprocessor technology, and large parts of the population spend their whole lives in the village where they grew up. Nor is there any real prospect that this will change in the foreseeable future.

The European population as a whole is growing by only about 0.6 per cent a year, a figure which is well below the world average of 1.8 per cent and which generally reflects its affluence and increasing sophistication. Growth is at its lowest in Germany (both the Eastern and Western halves), and in Hungary, all of which recorded negative rates between 1977 and 1990; in Turkey, Albania, Yugoslavia and Liechtenstein, on the other hand, populations increased by up to 23 per cent during the same period. In the Soviet Union, virtually all of the increase has been among the non-Russian and especially the Muslim peoples of the southern Republics, and for the first time since the October Revolution Russians now comprise less than half the population.

If we leave aside the Muslim states and those countries where contraception is still either illegal or unobtainable, we perceive a series of successive swings in the birth rate, most of which reflect the economic and social fortunes of their respective populations. The most notable, and of course the most completely documented, was the baby boom which occurred immediately after the end of the Second World War and during the early 1950s and 1960s; but other booms have occurred due to political factors (as, for example, in Albania or Romania, where premiums have at times been awarded to the parents of large families).

In most of Europe the baby boom ended in the late 1960s, and the recession-struck 1970s saw a noticeable drop in the numbers of pregnancies whose effects are already becoming increasingly apparent. In a few countries the effect is already so severe as to merit careful consideration by anyone looking at the future growth of their markets.

According to estimates from the European Commission, for example, the numbers of EC residents aged 15 to 25 are set to fall by 15 per cent between 1980 and 1995, bringing the cumulative fall since 1985 to 25 per cent - the worst effects being felt in West Germany and in Scandinavia (down by some 35 per cent over the ten-year period). For the Netherlands, the United Kingdom, Luxembourg and Belgium, too, the shortfall in the high-consuming 15-25 age band will be of the order of 20 per cent by the time 1995 arrives. Spain, Portugal and Italy can expect a steep relative decline in the younger age band of 5-14, reflecting the earlier onset of the decline in the birth rate.

For some countries (West Germany, Sweden, Denmark and Austria) the problem may prove even more acute in the long run. Labour shortages are already pushing up wage rates in Scandinavia, and the signs are that West Germany's dependency ratio (the ratio of over-65s to persons of working age) will exceed 1:1 by the year 2030.

In the shorter term, of course, the news is far from bad. The 25-45 age group whose numbers will be increasing between now and 1995 are among the most affluent consumers of all, having formed family units and started to consume household goods in large quantities as they reach the peak of their personal earnings potential. By the year 2000 they will be starting to consume more leisure goods and more health care goods and services.

It is no coincidence that Greece, Portugal, Spain and the Republic of Ireland, as the poorest and most devoutly Catholic (i.e. anti-contraception) countries in western Europe, were the least affected by the relative dearth of births in the 1970s - or that they will accordingly record some of the biggest overall population growths in 1985-1995 (6.82 per cent for Portugal, 6.67 per cent for Greece, and 4.15 per cent for Spain).

Nonetheless, the advent of economic prosperity in southern Europe during 1986-1990 has resulted in a very severe drop in marriage rates, coinciding with a correspondingly large increase in divorce rates. The legalisation of abortion (and, in France, the approval of the so-called

Introduction

"abortion pill") represent a major departure from Vatican doctrine in Catholic countries - excepting, of course, Ireland, where all divorce, abortion and contraception is illegal.

Generally speaking, couples tend to postpone the start of a family during times of either great hardship or relative affluence - the first for obvious reasons, the second because a life of greater social sophistication encourages it. Certainly, most West European couples are bearing their first children at a later age than, say, thirty years ago; French statistics show, for example, that the average age rose by nearly five years between the mid-1950s and the mid-1980s, and the trend holds true for all countries except Ireland, Greece and Portugal. The trend has if anything been more marked in eastern Europe, where the average childbearing age has risen since the late 1980s, but this may change in the near future if sociologists' predictions are confirmed.

Males account for about 51.3 per cent of all live births, compared with the female proportion of 48.7 per cent. In most European countries, males outnumber females up to the age of about 50, and thereafter females start to predominate. But with the improving standards of health care in most countries the balance of the sexes is lasting later into life than was hitherto the case - all of which means that the absolute numbers of men aged 60 or more are rising somewhat faster than the numbers of women - a factor which is bound to prove of significance in marketing terms as the century progresses.

During the 1970s and 1980s, paradoxically, this increasingly healthy and long-lived European population of elderly people was being encouraged to retire from its working careers at an ever earlier age. On the one hand this simply reflected a growing view in society that it was unacceptable for the elderly to have to work as long as was hitherto the case; on the other the pressures of unemployment also militated in favour of an earlier retirement which would allow employers to concentrate job opportunities at the lower end of the age scale. By the end of the decade, however, there was a growing feeling that the trend toward early retirement could go into reverse, as the falling numbers of younger people, together with real shortages of labour (especially in the northern part of the continent), threatened to push up the wage/price spiral to perhaps unsustainable levels.

4. Households

The relatively affluent spell of the last 20 years has been accompanied, predictably, by a steady increase in the numbers of households and a corresponding reduction in their size. Among members of the EC the average household size has shrunk from 2.9 to 2.7 persons since 1977, and the decline may be expected to continue during the 1990s; in the EFTA group, where family sizes are already relatively small because of a much earlier devolution of the family unit, the recent decline has been slower, and in the CMEA group the typical household has come down only quite gradually, from 2.9 persons to 2.8 persons.

In the smaller countries discussed by this report the decline has been of the order of 0.2 persons; but Albania, Gibraltar, Malta and Yugoslavia households still average more than 3 persons - while Turkey, afflicted by a population explosion and a difficult economic climate, has made almost no progress in reducing its average household size of 5.25 persons. Among its more developed European neighbours, Ireland too has been only barely able to keep its households increasing at a fast enough rate to match the growth of the population; with an average 3.86 members (1987), it has by far the largest household units in the northern continent.

One factor behind the overall growth in European households has been the sharp increase in the numbers of divorced and separated people. Single-member households of all types have been increasing sharply in number since the mid-1960s (except in Spain and in Ireland), and the numbers of single-parent family units have more than doubled in practically all countries. One-person households are most common in Norway, in West Germany and in Denmark; they are least common in the southern states (Turkey, Cyprus, Romania, Portugal and Greece); the United Kingdom, with 25 per cent single-member households in 1987, is in the middle range as far as Europe is concerned.

Generally speaking, European populations are still moving towards the major conurbations as jobs disappear on the land, and as improved communications make it easier to move away from the family home. There is evidence that the trend towards the large cities has all but stopped in Switzerland, Austria and some of the northern states; but France, Greece, Spain and Portugal are already experiencing some depopulation of rural districts, while in Italy the depopulation of the southern *Mezzogiorno* has become a major political issue.

5. Living Standards

European housing standards, while not yet on a par with those of the United States, are on the whole reasonably comfortable. Table 1604 shows that around 80 per cent of all dwellings have an indoor shower or bath of some description, with the major exceptions being in Spain and Portugal. A similar proportion have their own toilet, and in most countries at least 90 per cent have a direct water supply - the major exceptions being in Turkey, Portugal and Albania.

Introduction

Typically, European households spend about a fifth of their disposable incomes on housing, rates and water supply, and another 4-7 per cent on domestic fuels. Relatively few households own the premises in which they live, and in many countries the price of building land, especially in the urban areas, has long since risen beyond the reach of many people. The UK, with 58 per cent home ownership, tops the league of strongly industrialised European countries, with Italy (55 per cent ownership) and France (51 per cent) also all well ahead of the bottom runners, Luxembourg and the Netherlands (about 32 per cent).

Among the non-socialist countries of Europe, owner-occupation tends to be most common among either the very wealthy countries or the very poor, where land is inexpensive and where populations do not migrate much from one region to another. Greece, for example, has 86 per cent owner-occupiers, while Portugal has 70 per cent, Ireland has 60 per cent and Spain has 58 per cent - about the same as the UK.

6. Consumer Demand

Private consumption, as Table 0314 will confirm, typically accounts for between 50 and 60 per cent of gross domestic product in European countries, and in the non-socialist economies direct expenditure through the retail sector has usually accounted for about two thirds of this amount - the remainder going in rents, services, insurances and the like. Governments have always sought to boost private consumption when times were good and to restrain it, through high interest rates and other measures, when excessive purchasing threatened to push inflation too high. As such the moods of the consumer have become more important than ever in the calculations of finance ministers - who are often prevented by huge budget deficits from stimulating their economies with old-fashioned centralised spending.

In Britain, the frantic consumer boom occasioned by the 1988 tax concessions has proved much more difficult to stop than to start. Only in late 1990 were there any indications that the high interest rate strategy adopted by the central government was having any effect on consumer borrowing. In Italy, on the other hand, consumption levels are still on the increase, while in West Germany the prospect of reunification with the East seems to have occasioned, belatedly, a consumer revival which reversed the somewhat disappointing trends of the late 1980s. In Spain and Portugal, both of which experienced a major surge in consumption after joining the Common Market in 1986, consumption has now been throttled back by governments terrified by a growing trade deficit and rising inflation: both have taken specific action to curb borrowing for consumer durables.

In Sweden and in Norway, too, governments were still trying in 1990 to damp down the booming rate of private consumption - which shows every sign of engendering a return to high wage settlements and ensuing inflationary cycles unless something is done to prevent overheating.

In most of Europe, the rapid increase in numbers of households has been the main motive power behind sales of many household goods, especially durables. But in the next 15-20 years it seems likely that falling population levels among the 20-30 age group, together with rising costs, will have eroded the housing market, and durables manufacturers will have no option but to step up the rate of product innovation if they hope to achieve more than merely replacement sales.

Generally speaking, the experience of the minor markets in recent years has confirmed what one would expect: that consumer demand for certain items (notably food) rises disproportionately during the early stages of an economic revival, but that it tends to level off beyond a certain point of affluence as the purchasing of consumer goods, including durables, takes over. This is what we would expect to see happening in Spain and Portugal over the next ten to fifteen years.

Typically, as Tables 1102 and 1103 show, the European household spends about 20 per cent of its budget on buying foodstuffs (though the UK is a clear exception, spending not much more than half of this amount). In the less developed countries of the Mediterranean, of Eastern Europe and of Ireland, food accounts for a much larger proportion - sometimes as high as 45 per cent - and there is no immediate probability, in these slow-moving economies, of a major change here. Beverages tend to absorb 3-5 per cent of the household budget, depending on the very widely varying levels of indirect taxation on these products; in highly-taxed Ireland, for example, nearly 14 per cent of the budget goes on alcoholic and non-alcoholic drinks.

In the West at least, clothing and footwear typically account for between 5 and 7 per cent of all outgoings, but in poorer countries the proportion may in fact be higher - despite the fact that in some low-wage areas (Turkey, most of Greece, Portugal and parts of Italy), a significant proportion of clothing and footwear is either home-made or manufactured locally at very low cost.

The remaining, less absolutely central areas of consumption (household goods and services, leisure, transport and personal goods) are, inevitably, those which are most vulnerable to short-term cancellation or postponement, and as such they serve as valuable indicators of the strength of the economy and its perceived prospects.

Introduction

Viewed in this light, the signs are becoming more encouraging. Since the mid-1980s, volume sales of most such products have shown a strong recovery from the slump of 1981-1984; sales of durables such as cars (still running at all-time records in 1989), electrical goods and (in the northern countries) leisure and sports goods have exceeded all expectations

GUIDE TO USING THIS HANDBOOK

1. Scope of the Handbook

European Marketing Data and Statistics (EMDAS) is a statistical yearbook of business and marketing information. This edition features 350 pages of up-to-date and detailed marketing statistics on 24 principal subject sectors. These sectors are stored on a database of international marketing information and regularly updated by Euromonitor's research team.

The sections of EMDAS cover a wide variety of marketing topics, ranging from socio-economic trends and background information through to key consumer marketing parameters. The sections on advertising, finance and banking, tourism, energy, defence and the environment all include additional data for this edition. Key agro-industrial trends covering energy, automotives, industrial output and agricultural resources are included, in addition to the extensive section on economic indicators.

In EMDAS 1991, each statistical tabulation presents pan-European comparative information, either in the form of ten (in some cases eleven) year trendings, or single year data for the latest year available. All the countries are listed down the left-hand column, presented in three economic entities (EC, EFTA, CMEA) and "others". Where appropriate and available, regional totals and averages are included.

Where data is in values, units have been generally been left in national currencies. However the spreadsheets on which the data is stored facilitate calculations in US dollars. These are calculated only for the latest year available (usually 1988 and 1989) as fluctuations in exchange rates and contrasts in rates of inflation render year-on-year conversions meaningless.

In addition, calculations have been made where deemed appropriate to show European market shares by country, growth rates over a ten-year period, and per capita data. These permit easy cross comparisons between countries, regions and markets.

Using EMDAS 1991 is easy. Whatever topic is of interest, you simply look up the relevant tables (using the contents or index) and the table will show the relevant data for all countries. The heading shows the relevant section, title summary and title of the table, and unit. A guide to the sources used in the compilation of the data, and any relevant notes appear at the foot of the table.

User Guide

The aim of EMDAS is to locate in one handbook the essential statistical information relevant to European market planning. The handbook will save the busy marketeer or researcher hours of time trawling through statistics from many sources and provides a wealth of hard-to-get information drawn from the many reports and studies compiled by Euromonitor over the last 2-3 years - many based on trade interviews and original extrapolations. Business and librarians will find the handbook especially useful.

2. Subject Coverage

EMDAS 1991 is presented in 24 separate sections or "databases" which have all been specially compiled for Euromonitor. The subjects have been selected as those most appropriate for strategic planning and European market analysis, covering both background marketing parameters and detailed consumer market information. The 24 databases are discussed below.

01 Marketing Geography

This database features maps for each of the major European markets, showing standard and marketing regions, and arranged by economic grouping. Also included is a summary of basic data (political conditions, languages, etc) for each country covered, and some key facts and figures.

02 Demographic Trends and Forecasts

This database features 23 statistical compilations covering population trends, vital statistics, demographic analysis by age and sex, and population forecasts. Much of the data is in eleven-year trends, forming a basis for forecasting and projections.

03 Economic Indicators

This database features 14 tables of key economic data, again with several eleven-year trend tables. The main economic indicators are all covered, including GDP, GNP, inflation, money supply and exchange rates.

04 Finance and Banking

This section features six tabulations mainly showing data from 1981-1989 and covering bank assets, liabilities, claims and interest rates, as well as a table on credit card holders.

05 External Trade by Destination and Commodity

This section includes ten tables which give a cohesive and structured trade overview covering total imports and exports and external trade breakdowns by origin and commodity.

06 Labour Force Indicators

This database covers the key employment indicators including numbers employed, unemployed and hours of work. The structure of the labour force by industry sector and status is included for latest years available.

07 Industrial Resources and Output

This section provides key industrial indices for an eleven-year period and includes output tables covering some major industrial materials.

08 Energy Resources and Output

This section consists of 13 tables on energy supply and demand. Coverage extends to household energy consumption with most tables trended over eleven years. New information is included, in terms of new tables and conversions, to improve comparability of the data.

09 Defence

Tables in this section give key data on defence spending and personnel.

10 Environmental Data

This section includes six tables covering various environmental factors.

11 Consumer Expenditure Patterns

The presentation of this section comprises total consumer spending, a consolidated breakdown by product sector, and a series of tables analysing each major consumer sector. New 1988 data and estimates have been included and all the data are presented in eleven-year trends with growth rates and dollar comparisons.

12 Retailing and Retail Distribution

This section has drawn on Euromonitor's extensive European retail research in recent years, with 21 tables covering retail sales and channels and breakdowns for different retail sectors.

13 Advertising Patterns and Media Access

This section includes a broad range of data on advertising expenditure and the media.

14 Consumer Market Sizes

Per capita consumption and retail market sizes are included in 18 tables for 1989. The information for the main countries is drawn from Euromonitor's market information database, which formed the basis for the companion volume *Consumer Europe* (Euromonitor 1991) with information included for other countries where available. Coverage of minor markets and Eastern Europe will be expanded over future editions.

15 Consumer Prices and Costs

Trends in consumer prices and selected European living costs are included in five tables of data.

16 Households and Household Facilities

This section comprises nine tables of comparative statistics on households. Data on housing stock and household composition are included together with available data on household penetration.

17 Health and Living Standards

This database comprises five tables covering all major health indicators.

18 Literacy and Education

A range of literacy and educational statistics are included in this five-table section.

19 Agricultural Resources

This section presents key data on land use and the production of various agricultural produce. There are ten tables on the database, mostly including figures for 1988.

20 Telecommunications

This brief section features information on postal services and telecommunications.

21 Automotives

All automotive research data is incorporated in one complete database covering the circulation, manufacture and sales of cars, commercial vehicles and two-wheelers.

22 Transport Infrastructure

This 16-table database covers major movements in terms of the road, rail, air and shipping transport sectors.

23 Tourism and Travel

This database consists of nine tabulations covering tourism values and movements, tourist accommodation and its usage.

24 Cultural Indicators

This section includes six tables covering available data on libraries, museums, book publishing and cinemas.

3. Data Coverage

Each of the statistical compilations is presented in one of four data periods:

(1)   A ten-year trend table from 1979-1988, with data for each country drawn from the same consistent source. In some cases, some intermediary years have been excluded for reasons of space, mainly 1979 and 1981.

(2)   A different period trend, eg 1978-1988 (11-year trend) or a recent period (eg 1981-1989 or 1983-1988) where only certain periods are available.

(3)   Latest year available, with the years differing between countries. These are used where the information is drawn from occasional studies, eg a census, or where statistical offices vary in the speed of publishing statistics.

(4)   A single year, eg 1987 or 1988, where space does not permit trends or where an interactive range of information is provided (eg imports by origin, usage of GDP, etc).

The statistics in this volume are as available during the compilation period (June-August 1990). Figures for 1989 (in some cases provisional or estimates) have been included where possible. However consolidations across Europe tend to take time and much of the data is for 1988. Various one-off surveys cover earlier years only.

4. Country Coverage

This edition of EMDAS includes a total of 33 countries in both Western and Eastern Europe. These are grouped into four economic entities, as follows:

EC (EUROPEAN ECONOMIC COMMUNITY)

Belgium
Denmark
France
West Germany
Greece
Ireland
Italy
Luxembourg
Netherlands
Portugal
Spain
United Kingdom

EFTA (EUROPEAN FREE TRADE ASSOCIATION)

Austria
Finland
Iceland
Norway
Sweden
Switzerland

CMEA (COMMUNITY OF MUTUAL ECONOMIC ASSISTANCE)

Bulgaria
Czechoslovakia
East Germany
Hungary
Poland
Romania
USSR

OTHERS

Albania
Cyprus
Gibraltar
Liechtenstein
Malta
Monaco
Turkey
Yugoslavia

5. Sources

European Marketing Data and Statistics is based on extensive, on-going research into European markets and industries. A Europe-wide network of market analysts and researchers work to pull together available data on socio-economic patterns, market conditions and trends, living standards and background information relevant to business, export and market planning.

The principal sources used in the compilation of EMDAS are as follows:

-       International and European organisations, such as the United Nations, OECD, and the International Monetary Fund.

-       National Statistical Offices in each country.

-       Pan-European and national trade and industry associations.

-       Industry study groups and unofficial research publishers.

-       Euromonitor's own research publications, including one-off reports and statistical compilations.

-       Original research specially commissioned for the handbook, including consumer research, trade interviews and retail surveys.

A guide to the main sources used in the compilation of each table is included at the foot of each table. For reasons of space the main sources are only briefly cited; in some cases, many different reports and publications are used in the preparation of just one table. For example, we may have extracted data from publications by the National Statistical Offices for all the countries covered in order to compile one table. In other cases, statistical compilations are from secondary sources which have in turn used many different sources.

User Guide

A brief guide to the main sources used in each of the 24 databases follows.

01 Marketing Geography

Information mainly drawn from the business press, data from the yearbooks of the National Statistical Offices and various informal studies on the countries covered.

02 Demographic Trends and Forecasts

Drawn mainly from the statistical yearbooks of the National Statistical Offices supplemented with UN data and population forecasts.

03 Economic Indicators

The principal international sources are The World Bank and the International Monetary Fund. National Statistical Offices (yearbooks, national accounts) and economic bulletins by leading banks are also used.

04 Finance and Banking

The major source of comparative financial data is the International Monetary Fund ("International Financial Statistics".)

05 External Trade by Destination and Commodity

The International Monetary Fund, OECD and Eurostat (the Statistical Office of the European Community) track external trade flows in some detail. Statistical yearbooks are also utilised.

06 Labour Force Indicators

The primary international source is the International Labour Office, which publishes both a statistical yearbook and quarterly bulletins.

07 Industrial Resources and Output

Mainly drawn from UN and OECD publications. Various industry sectors are covered by associations as stated.

08 Energy Resources and Output

This compilation draws mainly on the UN and the OECD.

09 Defence

Sources include the International Monetary Fund, the CIA and the International Institute of Strategic Studies.

10 Environmental Data

Drawn largely from OECD sources.

11 Consumer Expenditure Patterns

Drawn from the national accounts of each country (generally published by the National Statistical Offices). Euromonitor estimates have been used to reach levels of consolidation.

12 Retailing and Retail Distribution

Drawn from a wide number of Euromonitor's own surveys and market reports on European retailing including *Retail Trade International* (Euromonitor 1989), *European Directory of Retailers and Wholesalers* (Euromonitor 1988), and also original research. Primary sources include retail trade censuses (various countries) by National Statistical Offices, retail trade associations, major retailers, etc.

13 Advertising Patterns and Media Access

Drawn from various media study groups, advertising associations and agents in various countries.

14 Consumer Market Sizes

Drawn from Euromonitor's consumer market database; primary sources include trade associations and industry leaders in all countries.

15 Consumer Prices and Costs

Mainly from the International Monetary Fund and the OECD; living costs from the International Labour Office and the Confederation of British Industry (CBI).

16 Households and Household Facilities

Compiled from various publications from National Statistical Offices, UN publications and incorporating Euromonitor estimates and calculations.

17 Health and Living Standards

The main sources are the World Health Organisation (yearbooks, various publications) and the OECD.

18 Literacy and Education

The main source is UNESCO with data from National Offices incorporated as available.

19 Agricultural Resources

Mainly based on the publications of the Food and Agricultural Organisation of the United Nations (FAO).

20 Telecommunications

Mainly based on UN data.

21 Automotives

Drawn from various motor trades organisations and compilations from the same.

22 Transport Infrastructure

Based on various UN publications; the International Civil Aviation Authority (ICAO); the International Road Federation; Union Internationale des Chemins de Fer (UIC) and Lloyds.

23 Tourism and Travel

A compilation drawn from the World Tourism Organisation (WHO), OECD and Euromonitor's own research, including *Travel and Tourism Data* (Euromonitor 1989).

24 Cultural Indicators

Mainly drawn from the UN, UNESCO and National Statistical Offices.

6. List of Abbreviations

BLEU	Belgo-Luxembourg Economic Union
CMEA	Council for Mutual Economic Assistance
ECE	Economic Commission for Europe
EEC	European Economic Community
EFTA	European Free Trade Association
Eurostat	Statistical Office of the European Communities
FAO	Food and Agricultural Organisation
GATT	General Agreement on Tariffs and Trade
IBRD	International Bank for Reconstruction and Development
ICAO	International Civil Aviation Organisation
ILO	International Labour Organisation
IMF	International Monetary Fund
OECD	Organisation for Economic Co-operation and Development
UN	United Nations
UNESCO	United Nations Educational, Scientific and Cultural Organisation
WHO	World Health Organisation
WTO	World Tourism Organisation

EAP	Economically Active Population
GDP	Gross Domestic Product
GNP	Gross National Product
RTA	Registered Tourist Arrivals
SITC	Standard International Trade Classification

Bn	billion
Mn	million
MT	metric tonne
000t	thousand tonnes
m3	cubic metre
m2	square metre
Gm	gramme
Kg	kilogramme
Km	kilometre
Km2	square kilometre
Hl	hectolitre
Gwh	gigawatt hoursKwh kilowatt hours
MW	megawatt
Twh	terawatt hours
TJ	terajoule
0	denotes less than 0.5 where no fraction given

7. European Map

KEY EUROPEAN MARKET INFORMATION SOURCES

1. Introduction

This section identifies the major information sources for researching the European market. The listings are not intended as exhaustive, but rather to list some of the main international and national organisations publishing statistics and locate some of the principal European libraries.

Readers are referred to several other Euromonitor publications for further information on European sources :

European Directory of Marketing Information Sources (Euromonitor, 1991)

This handbook presents information on official sources including further detail on National Statistical Offices, together with listings of market research companies, online databases, trade associations, trade journals, and general business contacts for the major countries of Western Europe.

Consumer Europe 1991 (Euromonitor 1991)

Primarily a handbook of consumer market data, this annual publication lists the major trade associations and trade journals publishing information on consumer markets across Western Europe.

European Directory of Non-official Statistical Sources (Euromonitor 1988)

This directory lists statistical information published by unofficial and semi-official organisations across Europe.

European Advertising, Marketing and Media Data (Euromonitor 1989)

This handbook examines advertising expenditure patterns, media availability and basic consumer marketing parameters across Western Europe and provides, in addition, an extensive directory section with details of the leading agency and media operators, advertisers and useful sources for further information.

2. Official Pan-European and International Organisations

Benelux Economic Union (L'Union Economique Benelux)
Address: Sécretariat Général, Rue de la Régence 39, B-1000 Brussels, Belgium
Telephone: (02) 5193811
Fax: (02) 5134206
Publications: *Benelux Review* (quarterly), *Benelux Info* (irregular), *Benelux Textes de Base*.

Council of Europe
Address: F-67006 Strasbourg Cedex, France
Obtaining publications: from sales agents; the UK agent is HMSO, and copies of publications can be ordered from HMSO bookshops. (London: 49 High Holborn, WC1V 6HB for callers only, PO Box 276, London SW8 5DT for mail order.)
Guides to publications: *Catalogue of publications* (available from Publicity Department (P9D), HMSO Books, St Crispins, Duke Street, Norwich NR3 1PD)
Contact points: all information about publications can be obtained from the Council of Europe Publications Section at the address above or from sales agents

Council for Mutual Economic Assistance - CMEA (COMECON)
Address: Prospekt Kalinina 56, Moscow 121205, USSR
Telephone: (095) 290 91 11
Telex: 411141
Publisher of statistical series: Permanent Commission for statistics
Publications: *Statistical Yearbook, Survey of CMEA Activities* (annual), *Economic Co-operation of the CMEA Member Countries* (monthly in Russian; also quarterly versions in English and Spanish), *International Agricultural Journal, Press Bulletin*; also books and press releases.

European Free Trade Association (EFTA)
Address: 9-11 rue de Varembe, CH-1211 Geneva 20, Switzerland
Telephone: (022) 7491111
Fax: (022) 7339291
Obtaining publications: as above; UK distributors are Gothard House Publications Ltd, Gothard House, Henley-on-Thames, Oxon RG9 1AJ
Guides to publications: no catalogue is published, but each edition of the quarterly *EFTA bulletin* carries a list of publications currently available. The bulletin is distributed free of charge and published in English, French, German and Scandinavian editions.
Contact points: EFTA, Press and Information Service, at address above

European Communities
Address: Office for Official Publications of the European Communities, BP 103, 2 rue Mercier, L-2985 Luxembourg
Telephone: 499281
Telex: 1324 PUBOF LU

Fax: 488573
Publisher of statistical series: main statistical series are published by Eurostat (qv). Publisher as above for other publications shown below.
Obtaining publications: publications are either priced, free, or for limited distribution; free publications may be obtained from the issuing institutions or, if published by the Information Offices, from those offices. The UK Information Offices are in London (8 Storey's Gate, London SW1P 3AT, telephone 071-2228122), Belfast (Windsor House, 9/15 Bedford Street, telephone 40708), Cardiff (4 Cathedral Road, Cardiff CF1 9SG, telephone 371631) and Edinburgh (9 Alva Street, Edinburgh EH2 4PH, telephone 2252058). Priced publications are obtainable from sales offices; UK sales offices are HMSO, and, as sub-agent, Alan Armstrong Ltd., 2 Arkwright Road, Reading RG2 0SQ, telephone 0734 751769
Guides to publications: *Annual Catalogue of Publications*, with quarterly updates. *The European Community as a publisher* (annual). Catalogues are available from sales offices. All catalogues are free of charge.
Contact points: Information Offices and Sales Offices

Eurostat (Statistical Office of the European Communities)
Address: BP 1907, rue Alcide de Gasperi, L-2929 Luxembourg
Telephone: 43014567
Telex: 3423 COMEUR LU
Publisher of statistical series: Office for Official Publications of the European Communities
Obtaining publications: directly from the Office for Official Publications of the European Communities, L-2985 Luxembourg, 2 rue Mercier, or through sales and subscription offices in individual countries; in the UK these are HMSO and, as sub-agent, Alan Armstrong Ltd, 2 Arkwright Road, Reading RG2 0SG, telephone 0743 751769.
Guides to publications: regular information on publications given in *Eurostat news* (quarterly); *Catalogue of Eurostat publications* (annual, free from sales and subscription offices. Eurostat publications are also included in the catalogues of the European Communities (qv).
Contact points: Eurostat at main address

Food and Agricultural Organisation of the United Nations
Address: Via delle Terme di Caracalla, 00100 Rome, Italy
Telephone: (06) 57971
Telex: 610181 FOODAGRI I
Fax: 57973152
Obtaining publications: from sales agents (HSMO in the UK) or from the Distribution and Sales Section of the FAO at the address above for countries without agents.
Guides to publications: *FAO books in print* (annual catalogue of FAO publications in English); *List of*

documents, listing publications in all languages expected to be of reasonably lasting nature.

General Agreement on Tariffs and Trade (GATT)
Address: Centre William Rappard, 154 rue de Lausanne, 1211 Geneva 21, Switzerland
Telephone: (022) 7395208
Telex: 412324 GATT CH
Fax: (022) 7314206
Guides to publications: GATT publications are included in the general *Catalogue of United Nations publications* (see main United Nations entry).

International Bank for Reconstruction and Development - IBRD (World Bank)
Address: 1818 H St NW, Washington, DC 20433, USA
Telephone: (202) 4771234
Telex: 248423
Guides to publications: World Bank Catalog of Publications.

International Civil Aviation Organisation (ICAO)
Address: 1000 Sherbrooke Street West, Suite 400, Montreal, Quebec, Canada H3A 2R2
Telephone: (514) 2858219
Telex: 24513
Obtaining publications: from the Document Sales Unit at the above address or from several addresses abroad (United Kingdom: Civil Aviation Authority., Printing and Publications Services, Greville House, 37 Gratton Road, Cheltenham, Gloucestershire GL50 2BN).

International Energy Agency
Address: 2 rue André-Pascal, 75775 Paris Cedex 16, France
Telephone: (1) 45248200
Telex: 620160 OCDE F
Publications: Energy policies and programmes of IEA countries (annual), *Annual oil market report, Quarterly oil and gas statistics, Annual oil and gas statistics, Energy prices and taxes* (quarterly)
Notes: IEA is an autonomous body within the framework of OECD; for details on obtaining publications, etc see OECD entry.

International Labour Organisation (ILO)
Address: 4 route des Morillons, 1211 Geneva 22, Switzerland
Telephone: (022) 7996111
Telex: 415647 ILO CH
Fax: (22) 7998571
Obtaining publications: from International Labour Office Publications at the above address or from branch offices in ca. 40 countries
Guides to publications: ILO Publications (quarterly in English, French, Spanish, German, Russian, Arabic and Chinese.

International Monetary Fund (IMF)
Address: 700 19th St NW, Room C-100, Washington DC 20431, USA
Telephone: (202) 623 7430

Telex: (RCA) 248331 IMF UR
Fax: (202) 623 7201
Obtaining publications: from address above. In the UK the publications maybe obtained from HMSO or Microinfo Ltd., telephone (0420) 86848.
Guides to publications: IMF publications are included in the general *Catalogue of United Nations publications* (see United Nations entry); there is also a publications brochure available from the above address.

International Telecommunication Union (ITU)
Address: Place des Nations, 1211 Geneva 20, Switzerland
Telephone: (022) 995111
Telex: 421000
Guides to publications: List of publications (twice a year)

Nordic Statistical Secretariat
Address: Postbox 2550, DK-2100 Copenhagen O, Denmark
Telephone: 298222
Publisher of statistical series: publishes jointly *Yearbook of Nordic Statistics* with the Nordic Council of Ministers.
Obtaining publications: through distributors: Denmark: Svensk-norsk boqimport, Postbox 1022, DK-1022 Copenhagen K; Finland: Government Printing Centre, Postbox 516, SF-00101 Helsinki 10; Norway: Universitetsforlaget, Avd. for offentlige publikasjoner, Postboks 8134 Dep., N-Oslo 1; Sweden: Liber distribution, Forlagsorder, S-16289 Stockholm; Iceland: Nordisk Rads delegation, Albingi, IS-Reykjavik.
Contact points: Nordic Statistical Secretariat, as above

OECD
Address: 2 rue André-Pascal, F-75775 Paris Cedex 16, France
Telephone: (1) 45248200 (orders (1) 45248167)
Telex: 620160 OCDE F
Obtaining publications: all orders should be addressed to OECD Publications Services at the main address above.
Guides to publications: OECD publications (annual catalogue) and quarterly supplements, Just out. News from OECD: monthly bulletin also lists publications appearing during the current month and is available regularly free on request.
Contact points: Publications Office

United Nations
Address: Palais des Nations, CH-1211 Geneva 10, Switzerland
Telephone: (022) 7346011 or 7310211
Telex: 289696
Obtaining publications: can be bought directly from the Sales Section in Geneva or from worldwide bookshops, agents or distributors (a list is available from the Sales Section, Geneva at the above address). The UK agent is HMSO, POB 276, London SW8 5DT (trade and mail orders only) or 49 High Holborn, London WC1V 6HB (callers only) and other HMSO bookshops.

Guides to publications: Catalogue of UN publications (annual, free, lists all publications currently in print of UN bodies and affiliated agencies whose publications are sold by the UN Sales Section. *UNDOC: current index (United Nations Documents Index)* is issued ten times a year and gives comprehensive coverage of UN documentation, on a subscription basis.
Contact points: Publishing Division/Sales Section at the Geneva address.

United Nations Conference on Trade and Development (UNCTAD)

Address: Palais des Nations, CH-1211 Geneva 10, Switzerland
Telephone: (022) 346011, 310211
Telex: 289696 CH
Obtaining publications: most UNCTAD documents are first issued as mimeographed documents, some of which are later reissued in printed from and become sales publications. Sales publications are obtained from the usual UN Sales Sections or agents (see main UN entry); occasional copies of mimeographed UNCTAD documents may be obtained from the UNCTAD Editorial Section at the address above (stocks permitting), quoting the document number. Subscription orders for mimeographed documents should be send directly to the Geneva Sales Section. The complete output of UNCTAD is also available on microfiche from UN Sales Sections.
Guides to publications: UNCTAD sales publications are included in the general *Catalogue of United Nations publications*. There is also an annual *Guide to UNCTAD publications* which contains entries in English, French and Spanish and is available from the UNCTAD Reference Unit, Conference Affairs Service, at the above address.

United Nations Educational, Scientific and Cultural Organisation (UNESCO)

Address: 7 place de Fontenoy, 75700 Paris, France
Telephone: (1) 45771610
Telex: 204461
Guides to publications: UNESCO publications are included in the general *Catalogue of United Nations publications* (see main UN entry).

The World Bank

Address: 1818 H Street NW, Washington, DC 20433, USA
Telephone: (202) 473 7561
Fax: (202) 473 8347
Obtaining publications: obtain directly from World Bank Publications, Box 7247-8619, Philadelphia, PA 19170-8619, USA.
Guides to publications: Index of publications available.

World Health Organisation (WHO)

Address: Avenue Appia, 1211 Geneva 27, Switzerland
Telephone: (022) 7912111
Telex: 415416
Fax: (22) 788 0401
Guides to publications: Catalogue of publications (free)

World Tourism Organisation (WTO)

Address: Capitan Haya 42, 28020 Madrid, Spain
Telephone: (91) 2792804, 2795107
Telex: 42188 OMT E
Guides to publications: Publications catalogue (annual, free)

3. National Statistical Offices

ALBANIA

State Planning Commission

Address: Tirana
Publisher of statistical series: N.I.S.H. Shtypshkronjave Mihal Duri (Mihal Duri State Printing House), Tirana
Obtaining publications: from state printing house above

AUSTRIA

Österreichisches Statistisches Zentralamt (Austrian Central Statistical Office)

Address: Hintere Zollamtsstrasse 2b, A-1033 Vienna
Telephone: (0222) 711 28/0
Telex: 0132600
Fax; 711 28/7728
Obtaining publications: orders to be sent to Österreichisches Statistisches Zentralamt, Informationsabteilung (address as above) or to Österreichischen Staatsdruckerei, Rennweg 12a, A-1037 Vienna, telephone (0222) 787631-39
Guides to publications: Publikationsangebot (half-yearly list of publications); there is also a booklet in English. *The Austrian Central Statistical Office,* published in 1978, which describes the history, legal basis, organisation etc.
Contact points: for enquiries and advice contact the Central Information Service (Informationsabteilung) at the address given above.

BELGIUM

Institut National de Statistique

Address: Rue de Louvain 44, B-1000 Brussels
Telephone: (02) 5139650 Ext. 306
Obtaining publications: from the above address; also on sale to callers at Place Albert 1er, 8e étage, B-6000 Charleroi, telephone (071) 328707 and Quai Marcellis 30, B-4020 Liège, telephone (041) 428070. Dutch language versions are on sale at Leuvenseweg 44, B-1000 Brussels, telephone (02) 5139650; Rubenslei 2, B-2018 Antwerp, telephone (03) 2311920; Coupure Rechts 620, B-9000 Ghent, telephone (091) 253273.
Guides to publications: L'Institut National de Statistique, (free); *Rapport des activités de l'Institut National de Statistique* (annual, free); *Catalogue des publications de l'Institut National de Statistique* plus monthly updatings (free).

BULGARIA

Central Statistical Office
Address: Council of Ministers, Panayot Volov St 2, Sofia
Telephone: 46-01
Telex: 22001

CYPRUS

Department of Statistics and Research
Address: Ministry of Finance, Nicosia
Telephone: (02) 303286
Telex: 3399
Fax: (02) 366080
Obtaining publications: from the Government Printing Office, Michael Karaoli Street, Nicosia; telephone (02) 40-2202, telex 3399 MINFIN CY
Guides to publications: Publications of the Department of Statistics and Research (priced); *Price list of recent publications of the Department of Statistics and Research* (free)

CZECHOSLOVAKIA

Federal Statistical Office
Address: Sokolovska 142, 18000 Prague 8
Telephone: (2) 814
Telex: 121197

DENMARK

Danmarks Statistik
Address: Sejrogade 11, DK-2100 Copenhagen O
Telephone: (31) 298222
Telex: 16236 DASTAT DK
Guides to publications: Vejviser i statistikken 198 (Guide to the statistics 1984); also annual report and work programme published each January, including information on scheduled new statistics and changes in current statistical series (free). There is also an annual list of publications in English, *Publications issued by Danmarks Statistik in 19...*
Contact points: for individual service for non-published statistics, and for general enquiries contact the Service Division. For individual monthly and quarterly data on exports/imports of particular commodities/groups and supply statistics (production plus imports minus exports) contact the External Trade Division.

EAST GERMANY

Central Statistical Office
Address: Council of Ministers, Klosterstrasse 47, 1020 Berlin
Telephone: 223
Telex: 1152337
Publisher of statistical series: Staatsverlag der DDR (Government Publishing Office), Otto Grotewohl Strasse 17, 1086 Berlin; telephone 2336336; telex 1152344

Obtaining publications: from Staatsverlag der DDR, see above

FINLAND

Central Statistical Office of Finland
Address: PO Box 504, SF-00101 Helsinki
Telephone: 1734535
Telex: 122656 TIKES SF
Obtaining publications: as above, or from Government Printing Centre, PO Box 516, SF-00101 Helsinki; also on sale at Government Printing Centre bookshops at Annankatu 44, Helsinki and Etelaesplanadi 4, Helsinki
Guides to publications: A catalogue, *Government statistics*, is published monthly and annually.
Contact points: for enquiries contact the Central Statistical Office Library, telephone 1734220, telex 122656

FRANCE

INSEE (Institut National de la Statistique et des Etudes Economiques)
Address: 18 boulevard Adolphe Pinard, Paris Cedex 14
Telephone: (1) 45401212
Telex: 204924 INSEEGD F
Obtaining publications: from INSEE at the above address, or if in France from the Observatoires Economiques Régionaux (Regional Economic Observatories), whose addresses appear in the INSEE catalogue; a network of 22 covers the whole of France.
Guides to publications: a detailed catalogue of publications is published annually. As well as the publications it gives details of all the functions and services of INSEE.
Contact points: INSEE Direction Générale at the above address or, if in France, the nearest regional economic observatory.

Ministère de l'Economie des Finances et du Budget, Direction Générale des Douanes et Droits Indirects, Centre de Renseignements Statistiques
Address: 192 rue Saint-Honoré, F-75001 Paris
Telephone: (1) 42615602
Guides to publications: Publications et adresses utiles (free)

GIBRALTAR

Statistical Department
Address: Government Secretariat, Gibraltar
Telephone: (0350) 70071
Telex: 2223

GREECE

National Statistical Service of Greece
Address: 14-16 Lycourgou Street, GR-10166 Athens
Telephone: (01) 32447846
Telex: 216734

HUNGARY

Kozponti Statisztikai Hivatal (Hungarian Central Statistical Office)
Address: Keleti Karoly u. 5-7, 1525 Budapest
Telephone: 135 8530
Telex: 224308

ICELAND

Statistical Bureau of Iceland
Address: Hverfisgata 8-10, 150 Reykjavik
Telephone: (91) 26699

IRELAND

Central Statistics Office
Address: St Stephen's Green House, Earlsfort Terrace, Dublin 2
Telephone: (01) 767531
Fax: (01) 682221
Obtaining publications: Personal purchases: Government Publications Sales Office, Sun Alliance House, Molesworth Street, Dublin 2, telephone (01) 710309. Trade and postal sales: Government Publications Office, Trade and Postal Sales, Bishop Street, Dublin 8, telephone (01) 781666. Fax (01) 780645
Guides to publications: Publication guide (annually) gives titles and descriptions of contents of publications and details of contact points for individual topics.
Contact points: there are two Statistical Divisions; for general information and information on economy and finance, agriculture, tourism, trade (imports/exports) and transport contact the main address as given above. For information on building and construction, demography, distribution and services, household budget, industry, labour and prices contact Central Statistics Office, Ardee Road, Rathmines, Dublin 6, telephone (01) 977144. Fax (01) 972360

ITALY

Istituto Centrale di Statistica (Istat)
Address: Via Cesare Balbo 16, I-00184 Rome
Telephone: (06) 4673 2384
Telex: 610338 ISTAT I
Publisher of statistical series: as above
Obtaining publications: from address above
Guides to publications: Catalogo 19.. (annual catalogue of publications with summaries of content)
Contact points: Centro Diffusione-Liberia Stat, Via Cesare Balbo 11a, 00184 Rome, telephone (06) 482 7666

LIECHTENSTEIN

Presse- und Informationsamt der Fürstlichen Regierung
Address: Regierungsgebäude, 9490 Vaduz
Telephone: (075) 66111
Telex: 889290

LUXEMBOURG

Service Central de la Statistique et des Etudes Economiques (STATEC)
Address: Boîte Postale 304 (19-21 boulevard Royal), L-2013 Luxembourg
Telephone: 4794-292/4794-276
Fax: 464289
Publisher of statistical series: STATEC
Obtaining publications: STATEC
Guides to publications: Répertoire analytique des publications du STATEC du 19e siècle à ce jour (annual); *Liste des publications du STATEC.*

MALTA

Central Office of Statistics
Address: Auberge d'Italie, Merchants Street, Valletta
Telephone: 224597
Telex: 1800

MONACO

Direction du Tourisme et des Congres
Address: Monte Carlo
Telephone: 304227
Notes: Monaco's external trade figures are included in those of France and are obtainable from INSEE (see France).

NETHERLANDS

Centraal Bureau voor de Statistiek (Netherlands Central Bureau of Statistics)
Address: Prinses Beatrixlaan 424, PO Box 959, NL-2270 AZ Voorburg
Telephone: (070) 3694341
Telex: 32692 CBS NL
Fax: (070) 3877429
(There is also an office at Kloosterweg 1, PO Box 4481, NL-6401 CZ Heerlen; telephone (045) 736666, telex 56724 CBS HR NL, fax (045) 727440)
Publisher of statistical series: Staatsuitgeverij, Christoffel Plantijnstraat 2, PO Box 20014, NL-2500 EA The Hague; telephone (070) 3789911
Obtaining publications: from publisher
Guides to publications: Systematic list of publications (last English edition 1988.). Annual Dutch edition, *Systematisch overzicht van de cbs-publikaties*, plus monthly updates of new publications.
Contact points: most subject fields covered at both offices, but Heerlen is the main base for foreign trade statistics, family and personal surveys, income and consumption, and Voorburg is the main base for agricultural statistics, prices, national accounts, population statistics and labour and wage statistics.

NORWAY

Statistisk Sentralbyrå (Central Bureau of Statistics)
Address: PO Box 8131 Dep, N-0033 Oslo 1
Telephone: (02) 864500

Telex: 11202
Fax: (02) 864973
Obtaining publications: Universitetsforlaget, Division for Publications, PO Box 2977, TOyen, -0608 Oslo 6, or local bookseller in any country. Subscriptions to weekly and monthly bulletins should be sent to the Central Bureau of Statistics.
Guides to publications: *Publications* (free annual brochure in English describing main series of publications); *Veiviser i norsk statistikk/Guide to Norwegian statistics* (free survey of official Norwegian statistics arranged by subject in Norwegian and English). There is also a historical survey in *Catalogue of Norwegian statistics and other publications published by the Central Bureau of Statistics 1828-1976*.
Contact points: Central Bureau of Statistics

POLAND

Glowny Urzad Statystyczny (Central Statistical Office)
Address: Al. Niepodlegosci 208, 00-925 Warsaw
Telephone: 252431
Telex: 814581

PORTUGAL

Instituto Nacional de Estatistica
Address: Avenida Antonio Jose de Almeida, P-1078 Lisbon CODEX
Telephone: (01) 802080 or 800364
Telex: 43719 PCDINE P
Obtaining publications: Imprensa Nacional - Casa da Moeda, R D Francisco Manuel de Melo 5, P-1000 Lisbon.
Guides to publications: current price lists available.
Contact points: INE, Servico de Documentacao at address above.

ROMANIA

Directia Centrala de Statistica (National Statistics Commission)
Address: Str. Stavropoleos 6, Bucharest
Telephone: 158200
Telex: 111153

SPAIN

Instituto Nacional de Estadistica
Address: Avenida de Generalismo 91, Madrid 16, Spain
Telephone: 5839100
Fax: 583 9486
Obtaining publications: Instituto Nacional de Estadistica, Paseo de la Castellana 183, 28046 Madrid, or, Libreria Lines-Chiel, Plaza Virgen del Romero 6, E-28027 Madrid
Guides to publications: *Publicaciones en existencia* (annual list of publications available); *Catalogo de la biblioteca del Instituto Nacional de Estadistica: Tomo I. Obras cientificas. Tomo II. Publicaciones estadisticas* (catalogue of the INE Library); *Catalogo descriptivo de las publicaciones estadisticas* (descriptive catalogue of statistical publications).
Contact points: main INE address. For enquiries from abroad there is a Servicio de Relaciones Internacionales.

Direccion General de Aduanas e Impuestos Especiales. Servicio de Publicaciones
Address: Guzman el Bueno 137, E-28071 Madrid
Publications: *Estadistica del comercio exterior. Comercio por productos y precios. Comercio por paises.* (annual)

SWEDEN

Statistiska Centralbyrån (Statistics Sweden)
Address: S-11581 Stockholm
Telephone: (08) 7834335
Telex: (54)5261 SWESTAT S
Fax: (08) 7834899
Obtaining publications: Statistics Sweden, Distribution, Box 902, S-70189 Orebo; telephone (019) 140320, telex 73170 SWESTAT S
Guides to publications: *Farska fakta och sorterade siffror* (free annual publications catalogue with summaries of contents, in Swedish only); *Arets tryck* (free annual list of the previous year's publications, with English introduction and titles translated into English).
Contact points: Information Service for postal or telephone enquiries on Swedish statistics or general enquiries on the SCB and its work; Distribution Section (at Orebo address) for information about publications.

SWITZERLAND

Bundesamt für Statistik/Office Fédéral de la Statistique/ Federal Statistical Office
Address: Hallwylstrasse 15, CH-3003 Berne
Telephone: (031) 618660
Telex: 32526 SLBBE CH
Fax: (031) 617856
Guides to publications: *Verzeichnis der Veröffentlichungen/Liste des publications, 1860-1985, Publiktionsverzeichnis/Liste des publications 1986-1989*

Eidg. Oberzolldirektion/ Direction générale des douanes/Directorate General of Customs, Trade Statistics Division
Address: Monbijoustrasse 40, CH-3003 Berne
Telephone: (031) 616525
Telex: 911100 CH
Guides to publications: sheet giving subscription details available

TURKEY

Economic Research Department
Address: Ankara
Telephone: (4) 118096

Telex: 42082
Guides to publications: subscriptions card available

UNION OF SOVIET SOCIALIST REPUBLICS

State Committee of Statistics of the USSR
Address: ul. Kirova 39, Moscow
Telephone: (095) 228 16 33

UNITED KINGDOM

Central Statistical Office
The CSO is the major collector of government statistics and also coordinates the Government Statistical Service, which embraces the statistics divisions of all major departments, and the Office of Population Censuses and Surveys, plus the CSO itself.
Address: Information Branch, (Press, Publications and Publicity), Room 65C/3, Government Offices, Great George Street, London SW1P 3AQ
Telephone: (071) 270 6363/6364
Publisher of statistical series: HMSO; some publications are published by individual Government departments - these are indicated where appropriate.
Obtaining publications: HMSO publications are obtainable from HMSO Publications Centre, PO Box 276, London SW8 5DT (mail and telephone orders only), telephone (071) 873 9090 (orders), (071) 873 0011 (general enquiries), telex 297138. Also from HMSO bookshops in London, Birmingham, Bristol, Manchester, Edinburgh and Belfast (postal orders and counter service, except for London, which is counter service only; London area postal orders should be sent to the HMSO Publications Centre at the address above). In many other large towns there is a bookseller who is an HMSO agent (for name of nearest agent ring HMSO general enquiries number above or consult Yellow Pages). Departmental publications are obtained from the departments and details are given with individual publications below.
Guides to publications: Government statistics: a brief guide to sources (free annual booklet, obtainable from the CSO at address above); *Guide to official statistics* (this is a substantial guide to official and significant non-official sources, arranged by topic with a keyword index); *HMSO publishes the CSO* (free CSO publications catalogue); *HMSO Books: guide to publications and services* (free brochure). Full HMSO catalogues are also available on subscription, including: *Daily list; Monthly catalogue; Annual catalogue; Consolidated indexes* (five-yearly indexes of HMSO publications). There are also free sectional lists updated at regular intervals, which are catalogues based on the divisions of responsibility between departments. Most HMSO titles are also listed on Prestel (Prestel number 50040) on the day of publication with details displayed for one week, and can be ordered via Prestel (further details from Bibliographic Services Manager, HMSO Books, 51 Nine Elms Lane, London SW8 5DR). Quarterly microfiche listings of all HMSO publications are also available on subscription, and online access to HMSO's

bibliographic database is available. Non-official guides include the following: *Directory of British official publications: a guide to sources,* 2nd ed, Mansell Publishing, 1984; *Catalogue of British official publications not published by HMSO,* published by Chadwyck-Healey of Cambridge every two months; *Reviews of United Kingdom statistical sources,* a series published by Pergamon Press covering statistics in various subject areas.
Contact points: for general publications and order enquiries see under heading for obtaining publications. For free HMSO catalogues/information leaflets contact HMSO Books, Publicity Department, St Crispins, Duke Street, Norwich NR3 1PD, telephone (0603) 622211 ext 6498. For enquiries on statistics, departmental responsibilities and contact points are listed in *Government statistics: a brief guide to sources;* in case of difficulty in finding the right contact telephone or write to the CSO at the main address given above or at, Cardiff Road, Newport, Gwent NP9 1XG, telephone (0633) 812973, telex 497121, fax (0633) 812599

National Economic Development Office (NEDO)
National Economic Development Council (NEDC)
Economic Development Committees (EDCs)
These bodies together form Neddy, and are included here although they are not government bodies, but organisations which bring together government, management and trade unions.
Address: Millbank Tower, Millbank, London SW1P 4QX
Telephone: (071) 217 4000
Obtaining publications: from NEDO Books at the address above, telephone (071) 217 4036/4037. Most publications are priced.
Guides to publications: Neddy books and videos (annual catalogue of all reports, videos and films available from Neddy, with a six-month supplement).
Contact points: NEDO Books for enquiries on publications; otherwise individual bodies forming Neddy.

WEST GERMANY

Statistisches Bundesamt
Address: Gustav-Stresemann-Ring 11, D-6200 Wiesbaden 1
Telephone: (06121) 751
Telex: 4186511 STB D
Fax: (0611) 753425
Also offices in West Berlin and Düsseldorf: Zweigestelle Berlin, Kurfürstenstrasse 87, D-1000 Berlin 30; telephone (030) 260030; fax (030) 26003-734. Aussenstelle Düsseldorf, Hüttenstrasse 5a, D-4000 Düsseldorf 1; telephone (0211) 38411-0; fax (0211) 38411-28
Publisher of statistical series: Verlag metzler-Poeschel, Kernerstrasse43, D-7000 Stuttgart 10
Obtaining publications: from booksellers or direct from the publishers Verlag Metzler-Poeschel, Delivery: Messrs Herman Leins, Holzwiesenstr. 2, Postfach 7, D-7408 Kusterdingen. Telephone: (07071) 33046, fax (07071) 33653.

Guides to publications: Veröffentlichungsverzeichnis. Stand 1. Januar 19.. (annual list of publications, also available in English and French versions); *Das Arbeitsgebiet der Bundesstatistik* (much more detailed survey of the work of the Federal Statistical Office and guide to publications, also available in abridged English version; English version entitled *Survey of German Federal Statistics*). In addition, all new publications are announced weekly in the *Bundesanzeiger* (Federal Advertiser), and in *Statistischer Wochendienst* (Information on statistics weekly), and monthly in *Wirtschaft und Statistik* (Economics and statistics).
Contact points: Allgemeiner Auskunftsdienst (General Information Service)

YUGOSLAVIA

Savezni Zavod za Statistiku (Federal Statistical Office)
Address: Kneza Milosa 20, 11000 Belgrade
Telephone: 681999
Telex: 11317
Fax: (11) 642368

4. Major Business Libraries

ALBANIA

National Library
Address: Tirana
Telephone: 5887
Stock: over 800,000 volumes

AUSTRIA

Ministerialbibliothek des Bundesministeriums für Finanzen (Library of the Ministry of Finance)
Address: Himmelpfortgasse 4, A-1015 Vienna
Telephone: (01) 51433/1247
Stock: covers economy, law, administration, taxes and customs, banking relating to Austria and Germany. Material in German. 270,000 books, 550 journals, Austrian company annual reports, Austrian company directories, trade journals and statistics

Österreichische Nationalbibliothek
Address: Josefsplatz 1, A-1015 Vienna
Telephone: (01) 525255/524686
Telex: 12624 OENB A
Stock: includes all publications published or printed in Austria, and literature published abroad concerning Austria or written by Austrian authors. 2,490,000 volumes of printed books and 10,475 current periodicals

Österreichisches Statistisches Zentralamt Bibliothek
Address: Hintere Zollamtsstrasse 2b, PO Box 9000, A-1033 Vienna

Telephone: (01) 71128/7800/7804
Fax: (01) 71128/7728
Telex: 132600
Stock: stocks official statistics of Austria and other countries. 170,000 volumes and microfiche

Universitätsbibliothek Graz
Address: Universitätsplatz 3, A-8010 Graz
Telephone: (0316) 3803100
Telex: 311662 UBGRZ
Stock: general collections, particularly scientific. Stock mainly in German and English with international and European coverage. 1,107,774 books, 4,148 journals, 50 national and international newspapers, annual reports for European countries, German and Austrian company and trade directories, international statistics

Wiener Stadt- und Landesbibliothek
Address: Rathaus, 4. Stiege, 1. Stock, Zimmer 333, A-1082 Vienna
Telephone: (01) 42800/42809

Zentrale Verwaltungsbibliothek und Dokumentation für Wirtschaft und Technik, Vertragsbibliothek der Europäischen Gemeinschaften
Address: Stubenring 1, A-1011 Vienna
Telephone: (01) 711005481
Stock: covers the EC and trade and commerce. Material mainly in German. 165,000 volumes, 360 journals, Austrian official statistics

BELGIUM

Antwerp University Library
Address: St.-Ignatius University Faculties, Prinsstraat 9, B-2000 Antwerp
Telephone: (03) 2316660/69
Telex: 33599 UFSIA B
Stock: 435,000 volumes, including periodicals, 3,600 current periodicals and annuals. Collections related to the four university faculties (Philosophy and letters, Law, Political and social sciences, Applied economic sciences), particularly strong in applied economic sciences, including marketing and business information.

Bibliotheek voor Hedendaagse Dokumentatie
Address: Parklaan 2, B-2700 Sint Niklaas
Telephone: (03) 7765063
Fax: (03) 7780785
Stock: private and independent library on social, economic and political matters with a special collection on science, technology and industry. Stock is international in coverage and 80% in English. 120,000 books, 4,100 journals and newspapers, 400 trade journals, 2,000 annual reports, company and trade directories, and audio-visual material

Bibliothèque Fonds Quetelet (Central Library of the Ministry of Foreign Affairs)
Address: Rue de l'Industrie 6, B-1040 Brussels
Telephone: (02) 5111930

Stock: covers economic and social sciences. 700,000 volumes, 7,000 journals

Bibliothèque Royale Albert I
Address: Boulevard de l'Empereur 4, B-1000 Brussels
Telephone: (02) 5195357
Stock: all publications produced in Belgium and Belgian and foreign publications in all fields of knowledge. Section on official documents includes publications of the UN and some of its agencies, the European Community, the OECD, Council of Europe and Benelux. National official publications are held in the general reading room.

Institut National de Statistique, Service des Renseignements et de la Documentation Générale
Address: Rue de Louvain 44, B-1000 Brussels
Telephone: (02) 5139650
Stock: all Belgian official statistical publications. Material in French and Dutch

Rijksuniversitair Centrum Antwerpen-Bibliotheek (RUCA)
Address: Middelheimlaan 1, B-2020 Antwerp
Telephone: (03) 2180790
Fax: (03) 2180652
Stock: about 70,000 volumes on general, business, industrial and transport economics, foreign trade, management, accountancy; special collection covering the Third World. Material in Dutch, English, French and German. 100 trade journals, 1,000 other periodicals, company and trade directories on Benelux and Germany, national and European statistical publications; national and international financial newspapers (last 5 years)

BULGARIA

Centre for Scientific, Technical and Economic Information
Address: 1113 Sofia, V. Lenin 125
Stock: collections on industry and agriculture

Cyril and Methodius National Library
Address: Boul. Tolbouhin 11, 1504 Sofia
Telephone: 882811
Telex: 22432
Stock: largest public scientific library in Bulgaria with over 2.5 million volumes; serves as the national bibliographic and information centre. Stock includes over 1.6 million books and periodicals.

Sofia City and District State Archives
Address: Ul. Vitosa 2, 1000 Sofia
Stock: ca. 340,000 dossiers.

Sofia University Library
Address: Boul. Ruski 15, 1504 Sofia
Telephone: 443719
Stock: ca. 1.3 million volumes

CYPRUS

American Center Library
Address: 33B Homer Avenue, Nicosia
Stock: lending and reference library with ca. 6,000 volumes

British Council Library
Address: PO Box 5654, Museum St 3, Nicosia
Telephone: 442152
Telex: 3911
Stock: ca. 25,000 volumes and periodicals

CZECHOSLOVAKIA

Knihovny Fakult a Ustavu Univerzity Karlovy (Charles University Libraries)
Address: Ovocny trh 5,11636 Prague 1
Stock: 2.7 million volumes, including ca. 10,000 periodicals

Statni Knihovna Ceske Socialisticke Republiky (State Library of the Czech Socialist Party)
Address: Klementinum 190, 11001 Prague 1
Telephone: 266541
Telex: 121207
Stock: central Czech research library with ca. 5.5 million volumes; collection of microfilms. Incorporates the Central Economic Library with 780,000 volumes.

Statni Technicka Knihovna (State Technical Library)
Address: Klementinum 190, 11307 Prague
Telephone: 265721
Telex: 122214
Stock: includes over 500,000 items of trade literature, 4,000 periodicals, microfiche and microfilm collections.

DENMARK

Danmarks Statistik
Address: The Library, Sejrogade 11, Postboks 2550, DK-2100 Copenhagen
Telephone: 31298222
Fax: 31184801
Telex: 16236
Stock: covers official statistics from all countries and from the most important international organisations. 185,000 books

Gentofte Kommunebibliotek (Municipal Library of Gentofte, County Library, County of Copenhagen)
Address: Ahlmanns Alle 6, DK-2900 Hellerup
Telephone: 31627500
Telex: 19887
Stock: book collection of approximately 700,000 volumes, including a good collection of economic literature

Handelshojskolens Bibliotek (Copenhagen School of Economics and Business Administration Library)
Address: Rosenörns Alle 31, DK-1970 Copenhagen C
Telephone: 31396677

Stock: covers accounting, advertising, banking and finance, computer science, foreign trade, law, marketing, statistics etc. Over 200,000 volumes and 3,000 periodicals

Handelshojskolens Bibliotek - Århus (Library of the Århus Business School)
Address: Fuglesangsallé 4, DK-8210 Århus V
Telephone: 86155588
Fax: 4586150188
Stock: covers marketing, foreign trade, management, economics, statistics and company information. Material in Danish and English, international in coverage but with the emphasis on Europe. 140,000 books, 800 journals, company reports, statistics, EC publications

Kongelige Bibliotek, Det (The Royal Library)
Address: Postboks 2149, DK-1016 Copenhagen K
Telephone: 33930111
Fax: 33329846
Telex: 15009
Stock: Danish national library, university library and principal research library for the humanities, social sciences and theology. Collections include all literature printed or published in Denmark as well as foreign literature about Denmark. The Office of International Publications has collections from the EC, UN, GATT, ILO, NATO, OECD, Unesco and the Council of Europe

EAST GERMANY

Deutsche Staatsbibliothek
Address: Unter den Linden 8, 1086 Berlin
Telephone: 20780
Telex: 112757
Stock: ca. 6.6 million volumes including 10,700 periodicals

Universitätsbibliothek der Technischen Universität
Address: Mommsenstrasse 13, 8027 Dresden
Telephone: 4634308
Telex: 02278
Stock: ca. 1.3 million volumes including 5,300 periodicals and collection of 60,000 industrial and commercial literature

Deutsche Bücherei
Address: Deutscher Platz, 7010 Leipzig
Telephone: 88120
Telex: 51562
Stock: ca. 8 million volumes

FINLAND

Central Statistical Office (Library of Statistics)
Address: POB 504, SF-00101 Helsinki
Telephone: (90) 17342220
Fax: (90) 17342279
Teletex: 1002111 TILASTO SF
Stock: Finnish and foreign national statistics and

statistics from international organisations; collection of Old Russian statistics 1847-1917. Material mostly in Finnish, Swedish, English, French, Spanish, Italian, German, Russian. 220,000 volumes, 1,300 Finnish periodicals, 3,500 foreign periodicals, annual reports of Finnish companies, 29,000 microfiches

Helsingin Kauppakorkeakoulun Kirjasto (Helsinki School of Economics Library)
Address: Runeberginkatu 22-24, SF-00100 Helsinki
Telephone: (90) 4313425
Fax: (90) 4313539
Telex: 122220 ECON SF
Stock: the library is the national resource centre for economics and business sciences. 240,000 books, 1,600 periodicals, company and trade directories, company reports, dissertations and statistics. International in coverage with an emphasis on the English language

FRANCE

Bibliothèque de la Direction Générale de l'INSEE
Address: 18 boulevard Adolphe Pinard, F-75675 Paris Cedex 14
Telephone: (1) 45401212
Telex: 204924 INSEE F
Stock: this is the library of the national statistical service. There are 12,000 linear meters of statistical and economic material and related subjects.

Bibliothèque nationale et universitaire de Strasbourg
Address: 5 rue du Maréchal Joffre, BP 1029/F, F-67070 Strasbourg Cedex
Telephone: 88360068
Stock: covers all disciplines

Centre d'enseignement supérieur des affaires
Address: 1 rue de la Libération, F-78350 Jouy-en-Josas
Telephone: 39568000
Telex: 697942
Stock: about 45,000 volumes and 480 current periodicals

Centre Georges Pompidou, Bibliothèque publique d'information
Address: rue Beaubourg, F-75191 Paris Cedex 04
Telephone: (1) 47741233
Telex: 212726 CNACGP F
Stock: about 360,000 volumes covering all disciplines, and about 2,100 current periodicals, of which about 30% are foreign. Relevant sections include business management, industry, statistics, official publications, demography, economics, as well as a reference section containing directories etc.

Chambre de Commerce et d'Industrie, Centre de Documentation/ Bibliothèque
Address: Palais de la Bourse, La Canebière, PO Box 1856, F-13222 Marseille
Telephone: 91919151

Fax: 91914225
Telex: 410091
Stock: covers law, marine transport, economics, management, commerce and finance. Material mainly in French, relating to France and Africa. 120,000 books, several hundred journals, French company reports, market research reports, company and trade directories, statistical publications

Chambre de Commerce et d'Industrie de Marseille, Centre International d'Information
Address: 2 Rue Henri Barbusse, F-13241 Marseille Cedex 01
Telephone: 91393357
Telex: 441247 COMERIM
Fax: 91393360
Stock: covers international trade. 2,500 books, 590 journals, newspapers, annual reports, market research reports, company and trade directories, statistical publications

Cours des Comptes, Bibliothèque (Library of the Audit Office)
Address: 13 rue Cambon, F-75100 Paris
Telephone: (1) 42989714
Stock: about 50,000 volumes and 700 periodicals on finance, law and economics

Université de Paris IX-Dauphine Bibliothèque
Address: Place du Maréchal de Lattre de Tassigny, F-75775 Paris Cedex 16
Telephone: (1) 45051410
Stock: covers economics, management, mathematics, data processing and social sciences. Material in French and English. 90,000 books, 2,000 journals, national and international newspapers, French company reports, company and trade directories, statistical publications, audiovisual material and computer programs

GIBRALTAR

Gibraltar Library Service
Address: 308 Main Street, Gibraltar
Telephone: 78000
Stock: ca. 30,000 volumes

GREECE

American Library
Address: 22 Massalias St, GR-10680 Athens
Telephone: (01) 3637740/3638114
Fax: (01) 3642986
Stock: covers social sciences, arts and humanities, international relations, technology. Material mainly in English. 12,000 books, 160 journals, newspapers, statistical publications

Athens Graduate School of Economics and Business Sciences
Address: 76 Patission Street, GR-10434 Athens
Telephone: (01) 8237361/8237345/8221456
Telex: 225363 ASOE GR
Stock: 50,000 titles and 450 current periodicals on

economics, business, mathematics, statistics, econometrics, operational research, business administration and law. Includes serial publications of the national statistical organisation and international organisations (EEC, OECD, UN, ILO and IMF).

ESYE (National Statistical Service of Greece Library)
Address: 14-16 Lycourgou, (3rd Floor), GR-10552 Athens
Telephone: (01) 3241102
Fax: (01) 322205
Telex: 216734
Stock: covers statistical data, statistical theory, demography, economics. Material mainly in Greek. 4,500 - 5,000 volumes and ca. 2,000 statistical series including all Greek statistical publications, those from several foreign countries and international organisations; 160 journals mainly on statistics and demography, 5 local newspapers, microforms

National Library of Greece
Address: 32 Panepistimiou Street, Athens
Telephone: (01) 3614413
Stock: aims to cover every field of knowledge

HUNGARY

Kozponti Statisztikai Hivatal Konyvtar es Dokumentacios Szolgalat (Library and Documentation Service of the Central Statistical Office)
Address: Keleti Karoly u. 5,1024 Budapest
Telephone: 1358530
Telex: 224308
Stock: exchange centre for official statistical publications; ca. 580,000 books and periodicals

Marx Karoly Kozgazdasagtudomanyi Egyetem Kozponti Konyvtara (Central Library of the Karl Marx University of Economic Sciences)
Address: Zsil u. 2, 1093 Budapest
Telephone: 1175827
Telex: 224186
Stock: ca. 530,000 volumes

Orszaggyulesi Konyvtar (Library of the Hungarian Parliament)
Address: Kossuth Lajos-ter 1-3, 1357 Budapest
Telephone: 1125273
Telex: 227463
Stock: 600,000 volumes; UN depository library

Orszagos Muszaki Informacios Kozpont es Konyvtar (National Technical Information Centre and Library)
Address: Muzeum u. 17, 1428 Budapest
Telephone: (36) 1382300
Telex: 224944
Stock: ca. 450,000 volumes and 6,000 current periodicals

Orszagos Szechenyi Konyvtar (National Szechenyi Library)
Address: Budavari Palota F-epulet, 1827 Budapest
Telephone: 556167
Telex: 224226
Stock: ca. 2.4 million books and periodicals and ca. 4 million manuscripts, maps, prints, microfilms etc

ICELAND

Landsbokasafn Islands (National Library of Iceland)
Address: Reykjavik
Stock: ca. 380,000 volumes

IRELAND

Central Statistics Office Library
Address: St Stephen's Green House, Earlsfort Terrace, Dublin 2
Telephone: (01) 767531
Fax: (01) 682221
Stock: statistics on demography, agriculture, industry, economics, finance, distribution and tourism. 1,500 books, Irish, EC and OECD statistics, Irish company reports

Dublin Public Libraries, Business Information Centre
Address: ILAC, Henry Street, Dublin 1
Telephone: (01) 733996
Fax: (01) 721451
Telex: 33287
Stock: general coverage of business. Material in English with wide international coverage. 15,000 books, 300 journals, national and international newspapers, Irish and some UK trade journals, Irish and some international statistics, company and trade directories, annual reports and press cuttings for Irish companies, some market research and stockbrokers' reports

Economic and Social Research Institute
Address: 4 Burlington Road, Dublin 4
Telephone: (01) 760115
Stock: Holdings of about 45,000 items cover economics, sociology, statistics, social psychology and include books, periodicals, annual reports etc of national and international origin

James Hardiman Library
Address: University College, Galway
Telephone: (091) 24411
Telex: 28831 UNIG EI
Stock: about 200,000 volumes covering arts, commerce, law, medicine, science and engineering

Trinity College Library Information Service
Address: Trinity College Library, College Street, Dublin 2
Telephone: (01) 772941
Telex: 25442 TCD EI
Stock: access to entire College library, which includes British and Irish copyright intake. Official publications:

Irish, British, EEC and the majority of UN publications. Many well known indexing services and a worldwide range of company directories.

University College Dublin Library
Address: Belfield, Dublin 4
Telephone: (01) 693244
Telex: 93207
Stock: about 750,000 books and pamphlets and 8,000 current periodical titles. Holdings include an extensive collection of books and periodicals on business studies, including annual reports of Irish companies, McCarthy's Information Service (Industry section and small Irish company section), Extel UK listed companies service, collection of UCD MBS/MBA theses.

ITALY

Biblioteca Nazionale Braidense
Address: Via Brera 28, I-20121 Milan
Telephone: (02) 808345
Fax: (02) 72023910
Stock: general stock covering all disciplines. Material mainly in Italian. Ca. 1 million volumes, local and main national newspapers, microforms of catalogues and newspapers

Biblioteca Nazionale Centrale di Firenze
Address: Piazza Cavalleggeri 1, I-50122 Florence
Telephone: (055) 244441/42/43
Stock: large general collection including section on economic sciences and separate periodicals room. Subject catalogue with 30,000 main headings.

Biblioteca Nazionale Centrale Vittorio Emanuele II
Address: Viale Castro Pretorio 105, I-00185 Rome
Telephone: (06) 4989
Stock: the library is a general one, but with a biais towards the humanities and literature; it is a copyright library, receiving all Italian publications by legal deposit. Holds about 4 million volumes, including books, periodicals and newspapers.

Biblioteca Nazionale Vittorio Emanuele III
Address: Palazzo Reale, I-80100 Naples
Telephone: (081) 402842
Stock: economic and business material contained in "Sezione Moderna"

LUXEMBOURG

Bibliothèque Nationale
Address: 37 Boulevard F.-D.-Roosevelt, L-2450 Luxembourg
Telephone: 26255
Stock: 600,000 volumes, mainly concerning humanities. Special Luxemburgensia collection (approximately 150,000 volumes). 2,300 foreign periodicals and 1,000 Luxembourg periodicals.

Bibliothèque de la Ville
Address: 26 Rue E.-Mayrisch, Esch-sur-Alzette
Telephone: 547383/495
Stock: literature in French, German, English and Italian, all disciplines, Luxemburgensia

Centre Universitaire - Bibliothèque
Address: 162A Avenue de la Faiencerie, L-1511 Luxembourg
Telephone: 21621
Stock: total stock of about 100,000 books and periodicals covering literature, philosophy, history, social sciences,
economics, law, linguistics, natural sciences, generalia and dictionaries, etc.

MALTA

National Library of Malta
Address: Old Treasury Street, Valletta
Telephone: 224338

University of Malta Library
Address: Msida
Telephone: 314306
Telex: 407
Stock: ca. 300,000 volumes

MONACO

Bibliothèque Louis Notari
Address: 8 rue Louis Notari, Monte Carlo
Telephone: 309509
Stock: ca. 150,000 volumes

NETHERLANDS

Central Bureau of Statistics Library
Address: Prinses Beatrixlaan 428, PO Box 959, NL-2270 AZ Voorburg
Telephone: (070) 3694341
Fax: (070) 3694341
Telex: 32692 CBS NL
Stock: economic and social statistics from all over the world

Erasmus University Library Rotterdam
Address: Burgemeester Oudlaan 50, PO Box 1738, NL-3000 DR Rotterdam
Telephone: (010) 525511
Stock: 600,000 volumes. Strong emphasis on economics, management and law. Also sociology, political sciences, history and philosophy. Separate reading rooms for economics, statistics and periodicals

Gemeente Bibliotheek Rotterdam, afd.
Bedrijfsinformatie (City Library Rotterdam, Business Information Department)
Address: Hoogstraat 110, NL-3011 PV Rotterdam
Telephone: (010) 4338911
Fax: (010) 4338338
Stock: provides business information for small and

medium sized businesses. Material in Dutch and English, covering the Western world, Japan and China. 1,500 books, 150 journals, Dutch trade journals, national and international newspapers, Dutch official statistics, company and trade directories, microforms (Dutch company reports, American telephone directories)

Koninklijke Bibliotheek (Royal Library - National Library of the Netherlands)
Address: PO Box 90407, 2509 LK The Hague
Telephone: (070) 3140911
Fax: (070) 3140450
Telex: 34402 KBNL
Stock: the Royal Library is a research library which concentrates on the humanities: social sciences, law, history, art, language and literature, theology, philosophy, bibliography and library science. 3 million volumes

Netherlands Foreign Trade Agency (EVD)
Address: 151 Bezuidenhoutseweg, NL-2594 AG The Hague
Telephone: (070) 3798933
Telex: 31099 ECOZA NL
Stock: 150,000 monographs and reports, 1,800 periodicals, 3,800 directories

The Hague Public Library
Address: Bilderdijkstraat 1, NL-2513 CM The Hague
Telephone: (070) 3469235
Stock: general stock including 780,000 volumes of adult books

NORWAY

Bergen University Library
Address: N-5000 Bergen
Telephone: (05) 212500
Telex: 42690 UBB N
Stock: about 1,200,000 volumes on humanities, science, medicine, social sciences and law

Norges Handelshöyskole Biblioteket (Library of the Norwegian School of Economics and Business Administration)
Address: Helleveien 30, N-5035 Bergen Sandviken
Telephone: (05) 959222
Fax: (05) 258100
Stock: covers accounting, auditing, data processing, finance, industrial economics, labour relations, management, statistics, petroleum economics. Material mainly in English and Scandinavian languages. 225,000 books, 1,200 journals, Norwegian and some international statistics, company and trade directories, Norwegian company information

Norges Tekniske Universitetsbibliotek (The Technical University Library of Norway)
Address: N-7034 Trondheim
Telephone: (07) 595110
Telex: 55186 NTHHBN

Fax: (07) 595103
Stock: science and technology, industrial economics, art and architecture. Material mainly in English. 1 million books, 8,000 journals, local, national and international newspapers, patents, standards and microforms

Statistisk Sentralbyrå, Biblioteket (Central Bureau of Statistics Library)
Address: PO Box 8131 Dep, N-0033 Oslo 1
Telephone: (02) 413820
Stock: approximately 160,000 volumes. Main subjects: economics, statistics, demography, with a special collection of statistical publications

POLAND

Biblioteka Glowna Politechniki Lodzkiej (Central Library of Lodz Technical University)
Address: Zeromskiego 116, 90543 Lodz
Stock: ca. 225,000 volumes and 98,000 periodicals covering most disciplines

Biblioteka Narodowa (National Library)
Address: Ul. Hankiewicza 1, 00973 Warsaw
Telephone: 224621
Telex: 817183
Stock: ca. 4 million volumes including periodicals; also houses the Bibliographical Institute and the Institute of Books and Public Reading

Biblioteka Sejmowa (Library of the Polish Parliament)
Address: ul. Wiejska 4, 00902 Warsaw
Telephone: 288545
Telex: 812544
Stock: ca. 225,000 volumes including 65,800 periodicals; covers official publications, economic, social, legal and political collections, international publications

Biblioteka Szkoly Glownej Planowania i Statystyki (Library of the Central School of Planning and Statistics)
Address: ul. Rakowiecka 22B, 02521 Warsaw
Telephone: 495098
Stock: ca. 600,000 volumes including 156,500 periodicals

Centralna Biblioteka Statystyczna (Central Statistical Library)
Address: Al. Niepodleglosci 208, 00925 Warsaw
Telephone: 250345
Telex: 816059
Stock: 350,000 volumes; emphasis on scientific, economic and social statistics

PORTUGAL

Biblioteca Nacional
Address: Campo Grande 83, P-1751 Lisbon Codex
Telephone: (01) 767639/764720

Fax: (01) 733607
Telex: 62803 BN P
Stock: general library but good coverage in social sciences and the humanities. Material mainly in Portuguese, covering Portugal. 2 million books, 50,000 journals, Portuguese official statistics, Portuguese company and trade directories

Instituto de Apoio às Pequenas e Médias Empresas e ao Investimento, Euro Info Centre
Address: Rua do Valasco 19C, P-7000 Evora
Telephone: (066) 21875/6
Fax: (066) 29781
Stock: covers EC matters concerning small and medium sized enterprises, international co-operation, grants and loans and technology transfer. EC and Eurostat publications, Portuguese company reports

Instituto Nacional de Estatistica Biblioteca
Address: Instituto Nacional de Estatistica Serviço de Documentaçao, Avenida Antonio José de Almeida, P-1078 Lisbon Codex
Telephone: (01) 8470050
Fax: (01) 8489480
Telex: 63738 PCDINE P
Stock: holds all publications of the National Statistical Institute

Porto Biblioteca Publica Municipal (Oporto Public Municipal Library)
Address: Passeio de S. Lazaro, P-4099 Porto Codex
Telephone: (02) 572147/565361/573147
Stock: about 1,300,000 volumes on all subjects, as this library receives the Portuguese copyright intake

ROMANIA

Biblioteca Centrala de Stat (Central State Library)
Address: Str. Ion Ghica 4, Bucharest
Stock: ca. 7.9 million volumes; acts as Copyright Deposit and Centre of Bibliographical Information

Biblioteca Institutului National de Informare si Documentare (Library of the National Institute for Information and Documentation)
Address: Str. Cosmonautilor 27-29, Sector 1, 70141 Bucharest
Telephone: 134010
Telex: 11247
Stock: ca. 650,000 volumes including 88,000 periodicals

SPAIN

Instituto de Estudios Fiscales Biblioteca
Address: Paseo del Prado 6, E-28014 Madrid
Telephone: (91) 2228519
Stock: 48,426 books, 11,720 pamphlets and 803 periodicals on public finance, economics and law, comparative fiscal law. Collections include foreign tax and trade briefs, guides to European taxation - taxation

of companies in Europe, taxation of patents royalties, dividends, interest in Europe etc

Instituto de Información en Ciencias Sociales y Humanidades (ISOC) del C.S.I.C. (Institute for Information and Documentation in Social Sciences and Humanities)
Address: Vitrubio 4, E-28006 Madrid
Telephone: (91) 4110244
Fax: (91) 5645069
Stock: covers all social sciences and humanities, including business and economics. Holds all Spanish journals in the social sciences and humanities field since 1975. 2,000 journal titles, 600 in the field of economics and business

Ministerio de Hacienda, Archivo Central y Biblioteca
Address: Calle de Alcala 11, E-28014 Madrid
Telephone: (91) 4682000
Stock: covers economics, finance and law

SWEDEN

Malmö Stadsbibliotek
Address: Regementsgatan 3, S-211 Malmö
Telephone: 77810
Stock: public library but with good coverage of business information and local information. 925,994 volumes, 1,650 journals, trade journals, statistics, Swedish company reports, company and trade directories

Riksdagsbiblioteket (Library of the Swedish Parliament)
Address: Riksdagen, S-10012 Stockholm
Telephone: (08) 7864000
Fax: (08) 218878
Telex: 10184 PARLBIB S
Stock: about 500,000 volumes and 2,600 periodical titles, of which 1,300 are from abroad. Specialises in political, economic and social sciences, and coverage includes economics, business and industry. Special collections include official publications, publications issued by the UN and its specialised agencies, the OECD, the Council of Europe, the Nordic Council, the EC and other international organisations.

Statistika Centralbyrån Biblioteket (Statistics Sweden, Library)
Address: Karlavägen 100, S-11581 Stockholm
Telephone: (08) 7835066
Fax: (08) 6615261
Telex: 15261 SWESTAT
Stock: covers official statistics from over 170 countries throughout the world. Also contains non-official statistics for Sweden. Material in all national languages.

Stockholms Stadsbibliotek (Stockholm Public Library)
Address: Box 6502, S-11383 Stockholm
Telephone: (08) 236600
Telex: 19478 STOCTEK S

Stock: about 2 million books, 160,000 AV-media, 1,500 newspapers and periodicals covering all subjects

SWITZERLAND

Bundesamt für Statistik, Bibliothek/ Office Fédéral de la Statistique, Bibliothèque (Federal Statistical Office Library)
Address: Hallwylstrasse 15, CH-3003 Bern
Telephone: (031) 618628
Telex: 32526 SIBBE CH
Fax: (031) 617856
Stock: covers statistics, economics, social sciences, applied sciences and the environment. 200,000 books, 2,700 journals

Schweizerische Landesbibliothek/ Bibliothèque Nationale Suisse
Address: Hallwylstrasse 15, CH-3003 Bern
Telephone: (031) 618911
Telex: 32526 SLBBE CH
Stock: about 1.5 million items of 'Helvetica': books and periodicals written by Swiss authors, both in the original language and in translation, all books dealing with Switzerland, the entire book production of the country. This includes journals and periodicals, including those of institutions and firms, and official publications; there is a periodicals catalogue and a catalogue of official publications.

Universität Zürich, Zentrale für Wirtschaftsdokumentation
Address: Wiesenstrasse 9, CH-8008 Zürich
Telephone: (01) 3835850
Stock: covers economics, energy, labour market, industry, science, technology, finance, banking, insurance, accountancy, regional development, transport and tourism. Material in German, English and French, worldwide in coverage. 15,000 books, 270 journals, 3,000 Swiss company reports, 500 foreign company reports, OECD statistical publications, 130,000 press cuttings

Zentralbibliothek Zürich, Kantons-, Stadt- und Universitätsbibliothek (Zurich Central Library, Canton, City and University Library)
Address: Zähringerplatz 6, CH-8025 Zürich
Telephone: (01) 2617272
Fax: (01) 2620373
Stock: all subjects covered in university curriculi. Material mainly in German, English, French and Italian. 2.45 million volumes, ca. 9,000 current periodicals, 150 newspapers (mostly local), general trade directories covering Switzerland and major European countries, statistical yearbooks of main European countries and international organisations. Microfilm collection: The Goldsmiths'-Kress library of economic literature; Saitzew collection: historic literature on economic theory

TURKEY

Bogazici University Library
Address: P.K. 2, Bebek, Istanbul
Telephone: 1631500 ext 739
Telex: 26411 BOUN TR
Stock: 200,000 volumes on all subjects; special collection on the Near East

National Library
Address: 06490 Bahcelievler, Ankara
Telephone: 90 9 4 2224158
Stock: depository library; open to researchers and students

UNION OF SOVIET SOCIALIST REPUBLICS

Krupskaya N.K., State Public Library of the Moldavian SSR
Address: Kievskaya ul. 78-a, 277612 Kishinev
Telephone: 221475
Stock: ca. 3 million volumes; national and principal depository library of the Moldavian SSR

State V.I. Lenin Library of the USSR
Address: 3 Pr. Kalinina, 101000 Moscow
Telephone: 2024056
Telex: 411167
Stock: ca. 28 million books, periodicals and serials; complete files of newspapers in all the languages of the Soviet Union and over 150 foreign languages

State Public Scientific and Technical Library
Address: Kuznetsky Most 12, 103031 Moscow
Telephone: 2287379
Stock: ca. 10 million books, periodicals, etc; special collections of industrial company catalogues

UNITED KINGDOM

Aberdeen City Libraries, Commercial and Technical Department
Address: Central Library, Rosemount Viaduct, Aberdeen AB9 1GU, Scotland
Telephone: (0224) 634622
Fax: (0224) 641985
Electronic mail: Mailbox MNU 421
Stock: all business and technical subjects covered. Stock size about 30,000 including: company and trade directories (UK and international); statistics, including official publications of UK Government, OECD, UN, EEC, USA and non-official statistics for specific industries, eg oil and gas; Extel and McCarthy card services, annual reports of oil and gas companies and nationalised industries, CRO microfiche for companies operating in Grampian.

Advertising Association Information Centre
Address: Abford House, 15 Wilton Road, London SW1V 1NJ
Telephone: (071) 828 2771
Stock: reference section, mainly on the UK. Over 3,000 volumes including current works on advertising, marketing, sales promotion, media and public relations; statistics on a wide range of topics, especially advertising and economics; over 150 English language periodicals on advertising, marketing and related subjects; over 300 press cuttings files

Birmingham Library Services
Address: Central Library, Chamberlain Square, Birmingham B3 3HQ
Telephone: (021) 235 4531 (Business Information), (021) 235 4545 (Social Sciences), (021) 235 4537 (Science and Technology)
Telex: 337655 BIRLIB G
Stock: statistics and market research collection (6,680), annual reports (3,700), foreign and specialised directories (7,000), patents (over 5 million), standards and government publications

British Institute of Management (BIM)
Address: Management Information Centre, Cottingham Road, Corby, Northants NN17 1TT
Telephone: (0536) 204222
Fax: (0536) 201651
Stock: 70,000 books and pamphlets and 40,000 indexed journal articles on management, directories of management education and audiovisual aids for managers

British Library Business Information Service
Address: 25 Southampton Buildings, Chancery Lane, London WC2A 1AW
Telephone: 01-323 7454 (free service), 01-323 7979 (priced service)
Telex: 266959 SCIREF G
Stock: business material held at the Science Reference and Information Service (formerly the Science Reference Library), where the Business Information Service is based, includes 2,000 trade directories, 2,500 market research reports, product literature and annual reports from 25,000 companies, and 5,000 trade and business journals; British and foreign company information, including Extel, McCarthy and Moody services; supplementary material at the Official Publications and Social Sciences Service (Great Russell Street), which holds all UK and major overseas statistical series, complementing the Export Market Information Centre, formerly the Statistics and Market Intelligence Library (see separate entry for EMIC).

British Library of Political and Economic Science
Address: 10 Portugal Street, London WC2A 2HD
Telephone: (071) 955 7229
Stock: about 3 million separate items. Covers social sciences in widest use of the term. Research collections emphasise economics, politics and sociology. Important collections of statistics, particularly government and inter-governmental, from all over the world. Special collections of bank reports and trade union annual reports

Central Statistical Office Library
Address: Room 1.001, Government Buildings, Cardiff Road, Newport NP9 1XG, Wales
Telephone: (0633) 812973
Fax: (0633) 812599
Telex: 497121
Stock: about 300 serial titles and 1,000 monographs. Complete collection of own *Business Monitor* statistical publications and many other official UK statistical titles. Periodicals and monographs on statistical methodology, automatic data processing and public administration. Collection of UK trade directories.

City Business Library (Corporation of London)
Address: 106 Fenchurch Street, London EC3M 5JB
Telephone: (071) 638 8215 (Enquiries);
(071) 480 7638 (recorded information)
Telex: 9312130747 CB G
Telecom Gold: 74:HAY 3004
Stock: public library covering all aspects of business information, with special emphasis on company data (UK and overseas) and market research materials (principally domestic consumer). Stock includes directories, card services, periodicals, newspapers, quoted company annual reports

City University Business School Library
Address: Level 14, Frobisher Crescent, Barbican, London EC2B 8HB
Telephone: (071) 920 0111 x 2268/9
Fax: (071) 588 2756
Telex: 263896
Stock: approximately 25,000 primarily theoretical and academic monographs on business studies subjects, shipping and arts administration. Small collection of basic educational and business reference works. About 400 current journal titles. Stock includes recent acquisitions from the Market Research Society collection

Export Market Information Centre - EMIC (*formerly Statistics and Market Intelligence Library*)
Address: Department of Trade and Industry, 1-19 Victoria Street, London SW1H 0ET (entrance to EMIC in Abbey Orchard Street)
Telephone: (071) 215 5444/5
Fax: (071) 215 4231
Telex: 8811074/5 DTHQ G
Stock: The Export Market Information Centre is provided by the DTI to give access for British exporters and potential exporters to a wide collection of detailed overseas official statistics, trade directories, development plans and other published information on overseas (i.e. non-UK) markets. Resources available include the British Overseas Trade Information System (BOTIS), the DTI's own database for information on products and markets, overseas agents, distributors and importers, export opportunities, promotional events, and for an index to other published information available for reference in EMIC

Financial Times Business Research Centre (*formerly FT Business Information Service*)
Address: Number One Southwark Bridge, London SE1 9HL
Telephone: (071) 873 3000
Fax: (071) 873 3069
Telex: 8811506
Stock: access to the stock of the Financial Times library covering current affairs, companies, industries and markets, statistics, personalities and international business and commerce; over 60,000 Company Files and 25,000 Personality files and information by subject and country. Access to a variety of external sources

Holborn Library, London Borough of Camden
Address: 32-38 Theobalds Road, London WC1X 8PA
Telephone: (071) 405 2705/9
Stock: business, employment and legal information. Company information includes: 3,000 + company annual reports (MIRAC), UK Extel cards, CRO microfiche index, trade directories, UK and foreign telephone directories, *Research index*. Marketing information: *Marketing surveys index, Reports index*, Jordans surveys, Keynotes, Mintel, *Retail business*. Statistics including *Business monitor* series. Newspapers and periodicals

Liverpool City Libraries, Commercial and Social Sciences Library
Address: Central Libraries, William Brown Street, Liverpool L3 8EW
Telephone: (051) 225 5434/5435/5436
Fax: (051) 207 1342
Telex: 629500
Stock: contains EC, HMSO, OECD and UN collections, large range of UK and overseas directories, statistical, shipping and law collections. 100,000 books, 500 journals, 300 trade journals, UK company reports, market research reports, UK, European and USA trade directories, local and national newspapers. Special company information service including Extel and McCarthy cards, Prestel and Teletext, Companies House directory on microfiches

London Business School/ LBS Information Service
Address: Sussex Place, Regent's Park, London NW1 4SA
Telephone: (071) 262 5050; (071) 724 2300 (LBS Information Service)
Telex: 27461
Fax: 01-724 7875
Stock: about 25,000 volumes covering all aspects of management and business in the private and public sectors as well as related parts of economics, law, politics, the behavioural sciences, information technology and the sciences generally. Also about 500 periodical titles, 150 of the most important British, European and international published statistical series and 15 daily and weekly newspapers. Collection of company information, including annual reports of all British publicly quoted companies and 500 European companies, Extel cards, McCarthy's press cuttings

services and directories and handbooks. Market research reports, government publications, information files on subjects and countries

London Chamber of Commerce and Industry
Address: 69 Cannon Street, London EC4N 5AB
Telephone: (071) 248 4444
Fax: (071) 489 0391
Telex: 888941 LCCI G
Stock: 1,000 trade magazines, 1,500 British and foreign trade directories, extensive collections of UK and foreign government trade regulations, trade statistics worldwide, economic background to most countries of the world, British company information, market research reports and openings for trade worldwide

Manchester Business School, University of Manchester
Address: Booth Street West, Manchester M15 6PB
Telephone: (061) 275 6499
Fax: (061) 273 7732
Telex: 668354
Stock: 30,000 books on all aspects of management and business as well as related aspects of sociology, economics, law, politics and information technology. 800 periodicals. Collection of company information including annual reports of 3,000 British and European companies, Extel cards, McCarthy's Press service and MIRAC. Online access to Textline, Datastar, Dialog, Dun & Bradstreet, Pergamon and other hosts. CD-ROM products include FAME (UK company financial data) and ABI/Inform (international bibliographic database). Market research reports, government publications, and information files

Manchester Commercial Library and Information Service
Address: Central Library, St Peters Square, Manchester M2 5PD
Telephone: (061) 236 9422 ext 283/284, (061) 228 0641/2
Telex: 667149
Stock: comprehensive stock covering all aspects of business information. Approximately 7,500 trade and telephone directories (UK and foreign); company information including card services, Business Ratios, Financial Surveys and in-house database of Manchester companies; large collection of UK, foreign and international statistics; large collection of trade magazines and financial newspapers; fully indexed collection of market reports; maps and travel information; information files on products, industries and services; European Communities information; trade names; import/export tariffs. Patents, standards, government publications and wide range of other information are available in the Central Library building

National Institute of Economic and Social Research
Address: 2 Dean Trench Street, Smith Square, London SW1P 3HE
Telephone: (071) 222 7665

Stock: 30,000 - 40,000 volumes and 500 serials on economics, especially statistics

National Library of Scotland
Address: George IV Bridge, Edinburgh EH1 1EW, Scotland
Telephone: (031) 226 4531
Telex: 72638 NLSEDI G
Stock: approximately 5 million volumes and pamphlets, and large collections of maps and manuscripts. A copyright deposit library with the right to claim copies of all British and Irish publications. Government publications are acquired and a wide range of foreign books is purchased.

National Library of Wales
Address: Aberystwyth, Dyfed, SY23 3BU, Wales
Telephone: (0970) 623816
Telex: 35165
Fax: (0970) 615709
Stock: collections include 2.5 million volumes and bound periodicals and 6,000 current periodicals. The library is entitled to receive copies of most published material originating within the UK and has an extensive stock of technical, scientific and business-related books and journals, including annual editions of trade directories. It is a deposit library for government publications and for the publications of international agencies such as the UN, UNESCO, and the EEC. Important publications from other countries are purchased

Newcastle upon Tyne City Libraries, Business and Technical Library
Address: Central Library, PO Box 1DX, Princess Square, Newcastle upon Tyne NE99 1DX
Telephone: (091) 261 0691
Fax: (091) 2611435
Telex: 53373 LINCLE G
Stock: an inhouse index to most of the marketing periodicals published in Britain; most UK directories and extensive coverage for Europe, North America, Japan, Australasia, South Africa, Middle East; large economic report files for every country in the world; all Extel and McCarthy card services; large collection of UK marketing periodicals.

Northern Ireland Department of Economic Development
Address: Netherleigh, Massey Avenue, Belfast BT4 2JP, Northern Ireland
Telephone: (0232) 63244 ext 2374/2286
Stock: covers commerce, economics, energy, mineral development, industrial development, public administration, training, industrial relations, factory inspection, tourism. Around 500 periodical titles held

Nottinghamshire County Library, Business Library
Address: Angel Row, Nottingham NG1 6HP
Telephone: (0602) 476332
Fax: (0602) 504207
Telex: 37662

Prestel Mailbox: 602412178
Stock: current or recent editions of most UK directories; telephone and general trade directories for principal industrial centres worldwide. Statistics: a large collection of UK official series and some others and a smaller collection of overseas material, mainly UN, OECD, and ECC. These basic resources backed by about 500 periodicals and a stock of about 20,000 current volumes in the social sciences, science and technology

Office of Population Censuses and Surveys Library
Address: St Catherines House, 10 Kingsway, London WC2B 6JP
Telephone: (071) 242 0262 ext 2235
Stock: collection of 50,000 books and pamphlets and 400 periodical titles. Main subject areas include demography, vital registration, epidemiology, survey methodology and computing. All published Census data for the UK from 1801 and some unpublished data, eg Small Area Statistics. Other collections include Social Survey reports, foreign censuses and statistical series and international statistics.

Sheffield City Libraries and Information Services: Business Library, Science and Technology Library
Address: Central Library, Surrey Street, Sheffield S1 1XZ
Telephone: (0742) 734736-8
Fax: (0742) 735009
Telex: 54243 SHFLIB G
Stock: includes company annual reports, Extel services, CRO indexes and directory, general and specialised trade directories for UK and abroad; collection of detailed local company information; foreign company data; UK and foreign telephone, telex and fax directories; lists of professional and trade services; wide range of business journals

Small Firms and Tourism Division, Department of Employment
Address: Room 112, Steel House, Tothill Street, London SW1H 9NF
Telephone: (071) 273 4941 (Headquarters), Freefone Enterprise for local offices
Stock: information and advice on the establishment of a business and on the running of an existing business

Welsh Office Library
Address: Crown Building, Cathays Park, Cardiff CF1 3NQ, Wales
Telephone: (0222) 823683/825449
Telex: 498228
Stock: general administration of Wales covering central and local government, education, National Health Service, agriculture, industry, economic planning, transport, highways and physical planning

Westminster Central Reference Library
Address: St Martins Street, London WC2 7HP
Telephone: (071) 798 2034/5
Fax: (071) 798 2040

Stock: covers commercial information and official publications. 100,000 books, 700 journals, market research reports, company and trade directories, statistical collection, national newspapers

WEST GERMANY

Deutsche Bibliothek
Address: Zeppelinalle 4-8, D-6000 Frankfurt am Main
Telephone: (069) 75661
Telex: 416643 DEUBI
Fax: (069) 7566476
Stock: stocks all post-war material published in Germany, German language material published abroad, all translations of German works and all material about Germany printed abroad. 3 million books, 66,500 journals, 370 newspapers

Handelskammer Hamburg Commerzbibliothek
(Library of the Hamburg Chamber of Commerce)
Address: Adolphsplatz, Börse, D-2000 Hamburg 11
Telephone: (040) 36138-371
Telex: 211250 HKHMB D
Stock: about 160,000 books on economics, politics, German law, business administration, sociology, history (especially of Hamburg), annual reports of firms, especially German ones, anniversary books of firms, about 400 journals and all German statistical office publications, microfiches, video tapes. Material in German, French and English

Ifo-Institut für Wirtschaftsforschung Bibliothek (Ifo Institute for Economic Research)
Address: Poschingerstrasse 5, Postfach 860460, D-8000 Munich
Telephone: (089) 92240
Telex: 522269
Fax: (089) 985369
Stock: covers the national and international economy, industry, agriculture, technology, transportation, construction, labour market, the environment, trade and distribution. Special collections on developing countries and Japan. Material mainly in German and English, international in coverage. 100,000 books, 1,300 journals, 1,500 statistical publications, German annual reports

Informationszentrum Sozialwissenschaften
Address: Lennestrasse 30, D-5300 Bonn 1
Telephone: (0228) 22810
Stock: central information and documentation centre for social sciences in West Germany, and national focal point for ECSSID (European Cooperation in Social Science Information and Documentation). Coverage includes sociology of industry and trade and economics.

Institut für Arbeitsmarkt- und Berufsforschung
(Institute for Labour Market and Occupational Research)
Regensburgerstrasse 104, D-8500 Nuremberg
Telephone: (0911) 171

Stock: main subjects covered: labour market and occupational research, economics, industrial relations, labour market policy. Computerised database contains 3,800 documents

Institut für Seeverkehrswirtschaft und - Logistik, Bibliothek (Library of the Institute of Shipping Economics)
Address: Am Dom 5A, D-2800 Bremen
Telephone: (0421) 36805-0
Stock: covers shipping, sea ports, seaborne trade

Institut für Weltwirtschaft Kiel, Bibliothek (Central National Library of Economics in the Federal Republic of Germany)
Address: Düsternbrooker Weg 120, Postfach 4309, D-2300 Kiel 1
Telephone: (0431) 884436
Fax: (0431) 85853
Telex: 292479 WELTWD
Stock: covers international economics, statistics and business administration. Material is in all languages and international in coverage. 800,000 books, 19,000 journals, comprehensive international statistical collection, international company information, small collections for the most important countries of market research reports, stockbroker reports, trade journals and company and trade directories

Institut für Wirtschaftsforschung-Hamburg (HWWA), Bibliothek (Institute of Economic Research)
Address: Neuer Jungfernstieg 21, D-2000 Hamburg 36
Telephone: (040) 3562219
Fax: (040) 351900
Telex: 211458 HWWA D
Stock: the HWWA Library is one of the largest specialised libraries for economic and social sciences. Collections on national and international statistical material are especially extensive, as well as the stocks of branches and product oriented periodicals, address books of firms and branches and special volumes. Total of 600,000 volumes including 280,000 annual reports of companies; annual addition: 20,000 volumes; 80 newspapers, 3,500 magazines and reviews, 9,000 yearbooks, 3,500 annual reports of companies, microforms

Osteuropa-Institut München, Bibliothek
Address: Scheinerstrasse 11, D-8000 Munich 80
Telephone: (089) 983821/987341
Stock: covers the economics, history and law of Eastern Europe. 140,000 volumes, 600 journals, newspapers, statistical publications and company information

Rheinisch-Westfälisches Institut für Wirtschaftsforschung, Bibliothek
Address: Hohenzollernstrasse 1/3, D-4300 Essen 1
Telephone: (0201) 233171
Fax: (0201) 238668
Stock: covers economics. Material mainly in German, covering Germany, Europe and the USA. 58,000 books,

300 journals, statistical publications and German company information

Staatsbibliothek Preussischer Kulturbesitz (State Library of the Prussian Cultural Foundation)
Address: Potsdamer Strasse 33, Postfach 1407, D-1000 Berlin 30
Telephone: (030) 2661
Fax: (030) 2662814
Telex: 183160 STAAB D
Stock: general coverage with special collections on Eastern Europe, Orient, East Asia and official publications. 4 million volumes, 600 newspapers, 30,000 journals, 850,000 microforms

Statistisches Bundesamt, Bibliothek (Library of the Federal Statistical Office of the Federal Republic of Germany)
Address: Gustav-Stresemann-Ring 11, Postfach 5528, D-6200 Wiesbaden 1
Telephone: (06121) 751
Fax: (06121) 7534225
Telex: 4186511 STBD
Stock: national and international statistical publications, covering economic and social life. 396,000 volumes

YUGOSLAVIA

Biblioteka Matice srpske (Yugoslav National Library)
Address: Ul. Matice srske 1, 21000 Novi Sad
Telephone: (021) 615599
Telex: 64367
Fax: 28574
Stock: ca. 700,000 volumes including 164,000 periodicals; national copyright and deposit library and depository library for FAO and UNESCO publications

Centraina ekonomska Knjiznica (Central Economic Library)
Address: Kardelijeva ploscad 17, Ljublijana
Telephone: (061) 345161
Stock: 145,300 volumes and periodicals, ca. 750 current periodicals

Nacionaina i Sveucilisna Biblioteka (National and University Library)
Address: Marulicav trg 21, Zagreb
Telephone: (041) 426322
Telex: 22206
Fax: 426676
Stock: ca. 1.4 million volumes, 340 volumes of periodicals, 4,000 microfilms, collections of prints, maps, records and scores; federal deposit and copyright library

Narodna Biblioteka Srbije (National Library of Serbia)
Address: Skerliceva 1, Belgrade
Telephone: (011) 451281
Telex: 12208
Stock: over 950,000 volumes, including 190,000

periodicals and 96,850 volumes of newspapers; federal deposit and copyright library

Narodna in Univerzitetna Knjiznica (National and University Library)
Address: Turjaska 1, 61000 Ljubljana
Telephone: (061) 332847
Telex: 32285
Stock: ca. 1.6 million volumes; federal copyright and depository library

5. Foreign Trade and Export Departments

ALBANIA

Albkontroll
Address: Bul. Enver Hoxha 45, Durres
Telephone: 23-45
Telex: 2181
Notes: Export/import control body with branches throughout Albania.

Ministry of Foreign Trade
Address: Ministria e Tregetise te Jashtme, Tirana
Telex: 2152

AUSTRIA

Bundesministerium für Auswärtige Angelegenheiten (Federal Ministry of Foreign Affairs)
Address: Wirtschaftspolitische Sektion, Ballhausplatz 2, A-1014 Vienna
Telephone: (01) 66150
Telex: 13710 AAWN A

Ministry of Trade and Industry, Export/Import Licensing Office (Zentralstelle Aussenhandel u. Zoll)
Address: A-1030 Vienna, Landstrasser Hauptstrasse 55-57
Telephone: (01) 71102-0
Telex: 131300
Fax: (01) 71102-352

Österreichische Exportfonds
(Austrian Export Fund)
Address: Gottfried-Keller-Gasse 1, A-1030 Vienna
Telephone: (01) 731213
Telex: 132846

Zoll-und Verbrauchsteuersektion (Customs and Excise Department)
Address: Bundesministerium für Finanzen, Himmelpfortgasse 4 & 8-9, A-1011 Vienna
Telephone: (0222) 5333

BELGIUM

Administration des Douanes et Accises (Customs and Excise Department)
Address: Sité Administrative d l'Etat, Tour Finances, Boîte 37, Boulevard du Jardin Botanique, B-1010 Brussels
Telephone: (02) 2102111

Ministère du Commerce Extérieur (Ministry of Foreign Trade)
Address: 2 Rue des Quatres Bras B-1000 Brussels
Telephone: (02) 5168311

Ministère des Relations Extérieures (Ministry of External Relations)
Address: 2 Rue des Quatre Bras, B-1000 Brussels
Telephone: (02) 5168211
Telex: 23979

Office Belge du Commerce Extérieur (Belgian Overseas Trade Office)
Address: World Trade Centre, 162 Boulevard Emile Jacqmain, B-1000 Brussels
Telephone: (02) 2194450
Telex: 21502
Notes: The Belgian Overseas Trade Office is the official organisation for the promotion of foreign trade under the Ministry of Foreign Trade. The Centre publishes trade opportunities.

Office National du Dacroire (Export Credit Guarantee Office)
Address: 40 Square de Meeûs, B-1040 Brussels
Telephone: (02) 5116580

BULGARIA

Bulgarian Chamber of Commerce and Industry
Address: Bul. Stamboliisky 11a, 1040 Sofia
Telephone: 87 26 31
Telex: 22374
Notes: Promotes business contacts between Bulgarian and foreign companies and organizations.

Ministry of Foreign Economic Relations
Address: Sofiska Komuna St.12, 1000 Sofia
Telephone: 87 48 11
Telex: 22530
Notes: Foreign trade is a state monopoly and is conducted through highly specialised state foreign trade organisations.

CYPRUS

Ministry of Commerce and Industry
Address: 6 Andreas Araouzos St, Nicosia
Telephone: (02) 403441
Telex: 2283
Fax: (02) 366120

CZECHOSLOVAKIA

Ceskoslovenska obchodni a prumyslova komora (Czechoslovak Chamber of Commerce and Industry)
Address: Argentinska 38, 170 05 Prague
Telephone: (2) 8724111
Telex: 121862

Notes: The membership comprises all the country's foreign trade organisations as well as most of the industrial enterprises and research institutes.

Ministry of Foreign Trade
Address: Prague

DENMARK

Direktoratet for Toldvæsenet (Customs and Excise Department)
Address: Amaliegade 44, DK-1256 Copenhagen K
Telephone: (33) 157300

Industriministeriet (Ministry of Industry)
Address: Slotsholmsgade 12, DK-1216 Copenhagen K
Telephone: (33) 923350
Telex: 22373
Notes: The Trade Department of the Ministry of Industry also deals with foreign trade.

Udenrigsministeriets Handelsafdeling (The Trade Department of the Ministry of Foreign Affairs)
Address: Asiatisk Plads 2, DK-1448 Copenhagen K
Telephone: (31) 920000
Telex: 31292 ETR DK
Fax: (31) 540533
Notes: The Department promotes Danish export, collects information on foreign commerce and economies and assists in establishing contacts between Danish and foreign enterprises. Foreign companies interested in making contacts with Danish companies or finding out more about Danish export products should contact the nearest Danish diplomatic or consular office. The Department publishes *The Foreign Office Journal* which carries trade enquiries from foreign companies free of charge, and *Denmark Review/Business News from Denmark*.

EAST GERMANY

Internationales Handelszentrum (International Trade Centre)
Address: Friedrichstrasse, 1086 Berlin
Telephone: 20960
Telex: 114381
Notes: Houses the offices of foreign companies operating in East Germany and the Association of Foreign Trade Agencies and Brokers. Holds foreign trade negotiations. Organises conferences and exhibitions.

Kammer für Aussenhandel der Deutschen Demokratischen Republik (Foreign Trade Chamber)
Address: Schönholzer Strasse 10-11, 1100 Berlin
Telephone: 48220
Telex: 114840
Fax: 4828408
Notes: The membership comprises all the foreign trade organisations and the leading industrial companies, financial institutions etc.

Ministerium für Aussenhandel (Ministry of Foreign Trade)
Address: Unter dem Linden 44-60, 1080 Berlin
Telephone: 2330
Telex: 1152361
Notes: Foreign trade is has hitherto been a state monopoly and is conducted through specialised trade organisations. Following reunification the Ministry will be combined with that of the Federal Republic.

FINLAND

Finnish Foreign Trade Association
Address: PO Box 908, Arkadiankatu 4-6 B, SF-00101 Helsinki 10
Telephone: (90) 69591
Telex: 121696 TRADE SF
Fax: (90) 6940028
Notes: The FFTA, the central organisation for export promotion, is a semi-official organisation supported by the Confederation of Finnish Industry and 800 affiliated companies. It has 8 regional centres.
The FFTA will supply foreign clients with information about:
- Finnish industries and relevant suppliers. A database, VIESTO, holds information about Finnish industrial exporters, contractors, sub-contractors and consultants, including detailed data on their products, services and market-orientation.
- general market conditions
- business opportunities in Finland
The FFTA provides Finnish exporters with:
- market information
- advice on marketing and legal matters
- advice on regulations in foreign trade
- project export services
- sales campaigns and publicity abroad
The FFTA publishes a book, *Finland as a Trading Partner. The Finnish Trade Review* is published 8 times annually and each issue is available in several languages, including English. Commercial Secretaries in the diplomatic corps are under the administration of the Ministry for Foreign Affairs, but the trade related work is co-ordinated by the Finnish Foreign Trade Association. Finnish and foreign companies can communicate with the Commercial Secretaries either direct or through the FFTA. The Commercial Secretaries supply information on market and sales opportunities and assist companies in marketing.

Handels- & Industriministeriet (Ministry of Trade and Industry)
Address: Commercial Department, Aleksanterikatu 10, SF-00171 Helsinki 17
Telephone: (90) 1601
Telex: 124645

Ministeriet för Utrikesärenden (Ministry of Foreign Affairs)
Address: Herikasarmi, Pl 176 SF-00161 Helsinki
Telephone: (90) 1601
Telex: 124636

Tullihallitus (Customs and Excise Department)
Address: Erottaja 2-4, SF 00101 Helsinki
Telephone: (90) 6141

Vientitakuulaitos (Export Guarantee Board)
Address: Eteläranta 6, Box 187, SF-00130 Helsinki
Telephone: (90) 661811
Telex: 121778

FRANCE

Centre Français du Commerce Extérieur
Address: 10 avenue d'Iéna, F-75783 Paris 16
Telephone: (1) 45053000
Telex: 611934 F
Fax: (1) 45053979
Notes: Centre for the promotion of French foreign trade. Maintains close contacts with industry and commerce. Publicises trade opportunities.

Service de Renseignements Douaniers (Customs Information Service)
Address: 182 rue St-Honore, F75001 Paris
Telephone: (1) 42603590 (office); (1) 42615602 (overseas trade statistics)

Direction Nationale des Statistiques de Commerce Extérieur (Directorate for Foreign Trade Statistics)
Address: 192 rue St. Honoré, F-75056 Paris
Telephone: (1) 42603300
Telex: 230061 DOUSTAT

Ministère du Commerce et de l'Artisanat (Ministry of Commerce and Small Businesses)
Address: Administration Centrale, 80 rue de Lille, F-75007 Paris
Telephone: (1) 45562424
Fax: (1) 47530834

Ministère du Commerce Extérieur (Ministry of Foreign Trade)
Address: 41 quai Branly, F-75007 Paris
Telephone: (1) 45507111
Telex: 205885 F
Fax: (1) 45559542

Ministère des Relations Extérieures (Ministry of Foreign Affairs)
Address: 37 quai d'Orsay, F-75000 Paris
Telephone: (1) 45559540
Telex: 202329 F
Fax: (1) 47534753

GIBRALTAR

Gibraltar Chamber of Commerce
Address: 30 Main Street, POB 29, Gibraltar
Telephone: (0350) 78376

GREECE

Athens Chamber of Commerce & Industry
Address: 7-9 Academias Street, GR-10671, Athens
Telephone: (01) 3624280
Telex: 215707 EBEA GR
Notes: The Athens Chamber of Commerce and Industry is a semi-governmental institution under the supervision of the Ministry of Commerce. It deals with all sorts of trade related enquiries and any approaches to other chambers will be referred to the Athens Chamber. It publishes a monthly report and a bi-annual journal, *Trade with Greece*.

Customs and Excise Department
Address: 6 Marni Street, Athens
Telephone: (01) 5223910

Directorate of Foreign Commerce
Address: Ministry of Commerce, Kaningos Square, Athens
Telephone: (01) 3616241
Telex: 215282/219033

Ministry of Foreign Affairs (Foreign Trade Departments and Export Advisory Bodies)
Address: Zalokosta 2, Athens
Telephone: (01) 3610581
Telex: 216593

HUNGARY

Magyar Gazdasagi Kamara (Hungarian Chamber of Commerce)
Address: PO Box 106, 1389 Budapest
Telephone: 1533 333
Telex: 224745
Fax: 153 1285
Notes: Promotes foreign trade. Membership includes all Hungarian foreign trade organisations.

Ministry of Foreign Affairs
Address: Bem Rkp. 47, 1027 Budapest
Telephone: 135-0100
Telex: 225571

Ministry of Trade
Address: Honved u. 13/15, 1055 Budapest
Telephone: 153-0000
Telex: 225578
Fax: 153 2794

ICELAND

Customs Department (Head Office)
Address: Tryggvagata 19, Reykjavik
Telephone: (91) 18500
Telex: 2128 CUSTOM IS

Iceland Chamber of Commerce
Address: Hus Verzlunarinnar, v. 103 Reykjavik
Telephone: (91) 83088
Telex: 2316

Ministry of Commerce
Address: Arnarhvali, 150 Reykjavik

Telephone: (91) 25000
Telex: 2092

IRELAND

An Roinn Gnothaí Eachtracha (Department of Foreign Affairs)
Address: 80 St. Stephen's Green, Dublin 2
Telephone: (01) 780822
Telex: 25300

An-Roinn Tionscail, Agus Trachtala Turasóireachta (Department of Industry, and Commerce)
Address: Kildare Street,
Dublin 2
Telephone: (01) 614444
Telex: 93478
Fax: (01) 762654

Córas Trachtala (CTT) (Irish Export Board)
Address: Merrion Hall, Strand Road, Sandymount,
Dublin 4
Telephone: (01) 695011
Telex: 25337 CTT EI
Notes: The CTT is the state organisation for the promotion and development of exports. The organisation has regional offices in Cork, Limerick, Waterford and Sligo as well as 20 overseas offices. The CTT provides a variety of services and incentives to exporters and companies which are planning to enter the export market. A range of services is also available for foreign buyers and importers.

Customs and Excise Department
Address: Office of Revenue Commissioners, Dublin Castle, Dublin 2
Telephone: (01) 792777
Telex: 93479 REV EI
Fax: (01) 711826

ITALY

Direzione Generale delle Dogane e Imposte Indirette (Customs and Excise Department)
Address: Viale America, I-00100 Rome
Telephone: (06) 5997/5924931

Istituto Nazionale per Il Commercio Estero (ICE) (Institute for Foreign Trade)
Address: Viale Liszt 21, I-00144 Rome
Telephone: (06) 5992
Telex: 610160/610178 ICERM I
Publications: Esportare (fortnightly), *Informazioni per il Commercio Estero* (daily), *Notiziaro ortofrutticolo* (monthly), *Quality* (quarterly), *Pubblicazioni technico informative.*
Notes: ICE is the government agency responsible for the promotion of exports. It runs a network of ICE offices overseas.

Ministero del Commercio Estero (Ministry of Foreign Trade)
Address: Viale America, I-00144 Rome
Telephone: (06) 5993
Telex: 610471 MINCOMES I

LIECHTENSTEIN

Industrie und Handelskammer (Chamber of Commerce and Industry)
Address: Postfach 232, 9490 Vaduz
Telephone: (075) 22744

LUXEMBOURG

Administration des Douanes (Customs and Excise Department)
Address: 4-6 rue du Saint Esprit, L-1475 Luxembourg
Telephone: 20951

Ministère des Affaires Etrangères, du Commerce Extérieur et de la Coopération (Ministry of Foreign Affairs, Foreign Trade and Co-operation)
Address: 5 Rue Notre-Dame, L-2240 Luxembourg
Telephone: 4781
Telex: 3405

MALTA

Department of Trade
Address: Lascaris, Valletta
Telephone: 22441
Telex: 1106
Fax: 606800
Notes: Deals with import, export, trade licenses, etc and promotes foreign trade relations.

Ministry of Finance
Address: St. Calcedonius Sq., Floriana
Telephone: 220437
Telex: 1512
Fax: 229925

NETHERLANDS

Customs and Excise Departments
Information about clearance of goods can be obtained from:

Inspectie der Invoerrechten en Accijnzen
Address: Leeuwendalersweg 21, NL-1055 JE Amsterdam
Telephone: (020) 864441

Inspectie der Invoerrechten en Accijnzen
Address: Westzeekijk 387, NL-3024 EK Rotterdam
Telephone: (010) 4765144

Inspectie der Invoerrechten en Accijnzen
Address: Waldorpstraat 440, NL-2521 CH, The Hague
Telephone: (070) 3889380

Ontvangstkantoor der Invoerrechten en Accijnzen
Address: Stationsgebouw, Stationsweg 1, NL-3151 HR
Hoek van Holland
Telephone: (01747) 2370

Directoraat-Generaal voor de Buitenlandse Economische Betrekkingen (Directorate-General for Foreign Economic Affairs)
Address: Bezuidenhoutseweg 30, NL-2594 AV The Hague
Telephone: (070) 3798911

Economische Voorlichtingsdienst, EVD (The Netherlands Foreign Trade Agency)
Address: Bezuidenhoutseweg 151, NL-2594 AG, The Hague
Telephone: (070) 3798933
Telex: 31099
Notes: The EVD is the information and export promotion department of the Ministry of Economic Affairs. The EVD collaborates with governmental, semi-governmental and private organisations, such as embassies, the Netherlands Council for Trade Promotion (see below), domestic and bilateral chambers of commerce and the Ministry of Agriculture and Fisheries. The EVD's function is to support Dutch exports and to supply information on domestic and international economic and commercial developments. The EVD helps trade and industry by finding and exploring new and traditional markets, setting up contracts with foreign companies, promoting Dutch trade and industry in general, supplying information about developments of foreign markets and legislation, and providing an extensive library service. The EVD also produces a *Foreign Trade and Economic Abstracts Database*
Publications include: Export Magazine, Export Agenda, as well as sector bulletins and a foreign projects bulletin.

Nederlands Centrum voor Handelsbevordering, NCH (Netherlands Council for Trade Promotion)
Address: Kettingstraat 2, PO Box 10, NL-2501 CA
The Hague
Telephone: (070) 3478234
Telex: 32306 NCH NL
Notes: The NCH is a private non-profitmaking organisation which aims to assist exports. The NCH collaborates with domestic and foreign governmental and private organisations. It organises and participates in exhibitions abroad, carries out surveys of foreign markets, organises conferences, seminars, etc. and runs an international market intelligence service. The NCH also houses the offices of the following bilateral chambers of commerce: Kamer Griekenland (Greece), Kamer Ierland (Ireland), Kamer Denemarken/IJsland (Denmark/Iceland), Kamer Finland (Finland), Kamer Noorwegen (Norway), Kamer Zweden (Sweden), Kamer Portugal (Portugal).

Central Service for Imports and Exports
Address: Engelse Kamp 2, NL-9722 AX, Groningen
Telephone: (050) 239111

NORWAY

Departementet for Handel og Skipsfart (Ministry of Commerce and shipping)
Address: Victoria terrasse 7, N-0030 Oslo 1
Telephone: (02) 314050
Telex: 18670

The Export Council of Norway
Address: Drammensveien 40, N-0255 Oslo 2
Telephone: (02) 437700
Telex: 18532
Fax: (02) 552628
Notes: The Export Council of Norway is part of the Norwegian Foreign Office Overseas Services. It has offices in 34 countries and is represented through embassies and consulates elsewhere. The Council provides a full range of professional services for existing and potential trading partners. This includes promoting contracts between Norwegian exporters and foreign customers and supplying extensive and up-to-date information and advice on the products of the country.

Finans- og tolldepartementet (Customs and Excise Department)
Address: Akersgatan 42, N-0030 Oslo 1
Telephone: (02) 119090
Telex: 72095

Utenriksdepartementet (Ministry of Foreign Affairs)
Address: 7 Juni plassen 1, Boks 8114, N-0030 Oslo 1
Telephone: (02) 204170
Telex: 71004

POLAND

Ministry of Foreign Economic Co-operation
Address: Pl. Trzech Krzyzy 5, 00950 Warsaw
Telephone: 693 5000
Telex: 814501
Fax: 286808

Polska Izba Handlu Zagranicznego (Polish Chamber of Foreign Trade)
Address: Trebacka 4, PO Box 361, 00950 Warsaw
Telephone: 260221
Telex: 814361

PORTUGAL

Alfandega de Lisboa (Customs and Excise Department)
Address: Terreiro du Trigo, Lisbon
Telephone: (01) 866176

Instituto do Comércio Externo (ICEP) (Foreign Trade Institute)
Address: Avenida 5 de Outubro 101, P-1000 Lisbon

Telephone: (01) 730103
Telex: 16498 ICEP P
Notes: ICEP's function is to promote Portuguese exports

Instituto do Investimento Estrangeiro (IIE) (Overseas Investment Institute)
Address: Avenida da Liberdade 258, P-1200 Lisbon
Telephone: (01) 570607
Telex: 14712
Notes: The Institute provides support and guidance to foreign investors and foreign exporters of technology.

Ministry of Foreign Affairs
Address: Largo do Rilvas, P-1351 Lisbon
Telephone: (01) 601028
Telex: 12276

Direccao-Geral do Comercio Externo (General Directorate of Overseas Trade)
Address: Av. da Republica 79, P-1000 Lisbon
Telephone: (01) 730993
Telex: 13418

ROMANIA

Ministry of Foreign Trade
Address: bd. Republicii 14, Bucharest
Telephone: 166850
Telex: 11220

SPAIN

Consejo Asesor de Exportación (CAE) (Export Advisory Board)
Address: Alcalá 9, Madrid 14
Telephone: (91) 2326124

Customs and excise (Head office)
Address: Guzman el Bueno 125, Madrid
Telephone: (91) 2543200
Telex: 23058

Information Centre of Foreign Trade - CEDIN (Ministry of Economy, Finance and Trade)
Address: Ministerio de Economía Hacienda y Comercio,Paseo de la Castellana 162, E28046 Madrid
Telephone: (91) 2590807
*Telex:*44185

Instituto Nacional de Fomento de la Exportación (INFE)
Address: Paseo de la Castellana 14, E-28046 Madrid 1
Telephone: (91) 4311240
Telex: 47392 IEC E
Notes: INFE is a state institute. Its function is to promote Spanish exports.

Ministerio de Asuntos Exteriores (Ministry of Foreign Affairs)
Address: Plaza de la Provincia 1, E-28012 Madrid
Telephone: (91) 2658605
Telex: 27739/22645

SWEDEN

Generaltullstyrelsen (Customs and Excise, Department)
Address: Box 2267, S-10316 Stockholm
Telephone: (08) 7897300

Industridepartementet (Ministry of Commerce)
Address: Fredsgatan 8, S-10333 Stockholm
Telephone: (08) 7631000
Telex: 14180

Sveriges Allmanna Exportforening (General Export Association)
Address: Storgatan 19, Box 5501, S-11485 Stockholm
Telephone: (08) 783800

Swedish Trade Council
Address: Storgatan 19, Box 5513, S-11485 Stockholm
Telephone: (08) 7838500
Telex: 19620 EXPORT S
Fax: (08) 6629093
Contacts: Bo Hampus Israelsson (president)
Notes: The Swedish Trade Council is a semi-official organisation. It is the central organisation for planning, co-ordination, marketing and promotion for Swedish export companies. The STC also assists the less experienced export trader with advice, in collaboration with the 24 Regional Development Funds and the 12 Chambers of Commerce. The STC has 30 Swedish trade offices around the world. The operative part of the STC's international organisation includes the commercial sections of Swedish embassies and consulates. The Council publishes *The Swedish Export Directory Buyer's Guide to Sweden*.

Utrikesdepartementet (Ministry of Foreign Affairs)
Address: Handelsavdelingen, Gustav Adolfstorg 1, Box 16121,
S-10323 Stockholm
Telephone: (08) 7866000
Telex: 10590/19350

SWITZERLAND

Federal Department of Finance
Address: Bundeshaus, Bundesgasse 3, CH-3003 Bern
Telephone: (031) 616111

Internationales Handelszentrum (International Trade Centre)
Address: 54-56 rue de Montbrullant, CH-1202 Geneva; Box Palais des Nations CH-1211 Geneva 10
Telephone: (022) 346021
Telex: 289052

Federal Department of Foreign Affairs
Address: Bundeshaus-West, Bundesgasse, CH-3003 Bern
Telephone: (031) 612111

Information Sources

Oberzolldirektion (Customs and Excise Department)
Address: Monbijoustrasse 40, CH-3003 Bern
Telephone: (031) 616511

**Schweizerische Zentrale für Handelsförderung
(Swiss Office for the Development of Trade)**
Address: Stampfenbachstrasse 85, CH-8035 Zürich
Telephone: (01) 3632250
Telex: 53111 OSEC CH
and
Address: Avant-Poste 4, CH-1005 Lausanne
Telephone: (021) 203231
Telex: 25425
Notes: The SODT is a semi-official organisation which
collaborates closely with the Swiss government and
various economic associations. Its aim is to promote
trade relations with foreign countries by bringing
together foreign and Swiss companies and agents,
advising on buyers, partners for joint ventures and
licences, providing addresses of Swiss suppliers,
providing information about the Swiss market,
organising industrial exhibitions abroad, technical
symposia and participation in exhibitions.
SODT publishes the following books and journals
which are available from all Swiss embassies,
consulates and chambers of commerce:
Swiss Export Products and Services (book), *How to
Export to Switzerland* (book), *Partner* (book), *Textiles
suisses* (journal), *Textiles suisses - Intérieur* (journal),
Swiss economic news (journal). The SODT has over
2000 members involved in foreign trade.

TURKEY

Foreign Trade Association of Turkey
Address: Otim Binasi, A Blok Kat 4, Besiktas, Istanbul
Telephone: (1) 1723828
Telex: 26689 FTAT TR

IGEME (Export Promotion Research Centre)
Address: Mithatpasa Cad. 60, Kizilay, Ankara
Telephone: (41) 172223
Telex: 4228 IGM TR

Ministry of Industry and Commerce
Address: Sanayi ve Ticaret Bakanligi, Ankara
Telephone: 2292834
Telex: 44598

**Union of Chambers of Commerce, Industry,
Maritime Commerce and Commodity Exchanges**
Address: Atatürk Bulv. 149, Bakanliklar, Ankara
Telephone: (4) 1177700
Telex: 42343

UNION OF SOVIET SOCIALIST REPUBLICS

Bank for Foreign Trade of the USSR
Address: Kopievsky Per. 3/5, Moscow 103009
Telephone: 2466973
Telex: 411174/8

Notes: Apart from normal banking operations, accepts
foreign currency from its clients, as well as precious
metals, securities and other valuables for custody.
Fulfils encashment, letter-of-credit and remittance
commisions of its clients and correspondence involved
in account-settling and credit operations in export and
import trade and services, as well as in account-settling
in non-commercial operations; grants and accepts
credits; guarantees financial liabilities to Soviet and
foreign juristic persons.

Ministry of Foreign Economic Relations
Address: Smolenskaya-Sennaya Pl. 32/34, Moscow
121200
Telephone: (095) 2441947
Telex: 411291/2

USSR Chamber of Commerce and Industry
Address: ul. Kuibysheva 6, Moscow 103684
Telephone: (095) 2210811
Telex: 411126
Notes: Promotes trade, economic, scientific and
technological exchanges between the Soviet Union
and other countries; organises exhibitions, seminars
etc and through the Soviet state exhibition
organisations. Registers patented inventions,
trademarks etc. Presides over arbitration disputes;
inspects goods for import and export; provides
translation services.

UNITED KINGDOM

Overseas Trade Division (OTD)
Address: Department of Trade and Industry, 1 Victoria
Street, London SW1H 0ET
Telephone: (071) 2155000
Telex: 27366
Fax: (071) 2155611
Notes: The OTD was set up to help British exporters. Its
members are drawn from experienced exporters in
commerce and industry. The OTD's responsibilities
are:
- to advice the government on strategy for overseas
trade
- to direct and develop the government export
promotion services on behalf of the Secretary of State
for Trade and Industry
- to encourage and support industry and commerce in
overseas trade with the aid of appropriate
governmental and non-governmental organisations at
home and overseas
- to contribute to the exchange of views between
government and industry and commerce in the field of
overseas trade and to search for solutions to problems.
(See also the Export Market Information Centre in the
chapter on libraries and information services)
*Publications include: Hints to Exporters, Country
Profiles, Sector Reports*
Customs and Excise Department
Address: King Beam House, Mark Lane, London EC3
Telephone: (071) 6261515

Department of Trade and Industry
Address: 1 Victoria Street, London SW1H 0ET
Telephone: (071) 2157877
Telex: 8811074

Foreign and Commonwealth Office
Address: Downing Street, London SW1A 2AL
Telephone: (071) 2333000
Telex: 297711

WEST GERMANY

**Abteilung III-Zölle, Verbrauchssteuern, Monopole
(Customs and Excise Department)**
Address: Bundesministerium der Finanzen (Ministry of
Finance), Graurheindforstrasse 108, D-5300 Bonn
Telephone: (0228) 682-1
Telex: 886645

Auswärtiges Amt (Ministry of Foreign Affairs)
Address: Adenauerallee 99-103, D-5300 Bonn
Telephone: (0228) 170
Telex: 886591

**Bundesstelle für Aussenhandelsinformation
(Foreign Trade Information Office)**
Address: Blaubach 13, Postfach 108007, D-5000
Cologne
Telephone: (0221) 233011
Telex: 882735
Notes: Official information office under the German
Ministry of Industry dealing with all foreign trade
enquiries. Together with the Bundesverband der
Deutschen Industrie (Federation of German Industry)
the Trade Information Office publish *Nachrichten für
den Aussenhandels* (foreign trade information bulletin),
Auslands-Anfragen (enquiries from abroad).

YUGOSLAVIA

Federal Secretariat for Foreign Economic Relations
Address: Omladinskih brigada 1, 11070 Belgrade
Telephone: (011) 195444
Telex: 12110

Institut za Spoljnu Trgovinu (Foreign Trade Institute)
Address: Mose Pijade 8, 11000 Belgrade
Telephone: 339041

**Privredna Komora Jugoslavije (Federal Chamber of
Economy)**
Address: Terazije 23, Po Box 1003, 11000 Belgrade
Telephone: (011) 339461
Telex: 11638
Fax: (011) 631928
Notes: Promotes economic and commercial relations
with other countries.

MARKETING GEOGRAPHY

This section has been compiled from recent press articles on European countries and current available information. The standard regions are extracted from regional data published by National Statistical Offices, and the marketing maps from Nielsen and national advertising data sources.

THE REUNIFICATION OF EAST AND WEST GERMANY: AN IMPORTANT NOTE

The reunification of East Germany with the Federal Republic of Germany on Oct. 3, 1990, marks, of course, the transition of East Germany from the Council for Mutual Economic Assistance (CMEA, or Comecon) to the European Community, and indeed the end of its existence as a separate state. For the purposes of this year's volume, however, it was nevertheless felt to be more appropriate to identify and to categorise East Germany in its former capacity as an East European state, for the following reasons:

Firstly, the statistical scope of the volume extends only as far as the beginning of January 1990, a time when East Germany remained both a sovereign state and a member of the CMEA.

Secondly, at the time of going to press the great bulk of statistical data on the country was still originating from the East German Government in East Berlin, or from the CMEA group itself, and virtually none from the European Community; nor, indeed, was there much information available from the Federal Republic. While this situation will doubtless be rectified in the coming year, it was clearly both more convenient and more logical, for the purposes of this year's volume, to retain the separate identification of the country.

It is apparent, moreover, that many of the features which have hitherto distinguished East Germany from the Federal Republic will continue to have a statistical relevance in the short term - in other words, that the former country will remain, for perhaps some years, a tangibly distinct marketing region, with a markedly different lifestyle from the more affluent norms more commonly seen in the West of the country.

Future editions of this and other statistical compilations from Euromonitor will, of course, refer to the former East German state in the context of its membership not only of the enlarged Germany but of the European Community.

October 1990

Belgium/Luxembourg

Population	9,980,000 (1990)
Urban population	96%
Land area	11,781 sq m
Languages	Dutch (Flemish) and French (Walloon), with German minority
Religion	Mostly Roman Catholic
Currency	Belgium Franc (= 100 centimes)
Head of state	HM King Baudouin (1951)
Head of government	Wilfried Martens
Ruling party	Christian Democrat parties of French and Dutch speakers lead a complex coalition
Main urban areas	Brussels (capital, 970,346 in early 1988)
	Antwerp (476,044)
	Ghent (232,620)
	Charleroi (210,000)
	Liège (200,312)
	Bruges (117,857)

Population	375,000 (1989)
Land area	998 sq m
Languages	French (official); Letzeburgesch is the local French dialect, German is also widely spoken as a first language
Religion	Roman Catholic
Currency	Luxembourg Franc (equivalent to the Belgian Franc which is also legal tender)
Head of state	HRH Grand Duke Jean (1964)
Head of government	Jacques Santer
Ruling party	Christian Socialist (in coalition)
Main urban area	Luxembourg (capital, 88,400)

The Kingdom of Belgium, established in 1830, is officially bi-lingual, with the northern and western provinces (Flanders, Antwerp, Limbourg and northern Brabant) being Dutch-speaking and the southern provinces French-speaking. About 85% of the inhabitants of Brussels speak French. 9% of the population are foreigners. Geographically, the country is divided into two by the river Meuse, with the south eastern third of the country, the Ardennes, having poorer soils than the lower lands north and west of the river.

With little in the way of natural resources, except coal, the country relies heavily on agriculture. The major crops are potatoes, sugar beet, wheat and barley. Dairy cattle and pigs are the main livestock.

raw and processed materials to the industrial areas of Germany via the Rhine. Petrochemicals are therefore a large part of this trade, as well as cement, steel products and processed foodstuffs. Heavy industry, especially in Wallonia, suffered badly in the 1980s, but some recovery has been in evidence since the start of 1990.

Belgium has an economic union with Luxembourg, dating back to 1922, and since 1960 a customs union with the Netherlands. It was a signatory of the 1990 Schengen agreement on the mutual abolition of border controls.

Marketing regions

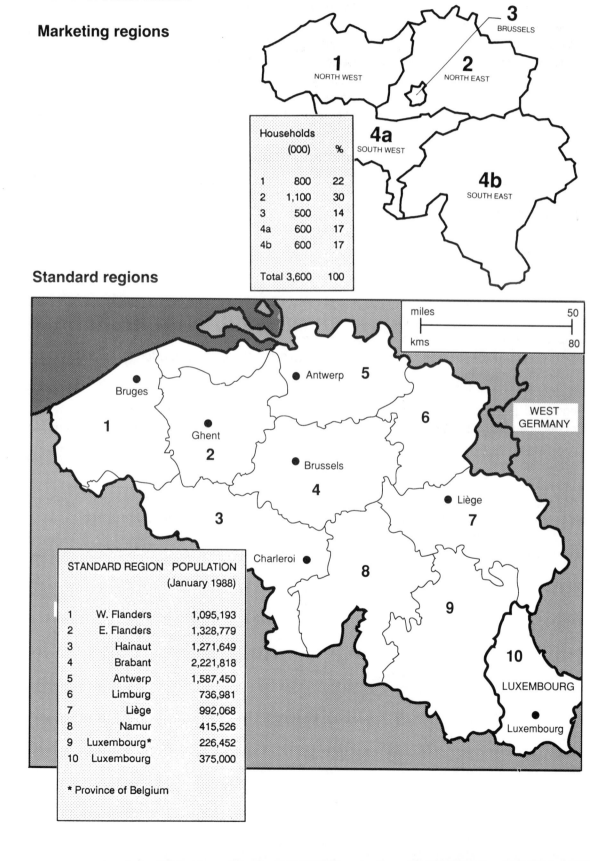

Households		
	(000)	%
1	800	22
2	1,100	30
3	500	14
4a	600	17
4b	600	17
Total	3,600	100

Standard regions

STANDARD REGION		POPULATION (January 1988)
1	W. Flanders	1,095,193
2	E. Flanders	1,328,779
3	Hainaut	1,271,649
4	Brabant	2,221,818
5	Antwerp	1,587,450
6	Limburg	736,981
7	Liège	992,068
8	Namur	415,526
9	Luxembourg*	226,452
10	Luxembourg	375,000

* Province of Belgium

Denmark

Population	5,135,000 (1990)
Urban population	86%
Land area	16,629 sq m
Language	Danish
Currency	Kroner (=100 ore)
Head of state	Queen Margrethe II (1972)
Head of government	Poul Schlüter
Ruling party	Conservative (in coalition)
Main urban areas	Copenhagen (capital, 469,523; 1,547,357 including suburbs)
	Arhus (195,152)
	Odense (137,286)
	Aalborg (113,650)
	Esbjerg (71,112)
	Randers (55,563)

The Jutland peninsula, which forms the bulk of the country's land area, has sandy soil, especially in the west, and consequently much of the available arable land is given over to livestock. Pigs and dairy cattle are the main animals, and the export of bacon and dairy products provides a large portion of the country's income.

Although best known as an agricultural country, Denmark's farming produce supports an expanding industrial base which in 1989 produced nearly 28% of GDP. Barley, for example, supplies a large brewing industry, while pig products are exported all over the world. Other industrial products include agricultural machinery, cement and food products. There is also a significant shipbuilding industry.

Centres of population are concentrated on the numerous islands to the east of Jutland, with Copenhagen facing the Swedish industrial city of Malmö across the Oresund. A system of bridges and causeways links many of the islands, aiding communication and transport, and more are being built.

The Kingdom also includes the Faroe Islands and Greenland, both of which have some degree of autonomy from the Danish parliament. There is some optimism that Greenland may hold reserves of valuable ores, although extraction is likely to be expensive; at present its 55,171 inhabitants (1989 estimate) rely mainly on fishing.

Marketing regions

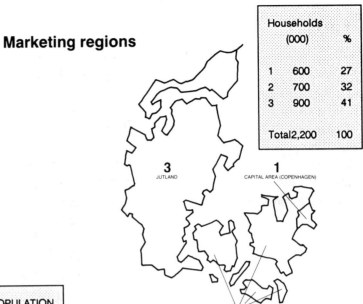

	Households (000)	%
1	600	27
2	700	32
3	900	41
Total	2,200	100

3 JUTLAND

1 CAPITAL AREA (COPENHAGEN)

2 ISLANDS (EXCLUSIVE OF COPENHAGEN)

Standard regions

	STANDARD REGION	POPULATION (1989)
1	N/W Jutland	1,170,000
2	S/SE Jutland	960,000
3	Fyn, Lolland, Bornholm	820,000*
4	Sjaelland	468,000
5	Kobenhavn	1,712,000

* (incl. part of Sjaelland Island)

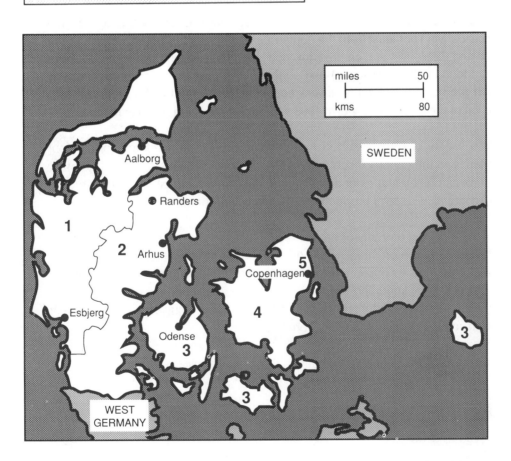

France

Population	57,580,000 (1989)
Urban population	73%
Land area	211,208 sq m
Language	French
Religion	Roman Catholic
Currency	Franc (= 100 centimes)
Head of state	President François Mitterrand (1981)
Head of government	Michel Rocard
Ruling party	Socialist Party
Main urban areas	Paris (capital, 2,188,918)
	Lyon (1,221,000)
	Marseille (1,111,000)
	Lille (936,000)
	Bordeaux (640,000
	Toulouse (541,000)

France is the largest country in Western Europe, and has a population which is predominantly rural in character and is widely spread. Consumer markets are, therefore, highly regionalised, although the concentration of population in the Ile de France (the area around Paris) makes it by far the most important area in marketing terms.

Compared with the cosmopolitan nature of Paris, the southern cities show a decided Mediterranean influence, deriving not least from the numerous immigrants from North Africa. In the south-west, Bordeaux and Toulouse are centres for new high-tech industries, whereas more traditional industries are found in the east (Lyon) and north (Lille). Dependence on heavy industry in the Pas de Calais in the north has created severe economic problems for the area in recent years, but the completion of the Channel Tunnel in 1993 seems likely to bring benefits to the area.

The country supports a variety of climate and soil conditions, producing a number of different crops. Of great importance to the country's economy is the number of vineyards, although other alcoholic beverages such as brandy and cider are also important on a regional basis. Livestock is important to the rural economy, with dairy production particularly important.

France possesses a corresponding diversity of natural resources: natural gas deposits have been exploited in the south-west, and iron ore, coal, uranium and bauxite are also plentiful. France was also one of the first major markets to obtain energy supplies outside the framework provided by the international oil companies: by importing natural gas from the USSR and from its own former colonies, notably Algeria. It has also adopted nuclear energy more enthusiastically than other western nations, deriving some 40% of its electricity from this source.

France is a signatory of the 1990 Schengen agreement on the mutual abolition of border controls.

Marketing regions

Households		
	(millions)	%
1	3.9	20
2	2.3	12
3	1.8	9
4	1.6	8
5	2.0	10
6	1.8	9
7	1.9	10
8	2.4	13
9	1.8	9
Total	19.5	100

Standard regions

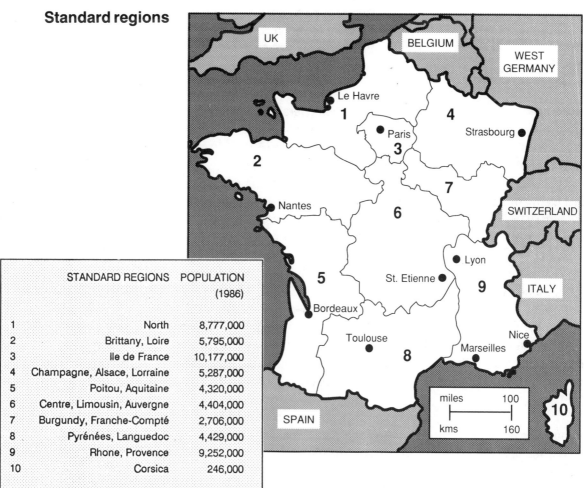

	STANDARD REGIONS	POPULATION
		(1986)
1	North	8,777,000
2	Brittany, Loire	5,795,000
3	Ile de France	10,177,000
4	Champagne, Alsace, Lorraine	5,287,000
5	Poitou, Aquitaine	4,320,000
6	Centre, Limousin, Auvergne	4,404,000
7	Burgundy, Franche-Compté	2,706,000
8	Pyrénées, Languedoc	4,429,000
9	Rhone, Provence	9,252,000
10	Corsica	246,000

Federal Republic of Germany

Population	62,285,000
Urban population	86%
Land area	95,976 sq m
Religions	Protestant (41.6%), Roman Catholic (42.9%), Jewish (0.5%)
Currency	Deutschmark (= 100 pfennig)
Head of state	President Dr Richard von Weizsäcker (1984)
Head of government	Dr Helmut Kohl
Ruling party	Christian Democrat (in coalition with Free Democrats); elections due in October 1990
Main urban areas	West Berlin (2,012,700 in June 1987 census)
	Hamburg (1,592,700)
	Munich (1,188,800)
	Cologne (927,500)
	Essen (623,000)
	Frankfurt am Main (618,500)
	Dortmund (583,600)
	Düsseldorf (563,400)
	Stuttgart (552,300)
	Bremen (533,400)
	Duisberg (525,200)
	Hanover (517,900)
	Bonn (capital, 276,500)

The scheduled reunification of West Germany, the Federal Republic, with the German Democratic Republic in October 1990 means that the biggest industrial power in Europe also becomes the most populous; with a total population increasing from 62 to 79 million, the country's EC partners face a period of economic adjustment in their dealings with the country. Moreover, the authorities of what is currently West Germany will need to make vast investments, both social and economic, as East Germany adds its five administrative regions to the 11 in the Federal Republic. West Berlin will eventually take over from Bonn as the capital of a reunited Germany, although the necessary legislation had still to be finalised in September 1990.

The industrial heartland of the present West Germany is the Ruhr, a vast conurbation stretching along the Ruhr valley and up the Rhine as far as Cologne. The Rhine provides a transport link for the supply of raw materials and the export of finished goods. The area itself is rich in mineral resources, particularly coal, lignite and ire ore, and there are further important coal reserves further west in the Saarland. There is, however, a lack of other energy resources. Some natural gas has been exploited close offshore in the North Sea and on land in the north of the country, but much of the country's oil requirements have to be imported, largely through the Netherlands.

The northern cities of Hamburg and Bremen also support metalworking industries, and there are numerous shipyards along the North Sea and Baltic coastlines. In the south of the country, there are lighter manufacturing centres in Bavaria and the upper Rhine valley. Frankfurt, situated in the

Main valley east of the Rhine, is the country's financial centre.

The agricultural areas of the north have comparatively poor soil for northern Europe, and the main crops are potatoes, barley, wheat, rye and oats. Apples are grown in large quantities, and the Rhine valley provides a good setting for vineyards. Livestock are predominantly cattle (largely dairy) and pigs.

The main concentration of population is in the west, close to the Dutch border, in the Ruhr region, and also along the Rhine valley as far as the French border near Karlsruhe. Elsewhere centres of population are more widely spread. There is a clear cultural division between the mainly Protestant northern states and the predominantly Catholic states of Bavaria and Baden-Württemburg.

Marketing regions

Households (000, 1987 census)		%
1	5,216	19.9
2	7,195	27.4
3a	4,291	16.4
3b	4,529	17.3
4	3,900	14.9
5	1,091	4.2
Total	26,218	100.0

Standard regions

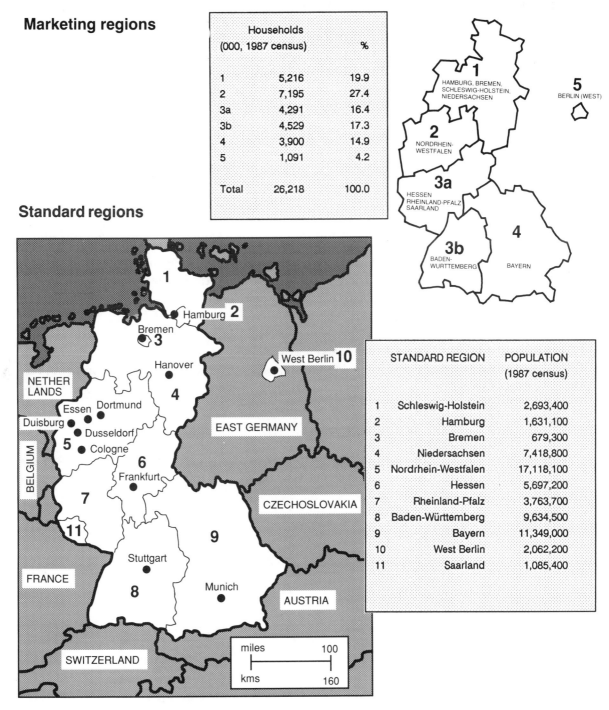

STANDARD REGION	POPULATION (1987 census)
1 Schleswig-Holstein	2,693,400
2 Hamburg	1,631,100
3 Bremen	679,300
4 Niedersachsen	7,418,800
5 Nordrhein-Westfalen	17,118,100
6 Hessen	5,697,200
7 Rheinland-Pfalz	3,763,700
8 Baden-Württemberg	9,634,500
9 Bayern	11,349,000
10 West Berlin	2,062,200
11 Saarland	1,085,400

Greece

Population	10,105,000 (1990)
Urban population	60%
Land area	50,944 sq m
Language	Greek
Religion	Greek Orthodox
Currency	Drachma (= 100 leptae)
Head of state	President Christos Sartzetakis (1985)
Head of government	Iannis Tzannetakis
Ruling party	New Democracy Party
Main urban area	Athens (capital, 3,449,735 in 1981 census)
	Salonika (Thessaloniki, 759,551)
	Patras (166,280)
	Volos (115,545)
	Larissa (110,167)
	Candia (Iraklion, on Crete) (110,137)

Development in modern Greece has been hampered by the dual disadvantages of poor agricultural and natural resources, and of the country's relatively isolated geographical position: it is the only EC member state which has no borders with other EC members.

The hot climate and parched soils are poor for cereal crops (although wheat and rice are grown), favouring fruits such as olives, peaches, oranges, lemons and grapes. Fresh and dried fruits are an important part of Greece's exports. There is some exploitation of bauxite resources, as well as magnesium ore and oil, and the country has set up petroleum refineries to serve its domestic market - although much of its crude oil is imported.

The country's mountainous topography, and the scattering of island communities, imposes a physical restriction on communications and transport. Moreover, a great deal of investment has been necessitated by the development of the electricity system, and by the broadening of the irrigation programmes. Regional aid from the European Community is a major source of development capital at present.

The Greek economy has had to rely on tourism to provide a large part of its income, but there are signs that growth in this sector is beginning to slow down, with tourists from western European countries venturing further afield.

Marketing regions

	Households (000)	%
1	1,050	37
2	220	8
3	550	19
4	550	19
5	470	17
Total	2,840	100

Standard regions

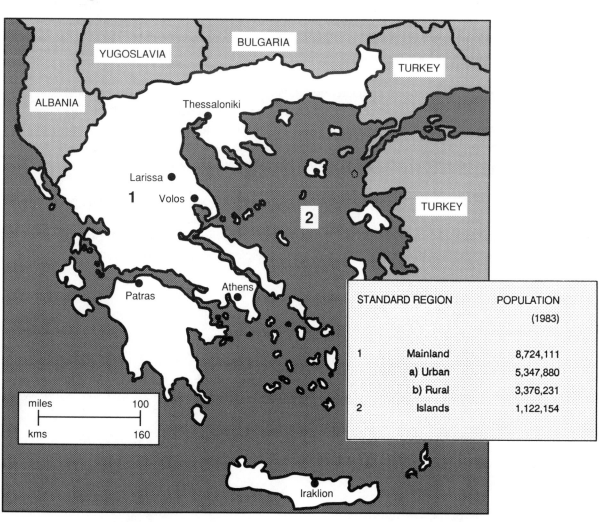

STANDARD REGION		POPULATION (1983)
1	Mainland	8,724,111
	a) Urban	5,347,880
	b) Rural	3,376,231
2	Islands	1,122,154

Irish Republic

Population	3,521,000 (1989)
Urban population	57%
Land area	27,136 sq m
Language	Irish, English
Religions	Catholic (93%). Church of Ireland (3%), Presbyterian (0.4%)
Currency	Punt (= 100 pence)
Head of state	President Patrick J Hillery (1976)
Head of government	Charles J Haughey
Ruling party	Fianna Fail
Main urban areas	Dublin (capital, 920,956, including county)
	Cork (173,694)
	Limerick (76,557)
	Galway (47,104)

Ireland is a largely low-lying island, exposed to the Atlantic ocean and dominated by a wet climate. The Irish Republic, the southern part of the island, was left when the United Kingdom partitioned Ireland in 1921. The economy is still largely dependent on farming, with potatoes and barley the dominant crops, and with an important dairy and cattle sector.

There is relatively little indigenous manufacturing industry, but considerable growth has been seen in the export-orientated assembly of high-technology and other goods on behalf of Japanese, American and West European companies - all attracted by the generous incentives offered by the Government. However, the growth has failed to stem the increase in unemployment which has driven thousands of people into emigration, and in 1990 the population was actually shrinking.

The UK remains the country's most important trading partner, although this position has declined somewhat since Ireland's accession to the EC. Food and food products make up the largest part of the country's exports, although the recent development of oil reserves in the Irish Sea has also made a contribution to trade. Manufactured goods and chemicals are the major imports.

Marketing regions

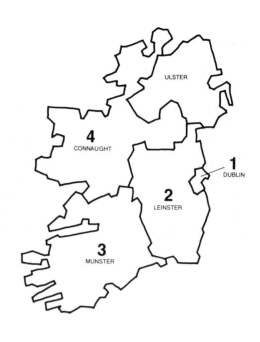

Households		
	(000)	%
1	455	52
2	251	29
3	106	12
4	58	7
Total	870	100

Standard regions

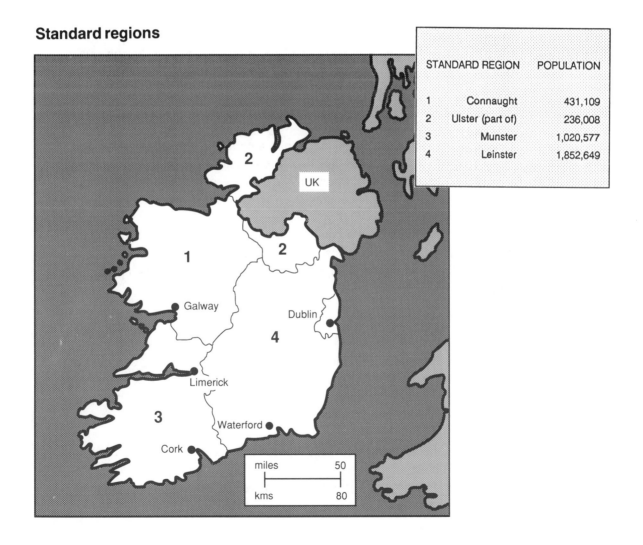

	STANDARD REGION	POPULATION
1	Connaught	431,109
2	Ulster (part of)	236,008
3	Munster	1,020,577
4	Leinster	1,852,649

Italy

Population	58,047,000 (1990)
Urban population	67%
Land area	116,304 sq m
Language	Italian
Currency	Lira
Head of state	President Francesco Cossiga (1985)
Head of government	Giulio Andreotti
Ruling party	Christian Democrats (in coalition with Socialist Party)
Main urban areas	Rome (capital, 2,816,474 in January 1989)
	Milan (1,464,127)
	Naples (1,202,582)
	Turin (1,012,180)
	Palermo (731,483)
	Genoa (714,641)
	Bologna (422,204)
	Florence (417,487)

The size and shape of Italy imply a diversity in all areas of economic life, but broadly speaking the country can be regarded as having two distinct areas: to the north of Rome lie the prosperous industrial areas and fertile arable land: to the south (the Mezzogiorno) the climate is harder with correspondingly poorer agriculture.

Milan is the main industrial centre, with steel, machine tool and automobile industries, and is also the hub of the Lombardy region, which houses much of the country's financial and banking services. West of Milan lies Turin, where 75% of the country's cars are made, and the Piedmont region, where the country's textile industry is concentrated.

In the north-east there has in recent years been some development of light industry, especially in Verona, Trieste and around Venice. Similarly, in Tuscany and Emilia, regions of special agricultural importance, industry has developed: in Florence (leather), in Bologna (food processing), and in numerous smaller towns.

South of Rome, social conditions are different, with higher unemployment and lower standards of living. The Government is attempting to encourage industry around Naples and on the Adriatic coast around Bari. There are some industrial plants, notably oil refineries in the east and a steelworks at Taranto. But the soil quality in the south is poor, and agriculture concentrates on fruits (olives, oranges, tomatoes) and nuts. For many southern regions tourism is an important part of the economy, particularly in Sicily and on the Adriatic coast.

The overall Italian economy seems to have recovered from problems of inflation, balance of payments deficits and industrial unrest, which were largely responsible for the poor growth of the 1970s, and there is considerable optimism about the expansion of the country's consumer economy. Unemployment remains a problem, however, particularly in the south.

Marketing regions

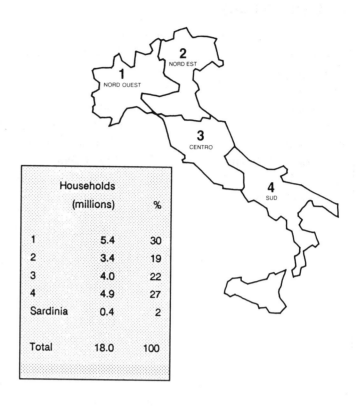

Households		
	(millions)	%
1	5.4	30
2	3.4	19
3	4.0	22
4	4.9	27
Sardinia	0.4	2
Total	18.0	100

Standard regions

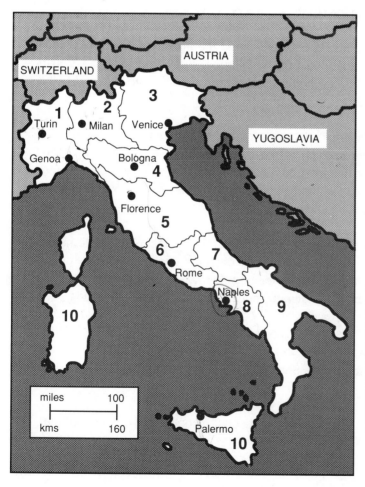

	STANDARD REGION	POPULATION
		(1989)
1	Valle d'Aosta, Piedmont,	
	Liguria	6,218,934
2	Lombardia	8,898,951
3	Friuli, Veneto, Trentino	6,470,988
4	Emilia-Romagna	3,921,281
5	Marche, Umbria, Toscana	5,814,065
6	Lazio	5,156,053
7	Abruzzi and Molise	1,597,903
8	Campania	5,773,067
9	Calabria, Basilicata,	
	Puglia	6,833,324
10	Sicilia, Sardinia	6,820,125

Netherlands

Population	14,842,300 (1990)
Urban population	88%
Land area	15,770 sq m
Language	Dutch
Currency	Florin or Guilder (= 100 cents)
Head of state	HM Queen Beatrix (1980)
Head of government	Ruud Lubbers
Ruling party	Christian Democrats and Labour Party (in coalition)
Main urban areas	Amsterdam (capital, 694,680 at January 1989)
	Rotterdam (572,642)
	The Hague (seat of government, 445,127)
	Utrecht (229,326)
	Eindhoven (190,736)
	Groningen (167,788)
	Tilburg (155,110)
	Haarlem (149,198)

With 352 persons per square kilometre, the Netherlands is the most densely populated major European nation. Most of the population live in the southern half of the country, but there has been an increase too in the areas reclaimed from the North Sea in recent decades.

Arable land, especially in the reclaimed areas, is very fertile, and the agricultural sector is highly productive, with potatoes, wheat, rye and sugar beet the main crops, and with dairy cattle, poultry and pigs as the main livestock. There is a large horticultural sector exporting flowers and bulbs, and an important fishing industry.

The importance of the Netherlands lies in its position as a trading nation, which for centuries has provided much of the nation's wealth. Its position at the mouth of the rivers Rhine, Maas and Scheldt allows it to act as an entrepôt for materials moving into West Germany and other central European countries, and industries such as oil and petrochemical refining have grown up to take advantage of this trade, as has a large banking and financial services sector.

There are few metal deposits, but there is some coal mining, and during the 1980s large natural gas reserves were exploited in the north of the country and offshore. Lacking its own iron ore resources, there is little heavy industry: rather, manufacturing activity centres on electrical and mechanical engineering, automobiles, aircraft and defence equipment, and consumer goods.

The Netherlands has three of the largest consumer product companies in Europe: Royal Dutch Shell (oil, plastics and petrochemicals), Unilever (household and personal products), Philips (domestic appliances and consumer electronics). Shell and Unilever are both co-owned by UK interests.

The country was a signatory of the 1990 Schengen agreement on the abolition of border controls.

Marketing regions

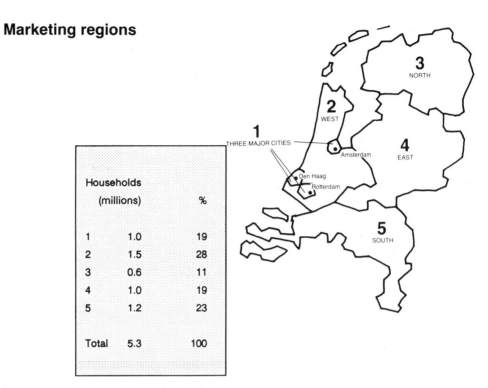

Households (millions)		%
1	1.0	19
2	1.5	28
3	0.6	11
4	1.0	19
5	1.2	23
Total	5.3	100

Standard regions

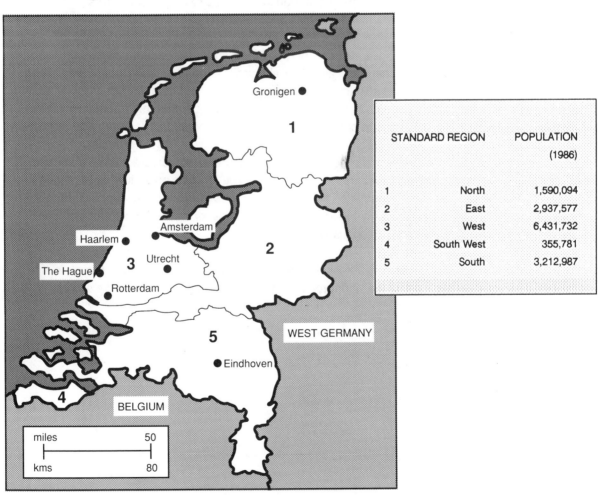

STANDARD REGION		POPULATION (1986)
1	North	1,590,094
2	East	2,937,577
3	West	6,431,732
4	South West	355,781
5	South	3,212,987

Portugal

Population	10,350,000 (1990)
Urban population	34%
Land area	34,317sq m
Language	Portuguese
Currency	Escudo (= 100 centavos)
Head of state	Dr Mario Lopes Soares (1986)
Head of government	Dr Anibal Cavaco Silva
Ruling party	Social Democrat Party
Main urban areas	Lisbon (capital, 807,937 in 1981 census)
	Oporto (327,368)
	Amadora (95,518)
	Setubal (77,885)
	Coimbra (74,616)
	Braga (63,033)

Since the late 1970s Portugal has emerged from a period of political upheaval, and with its accession to the EC and increasing revenues from tourism, appears to be growing into a profitable and expanding economy.

Development assistance is helping a variety of industries, notably textiles, footwear, food processing and wood products. There are also two shipyards, and a modern steelworks. The industrial sector as a whole is as yet still underdeveloped, however, and manufactured goods and raw materials make up a large part of the country's imports. A burgeoning trade deficit has necessitated strict controls on lending to consumers.

Because of the nature of the soil and the hot climate, agricultural products are mainly fruits and potatoes. Cereal crops are largely imported. Its seaboard situation has given it a large, though comparatively unorganised, fishery industry. There are a number of small mineral deposits, but the country lacks coal and oil reserves. It has begun to make use of its hydro-electric potential, however, which is helping the growth of industry.

In recent years tourism has become extremely important, particularly in the Algarve region in the far south, where as much as 90% of the workforce is directly or indirectly involved in the sector.

Marketing regions

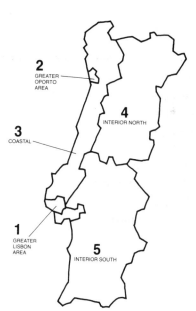

Households		
	(000)	%
1	700	20
2	300	9
3	1,200	35
4	600	18
5	600	18
Total	3,400	100

Map labels:
- 2 GREATER OPORTO AREA
- 4 INTERIOR NORTH
- 3 COASTAL
- 1 GREATER LISBON AREA
- 5 INTERIOR SOUTH

Standard regions

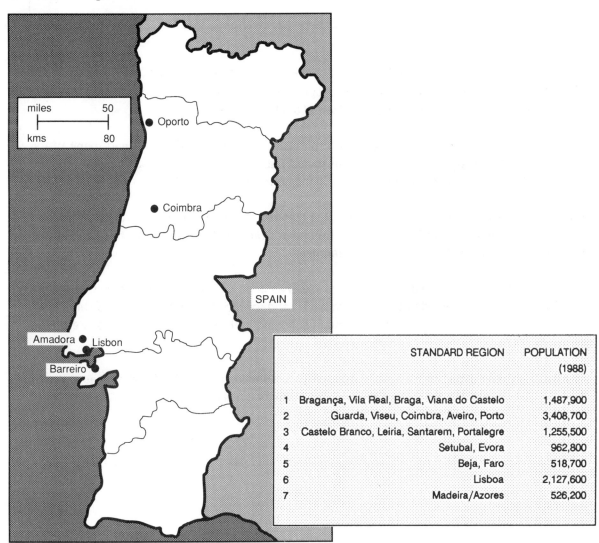

miles 50
kms 80

● Oporto

● Coimbra

SPAIN

Amadora ● Lisbon
Barreiro

	STANDARD REGION	POPULATION
		(1988)
1	Bragança, Vila Real, Braga, Viana do Castelo	1,487,900
2	Guarda, Viseu, Coimbra, Aveiro, Porto	3,408,700
3	Castelo Branco, Leiria, Santarem, Portalegre	1,255,500
4	Setubal, Evora	962,800
5	Beja, Faro	518,700
6	Lisboa	2,127,600
7	Madeira/Azores	526,200

Spain

Population	39,242,000 (1990)
Urban population	76%
Land area	194,897 sq m
Languages	Spanish (Castilian, Catalan, Galician), Basque
Currency	Peseta (= 100 centimos)
Head of state	King Juan Carlos I (1975)
Head of government	Felipe Gonzalez Marquez
Ruling party	Socialist Workers' Party (PSOE)
Main urban areas	Madrid (capital, 3,188,297)
	Barcelona (1,754,900)
	Valencia (751,734)
	Seville (643,833)
	Zaragoza (590,750)
	Malaga (503,251)
	Bilbao (433,030)

The interior of Spain is dominated by a relatively fertile plain allowing the cultivation of a variety of fruits (olives, grapes, citrus fruits, tomatoes, peppers, etc), as well as nuts cereals, hemp and flax/ The export of food products is an important part of the Spanish economy.

Spain also has numerous mineral deposits, but these are becoming depleted and many of the more accessible reserves have already been mined out. Coal, oil, iron and other metal ores are found throughout the country, and particularly in the north-east.

The main industrial centres are on the east coast (centred on Barcelona) and north coast (around Bilbao); since the accession of Spain to the European Community in 1986 there has been strong interest from foreign investors in Spanish enterprises.

The consumer boom in Spain since the start of 1987 has been one of the strongest seen anywhere in Europe, with a pronounced shift away from basics and towards luxury goods. In 1989 and 1990, however, the Government was forced to restrain spending in the face of growing pressure on the trade balance.

Tourism is an integral part of the Spanish economy, contributing around 1,500 billion Ptas a year to the balance of payments. British tourists comprise more than half of the country's foreign visitors.

Marketing regions

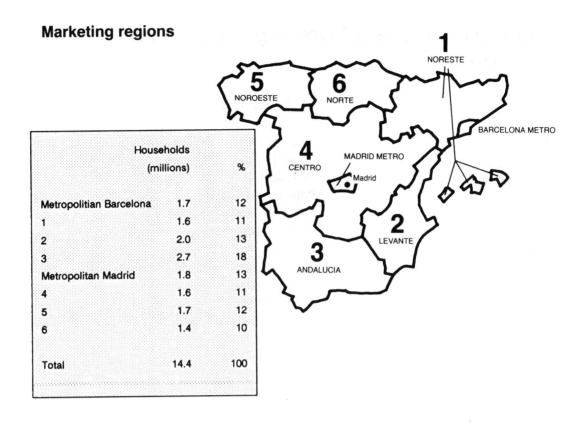

	Households (millions)	%
Metropolitian Barcelona	1.7	12
1	1.6	11
2	2.0	13
3	2.7	18
Metropolitan Madrid	1.8	13
4	1.6	11
5	1.7	12
6	1.4	10
Total	14.4	100

Standard regions

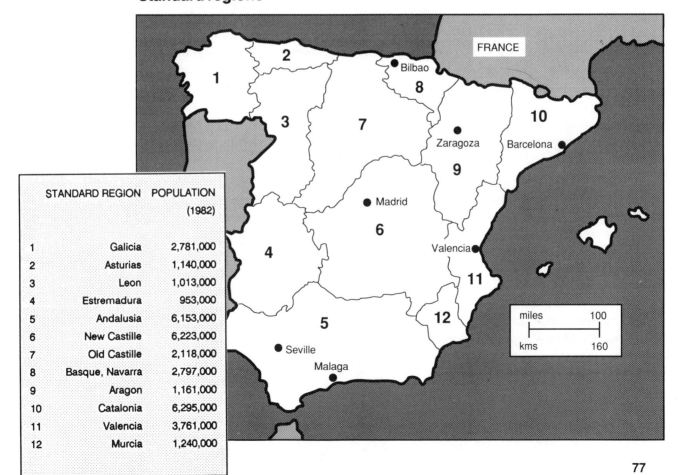

	STANDARD REGION	POPULATION (1982)
1	Galicia	2,781,000
2	Asturias	1,140,000
3	Leon	1,013,000
4	Estremadura	953,000
5	Andalusia	6,153,000
6	New Castille	6,223,000
7	Old Castille	2,118,000
8	Basque, Navarra	2,797,000
9	Aragon	1,161,000
10	Catalonia	6,295,000
11	Valencia	3,761,000
12	Murcia	1,240,000

United Kingdom of Great Britain and Northern Ireland

Population	57,397,000 (1990)
Urban population	92%
Land area	93,005 sq m
Language	English
Religion	Protestant
Currency	Pound (= 100 pence)
Head of state	HM Queen Elizabeth II (1952)
Head of government	Margaret Thatcher
Ruling party	Conservative Party
Main urban areas	Greater London (capital, 6,735,000)
	Birmingham (974,000)
	Leeds (710,000)
	Glasgow (703,000)
	Sheffield (528,000)
	Liverpool (470,000)
	Bradford (464,000)
	Manchester (446,000)
	Edinburgh (433,000)
	Bristol (378,000)

Britain's position as a wealthy nation was derived initially from the fertile agricultural land, particularly in the east of England, and subsequently from the development of heavy industry in the Midlands and the north of the country. Its imperial possessions in the eighteenth and nineteenth centuries enabled further growth in manufacturing industry by providing raw materials, and its position as a major trading nation helped to make London the world's leading financial centre.

Although many of these factors are now less relevant, the country is managing to replace much of its lost industrial base with new high-tech and light industries. London remains one of the three main financial centres in a vastly expanded global market, and relies on its heavy services income from abroad to offset its equally heavy trade deficits. Agriculture remains extremely efficient, and in the 1970s and 1980s large reserves of hydrocarbons in the North Sea have been exploited to provide another significant source of income.

Over-borrowing by consumers in the late 1980s, combined with a high interest rate policy and a continuing trade deficit, has braked the economy in the early 1990s. The effects have not been felt equally across the country, however: traditional manufacturing areas in the north and the Midlands have been worst affected, while the south in general and Greater London in particular remain more affluent. The completion of the Channel Tunnel to France, scheduled for 1993, will further add to the pressures in the region although it will generate considerable wealth as well.

Marketing regions

	Households (millions)	%
1	4.3	22
2	1.2	6
3	1.5	8
4	2.0	10
5	2.9	15
6	2.7	14
7	2.1	11
8	1.0	5
9	1.8	9
Total	19.5	100

Standard regions

	STANDARD REGION	POPULATION (000, mid-1988)
1	North	3,071
2	Yorks, Humberside	4,913
3	E. Midlands	3,970
4	E. Anglia	2,034
5	South East	17,344
6	South West	4,634
7	W. Midlands	5,207
8	North West	6,364
9	Wales	2,857
10	Scotland	5,094
11	N. Ireland	1,578

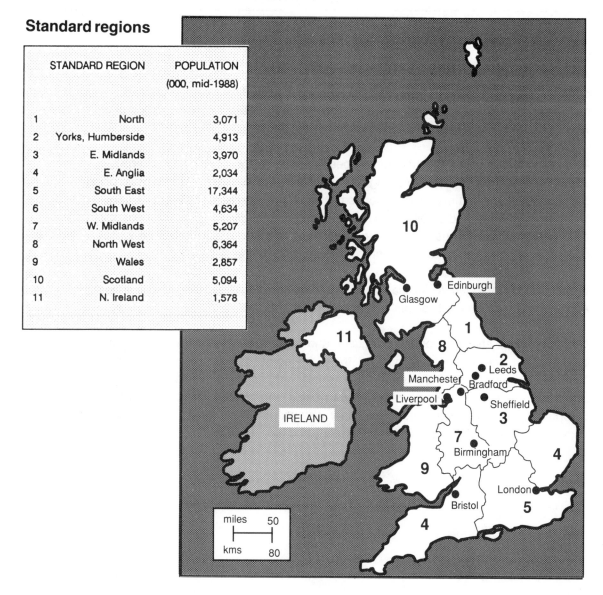

Austria

Population	7,650,000 (1990)
Urban population	56%
Land area	32,374 sq m
Language	German (minorities speak Slovene and Croat)
Religion	Roman Catholic
Currency	Schilling (= 100 Groschen)
Head of state	President Dr Kurt Waldheim (1986)
Head of government	Dr Franz Vranitzky
Ruling party	Socialist Party of Austria, in coalition with the National People's Party
Main urban areas	Vienna (capital, 1,531,346 in 1981 census)
	Graz (243,166)
	Linz (199,910)
	Salzburg (139,426)
	Innsbruck (117,287)
	Klagenfurt (87,321)

Although a mountainous country, Austria's climate sustains a variety of crops and fruit, including potatoes, sugar beet, wheat, barley, apples and pears, as well as a large number of vineyards. The main livestock animals are dairy cows, pigs and chickens. With a large proportion of land forested, wood and timber-derived products are also important.

Austria's industrial sector has traditionally been dominated by state-owned enterprises, especially in the important machine tool and engineering sector, but 1987-90 saw moves to privatise these often cumbersome and loss-making concerns. Natural resources include brown coal, magnesium and aluminium ores, and small quantities of oil and natural gas. The terrain lends itself to hydro-electric production; the use of nuclear power was rejected in a referendum in 1987, and the country's only nuclear reactor at Zwentendorf is currently being dismantled.

Tourism is very important to Austria - foreign currency earnings from over 15 million foreign visitors were equivalent to over 25% of total federal income in 1988.

Although Austria shares a common language and heritage with West Germany, which represents its overwhelmingly major trade partner, there are some marked differences, due not only to Austria's adherence to Catholicism, but also its links with, and its proximity to, the eastern Slavonic countries of the Warsaw Pact. In July 1989 Austria submitted a formal application to join the European Community; negotiations are under way with Brussels for an improvement in the road links on which through traffic from West Germany and Italy depends.

Marketing regions

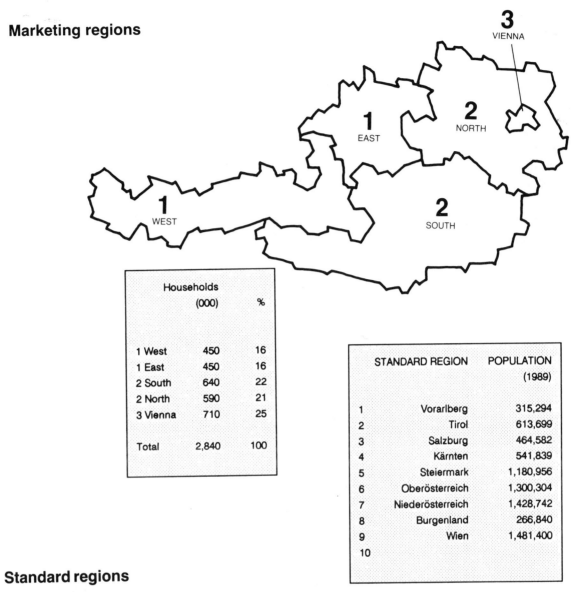

Households		
	(000)	%
1 West	450	16
1 East	450	16
2 South	640	22
2 North	590	21
3 Vienna	710	25
Total	2,840	100

STANDARD REGION		POPULATION (1989)
1	Vorarlberg	315,294
2	Tirol	613,699
3	Salzburg	464,582
4	Kärnten	541,839
5	Steiermark	1,180,956
6	Oberösterreich	1,300,304
7	Niederösterreich	1,428,742
8	Burgenland	266,840
9	Wien	1,481,400
10		

Standard regions

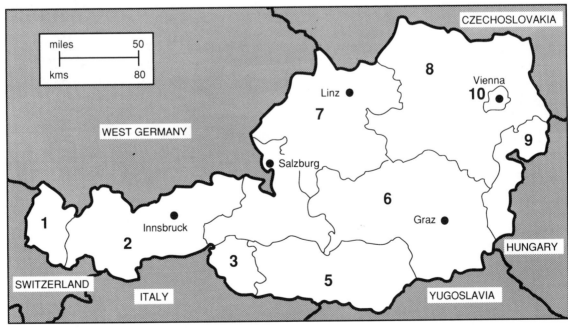

Finland

Population	4,963,000 (1990)
Urban population	64%
Land area	137,851 sq m
Language	Finnish (93.5%), Swedish (6.3%), Lapp (0.2%)
Religions	Lutheran (90%), Greek Orthodox
Currency	Markkas (= 100 pennia)
Head of state	President Dr Mauno Koivisto (1982)
Head of government	Harri Holkeri
Ruling party	National Coalition Party leads a four-party coalition
Main urban areas	Helsinki (capital, 489,965 in January 1989)
	Tampere (171,068)
	Espoo (167,734)
	Turku (159,917)
	Vantaa (151,157)
	Oulu (98,933)
	Lahti (93,251)

Although most of its economy derives from activities in the southern portion of the country, Finland also possesses huge natural resources in the forests which cover some 65% of the land area in the north and centre.

Much of the country's industry centres on processing of wood products, which make up some 40% of exports. Engineering, shipbuilding and chemical sectors have been growing in importance, however, and the country also produces a large quantity of consumer goods, particularly textiles and footwear, and also plastics, electronic equipment, glassware and ceramics. By 1990 engineering and industrial goods will account for 61% of total exports.

The country's agricultural sector is limited by the amount of arable land available, and by the poor nature of the soil, which favours livestock rather than crops.

The main centres of population are in the south, notably in Helsinki and in other major cities on the coast. Improvements in communication links have, however, encouraged a spread of the population into the interior of the country, where there are numerous lakes. Further north the population is more thinly spread, being concentrated on the coast.

Finland faces a serious shortage of labour in the 1990s, due to the low birth rates of previous decades, and this is likely to spin off into wage/price pressures. The country is also painfully aware of the likely impact of the Single European Market on its trade with EC members, but has so far been unable to mobilise industry for change.

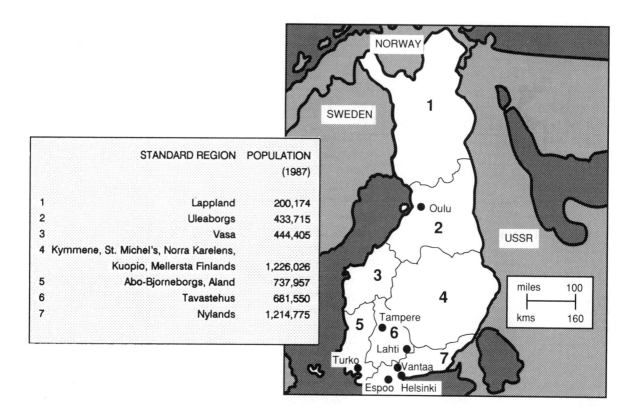

	STANDARD REGION	POPULATION (1987)
1	Lappland	200,174
2	Uleaborgs	433,715
3	Vasa	444,405
4	Kymmene, St. Michel's, Norra Karelens, Kuopio, Mellersta Finlands	1,226,026
5	Abo-Bjorneborgs, Aland	737,957
6	Tavastehus	681,550
7	Nylands	1,214,775

Iceland

Population	251,690 (January 1989)
Urban population	89%
Land area	39,768 sq m
Language	Icelandic
Currency	Krona (= 100 aurar)
Head of state	Vigdis Finnbogadottir (1980)
Head of government	Steingrimur Hermansson
Ruling party	Progressive Party heads a three-party coalition
Main urban areas	Reykjavik (capital, 91,497)
	Kopavogur (14,687)
	Akureyri (13,761)
	Hafnarfjordur (13,425)
	Keflavik (6,980)

Being geographically isolated from the rest of Western Europe, Iceland's economy relies to a large extent on its fishing industry. In recent years the country's natural energy resources have begun to be more widely exploited: in addition to hydro-electric generation the potential for geothermal power is only now beginning to be realised. The abundance of such energy sources has increased the feasibility of building an industry based on energy-intensive manufacturing, although virtually all raw materials need to be imported.

There is almost no arable land in Iceland, but sheep are reared in large numbers on lowland pasture. Apart from fish and lamb, virtually all other foodstuffs are imported.

Transport poses a problem for the country: there are no railways, and most main roads (few of which are metalled) are impassable in winter. Consequently, all the main towns are situated on the coast, and transport is effected by sea.

Norway

Population	4,233,000 (1990)
Urban population	73%
Land area	149,282 sq m
Language	Norwegian
Currency	Krone (= 100 ore)
Head of state	King Olav V (1957)
Head of government	Gro Harlem Brundtland
Ruling party	Labour
Main urban areas	Oslo (capital, 451,818 in January 1990)
	Bergen (211,866)
	Trondheim (137,408)
	Stavanger (97,716)
	Kristiansand (64,926)
	Drammen (51,892)

Norway's mountainous terrain and craggy coastline make overland transport extremely difficult. Except for the southern areas around Oslo, where the land is somewhat flatter, towns are located on the coast.

Until the 1970s the economy was founded on the fishery industry, which benefited from the warm Gulf Stream feeding the coastal waters. However, the discovery of oil and gas reserves in the Norwegian sector of the North Sea dramatically altered the nature of the economy. In the early 1980s the sector directly employed 18% of the total workforce, and shipbuilders turned to producing drilling equipment, creating a corresponding growth in other service industries. Meanwhile, the exploitation of hydro-electric power also enabled the growth of energy-intensive industries.

By 1985, however, it was clear that this situation could not last. Falling oil revenues, increasing government debts and widespread overspending by consumers had created a threatening economic crisis which has only just been held off by repeated devaluation of the currency and harsh austerity budgets. Labour shortages are a recurrent feature of the Norwegian economy and these periodically push the wage/price spiral to levels which endanger the external trade balance.

The country has a number of mineral deposits, although the terrain makes extraction expensive. Aluminium, molybdenum and titanium are exported in significant quantities. Agricultural production is assisted by the Gulf Stream, although the growing season is short. Potatoes and barley are the main crops, and forestry is also important. Sheep and pigs are kept, but the livestock sector is dominated by the fishery industry.

Marketing regions

	Households	
	(000)	%
1	200	13
2	400	27
3	300	20
4	300	20
5	200	13
6	100	7
Total	1,500	100

Standard regions

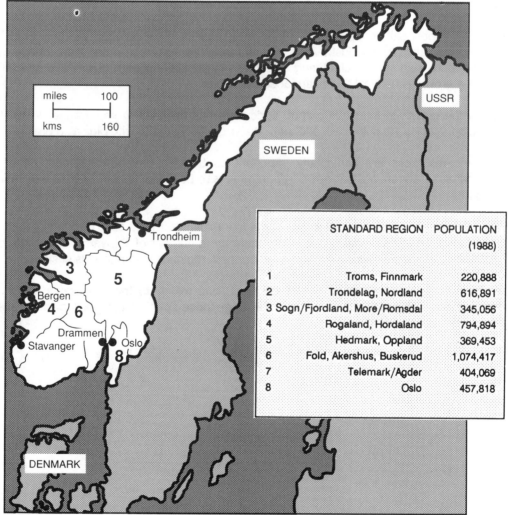

STANDARD REGION	POPULATION
	(1988)
1 Troms, Finnmark	220,888
2 Trondelag, Nordland	616,891
3 Sogn/Fjordland, More/Romsdal	345,056
4 Rogaland, Hordaland	794,894
5 Hedmark, Oppland	369,453
6 Fold, Akershus, Buskerud	1,074,417
7 Telemark/Agder	404,069
8 Oslo	457,818

85

Sweden

Population	8,553,981 (January 1990)
Urban population	83%
Land area	173,732 sq m
Language	Swedish
Religion	Lutheran (95%)
Currency	Krona (= 100 ore)
Head of state	King Carl XVI Gustav (1973)
Head of government	Ingvar Carlsson
Ruling party	Social Democratic Labour Party
Main urban areas	Stockholm (capital, 1,666,810)
	Göteborg (431.521)
	Malmö (230,838)
	Uppsala (159,962)
	Orebro (119,066)
	Norrköping (119,001)
	Vasteras (118,602)

Sweden's profitable industrial sector stems from the country's abundance of natural resources, especially forests, mineral deposits and hydro-electric power.

Forests cover almost half of the country's land area, and have encouraged the growth of large timber, wood pulp and paper industries. Its mineral resources include iron ore, lead, zinc, sulphur, uranium and aluminium. Its manufacturing industries are generally of high quality and specialised, and there is a growing chemical and pharmaceutical sector.

Because of the growth in industrial output, agriculture has declined in importance. A variety of cereals and vegetables are cultivated, and there is a large dairy sector, with pigs also preferred.

Hydro-electric resources are particularly important as Sweden has no significant oil or gas deposits, and as its current nuclear power programme is to be discontinued by 2010 as a result of a referendum.

The main concentrations of population are in the low midlands to the east (around Stockholm), and further south on the Kattegat coast, where there are a number of shipyards. Unlike the other Nordic countries, there are towns throughout the northern regions, as transport is easier.

Sweden faces a recurrent shortage of skilled labour, due mainly to low birth rates in previous decades, and this has periodically worsened the wage/price spiral to the point of necessitating devaluations of the national currency.

Marketing regions

	Households (000, 1985)	%
1	640	17.4
2	650	17.7
3	750	20.4
4	900	24.5
5	730	19.9
Total	3,670	100.0

Standard regions

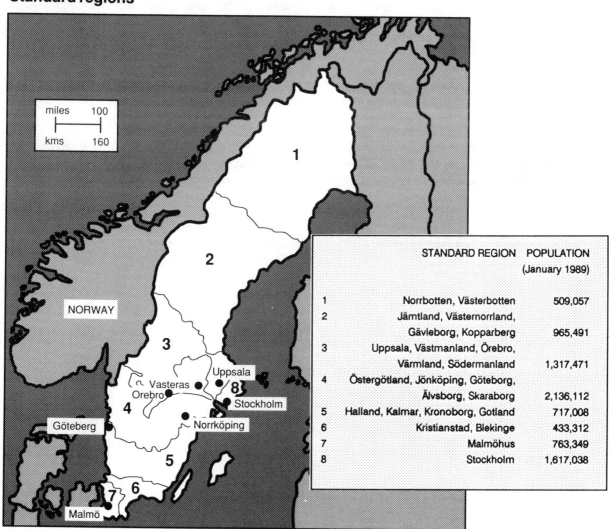

	STANDARD REGION	POPULATION (January 1989)
1	Norrbotten, Västerbotten	509,057
2	Jämtland, Västernorrland, Gävleborg, Kopparberg	965,491
3	Uppsala, Västmanland, Örebro, Värmland, Södermanland	1,317,471
4	Östergötland, Jönköping, Göteborg, Älvsborg, Skaraborg	2,136,112
5	Halland, Kalmar, Kronoborg, Gotland	717,008
6	Kristianstad, Blekinge	433,312
7	Malmöhus	763,349
8	Stockholm	1,617,038

Switzerland

Population	6,660,000 (1990)
Urban population	58%
Land area	15,943 sq m
Languages	German, French, Italian, Romansch
Religion	Roman Catholic (47.6%), Protestant (44.3%)
Currency	Swiss Franc (=100 centimes)
Head of state	Arnold Koller (1990); Flavio Cotti (1991)
Main urban areas	Zurich (349,052: 1988 average)
	Basel (172,294)
	Geneva (166,925)
	Berne (capital, 136,631)
	Lausanne (125,558)

Switzerland occupies a unique position within Europe: as a universally recognised neutral confederation of 26 cantons, and as a particularly important financial centre. Banking, insurance and other financial services are vital to the country's economy, and its advantageous tax rates have also attracted international businesses, particularly those involved in commodity trading.

The country itself is largely mountainous, and its heavily subsidised farming sector is contained in the valleys and the flatter country to the north. Despite the high altitude a wide variety of cereals and other crops are grown, and there are a large number of dairy herds. There is also a vigorous wine industry.

The country has few mineral reserves, but a plentiful supply of hydro-electrical power, and sustains a manufacturing industry on the basis of imported raw materials, exporting finished goods, particularly in the electrical and mechanical engineering, clocks and watches, pharmaceuticals, textiles and woodworking fields.

Industry and population are concentrated in the north of the country, notably in the valley of the river Aare, a tributary of the Rhine which is used a means of transporting raw materials.

Marketing regions

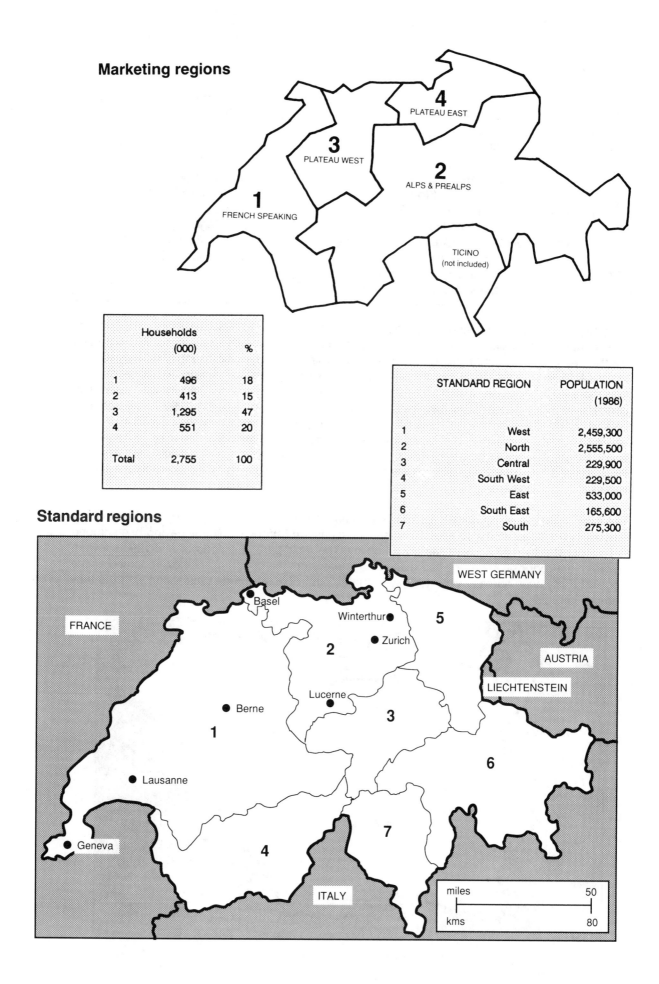

	Households	
	(000)	%
1	496	18
2	413	15
3	1,295	47
4	551	20
Total	2,755	100

	STANDARD REGION	POPULATION
		(1986)
1	West	2,459,300
2	North	2,555,500
3	Central	229,900
4	South West	229,500
5	East	533,000
6	South East	165,600
7	South	275,300

Standard regions

89

Bulgaria

		Main urban areas:
Population	9,065,000 (1990)	
Urban population	67%	
Land area	42,823 sq m	Sofia (capital, 1,128,859)
Language	Bulgarian	Plovdiv (356,596)
Religion	Bulgarian Orthodox	Varna (305,891)
Currency	Lev (= 100 Stotinki)	Ruse (190,450)
Head of state	Acting President Petar	Burgas (197,555)
	Mladenov resigned July 1990	Stara Zagora (156,441)
Head of government	Andrei Lukanov (acting Prime	Pleven (133,737)
	Minister, June 1990)	Tolbukhin (111,037)
Ruling party	Socialist Party (formerly the	
	Bulgarian Communist Party)	

Bulgaria is a largely mountainous country, with most of the centres of population and industry concentrated in the valleys of the Danube (which forms the border with Romania to the north) and the river Maritsa to the south, and on the Black Sea coast in the east. The country has worked hard to establish an industrial base, but it is still significantly dependent on the agricultural sector; it is also more strongly dependent on trade with the troubled Soviet Union than its East European partners, and the transition to hard-currency trading with that country in 1990 is expected to present severe difficulties. Agricultural products still provide a major part of the country's exports. The main crops are wheat, maize, barley and tomatoes, and the wine industry is gaining in importance as an export industry. Although there is some growth in foreign investment from the West, the country is hard pressed to keep abreast of its less heavily indebted competitors when it comes to attracting capital.

The removal of the communist head of state Todor Zhivkov in October 1989 marked one of the most decisive stages in the spread of *perestroika* in eastern Europe - Bulgaria having been among the strongest adherents of old-style Soviet policy. The multi-party elections of mid-1990 showed, however, that opposition groups had made little impression: the communists, now renamed as the Socialist Party, won an easy victory. Only in the autumn of 1990 did dissatisfaction with the new leaders start to show.

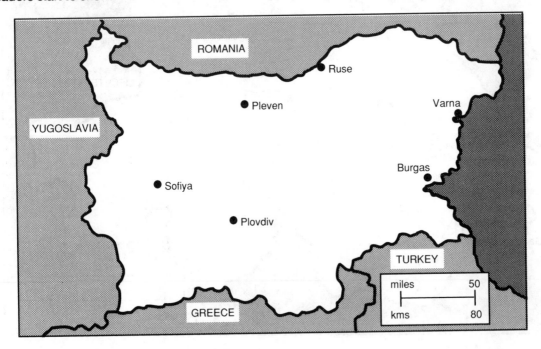

Czechoslovakia

Population	15,654,000 (1990)	Main urban areas:
Urban population	67%	
Land area	49,370 sq m	Prague (capital, 1,211,207)
Languages	Czech, Slovak	Bratislava (435,710)
Currency	Koruna (= 100 Heller)	Brno (389,789)
Head of state	Vaclav Havel (1990)	Ostrava (330,602)
Head of government	Marian Calfa	Kosice (232,362)
Ruling party	Civic Forum/Public Against Violence	Plzen (174,625)

Czechoslovakia comprises a federation of two republics, the Czech lying to the west and including some two thirds of the population and a majority of the country's industry, and the Slovak to the east. Each has its own regional parliament and government. Having been a hard-line Soviet satellite since the ending of the liberal Prague Spring in 1968, Czechoslovakia has adapted relatively quickly to the realities of the multi-party democracy. Less successful, however, have been the government's efforts to wind down the crippling state subsidies with which consumer purchasing power was still buoyed up in mid-1990; by August it was clear that the economic problems caused by price decontrol would be worse than expected.

Overall the country is highly productive: although there is a large proportion of fertile arable land, Czechoslovakia has long been industrialised, and specialises in heavy industries. There is also, however, a significant small business and crafts sector. Although there is little in the way of metallic ores, the country has large resources of coal and lignite, and has built an important base in ferrous metal industries. There are significant deposits of silver and manganese ores. The main agricultural products are potatoes, wheat and barley, and the extensive area under forest produces abundant quantities of wood and wood products.

Until 1990 Czechoslovakia had no private enterprises at all, having progressively eliminated them in the 1960s and 1970s. The population has, however, adapted extremely well to the introduction of the profit principle, and has had no difficulty in attracting investment capital from the West.

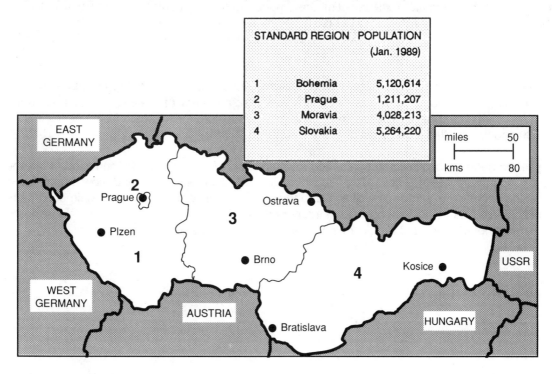

STANDARD REGION	POPULATION (Jan. 1989)
1 Bohemia	5,120,614
2 Prague	1,211,207
3 Moravia	4,028,213
4 Slovakia	5,264,220

German Democratic Republic

(Please see explanatory notes in introduction)

Population	16,200,000 (1990)
Urban population	77%
Land area	41,768 sq m
Language	German
Currency	Deutschmark (= 100 pfennig), after currency union with West Germany in July 1990
Head of state	
Head of government	Lothar de Maizière
Ruling party	Christian Democrats lead a coalition with Social Democrats; elections due October 1990
Main urban areas	East Berlin (capital, 1,284,535)
	Leipzig (545,307)
	Dresden (518,057)
	Karl-Marx-Stadt* (311,765)
	Magdeburg (290,579)
	Rostock (253,990)
	Halle (236,044)

* Shortly due to revert to its traditional name of Chemnitz.

The German Democratic Republic's scheduled reunification with the Federal Republic in October 1990 marks the ending of a split which started after the Second World War, and which was confirmed by the separate 1949 constitutions imposed by the occupying powers, and by the subsequent erection of the Berlin Wall in 1961. The reunification was formalised in September 1990 with the signing in Moscow of a settlement treaty which laid down the terms of the future unified state.

The country, which is due to be incorporated as five regions of the Federal Republic, is far smaller than its western neighbour, with a population of just over a quarter of West Germany's. As in the West, low birth rates have resulted in a shrinking population, quite apart from the estimated 400,000 people who fled to the West after the Hungarian/Austrian border was opened in mid-1989.

Despite the depredations inflicted by the occupying Soviet forces after the Second World War, the country spent the 1960s and 1970s rebuilding its industrial economy and now maintains a flourishing engineering sector as well as light industries such as optical and electronic equipment manufacturing. The country is, however, largely dependent on imports of raw materials from the USSR, most notably fuel, and it lacks much in the way of metal ore resources.

The country is self-sufficient in food, having an abundance of fertile arable land. Agriculture is collectivised, and the main crops are potatoes, rye, barley, and wheat. As with West Germany, cattle and pits predominate in livestock terms.

The currency union with West Germany in July 1990 prompted a major rush for Western goods which has hit local industries unable to compete with their counterparts in the West. At the same time the abolition of most state price subsidies has sent inflation to very high levels, and as the hitherto exclusively state-owned industries are told to become financially independent, unemployment has reached levels of 12-15 per cent. A massive programme of privatisation has attracted ready offers from investors in the Federal Republic.

		STANDARD REGION POPULATION (June 1988)
1	North: Neubrandenburg, Rostock, Schwerin	2,132,184
2	East: Frankfurt, Cottbus	1,598,508
3	West: Magdeburg, Potsdam	2,373,277
4	Central: Halle, Leipzig	3,137,381
5	South West: Erfurt, Gera, Suhl	2,531,859
6	South East: Dresden, Karl-Marx-Stadt/Chemnitz	3,616,888
7	East Berlin	1,284,535

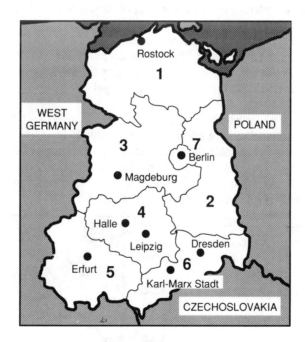

Hungary

Population	10,610,000 (1990)
Urban population	56%
Land area	35,919 sq m
Language	Magyar
Religions	Catholic (65%), Calvinist (30%)
Currency	Forint (= 100 filler)
Head of state	President Arpad Goncz (Interim President, 1990)
Head of government	Jozsef Antall (1990)
Ruling party	Democratic Forum heads a coalition with Smallholders' Party and Christian Democrats
Main urban areas	Budapest (capital, 2,115,000)
	Debrecen (220,000)
	Miskolc (208,000)
	Szeged (189,000)
	Pécs (183,000)

The opening of Hungary's border with Austria in May 1989 marked the first major practical stage in the liberalisation of East European regimes. The massive outflow of East Germans, Czechoslovakians and Hugarians which followed forced the pace of political change elsewhere in the region - most notably in East Germany, where the Berlin Wall was breached in November in an effort to attract the refugees back to their homeland.

Hungary has long maintained a relatively liberal economy, allowing private enterprise to operate alongside its state-run activities; the country was, then, ideally equipped to attract foreign investment capital from the start, and it has been quick to introduce Western-style banking and stockbroking activities. Moreover, liberal cultural and political traditions paved the way for an easy return to multi-party democracy. The country has yet to cope with its hard currency debts, however, which have hindered the expansion in national or personal income, and industry is expected to under-perform for some years yet.

Hungary has nevertheless made major strides in its industrial development, with engineering to the fore. Although well equipped with fuel reserves, in the form of brown coal and natural gas, there is little in the way of metallic deposits, however, and much of the country's raw material requirements are met from imports, largely from the USSR, Czechoslovakia and East Germany. The main agricultural crops are wheat and maize, and the climate also supports a vigorous wine industry. Pigs and sheep dominate the livestock sector.

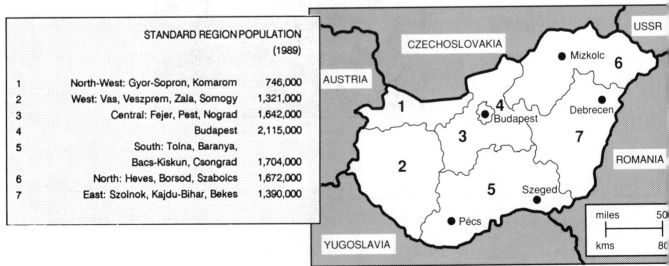

	STANDARD REGION POPULATION	(1989)
1	North-West: Gyor-Sopron, Komarom	746,000
2	West: Vas, Veszprem, Zala, Somogy	1,321,000
3	Central: Fejer, Pest, Nograd	1,642,000
4	Budapest	2,115,000
5	South: Tolna, Baranya, Bacs-Kiskun, Csongrad	1,704,000
6	North: Heves, Borsod, Szabolcs	1,672,000
7	East: Szolnok, Kajdu-Bihar, Bekes	1,390,000

Poland

Population	37,928,000 (1986)
Urban population	61%
Land area	120,725 sq m
Language	Polish
Currency	Zloty (= 100 groszy)
Head of state	General Wojciech Jaruzelski
Head of government	Tadeusz Mazowiecki
Ruling party	Coalition led by Solidarity activists
Main urban areas	Warsaw (capital, 1,651,200 in 1989)
	Lodz (851,500)
	Krakow (743,700)
	Wroclaw (637,400)
	Poznan (586,500)
	Gdansk (461,500)
	Szczecin (409,500)
	Bydgoszcz (377,900)
	Katowice (365,800)

Poland, one of the most heavily industrialised countries of Eastern Europe, supports a large number of heavy industries, including steelworks, shipbuilding, cement works and chemicals. The nation's economy is based on its plentiful supplies of coal, and on iron ore deposits.

Poland was among the major forerunners of *perestroika* in Eastern Europe, installing non-communist politicians in high offices as long ago as the mid-1980s. The victory of non-communist opposition parties in elections held in mid-1980 was followed by the installation of a government sympathetic to the trade union Solidarity, although the President is still constitutionally required to belong to the Communist Party. Constitutional changes are expected in 1991 to end this anomaly.

Poland took bold action at the end of 1989 to liberalise price mechanisms and to remove state subsidies; although rampant inflation followed, it had settled within months to near-stable levels. Privatisation of all state industries is under way, but the high unemployment necessitated by the drive toward efficiency has caused severe personal hardship. At the same time the drive toward reducing industrial pollution has been vigorously enforced, driving some of the largest producers out of business.

Although Poland has vast agricultural areas the land is not particularly fertile, and food products often have to be imported. The main crops are beets, rye, wheat and barley, with livestock of all kinds. Coal mining is of major importance to the export economy.

	STANDARD REGION	POPULATION
		(January 1989)
1	Szczecin, Koszalin, Slupsk, Pila, Zielona Gora, Gorzow	3,481,800
2	Gdansk, Elbiag, Torun, Bydgoszcz, Wloclawek, Plock, Konin	5,070,100
3	Olsztyn, Suwalki, Ciechanow, Ostroleka, Lomza, Bialystok, Siedlce, Biala Podlaska	3,997,200
4	Warsaw	2,412,900
5	Jelenia Gora, Legnica, Leszno, Poznan, Walbrzych, Wroclaw, Kalisz, Opole	5,286,700
6	Sieradz, Lodz, Skiernewice, Piotrkow, Radom, Lublin, Chelm	4,593,800
7	Kielce, Tarnobrzeg, Zamosc, Tarnow, Rzeszow, Przemysl, Nowy Sacz, Krosno	5,149,000
8	Czestochowa, Katowice, Krakow, Bielsko-Biala	6,813,600

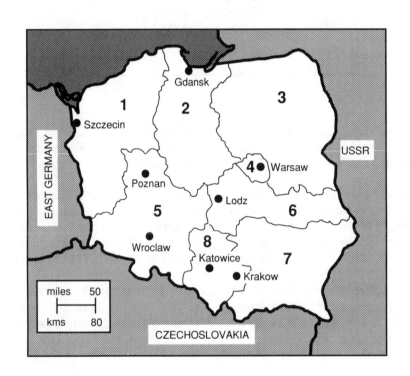

Romania

Population	22,828,000 (1990)
Urban population	49%
Land area	91,699 sq m
Language	Romanian
Religions	Romanian Orthodox, Roman Catholic
Currency	Leu (= 100 Bani)
Head of state	Ion Iliescu (June 1990)
Head of government	Petre Roman
Ruling party	National Salvation Front
Main urban areas	Bucharest (capital, 1,989,823)
	Brasov (351,493)
	Constanta (327,676)
	Timisoara (325,272)
	Iasi (313,060)
	Cluj-Napoca (310,017)
	Galati (295,372)

Romania was the last East European member of the CMEA group to initiate a policy of political change, forcibly removing the Communist president Nicolae Ceausescu in December 1989 and installing in his place an ad hoc alliance of opposition groups. The Ceausescu regime was toppled amid considerable bloodshed as its troops resisted the masses, and the process of recrimination which followed was reflected in continuing political instability throughout the first half of 1990.

Romania's agricultural areas are among the most fertile in eastern Europe. Wallachia (the valley of the Danube) in the south, Moldavia (Siret valley) in the north, and the Transylvanian lowlands to the west support a variety of cereal and beet crops, as well as cattle and sheep rearing, and flax and hemp. The Carpathian and Transylvanian mountains sustain an important forestry sector, and there are vineyards and orchards in the valleys. Nevertheless, productivity has been poor since the early 1980s, with a serious lack of investment.

Coal, oil, natural gas, iron ore, bauxite and other metal ores are found in quantities, and a number of heavy industries have been developed. A drive by the Ceausescu government to eliminate the country's foreign debts resulted, however, in serious under-investment while simultaneously depriving the population of Romania's food products; major food shortages have resulted.

The deposed Ceausescu government's plans to demolish over 7,000 villages, mainly occupied by ethnic Hungarians, have now been dropped; hostility toward the country's Hungarians continues, however, and there were bitter confrontations in Transylvania during early 1990.

All Romanian statistics are open to qualification, having been deliberately tampered with since the mid-1980s. While data presented in this volume is given in good faith, this fact should always be borne in mind.

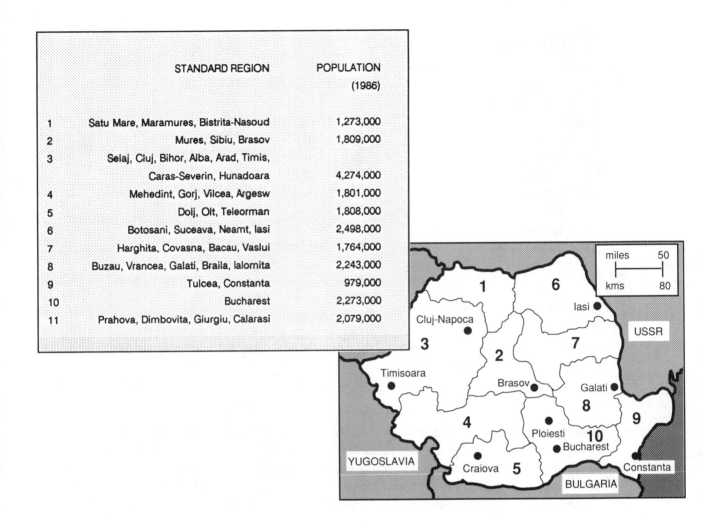

	STANDARD REGION	POPULATION (1986)
1	Satu Mare, Maramures, Bistrita-Nasoud	1,273,000
2	Mures, Sibiu, Brasov	1,809,000
3	Selaj, Cluj, Bihor, Alba, Arad, Timis, Caras-Severin, Hunadoara	4,274,000
4	Mehedint, Gorj, Vilcea, Argesw	1,801,000
5	Dolj, Olt, Teleorman	1,808,000
6	Botosani, Suceava, Neamt, Iasi	2,498,000
7	Harghita, Covasna, Bacau, Vaslui	1,764,000
8	Buzau, Vrancea, Galati, Braila, Ialomita	2,243,000
9	Tulcea, Constanta	979,000
10	Bucharest	2,273,000
11	Prahova, Dimbovita, Giurgiu, Calarasi	2,079,000

Union of Soviet Socialist Republics

Population	284,300,000 (1990)
Urban population	65.6%
Land area	8,649,461 sq m
Language	Russian (numerous dialects and regional languages)
Currency	Rouble (= 100 kopeks)
Head of state and party	Mikhail Gorbachev (1985)
Chairman of Council	Nikolai Ryzhkov (1985)
Ruling party	Communist Party
Main urban areas	Moscow (capital, 8,967,000 in 1989)

Leningrad (5,020,000)	Minsk (1,612,000)
Kiev (2,602,000)	Kharkov (1,611,000)
Tashkent (2,079,000)	Gorky (1,438,000)
Baku (1,757,000)	Novosibirsk (1,436,000)
	Sverdlovsk (1,367,000)

Although the Soviet Union has made immense progress in terms of industry and agriculture since the overthrow of the quasi-feudal rule of the Czars some 80 years ago, progress has been hampered over the years by inefficiency, favouritism and corruption, and a lack of industrial willpower engendered by the absence of a profit principle. At the same time, for many years the USSR's position as leader and guardian of the Warsaw Pact group entailed vast expenditure on defence which is only now being restrained.

Reforms proposed by President Gorbachev in 1986-1988, and partially implemented, have re-introduced the concept of private enterprise to this hitherto exclusively collectivist state. At the same time the tentative winding down of state subsidies on consumer goods has begun; there has, however, been a consumer backlash against the necessary price increases, which has been exploited by separatist and nationalist factions among the republics which make up the union. In late 1990 it was clear that Gorbachev faced a real threat of political defeat, and this has forced him into renewed negotiations with some of his staunchest political critics.

The USSR contains a wealth of natural resources, including the world's largest reserves of oil, natural gas and coal, which are widely spread throughout the county. All kinds of metal ores are found, particularly in the Ural mountains, and 40% of the land is forested.

Overall agricultural efficiency is poor, however, and agricultural development has not been as rapid as the industrial sector. Lack of incentives for collective and state farmers, and poor planning, hindered by the logistical problems of transportation, are blamed, and a succession of poor harvests due to drought have also had an effect. In 1990 the Soviet Union was late in paying instalments on some hard-currency debts; it declared that it would charge its East European allies the current market prices for oil, and that from 1991 it would insist on payment in hard currency for all such transactions.

	STANDARD REGION	POPULATION (1989)
1	Latvia, Estonia, Lithuania	7,944,000
2	Byelorussia	10,200,000
3	Ukraine, Moldavia	56,045,000
4	Armenia, Georgia, Azerbaijan	15,761,000
5	Kazakhstan, Turkmenistan, Tadzikistan, Uzbekistan, Kirghizia	15,761,000
6	Russia	147,386,000

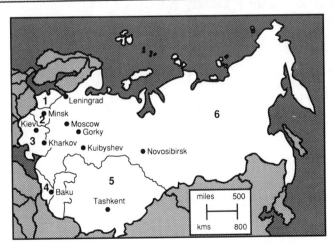

Albania

Population	3,200,000 (1990)
Urban population	34%
Land area	11,099 sq m
Language	Albanian (dialects: Gheg, Tosk)
Currency	Lek (= 100 Quindarkas)
Head of state	Chairman Ramiz Alia (1982)
Head of government	Adil Carcani
Ruling party	Albanian Party of Labour
Main urban areas	Tirana (capital, 225,700 in 1987)
	Durres (78,700)
	Elbassan (78,300)
	Shkodra (76,300)
	Vlora (67,600)
	Korca (61,500)

Independent since 1912, and a republic since 1946, Albania is a small and isolated communist country on the Adriatic coast. The country has pursued a Stalinist, isolationist policy since its liberation from Italian occupation in 1944, and it has only recently begun to encourage external contact, through trade and tourism, especially with Yugoslavia.

Much of the country's land area is mountainous, with arable land confined to coastal areas and the Koritza Basin. Land reclamation projects have increased the area under cultivation, the main crops being maize, wheat and sugar beet. Sheep and goats are the natural livestock for such an environment, and chickens are also kept in large quantities.

Around 50% of the country is forested, and forest products are an important factor in the economy. Other natural resources include chrome (of which Albania has the world's fourth largest resources) and a small amount of petroleum.

The main products of the nation's industry (which is wholly nationalised) are food products, textiles, oil products and cement. Under current plans more attention is being placed on building the country's engineering industries.

Cyprus

Population	730,000 (1990)
Urban population	50%
Land area	3,572 sq m
Languages	Greek (78%), Turkish (18%), Armenian
Currency	Cyprus pound (= 100 cents)
Head of state	President Georgios Vassilliou (1988)
Ruling party	Democratic Rally (in coalition)
Main urban areas	Nicosia (capital, 149,100*)
	Limassol (107,200)
	Larnaca (48,300)
	Famagusta (39,500)

* plus 37,400 in the Turkish sector

Recent Cypriot history has been dominated by the 1974 invasion from Turkey, followed by the partition of the island which left the north sector under the protection of Turkish forces. Turkey has declared this zone a separate state, but it is not recognised as such by any other country.

The country's economy is dominated by the agricultural sector, which provides much of its exports - mainly citrus and vine fruit and products. There is little potential for further growth in this area, and the government has attempted to promote the island as a natural trading station between the West and the Middle East, a policy which appears to be bearing fruit with the installation of a number of international companies' offices.

The need to import much of its raw materials and manufactured goods means that the country's visible trade balance is regularly in deficit, being offset by income from tourism and British and United Nations service personnel stationed on the island. Cyprus entered a customs union with the European Community in 1988.

Gibraltar

Population	29,700 (1990)
Land area	2.25 sq m
Language	English
Head of state	HM Queen Elizabeth II, represented by the Governor
Chief minister	Joe Bossano

Gibraltar's importance to the United Kingdom over nearly three centuries has been as a strategic naval base covering access to the Mediterranean Sea. More recently, its low rates of duty have given it a position as a favoured shopping area and merchant marine base, enhanced by the promotion of tourism.

The reopening in 1986 of the border with Spain has done much to boost the colony's economy. Meanwhile Gibraltar is becoming increasingly important as a centre for financial services related to Mediterranean trade and investment.

Liechtenstein

Population	27,800 (1990)
Land area	61. sq m
Language	German
Currency	Swiss Franc (other currencies are widely accepted)
Head of state	Prince Franz Josef II (1938) (titular)
	Crown Prince Hans Adam (1984) (acting)
Head of government	Hans Brunhart
Ruling party	Patriotic Union Party
Main urban areas	Vaduz (capital, 4,200)

Liechtenstein operates under a customs union with Switzerland, which also represents the principality in diplomatic matters.

The country's economy, once predominantly agricultural in character, has seen a major expansion of light and high-tech industries, and Liechtenstein has acquired a new status as a centre for offshore banking and financial activities. Agriculture is still important, however, and based largely on the rearing of livestock. Tourism has also been developed.

Malta

Population	355,000 (1990)
Urban population	85%
Land area	94.9 sq m
Languages	Maltese, English
Religion	Roman Catholic
Currency	Maltese Lira (= 100 cents)
Head of state	Vincent Tabone (1989)
Head of government	Dr Edward Fenech Adami
Ruling party	Nationalist Party
Main urban areas	Valletta (capital, 9,239 in 1987)
	Birkirkara (20,490)
	Sliema (13,604)

The Maltese economy is remarkably strong for such a small state, and is based on a balance of three areas. The agricultural sector, significant in employment terms, produces a variety of fruit, root crops and legumes, as well as wine and horticultural products. The main industry is shipping and ship repair, but there is also a wide variety of manufacturing industry, producing textiles, clothing, food products, plastics and chemicals. The growth area is now tourism.

Following the election in 1987 of Dr Adami, Malta has made renewed efforts to repair its relations with Western Europe and the United States (hitherto damaged by its close links with the Government of Libya), and it has been trying to attract foreign investment as well as strengthening its relations with the European Community, with which it has an Association Agreement.

Monaco

Population	28,000 (1990)
Urban population	100%
Land area	0.7 sq m
Language	French
Currency	French Franc
Head of state	HSH Sovereign Prince Rainier III
Head of government	Jean Ausseil
Main urban areas	Monaco-ville (1,443)

Monaco's income derives almost exclusively from tourism, and in particular from the Monte Carlo Casino. There is no agriculture - the whole of the principality being built up. Visitors number over 250,000 annually - nearly ten times the population.

Turkey

Population	56,028,000 (1990)
Urban population	46%
Land area	301,380 sq m
Language	Turkish
Religion	Islam (99%)
Currency	Lira (= 100 Kuru)
Head of state	General Kenan Evren (1980)
Head of government	Turgut Özal
Ruling party	Motherland Party
Main urban areas	Istanbul (5,482,985 at 1985 census)
	Ankara (capital, 3,306,327)
	Izmir (2,317,829)
	Adana (1,725,940)
	Bursa (1,324,015)
	Eskisehir (597,397)

Agriculture is the most important sector in the Turkish economy, employing 50% of the workforce and contributing 16% of GDP. Wheat is the major crop, grown on the arid tablelands of Anatolia. Other important crops, cultivated in the coastal areas, include barley, grapes, olives and citrus fruits. Around Izmir there are tobacco farms, and also sultana and fig cultivation. Adana is the centre of cotton cultivation. The foothills of Anatolia are widely afforested, although there is concern that depletion of forest resources is proceeding too rapidly.

Turkey has abundant natural resources, many of which are relatively unexploited. Lignite and hard coal are produced in great quantities, as are ores of iron, copper, chrome and boron. Indigenous industries are centred on the exploitation of these resources, and the processing of its agricultural produce.

Turkey has relatively minor energy resources, although there is a great deal of potential for hydro-electric schemes. It has also developed a thriving trade as an entrepôt for the export of oil and gas from Iraq and other Middle Eastern countries via Ceyhan, where there are refineries and petrochemical plants. However, the invasion of Kuwait by Iraq in August 1990, and the ensuing onset of economic sanctions, have been a serious blow for the country's trade prospects; meanwhile the costs of arming for potential conflict with Iraq further added to the country's worries in the autumn of 1990.

Turkey continues to suffer grave economic problems, the most serious being high inflation and low investment. Unemployment is high, and there is a persistent current account deficit, although this has been reduced in recent years. The government has applied to be considered for membership of the EC, which would presumably assist the country to take advantage of its resources to help stabilise the economy but which has aroused strong protests from Greece. An unstable political scene has also been a problem, and the EC members would obviously like to see evidence that such disturbances are now over before allowing Turkey's accession.

	STANDARD REGION	POPULATION
		(1985 census)
1	Edirne, Kirklareli, Tekirdag	1,089,457
2	Kocaeli, Sakarya	1,352,745
3	Bolu, Zonguldak	1,549,723
4	Izmir, Aydin	3,061,248
5	Rize, Trabzon, Giresun, Ordu, Samsun	3,535,118
6	Adana, Hatay	2,728,192
7	Central region	31,474,990
8	Istanbul	5,842,990

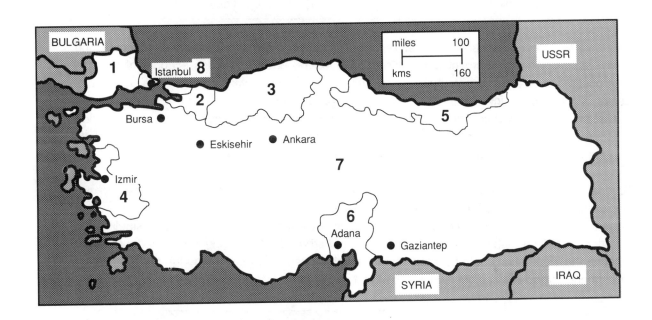

Yugoslavia

Population	23,814,000 (1990)
Urban population	46%
Land area	98,766 sq m
Languages	Serbo-Croat, Slovenian, Macedonian, and several other minor Slavonic, Romance and Magyar dialects
Religion	Orthodox, Catholic, Islamic
Currency	Dinar
Head of state	Borislav Jovic (1990); Stipe Suvar (1991)
Head of party	Milan Pancevski (elections December 1989)
Head of government	Ante Markovic
Ruling party	League of Communists of Yugoslavia
Main urban areas	Belgrade (capital, 1,470,073 at 1981 census)
	Zagreb (768,700) Sarajevo (448,519)
	Skopje (506,547) Ljubljana (305,211)

As a diverse collection of heterogeneous republics, Yugoslavia displays a variety of economic and social regions. The government is organised on a federal basis and takes account of regional differences. Unusually in a communist state, private ownership is widespread in the agricultural sector. A great deal of investment has been made in building the country's manufacturing industry, but attention has now been turned towards developments in the mining, energy and transport sectors. Yugoslavia's industry is based on its large reserves of coal and metal ores, particularly iron, bauxite, copper and mercury, located in the central and southern areas.

Rampant inflation in 1988-1989, which was met with draconian measures to control private sector borrowing and spending, prompted a series of political crises. A wage freeze, combined with a currency reform in January 1990 devaluing the Dinar by a factor of 1,000, helped to stabilise the situation. In 1990 a major resurgence of regional and ethnic conflict brought serious doubt about whether the Federation could hold together for much longer. As a result, although open to foreign investment, Yugoslavia has been unable to attract strong interest from foreign partners.

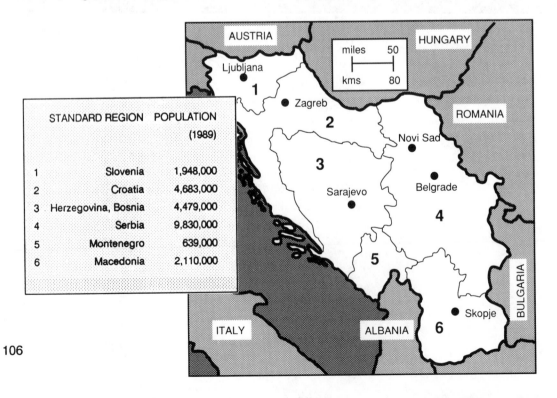

	STANDARD REGION	POPULATION (1989)
1	Slovenia	1,948,000
2	Croatia	4,683,000
3	Herzegovina, Bosnia	4,479,000
4	Serbia	9,830,000
5	Montenegro	639,000
6	Macedonia	2,110,000

	1977	1978	1979	1980	1981	1982	1983	1984	1985
EEC members									
Belgium	9822	9830	9837	9847	9852	9856	9856	9853	9903
Denmark	5088	5104	5117	5123	5122	5118	5114	5112	5114
France	53145	53376	53606	53880	54182	54480	54729	54947	54621
West Germany	61396	61310	61337	61561	61666	61638	61421	61181	61015
Greece	9268	9360	9449	9643	9729	9790	9847	9896	9935
Ireland	3272	3314	3368	3401	3440	3483	3508	3535	3552
Italy	55929	56127	56292	56416	56502	56639	56836	56983	57128
Luxembourg	361	362	363	364	365	366	366	366	366
Netherlands	13853	13937	14030	14144	14246	14310	14362	14420	14484
Portugal	9736	9796	9841	9884	9855	9930	10009	10164	10229
Spain	36351	36775	37183	37430	37654	37935	38228	38333	38602
United Kingdom	56179	56167	56228	56314	56378	56335	56377	56488	56125
EEC total	314400	315458	316651	318007	318991	319880	320653	321278	321074
EFTA members									
Austria	7568	7562	7549	7549	7565	7574	7552	7552	7555
Finland	4739	4753	4765	4780	4800	4827	4856	4882	4908
Iceland	222	224	226	228	231	234	237	239	241
Norway	4043	4059	4073	4086	4100	4115	4128	4141	4152
Sweden	8252	8276	8294	8310	8320	8325	8329	8337	8350
Switzerland	6327	6333	6351	6385	6429	6467	6505	6442	6374
EFTA total	31151	31207	31258	31338	31445	31542	31607	31593	31580
CMEA members									
Bulgaria	8804	8814	8826	8862	8891	8917	8940	8961	8957
Czechoslovakia	15030	15137	15237	15311	15320	15369	15414	15458	15500
East Germany	16765	16756	16745	16737	16736	16697	16699	16671	16644
Hungary	10637	10673	10698	10711	10712	10706	10689	10668	10649
Poland	34698	35010	35257	35578	35902	36227	36571	36914	37203
Romania	21658	21855	22048	22201	22353	22478	22553	22625	23017
USSR	259029	261253	263425	265542	267722	270042	272500	275066	278618
CMEA total	366621	369498	372236	374942	377636	380436	383366	386363	390588
Others									
Albania	2508	2563	2617	2671	2725	2783	2841	2901	2962
Cyprus	613	616	620	627	634	641	649	657	665
Gibraltar	30	29	30	30	30	29	29	29	30
Liechtenstein	24	25	26	26	26	26	26	28	28
Malta	332	340	347	364	364	360	377	380	383
Monaco	25	25	25	26	26	26	27	27	27
Turkey	41768	42640	43530	44438	45366	46312	46279	48265	49272
Yugoslavia	21775	21968	22166	22394	22471	22642	22801	22963	23123
Total	67075	68206	69361	70576	71642	72819	73029	75250	76490
European total	779247	784369	789506	794863	799714	804677	808655	814484	819732

Source: UN Demographic Yearbook/UN Population and Votal Statistics Report/IMF

Database name: Demographic Trends and Forecasts
Sector name: Total Population   Table No: 0201

Title: Trends in Total Population 1977-1989: International Estimates

Unit: 000s

	1986	1987	1988	1989	% growth 1977-89	% share 1977	% share 1989
EC members							
Belgium	9913	9918	9874	9926	1.06	1.26	1.19
Denmark	5121	5127	5138	5143	1.08	0.65	0.62
France	55392	55632	55858	56130	5.62	6.82	6.72
West Germany	61048	61171	61319	61601	0.33	7.88	7.37
Greece	9966	9992	10027	10074	8.70	1.19	1.21
Ireland	3537	3543	3538	3529	7.85	0.42	0.42
Italy	57221	57355	57422	57744	3.25	7.18	6.91
Luxembourg	363	367	372	372	3.05	0.05	0.04
Netherlands	14563	14661	14725	14812	6.92	1.78	1.77
Portugal	10291	10350	10279	10319	5.99	1.25	1.23
Spain	38668	38832	38996	39160	7.73	4.66	4.69
United Kingdom	56763	56891	57065	57244	1.90	7.21	6.85
EC total	322846	323839	324613	326054	3.71	40.35	39.01
EFTA members							
Austria	7565	7573	7574	7594	0.34	0.97	0.91
Finland	4918	4932	4954	4963	4.73	0.61	0.59
Iceland	243	246	248	251	13.06	0.03	0.03
Norway	4169	4187	4192	4238	4.82	0.52	0.51
Sweden	8370	8399	8396	8463	2.56	1.06	1.01
Switzerland	6504	6538	6558	6598	4.28	0.81	0.79
EFTA total	31769	31875	31922	32107	3.07	4.00	3.84
CMEA members							
Bulgaria	8959	8970	8995	9030	2.57	1.13	1.08
Czechoslovakia	15534	15573	15600	15627	3.97	1.93	1.87
East Germany	16624	16641	16650	16648	-0.70	2.15	1.99
Hungary	10627	10613	10626	10639	0.02	1.37	1.27
Poland	37456	37664	37703	37742	8.77	4.45	4.52
Romania	23174	22936	22900	22864	5.57	2.78	2.74
USSR	280144	283100	283500	283900	9.60	33.24	33.97
CMEA total	392518	395497	395974	396450	8.14	47.05	47.44
Others							
Albania	3022	3083	3130	3177	26.67	0.32	0.38
Cyprus	673	680	700	720	17.46	0.08	0.09
Gibraltar	30	30	30	30	0.00	0.00	0.00
Liechtenstein	27	28	29	30	25.00	0.00	0.00
Malta	385	344	347	350	5.41	0.04	0.04
Monaco	27	27	28	28	12.00	0.00	0.00
Turkey	50301	51350	52243	53136	27.22	5.36	6.36
Yugoslavia	23271	23411	23535	23659	8.65	2.79	2.83
Total	77736	78953	80042	81130	20.95	8.61	9.71
European total	824869	830164	832551	835740	7.25	100.00	100.00

Database name: Demographic Trends and Forecasts
Sector name: Total Population   Table No: 0202

Title: Trends in Total Population 1977-1990 : National Estimates for January 1st

Unit: 000s

	1977	1980	1981	1982	1983	1984	1985	1986	1987	1988	1989	1990	Not
EC members													
Belgium	9823	9855	9863	9855	9858	9853	9857	9865	9876	9881	9928	9980	
Denmark	5080	5122	5124	5199	5116	5112	5111	5116	5125	5129	5130	5135	
France	53019	53731	54029	54335	54626	54831	55062	55278	55510	55750	56017	57580	
West Germany	61442	61439	61658	61713	61546	61307	61049	61020	61238	61715	62000	62285	
Greece	9308	9643	9729	9790	9847	9896	9919	9950	9978	10000	10058	10105	a
Ireland	3262	3401	3443	3480	3504	3529	3540	3537	3542	3539	3530	3521	a
Italy	56123	57000	56479	56537	57342	56933	57080	57202	57291	57399	57723	58047	
Luxembourg	361	364	365	366	366	366	366	367	370	372	375	375	
Netherlands	13814	14091	14209	14286	14340	14394	14454	14530	14615	14715	14805	14892	
Portugal	9403	9714	9819	9892	9969	10050	10129	10185	10230	10304	10310	10350	
Spain	36155	37242	37520	37856	38067	38280	38495	38549	38750	38910	39082	39242	
United Kingdom	56190	56330	56352	56306	56347	56460	56618	56763	56847	57017	57218	57397	
EC total	313980	317932	318590	319615	320928	321011	321680	322362	323372	324731	326176	328909	
EFTA members													
Austria	7568	7549	7555	7574	7552	7553	7558	7566	7576	7598	7624	7650	b
Finland	4731	4771	4788	4812	4842	4870	4894	4911	4932	4950	4954	4963	
Iceland	221	227	229	233	236	238	241	242	246	249	253	255	
Norway	4035	4079	4092	4107	4123	4134	4146	4159	4175	4198	4221	4233	
Sweden	8236	8303	8318	8323	8327	8331	8343	8358	8381	8414	8459	8527	
Switzerland	6298	6314	6335	6373	6410	6428	6456	6485	6523	6567	6620	6660	
EFTA total	31089	31243	31317	31422	31490	31554	31638	31721	31833	31976	32131	32288	
CMEA members													
Bulgaria	8804	8862	8891	8917	8940	8961	8960	8950	8970	8995	9030	9065	b
Czechoslovakia	15030	15311	15320	15369	15414	15458	15500	15519	15573	15600	15627	15654	b
East Germany	16767	16740	16740	16706	16706	16709	16671	16655	16641	16650	16648	16200	
Hungary	10615	10710	10713	10711	10700	10679	10657	10640	10607	10620	10633	10610	
Poland	34528	35414	35735	36062	36399	36745	37063	37341	37811	37850	37889	37928	
Romania	21660	22201	22353	22478	22553	22625	22725	22860	22936	22900	22864	22828	b
USSR	259029	265542	267722	270042	272540	275066	277537	280144	283100	283500	283900	284300	a
CMEA total	366433	374780	377474	380285	383252	386243	389113	392109	395638	396115	396591	396585	
Others													
Albania	2508	2671	2725	2783	2841	2901	2962	3022	3083	3130	3177	3200	a
Cyprus	613	623	631	637	645	653	662	669	680	700	720	730	
Gibraltar	30	30	30	29	29	29	28	29	30	30	30	30	
Liechtenstein	24	26	25	26	26	27	27	27	28	29	30	30	
Malta	311	323	326	328	332	338	340	343	346	349	352	355	
Monaco	25	26	26	27	27	27	27	27	27	28	28	28	
Turkey	41768	44438	45540	46688	47864	49070	50664	52150	53250	54176	55102	56028	a
Yugoslavia	21780	22304	22471	22642	22805	22966	23118	23270	23442	23566	23690	23814	a
Total	67059	70441	71774	73160	74569	76011	77828	79537	80886	82008	83129	84215	
European total	778561	794396	799155	804482	810239	814819	820259	825729	831729	834830	838027	841997	

Source: National Statistical Offices : all countries
Notes: Non-EEC data for 1988 are Euromonitor estimates
     a   Mid-year
     b   Annual average

Database name: Demographic Trends and Forecasts
Sector name: Total Population

Table No: 0203

Title: Total Population: Latest Official Census Year

Unit: 000s

	Year	Total	Male	Female	0-14	15-64	65+
EC members							
Belgium	1981	9849	4810	5038	1972	6462	1415
Denmark	1981	5124	2528	2596	968	3151	1005
France	1982	54335					
West Germany	1987						
Greece	1981	9740	4780	4960			
Ireland	1986	3541	1770	1771	1025	2131	385
Italy	1981	56557	27506	29051	12128	36944	7485
Luxembourg	1981	365	178	187	67	248	50
Netherlands	1971	13060					
Portugal	1981	9833	4738	5095			
Spain	1981	37746	18530	19216	9686	20189	7871
United Kingdom	1981	55089	26803	28286	11455	35465	8169
EC total							
EFTA members							
Austria	1981	7555	3572	3983	1511	4898	1146
Finland	1980	4785	2313	2472	967	3242	576
Iceland	1970	205	104	101			
Norway	1980	4091	2027	2064	1215	2040	836
Sweden	1980	8320	4122	4198	1585	5357	1377
Switzerland	1980	6366	3115	3251	1222	4262	882
CMEA members							
Bulgaria	1985	8948					
Czechoslovakia	1980	15283	7441	7842			
East Germany	1981	16706	7849	8857			
Hungary	1980	10710	5189	5521	2341	6539	1830
Poland	1984	37026	18026	19000			
Romania	1977	21560	10626	10934			
USSR	1979	262436	122329	140107			
Others							
Albania	1960	1626	835	791			
Cyprus	1982	643	320	323	161	413	69
Gibraltar	1981	26	13	14	6	18	3
Liechtenstein	1981	26	13	13			
Malta	1985	346	170	176	83	229	34
Monaco	1982	27	13	14			
Turkey	1985	50664	25072	24992	18391	30145	2128
Yugoslavia	1981	22425	11084	11341	5488	14804	2133

Source: UN Population & Vital Statistics Report/National Statistical Offices

Database name: Demographic Trends and Forecasts
Sector name: Vital Statistics

Table No: 0204

Title: Number of Live Births 1977-1989

Unit: 000s

	1977	1980	1981	1982	1983	1984	1985	1986	1987	1988	1989	Notes
EEC members												
Belgium	121.9	124.4	123.8	120.3	117.4	115.7	114.0	117.0	118.0	115.5	119.1	
Denmark	61.9	57.3	53.1	52.7	50.8	51.8	54.0	55.4	56.4	58.8	61.5	
France	744.7	800.4	805.5	797.2	748.8	760.5	769.1	778.9	767.7	770.8	757.8	
West Germany	582.3	620.7	624.6	621.2	594.2	584.2	584.8	624.4	642.3	677.3	677.4	
Greece	143.7	148.1	141.0	137.3	132.6	126.8	116.7	112.3	105.9	107.3	106.8	
Ireland	68.9	74.1	72.2	70.8	67.1	64.2	62.2	61.4	58.8	54.3	53.3	
Italy	741.1	640.4	621.8	617.5	600.3	586.0	576.2	580.0	550.6	568.5	571.7	
Luxembourg	4.1	4.2	4.4	4.3	4.2	4.2	4.1	4.3	4.2	4.5	4.5	
Netherlands	173.3	181.3	178.6	172.1	170.2	174.4	178.2	185.0	186.2	185.5	189.6	
Portugal	181.1	158.4	152.1	151.0	144.3	136.9	130.5	128.0	124.2	118.2	113.5	
Spain	661.1	565.4	532.3	509.7	477.3	465.7	451.0	434.0	425.0	409.5	411.2	
United Kingdom	657.0	753.7	730.8	719.2	721.5	729.6	750.7	755.0	773.7	781.8	790.0	
EEC total	4141.1	4128.2	4040.0	3973.2	3828.7	3800.0	3791.3	3835.7	3813.1	3852.0	3856.2	
EFTA members												
Austria	85.6	90.9	93.9	94.8	90.1	89.2	86.6	86.3	86.3	88.0	88.8	
Finland	65.7	63.1	63.5	66.1	66.9	65.1	63.0	60.8	59.2	63.4	64.0	
Iceland	4.0	4.5	4.3	4.3	4.4	4.1	3.8	3.9	4.2	4.7	4.7	
Norway	50.9	51.0	50.7	51.2	49.9	50.3	51.4	52.5	54.0	57.5	59.2	
Sweden	96.1	97.1	94.1	92.7	91.8	93.9	98.3	102.0	104.7	112.1	115.9	
Switzerland	72.8	73.7	73.7	74.9	73.7	74.7	74.7	76.3	76.5	80.3	79.8	
EFTA total	375.0	380.2	380.3	384.2	376.8	377.3	377.8	381.7	384.9	406.0	412.5	
CMEA members												
Bulgaria	141.7	128.9	124.4	124.2	123.0	122.3	117.9	120.4	115.7			
Czechoslovakia	281.3	248.9	237.7	234.4	229.5	227.8	225.2	220.0	214.9			
East Germany	223.2	245.1	237.5	240.1	233.8	228.1	227.4	222.3	226.3	214.8		
Hungary	177.6	148.7	142.9	133.6	127.3	125.3	129.9	128.5	125.2	124.3		
Poland	662.6	692.8	678.7	702.4	720.8	699.0	677.6	634.7	606.4	584.4	562.4	
Romania	424.0	398.9	381.1	344.4	321.5	350.7	358.8	361.0	365.0			
USSR	4693.4	4851.4	4961.4	5100.3	5391.9	5386.9	5374.4	5614.7	5605.4			
CMEA total	6603.6	6714.7	6763.7	6879.2	7147.6	7140.2	7111.2	7301.6	7258.9			
Others												
Albania	70.0	70.7	72.2	77.2	73.8	79.2	77.5	77.5				
Cyprus	11.3	12.8	13.1	13.5	14.6	13.5	13.0	13.1	12.7			
Gibraltar	0.5	0.6	0.5	0.6	0.5	0.5	0.5	0.5	0.5	0.5		
Liechtenstein	0.3	0.4	0.4	0.4	0.3	0.4	0.4	0.4				
Malta	5.9	5.8	5.5	6.1	5.7	5.6	5.4	5.4	5.5	5.5		
Monaco	0.2	0.5	0.5	0.5	0.5	0.5	0.5	0.5				
Turkey	650.0	650.0	650.0	650.0	650.0	650.0	650.0	650.0				a
Yugoslavia	384.6	382.1	369.0	378.8	379.3	376.4	367.5	358.3	358.2	355.4	338.3	
Total	1122.9	1122.9	1111.2	1127.1	1124.8	1126.1	1114.8	1105.7				
European total	12242.7	12346.0	12295.2	12363.7	12477.9	12443.7	12395.2	12624.6				

Source: UN Demographic Yearbook/UN Population & Vital Statistics Report
Notes: Figures of 0 signify totals less than 0.5
a   Euromonitor estimate

Database name: Demographic Trends and Forecasts
Sector name: Vital Statistics

Table No: 0205

Title: Number of Deaths 1977-1989

Unit: 000s

	1977	1980	1981	1982	1983	1984	1985	1986	1987	1988	1989
EEC members											
Belgium	112.7	113.7	112.3	112.5	114.8	109.7	110.8	110.5	106.1	110.6	112.2
Denmark	50.5	55.9	56.4	55.4	57.2	57.1	58.4	58.1	58.0	59.0	59.4
France	536.2	547.1	554.8	543.1	559.7	540.6	552.5	546.9	528.5	525.1	527.6
West Germany	704.9	714.1	722.2	715.9	718.3	696.1	703.4	699.6	687.0	687.5	692.7
Greece	83.8	87.3	86.3	86.3	90.6	88.5	92.1	91.5	95.9	93.3	92.7
Ireland	33.6	33.5	32.9	32.5	33.0	32.2	31.9	33.6	31.0	31.6	31.4
Italy	546.7	554.5	545.3	535.0	564.0	535.0	547.0	542.0	533.4	534.0	548.6
Luxembourg	4.1	4.1	4.1	4.1	4.1	4.1	3.9	4.0	4.0	3.7	4.0
Netherlands	110.1	114.3	115.5	117.3	117.8	119.8	122.4	125.0	121.7	123.7	127.4
Portugal	96.2	95.0	95.9	92.6	96.4	97.2	97.3	97.3	96.3	98.7	97.0
Spain	294.3	287.6	286.4	282.3	296.2	295.4	295.5	306.0	310.0	312.0	313.3
United Kingdom	655.1	661.5	658.0	662.8	659.1	644.9	670.6	660.7	637.2	650.5	669.8
EEC total	3228.2	3268.6	3270.1	3239.6	3311.1	3220.6	3285.8	3275.2	3209.1	3229.6	3275.9
EFTA members											
Austria	92.4	92.4	92.7	91.3	93.0	88.5	89.0	86.5	84.9	83.3	83.4
Finland	44.1	44.4	44.4	43.4	45.4	45.1	48.2	47.1	47.8	49.0	47.6
Iceland	1.4	1.5	1.7	1.6	1.7	1.6	1.7	1.7	1.7	1.8	
Norway	39.8	41.3	41.9	41.5	42.2	42.5	44.2	40.8	44.8	45.4	45.0
Sweden	88.2	91.8	92.0	90.7	90.8	90.5	94.0	93.0	93.2	96.7	92.0
Switzerland	55.7	59.1	59.8	59.2	60.8	58.6	59.6	60.1	59.5	60.6	60.7
EFTA total	321.6	330.6	332.4	327.7	333.9	326.8	336.6	329.1	332.0	336.9	328.7
CMEA members											
Bulgaria	94.4	98.0	95.4	100.3	102.2	101.4	107.4	101.8	107.6		
Czechoslovakia	173.4	186.1	180.0	181.2	186.9	183.9	182.6	184.0	179.1		
East Germany	226.2	238.3	232.2	228.0	222.7	221.2	225.4	223.5	214.7		
Hungary	132.0	145.4	144.8	144.3	148.6	146.7	147.4	146.4	142.2		
Poland	313.0	350.2	328.9	334.9	349.4	364.9	381.5	376.3	376.6		
Romania	208.7	231.9	224.6	224.1	233.9	233.7	246.7	242.0			
USSR	2494.7	2743.8	2742.1	2723.6	2822.6	2964.9	2947.1	2741.2	2802.7		
CMEA total	3642.4	3993.6	3948.1	3936.3	4066.4	4216.7	4238.1	4015.3	3822.9		
Others											
Albania	16.5	17.0	18.0	16.5	17.4	16.7	17.2	17.0			
Cyprus	5.5	5.8	5.3	5.4	5.6	5.3	5.7	5.3	6.1		
Gibraltar	0.2	0.3	0.2	0.2	0.3	0.3	0.3	0.3	0.2	0.3	
Liechtenstein	0.1	0.2	0.2	0.2	0.2	0.2	0.2	0.2			
Malta	2.9	3.2	3.1	3.1	3.1	2.9	2.8	2.8	2.9	2.7	
Monaco	0.3	0.5	0.6	0.4	0.4	0.4	0.4	0.4			
Turkey	122.7	130.1	136.1	130.7	134.7	136.3	141.3	133.1			
Yugoslavia	182.8	197.4	201.2	203.3	219.3	213.1	211.0	212.0	215.4	211.8	215.3
Total	331.0	354.4	364.6	359.8	381.0	375.1	378.9	371.1	224.5	214.8	215.3
European total	7523.2	7947.2	7915.3	7863.4	8092.3	8139.2	8239.5	7990.7	7588.5	3781.3	3820.0

Source: UN Demographic Yearbook/UN Population & Vital Statistics/National Statistical Offices

Title: Birth Rates 1977-1989

Unit: Per 000 inhabitants

	1977	1980	1981	1982	1983	1984	1985	1986	1987	1988	1989	Note
EC members												
Belgium	12.4	12.6	12.6	12.2	11.9	11.7	11.5	11.8	11.9	11.7	12.0	
Denmark	12.2	11.2	10.4	10.3	9.9	10.1	10.6	10.8	11.0	11.5	12.0	
France	14.0	14.9	14.9	14.6	13.7	13.8	14.1	14.1	13.8	13.8	13.5	
West Germany	9.5	10.1	10.1	10.1	9.7	9.5	9.6	10.2	10.5	11.0	11.0	
Greece	15.5	15.4	14.5	14.0	13.5	12.8	11.7	11.3	10.6	10.7	10.6	
Ireland	21.1	21.8	21.0	20.3	19.1	18.2	17.5	17.4	16.6	15.3	15.1	
Italy	13.1	11.4	11.0	10.9	10.6	10.3	10.1	9.7	9.6	9.9	9.9	
Luxembourg	11.2	11.4	12.1	11.8	11.4	11.5	11.2	11.7	11.5	12.1	12.0	
Netherlands	12.5	12.8	12.5	12.0	11.9	12.1	12.3	12.7	12.7	12.6	12.8	
Portugal	18.6	16.0	15.4	15.2	14.4	14.2	12.8	12.4	12.0	11.5	11.0	
Spain	18.0	15.2	14.1	13.6	12.7	12.3	11.7	11.2	10.9	10.5	10.5	
United Kingdom	11.8	13.4	13.0	12.8	12.8	12.9	13.3	13.3	13.6	13.7	13.8	
EC total	13.1	13.0	12.7	12.4	12.0	11.9	11.8	11.8	11.8	11.9	11.8	
EFTA members												
Austria	11.4	12.0	12.4	12.5	11.9	11.8	11.6	11.5	11.4	11.5	11.6	
Finland	13.9	13.2	13.2	13.7	13.8	13.3	12.8	12.4	12.0	12.8	12.9	
Iceland	18.0	19.8	18.8	18.5	18.4	17.2	15.8	15.6	16.9	19.0		
Norway	12.6	12.5	12.4	12.5	12.1	12.1	12.4	12.6	13.0	13.7	14.0	
Sweden	11.6	11.7	11.3	11.1	11.0	11.3	11.8	12.2	12.5	13.3	13.7	
Switzerland	11.5	11.5	11.5	11.6	11.3	11.5	11.4	11.7	11.8	12.3	12.1	
EFTA average	12.1	12.1	12.1	12.2	11.9	11.9	11.9	12.0	12.1	12.7	12.8	
CMEA members												
Bulgaria	16.1	14.5	14.0	13.9	13.8	13.6	13.2	13.2	12.9			
Czechoslovakia	18.7	16.3	15.5	15.2	14.9	14.7	14.5	14.2	13.8			
East Germany	13.3	14.6	14.2	14.4	14.0	13.7	13.3	13.4	13.6	12.9		
Hungary	16.7	13.9	13.3	12.5	11.9	11.7	12.2	12.1	11.8	11.7		
Poland	19.1	19.5	18.9	19.4	19.7	18.9	18.2	16.9	16.1	15.5	14.9	
Romania	19.6	18.0	17.0	15.3	14.3	15.5	15.8	15.6	15.9			
USSR	18.1	18.3	18.5	18.9	19.8	19.6	19.4	19.9	19.8			
CMEA average	18.0	17.9	17.9	18.1	18.7	18.5	18.3	18.5	18.4	14.2	14.9	
Others												
Albania	28.5	26.5	26.5	27.8	26.0	27.3	26.2	25.3				
Cyprus	18.3	20.4	19.6	20.8	20.7	20.6	19.5	19.5	18.7			
Gibraltar	16.8	18.5	17.2	19.2	17.5	17.6	17.3	17.4	17.9	16.7		
Liechtenstein	12.5	15.4	14.4	14.6	13.2	12.5	12.5	13.0				
Malta	17.9	16.0	15.0	16.9	17.6	17.0	16.8	15.8	15.9	15.8		
Monaco	7.5	20.6	19.8	20.2	19.6	19.6	19.8	19.9				
Turkey	14.9	14.6	14.3	14.0	14.0	13.5	13.2	12.9				
Yugoslavia	17.7	17.1	16.4	16.7	16.6	16.4	15.9	15.4	15.3	15.1	14.3	
Average	16.4	15.9	15.5	15.5	15.4	15.0	14.6	14.2	15.4	15.1		
European average	15.7	15.6	15.4	15.4	15.5	15.3	15.2	15.2	15.3	12.4		

Source: United Nations/National Statistical Offices
Notes: a 1980 = UN estimates for 1975-80
        1985 = UN estimates for 1980-85

114

Database name: Demographic Trends and Forecasts
Sector name: Vital Statistics   Table No: 0207

Title: Death Rates 1977-1989

Unit: Per 000 inhabitants

	1977	1980	1981	1982	1983	1984	1985	1986	1987	1988	1989	Notes
EC members												
Belgium	11.5	11.5	11.4	11.4	11.6	11.1	11.2	11.2	10.7	11.2	11.3	
Denmark	9.9	10.9	11.0	10.8	11.2	11.2	11.4	11.3	11.3	11.5	11.6	
France	10.1	10.2	10.2	10.0	10.2	9.8	10.1	9.9	9.5	9.4	9.4	
West Germany	11.5	11.6	11.7	11.6	11.7	11.4	11.5	11.5	11.2	11.2	11.2	
Greece	9.0	9.1	8.9	8.8	9.2	8.9	9.3	9.2	9.6	9.3	9.2	
Ireland	10.3	9.8	9.6	9.3	9.4	9.1	9.0	9.5	8.8	8.9	8.9	
Italy	9.8	9.8	9.7	9.4	9.9	9.3	9.6	9.5	9.3	9.3	9.5	
Luxembourg	11.3	11.3	11.2	11.3	11.3	11.1	11.0	10.8	10.9	10.0	10.7	
Netherlands	7.9	8.1	8.1	8.2	8.2	8.3	8.4	8.6	8.3	8.4	8.6	
Portugal	9.9	9.6	9.7	9.3	9.6	9.6	9.6	9.4	9.3	9.6	9.4	
Spain	8.1	7.7	7.8	7.5	7.9	7.8	8.0	7.9	8.0	8.0	8.0	
United Kingdom	11.7	11.7	11.7	11.8	11.7	11.4	11.8	11.7	11.2	11.4	11.7	
EC total	10.3	10.3	10.3	10.1	10.3	10.0	10.2	10.2	9.9	9.9	10.0	
EFTA members												
Austria	12.2	12.2	12.3	12.1	12.3	11.7	11.8	11.4	11.2	11.0	10.9	
Finland	9.3	9.3	9.2	9.0	9.3	9.2	9.8	9.6	9.7	9.9	9.6	
Iceland	6.5	6.7	7.2	6.8	7.0	6.6	7.0	6.8	6.9	7.3		
Norway	9.8	10.1	10.2	10.1	10.2	10.3	10.6	9.8	10.7	10.8	10.6	
Sweden	10.7	11.0	11.1	10.9	10.9	10.9	11.3	11.1	11.1	11.4	10.8	
Switzerland	8.8	9.3	9.3	9.2	9.3	9.1	9.2	9.2	9.2	9.2	9.2	
EFTA average	10.3	10.5	10.6	10.4	10.5	10.4	10.6	10.3	10.4	10.5	10.3	
CMEA members												
Bulgaria	10.7	11.1	10.7	11.2	11.4	11.3	12.0	11.4	12.0			
Czechoslovakia	12.2	12.6	12.2	11.1	12.3	11.9	11.8	11.8	11.5			
East Germany	13.5	14.2	13.9	13.7	13.3	13.3	13.5	13.4	12.9			
Hungary	12.4	13.6	13.5	13.5	13.9	13.8	13.8	13.8	13.4			
Poland	9.0	9.8	9.2	9.2	9.6	9.9	10.3	10.0	10.0			
Romania	9.6	10.4	10.0	10.0	10.4	10.3	10.9	10.4				
USSR	9.6	10.3	10.2	10.1	10.4	10.8	10.6	9.7	9.9			
CMEA average	9.9	10.6	10.4	10.3	10.6	10.9	10.9	10.2	10.3			
Others												
Albania	6.8	6.4	6.6	5.9	6.1	5.7	5.8	5.7				
Cyprus	9.1	9.3	8.4	8.5	8.6	8.0	8.5	8.4	8.9			
Gibraltar	8.2	9.5	7.8	7.6	8.6	9.2	9.6	9.9	7.3	10.0		
Liechtenstein	6.1	6.9	6.3	6.4	5.7	5.7	5.8	6.1				
Malta	8.6	8.8	8.4	8.5	8.3	7.6	7.4	7.3	8.4	7.8		
Monaco	20.6	21.1	21.3	17.2	16.6	16.6	16.3	16.1				
Turkey		10.2					9.4					a
Yugoslavia	8.4	8.8	9.0	9.0	9.6	9.3	9.1	9.1	9.2	9.0	9.1	
Average	8.3	9.6	8.7	8.7	9.2	8.9	9.2	8.7	9.2	9.0	9.2	
European average	10.0	10.4	10.3	10.2	10.5	10.4	10.5	10.1	10.1	9.9	10.0	

Source: United Nations/National Statistical Offices
Notes: a 1980 = UN estimate for 1975-80; 1985 = UN estimate for 1980-85

115

Database name: Demographic Trends and Forecasts
Sector name: Vital Statistics

Table No: 0208

Title: Infant Mortality Rate 1977-1988

Unit: Per 000 live births

	1977	1980	1981	1982	1983	1984	1985	1986	1987	1988	Notes
EC members											
Belgium	13.6	12.1	11.5	11.7	11.2	10.7	9.4	9.7	9.7	9.6	
Denmark	8.7	8.4	7.9	8.2	7.7	7.7	7.9	8.2	8.3	7.6	
France	11.4	10.0	9.7	9.5	9.1	8.3	8.3	8.0	7.8	8.0	
West Germany	15.5	12.6	11.6	10.9	10.3	9.6	8.9	8.7	8.3	8.4	
Greece	20.4	17.9	16.3	15.1	14.6	14.1	14.0	12.3	11.7	12.0	
Ireland	15.5	11.1	10.3	10.5	10.1	9.6	8.8	8.7	7.4	9.2	
Italy	18.1	14.6	14.1	13.0	12.3	11.4	10.5	9.8	9.6	9.6	
Luxembourg	10.6	11.5	13.8	12.1	11.2	11.7	9.0	9.7	9.4	9.5	
Netherlands	9.5	8.6	8.3	8.3	8.4	8.3	8.0	7.7	7.6	7.5	
Portugal	30.3	24.3	21.8	19.8	19.3	16.7	17.8	15.8	14.2	13.6	
Spain	16.0	12.3	12.5	11.3	10.9	9.9	8.5	8.8	8.5		
United Kingdom	14.1	12.1	11.2	11.0	10.5	9.6	9.3	9.5	9.1	9.0	
EC total	15.2	12.6	12.1	11.4	10.9	10.0	9.5	9.2	8.9	9.0	
EFTA members											
Austria	16.8	14.3	12.7	12.8	11.9	11.4	11.0	10.3	9.8	8.1	
Finland	9.1	7.6	6.5	6.0	6.2	6.5	6.3	5.8	6.3		
Iceland						6.1			3.4	6.2	
Norway	9.2	8.1	7.5	8.1	7.9	8.3	8.5	7.8	8.0	8.1	
Sweden	8.0	6.9	6.9	6.8	7.0	6.4	6.7	5.9	5.7	5.8	
Switzerland	9.8	9.1	7.6	7.7	7.5	7.1	6.9	6.9	6.8	6.8	
EFTA average	10.8	9.4	8.5	8.5	8.3	8.0	8.0	7.4	7.3	7.1	
CMEA members											
Bulgaria	24.0	20.2	18.9	18.2	16.5	16.1	15.8	14.5	15.0	14.5	
Czechoslovakia	19.7	18.4	16.9	16.2	15.7	15.3	14.0	13.5	13.1	13.2	
East Germany	13.1	12.1	12.3	11.4	10.7	10.0	9.8	9.2	8.5	9.0	
Hungary	26.2	23.2	20.8	20.0	19.0	20.4	20.4	18.9	17.4	18.0	
Poland	24.6	21.3	20.6	20.2	19.2	19.2	18.5	17.5	17.5	17.5	
Romania	31.2	29.3	28.6	28.0	23.4	23.4	25.6				
USSR		28.0					25.1	25.1	25.1	25.1	a
CMEA average	23.6	26.0	20.3	19.7	18.1	18.0	23.1	22.7	22.6	22.7	
Others											
Albania		50.0					44.8				a
Cyprus	13.0	12.0					16.5	11.5	11.0	11.0	a
Gibraltar											
Liechtenstein											
Malta	13.8	15.2	11.0	14.9	14.9	11.7	13.6	10.1	7.3	8.0	
Monaco											
Turkey							92.1				
Yugoslavia	35.6	31.4	30.8	30.3	31.6	28.9	28.8	27.3	25.1	24.5	
Average	34.7	32.6	30.5	30.1	31.3	28.6	70.1	26.6	24.5	23.9	
European average	17.8	19.9	14.6	14.0	13.3	12.6	21.6	16.4	16.1	16.6	

Source: United Nations/National Statistical Offices
Notes: Rates are number of deaths of infants under one year per '000 live births
    a   1980 = UN estimate for 1975-1980
        1985 = UN estimate for 1980-1985

Database name: Demographic Trends and Forecasts
Sector name: Vital Statistics   Table No: 0209

Title: Marriage Rate 1977-1989

Unit: Per 000 inhabitants

	1977	1978	1979	1980	1981	1982	1983	1984	1985	1986	1987	1988	1989
EC members													
Belgium	7.0	6.8	6.7	6.7	6.5	6.3	6.1	6.0	5.8	5.8	5.7	5.5	
Denmark	6.3	5.6	5.4	5.2	5.0	4.8	5.3	5.6	5.8	6.0	6.1	6.3	6.0
France	6.9	6.7	6.4	6.2	5.8	5.7	5.5	5.1	4.9	4.8	4.7	4.9	
West Germany	5.8	5.4	5.6	5.9	5.8	5.9	6.0	6.0	6.0	6.1	6.3	6.5	6.4
Greece	8.2	7.7	8.3	6.5	7.3	6.9	7.2	5.5	6.4	5.8	6.6	5.2	
Ireland	6.1	6.4	6.2	6.4	6.0	5.8	5.5	5.2	5.3	5.2	5.1	5.1	5.1
Italy	6.2	5.8	5.7	5.7	5.6	5.5	5.3	5.2	5.2	5.2	5.3	5.5	
Luxembourg	6.1	5.9	5.7	5.9	5.5	5.7	5.4	5.4	5.3	5.1	5.3	5.5	
Netherlands	6.7	6.4	6.1	6.4	6.0	5.8	5.5	5.7	5.7	6.0	6.0	6.0	
Portugal	9.4	8.5	8.3	7.4	7.7	7.4	7.5	6.9	6.7	6.8	7.0	7.0	
Spain	7.0	7.0	6.6	5.7	5.4	5.1	5.1	5.2	5.0	5.3			
United Kingdom	7.2	7.4	7.4	7.4	7.1	7.0	6.9	7.0	6.9	6.9	7.0	6.7	
EC total	6.7	6.5	6.4	6.3	6.1	6.0	5.9	5.8	5.7	5.7	5.9	5.9	6.3
EFTA members													
Austria	6.0	5.9	6.1	6.1	6.3	6.3	7.4	6.1	5.9	6.0	5.0	4.7	5.6
Finland	6.5	6.3	6.1	6.1	6.3	6.3	6.0	5.8	5.8	5.3	5.3	5.3	
Iceland	7.1	7.1	6.4	5.7	5.9	5.6	5.9	5.9	5.4				
Norway	5.9	5.8	5.7	5.4	5.4	5.3	5.0	5.0	5.0	5.2	5.2	5.2	
Sweden	4.9	4.6	4.5	4.5	4.5	4.4	4.3	4.4	4.5	4.6	5.0	5.2	12.8
Switzerland	5.2	5.1	5.3	5.6	5.6	5.8	5.9	6.0	6.0	6.2	6.5	6.8	
EFTA average	5.6	5.4	5.5	5.5	5.6	5.6	5.7	5.4	5.4	5.5	5.4	5.4	9.4
CMEA members													
Bulgaria	8.5	8.1	7.9	7.9	7.5	7.5	7.5	7.3	7.2				
Czechoslovakia	9.1	8.9	8.3	7.7	7.6	7.6	7.8	7.8	7.7	7.6	7.6	7.5	
East Germany	8.8	8.4	8.2	8.0	7.7	7.5	7.5	8.0	7.9	8.0	8.2		
Hungary	9.1	8.7	8.1	7.5	7.2	7.1	7.1	7.0	6.9	6.5	6.2		
Poland	9.4	9.3	9.0	8.6	9.0	8.7	8.4	7.7	7.2	7.0	6.5	6.8	
Romania	9.2	9.2	9.0	8.2	8.2	7.8	7.3	7.3	7.3				
USSR	10.7	10.7	10.9	10.3	10.4	10.3	10.4	9.6	9.7				
CMEA average	10.2	10.2	10.2	9.7	9.7	9.6	9.6	9.0	9.0	7.3	7.0	7.0	
Others													
Albania	8.0	8.0	8.0	8.1	8.5	9.0	9.0	9.1	8.5				
Cyprus	9.7	9.7	12.0	8.1	11.3	10.6	11.2	8.0	10.2	10.3			
Gibraltar	15.3	16.9	15.4	14.4	14.4	13.8	14.8	13.9	14.0	14.0	14.1	14.0	
Liechtenstein	12.2	11.4	11.8	13.7	12.6	12.3	13.7	14.0	14.0				
Malta	20.3	18.5	17.2	17.4	17.4	16.9	16.3	15.2	14.2	14.0	14.2	14.7	
Monaco	7.0	7.0	7.1	6.5	7.3	7.3	7.3	7.3	7.3				
Turkey	3.4	3.6	3.8	3.7	3.8	3.6	3.7	3.8	3.8				
Yugoslavia	8.2	8.1	8.0	7.7	7.7	7.6	7.5	7.3	7.0			6.9	6.7
Average	5.3	5.4	5.5	5.3	5.3	5.2	5.2	5.2	5.1	11.7	7.0	6.8	
European average	8.2	8.1	8.1	7.7	7.7	7.6	7.6	7.2	7.2	6.0	6.1	6.1	6.9

Source: United Nations/National Statistical Offices
Notes: Rates are the number of legal (recognised) marriages performed and registered per '000 mid-year population

Database name:	Demographic Trends and Forecasts					Table No:	0210
Sector name:	Vital Statistics						

Title: Divorce Rate 1977-1989

Unit: Per 000 inhabitants

	1977	1978	1979	1980	1981	1982	1983	1984	1985	1986	1987	1988	1989
EEC members													
Belgium	1.3	1.4	1.4	1.5	1.6	1.6	1.8	1.9	1.9	1.9	1.9	2.0	
Denmark	2.6	2.6	2.6	2.7	2.8	2.9	2.9	2.8	2.8	2.8	2.8	3.0	
France	1.4	1.5	1.7	1.5	1.6	1.7	1.8	1.9	2.0	2.0	2.2		
West Germany	1.2	0.5	1.3	1.6	1.8	1.9	2.0	2.1	2.0	2.0	2.1		2.1
Greece	0.5	0.5	0.5	0.7	0.7	0.6	0.6	0.9	0.8	0.8	0.9		
Ireland													
Italy	0.2	0.2	0.2	0.2	0.2	0.3	0.2	0.3	0.3	0.3	0.5		
Luxembourg	1.2	1.5	1.2	1.6	1.4	1.7	1.6	1.7	1.8	1.9	2.0		
Netherlands	1.6	1.6	1.7	1.8	2.0	2.2	2.3	2.4	2.3	2.4	2.4	2.4	
Portugal		0.7	0.6	0.6	0.7	0.6	0.8	0.7	0.8	0.8	0.8		
Spain					0.3	0.6	0.5	0.5	0.2	0.2	0.2		
United Kingdom	2.5	2.7	2.6	2.8	2.8	2.8	2.9	2.8	3.1	3.0	3.1	3.1	
EEC average	1.3	1.2	1.4	1.5	1.4	1.5	1.6	1.6	1.6	1.6	1.7	2.5	
EFTA members													
Austria	1.6	1.7	1.7	1.8	1.8	1.9	1.9	2.0	2.0	2.0	2.0	2.0	2.0
Finland	2.1	2.2	2.1	2.0	2.0	2.0	2.0	2.0	2.0				
Iceland	1.8	1.8	1.7	1.9	2.0	1.8	2.1	1.9	2.2				
Norway	1.5	1.5	1.6	1.6	1.7	1.7	1.9	1.9	1.9				
Sweden	2.5	2.5	2.5	2.4	2.4	2.5	2.5	2.4	2.3	2.2	2.2	2.1	2.2
Switzerland	1.7	1.7	1.6	1.7	1.7	1.8	1.8	1.7	1.8				
EFTA average	1.9	1.9	2.0	1.9	2.0	2.0	2.1	2.0	2.0	2.1	2.1	2.1	2.1
CMEA members													
Bulgaria	1.5	1.5	1.4	1.5	1.5	1.5	1.6	1.5	1.7				
Czechoslovakia	2.1	2.2	2.1	2.2	2.3	2.2	2.4	2.4	2.5				
East Germany	2.6	2.6	2.7	2.7	2.9	3.0	3.0	3.0	3.1				
Hungary	2.6	2.7	2.6	2.6	2.6	2.7	2.7	2.7	2.7				
Poland	1.2	1.0	1.1	1.1	1.1	1.3	1.3	1.4	1.3				
Romania	1.2	1.5	1.6	1.5	1.5	1.5	1.5	1.5					
USSR	3.5	3.5	3.6	3.5	3.5	3.3	3.5	3.4					
CMEA average	3.0	3.0	3.1	3.0	3.0	2.9	3.0	3.0	2.1				
Others													
Albania			0.7	0.8	0.8	0.8	0.8	0.8	0.8				
Cyprus	0.2	0.3	0.3	0.3	0.3	0.3	0.4	0.4	0.5	0.5	0.5	0.6	
Gibraltar					0.4								
Liechtenstein													
Malta													
Monaco			2.2	1.9	2.5		1.4						
Turkey	0.3	0.3	0.3	0.4	0.3	0.4	0.4						1.0
Yugoslavia	1.1	1.1	1.0	1.0	1.0	1.0	0.9	0.9	0.9	1.0	1.0	1.0	
Average	0.6	0.6	0.6	0.6	0.6	0.6	0.6	0.9	0.9	1.0	1.0	1.0	
European average	2.1	2.1	2.2	2.2	2.1	2.1	2.2	2.3					

Source: United Nations/National Statistical Offices

Notes: Rates are number of final divorce decrees granted under civil law per '000 mid-year population

Database name: Demographic Trends and Forecasts
Sector name: Vital Statistics   Table No: 0211

Title: Total Fertility Rate 1977-1988

Unit: Children born per female

	1977	1980	1981	1982	1983	1984	1985	1986	1987	1988
EC members										
Belgium	1.8	1.8	1.7	1.6	1.6	1.6	1.6	1.5	1.6	1.6
Denmark	1.7	1.8	1.8	1.9	1.4	1.4	1.4	1.5	1.5	1.6
France	1.9	1.9	1.9	1.9	1.8	1.8	1.8	1.8	1.8	1.8
West Germany	1.4	1.5	1.5	1.4	1.4	1.4	1.3	1.3	1.4	1.4
Greece	2.3	2.3	2.3	2.3	2.1	2.1	2.0	1.6	1.7	1.7
Ireland	3.3	3.2	3.1	3.0	2.8	2.6	2.5	2.4	2.3	2.3
Italy	2.1	1.7	1.6	1.6	1.5	1.5	1.4	1.5	1.3	1.3
Luxembourg	1.5	1.5	1.6	1.5	1.4	1.4	1.4	1.4	1.4	1.4
Netherlands	1.6	1.6	1.5	1.4	1.5	1.5	1.5	1.6	1.6	1.7
Portugal	2.5	2.2	2.1	2.1	2.0	1.9	1.7	1.6	1.6	1.6
Spain	2.6	2.2	2.1	1.9	1.8	1.7	2.0	1.7	1.6	1.6
United Kingdom	1.7	1.8	1.7	1.8	1.8	1.8	1.8	1.8	1.8	1.7
EC total	1.9	1.8	1.8	1.7	1.7	1.7	1.6	1.6	1.6	1.6
EFTA members										
Austria	1.6	1.7	1.7	1.6	1.6	1.6	1.7	1.5	1.5	1.5
Finland	1.7	1.7	1.6	1.6	1.8	1.7	1.7	1.7	1.6	1.6
Iceland		2.4	2.3	2.2	2.1	2.0	1.9	1.9	2.1	2.3
Norway	1.8	1.9	1.8	1.7	1.7	1.7	1.7	1.7	1.7	1.8
Sweden	1.7	1.7	1.7	1.7	1.7	1.6	1.7	1.8	1.8	2.0
Switzerland	1.5	1.6	1.8	1.9	1.9	1.5	1.5	1.5	1.6	1.5
EFTA average	1.6	1.7	1.7	1.7	1.7	1.6	1.7	1.6	1.6	1.7
CMEA members										
Bulgaria	2.2	2.2	2.2	2.1	2.0	2.0	2.0	2.0	2.0	2.0
Czechoslovakia	2.4	2.3	2.3	2.2	2.1	2.0	2.1	2.1	2.0	2.0
East Germany	1.8	1.8	1.9	1.9	1.9	1.8	1.8	1.7	1.6	1.6
Hungary	2.2	2.1	2.0	2.0	1.8	1.7	1.7	1.8	1.8	1.8
Poland	2.3	2.3	2.3	2.3	2.4	2.3	2.3	2.3	2.2	2.1
Romania	2.6	2.5	2.5	2.4	2.4	2.2	2.1	2.1	2.1	2.1
USSR	2.4	2.3	2.4	2.4	2.4	2.3	2.3	2.4	2.3	2.2
CMEA average	2.4	2.3	2.4	2.3	2.3	2.2	2.2	2.3	2.2	2.1
Others										
Albania	4.2	3.9	3.8	3.6	3.6	3.4	3.4	3.3	3.3	
Cyprus	2.3	2.5	2.4	2.5	2.5	2.5	2.4	2.4	2.3	2.3
Gibraltar										
Liechtenstein										
Malta										
Monaco										
Turkey	4.3	4.4	4.6	4.1	4.1	3.9	3.9	3.7	3.8	
Yugoslavia	2.2	2.2	2.2	2.0	2.1	2.1	2.1	2.0	2.0	
Average	3.6	3.7	3.8	3.4	3.4	3.3	3.3	3.2	3.2	
European average	2.3	2.2	2.2	2.2	2.1	2.1	2.1	2.1	2.0	

Source: World Bank
Notes: Rate represents the number of children that would be born per woman,
if she were to live to the end of her childbearing years and bear children at each
age in accordance with prevailing age-specific fertility rates

Database name: Demographic Trends and Forecasts
Sector name: Vital Statistics   Table No: 0212

Title: Life Expectancy: Latest Period Available

Unit: Years

	Period	Male	Female
EC members			
Belgium	1980-85	70.4	77.2
Denmark	1986-87	71.8	77.6
France	1987	72.0	80.3
West Germany	1984-86	71.5	78.1
Greece	1980-85	72.1	76.0
Ireland	1980-85	70.4	75.7
Italy	1984	71.6	78.1
Luxembourg	1985-87	70.6	77.9
Netherlands	1985-86	73.0	79.6
Portugal	1987	70.7	77.5
Spain	1980-85	72.8	78.9
United Kingdom	1984-86	71.7	77.5
EC total			
EFTA members			
Austria	1988	72.0	78.6
Finland	1985	70.7	78.5
Iceland	1983-84	74.0	80.2
Norway	1984-85	72.8	79.5
Sweden	1988	74.0	80.0
Switzerland	1984-85	73.5	80.0
CMEA members			
Bulgaria	1980-85	68.4	74.4
Czechoslovakia	1984	67.1	74.3
East Germany	1985	69.5	75.4
Hungary	1985	65.6	73.6
Poland	1985	66.5	74.8
Romania	1980-85	66.9	72.5
USSR	1984-85	62.9	72.7
Others			
Albania	1984-85	68.5	73.8
Cyprus	1980-85	72.5	77.5
Gibraltar	1980-81	71.4	75.5
Liechtenstein			
Malta	1985	70.8	76.0
Monaco			
Turkey	1980-85	60.0	63.3
Yugoslavia	1980-85	67.9	73.8

Source: United Nations/World Bank

	1977	1980	1981	1982	1983	1984	1985	1986	1987	1988	1989
EC members											
Belgium	322.2	323.0	323.2	323.3	323.3	323.2	324.9	325.2	325.3	325.4	325.6
Denmark	118.5	119.3	119.2	119.2	119.1	119.1	119.1	119.3	119.4	119.7	119.8
France	97.6	98.9	99.5	100.1	100.5	100.9	100.3	101.7	102.2	102.6	103.1
West Germany	246.6	247.3	247.7	247.6	246.7	245.7	245.1	245.2	245.7	246.3	247.4
Greece	70.9	73.8	74.4	74.9	75.3	75.7	76.0	76.2	76.4	76.7	77.1
Ireland	47.2	49.1	49.6	50.2	50.6	51.0	51.2	51.0	51.1	51.0	50.9
Italy	186.3	187.9	188.2	188.7	189.3	189.8	190.3	190.6	191.1	191.3	192.3
Luxembourg	140.0	141.2	141.6	141.9	141.9	141.9	141.9	140.8	142.3	144.3	144.3
Netherlands	341.2	348.4	350.9	352.5	353.7	355.2	356.7	358.7	361.1	362.7	364.8
Portugal	106.4	108.0	107.7	108.5	109.4	111.1	111.8	112.5	113.1	112.3	112.8
Spain	72.9	75.1	75.5	76.1	76.7	76.9	77.4	77.5	77.9	78.2	78.5
United Kingdom	230.1	230.7	230.9	230.7	230.9	231.4	229.9	232.5	233.0	233.7	234.5
EC average	180.4	181.3	181.7	181.8	181.8	181.9	181.6	182.5	183.0	183.4	184.2
EFTA members											
Austria	90.2	90.0	90.2	90.3	90.0	90.0	90.0	90.2	90.3	90.3	90.5
Finland	14.1	14.2	14.3	14.4	14.4	14.5	14.6	14.6	14.7	14.7	14.8
Iceland	2.2	2.3	2.3	2.3	2.3	2.4	2.4	2.4	2.4	2.5	2.5
Norway	12.5	12.6	12.7	12.7	12.8	12.8	12.8	12.9	12.9	13.0	13.1
Sweden	18.4	18.5	18.6	18.6	18.6	18.6	18.6	18.7	18.7	18.7	18.9
Switzerland	153.4	154.8	155.9	156.8	157.7	156.2	154.5	157.7	158.5	159.0	160.0
EFTA average	61.7	62.0	62.3	62.6	62.8	62.2	61.6	62.6	62.9	63.0	63.3
CMEA members											
Bulgaria	79.5	80.0	80.3	80.5	80.7	80.9	80.9	80.9	81.0	81.2	81.5
Czechoslovakia	118.4	120.6	120.7	121.1	121.4	121.8	122.1	122.4	122.7	122.9	123.1
East Germany	154.9	154.6	154.6	154.3	154.3	154.0	153.8	153.6	153.8	153.8	153.8
Hungary	114.7	115.5	115.5	115.4	115.3	115.0	114.8	114.6	114.4	114.6	114.7
Poland	112.0	114.8	115.9	116.9	118.0	119.2	120.1	120.9	121.6	121.7	121.8
Romania	92.0	94.3	95.0	95.5	95.8	96.1	97.8	98.4	97.4	97.3	97.1
USSR	11.7	12.0	12.1	12.2	12.3	12.4	12.6	12.7	12.8	12.8	12.8
CMEA average	41.5	42.0	42.1	42.2	42.3	42.4	42.6	42.7	42.6	42.6	42.6
Others											
Albania	89.2	95.0	96.9	99.0	101.0	103.2	105.3	107.5	109.7	111.3	113.0
Cyprus	66.6	68.1	68.9	69.6	70.5	71.4	72.2	73.1	73.9	76.1	78.2
Gibraltar	5000.0	5000.0	5000.0	4833.3	4833.3	4833.3	5000.0	5000.0	5000.0	5000.0	5000.0
Liechtenstein	159.2	172.5	172.5	172.5	172.5	185.7	185.7	179.1	185.7	192.4	199.0
Malta	1075.9	1179.6	1179.6	1166.6	1221.7	1231.5	1241.2	1247.7	1114.8	1124.5	1134.1
Monaco	16778.5	17449.6	17449.6	17449.6	18120.8	18120.8	18120.8	18120.8	18120.8	18791.9	18791.9
Turkey	54.6	58.1	59.3	60.5	60.5	63.1	64.4	65.8	67.1	68.3	69.5
Yugoslavia	85.9	88.3	88.6	89.3	89.9	90.6	91.2	91.8	92.4	92.8	93.3
Average	79.7	83.5	84.1	84.7	86.0	87.4	88.4	89.3	89.0	90.3	91.1
European average	101.6	102.2	102.4	102.4	102.4	102.4	102.0	102.6	102.5	102.9	103.4

Source: Euromonitor calculations

Database name: Demographic Trends and Forecasts
Sector name: Urbanisation

Table No: 0214

Title: Urban Population, City Population 1985, Growth Rates 1975-1980, 1980-1985

	Urban Population '000	% of Total Population	% in Largest City	% In Cities Over 500,000	Cities Over 500,000	Average Annual Growth Rates 1975-80	1980-85	Notes
EC members								
Belgium	9535	96.3	10.0		3	0.3	0.3	
Denmark	4402	85.9	27.8	27.8	1	0.8	0.4	
France	40114	73.4	21.6	29.6	6	0.4	0.4	
West Germany	52077	85.5	4.2	17.1	12	0.2	0.1	a
Greece	5939	60.1	45.1	55.6	2	2.1	1.3	
Ireland	2058	57.0	49.1	49.1	1	1.8	1.8	
Italy	38592	67.4	18.7	48.0	6	0.7	0.4	
Luxembourg	294	81.0	27.1			1.1	0.8	
Netherlands	12818	88.4	7.1	24.3	4	0.5	0.5	
Portugal	3181	31.2	60.5	60.5	1	2.1	1.8	
Spain	29210	75.8	11.0	23.5	6	1.9	1.4	
United Kingdom	51351	91.5	20.2	36.4	5	0.2	0.3	
EC average								
EFTA members								
Austria	4211	56.1	39.4	39.4	1	0.5	0.5	
Finland	3130	64.0	34.3	34.3	1	1.9	1.9	
Iceland	217	89.4	59.8			1.2	1.5	
Norway	3016	72.8	21.3	21.3	1	1.1	0.9	
Sweden	6968	83.4	22.1	30.5	2	0.4	0.2	
Switzerland	3712	58.2	19.2	19.2	1	0.2	0.6	
CMEA members								
Bulgaria	6031	66.5	23.9	23.9	1	2.0	1.7	
Czechoslovakia	10180	65.3	11.3	11.3	1	1.7	1.3	a
East Germany	12903	77.0	9.3	17.6	3	0.1	0.2	a
Hungary	6017	56.2	34.2	34.2	1	1.7	1.0	a
Poland	22686	61.0	7.3	19.6	5	1.9	1.9	a
Romania	11289	49.0	19.7	19.7	1	1.7	1.1	
USSR	182867	65.6	4.9	32.8	54			a
Others								
Albania	1038	34.0	26.0			2.8	2.6	
Cyprus	331	49.5	57.4			2.0	2.5	
Gibraltar	31	100.0	100.0			1.4	1.3	
Liechtenstein	7	23.5	71.4			2.4	2.8	
Malta	327	85.3	4.7			1.9	1.3	
Monaco	27	100.0	100.0			0.8	0.8	
Turkey	22633	45.9	9.0	31.3	5	2.8	2.2	
Yugoslavia	10714	46.3	10.2	16.7	2	2.8	2.5	

Source: UN Prospects of World Urbanisation/Demographic Yearbook/Statistical Offices
Notes: Data on cities refer to urban agglomerations
a Data on cities refer to cities proper

| Database name: | Demographic Trends and Forecasts | | | | | | | | | | |
| Sector name: | Demographic Analysis | | | | Table No: | 0215 | | | | | |

Title: Number of Males 1977-1989: National Estimates at January 1st

Unit: 000s

	1977	1980	1981	1982	1983	1984	1985	1986	1987	1988	1989
EC members											
Belgium	4809	4810	4812	4813	4813	4810	4812	4812	4816	4840	4878
Denmark	2513	2529	2528	2524	2521	2518	2517	2521	2526	2528	2536
France	25950	26247	26381	26530	26662	26751	26852	26948	27053	27162	27374
West Germany	29263	29317	29481	29523	29428	29306	29180	29190	29285	29350	29574
Greece	4517	4703	4764	4797	4829	4854	4879	4894	4909	4920	4963
Ireland	1640	1705	1724	1745	1755	1776	1771	1768	1770	1768	1769
Italy	27538	27840	27901	27947	27589	27679	27740	27792	27833	27890	28132
Luxembourg	179	178	178	178	178	178	178	179	180	181	183
Netherlands	6875	6994	7049	7082	7103	7124	7150	7185	7224	7275	7341
Portugal	4592	4687	4731	4767	4804	4846	4887	4916	4940	4960	4978
Spain	17711	18273	18414	18580	18689	18798	18908	18934	19037	19123	19265
United Kingdom	27269	27412	27408	27426	27428	27476	27537	27615	27692	27750	27931
EC total	152856	154695	155371	155912	155799	156116	156411	156754	157265	157747	158924
EFTA members											
Austria	3548	3551	3581	3600	3577	3578	3582	3589	3601	3610	3633
Finland	2286	2307	2315	2328	2343	2357	2369	2378	2389	2400	2409
Iceland	112	114	116	117	119	120	121	122	124	125	127
Norway	2003	2022	2028	2034	2040	2046	2050	2056	2060	2065	2083
Sweden	4093	4116	4120	4119	4117	4116	4121	4127	4145	4155	4190
Switzerland	3069	3073	3082	3102	3121	3130	3145	3160	3202	3230	3266
EFTA total	15111	15183	15242	15300	15317	15347	15388	15432	15521	15585	15708
CMEA members											
Bulgaria	4385	4409	4422	4434	4443	4450	4456	4448	4440	4475	4506
Czechoslovakia	7296	7446	7444	7471	7496	7517	7537	7558	7586	7650	7639
East Germany	7813	7847	7864	7852	7868	7867	7870	7881	7913	8120	8143
Hungary	5162	5189	5188	5185	5177	5164	5149	5138	5188	5200	5222
Poland	16805	17254	17411	17572	17741	17914	18073	18211	18370	18450	18524
Romania	10677	10953	11030	11092	11129	11165	11214	11261	11340	11395	11343
USSR	120548	123953	125100	126317	127626	128958	130273	131721	133283	135010	135606
CMEA total	172686	177051	178459	179923	181480	183035	184572	186218	188120	190300	190984
Others											
Albania		1379	1406	1436	1466	1496	1526	1550	1575	1600	1629
Cyprus	306	309	313	316	321	325	329	333	339	343	354
Gibraltar	16	15	15	15	15	15	14	15	15	15	15
Liechtenstein											
Malta	147	154	155	156	158	160	161	168	169	170	172
Monaco											
Turkey											
Yugoslavia			11084								
total	469	1857	12973	1923	1960	1996	2030	2066	2098	2128	2170
European total	341122	348786	362045	353058	354556	356494	358401	360470	363004	365760	367786

Source: National Statistical Offices : all countries
Note: Non-EEC data for 1989 are Euromonitor estimates

Database name: Demographic Trends and Forecasts
Sector name: Demographic Analysis   Table No: 0216

Title: Number of Females 1977-1989: National Estimates at January 1st

Unit: 000s

	1977	1980	1981	1982	1983	1984	1985	1986	1987	1988	1989
EC members											
Belgium	5014	5045	5051	5042	5045	5043	5045	5053	5060	5041	5050
Denmark	2567	2593	2596	2675	2595	2594	2594	2595	2599	2601	2594
France	27069	27484	27648	27805	27964	28080	28210	28330	28457	28588	28643
West Germany	32179	32122	32177	32190	32118	32001	31869	31830	31953	32365	32426
Greece	4791	4940	4965	4993	5018	5042	5040	5056	5069	5080	5095
Ireland	1622	1696	1719	1735	1749	1753	1769	1769	1772	1771	1761
Italy	28585	29160	28578	28590	29753	29254	29340	29410	29458	29509	29591
Luxembourg	182	186	187	188	188	188	188	188	190	191	192
Netherlands	6939	7097	7160	7204	7237	7270	7304	7345	7391	7440	7464
Portugal	4811	5027	5088	5125	5165	5204	5242	5269	5290	5344	5332
Spain	18444	18969	19106	19276	19378	19482	19587	19615	19713	19787	19817
United Kingdom	28921	28918	28944	28880	28919	28984	29081	29148	29155	29267	29287
EC total	161124	163237	163219	163703	165129	164895	165269	165608	166107	166984	167252
EFTA members											
Austria	4020	3998	3974	3974	3975	3975	3976	3977	3975	3988	3991
Finland	2445	2464	2473	2484	2499	2513	2525	2533	2543	2550	2545
Iceland	109	113	113	115	117	118	120	120	122	124	126
Norway	2032	2057	2064	2073	2083	2088	2096	2103	2115	2133	2138
Sweden	4143	4187	4198	4204	4210	4215	4222	4231	4236	4259	4269
Switzerland	3229	3241	3253	3271	3289	3298	3311	3325	3321	3337	3354
EFTA total	15978	16060	16075	16121	16173	16207	16250	16289	16312	16391	16423
CMEA members											
Bulgaria	4419	4453	4469	4483	4497	4511	4504	4502	4530	4520	4524
Czechoslovakia	7734	7865	7876	7898	7918	7941	7963	7961	7987	7950	7988
East Germany	8954	8893	8876	8854	8838	8842	8801	8774	8728	8530	8505
Hungary	5453	5521	5525	5526	5523	5515	5508	5502	5419	5420	5411
Poland	17723	18160	18324	18490	18658	18831	18990	19130	19441	19400	19365
Romania	10983	11248	11323	11386	11424	11460	11511	11599	11596	11505	11521
USSR	138481	141589	142622	143725	144914	146108	147264	148423	149817	148490	148294
CMEA total	193747	197729	199015	200362	201772	203208	204541	205891	207518	205815	205607
Others											
Albania		1292	1319	1347	1375	1405	1436	1472	1508	1530	1548
Cyprus	307	314	318	321	324	328	333	336	341	357	366
Gibraltar	14	15	15	14	14	14	14	14	15	15	15
Liechtenstein											
Malta	164	169	171	172	174	178	179	175	177	179	180
Monaco											
Turkey											
Yugoslavia			11387								
Total	485	1790	13210	1854	1887	1925	1962	1997	2041	2081	2109
European total	371334	378816	391519	382040	384961	386235	388022	389785	391978	391271	391391

Source: National   National Statistical Offices: all countries
Notes: Non-EEC data for 1989 are Euromonitor estimates

Database name: Demographic Trends and Forecasts
Sector name: Demographic Analysis   Table No: 0217

Title: Number of Children Aged 0-14 Years 1977-1989: National Estimates at January 1st

Unit: 000s

	1977	1980	1981	1982	1983	1984	1985	1986	1987	1988	1989
EC members											
Belgium	2118	1971	1973	1947	1917	1897	1874	1844	1874	1803	
Denmark	1133	1081	1055	1020	992	969	951	935	901	895	890
France	12388	12002	12024	11966	11924	11832	11744	11652	11539	11425	
West Germany	12664	11363	11003	10604	10177	9738	9341	9126	9045	8964	
Greece	2181	2213	2187	2170	2142	2120	2094	2071	2027	1983	
Ireland	1004	1034	1042	1051	1054	1050	1046	1041	1025	1009	
Italy	13223	12699	12402	12078	11778	11497	11178	10877	10548	10219	
Luxembourg	70	69	68	67	66	64	63	63	63	62	
Netherlands	3380	3184	3134	3074	3003	2930	2850	2788	2753	2719	
Portugal	2710	2601	2505	2477	2458	2435	2410	2369	2323	2269	
Spain	9738	9693	9646	9540	9393	9246	9100	8781	8650	8486	
United Kingdom	12709	11801	11718	11490	11284	11102	11012	10815	10773	10761	
EC total	73318	69711	68757	67484	66188	64880	63663	62362	61520	60593	
EFTA members											
Austria	1673	1540	1508	1473	1439	1405	1378	1358	1339	1320	
Finland	1017	976	965	957	952	950	952	952	952	956	960
Iceland	65	63	63	63	63	63	63	63	63	63	63
Norway	945	912	899	885	871	854	837	824	808	805	801
Sweden	1695	1641	1615	1586	1556	1534	1521	1512	1502	1505	1508
Switzerland	1358	1248	1234	1210	1188	1166	1149	1134	1046	958	
EFTA total	6753	6380	6284	6174	6069	5972	5900	5843	5710	5607	
CMEA members											
Bulgaria	1955	1960	1964	1969	1972	1960	1946	1865	1905	1905	
Czechoslovakia	3561	3703	3718	3736	3757	3774	3781	3781	3766	3751	
East Germany		3102	3162	3141	3133	3127	3114	3100	3209	3319	
Hungary		2475	2480	2470	2460	2450	2460	2330	2290	2233	
Poland	8237	8550	8707	8861	9047	9243	9400	9558	9600	9642	
Romania	5560	5922		6069	5814	5664	5603	5400	5300	5200	
USSR		64650					68948	69500	70000	70500	
Others											
Albania		1047									
Cyprus	153	155	156	159	162	166	168	171	173	177	
Gibraltar											
Liechtenstein											
Malta										83	
Monaco											
Turkey							19010				
Yugoslavia			5488								

Source: National Statistical Offices: all countries

Database name: Demographic Trends and Forecasts
Sector name: Demographic Analysis

Table No: 0218

Title: Number of Persons of Working Age (15-64 Years) 1977-1989: National Estimates at January 1st

Unit: 000s

	1977	1980	1981	1982	1983	1984	1985	1986	1987	1988	198
EC members											
Belgium	6328	6457	6461	6507	6564	6609	6637	6636	6646	6655	
Denmark	3251	3306	3328	3351	3370	3381	3394	3404	3440	3442	344
France	33362	34050	34539	35053	35505	35901	36262	36394	36577	36761	
West Germany	39646	40513	41120	41739	42196	42588	42727	42768	42891	43015	
Greece	5890	6116	6237	6297	6375	6443	6503	6531	6600	6668	
Ireland	1905	1995	2023	2050	2072	2100	2114	2147	2132	2135	
Italy	35835	36690	36335	36694	38168	38159	38631	38854	39293	39396	
Luxembourg	244	246	247	250	250	254	255	257	259	260	
Netherlands	8920	9292	9433	9544	9649	9756	9874	9972	10064	10156	
Portugal	6032	6264	6190	6270	6344	6434	6518	6582	6643	6706	
Spain	22616	23520	23783	23987	24261	24536	24810	25111	25345	25561	
United Kingdom	35263	36043	36162	36390	36648	36934	37134	37268	37325	37422	
EC total	199292	204492	205858	208132	211402	213095	214859	215924	217215	218178	
EFTA members											
Austria	4697	4804	4897	4991	5027	5069	5097	5108	5123	5138	
Finland	3190	3227	3246	3269	3294	3316	3336	3341	3346	3345	33
Iceland	136	142	144	147	149	151	153	154	157	160	16
Norway	2526	2568	2585	2605	2623	2641	2663	2675	2705	2720	27
Sweden	5267	5317	5341	5359	5376	5387	5397	5392	5411	5429	54
Switzerland	4118	4194	4222	4278	4331	4367	4404	4438	4465	4493	
EFTA total	19934	20252	20435	20649	20800	20931	21050	21108	21207	21283	
CMEA members											
Bulgaria	5866	5862	5865	5903	5954	6004	6003	6068	5981	5984	
Czechoslovakia	9623	9680	9715	9798	9884	9969	10016	10023	10043	10063	
East Germany			10581	10620	10688	10758	10776	10799	11220	11640	
Hungary		6452	6430	6406	6394	6382	6380	6368	7002	7002	
Poland	22898	23254	23439	23635	23826	24018	24100	24258	24400	24542	
Romania	13932	13998	14100	14172	14583	14721	14969	15000	15050	15100	
USSR		174233					182714	184800	186900	189000	
Others											
Albania		1509									
Cyprus	398	412	416	422	417	421	426	431	436	440	
Gibraltar											
Liechtenstein											
Malta									227		
Monaco											
Turkey							29432				
Yugoslavia			14948								

Source: National Statistical Offices: all countries

Database name: Demographic Trends and Forecasts
Sector name: Demographic Analysis   Table No: 0219

Title: Number of Persons Aged 65 Years and Over 1977-1989: National Estimates at January 1st

Unit: 000s

	1977	1980	1981	1982	1983	1984	1985	1986	1987	1988	1989
EC members											
Belgium	1378	1414	1416	1401	1377	1347	1347	1379	1402	1418	
Denmark	697	735	741	748	755	762	766	777	791	793	796
France	7223	7535	7466	7316	7197	7098	7057	7232	7565	7476	
West Germany	9133	9563	9535	9370	9173	8981	8981	9127	9283	9439	
Greece	1157	1259	1275	1293	1304	1309	1323	1348	1352	1375	
Ireland	353	364	368	370	372	373	377	378	384	394	
Italy	7065	7611	7742	7765	7396	7273	7271	7490	7689	7887	
Luxembourg	48	49	50	49	49	48	48	48	49	50	
Netherlands	1514	1615	1642	1668	1688	1709	1730	1769	1805	1840	
Portugal	957	1018	1124	1145	1167	1181	1201	1234	1265	1295	
Spain	3801	4029	4091	4329	4413	4498	4584	4653	4756	4868	
United Kingdom	7987	8478	8440	8497	8452	8424	8472	8680	8750	8883	
EC total	41313	43670	43890	43951	43343	43003	43157	44115	45090	45720	
EFTA members											
Austria	1148	1161	1151	1123	1090	1077	1081	1095	1114	1133	
Finland	524	568	577	586	596	604	606	618	639	645	651
Iceland	21	22	23	23	23	24	24	25	26	26	26
Norway	565	598	608	617	629	639	646	660	678	681	684
Sweden	1274	1345	1362	1378	1395	1410	1425	1454	1493	1499	1505
Switzerland	823	871	879	885	891	895	903	918	933	1000	
EFTA total	4355	4565	4600	4612	4624	4649	4685	4770	4883	4984	
CMEA members											
Bulgaria	983	1040	1062	1045	1014	997	1011	1017	1054	1090	
Czechoslovakia	1846	1928	1887	1835	1773	1715	1703	1715	1712	1786	
East Germany			2996	2994	2885	2824	2781	2756	2230	1691	
Hungary		1516	1522	1536	1546	1556	1558	1570	1470	1369	
Poland	3393	3610	3589	3566	3526	3484	3500	3525	3545	3519	
Romania	2168	2281		2237	2156	2155	2153	2160	2165	2170	
USSR		26659					25873	26000	26500	27000	
CMEA total	8390	37034	11056	13213	12900	12731	38579	38743	38675	38625	
Others											
Albania		118									
Cyprus	63	62	66	65	69	70	71	71	71	71	
Gibraltar											
Liechtenstein											
Malta									34		
Monaco											
Turkey											
Yugoslavia			2035								
Total	63	180	2101	65	69	70	71	71	105	71	
European total	54121	85449	61647	61841	60936	60453	86492	87699	88754	89399	

Source: National Statistical Offices: all countries

Database name: Demographic Trends and Forecasts
Sector name: Demographic Analysis   Table No: 0220

Title: Demographic Breakdown by Age Group : Latest Official Estimates at January 1st

Unit: 000s

	Year	0-4	5-9	10-14	15-19	20-24	25-29	30-34	35-39	40-44
EC members										
Belgium	1988	579.8	611.7	611.0	697.1	777.6	797.5	757.9	715.5	647.1
Denmark	1989	278.0	276.5	335.0	366.4	413.5	386.3	371.5	372.9	419.6
France	1988	3714.3	3852.5	3858.2	4301.1	4287.4	4208.1	4216.3	4359.2	3605.5
West Germany	1987	3004.2	2963.5	3077.2	4518.9	5396.9	4942.4	4358.3	4152.1	3762.2
Greece	1987	616.5	712.5	698.2	758.4	739.1	705.9	678.9	654.6	604.8
Ireland	1988	307.1	351.7	342.9	336.0	275.3	253.0	245.6	232.0	208.9
Italy	1988	2886.9	3242.4	4089.2	4571.8	4865.4	4386.6	4039.4	3902.4	3666.6
Luxembourg	1987	21.1	21.0	20.4	24.9	30.1	31.3	30.6	28.3	25.2
Netherlands	1988	896.2	890.4	931.9	1203.6	1270.1	1259.2	1177.3	1155.7	1095.9
Portugal	1988	658.6	750.2	859.7	863.1	864.5	809.8	707.8	660.0	591.8
Spain	1988	2420.7	2801.9	3263.0	3284.6	3306.3	3053.7	2658.0	2457.7	2347.0
United Kingdom	1988	3747.4	3619.0	3394.4	4249.5	4727.7	4495.1	3892.3	3847.3	4005.5
EFTA members										
Austria	1987	440.1	440.3	458.6	581.4	656.6	622.6	531.3	513.3	474.4
Finland	1989	311.0	325.3	323.6	304.2	363.8	377.8	391.2	417.9	413.4
Iceland	1989	20.8	22.0	20.4	21.2	22.0	22.0	20.5	18.3	15.5
Norway	1989	267.0	258.4	275.8	327.6	338.0	318.5	316.6	305.5	313.5
Sweden	1989	516.3	481.2	510.5	560.3	622.6	568.8	574.3	601.9	673.8
Switzerland	1987	370.3	366.2	388.5	472.6	526.1	505.8	490.6	501.8	493.6
CMEA members										
Bulgaria	1988	593.1	626.4	685.3	624.9	573.5	614.7	640.3	688.2	600.0
Czechoslovakia	1987	1121.0	1289.0	1356.0	1082.0	1098.0	1082.0	1246.0	1243.0	1032.0
East Germany	1987	1123.2	1158.0	928.1	1124.2	1358.6	1370.4	1271.5	1132.6	879.5
Hungary	1988	624.2	739.0	870.1	736.3	657.3	677.9	901.1	817.5	706.4
Poland	1986	3406.0	3148.5	3003.5	2514.7	2698.7	3261.7	3333.0	2858.8	1801.9
Romania	1985	1722.7	1984.2	1895.8	1994.3	1413.8	1736.3	1751.1	1466.4	1234.4
USSR										
Others										
Albania	1980	406.1	336.5	304.5	293.8	259.1	195.1	164.3	144.3	126.7
Cyprus	1988	64.4	61.2	50.9	50.5	55.5	60.8	54.8	47.9	46.6
Gibraltar										
Liechtenstein										
Malta	1987	27.5	28.1	27.0	23.9	25.9	28.6	27.5	29.3	24.2
Monaco										
Turkey	1985	6078.0	6739.0	6193.0	5407.0	4784.0	4041.0	3374.0	2787.0	2208.0
Yugoslavia	1981	1862.7	1837.3	1787.9	1845.1	1860.3	1894.1	1695.1	1263.9	1491.7

Source: National Statistical Offices: all countries

Database name: Demographic Trends and Forecasts
Sector name: Demographic Analysis   Table No: 0220

Title: Demographic Breakdown by Age Group: Latest Official Estimates at January 1st

Unit: 000s

	Year	45-49	50-54	55-59	60-64	65-69	70-74	75-79	80-84	85-89	90+	Notes
EC members												
Belgium	1988	535.2	567.3	597.5	562.4	450.1	329.2	310.4	201.2	127.2		
Denmark	1989	331.1	278.5	252.8	252.0	242.9	202.2	168.0	107.1	53.6	21.9	
France	1988	2830.2	2996.8	3080.7	2875.6	2299.8	1581.6	1723.7	1160.6	586.9	122.9	
West Germany	1987	4901.0	3944.9	3604.2	3310.5	2524.6	2431.0	2212.4	1352.9	573.5	188.7	
Greece	1987	617.4	689.7	651.3	499.6	393.8	380.4	294.7	185.3	97.7		a
Ireland	1988	167.3	150.7	141.9	136.4	131.8	108.3	80.2	43.8	26.4		b
Italy	1988	3711.2	3515.0	3467.8	3270.1	2499.2	2006.9	1774.1	997.5	453.0	156.6	
Luxembourg	1987	23.3	22.5	23.6	18.7	14.3	13.6	11.3	10.0			
Netherlands	1988	844.0	752.3	726.5	671.6	589.5	476.1	368.7	239.6	166.2		
Portugal	1988	552	573.9	561.9	521.8	427.7	352.8	279.2	156.4	79.2		
Spain	1988	2026.7	2202.2	2234.0	1990.5	1608.3	1259.5	1000.9	622.0	377.3		
United Kingdom	1988	3209.1	3055.0	3000.0	2940.1	2865.1	2165.8	1860.3	1196.2	795.7		a
EFTA members												
Austria	1987	531.3	380.4	414.9	416.6	324.5	267.4	264.4	165.2	70.7	21.7	
Finland	1989	294.7	270.3	260.1	250.1	209.6	168.6	140.9	84.9	35.6	11.5	
Iceland	1989	11.8	10.4	10.9	9.7	8.5	6.6	5.0	3.4	1.9	0.9	
Norway	1989	226.6	189.6	193.1	205.0	212.9	179.0	139.5	88.6	45.1	18.4	
Sweden	1989	540.3	441.2	423.4	439.5	458.7	380.6	319.9	207.4	100.1	37.8	
Switzerland	1987	412.3	384.9	353.5	324.1	270.7	240.6	204.4	132.9	63.0	21.4	
CMEA members												
Bulgaria	1988	529.9	579.1	575.8	557.2	415.2	256.8	238.9	125.7	41.9	11.5	
Czechoslovakia	1987	826.0	784.0	834.0	816.0	529.0	476.0	415.0	219.0	73.0		
East Germany	1987	1277.0	1106.2	934.5	765.0	661.0	487.8	558.8	346.2	140.5	36.0	
Hungary	1988	660.0	615.9	632.9	597.0	480.0	318.1	318.0	164.6	68.4	19.9	
Poland	1986	2029.4	2069.0	2004.4	1685.6	1009.6	1039.7	821.2	654.8			
Romania	1985	1502.7	1435.7	1326.3	1107.7	588.3	731.9	491.2	249.4	92.5		a
USSR												
Others												
Albania	1980	109.4	93.6	69.3	53.6	117.5						
Cyprus	1988	36.4	33.2	28.7	25.9	21.7	20.6	16.6	11.8			
Gibraltar												
Liechtenstein												
Malta	1987	17.9	18.1	16.0	15.2	12.0	8.9	7.3	3.9	2.0		
Monaco												
Turkey	1985	2009.0	2043.0	1649.0	1130.0	2126.0						c
Yugoslavia	1981	1543.8	1433.6	1126.1	650.7	700.8	639.4	694.3				d

Source: National Statistical Offices: all countries
Notes: Last figure for each country includes people of all older age groups
            a   Mid-year
            b   Annual average
            c   Does not include 167,400 people of unknown age
            d   Does not include 98,100 people of unknown age

Database name: Demographic Trends and Forecasts
Sector name: Demographic Analysis   Table No: 0221

Title: Demographic Breakdown by Age Group: Latest Official Estimates at January 1st

Unit: Percentage of the population

	Year	0-4	5-9	10-14	15-19	20-24	25-29	30-34	35-39	40-44
EC members										
Belgium	1988	5.9	6.2	6.2	7.1	7.9	8.1	7.7	7.2	6.6
Denmark	1989	5.4	5.4	6.5	7.1	8.1	7.5	7.2	7.3	8.2
France	1988	6.7	6.9	6.9	7.7	7.7	7.6	7.6	7.8	6.5
West Germany	1987	4.9	4.8	5.0	7.4	8.8	8.1	7.1	6.8	6.1
Greece	1987	6.2	7.1	7.0	7.6	7.4	7.1	6.8	6.6	6.1
Ireland	1988	8.7	9.9	9.7	9.5	7.8	7.1	6.9	6.6	5.9
Italy	1988	5.0	5.6	7.1	8.0	8.5	7.6	7.0	6.8	6.4
Luxembourg	1987	5.7	5.7	5.5	6.7	8.1	8.5	8.3	7.6	6.8
Netherlands	1988	6.1	6.1	6.3	8.2	8.6	8.6	8.0	7.9	7.4
Portugal	1988	6.4	7.3	8.4	8.4	8.4	7.9	6.9	6.4	5.8
Spain	1988	6.2	7.2	8.4	8.4	8.5	7.8	6.8	6.3	6.0
United Kingdom	1988	6.6	6.3	5.9	7.4	8.3	7.9	6.8	6.7	7.0
EFTA members										
Austria	1987	5.8	5.8	6.1	7.7	8.7	8.2	7.0	6.8	6.3
Finland	1989	6.3	6.6	6.5	6.1	7.3	7.6	7.9	8.4	8.3
Iceland	1989	8.3	8.7	8.1	8.4	8.7	8.7	8.1	7.3	6.2
Norway	1989	6.3	6.1	6.5	7.8	8.0	7.5	7.5	7.2	7.4
Sweden	1989	6.1	5.7	6.0	6.6	7.4	6.7	6.8	7.1	8.0
Switzerland	1987	5.7	5.6	6.0	7.2	8.1	7.8	7.5	7.7	7.6
CMEA members										
Bulgaria	1988	6.6	7.0	7.6	7.0	6.4	6.8	7.1	7.7	6.7
Czechoslovakia	1987	7.2	8.3	8.7	7.0	7.1	7.0	8.0	8.0	6.6
East Germany	1987	6.7	7.0	5.6	6.7	8.2	8.2	7.6	6.8	5.3
Hungary	1988	5.9	7.0	8.2	6.9	6.2	6.4	8.5	7.7	6.7
Poland	1986	9.1	8.4	8.0	6.7	7.2	8.7	8.9	7.7	4.8
Romania	1985	7.6	8.7	8.3	8.8	6.2	7.6	7.7	6.5	5.4
USSR										
Others										
Albania	1980	15.2	12.6	11.4	11.0	9.7	7.3	6.1	5.4	4.7
Cyprus	1988	9.4	8.9	7.4	7.3	8.1	8.8	8.0	7.0	6.8
Gibraltar										
Liechtenstein										
Malta	1987	8.0	8.2	7.9	7.0	7.5	8.3	8.0	8.5	7.0
Monaco										
Turkey	1985	12.0	13.3	12.2	10.7	9.5	8.0	6.7	5.5	4.4
Yugoslavia	1981	8.3	8.2	8.0	8.3	8.3	8.5	7.6	5.7	6.7

	Year	45-49	50-54	55-59	60-64	65-69	70-74	75-79	80-84	85-89	90+	Total
EC members												
Belgium	1988	5.4	5.7	6.1	5.7	4.6	3.3	3.1	2.0	1.3		100.0
Denmark	1989	6.5	5.4	4.9	4.9	4.7	3.9	3.3	2.1	1.0	0.4	100.0
France	1988	5.1	5.4	5.5	5.2	4.1	2.8	3.1	2.1	1.1	0.2	100.0
West Germany	1987	8.0	6.4	5.9	5.4	4.1	4.0	3.6	2.2	0.9	0.3	100.0
Greece	1987	6.2	6.9	6.5	5.0	3.9	3.8	3.0	1.9	1.0		100.0
Ireland	1988	4.7	4.3	4.0	3.9	3.7	3.1	2.3	1.2	0.7		100.0
Italy	1988	6.5	6.1	6.0	5.7	4.3	3.5	3.1	1.7	0.8	0.3	100.0
Luxembourg	1987	6.3	6.1	6.4	5.1	3.9	3.7	3.1	2.7			100.0
Netherlands	1988	5.7	5.1	4.9	4.6	4.0	3.2	2.5	1.6	1.1		100.0
Portugal	1988	5.4	5.6	5.5	5.1	4.2	3.4	2.7	1.5	0.8		100.0
Spain	1988	5.2	5.7	5.7	5.1	4.1	3.2	2.6	1.6	1.0		100.0
United Kingdom	1988	5.6	5.4	5.3	5.2	5.0	3.8	3.3	2.1	1.4		100.0
EFTA members												
Austria	1987	7.0	5.0	5.5	5.5	4.3	3.5	3.5	2.2	0.9	0.3	100.0
Finland	1989	5.9	5.5	5.2	5.0	4.2	3.4	2.8	1.7	0.7	0.2	100.0
Iceland	1989	4.7	4.1	4.3	3.9	3.4	2.6	2.0	1.4	0.8	0.4	100.0
Norway	1989	5.4	4.5	4.6	4.9	5.0	4.2	3.3	2.1	1.1	0.4	100.0
Sweden	1989	6.4	5.2	5.0	5.2	5.4	4.5	3.8	2.5	1.2	0.4	100.0
Switzerland	1987	6.3	5.9	5.4	5.0	4.1	3.7	3.1	2.0	1.0	0.3	100.0
CMEA members												
Bulgaria	1988	5.9	6.4	6.4	6.2	4.6	2.9	2.7	1.4	0.5	0.1	100.0
Czechoslovakia	1987	5.3	5.1	5.4	5.3	3.4	3.1	2.7	1.4	0.5		100.0
East Germany	1987	7.7	6.6	5.6	4.6	4.0	2.9	3.4	2.1	0.8	0.2	100.0
Hungary	1988	6.2	5.8	6.0	5.6	4.5	3.0	3.0	1.6	0.6	0.2	100.0
Poland	1986	5.4	5.5	5.4	4.5	2.7	2.8	2.2	1.8			100.0
Romania	1985	6.6	6.3	5.8	4.9	2.6	3.2	2.2	1.1	0.4		100.0
USSR												
Others												
Albania	1980	4.1	3.5	2.6	2.0	4.4						100.0
Cyprus	1988	5.3	4.8	4.2	3.8	3.2	3.0	2.4	1.7			100.0
Gibraltar												
Liechtenstein												
Malta	1987	5.2	5.3	4.7	4.4	3.5	2.6	2.1	1.1	0.6		100.0
Monaco												
Turkey	1985	4.0	4.0	3.3	2.2	4.2						100.0
Yugoslavia	1981	6.9	6.4	5.0	2.9	3.1	2.9	3.1				100.0

Source: National Statistical Offices: all countries
Notes: Last figure for each country includes people of all older age groups

Database name: Demographic Trends and Forecasts
Sector name: Population Forecasts

Table No: 0222

Title: Official Population Projections 1990-2020

Unit: 000s

	1990	1995	2000	2005	2010	2020	% increase 1990-2020
EC members							
Belgium	9938	9980	10034	10046	10040	9974	0.36
Denmark	5120	5129	5139	5137	5085	5038	-1.60
France	56173	57188	58196	58889	59430	60229	7.22
West Germany	61039	60701	60318	59511	58407	55889	-8.44
Greece	10047	10124	10193	10247	10249	10139	0.92
Ireland	3720	3900	4086	4462	4462	4808	29.25
Italy	57322	57591	57881	57771	57290	55785	-2.68
Luxembourg	367	368	368	366	363	355	-3.27
Netherlands	14752	15008	15207	15301	15318	15225	3.21
Portugal	10285	10429	10587	10717	10809	10912	6.10
Spain	39333	40060	40812	41420	41831	42366	7.71
United Kingdom	56926	57268	57509	57562	57560	57630	1.24
EC total	325022	327746	330330	331429	330844	328350	1.02
EFTA members							
Austria	7492	7479	7461	7406	7339	7173	-4.26
Finland	4975	5030	5076	5108	5132	5148	3.48
Iceland	253	264	274	283	291	305	20.55
Norway	4212	4271	4331	4378	4416	4485	6.48
Sweden	8339	8326	8322	8305	8275	8205	-1.61
Switzerland	6521	6552	6553	6508	6434	6247	-4.20
EFTA total	31792	31922	32017	31988	31887	31563	-0.72
CMEA members							
Bulgaria	9010	9036	9071	9077	9059	8985	-0.28
Czechoslovakia	15667	15874	16179	16478	16715	17061	8.90
East Germany	16149	16118	16118	16121	16118	15863	-1.77
Hungary	10552	10509	10531	10519	10459	10291	-2.47
Poland	38423	39365	40366	41462	42553	44333	15.38
Romania	23272	23816	24346	24731	25013	25521	9.66
USSR	287991	298000	307737	317266	326415	343212	19.17
CMEA total	401064	412718	424348	435654	446332	465266	16.01
Others							
Albania	3245	3521	3795	4061	4316	4792	47.67
Cyprus	701	734	765	795	826	882	25.82
Gibraltar							
Liechtenstein							
Malta	353	360	366	373	379	388	9.92
Monaco							
Turkey	55616	61151	66622	71800	76641	85342	53.45
Yugoslavia	23849	24471	25026	25481	25822	26211	9.90
Total	83764	90237	96574	102510	107984	117615	40.41
European total	841642	862623	883269	901581	917047	942794	12.02

Source: UN World Population Prospects (1988 base)
Notes: Allowance has been made for an emigration of 500,000 East Germans to what is, in 1990, the still separate state of West Germany

Database name: Demographic Trends and Forecasts
Sector name: Population Forecasts

Table No: 0223

Title: Projected Demographic Population by Age and Sex 1995: Official Forecasts

Unit: 000s

	Total	Male	Female	0-14	15-64	65+	Notes
EC members							
Belgium	9729	4747	4982	1766	6404	1559	
Denmark	5108	2507	2601	849	3455	804	
France	56338	27756	28582	11194	37338	7807	a
West Germany	59983	29118	30864	9502	41004	9477	a
Greece	10168	5053	5115	2347	6434	1387	
Ireland	4083	2051	2032	1161	2533	389	a
Italy	57506	27960	29546	9307	39071	9128	
Luxembourg	373	182	191	71	253	49	
Netherlands	15028	7413	7615	2653	10325	2050	
Portugal	10819	5273	5547	2129	7263	1427	
Spain	40022	19706	20316	7647	26745	5630	
United Kingdom	58144	28483	29661	11593	37385	9166	
EC total	327301	160249	167052	60219	218210	48873	
EFTA members							
Austria	7621	3661	3960	1328	5094	1199	
Finland	5054	2467	2588	941	3383	731	
Iceland	256	129	128	57	170	29	
Norway	4273	2109	2163	784	2788	701	
Sweden	8498	4188	4309	1502	5472	1524	
Switzerland	6382	3115	3266	1036	4347	999	a
EFTA total	32084	15669	16414	5648	21254	5183	
CMEA members							
Bulgaria	9392	4656	4737	2006	6069	1318	a
Czechoslovakia	16155	7896	8259	3461	10746	1949	a
East Germany	16998	8231	8767	3447	11362	2189	a
Hungary	10661	5146	5516	1959	7172	1530	a
Poland	39600	19324	20276	9410	25786	4404	
Romania	24690	12214	12476	5840	16045	2805	a
USSR	303517	145752	157765	74801	195059	33657	
CMEA total	421013	203219	217796	100924	272239	47852	
Others							
Albania	3759	1903	1856	1235	2322	202	a
Cyprus	734	367	366	186	477	71	a
Gibraltar							
Liechtenstein							
Malta	361	174	187	82	243	36	b
Monaco							
Turkey	64485	32997	31488	21625	39720	3140	b
Yugoslavia	24908	12399	12509	5326	16874	2708	
European total	874645	426977	447668	195245	571339	108065	c

Source: National Statistical Offices/UN World Population Prospects
Notes:
a UN estimates (medium variant)
b Euromonitor estimates
c Excluding Gibraltar, Liechtenstein and Monaco (combined population about 95,000)

TABLE 0202: POPULATION DEVELOPMENT
Millions

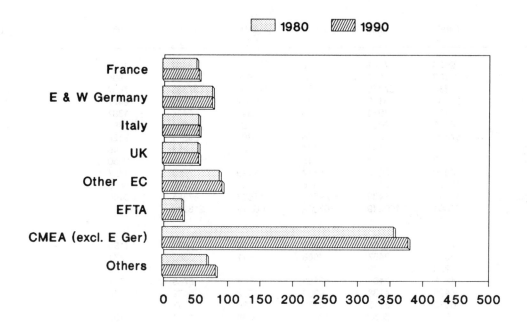

TABLE 0222: POPULATION FORECASTS
Millions

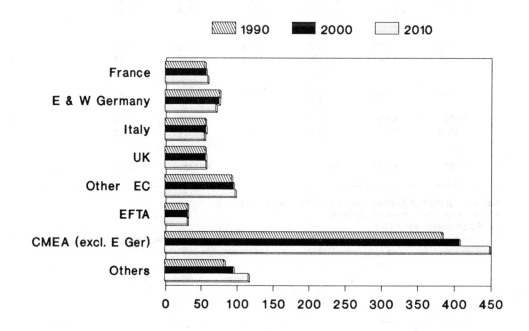

134

TABLE 0204: BIRTHS 1980-1989
Thousands

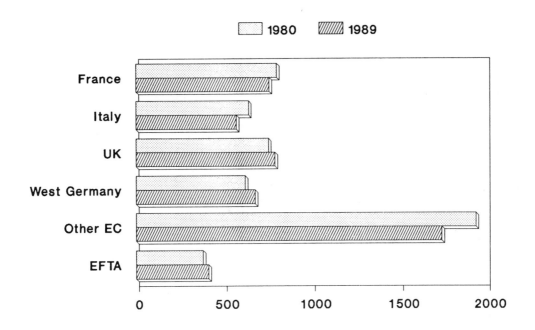

TABLE 0205: DEATHS 1980-1989
Thousands

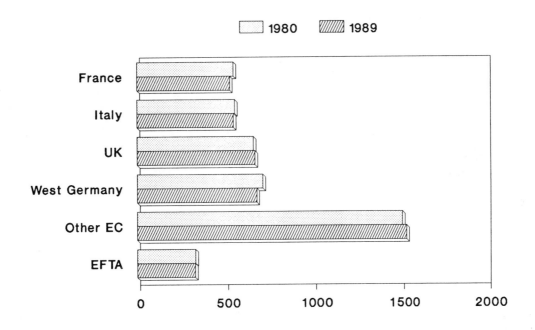

03
ECONOMIC INDICATORS

	1977	1978	1979	1980	1981	1982	1983	1984	1985
EC members									
Belgium	2842	3058	3266	3519	3659	3979	4221	4541	4855
Denmark	279	311	347	374	408	464	513	565	615
France	1918	2183	2481	2808	3165	3626	4007	4362	4700
West Germany	1198	1285	1392	1479	1541	1598	1675	1756	1831
Greece	964	1161	1429	1711	2050	2575	3079	3806	4618
Ireland	6	7	8	9	11	13	15	16	18
Italy	190	222	270	390	468	545	633	727	813
Luxembourg	118	129	138	148	162	182	198	222	240
Netherlands	275	297	316	337	353	369	381	400	418
Portugal	626	787	991	1232	1465	1848	2279	2806	3536
Spain	9178	11231	13131	15185	16989	19567	22235	25121	27889
United Kingdom	146	168	197	230	254	276	304	324	355
EC total									
EFTA members									
Austria	796	842	919	995	1056	1134	1202	1285	1367
Finland	130	144	167	193	218	245	274	310	337
Iceland	4	6	9	15	24	38	66	87	119
Norway	192	213	239	285	328	362	402	453	500
Sweden	370	412	462	525	573	628	710	794	866
Switzerland	146	152	159	170	185	196	204	214	228
EFTA total									
CMEA members									
Bulgaria	17	17	19	21	22	23	24	25	26
Czechoslovakia	411	434	456	483	470	491	503	534	549
East Germany	164	176	179	187	196	202	210	222	232
Hungary	582	630	682	721	780	848	896	979	1034
Poland				2511	2753	5546	6924	8576	10367
Romania	436	468	497	512	522	537	557	600	660
USSR	413	420	433	454	478	513	536	559	569
CMEA total									
Others									
Albania									
Cyprus	0	1	1	1	1	1	1	1	1
Gibraltar									
Liechtenstein									
Malta	0	0	0	0	0	0	0	0	0
Monaco									
Turkey	860	1273	2182	4328	6414	8578	11532	18212	27552
Yugoslavia	734	902	1165	1553	2208	2925	4084	6654	11951
Total									
European total									

Source:　　International Monetary Fund/Comecon/National Statistical Offices
Notes:　　Values of 0 denote less than 500 million units
　　　　a　'000 billion lire
　　　　b　Net material product
　　　　c　Dollar and percentage growth values based on 1988 results

Database name: Economic Indicators
Sector name: Gross Domestic Product

Table No: 0301

Title: Trends in Total Gross Domestic Product 1977-1989

Unit: National currencies (billions)

	1986	1987	1988	1989	% growth 1977-1989	% share 1989	Total $ billion 1989	$ per capita 1989	Notes
EC members									
Belgium	5117	5322	5657	5912	108	2.2	150.0	15115	
Denmark	667	696	724	733	163	1.5	100.3	19497	
France	5053	5301	5658	5845	205	13.5	916.1	16322	
West Germany	1931	2006	2111	2187	83	17.2	1163.3	18884	
Greece	5480	6256	7446	7617	690	0.7	46.9	4655	
Ireland	19	20	21	22	286	0.5	31.2	8846	
Italy	896	980	1079	1116	487	12.0	813.4	14085	a
Luxembourg	253	224	236	244	107	0.1	6.2	16646	
Netherlands	429	432	451	470	71	3.3	221.6	14963	
Portugal	4419	5187	5868	6150	882	0.6	39.1	3785	
Spain	31948	35715	39618	41559	353	5.2	351.1	8965	
United Kingdom	381	417	462	473	224	11.5	775.7	13550	
EC total					293	68.2	4614.8	14154	
EFTA members									
Austria	1441	1488	1550	1612	103	1.8	121.8	16044	
Finland	360	394	414	435	235	1.5	101.4	20425	
Iceland	159	208	255	294	7250	0.1	5.2	20534	
Norway	514	562	583	640	233	1.4	92.7	21872	
Sweden	946	1021	1114	1136	207	2.6	176.2	20821	
Switzerland	244	255	269	287	97	2.6	175.4	26590	
EFTA total					257	9.9	672.7	20952	
CMEA members									
Bulgaria	27	29	32			0.3	18.8	2085	b,c
Czechoslovakia	562	575	589			0.9	62.7	4010	b,c
East Germany	238	254	261			2.1	139.6	8384	b,c
Hungary	1089	1226	1406			0.4	27.9	2622	c
Poland	12953	16940	29629			1.0	68.8	1824	c
Romania	730	765	800			0.8	56.0	2451	c
USSR	576	585	611			14.8	998.4	3517	c
CMEA total					176	20.3	1372.2	3461	
Others									
Albania									
Cyprus	2	2	2			0.1	4.3	5958	c
Gibraltar									
Liechtenstein									
Malta	1	1	1			0.0	3.0	8646	c
Monaco									
Turkey	39288	58299	100411	101516		1.0	706.0	1329	c
Yugoslavia	23400	52340	158328	159595		0.4	30.4	1284	c
Total					122	1.6	743.7	1335	
European total					250	100.0	7403	8858	

Source: International Monetary Fund/Comecon/National Statistical Offices
Notes:
a '000 billion lire
b Net material product
c Dollar and percentage growth values based on 1988 results

Database name: Economic Indicators
Sector name: Gross National Product

Table No: 0302

Title: Trends in Gross National Product 1977-1988

Unit: National currencies (billions)

	1977	1978	1979	1980	1981	1982	1983	1984
EC members								
Belgium	3231	3328	3384	3501	3635	3940	4168	4492
Denmark	276	306	340	365	395	447	494	541
France					3181	3625	3932.0	4338
West Germany	1199	1292	1397	1485	1545	1597	1680	1770
Greece	994	1194	1472	1768	2109	2632	3110	3806
Ireland	6	7	8	9	11	12	14	15
Italy	190	222	271	339	399	467	627	721
Luxembourg	121	134	147	164	166	189	207	233
Netherlands	275	296	315	336	352	368	382	400
Portugal	619	772	969	1199	1439	1745	2160	2628
Spain	9116	11143	13052	15072	16751	19283	21877	24724
United Kingdom	146	169	198	230	255	277	307	329
EC total								
EFTA members								
Austria	789	834	911	986	1047	1125	1193	1270
Finland	128	141	164	189	214	240	269	301
Iceland	4	6	8	15	24	37	63	83
Norway	156	171	192	234	317	350	389	439
Sweden	369	411	461	521	564	614	688	774
Switzerland	152	158	165	177	194	205	214	226
EFTA total								
CMEA members								
Bulgaria	17	17	19	21	22	23	24	25
Czechoslovakia	411	434	456	483	470	491	503	534
East Germany	164	176	179	187	196	202	210	222
Hungary	477	515	556	583	635	696	738	804
Poland				1992	2160	4753	5924	7182
Romania	436	468	497	512	522	537	557	600
USSR	413	420	433	454	478	513	536	559
CMEA total								
Others								
Albania								
Cyprus	0	1	1	1	1	1	1	1
Gibraltar								
Liechtenstein								
Malta	0	0	0	0	0	1	0	1
Monaco								
Turkey	873	1291	2200	4435	6554	8722	11551	18375
Yugoslavia			1353	1814	2513	3283	4399	6876
Total								
European total								

Source: International Monetary Fund/Comecon/National Statistical Offices

Database name: Economic Indicators
Sector name: Gross National Product

Table No: 0302

Title: Trends in Gross National Product 1977-1988

Unit: National currencies (billion)

	1985	1986	1987	1988	% growth 1977-1988	% share 1988	Total $ billion 1988	$ per capita 1988	Notes
EC members									
Belgium	4792	5064	5278	5604	73	2.2	152.4	15436	
Denmark	589	639	668	695	152	1.5	103.2	20093	
France			5283	5463		13.4	917.1	16418	
West Germany	1844	1945	2018	2122	77	17.7	1208.3	19705	
Greece	4584	5412	6192	7390	643	0.8	52.1	5195	
Ireland	16	17	18	19	239	0.4	27.2	7684	
Italy	808	893	974	1055	455	11.9	810.5	14116	a
Luxembourg	251	261	271	281	132	0.1	7.6	20527	
Netherlands	419	428	431	449	63	3.3	227.2	15427	
Portugal	3340	4267	5054	5744	828	0.6	39.9	3882	
Spain	27558	31649	35407	39190	330	4.9	336.4	8627	
United Kingdom	358	386	422	468	221	12.2	833.8	14611	
EC total						69.0	4715.8	14527	
EFTA members									
Austria	1347	1421	1475	1529	94	1.8	123.8	16349	
Finland	331	355	388	421	229	1.5	100.7	20317	
Iceland	114	152	202	246	6050	0.1	5.7	23061	
Norway	491	505	554	569	265	1.3	87.3	20828	
Sweden	845	926	1005	1094	196	2.6	178.5	21266	
Switzerland	242	256	266	283	86	2.8	193.4	29490	
EFTA total						10.1	689.5	21598	
CMEA members									
Bulgaria	26	27	29	31	88	0.3	18.3	2034	b
Czechoslovakia	549	562	575	589	43	0.9	62.7	4017	b
East Germany	232	238	254	261	59	2.0	139.6	8383	b
Hungary	842	881	1000	1152	142	0.3	22.9	2151	
Poland	8586	10697	14013	24995		0.8	58.1	1540	b
Romania	660	730	765	800	83	0.8	56.0	2447	b
USSR	569	576	585	611	48	14.6	998.4	3522	b
CMEA total						19.8	1355.8	3424	
Others									
Albania									
Cyprus	2	2	2	2	365	0.1	4.3	6129	
Gibraltar									
Liechtenstein									
Malta	1	1	1	1	286	0.0	3.0	8720	
Monaco									
Turkey	27789	39310	58390	99992	11354	1.0	70.3	1346	
Yugoslavia	12242	23820	54303	1661700					
Total						1.1	77.6	970	
European total						100.0	6838.7	8214	

Source: International Monetary Fund/Comecon/National Statistical Offices
Notes: Values of 0 denote less than 500 million units
            a   '000 billion lire
            b   Net material product

Database name: Economic Indicators
Sector name: Gross Domestic Product

Table No: 0303

Title: Trends in Total Gross Domestic Product 1977-1989

Unit: Current US dollars (billions)

	1977	1980	1981	1982	1983	1984	1985
EC members							
Belgium	79.3	120.3	98.5	87.1	82.6	78.6	81.8
Denmark	46.5	66.4	57.3	55.7	56.1	54.6	58.0
France	390.3	664.5	582.4	551.7	525.8	499.1	523.1
West Germany	515.9	813.7	681.9	658.5	656.0	617.0	621.9
Greece	26.2	40.1	37.0	38.5	35.0	33.8	33.4
Ireland	9.9	19.3	18.4	19.0	18.3	17.7	19.2
Italy	215.3	455.4	411.7	403.0	416.8	413.8	426.2
Luxembourg	3.3	5.1	4.4	4.0	4.3	4.2	4.3
Netherlands	112.0	169.5	141.5	138.2	133.5	124.7	125.9
Portugal	16.4	24.6	23.8	23.3	20.6	19.2	20.8
Spain	120.8	211.8	184.0	178.1	155.0	156.3	164.0
United Kingdom	254.8	535.0	515.1	483.1	461.2	433.0	460.2
EC total	1790.8	3125.7	2755.9	2640.2	2565.1	2451.8	2538.8
EFTA members							
Austria	48.2	76.9	66.3	66.5	66.9	64.2	66.1
Finland	32.3	51.7	50.5	50.8	49.2	51.6	54.4
Iceland	2.0	3.1	3.3	3.1	2.7	2.7	2.9
Norway	36.1	57.7	57.1	56.1	55.1	55.5	58.2
Sweden	82.6	124.1	113.2	100.0	92.6	96.0	100.7
Switzerland	60.7	101.5	94.2	96.5	97.2	91.1	92.8
EFTA total	261.8	415.0	384.6	373.0	363.6	361.1	374.9
CMEA members							
Bulgaria	18.5	23.9	23.8	24.1	24.1	24.7	24.7
Czechoslovakia	41.1	40.0	40.0	39.6	39.3	44.1	48.6
East Germany	123.0	102.7	86.7	83.1	82.4	71.6	89.2
Hungary	14.2	22.2	22.7	23.1	21.0	24.4	20.6
Poland	0.9	56.7	53.7	65.4	75.5	75.4	70.5
Romania	21.8	28.4	34.8	35.8	32.4	28.2	38.5
USSR	560.4	699.5	664.8	706.6	721.4	685.0	679.0
CMEA total	779.9	973.5	926.5	977.7	996.1	953.5	971.1
Others							
Albania							
Cyprus	1.0	2.1	2.1	2.1	2.1	2.2	2.8
Gibraltar							
Liechtenstein							
Malta	0.6	1.1	1.1	1.1	1.1	1.0	1.0
Monaco							
Turkey	47.8	56.9	57.7	52.8	51.1	49.7	52.8
Yugoslavia	40.1	63.0	63.1	58.2	44.0	43.5	44.2
Total	89.5	123.2	124.0	114.2	98.3	96.4	100.9
European total	2922.0	4637.4	4191.1	4105.1	4023.1	3862.9	3985.7

Source: Euromonitor
Notes: a Dollar values calculated from 1988 data

Database name: Economic Indicators
Sector name: Gross Domestic Product

Table No: 0303

Title: Trends in Total Gross Domestic Product 1977-1989

Unit: Current US dollars (billions)

	1986	1987	1988	1989	% growth 1977-88	% share 1977	% share 1989	Notes
EC members								
Belgium	114.5	142.6	153.9	150.0	94.0	2.7	2.8	
Denmark	82.4	101.8	107.5	100.3	131.4	1.6	1.9	
France	729.6	881.9	949.8	916.1	143.3	13.4	17.3	
West Germany	889.2	1116.1	1202.0	1163.3	133.0	17.7	22.0	
Greece	39.1	46.2	52.5	46.9	100.5	0.9	0.9	
Ireland	25.5	29.8	30.0	31.2	202.0	0.3	0.6	
Italy	601.0	756.1	829.0	813.4	285.0	7.4	15.4	
Luxembourg	5.0		6.4	6.2	94.8	0.1	0.1	
Netherlands	175.1	213.3	228.2	221.6	103.6	3.8	4.2	
Portugal	29.5	36.8	40.8	39.1	149.3	0.6	0.7	
Spain	228.1	289.2	340.1	351.1	181.5	4.1	6.6	
United Kingdom	558.9	683.4	823.1	775.7	223.0	8.7	14.7	
EC total	3478.1	4297.1	4763.3	4614.8	166.0	61.3	87.3	
EFTA members								
Austria	94.4	117.7	125.5	121.8	160.6	1.6	2.3	
Finland	71.0	89.6	99.0	101.4	206.8	1.1	1.9	
Iceland	3.9	5.4	5.9	5.2	194.8	0.1	0.1	
Norway	69.5	83.4	89.5	92.7	148.0	1.2	1.8	
Sweden	132.8	161.0	181.8	176.2	120.2	2.8	3.3	
Switzerland	135.6	171.0	183.8	175.4	202.6	2.1	3.3	
EFTA total	507.2	628.2	685.5	672.7	161.8	9.0	12.7	
CMEA members								
Bulgaria	22.4	22.3	18.8		2.0	0.6		a
Czechoslovakia	57.9	61.2	62.7		52.5	1.4		a
East Germany	119.0	149.4	139.6		13.5	4.2		a
Hungary	23.8	26.1	27.9		96.3	0.5		a
Poland	73.9	63.9	68.8		7281.3	0.0		a
Romania	45.2	52.6	56.0		157.0	0.7		a
USSR	818.2	915.6	998.4		78.2	19.2		a
CMEA total	1160.4	1291.1	1372.2		75.9	26.7		
Others								
Albania								
Cyprus	3.0	5.0	4.3		329.0	0.0		a
Gibraltar								
Liechtenstein								
Malta	2.5	2.9	3.0		432.3	0.0		a
Monaco								
Turkey	58.2	68.0	70.6		47.8	1.6		a
Yugoslavia	61.7	71.0	30.4		-24.3	1.4		a
Total	125.5	146.9	108.3		21.0	3.1		a
European total	5271.3	6363.2	6929.3	5287.5	137.1	100.0	100.0	

Source: Euromonitor
Notes: a Dollar values calculated from 1988 data

Database name: Economic Indicators
Sector name: Gross Domestic Product

Table No: 0304

Title: Trends in Total Gross National Product 1977-1988

Unit: Current US dollars (billions)

	1977	1978	1979	1980	1981	1982	1983	1984
EC members								
Belgium	90.1	105.7	115.4	119.7	97.9	86.2	81.5	77.7
Denmark	46.0	55.5	64.6	64.8	55.5	53.6	54.0	52.2
France					585.3	551.6		
West Germany	516.3	643.2	762.2	817.0	683.6	658.1	658.0	621.9
Greece	27.0	32.5	39.7	41.5	38.1	39.4	35.3	33.8
Ireland	9.8	12.5	15.6	18.5	17.5	17.7	16.8	15.9
Italy	215.3	261.6	326.2	395.8	351.0	345.3	412.8	410.4
Luxembourg	3.4	4.3	5.0	5.6	4.5	4.1	4.0	4.0
Netherlands	112.0	136.8	157.0	169.0	141.1	137.8	133.8	124.7
Portugal	16.2	17.6	19.8	24.0	23.4	22.0	19.5	18.0
Spain	120.0	145.3	194.4	210.2	181.4	175.5	152.5	153.8
United Kingdom	254.8	324.4	420.1	535.0	517.1	484.9	465.7	439.7
EC total	1411.0	1739.3	2120.1	2401.1	2696.4	2576.3	2034.1	1952.1
EFTA members								
Austria	47.7	57.4	68.1	76.2	65.7	65.9	66.4	63.5
Finland	31.8	34.2	42.1	50.7	49.6	49.8	48.3	50.1
Iceland	2.0	2.2	2.3	3.1	3.3	3.0	2.5	2.6
Norway	29.3	32.6	37.9	47.4	55.2	54.2	53.3	53.8
Sweden	82.3	91.0	107.5	123.2	111.4	97.7	89.7	93.6
Switzerland	63.2	88.4	99.2	105.6	98.8	101.0	101.9	96.2
EFTA total	256.4	305.8	357.2	406.2	384.0	371.7	362.2	359.7
CMEA members								
Bulgaria	18.5	18.4	21.7	23.9	23.8	24.1	24.1	24.7
Czechoslovakia	72.5	75.0	85.7	40.0	40.0	39.6	39.3	44.1
East Germany	437.1	400.6	355.8	102.7	86.7	83.1	82.4	71.6
Hungary	11.6	13.6	15.6	17.9	18.5	19.0	17.3	20.1
Poland				45.0	42.1	56.0	64.6	63.2
Romania				28.4	34.8	35.8	32.4	28.2
USSR	560.4	613.1	665.1	699.5	664.8	706.6	721.4	685.0
CMEA total	1100.1	1120.8	1144.0	957.5	910.7	964.2	981.5	936.9
Others								
Albania								
Cyprus								
Gibraltar								
Liechtenstein								
Malta				1.2	1.2	1.2	1.1	2.2
Monaco								
Turkey	48.5	53.2	70.8	58.3	58.9	53.7	51.2	50.1
Yugoslavia				73.6	71.9	65.3	47.4	45.0
Total	48.5	53.2	70.8	133.2	132.0	120.2	99.8	97.3
European total	2816.0	3219.1	3692.0	3898.0	4123.2	4032.4	3477.6	3346.0

Source: Euromonitor

Title: Trends in Total Gross National Product 1977-1988

Unit: Current US dollars (billions)

	1985	1986	1987	1988	% growth 1977-88	% share 1977	% share 1988
EC members							
Belgium	80.7	113.4	141.4	152.4	69.1	3.6	2.2
Denmark	55.6	79.0	97.7	103.2	124.5	1.8	1.5
France			878.9	917.1			13.4
West Germany	626.4	895.7	1122.7	1208.3	134.0	20.7	17.7
Greece	33.2	38.7	45.7	52.1	93.0	1.1	0.8
Ireland	17.1	22.8	26.8	27.2	178.1	0.4	0.4
Italy	423.6	599.0	751.5	810.5	276.4	8.6	11.9
Luxembourg	4.2	5.8	7.3	7.6	126.2	0.1	0.1
Netherlands	126.2	174.7	212.8	227.2	102.7	4.5	3.3
Portugal	19.6	28.5	35.9	39.9	146.8	0.6	0.6
Spain	162.1	226.0	286.7	336.4	180.3	4.8	4.9
United Kingdom	464.1	566.2	691.6	833.8	227.2	10.2	12.2
EC total	2012.6	2749.8	4298.9	4715.8	234.2	56.6	69.0
EFTA members							
Austria	65.1	93.1	116.7	123.8	159.4	1.9	1.8
Finland	53.4	70.0	88.3	100.7	216.8	1.3	1.5
Iceland	2.7	3.7	5.2	5.7	184.4	0.1	0.1
Norway	57.1	68.3	82.2	87.3	197.9	1.2	1.3
Sweden	98.2	130.0	158.5	178.5	116.9	3.3	2.6
Switzerland	98.5	142.3	178.4	193.4	205.8	2.5	2.8
EFTA total	375.1	507.4	629.3	689.5	168.9	10.3	10.1
CMEA members							
Bulgaria	24.7	22.4	22.3	18.3	-0.9	0.7	0.3
Czechoslovakia	48.6	57.9	61.2	62.7	52.5	1.6	0.9
East Germany	89.2	119.0	149.4	139.6	13.5	4.9	2.0
Hungary	16.8	19.2	21.3	22.9	96.3	0.5	0.3
Poland	58.3	61.1	52.9	58.1			0.8
Romania	38.5	45.2	52.6	56.0	157.0	0.9	0.8
USSR	679.0	818.2	915.6	998.4	78.2	22.5	14.6
CMEA total	955.2	1143.0	1275.2	1355.8	74.6	31.1	19.8
Others							
Albania							
Cyprus		1.7	4.0	4.0			0.1
Gibraltar							
Liechtenstein							
Malta	2.1	2.5	2.9	3.0	393.2	0.0	0.0
Monaco							
Turkey	53.2	58.3	68.1	70.3	45.0	1.9	1.0
Yugoslavia	45.3	62.8	73.7				
Total	100.7	125.3	148.7	77.3	57.4	2.0	1.1
European total	3443.6	4525.5	6352.1	6838.4	174.3	100.0	100.0

Source: Euromonitor

Database name: Economic Indicators
Sector name: Money Supply   Table No: 0305

Title: Trends in Money Supply 1977-1989

Unit: National currencies (billions)

	1977	1980	1981	1982	1983	1984	1985	1986	1987	1988	1989	Total $ billion 1989	Note
EC members													
Belgium	741.0	806.1	823.5	855.8	929.8	932.5	962.4	1037.3	1086.0	1145.9	1150.1	29.2	
Denmark	58.9	83.2	93.0	105.2	114.2	153.8	195.8	215.0	235.4	250.5			
France	508.0	671.0	858.0	942.0	970.0	1309.0	1327.0	1407.0	1471.0	1532.0	1633.0	256.0	
West Germany	198.6	243.4	239.6	256.7	278.2	294.8	314.5	340.2	365.7	408.3	431.6	229.6	a
Greece	186.6	303.8	377.4	459.1	525.6	630.9	743.3	896.0	1000.0	1011.8			
Ireland	1.1	1.7	1.7	1.8	2.1	2.3	2.3	2.4	2.6	2.8	3.1	4.4	b
Italy	96.9	171.3	188.1	219.6	244.6	275.1	303.5	335.9	360.8	388.2	432.1	314.9	c
Luxembourg													
Netherlands	57.8	65.6	64.0	72.3	79.7	85.0	90.8	97.2	103.7	111.3	119.0	56.1	
Portugal	286.0	504.6	549.4	637.0	687.3	799.4	1017.6	1413.4	1581.8	1791.1			
Spain	2836.0	4098.0	4630.0	4850.0	5277.0	5746.0	6589.0	7580.0	8899.0	10573.0	12177.0	102.9	b,d
United Kingdom	23.5	31.0	36.5	40.7	42.5	48.1	56.7	69.3	153.5	169.9	194.3	318.6	d,e
EFTA members													
Austria	127.3	145.1	141.6	153.3	170.4	176.4	181.9	193.5	213.5	232.2	244.0	18.4	
Finland	9.9	15.0	17.2	19.9	21.4	24.9	27.7	27.8	30.3	35.9	40.1	9.3	
Iceland	0.3	1.0	1.6	2.1	3.7	7.7	15.2	22.6	34.5	44.2	55.9	1.0	j
Norway	37.0	45.6	52.4	58.8	65.9	82.0	98.7	101.8	152.6	187.1	313.5	45.4	
Sweden	49.6	79.4	85.7	80.0	86.8	95.7	102.8	112.2	115.4	116.9	119.2	18.5	d
Switzerland	56.4	68.3	64.8	69.4	75.8	75.9	73.9	75.5	85.9	87.8	85.4	52.2	f
CMEA members													
Bulgaria													
Czechoslovakia													
East Germany													
Hungary	117.1	160.7	177.6	196.8	203.1	212.9	243.0	289.1	306.1	311.5			g
Poland		910.3	1115.5	1590.0	1747.0	2001.0	2449.0	2989.0	3785.0	5748.0	7991.0	5.6	
Romania	84.2	114.5	135.4	167.0	156.3	162.3	174.5	179.7	172.2				h
USSR													
Others													
Albania													
Cyprus	0.1	0.2	0.2	0.2	0.2	0.3	0.3	0.3	0.3	0.4	0.4	0.8	
Gibraltar													
Liechtenstein													
Malta	0.2	0.3	0.3	0.3	0.3	0.3	0.3	0.3	0.4	0.4	0.4	1.1	
Monaco													
Turkey	210.3	719.8	969.3	1342.7	2090.0	2487.0	3468.0	5432.0	8960.0	11956.0	16258.0	7.7	
Yugoslavia	247.1	451.7	568.5	727.1	874.0	1251.9	1820.0	3829.8	7644.0	24070.0	********	1.7	

Source: International Monetary Fund/UN/OECD
Notes: a   New series starting 1985   e   New series starting 1981
            b   New series starting 1982   f   New series starting 1984
            c   '000 billion lire   g   New series starting 1978 and 1986
            d   New series starting 1983   h   New series starting 1980
                                                  i   New series starting 1988

Database name: Economic Indicators
Sector name: Inflation Rates — Table No 0306

Title: Annual Rates of Inflation 1979-1989

Unit: % growth

	1979	1980	1981	1982	1983	1984	1985	1986	1987	1988	1989	Notes
EC members												
Belgium	4.5	6.6	7.6	8.7	7.7	6.3	4.9	1.3	1.6	1.2	3.1	
Denmark	9.6	12.3	11.7	10.1	6.9	6.3	4.7	3.7	4.0	4.6	4.8	
France	10.8	13.3	13.4	11.8	9.6	7.4	5.8	2.5	3.3	2.7	3.5	
West Germany	4.1	5.4	6.3	5.3	3.3	2.4	2.2	-0.1	0.2	1.3	2.8	
Greece	19.0	24.9	24.5	21.0	20.2	18.4	19.3	23.0	16.4	13.5	13.7	
Ireland	13.2	18.2	20.4	17.1	10.5	8.6	5.4	3.8	3.1	2.2	4.1	
Italy	14.8	21.3	19.5	16.5	14.6	10.8	9.2	5.9	4.7	5.0	6.2	
Luxembourg	4.5	6.3	8.1	9.4	8.7	5.6	4.1	0.3	-0.1	1.5	3.4	
Netherlands	4.2	6.5	6.7	5.9	2.8	3.3	2.2	0.1	-0.7	0.7	1.1	
Portugal	23.6	16.6	20.0	22.7	25.1	28.9	19.6	11.7	9.4	9.6	12.6	
Spain	15.7	15.6	14.5	14.4	12.2	11.3	8.8	8.8	5.3	4.8	6.8	
United Kingdom	13.4	18.0	11.9	8.6	4.6	5.0	6.1	3.4	4.2	4.9	7.8	
EFTA members												
Austria	3.7	6.4	6.8	5.4	3.3	5.7	3.2	1.7	1.4	1.9	2.6	
Finland	7.5	11.6	12.0	9.6	8.4	7.1	5.9	2.9	4.1	5.1	6.6	
Iceland	45.5	58.5	50.6	49.1	86.1	30.8	32.0	21.9	17.7	25.8	20.8	
Norway	4.8	10.8	13.7	11.4	8.4	6.3	5.7	7.2	8.7	6.7	4.6	
Sweden	7.2	13.7	12.1	8.6	8.9	8.0	7.4	4.2	4.2	5.8	6.4	
Switzerland	3.6	4.0	6.5	5.7	3.0	2.9	3.4	0.8	1.4	1.9	3.2	
CMEA members												
Bulgaria	4.4	14.0	0.5	0.3	1.4	0.7	1.7	3.4	0.0	1.3	9.2	
Czechoslovakia	3.8	2.9	1.5	4.6	0.9	0.8	1.7	0.4	0.1	0.2	1.5	a
East Germany	0.3	0.4	0.2	0.0	0.0	0.2	-0.1	0.0	0.0	0.0	2.0	a
Hungary	8.9	9.1	4.6	6.9	7.3	8.3	7.0	5.3	8.7	15.8	17.0	b
Poland	7.1	9.4	21.2	100.8	22.1	15.4	14.6	17.7	25.2	60.0	244.5	
Romania	1.8	1.5	2.2	16.9	5.2	1.1	-0.4	-0.1	0.2			
USSR	1.0	1.1	1.3	3.3	0.6	-1.0	-2.0	1.9	1.9	2.3	2.3	
Others												
Albania												
Cyprus	9.5	13.5	10.6	6.4	5.0	6.0	5.0	1.2	2.8	3.4	3.8	
Gibraltar	16.3	11.9	8.3	9.3	5.1	6.7	6.0	3.6				
Liechtenstein	3.6	4.0	6.5	5.7	3.0	2.9	3.4	0.8	1.4			
Malta	7.1	15.8	11.5	5.8	-0.9	-0.4	-0.2	2.0	0.4	1.0	0.8	
Monaco												
Turkey	58.7	110.2	36.6	30.8	32.9	48.4	45.0	34.6	38.8	75.4	69.6	
Yugoslavia	21.2	30.9	39.8	31.5	40.2	54.7	72.3	89.8	120.8	194.1	1239.9	

Source: IMF/International Labour Office/UN/OECD/Euromonitor

Notes:
a Calculated from state retail price index
b Calculated from index of retail prices, service charges and fares

	1977	1980	1981	1982	1983	1984	1985	1986	1987	1988	1989	Total $ million 1989	Per capita $ 1989
EC members													
Belgium	489.0	613.9	667.1	706.7	757.0	792.0	849.0	878.0	894.0	898.0	892.6	22653	2282
Denmark	66.8	99.7	113.2	131.1	140.5	146.2	155.5	159.4	176.2	187.0	186.1	25458	4950
France	329.5	509.3	595.0	701.3	793.5	866.4	923.0	972.7	1017.0	1060.7	1086.2	170248	3033
West Germany	235.0	297.8	318.2	326.2	336.2	350.2	365.6	382.7	397.2	411.5	419.1	222926	3619
Greece	153.8	280.0	368.5	471.2	579.4	742.8	942.0	1067.2	1243.0	1533.1	1609.8	9911	984
Ireland	1.0	1.9	2.3	2.6	2.8	3.0	3.2	3.4	3.6	3.6	3.5	4967	1407
Italy	30.0	57.0	74.2	87.4	103.2	120.0	135.5	147.7	167.9	187.9	192.4	140223	2428
Luxembourg	16.3	22.2	24.7	26.1	27.6	29.8	32.3	35.5	37.3	38.2	38.8	985	2647
Netherlands	47.9	60.3	62.8	65.1	66.6	66.4	67.7	68.6	70.5	70.9	71.8	33857	2286
Portugal	87.8	182.6	225.9	276.2	348.4	405.5	501.9	598.6	685.0	766.1	786.8	4997	484
Spain	921.0	1929.3	2242.2	2619.5	3090.9	3448.3	3906.6	4470.0	5442.0	5671.0	5982.9	50540	1291
United Kingdom	29.5	49.0	55.5	60.5	65.9	69.9	74.0	79.7	85.5	91.9	91.6	150213	2624
EFTA members													
Austria	138.7	178.7	195.2	214.3	226.9	237.8	255.0	272.5	282.6	284.6	287.4	21722	2860
Finland	24.0	34.9	40.8	46.7	53.3	59.7	68.2	74.0	81.2	83.2	86.0	20041	4038
Iceland	0.4	2.5	4.0	6.6	11.6	14.1	20.1	27.3	36.8	47.5	55.2	968	3855
Norway	38.6	53.5	62.6	70.4	78.2	84.1	92.7	101.6	116.1	122.3	130.4	18886	4456
Sweden	102.8	151.4	167.4	182.7	203.5	221.1	239.2	257.9	272.1	289.1	292.6	45386	5363
Switzerland	19.2	21.7	23.5	25.6	27.4	28.5	30.9	32.3	33.0	35.0	37.1	22679	3437
CMEA members													
Bulgaria													
Czechoslovakia													
East Germany													
Hungary	57.8	74.1	79.1	84.2	90.9	95.3	104.6	116.0	126.3	160.0			
Poland		230.8	260.3	454.5	609.7	801.2	1022.9	1178.1	1516.0	2429.0			
Romania	35.5	42.7	42.7	44.9	49.5	53.4	54.0	56.0					
USSR													
Others													
Albania													
Cyprus	0.1	0.1	0.1	0.2	0.2	0.2	0.2	0.2	0.2	0.3			
Gibraltar													
Liechtenstein													
Malta		0.1	0.1	0.1	0.1	0.1	0.1	0.1	0.1	0.1			
Monaco													
Turkey	116.0	544.1	700.1	939.4	1175.5	1621.4	2368.4	3552.6	5254.3	5364.6			
Yugoslavia	72.6	291.0	380.9	499.6	643.0	931.6	1666.0	3348.0	7517.8	22520.0			

Source: International Monetary Fund
Notes: Italy: 000 billion lire

Database name: Economic Indicators
Sector name: Private Consumption Table No: 0308

Title: Trends in Private Consumption 1977-1989

Unit: National currencies (billions)

	1977	1980	1981	1982	1983	1984	1985	1986	1987	1988	1989	Total $ million 1989	$ Per capita 1989
EC members													
Belgium	1724.5	2171.9	2328.1	2545.2	2763.0	2961.0	3199.0	3300.0	3447.0	3588.0	3710.0	94153	9485
Denmark	158.9	208.8	228.6	255.6	280.0	307.9	337.2	366.8	377.7	386.2	384.3	52572	10222
France	1117.1	1653.3	1907.2	2200.8	2424.1	2639.2	2858.4	3042.8	3223.2	3401.2	3486.2	546418	9735
West Germany	683.2	840.8	887.9	918.1	964.2	1003.6	1038.3	1068.6	1112.8	1156.8	1213.7	645585	10480
Greece	634.9	1104.6	1383.1	1734.2	2053.6	2461.4	3025.5	3689.0	4290.3	5104.5	5257.6	32370	3213
Ireland	3.7	6.2	7.5	8.0	8.8	9.7	10.4	11.1	11.5	12.4	13.0	18448	5227
Italy	135.6	239.3	286.5	335.4	396.5	453.5	510.0	559.2	611.4	665.3	687.9	501348	8682
Luxembourg	61.1	78.1	86.3	95.8	104.2	112.6	120.5	126.6	132.1	136.4	141.2	3583	9633
Netherlands	164.3	205.8	213.2	221.8	229.9	236.8	247.7	256.2	263.2	268.3	277.7	130947	8841
Portugal	450.4	845.5	1045.4	1287.1	1577.9	1979.0	2388.6	2900.8	3414.0	3871.9	4019.0	25524	2473
Spain	6067.3	10080.4	11457.9	13143.3	14808.1	16370.0	18137.7	20435.7	22713.6	24948.0	26320.1	222336	5678
United Kingdom	86.3	137.2	152.7	167.5	185.9	198.9	217.0	239.2	2661.7	293.6	304.5	499344	8723
EFTA members													
Austria	456.9	552.5	596.5	640.2	694.8	733.0	774.9	801.8	830.3	874.8	927.0	70062	9226
Finland	72.5	104.0	118.0	134.2	149.6	165.7	181.7	195.2	213.6	224.3	233.3	54367	10954
Iceland	2.3	8.8	14.4	23.1	39.4	53.9	74.7	96.9	131.7	158.2	176.3	3091	12314
Norway	103.9	135.2	155.2	175.3	193.0	210.9	245.4	278.9	298.1	308.6	316.7	45869	10823
Sweden	198.9	271.8	301.0	336.6	371.9	407.3	447.9	492.8	541.5	590.9	598.0	92758	10960
Switzerland	92.9	108.3	116.0	122.4	127.3	133.6	140.6	144.9	150.2	157.0	165.6	101229	15342
CMEA members													
Bulgaria													
Czechoslovakia													
East Germany													
Hungary	334.0	441.2	477.7	515.1	551.2	600.5	649.3	695.5	778.5	860.7			
Poland		1679.5	2041.0	3476.7	4489.6	5427.6	6397.0	7916.8	10157.0	16916.0			
Romania	269.5	354.2	381.3	442.5	439.8	456.1	490.7	509.8					
USSR													
Others													
Albania													
Cyprus	0.3	0.5	0.6	0.7	0.7	0.8	0.9	1.0	1.1	1.2			
Gibraltar													
Liechtenstein													
Malta	0.2	0.3	0.3	0.3	0.3	0.3	0.3	0.3	0.4	0.4			
Monaco													
Turkey	573.3	2991.9	4513.9	6159.7	8527.0	13646.2	20150.3	27110.5	38690.3				
Yugoslavia	429.0	881.1	1226.4	1623.8	2242.9	3389.2	5951.0	11782.0	26440.9	79251.7			

Source: International Monetary Fund
Notes: Italy: 000 billion lire

Database name: Economic Indicators
Sector name: Government Finance

Table No: 0309

Title: Government Finance and International Liquidity: Latest Year

Unit: National currencies (billions)

	Year	Budget Revenue	Budget Expend-iture	Budget Surplus/ Deficit	Foreign Debt	1989 Gold Reserves (mn Troy Ounces)	1989 Foreign Exchange Reserves ($mn)	Notes
EC members								
Belgium	1987	2369.2	2757.8	-435.7	999.9	30.2	9760	
Denmark	1988	298.9	285.8	-	124.3	2.0	5782	
France	1988	2339.7	2431.6	-127.9	36.7	81.9	21868	a
West Germany	1988	604.2	634.3	-32.5	149.4	95.2	55862	f
Greece	1988	1936.0	3037.1	-1045.1		3.4	3106	
Ireland	1989	8.1	8.6	-0.5		0.4	3702	
Italy	1989	352.5	470.2	-133.7		66.7	44278	b
Luxembourg	1987	113.9	106.5	+8.1	3.3	0.4		
Netherlands	1988	229.4	250.1	-19.3		43.9	15027	
Portugal	1987	1805.7	2282.0	-554.2	72.5	16.1	9826	
Spain	1987	9847.5	10806.7	-1608.4	865.9	15.7	39558	
United Kingdom	1987	152.5	157.3	-3.2	18.5	19.0	31990	g
EFTA members								
Austria	1988	553.4	624.7	-79.1	130.8	21.2	7939	
Finland	1988	134.8	130.4	+1.2	26.3	2.0	4637	a
Iceland	1985	31.2	33.6	-4.7	25.6	0.1	332	
Norway	1988	267.7	251.2	-	11.1	1.2	12751	f
Sweden	1988	467.5	445.1	+23.8	110.1	6.1	8885	
Switzerland	1988	28.1	24.4	2.1	27.7	83.3	25070	c,d
CMEA members								
Bulgaria								
Czechoslovakia								
East Germany	1986	247.0	246.4	0.6				
Hungary	1987	652.0	702.1	-42.8	31.7	1.6	1867	d
Poland	1988	10966.1	11457.8	-673.0	67.3	0.5	2314	
Romania	1985	279.2	258.3	20.9		3.3	582	e
USSR								
Others								
Albania								
Cyprus	1988	0.5	0.6	0.1	0.5	0.5	1100	
Gibraltar	1986	177.9	192.3	-19.5	35.4	0.5	1260	
Liechtenstein								
Malta	1987	0.2	0.2			0.2	1254	
Monaco								
Turkey	1988	17587.3	21423.7	-3858.7	12751.1	3.8	4738	f
Yugoslavia	1987	3592.7	3576.1	+16.5		1.9	4136	

Source: International Monetary Fund/OECD
Notes:
a Foreign debt refers to foreign currency debt
b '000 billion lire
c Foreign debt refers to total debt
d Gold reserves and foreign exchange reserves in 1988
e Gold reserves and foreign exchange reserves in 1986
f Foreign debt in 1987
g Foreign debt in 1986

Database name: Economic Indicators
Sector name: Government Expenditure

Table No: 0310

Title: Government Expenditure by Object: Latest Year

Unit: National currencies (billions)

		A	B	C	D	E	F	G	H	I	Total
EC members											
Belgium	1987	91.5	134.1	336.8	51.0	1124.6	68.4	25.6	250.6	675.2	2757.8
Denmark	1986	18.8	13.1	23.0	3.4	101.6	3.3	4.3	18.3	69.3	255.1
France	1986	125.7	131.5	164.4	437.5	787.0	22.6			432.1	2100.8
West Germany	1986	23.3	52.1	3.6	106.5	286.6	2.3	0.6	41.4	68.3	584.7
Greece	1981	96.2	88.6	79.0	86.7	251.9	20.5	16.1	140.7	80.3	822.3
Ireland	1987	0.8	0.3	1.2	1.3	2.7	0.5	0.0	1.6	2.1	10.5
Italy	1988	37.9	18.4	41.9	57.2	191.9	2.9	4.9	58.0	136.8	549.9
Luxembourg	1987	10.3	2.0	9.6	2.3	51.4	1.7	1.5	17.7	9.5	106.5
Netherlands	1988	14.5	12.7	29.6	27.2	87.7	11.4	2.5	23.6	40.9	250.1
Portugal	1987	139.1	122.9	217.6	177.7	548.1	37.3	18.8	213.7	806.8	2282.0
Spain	1985	368.8	84.6	529.3	1212.0	3760.3	100.3	67.6	1125.0	1742.4	9564.7
United Kingdom	1987	5.2	19.8	3.5	21.3	45.7	2.9	0.7	10.8	47.4	157.3
EFTA members											
Austria	1988	30.7	16.5	58.1	79.9	279.7	17.2	4.1	70.6	67.9	624.7
Finland	1987	9.3	6.4	16.8	12.9	41.8	2.1	1.9	24.3	5.8	121.3
Iceland	1985	3.3		4.0	7.7	5.4	1.3	0.5	7.9	3.4	33.6
Norway	1987	10.9	19.1	18.9	24.7	80.6	2.5	2.8	44.8	25.7	230.0
Sweden	1988	18.9	30.5	40.8	5.0	224.6	16.5	3.1	35.5	70.2	445.1
Switzerland	1984	2.2	4.6	1.4	5.9	22.4	0.3	0.1	5.5	2.7	44.9
CMEA members											
Bulgaria											
Czechoslovakia											
East Germany	1986			12.8	13.0	34.1				186.5	246.4
Hungary	1988	140.0	38.0	16.8	13.8	217.4	9.8	14.2	275.7	66.3	792.0
Poland											
Romania	1985	1.9	12.1	4.6	2.0	56.6		0.6	143.3	37.2	258.3
USSR											
Others											
Albania											
Cyprus	1988	48.7	20.4	63.8	40.1	116.6	23.5	9.6	108.4	125.2	588.7
Gibraltar											
Liechtenstein											
Malta	1987	22.0	7.3	19.8	20.7	78.6	21.9	2.2	42.7	8.8	223.7
Monaco											
Turkey	1988	10550.8	2236.4	2728.2	509.0	265.4	389.8	2.1	4742.0		21423.7
Yugoslavia	1987	198.9	1970.8			401.1		7.4	584.8	413.1	3576.1

Source: IMF/United Nations/National Statistical Offices
Notes: Italy: 000 billion lire. Luxembourg, Cyprus and Malta: millions

A General public services
B Defence
C Education
D Health
E Social security and welfare
F Housing and community amenities
G Other community/social services
H Economic services
I Other purposes

Database name: Economic Indicators
Sector name: Gross Domestic Product

Table No: 0311

Title: Origin of Gross Domestic Product: Latest Available Year

Unit: National currencies (billions)

	Year	A	B	C	D	E	F	G	H	Total, inc Others	Notes
EC members											
Belgium	1987	110.6	20.4	1175.1	167.2	279.8	1136.6	414.9	2018.4	5323.0	a,g
Denmark	1987	28.3	5.1	115.0	6.9	40.4	86.8	48.1	362.4	693.0	
France	1987	185.0	33.3	1152.2	123.3	287.1	791.7	315.9	2400.1	5288.7	g
West Germany	1987	29.7		646.6		103.4		113.4	569.6	2009.1	
Greece	1987	875.0	100.4	971.0	167.9	341.1		444.3	2639.4	5539.1	h
Ireland	1986	1.6				1.0	2.3	1.0	12.6	18.5	
Italy	1987	40.3		227.4	49.5	54.3	184.9	58.6	364.7	979.7	b,d
Luxembourg	1986	5.9	0.2	62.9	4.8	12.9	35.4	12.5	86.0	220.5	g
Netherlands	1987	17.1	15.4	80.5	8.7	24.3	59.3	28.2	198.2	431.8	
Portugal	1986	328.7		1290.1	136.4	245.7	948.5	297.1	1173.9	4420.4	b
Spain	1986	1814.5		9301.6	1020.1	2226.6	6600.1	1781.6	9203.0	31947.5	b
United Kingdom	1986	5.9	12.8	81.3	9.4	20.1	45.8	23.7	174.7	373.7	g
EFTA members											
Austria	1987	48.6	6.4	390.4	49.2	99.6	230.9	86.3	570.1	1481.6	
Finland	1987	22.7	1.0	84.1	10.2	27.4	40.5	28.1	179.5	393.5	
Iceland	1986	15.8		25.5	6.2	10.2	14.4	9.7	77.2	158.9	
Norway	1987	19.3	51.7	83.0	22.7	36.0	68.4	45.7	230.1	556.9	
Sweden	1987	28.7	3.5	208.6	28.7	62.3	114.7	60.4	498.1	1005.2	
Switzerland	1985	8.2		58.6	5.0	17.3	44.1	14.8	80.0	228.0	
CMEA members											
Bulgaria	1986	4.1		16.7		2.6	1.2	1.8	0.6	26.9	b,c,e
Czechoslovakia	1987	43.2		350.0		62.4	96.1	20.4	2.5	574.7	b,c,e
East Germany	1987	31.3		164.6		20.0	22.6	14.0	9.6	262.1	b,c,e
Hungary	1987	112.5		401.8		105.2	114.6	74.9	15.8	999.6	b,c,e
Poland	1987	1849.2		6804.0		1801.0	2384.7	851.2	323.1	14013.2	b,c,e
Romania	1986									730.0	e
USSR	1987	122.6		268.6		74.7	97.1	36.6		599.6	b,c,e
Others											
Albania											
Cyprus	1988	0.1		0.3		0.2	0.4	0.2	0.8	2.0	
Gibraltar											
Liechtenstein											
Malta	1986			0.1			0.1		0.2	0.5	a,f
Monaco											
Turkey	1987	9743.4	1105.0	15171.9	2476.9	2373.6	10085.4	5580.6	11759.6	58296.4	a
Yugoslavia	1988	16435.9	3928.8	58951.1	3257.7	9110.7	11188.7	16276.2	27301.3	146450.4	

Source: OECD/United Nations/National Statistical Offices

Notes:
A Agriculture/forestry/fishing
B Mining & quarrying
C Manufacturing
D Electricity, gas and water
E Construction
F Wholesale and retail trade, restaurants and hotels
G Transport, storage and communications
H Others

a Restaurants and hotels included in
b C includes B
c C includes D
d '000 billion lire
e Data refer to net material product
f C includes E
g GDP total given by government diff
   significantly from external estimate
h H includes F

Database name: Economic Indicators
Sector name: Gross Domestic Product   Table No: 0312

Title: Origin of Gross Domestic Product : Latest Available Year

Unit: %

	Year	A	B	C	D	E	F	G	H	Total, inc Others	Notes
EC members											
Belgium	1987	2.1	0.4	22.1	3.1	5.3	21.4	7.8	37.9	100.0	a,g
Denmark	1987	4.1	0.7	16.6	1.0	5.8	12.5	6.9	52.3	100.0	
France	1987	3.5	0.6	21.8	2.3	5.4	15.0	6.0	45.4	100.0	
West Germany	1987	1.5		32.2		5.1		5.6	28.4	100.0	g
Greece	1987	15.8	1.8	17.5	3.0	6.2		8.0	47.7	100.0	
Ireland	1986	8.6	0.0			5.4	12.4	5.4	68.1	100.0	h
Italy	1987	4.1	0.0	23.2	5.1	5.5	18.9	6.0	37.2	100.0	b,d
Luxembourg	1986	2.7	0.1	28.5	2.2	5.9	16.1	5.7	39.0	100.0	
Netherlands	1987	4.0	3.6	18.6	2.0	5.6	13.7	6.5	45.9	100.0	g
Portugal	1986	7.4		29.2	3.1	5.6	21.5	6.7	26.6	100.0	
Spain	1986	5.7		29.1	3.2	7.0	20.7	5.6	28.8	100.0	b
United Kingdom	1986	1.6	3.4	21.8	2.5	5.4	12.2	6.4	46.7	100.0	b,g
EFTA members											
Austria	1987	3.3	0.4	26.3	3.3	6.7	15.6	5.8	38.5	100.0	
Finland	1987	5.8	0.3	21.4	2.6	7.0	10.3	7.1	45.6	100.0	
Iceland	1986	9.9		16.0	3.9	6.4	9.1	6.1	48.6	100.0	g
Norway	1987	3.5	9.3	14.9	4.1	6.5	12.3	8.2	41.3	100.0	
Sweden	1987	2.9	0.3	20.8	2.9	6.2	11.4	6.0	49.6	100.0	
Switzerland	1985	3.6		25.7	2.2	7.6	19.3	6.5	35.1	100.0	
CMEA members											
Bulgaria	1986	15.2		62.1		9.7	4.5	6.7	2.2	100.0	b,c,e
Czechoslovakia	1987	7.5		60.9		10.9	16.7	3.5	0.4	100.0	b,c,e
East Germany	1987	11.9		62.8		7.6	8.6	5.3	3.7	100.0	b,c,e
Hungary	1987	11.3		40.2		10.5	11.5	7.5	1.6	100.0	b,c,e
Poland	1987	13.2		48.6		12.9	17.0	6.1	2.3	100.0	b,c,e
Romania	1986									100.0	e
USSR	1987	20.4		44.8		12.5	16.2	6.1		100.0	b,c,e,
Others											
Albania											
Cyprus	1988	5.9		15.0		8.0	20.0	7.8	40.0	100.0	
Gibraltar											
Liechtenstein											
Malta	1986			25.4			11.7		39.1	100.0	a,f
Monaco											
Turkey	1987	16.7	1.9	26.0	4.2	4.1	17.3	9.6	20.2	100.0	a
Yugoslavia	1988	11.2	2.7	40.3	2.2	6.2	7.6	11.1	18.6	100.0	

Source: United Nations/National Statistical Offices
Notes: A   Agriculture/forestry/fishing
        B   Mining & quarrying
        C   Manufacturing
        D   Electricity, gas and water
        E   Construction
        F   Wholesale and retail trade, restaurants and hotels
        G   Transport, storage and communications
        H   Others

Title: Usage of Gross Domestic Product 1988

Unit: National currencies (billions)

	A	B	C	D	E	F	Total,incl. Others	Notes
EC members								
Belgium	843.8	3481.8	25.5	980.1	3990.9	3805.3	5516.7	
Denmark	188.1	388.7	-4.8	130.2	233.9	212.5	723.6	
France	1049.9	3416.7	45.7	1137.8	1217.0	1208.5	5658.6	
West Germany	411.5	1156.8	13.7	419.1	620.7	511.2	2110.6	
Greece	1533.1	5104.5	77.0	1292.6	1800.9	2263.9	7446.2	
Ireland	3.6	12.4	-0.2	3.6	13.5	11.6	21.3	
Italy	185.2	660.1	15.7	214.6	211.1	207.9	1078.9	a
Luxembourg	41.1	137.9	0.6	58.5	248.3	245.1	241.3	
Netherlands	70.9	268.3	-2.9	96.7	246.1	227.8	451.2	
Portugal	962.8	3909.2	169.8	1611.3	2129.5	2779.9	6002.8	
Spain	5670.8	24948.1	537.8	8903.0	7740.9	8182.6	39618.0	
United Kingdom	91.9	291.9	4.4	88.8	109.1	125.5	462.6	
EFTA members								
Austria	289.1	874.8	33.0	369.1	586.8	582.1	1570.6	
Finland	88.9	235.3	2.9	109.2	109.0	110.2	440.0	
Iceland	47.6	158.2	2.7	46.9	84.1	85.3	254.3	
Norway	122.6	308.8	-3.7	170.9	213.1	217.5	594.2	
Sweden	289.1	590.9	-2.0	219.1	361.9	345.0	1114.0	
Switzerland	34.2	157.9	4.4	71.5	97.6	96.8	268.8	
CMEA members								
Bulgaria								
Czechoslovakia								
East Germany								
Hungary	160.0	860.7	53.9	298.0	530.4	491.7	1411.3	
Poland	2429.0	16916.0	2994.0	6663.0	6745.0	5934.0	29629.0	
Romania	56.0	509.8	24.2	249.3	32.5		917.5	b
USSR								
Others								
Albania								
Cyprus	272.3	1209.9	42.0	463.2	960.4	1014.1	1976.5	c
Gibraltar								
Liechtenstein								
Malta	105.2	392.1	14.2	169.9			591.8	c
Monaco								
Turkey	8.7	65.0	0.0	24.2	24.1	21.5	100.4	a
Yugoslavia	22520.0	79251.7	31536.9	27192.8	46644.0	48061.0	148560.0	d

Source: United Nations/National Statistical Offices
A Government final consumption expenditure
B Private final consumption expenditure
C Increase in stocks
D Gross fixed capital formation
E Exports of goods and services
F Imports of goods and services

a '000 billion
b Usage of Gross National Product i
c Millions
d 1986 latest data available

Database name: Economic Indicators
Sector name: Gross Domestic Product

Table No: 0314

Title: Usage of Gross Domestic Product 1988

Unit: Proportion of total expenditure

	A	B	C	D	E	F	Total,incl. Others	Notes
EC members								
Belgium	15.3	63.1	0.5	17.8	72.3	69.0	100.0	
Denmark	26.0	53.7	-0.7	18.0	32.3	29.4	100.0	
France	18.6	60.4	0.8	20.1	21.5	21.4	100.0	
West Germany	19.5	54.8	0.6	19.9	29.4	24.2	100.0	
Greece	20.6	68.6	1.0	17.4	24.2	30.4	100.0	
Ireland	16.9	58.2	-0.9	16.9	63.4	54.5	100.0	
Italy	17.2	61.2	1.5	19.9	19.6	19.3	100.0	a
Luxembourg	17.0	57.1	0.2	24.2	102.9	101.6	100.0	
Netherlands	15.7	59.5	-0.6	21.4	54.5	50.5	100.0	
Portugal	16.0	65.1	2.8	26.8	35.5	46.3	100.0	
Spain	14.3	63.0	1.4	22.5	19.5	20.7	100.0	
United Kingdom	19.9	63.1	1.0	19.2	23.6	27.1	100.0	
EFTA members								
Austria	18.4	55.7	2.1	23.5	37.4	37.1	100.0	
Finland	20.2	53.5	0.7	24.8	24.8	25.0	100.0	
Iceland	18.7	62.2	1.1	18.4	33.1	33.5	100.0	
Norway	20.6	52.0	-0.6	28.8	35.9	36.6	100.0	
Sweden	26.0	53.0	-0.2	19.7	32.5	31.0	100.0	
Switzerland	12.7	58.7	1.6	26.6	36.3	36.0	100.0	
CMEA members								
Bulgaria								
Czechoslovakia								
East Germany								
Hungary	11.3	61.0	3.8	21.1	37.6	34.8	100.0	
Poland	8.2	57.1	10.1	22.5	22.8	20.0	100.0	
Romania	6.1	55.6	2.6	27.2	3.5		100.0	b
USSR								
Others								
Albania								
Cyprus	13.8	61.2	2.1	23.4	48.6	51.3	100.0	c
Gibraltar								
Liechtenstein								
Malta	17.8	66.3	2.4	28.7			100.0	c
Monaco								
Turkey	8.7	64.7		24.1	24.0	21.4	100.0	a
Yugoslavia	15.2	53.3	21.2	18.3	31.4	32.4	100.0	d

Source: United Nations/National Statistical Offices
A Government final consumption expenditure
B Private final consumption expenditure
C Increase in stocks
D Gross fixed capital formation
E Exports of goods and services

F Imports of goods and services
a '000 billion
b Usage of Gross National Product in 1986
c Millions
d 1986 latest data available

Database name: Economic Indicators
Sector name: Exchange Rates

Table No: 0315

Title: Exchange Rates Against US Dollar 1977-1990

Unit: National currency units per US dollar

	1977	1978	1979	1980	1981	1982	1983	1984
EC members								
Belgium	35.8	31.5	29.3	29.2	37.1	45.7	51.1	57.8
Denmark	6.0	5.5	5.3	5.6	7.1	8.3	9.1	10.4
France	4.9	4.5	4.3	4.2	5.4	6.6	7.6	8.7
West Germany	2.3	2.0	1.8	1.8	2.3	2.4	2.6	2.8
Greece	36.8	36.8	37.0	42.6	55.4	66.8	88.1	112.7
Ireland	0.6	0.5	0.5	0.5	0.6	0.7	0.8	0.9
Italy	882.4	848.7	830.9	856.4	1136.8	1352.5	1518.8	1757.0
Luxembourg	35.8	31.5	29.3	29.2	37.1	45.7	51.1	57.8
Netherlands	2.5	2.2	2.0	2.0	2.5	2.7	2.9	3.2
Portugal	38.3	43.9	48.9	50.1	61.6	79.5	110.8	146.4
Spain	76.0	76.7	67.1	71.7	92.3	109.9	143.4	160.8
United Kingdom	0.6	0.5	0.5	0.4	0.5	0.6	0.7	0.7
EFTA members								
Austria	16.5	14.5	13.4	12.9	15.9	17.1	18.0	20.0
Finland	4.0	4.1	3.9	3.7	4.3	4.8	5.6	6.0
Iceland	2.0	2.7	3.5	4.8	7.2	12.4	24.8	31.7
Norway	5.3	5.2	5.1	4.9	5.7	6.5	7.3	8.2
Sweden	4.5	4.5	4.3	4.2	5.1	6.3	7.7	8.3
Switzerland	2.4	1.8	1.7	1.7	2.0	2.0	2.1	2.3
CMEA members								
Bulgaria	0.9	0.9	0.9	0.9	0.9	1.0	1.0	1.0
Czechoslovakia						12.4	12.8	12.1
East Germany	1.3	1.5	1.8	1.8	2.3	2.4	2.6	3.1
Hungary	41.0	37.9	35.6	32.5	34.3	36.6	42.7	40.0
Poland	43.2	41.2	40.2	44.3	51.3	84.8	91.7	113.7
Romania	20.0	18.4	18.0	18.0	15.0	15.0	17.2	21.3
USSR	0.7	0.7	0.7	0.6	0.7	0.7	0.7	0.8
Others								
Albania	0.1	6.7	6.3	6.2	6.1	5.9	6.6	7.3
Cyprus	2.5	2.7	2.8	2.8	2.4	2.1	1.9	0.6
Gibraltar	0.6	0.5	0.5	0.4	0.5	0.6	0.7	0.7
Liechtenstein	2.4	1.8	1.7	1.7	2.0	2.0	2.1	2.3
Malta	0.4	0.4	0.4	0.3	0.4	0.4	0.4	0.5
Monaco	4.9	4.5	4.3	4.2	5.4	6.6	7.6	8.7
Turkey	18.0	24.3	31.1	76.0	111.2	162.6	225.5	366.7
Yugoslavia	18.3	18.6	19.0	24.6	35.0	50.3	92.8	152.8

Source: International Monetary Fund/National Statistical Offices

Database name: Economic Indicators
Sector name: Exchange Rates

Table No: 0315

Title: Exchange Rates Against US Dollar 1977-1990

Unit: National currency units per US dollar

	1985	1986	1987	1988	1989	Mid-1990	Unit of currency	Notes
EC members								
Belgium	59.4	44.7	37.3	36.8	39.4	34.3	Belgian Franc	
Denmark	10.6	8.1	6.8	6.7	7.3	6.4	Danish Kroner	
France	9.0	6.9	6.0	6.0	6.4	5.6	Franc	
West Germany	2.9	2.2	1.8	1.8	1.9	1.7	Deutsche Mark	
Greece	138.1	140.0	135.4	141.9	162.4	163.0	Drachma	
Ireland	0.9	0.7	0.7	0.7	0.7	0.8	Pound	
Italy	1907.4	1490.8	1296.1	1301.6	1372.1	1222.0	Lira	
Luxembourg	59.4	44.7	37.3	36.8	39.4	34.3	Luxembourg Franc	
Netherlands	3.3	2.5	2.0	2.0	2.1	1.9	Guilder	
Portugal	170.4	149.6	140.9	144.0	157.5	146.5	Escudo	
Spain	170.0	140.1	123.5	116.5	118.4	102.4	Peseta	
United Kingdom	0.8	0.7	0.6	0.6	0.6	0.6	Pound	
EFTA members								
Austria	20.7	15.3	12.6	12.3	13.2	11.7	Schilling	
Finland	6.2	5.1	4.4	4.2	4.3	6.8	Markka	
Iceland	41.5	41.1	38.7	43.0	57.0		Icelandic Krona	
Norway	8.6	7.4	6.7	6.5	6.9	6.4	Norwegian Krone	
Sweden	8.6	7.1	6.3	6.1	6.4	6.0	Swedish Kronor	
Switzerland	2.5	1.8	1.5	1.5	1.6	1.4	Swiss Franc	
CMEA members								
Bulgaria	1.0	1.2	1.3	1.7	2.1		Leva	
Czechoslovakia	11.3	9.7	9.4	9.4	10.0		Koruny	
East Germany	2.6	2.0	1.7	1.9	1.9		DDR Mark	
Hungary	50.1	45.8	47.0	52.5	59.1		Forint	
Poland	147.2	175.2	265.1	430.5	1439.2		Zloty	
Romania	17.1	16.2	14.6	14.3	14.9		Lei	
USSR	0.8	0.7	0.6	0.6	0.6		Rouble	
Others								
Albania	7.7	6.7	6.2	6.0	6.4		Lek	a
Cyprus	0.5	0.5	0.4	0.5	0.5		Cyprus Pound	
Gibraltar	0.8	0.7	0.6	0.6	0.6		Gibraltar Pound	
Liechtenstein	2.5	1.8	1.5	1.4			Swiss Franc	
Malta	0.5	0.4	0.3	0.3	0.3		Maltese Lira	
Monaco	9.0	6.9	6.0	6.0	6.4		French Franc	
Turkey	522.0	674.5	857.2	1422.3	2121.7		Turkish Lira	
Yugoslavia	270.2	379.2	737.0	5210.8	77619.0		Dinar	a

Source: International Monetary Fund/UN/National Statistics
Notes: Annual average market exchange rates
a   Mid-year exchange data

04
FINANCE AND BANKING

Database name: Finance and Banking
Sector name: Interest Rates
Title: Lending Rates 1980-1989
Unit: % per annum

Table No: 0401

	1980	1981	1982	1983	1984	1985	1986	1987	1988	1989	Notes
EC members											
Belgium	17.00	18.00	15.50	13.75	14.00	12.54	10.44	9.33	8.92	11.08	
Denmark	17.20	17.70	18.55	14.49	13.38	14.65	12.98	13.62	12.59	13.44	
France	18.73	20.77	20.33	18.95	18.85	17.77	16.38	15.82	15.65	16.01	
West Germany	12.04	14.69	13.50	10.05	9.82	9.53	8.75	8.36	8.33	9.94	
Greece	21.30	21.30	20.50	20.50	20.50	20.50	20.50	21.81	22.89	23.26	
Ireland	15.96	15.50	17.04	14.13	12.92	12.44	12.23	11.15	8.29	9.42	
Italy	19.03	18.36	17.37	22.27	20.38	13.36	15.93	13.58	13.57	14.21	
Luxembourg	9.25	9.63	10.00	9.38	9.25	8.75	7.75	7.19	6.71	7.25	
Netherlands	13.50	14.25	11.17	8.46	8.88	9.25	8.63	8.15	7.77	10.75	
Portugal	18.50	19.40	22.75	24.10	27.05	25.59					
Spain	16.85	15.26	14.98	15.00	16.58	13.52	12.19	16.36	12.43	15.84	
United Kingdom	16.17	13.25	11.79	9.79	9.65	12.29	10.83	9.63	10.29	13.92	
EFTA members											
Austria											
Finland	9.77	8.84	9.32	9.56	10.49	10.41	9.08	8.91	9.72	10.35	a
Iceland	45.00	40.00	46.00	42.80	22.80	32.60	18.80	26.60	30.30	28.00	
Norway	12.63	13.90	14.33	14.35	13.69	13.46	13.62	14.03	14.28	14.38	a
Sweden	15.12	17.50	16.09	15.07	15.53	16.72	14.18	12.99	13.32	14.36	a
Switzerland		5.56	5.98	5.49	5.49	5.43	5.46	5.24	5.07	5.85	
CMEA members											
Bulgaria											
Czechoslovakia											
East Germany											
Hungary	9.00	11.00	14.00	13.00	13.00	12.00	11.00	11.50	13.00	14.00	a
Poland	8.00	9.00	9.00	9.00	9.00	12.00	12.00	12.00	6.70	74.00	a
Romania											
USSR											
Others											
Albania											
Cyprus	9.00	9.00	9.00	9.00	9.00	9.00	9.00	9.00	9.00	9.00	a
Gibraltar											
Liechtenstein											
Malta	8.00	8.00	8.00	8.00	8.00	8.00	8.00	8.00	8.50	8.50	
Monaco											
Turkey	25.67	35.58	36.00	35.50	52.33	53.50	52.63	50.00			
Yugoslavia	11.50	12.00	21.00	38.00	44.50	71.50	82.00	111.25	455.17	4353.75	

Source: International Monetary Fund
Notes: a 1989 estimated

Database name: Finance and Banking
Sector name: Bank Reserves

Table No: 0402

Title: Reserves of Deposit Banks 1980-1989

Unit: National currencies (billions)

	1980	1981	1982	1983	1984	1985	1986	1987	1988	1989	Notes
EC members											
Belgium	19.5	17.1	17.0	16.9	21.7	20.0	22.9	21.6	20.9	19.9	a
Denmark	1.1	1.7	1.6	1.3	2.1	25.8	11.2	3.7	9.0		
France	47.0	28.0	38.0	28.0	36.0	68.0	54.0	67.0	114.0	87.0	
West Germany	70.4	66.5	69.0	69.5	75.6	78.3	80.2	83.6	89.0	96.8	
Greece	100.8	198.3	324.6	348.8	600.9	661.4	715.5	984.9	1150.0		
Ireland	0.5	0.4	0.4	0.4	0.5	0.5	0.6	0.6	0.6	0.7	
Italy	37110.0	41268.0	48502.0	56347.0	66988.0	818540.0	89384.0	97168.0	106742.0	116256.0	
Luxembourg		6.8	7.5	7.2	7.0	6.5	5.5	4.9	5.0		
Netherlands	1.0	1.0	1.6	1.6	1.9	2.1	2.1	2.1	2.2	2.6	
Portugal	112.3	186.2	256.0	297.0	287.0	273.0	256.0	352.0	424.0	1091.0	a
Spain	884.0	988.0	1292.0	3601.0	3649.0	3678.0	3789.0	5274.0	5285.0	6003.0	
United Kingdom	2.4	2.4	2.6	2.4	2.8	2.9	3.6	4.3	5.0	5.8	
EFTA members											
Austria	43.4	48.9	50.6	50.6	54.0	55.4	62.0	52.7	48.8	65.3	
Finland	4.0	3.3	4.0	6.0	10.4	12.2	11.6	18.6	24.0	27.9	a
Iceland			2.9	4.9	6.8	8.4	11.5	11.6	12.8	15.7	
Norway	1.4	1.4	1.5	2.0	2.2	2.7	3.3	3.9	2.7	2.7	
Sweden	5.7	8.5	8.4	4.8	5.3	7.7	13.9	15.4	18.8	19.0	a
Switzerland		15.4	17.9	18.6	15.8	15.8	17.2	18.7	9.3	8.6	
CMEA members											
Bulgaria											
Czechoslovakia											
East Germany											
Hungary	68.0	73.6	125.1	99.8	76.7	84.6	98.4	148.7	126.8		b
Poland		1275.8	1298.5	1351.1	1363.4	1314.3	1273.1	1151.0	3176.0	5859.0	a
Romania	81.3	86.1	78.3	67.9	43.6	26.6	7.1	3.6			
USSR											
Others											
Albania											
Cyprus	0.1	0.1	0.2	0.2	0.2	0.2	0.3	0.3	0.3	0.3	a
Gibraltar											
Liechtenstein			70.2	75.2	114.3						
Malta	76.5	76.8	58.4	55.7	58.1	127.2	127.6	113.2	103.6	86.4	
Monaco											
Turkey	219.5	429.2	592.2	827.1	1299.1	1833.8	2205.2	2806.0	5635.0	7193.8	a
Yugoslavia	322.5	440.9	658.3	1161.3	1774.8	2995.8	5406.5	17126.0	61950.0	399000.0	a

Source: International Monetary Fund
Notes: a 1989 figures estimated
b New series starting 1987

Database name: Finance and Banking
Sector name: Foreign Assets

Table No: 0403

Title: Foreign Assets of Deposit Banks 1980-1989

Unit: Million US dollars

	1980	1981	1982	1983	1984	1985	1986	1987	1988	1989	Notes
EC members											
Belgium	60680	69943	65748	66202	71607	92631	117926	149126	150374	153458	a
Denmark	4833	5265	5865	6654	7975	14158	16033	23920	24423		
France	148098	146491	151853	144460	145340	170900	202230	266410	265400	306360	a
West Germany	85171	84535	81729	74756	75232	112932	178478	232608	230045	295247	
Greece	1188	1666	1408	1386	1598	1980	1788	1870	2165	2800	a
Ireland			1020	1044	1164	1352	2119	2961	3125	5298	
Italy	31195	33069	30939	31498	33159	43214	52365	57098	59102		
Luxembourg	104755	114204	109709	103250	101710	130950	171700	226525	232022	246665	a
Netherlands	62625	66352	63921	58862	57520	72876	91099	115975	120572	146271	
Portugal	1739	1553	1532	1710	1850	2270	2320	3106	4285	4163	
Spain		14824	17361	15712	17524	20039	23817	25728	24571	27511	b
United Kingdom	350946	456318	499925	485210	489710	590070	715560	875710	883640	923990	c
EFTA members											
Austria	21711	22458	25039	25743	26515	36754	48900	58955	54604	58902	
Finland	2762	3231	4154	4777	6258	7671	14310	18825	20542	22242	
Iceland	35	35	41	41	40	58	61	106	99	109	
Norway	627	1882	2347	2540	2997	3644	6800	8507	6326	6509	
Sweden	8036	7515	6725	7122	6741	8943	10787	15023	14905	23153	a
Switzerland	66452	70672	69446	68374	62091	85244	116102	158534	140737	132779	d
CMEA members											
Bulgaria											
Czechoslovakia											
East Germany											
Hungary	177	73	66	129	182	363	685	636	733		
Poland	1477	2034	1713	1640	1896	2295	2371	2783	2795	2807	a
Romania	260	187	254	353	317	608	1770	1547			a
USSR											
Others											
Albania											
Cyprus	46	56	61	67	85	124	178	232	319	411	a
Gibraltar											
Liechtenstein											
Malta	159	145	141	125	118	157	199	260	308	425	
Monaco											
Turkey	547	794	950	992	2076	1994	2178	2425	3280	2969	a
Yugoslavia	1811	2166	1891	1896	2283	2676	2173	2037	2089	2638	a

Source: International Monetary Fund
Notes:
a 1989 figures estimated
b New series starting 1982
c New series starting 1985
d New series starting 1982 and again in 1984

162

Table No: 0404

Title: Foreign Liabilities of Deposit Banks 1980-1989

Unit: Million US dollars

	1980	1981	1982	1983	1984	1985	1986	1987	1988	1989	Notes
EC members											
Belgium	71953	83102	78374	80196	86376	112925	144838	184795	186432	193278	a
Denmark	4877	5271	5844	7104	8289	14852	16405	23440	25025		
France	133554	139433	146101	152020	156950	181200	210700	271430	279408	327900	a
West Germany	72093	66795	64692	57923	58224	75773	101288	131375	131000	159895	
Greece	4001	4676	4916	6600	6600	7590	9120	11410	11363	12233	a
Ireland			2082	2266	2326	2922	3933	4796	4960	5345	
Italy	44696	46411	41123	43790	47476	58593	76129	88478	92002		
Luxembourg	97263	106184	102158	94730	92880	117540	152480	197857	199670	218883	a
Netherlands	64353	65181	62732	56217	53052	65677	83456	108672	109884	121329	
Portugal	808	896	1366	1684	1766	1636	1516	1770	1992	2600	a
Spain	22856	26175	19349	19417	21209	20939	25409	33186	36998	43627	
United Kingdom	365601	471122	517063	532027	606172	539274	723818	779608	914963	1003617	
EFTA members											
Austria	24955	25538	26118	26355	28153	38026	50891	62440	59370	65949	
Finland	4566	4909	6293	7205	9441	12812	20531	32917	37756	42581	
Iceland	178	209	222	289	300	422	419	630	754	685	
Norway	2738	3439	3979	4336	5540	9164	13324	19972	19047	19353	
Sweden	12518	14100	13157	13980	13098	17199	23621	35051	43924	55010	a
Switzerland	47949	58606	56124	54517	49078	63396	82400	109973	102794	110325	
CMEA members											
Bulgaria											
Czechoslovakia											
East Germany											
Hungary	1752	1555	1312	1237	1284	1415	1851	1750	1833		
Poland	25318	27593	25544	24040	23394	26681	30754	35015	33198	31323	a
Romania	8381	9056	8034	7603	6460	6160	6213	6312			
USSR											
Others											
Albania											
Cyprus	148	174	212	249	286	365	463	600	715	713	a
Gibraltar											
Liechtenstein											
Malta	19	25	25	30	27	42	49	77	103	124	
Monaco											
Turkey	82	46	343	446	1693	2507	3990	6184	6274	6173	
Yugoslavia	8261	8986	8113	7866	8291	9615	11363	11757	11003	10420	a

Source: International Monetary Fund
Notes: a 1989 figures estimated

Database name: Finance and Banking
Sector name: Private Lending

Table No: 0405

Title: Bank Claims on the Private Sector 1980-1989

Unit: National currencies (billions)

	1980	1981	1982	1983	1984	1985	1986	1987	1988	1989	Notes
EC members											
Belgium	968.0	1021.3	1049.3	1101.3	1181.0	1222.3	1342.4	1493.8	1769.5	2051.8	a
Denmark	94.0	99.4	111.5	132.9	162.0	190.4	251.9	253.9	257.0		
France	1336.0	1502.0	1743.0	1931.0	1847.0	2229.0	2398.0	2400.0			
West Germany	1155.2	1238.7	1306.3	1399.4	1489.0	1594.6	1665.5	1726.1	1819.0	1952.7	
Greece	516.8	671.7	831.3	933.5	1078.0	1264.0	1524.0	1712.0	2050.0		
Ireland	2.9	3.5	3.7	4.1	4.5	4.3	4.7	5.0	6.3	7.7	
Italy	136717.0	153199.0	169876.0	203225.0	240607.0	268681.0	296400.0	321429.0	371690.0		
Luxembourg	111.8	123.9	144.6	204.5	218.4	224.9	259.7	280.2	323.6	366.7	a
Netherlands	224.8	236.8	242.4	250.5	259.5	270.9	290.7	306.4	375.1	399.9	b
Portugal	688.1	906.8	1167.0	1289.0	1500.0	1689.0	1893.0	2024.3	2380.9	2450.7	a
Spain	10714.0	12519.0	14724.0	15680.0	15832.0	16887.0	18356.0	21063.0	24545.0	28058.0	
United Kingdom	56.6	67.1	80.8	93.3	107.1	124.3	143.5	376.2	467.4	582.4	
EFTA members											
Austria	754.2	840.7	896.0	957.5	788.4	928.8	874.6	914.7	1018.2	1161.4	
Finland	90.3	103.9	123.9	146.1	170.5	203.2	231.0	271.5	346.8	390.6	a
Iceland	4.3	7.3	14.3	26.0	38.3	50.5	58.2	81.8	111.4	145.7	c
Norway	94.6	109.5	124.0	143.4	180.1	236.6	303.8	372.6	399.1	434.7	
Sweden	219.2	241.1	273.4	289.0	323.5	340.6	398.7	453.9	581.8	639.9	a,d
Switzerland	195.8	213.7	262.1	281.6	305.1	335.3	355.2	388.2	431.8	490.0	e
CMEA members											
Bulgaria											
Czechoslovakia											
East Germany											
Hungary	113.1	127.4	141.9	167.3	195.8	222.4	251.3	284.1	316.3		f
Poland	156.0	168.9	228.0	295.0	364.0	462.0	580.0	742.0	1104.0	1572.0	a
Romania		292.9	315.9	349.8	380.6	410.1	442.9	448.3			
USSR											
Others											
Albania											
Cyprus	0.4	0.5	0.5	0.6	0.7	0.8	0.9	1.0	1.2	1.3	a
Gibraltar											
Liechtenstein											
Malta	0	0.1	0.1	0.2	0.2	0.2	0.2	0.3	0.3	0.4	
Monaco											
Turkey	660.3	1231.3	1813.5	1707.9	3624.8	5725.3	8993.0	13992.0	20072.0	26294.0	
Yugoslavia	1396.6	1734.2	2164.0	2904.9	4328.4	6445.7	10915.9	24921.0	85073.0	534400.0	a

Source: International Monetary Fund
Notes: Figures of 0 signify totals less than 0.5
a 1989 figures estimated
b New series from 1988
c New series from 1989
d New series from 1983
e New series from 1982 and 1984
f New series from 1987

Database name:	Consumer Expenditure Patterns		
Sector name:	Personal Finance		Table No: 0406
Title:	Eurocard and Mastercard holders, and ATM machines		
Unit:	Thousands/numbers		

| | Eurocard/Mastercard (000s) | | ATMs |
	1987	1988	(number) 1986
EC members			
Belgium	107	184	723
Denmark	99	122	462
France	1423	1840	9480
West Germany	577	835	3300
Greece	33	64	70
Ireland	177	204	270
Italy	282	397	240
Luxembourg	17	29	30
Netherlands	130	186	240
Portugal	8	11	
Spain	256	450	830
United Kingdom	10497	12100	10845
EFTA members			
Austria	60	93	502
Finland	32	39	973
Iceland	19	26	
Norway	56	60	930
Sweden	32	39	1439
Switzerland	189	248	1321
CMEA members			
Bulgaria			
Czechoslovakia			
East Germany			
Hungary			
Poland			
Romania			
USSR			
Others			
Albania			
Cyprus		1	
Gibraltar			
Liechtenstein			
Malta			
Monaco			
Turkey	8	15	
Yugoslavia	25	25	

| Source: | Eurocard International/Euromonitor estimates |
| Notes: | ATM = Automated Teller Machines |

TABLE 0401: BANK LENDING RATES
Percent

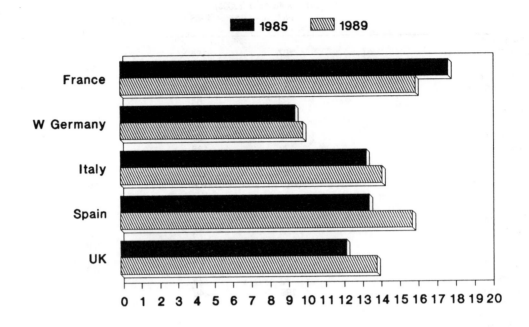

TABLE 0405: BANK LENDING EXPOSURE
Claims on the Private Sector ($ billion)

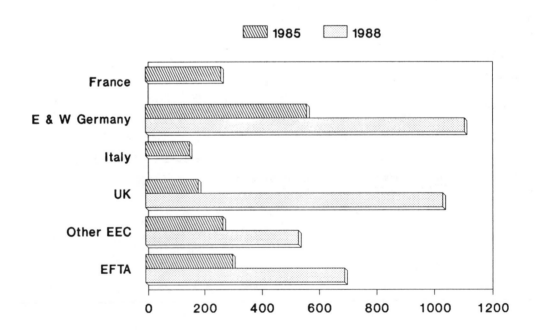

	1977	1978	1979	1980	1981	1982	1983	1984	1985
EC members									
Belgium	1404.5	1480.1	1730.7	2037.6	2240.3	2573.6	2736.1	3099.7	3218.0
Denmark	76.4	77.9	92.6	104.6	119.2	132.8	142.3	164.3	183.1
France	331.0	355.0	438.0	551.0	635.8	705.0	757.5	870.7	931.1
West Germany	227.7	235.8	282.7	331.4	357.3	365.2	378.5	421.4	451.1
Greece	223.1	254.7	315.8	400.8	437.0	589.3	749.3	959.3	1250.3
Ireland	2.9	3.5	4.6	5.2	6.3	6.5	7.0	8.5	9.0
Italy	39.6	44.7	60.1	80.4	99.8	110.2	113.3	139.8	156.3
Luxembourg									
Netherlands	106.7	109.9	129.2	147.0	157.8	161.1	167.6	188.3	204.0
Portugal	165.6	208.6	290.2	422.2	543.6	683.4	817.3	1052.3	1181.1
Spain	1257.1	1332.7	1596.3	2313.4	2808.5	3289.7	3944.1	4366.4	4786.1
United Kingdom	34.0	36.6	44.1	46.1	47.6	53.2	61.6	74.8	80.1
EC total									
EFTA members									
Austria	227.9	225.2	262.3	305.7	321.3	320.3	333.1	374.5	411.5
Finland	29.3	30.8	42.1	55.5	58.4	61.7	68.2	71.3	77.9
Iceland	1.1	1.7	2.6	4.4	6.8	10.6	18.7	24.3	34.2
Norway	66.9	58.7	67.7	81.8	87.8	97.8	95.8	110.3	129.2
Sweden	83.9	86.2	120.8	139.2	143.5	169.2	195.6	213.6	239.1
Switzerland	41.9	41.1	47.4	58.8	58.3	57.3	60.6	68.5	74.0
EFTA total									
CMEA members									
Bulgaria	6.0	6.8	7.4	8.3	10.0	11.0	12.0	12.8	14.0
Czechoslovakia	63.2	68.1	75.8	81.5	86.3	94.2	103.0	113.7	120.3
East Germany	49.9	50.7	56.4	63.0	67.0	69.9	76.2	83.5	86.7
Hungary	262.9	295.8	304.0	294.6	307.9	319.0	365.0	390.5	410.1
Poland	559.9	584.6	622.0	706.3	623.7	868.9	970.2	1209.7	1594.9
Romania	140.4	163.6	196.5	230.7	186.9	146.2	130.4	160.8	178.8
USSR	30.1	34.6	37.9	44.5	52.6	56.4	59.6	65.4	69.1
CMEA total									
Others									
Albania									
Cyprus	0.2	0.3	0.3	0.4	0.4	0.5	0.6	0.7	0.7
Gibraltar									0.1
Liechtenstein				0.4	0.4	0.4	0.4	0.4	0.4
Malta	0.2	0.2	0.2	0.3	0.3	0.3	0.3	0.3	0.3
Monaco									
Turkey	99.6	107.6	169.6	582.6	961.3	1389.2	2127.0	4035.0	5995.0
Yugoslavia	161.6	170.8	223.9	341.4	502.1	624.0	1062.5	1717.4	3049.6
Total									
European total									

Source: IMF International Financial Statistics/Comecon Foreign Trade Data/National trade statistics

Database name: External Trade by Destination and Commodity
Sector name: Total Imports

Table No: 0501

Title: Trends in Total Imports (fob) 1977-1988

Unit: National currencies (billions)

	1986	1987	1988	% growth 1978-1988	% share 1988	Total $ million 1988	$ per capita 1988	Notes
EC members								
Belgium	2969.8	3016.6	3284.7	133.9	6.2	89.3	9047.6	a
Denmark	176.6	166.4	170.4	123.1	1.8	25.3	4927.3	
France	867.4	920.5	1030.5	211.3	12.0	173.0	3097.0	
West Germany	402.9	409.6	439.8	93.1	17.4	250.4	4084.0	
Greece	1404.8	1404.8						
Ireland	8.8	8.7	9.7	235.4	1.0	13.9	3933.9	
Italy	138.7	151.3	168.4	325.3	9.0	129.4	2253.1	b
Luxembourg								
Netherlands	175.0	174.3	186.4	74.7	6.6	94.3	6405.7	
Portugal	1307.8	1781.8	2099.9	1168.1	1.0	14.6	1419.2	
Spain	4613.6	5688.6	6641.1	428.3	4.0	57.0	1461.9	
United Kingdom	81.0	89.6	100.7	196.2	12.5	179.4	3144.3	
EC total					71.3	1026.7		
EFTA members								
Austria	389.8	393.9	424.5	86.3	2.4	34.4	4539.0	
Finland	72.0	82.8	84.8	189.3	1.4	20.3	4090.7	
Iceland	41.7	55.7	62.7	5602.2	0.1	1.5	5879.9	
Norway	146.2	148.2	146.9	119.5	1.6	22.5	5375.7	
Sweden	227.2	251.6	273.0	225.4	3.1	44.6	5306.4	
Switzerland	72.8	74.4	81.8	95.2	3.9	55.9	8522.7	
EFTA total					12.4	179.1		
CMEA members								
Bulgaria	14.4	14.0	13.8	130.0	0.6	8.1	902.5	d
Czechoslovakia	125.4	127.3	129.1	104.3	1.0	13.7	880.4	c,d
East Germany	90.5	80.6	87.1	74.5	3.2	46.6	2797.4	b,c
Hungary	439.7	436.1	472.5	79.7	0.7	9.4	882.3	c
Poland	1964.0	2889.4	5252.1	838.0	0.8	12.2	323.6	c,e
Romania	170.9	129.6	118.5	-15.6	0.6	8.3	362.4	c,e
USSR	62.6	60.7	65.0	115.9	7.4	106.2	374.6	c
CMEA total					14.2	204.5		
Others								
Albania								
Cyprus	0.6	0.6	0.8	246.3	0.1	1.7	2440.5	
Gibraltar	0.1	0.1	0.1		0.0	0.3	8598.3	d
Liechtenstein	0.5							
Malta	0.3	0.4	0.4	101.6	0.1	1.2	3516.3	d
Monaco								
Turkey	7561.0	12360.0	20557.0	20539.6	1.0	14.5	276.7	
Yugoslavia	4111.1	8549.2	63050.7	38916.5	0.8	12.1	514.1	d
Total					2.1	29.7		e
European total					100.0	1440.1		

Source: IMF International Financial Statistics/Comecon Foreign Trade Data/National trade statistics
Notes:
a Belgium-Luxembourg Economic Union (BLEU)
b '000 billion lire
c Foreign-exchange currency
d Imports (cif)
e 1987 and 1988 figures calculated, in the absence of national data, from external dollar estimates

Database name: External Trade by Destination and Commodity
Sector name: Total Exports

Table No: 0502

Title: Trends in Total Exports (fob) 1977-1988

Unit: National currencies (billions)

	1977	1978	1979	1980	1981	1982	1983	1984	1985
EC members									
Belgium	1344.7	1410.3	1661.2	1890.4	2062.3	3393.2	2651.3	2992.1	3167.7
Denmark	60.4	65.3	77.3	95.7	114.3	128.1	146.7	165.3	179.6
France	319.2	357.6	428.0	490.6	576.7	633.1	723.1	851.0	906.9
West Germany	273.6	284.9	314.5	350.3	397.0	427.8	432.3	488.2	537.1
Greece	101.3	123.7	144.2	221.1	237.9	286.3	392.7	542.7	629.1
Ireland	2.5	3.0	2.5	4.1	4.8	5.7	6.9	8.9	9.7
Italy	40.0	47.5	59.9	66.7	86.0	99.2	110.6	129.0	149.7
Luxembourg									
Netherlands	107.2	108.2	127.7	147.0	170.8	176.8	184.4	210.7	225.6
Portugal	75.7	106.5	170.5	232.2	254.9	331.7	508.6	760.6	967.4
Spain	775.3	1001.4	1221.2	1493.2	1888.4	2258.0	2838.6	3778.1	4099.2
United Kingdom	32.0	35.4	40.6	47.4	50.7	55.6	60.5	70.5	78.3
EC total									
EFTA members									
Austria	161.8	176.1	206.3	226.2	251.8	266.9	277.1	314.5	354.0
Finland	30.9	35.2	43.4	52.8	60.3	63.0	69.9	80.9	84.1
Iceland	1.0	1.8	2.8	4.5	6.5	8.5	18.6	23.6	33.8
Norway	47.3	57.1	68.5	91.7	104.3	113.2	131.4	154.0	170.7
Sweden	85.7	98.2	118.2	130.7	144.9	168.1	210.5	242.8	260.5
Switzerland	42.0	41.8	44.1	49.6	52.9	52.7	53.8	60.6	66.7
EFTA total									
CMEA members									
Bulgaria	6.0	6.6	7.7	8.9	9.9	10.9	11.8	13.0	13.7
Czechoslovakia	58.2	63.6	70.2	80.2	87.7	95.3	103.8	114.2	119.8
East Germany	41.8	46.2	52.4	57.1	65.9	75.2	84.2	90.4	93.5
Hungary	238.6	240.7	282.1	281.0	299.5	324.5	374.1	414.0	424.6
Poland	430.3	503.7	566.0	628.6	547.9	951.2	1060.2	1336.1	1691.0
Romania	122.8	140.4	148.4	201.8	189.2	173.4	173.3	228.1	192.3
USSR	33.3	35.7	42.4	49.6	57.1	63.2	67.9	74.4	72.7
CMEA total									
Others									
Albania									
Cyprus	0.1	0.1	0.2	0.2	0.2	0.3	0.2	0.3	0.3
Gibraltar									
Liechtenstein				0.9	0.9	0.9	0.9	1.1	1.2
Malta	0.1	0.1	0.2	0.2	0.2	0.2	0.2	0.2	0.2
Monaco									
Turkey	31.3	55.4	75.7	221.5	530.7	937.3	1298.9	2608.3	4152.9
Yugoslavia	96.1	105.8	123.3	224.3	387.9	525.8	943.3	1603.0	2934.8
Total									
European total									

Source: IMF International Financial Statistics/Comecon Foreign Trade Data/National Trade Statistics

Database name: External Trade by Destination and Commodity
Sector name: Total Exports   Table No: 0502

Title: Trends in Total Exports (fob) 1977-1988

Unit: National currencies (billions)

	1986	1987	1988	% growth 1977-1988	% share 1989	Total $ million 1988	$ per capita 1989	Notes
EC members								
Belgium	3066.6	3100.1	3381.1	151.4	6.3	92.0	9313.1	a
Denmark	171.8	175.3	187.4	210.2	1.9	27.8	5417.4	
France	864.4	888.9	997.6	212.5	11.5	167.5	2998.1	
West Germany	526.4	527.4	567.7	107.5	22.3	323.3	5271.7	
Greece	790.0	881.0						
Ireland	9.4	10.7	12.3	392.0	1.2	17.6	4974.9	
Italy	145.3	144.8	167.4	318.5	8.9	128.6	2239.8	b
Luxembourg								
Netherlands	197.4	187.4	204.5	90.8	7.1	103.5	7026.9	
Portugal	1082.3	1311.0	1519.9	1907.8	0.7	10.6	1027.2	
Spain	3799.1	4195.6	4686.4	504.5	2.8	40.2	1031.6	
United Kingdom	73.0	79.8	81.5	154.6	10.0	145.2	2543.7	
EC total					72.7	1056.1	3253.5	
EFTA members								
Austria	342.3	342.4	382.8	136.6	2.1	31.0	4093.1	
Finland	82.7	87.5	91.7	196.6	1.5	21.9	4423.4	
Iceland	45.1	53.1	61.7	6067.4	0.1	1.4	5781.5	
Norway	134.9	144.5	143.9	204.2	1.5	22.1	5266.8	
Sweden	265.1	281.3	304.2	254.9	3.4	49.6	5913.0	
Switzerland	67.0	67.5	74.0	76.1	3.5	50.5	7706.4	
EFTA total					12.2	176.6	5532.6	
CMEA members								
Bulgaria	13.4	13.8	14.4	140.0	0.6	8.5	941.7	c
Czechoslovakia	121.7	125.3	132.8	128.2	1.0	14.1	905.6	c
East Germany	91.4	83.6	52.0	24.4	1.9	27.8	1669.7	c
Hungary	420.3	450.1	504.1	111.3	0.7	10.0	941.3	
Poland	2115.6	3234.0	6027.0	1300.7	1.0	14.0	371.3	
Romania	167.4	179.9	187.0	52.3	0.9	13.1	572.1	d,e
USSR	68.3	68.1	67.1	101.5	7.5	109.6	386.7	c,e
CMEA total					13.6	197.1	571.8	
Others								
Albania								
Cyprus	0.2	0.3	0.4	257.9	0.1	0.8	1096.8	
Gibraltar		0.1	0.0		0.0	0.1	2737.3	
Liechtenstein	1.2							
Malta	0.2	0.3	0.2	135.1	0.0	0.7	2050.1	
Monaco								
Turkey	5012.0	8844.0	11662.0	37158.8	0.6	8.2	156.9	
Yugoslavia	3975.2	84018.0	65656.1	68220.6	0.9	12.6	535.4	e
Total					1.5	22.4	203.8	
European total					100.0	1452.3	1744.3	

Source: IMF International Financial Statistics/Comecon Foreign Trade Data/National Trade Statistics
Notes: a   BLEU
          b   '000 billion lire
          c   Billion units foreign-exchange currency
          d   Calculated, in the absence of national data, from external dollar estimates

| Database name: | External Trade by Destination and Commodity | |
| Sector name: | External Trade by Destination | Table No: 0503 |

Title: Imports by Country of Origin 1988

Unit: US $ (millions)

	BLEU	France	West Germany	Italy	Nether- lands	UK	Total EEC	Norway	Sweden	Switzer- land	Total EFTA
EC members											
Belgium		14235.0	22591.0	3932.0	16396.0	7057.0	67460.0	530.0	1998.0	1744.0	5456.
Denmark	885.0	1309.0	6129.0	1039.0	1585.0	1858.0	13297.0	1171.0	3236.0	592.0	6189
France	16067.0		34645.0	20494.0	9097.0	12798.0	105742.0	1976.0	2958.0	4420.0	12302.
West Germany	17777.0	30271.0		22934.0	25932.0	17355.0	129774.0	3510.0	6132.0	11209.0	34428.
Greece	529.0	1372.0	3465.0	2281.0	1060.0	918.0	10303.0	55.0	242.0	280.0	932.
Ireland	326.0	635.0	1344.0	395.0	621.0	6514.0	10253.0	66.0	245.0	109.0	634.
Italy	6789.0	20618.0	30184.0		7933.0	7053.0	79782.0	421.0	1995.0	6121.0	12574.
Luxembourg											
Netherlands	14574.0	7584.0	26107.0	3745.0		7616.0	63933.0	1229.0	2204.0	1280.0	6614.
Portugal	680.3	1932.1	2283.7	1562.8	796.8	1375.2	11117.6	173.9	316.5	391.1	1231.
Spain	1983.0	8179.0	9799.0	5816.0	2080.0	4301.0	34430.0	232.0	1138.0	913.0	3249.
United Kingdom	8826.0	16716.0	31389.0	10352.0	14730.0		99374.0	5471.0	5996.0	6850.0	23433.
EFTA members											
Austria	923.0	1438.0	16274.0	3263.0	1021.0	906.0	24846.0	153.0	671.0	1611.0	2686.
Finland	533.0	858.0	3548.0	941.0	685.0	1419.0	9167.0	498.0	2811.0	405.0	3994.
Iceland	33.2	50.1	204.4	68.9	129.6	130.3	799.7	143.7	139.4	18.1	352.
Norway	586.0	774.0	3111.0	776.0	904.0	1793.0	10669.0		4078.0	382.0	5552.
Sweden	1470.0	2210.0	9591.0	1814.0	1837.0	3911.0	25232.0	2708.0		895.0	7389.
Switzerland	1932.0	5984.0	19382.0	5693.0	2367.0	3210.0	40381.0	261.0	1159.0		4057.
CMEA members											
Bulgaria	87.9	167.9	980.9	224.2	92.5	161.3	1844.6	65.0	56.6	137.9	452.
Czechoslovakia	100.4	255.2	1524.2	308.8	170.5	269.2	2813.0	37.3	130.8	269.1	953.
East Germany	166.7	385.1		289.6	292.5	209.1	1624.1	25.0	207.0	368.3	1211.
Hungary	138.0	185.1	1293.8	295.9	165.4	169.7	2355.6	14.3	136.5	239.5	1136.
Poland	137.0	318.0	1643.0	377.0	271.0	313.0	3265.0	79.0	217.0	200.0	887.
Romania	27.0	119.0	327.0	72.0	43.0	89.0	747.0	2.0	16.0	13.0	75.
USSR	582.0	2132.0	5904.0	2323.0	526.0	1009.0	13147.0	151.0	303.0	620.0	5702.
Others											
Albania							87.0				
Cyprus	37.3	93.0	172.1	191.1	49.1	257.9	1012.7	6.8	35.2	31.2	116.
Gibraltar	1.4	1.8	6.8	4.6	9.4	90.0	151.8		0.9	3.2	
Liechtenstein											
Malta	23.9	66.8	200.3	301.0	39.0	242.1	944.2	1.4	11.2	14.8	40.
Monaco											
Turkey	230.3	618.2	1836.4	769.7	295.8	587.5	4741.0	35.1	167.8	325.2	733.
Yugoslavia	160.0	568.0	2241.0	1373.0	239.0	296.0	5091.0	30.0	193.0	275.0	1147.

Source: OECD Foreign Trade Statistics/IMF Direction of Trade Statistics

Notes: Americas: all American countries except USA and Canada
Australasia: Australia and New Zealand
Asia: excluding Japan
a CMEA figures do not include USSR
b Calculated from figures expressed in Gibraltar pounds

European CMEA	Non-European CMEA	USA	Canada	Brazil	Americas	Total Africa	Japan	China	Asia	Australasia	Total inc others	Notes
1864.0	9.0	3895.0	630.0	517.0	1599.0	3443.0	2071.0	239.0	2507.0	544.0	92151.0	
705.0	3.0	1579.0	119.0	192.0	824.0	155.0	1106.0	316.0	1329.0	94.0	26388.0	
4704.0	78.0	13536.0	1290.0	1597.0	4128.0	8081.0	7354.0	1427.0	8541.0	1232.0	178863.0	
9082.0	86.0	16583.0	2064.0	2810.0	7562.0	6431.0	16150.0	2463.0	16718.0	1473.0	250554.0	
816.0	11.0	714.0	53.0	101.0	190.0	417.0	496.0	48.0	602.0	107.0	16384.0	
174.0		2484.0	142.0	60.0	137.0	189.0	755.0	57.0	538.0	32.0	15567.0	
5544.0	65.0	7715.0	968.0	1665.0	3766.0	6286.0	3498.0	1428.0	5944.0	1175.0	138518.0	
2076.0	76.0	7587.0	822.0	1092.0	2666.0	2575.0	3173.0	466.0	5116.0	444.0	99307.0	
102.8	10.3	735.3	166.8	273.0	704.2	856.0	593.8	63.6	508.2	62.4	16712.4	
1312.0	83.0	5404.0	263.0	939.0	3121.0	3141.0	3103.0	384.0	2808.0	340.0	60518.0	
2822.0	55.0	19351.0	3628.0	1318.0	3402.0	3750.0	11569.0	786.0	13456.0	2089.0	189349.0	
2238.0	5.0	1243.0	151.0	200.0	472.0	371.0	1873.0	162.0	1377.0	55.0	36377.0	
3172.0	4.0	1338.0	151.0	135.0	485.0	103.0	1557.0	120.0	807.0	91.0	21145.0	
108.3	0.1	121.6	6.8	5.8	12.1	3.7	112.8	3.9	42.1	33.4	1598.0	
527.0		1543.0	390.0	140.0	1016.0	724.0	1076.0	107.0	1083.0	103.0	22997.0	
1637.0	7.0	3472.0	350.0	309.0	932.0	182.0	2902.0	270.0	2098.0	177.0	45316.0	
671.0	16.0	3116.0	206.0	247.0	1290.0	822.0	2841.0	202.0	2053.0	87.0	56549.0	
		140.0	20.5	5132.4	234.8	57.1	176.1	47.1	175.9	12.8	4460.1	a
		60.6	10.3	83.6	305.1	63.4	53.1	404.3	643.0	71.9	7862.0	a
		120.0	54.0	183.1	337.8	58.4	167.7	340.5	576.7	38.2	7060.4	a
4096.6	36.7	210.0	10.0	160.5	284.5	115.9	135.1	157.1	391.5	19.7	9340.3	
9470.0	82.0	304.0	23.0	306.0	409.0	43.0	258.0	371.0	862.0	176.0	16773.0	
5408.0	216.0	203.0	42.0	26.0	48.0	117.0	53.0	357.0	522.0	86.0	9285.0	
		3045.0	1025.0	257.0	1327.0	597.0	3444.0	1626.0	5893.0	799.0	51585.0	
						2.0			22.0		232.0	
99.5	0.3	84.4	4.3	15.0	22.5	31.4	216.0	10.0	126.0	3.6	1857.5	
		11.0					21.6				206.8	a
32.7		128.8	1.5	11.4	21.1	7.0	37.9	8.9	65.5	5.3	1349.6	
691.2	4.9	1160.3	124.4	87.9	174.7	382.4	391.8	58.3	352.1	173.9	11284.1	
3584.0	6.0	725.0	29.0	115.0	326.0	289.0	175.0	68.0	309.0	109.0	13155.0	

Title: Imports by Country of Origin 1988

Unit: %

	BLEU	France	West Germany	Italy	Nether-lands	UK	Total EEC	Norway	Sweden	Switzer-land	Total EFTA
EC members											
Belgium		15.4	24.5	4.3	17.8	7.7	73.2	0.6	2.2	1.9	5.9
Denmark	3.4	5.0	23.2	3.9	6.0	7.0	50.4	4.4	12.3	2.2	23.5
France	9.0		19.4	11.5	5.1	7.2	59.1	1.1	1.7	2.5	6.9
West Germany	7.1	12.1		9.2	10.3	6.9	51.8	1.4	2.4	4.5	13.7
Greece	3.2	8.4	21.1	13.9	6.5	5.6	62.9	0.3	1.5	1.7	5.7
Ireland	2.1	4.1	8.6	2.5	4.0	41.8	65.9	0.4	1.6	0.7	4.1
Italy	4.9	14.9	21.8		5.7	5.1	57.6	0.3	1.4	4.4	9.1
Luxembourg											
Netherlands	14.7	7.6	26.3	3.8		7.7	64.4	1.2	2.2	1.3	6.7
Portugal	4.1	11.6	13.7	9.4	4.8	8.2	66.5	1.0	1.9	2.3	7.4
Spain	3.3	13.5	16.2	9.6	3.4	7.1	56.9	0.4	1.9	1.5	5.4
United Kingdom	4.7	8.8	16.6	5.5	7.8		52.5	2.9	3.2	3.6	12.4
EFTA members											
Austria	2.5	4.0	44.7	9.0	2.8	2.5	68.3	0.4	1.8	4.4	7.4
Finland	2.5	4.1	16.8	4.5	3.2	6.7	43.4	2.4	13.3	1.9	18.9
Iceland	2.1	3.1	12.8	4.3	8.1	8.2	50.0	9.0	8.7	1.1	22.1
Norway	2.5	3.4	13.5	3.4	3.9	7.8	46.4		17.7	1.7	24.1
Sweden	3.2	4.9	21.2	4.0	4.1	8.6	55.7	6.0		2.0	16.3
Switzerland	3.4	10.6	34.3	10.1	4.2	5.7	71.4	0.5	2.0		7.2
CMEA members											
Bulgaria	2.0	3.8	22.0	5.0	2.1	3.6	41.4	1.5	1.3	3.1	10.1
Czechoslovakia	1.3	3.2	19.4	3.9	2.2	3.4	35.8	0.5	1.7	3.4	12.1
East Germany	2.4	5.5		4.1	4.1	3.0	23.0	0.4	2.9	5.2	17.2
Hungary	1.5	2.0	13.9	3.2	1.8	1.8	25.2	0.2	1.5	2.6	12.2
Poland	0.8	1.9	9.8	2.2	1.6	1.9	19.5	0.5	1.3	1.2	5.3
Romania	0.3	1.3	3.5	0.8	0.5	1.0	8.0	0.0	0.2	0.1	0.8
USSR	1.1	4.1	11.4	4.5	1.0	2.0	25.5	0.3	0.6	1.2	11.1
Others											
Albania							37.5				
Cyprus	2.0	5.0	9.3	10.3	2.6	13.9	54.5	0.4	1.9	1.7	6.3
Gibraltar	0.7	0.9	3.3	2.2	4.6	43.5	73.4		0.4	1.6	
Liechtenstein											
Malta	1.8	4.9	14.8	22.3	2.9	17.9	70.0	0.1	0.8	1.1	3.0
Monaco											
Turkey	2.0	5.5	16.3	6.8	2.6	5.2	42.0	0.3	1.5	2.9	6.5
Yugoslavia	1.2	4.3	17.0	10.4	1.8	2.3	38.7	0.2	1.5	2.1	8.7

Source: OECD Foreign Trade Statistics/IMF Direction of Trade Statistics
Notes: Americas: all American countries except USA and Canada
         Australasia: Australia and New Zealand
         Asia: excluding Japan

European CMEA	Non-European CMEA	USA	Canada	Brazil	Americas	Total Africa	Japan	China	Asia	Austra-lasia	Total inc others
2.0	0.0	4.2	0.7	0.6	1.7	3.7	2.2	0.3	2.7	0.6	100.0
2.7	0.0	6.0	0.5	0.7	3.1	0.6	4.2	1.2	5.0	0.4	100.0
2.6	0.0	7.6	0.7	0.9	2.3	4.5	4.1	0.8	4.8	0.7	100.0
3.6	0.0	6.6	0.8	1.1	3.0	2.6	6.4	1.0	6.7	0.6	100.0
5.0	0.1	4.4	0.3	0.6	1.2	2.5	3.0	0.3	3.7	0.7	100.0
1.1		16.0	0.9	0.4	0.9	1.2	4.9	0.4	3.5	0.2	100.0
4.0	0.0	5.6	0.7	1.2	2.7	4.5	2.5	1.0	4.3	0.8	100.0
2.1	0.1	7.6	0.8	1.1	2.7	2.6	3.2	0.5	5.2	0.4	100.0
0.6	0.1	4.4	1.0	1.6	4.2	5.1	3.6	0.4	3.0	0.4	100.0
2.2	0.1	8.9	0.4	1.6	5.2	5.2	5.1	0.6	4.6	0.6	100.0
1.5	0.0	10.2	1.9	0.7	1.8	2.0	6.1	0.4	7.1	1.1	100.0
6.2	0.0	3.4	0.4	0.5	1.3	1.0	5.1	0.4	3.8	0.2	100.0
15.0	0.0	6.3	0.7	0.6	2.3	0.5	7.4	0.6	3.8	0.4	100.0
6.8	0.0	7.6	0.4	0.4	0.8	0.2	7.1	0.2	2.6	2.1	100.0
2.3		6.7	1.7	0.6	4.4	3.1	4.7	0.5	4.7	0.4	100.0
3.6	0.0	7.7	0.8	0.7	2.1	0.4	6.4	0.6	4.6	0.4	100.0
1.2	0.0	5.5	0.4	0.4	2.3	1.5	5.0	0.4	3.6	0.2	100.0
		3.1	0.5	115.1	5.3	1.3	3.9	1.1	3.9	0.3	100.0
		0.8	0.1	1.1	3.9	0.8	0.7	5.1	8.2	0.9	100.0
		1.7	0.8	2.6	4.8	0.8	2.4	4.8	8.2	0.5	100.0
43.9	0.4	2.2	0.1	1.7	3.0	1.2	1.4	1.7	4.2	0.2	100.0
56.5	0.5	1.8	0.1	1.8	2.4	0.3	1.5	2.2	5.1	1.0	100.0
58.2	2.3	2.2	0.5	0.3	0.5	1.3	0.6	3.8	5.6	0.9	100.0
		5.9	2.0	0.5	2.6	1.2	6.7	3.2	11.4	1.5	100.0
						0.9			9.5		100.0
5.4	0.0	4.5	0.2	0.8	1.2	1.7	11.6	0.5	6.8	0.2	100.0
		5.3					10.4				100.0
2.4		9.5	0.1	0.8	1.6	0.5	2.8	0.7	4.9	0.4	100.0
6.1	0.0	10.3	1.1	0.8	1.5	3.4	3.5	0.5	3.1	1.5	100.0
27.2	0.0	5.5	0.2	0.9	2.5	2.2	1.3	0.5	2.3	0.8	100.0

Database name: External Trade by Destination and Commodity
Sector name: External Trade by Destination   Table No: 0505

Title: Exports by Country of Destination 1988

Unit: US $ (millions)

	BLEU	France	West Germany	Italy	Nether-lands	UK	Total EEC	Norway	Sweden	Switzer-land	Total EFTA
EEC members											
Belgium		18406.0	17923.0	5744.0	13494.0	8582.0	68433.0	530.0	1410.0	2102.0	5558.0
Denmark	568.0	1569.0	4888.0	1296.0	1133.0	3236.0	13674.0	1938.0	3188.0	638.0	6869.0
France	14515.0		26335.0	19737.0	9014.0	15684.0	99254.0	692.0	2106.0	6642.0	11693.0
West Germany	24008.0	40647.0		29461.0	28035.0	30093.0	176036.0	2925.0	9492.0	19626.0	53933.0
Greece	247.0	622.0	1656.0	916.0	213.0	578.0	4663.0	21.0	103.0	71.0	583.0
Ireland	830.0	1708.0	2086.0	706.0	1309.0	6619.0	13895.0	226.0	353.0	243.0	1032.0
Italy	4393.0	21305.0	23229.0		3951.0	10298.0	73580.0	614.0	1669.0	6063.0	12424.0
Luxembourg											
Netherlands	15188.0	11090.0	27116.0	6623.0		11092.0	77127.0	966.0	1939.0	1912.0	7096.0
Portugal	338.1	1633.0	1566.1	430.9	634.1	1505.9	7670.1	184.6	431.1	230.5	1123.4
Spain	1370.0	7460.0	4844.0	3916.0	1976.0	3950.0	26491.0	153.0	393.0	691.0	1684.0
United Kingdom	7587.0	14741.0	16958.0	7319.0	9944.0		73109.0	1874.0	3914.0	3301.0	11623.0
EFTA members											
Austria	742.0	1434.0	10838.0	3249.0	809.0	1468.0	19811.0	212.0	624.0	2237.0	3336.0
Finland	429.0	1159.0	2355.0	590.0	794.0	2828.0	9605.0	750.0	3136.0	373.0	4511.0
Iceland	11.2	69.0	147.9	35.3	16.7	327.4	837.4	34.6	26.7	64.0	144.9
Norway	546.0	1645.0	2786.0	636.0	1550.0	5860.0	14677.0		2637.0	233.0	3465.0
Sweden	2052.0	2635.0	6014.0	1979.0	2386.0	5595.0	25972.0	4647.0		1175.0	9879.0
Switzerland	1126.0	4737.0	10592.0	4220.0	1413.0	3983.0	28384.0	336.0	937.0		3146.0
CMEA members											
Bulgaria	18.5	56.4	166.2	101.2	31.7	45.4	554.9	4.2	8.7	13.0	61.9
Czechoslovakia	84.6	225.9	1138.6	305.3	145.5	2634.4	2395.3	36.7	100.1	102.8	803.1
East Germany	179.9	415.4		192.7	179.1	223.4	1469.7	118.1	283.8	81.4	6804.0
Hungary	80.7	201.4	1085.1	419.2	117.2	187.1	2238.9	13.8	118.8	199.7	991.6
Poland	152.0	340.0	1506.0	407.0	267.0	532.0	3625.0	53.0	283.0	65.0	915.0
Romania	53.0	427.0	718.0	747.0	122.0	163.0	2435.0	96.0	47.0	16.0	236.0
USSR	1134.0	2548.0	3558.0	2850.0	1034.0	1178.0	13920.0	154.0	657.0	188.0	4078.0
Others											
Albania							91.0				
Cyprus	10.7	14.0	26.2	18.8	11.9	153.1	303.3	4.4	6.3	3.5	19.7
Gibraltar											
Liechtenstein											
Malta	21.9	29.6	190.6	124.2	15.0	93.8	482.6	0.6	6.6	3.3	12.5
Monaco											
Turkey	111.1	392.8	1634.5	696.8	219.2	491.5	3796.9	13.0	53.4	188.8	410.2
Yugoslavia	88.0	498.0	1466.0	1930.0	140.0	330.0	4763.0	22.0	112.0	110.0	768.0

Source: OECD Foreign Trade Statistics/IMF Direction of Trade Statistics
Notes: Americas: all American countries except USA and Canada
            Australasia: Australia and New Zealand
            Asia: excluding Japan

European CMEA	Non-European CMEA	USA	Canada	Brazil	Americas	Total Africa	Japan	China	Asia	Australasia	Total inc others	Notes
1145.0	25.0	4579.0	468.0	113.0	701.0	1984.0	1084.0	348.0	3811.0	309.0	92083	a
521.0	16.0	1595.0	194.0	30.0	742.0	532.0	1141.0	128.0	1005.0	186.0	27667	
3333.0	127.0	11755.0	2011.0	722.0	4899.0	10397.0	2740.0	915.0	6946.0	823.0	167765	
11187.0	117.0	26020.0	2759.0	1538.0	5553.0	7279.0	7461.0	2786.0	14641.0	2359.0	323375	
325.0		535.0	54.0		8.0	164.0	126.0	32.0	135.0	38.0	7560	
91.0		1443.0	184.0	24.0	188.0	287.0	362.0	17.0	329.0	165.0	18724	
3625.0	108.0	11385.0	1433.0	427.0	2673.0	4027.0	2423.0	1302.0	5467.0	1104.0	128441	b
1484.0	62.0	4402.0	593.0	170.0	1113.0	2171.0	888.0	262.0	3635.0	539.0	103040	
96.3	1.0	634.2	83.5	24.2	70.7	399.2	81.7	31.5	149.2	43.1	10623	
713.0	214.0	3164.0	468.0	89.0	1373.0	1927.0	478.0	218.0	1128.0	161.0	40335	
2136.0	63.0	18853.0	3634.0	541.0	2506.0	5065.0	3102.0	731.0	9961.0	2986.0	145136	
2804.0	8.0	1095.0	222.0	28.0	217.0	407.0	403.0	166.0	743.0	150.0	30998	
3590.0	21.0	1204.0	262.0	52.0	455.0	208.0	394.0	110.0	704.0	266.0	21754	
79.2		192.1	4.0	1.6	11.6	17.7	107.1	4.8	16.7	1.1	1431	
293.0	6.0	1376.0	278.0	65.0	404.0	358.0	423.0	67.0	530.0	135.0	22532	
1013.0	43.0	4897.0	812.0	187.0	875.0	683.0	887.0	224.0	2261.0	633.0	49862	
1704.0	31.0	4329.0	518.0	372.0	1463.0	980.0	2171.0	409.0	3730.0	446.0	50621	
		28.6	9.7	0.1	19.0	49.2	45.1	76.9	310.1	3.5	2457	c
		87.2	63.4	34.3	93.5	110.1	106.0	428.5	703.2	40.0	7355	c
		115.1	56.3	88.4	157.8	142.4	85.2	352.9	681.9	13.3	6482	c
4444.9	79.4	293.6	44.6	18.7	61.9	166.8	99.9	183.4	488.7	25.6	9944	
8883.0	93.0	379.0	64.0	168.0	204.0	195.0	105.0	303.0	594.0	23.0	17034	
5823.0	146.0	674.0	57.0	15.0	119.0	226.0	129.0	527.0	937.0	41.0	13953	
		590.0	114.0	29.0	250.0	611.0	2520.0	1638.0	4534.0	42.0	41328	c
29.4		15.3	2.0		3.0					35.0	235.0	
					4.1	12.3	3.3	0.3	13.1	0.6	709.0	
											40.1	d
14.7		68.2	2.2		0.2	4.8	0.6		26.0	0.7	697.7	
454.0	4.1	628.1	36.8	5.8	44.5	292.1	179.7	145.0	578.6	21.7	10080.9	
4041.0	36.0	767.0	66.0	14.0	120.0	420.0	87.0	92.0	350.0	41.0	12602	

Notes:
a BLEU
b Billion lire
c Million units foreign-exchange currency
d Calculated from data presented in Gibraltar pounds

Database name: External Trade by Destination and Commodity
Sector name: External Trade by Destination   Table No: 0506

Title: Exports by Destination 1988

Unit: %

	BLEU	France	West Germany	Italy	Nether- lands	UK	Total EEC	Norway	Sweden	Switzer- land	Total EFTA
EC members											
Belgium		20.0	19.5	6.2	14.7	9.3	74.3	0.6	1.5	2.3	6.0
Denmark	2.1	5.7	17.7	4.7	4.1	11.7	49.4	7.0	11.5	2.3	24.8
France	8.7		15.7	11.8	5.4	9.3	59.2	0.4	1.3	4.0	7.0
West Germany	7.4	12.6		9.1	8.7	9.3	54.4	0.9	2.9	6.1	16.7
Greece	3.3	8.2	21.9	12.1	2.8	7.6	61.7	0.3	1.4	0.9	7.7
Ireland	4.4	9.1	11.1	3.8	7.0	35.4	74.2	1.2	1.9	1.3	5.5
Italy	3.4	16.6	18.1		3.1	8.0	57.3	0.5	1.3	4.7	9.7
Luxembourg											
Netherlands	14.7	10.8	26.3	6.4		10.8	74.9	0.9	1.9	1.9	6.9
Portugal	3.2	15.4	14.7	4.1	6.0	14.2	72.2	1.7	4.1	2.2	10.6
Spain	3.4	18.5	12.0	9.7	4.9	9.8	65.7	0.4	1.0	1.7	4.2
United Kingdom	5.2	10.2	11.7	5.0	6.9		50.4	1.3	2.7	2.3	8.0
EFTA members											
Austria	2.4	4.6	35.0	10.5	2.6	4.7	63.9	0.7	2.0	7.2	10.8
Finland	2.0	5.3	10.8	2.7	3.6	13.0	44.2	3.4	14.4	1.7	20.7
Iceland	0.8	4.8	10.3	2.5	1.2	22.9	58.5	2.4	1.9	4.5	10.1
Norway	2.4	7.3	12.4	2.8	6.9	26.0	65.1		11.7	1.0	15.4
Sweden	4.1	5.3	12.1	4.0	4.8	11.2	52.1	9.3		2.4	19.8
Switzerland	2.2	9.4	20.9	8.3	2.8	7.9	56.1	0.7	1.9		6.2
CMEA members											
Bulgaria	0.8	2.3	6.8	4.1	1.3	1.8	22.6	0.2	0.4	0.5	2.5
Czechoslovakia	1.2	3.1	15.5	4.2	2.0	35.8	32.6	0.5	1.4	1.4	10.9
East Germany	2.8	6.4		3.0	2.8	3.4	22.7	1.8	4.4	1.3	105.0
Hungary	0.8	2.0	10.9	4.2	1.2	1.9	22.5	0.1	1.2	2.0	10.0
Poland	0.9	2.0	8.8	2.4	1.6	3.1	21.3	0.3	1.7	0.4	5.4
Romania	0.4	3.1	5.1	5.4	0.9	1.2	17.5	0.7	0.3	0.1	1.7
USSR	2.7	6.2	8.6	6.9	2.5	2.9	33.7	0.4	1.6	0.5	9.9
Others											
Albania							38.7				
Cyprus	1.5	2.0	3.7	2.7	1.7	21.6	42.8	0.6	0.9	0.5	2.8
Gibraltar											
Liechtenstein											
Malta	3.1	4.2	27.3	17.8	2.1	13.4	69.2	0.1	0.9	0.5	1.8
Monaco											
Turkey	1.1	3.9	16.2	6.9	2.2	4.9	37.7	0.1	0.5	1.9	4.1
Yugoslavia	0.7	4.0	11.6	15.3	1.1	2.6	37.8	0.2	0.9	0.9	6.1

Source: OECD Foreign Trade Statistics/IMF Direction of Trade Statistics
Notes: Americas: all American countries except USA and Canada
           Australasia: Australia and New Zealand
           Asia: excluding Japan

Database External Trade by Destination and Commodity
Sector na External Trade by Destination   Table No: 0506

Title: Exports by Destination 1988

Unit: %

European CMEA	Non-European CMEA	USA	Canada	Brazil	Americas	Total Africa	Japan	China	Asia	Austra-lasia	Total inc others
1.2	0.0	5.0	0.5	0.1	0.8	2.2	1.2	0.4	4.1	0.3	100.0
1.9	0.1	5.8	0.7	0.1	2.7	1.9	4.1	0.5	3.6	0.7	100.0
2.0	0.1	7.0	1.2	0.4	2.9	6.2	1.6	0.5	4.1	0.5	100.0
3.5	0.0	8.0	0.9	0.5	1.7	2.3	2.3	0.9	4.5	0.7	100.0
4.3		7.1	0.7		0.1	2.2	1.7	0.4	1.8	0.5	100.0
0.5		7.7	1.0	0.1	1.0	1.5	1.9	0.1	1.8	0.9	100.0
2.8	0.1	8.9	1.1	0.3	2.1	3.1	1.9	1.0	4.3	0.9	100.0
1.4	0.1	4.3	0.6	0.2	1.1	2.1	0.9	0.3	3.5	0.5	100.0
0.9	0.0	6.0	0.8	0.2	0.7	3.8	0.8	0.3	1.4	0.4	100.0
1.8	0.5	7.8	1.2	0.2	3.4	4.8	1.2	0.5	2.8	0.4	100.0
1.5	0.0	13.0	2.5	0.4	1.7	3.5	2.1	0.5	6.9	2.1	100.0
9.0	0.0	3.5	0.7	0.1	0.7	1.3	1.3	0.5	2.4	0.5	100.0
16.5	0.1	5.5	1.2	0.2	2.1	1.0	1.8	0.5	3.2	1.2	100.0
5.5		13.4	0.3	0.1	0.8	1.2	7.5	0.3	1.2	0.1	100.0
1.3	0.0	6.1	1.2	0.3	1.8	1.6	1.9	0.3	2.4	0.6	100.0
2.0	0.1	9.8	1.6	0.4	1.8	1.4	1.8	0.4	4.5	1.3	100.0
3.4	0.1	8.6	1.0	0.7	2.9	1.9	4.3	0.8	7.4	0.9	100.0
		1.2	0.4	0.0	0.8	2.0	1.8	3.1	12.6	0.1	100.0
		1.2	0.9	0.5	1.3	1.5	1.4	5.8	9.6	0.5	100.0
		1.8	0.9	1.4	2.4	2.2	1.3	5.4	10.5	0.2	100.0
44.7	0.8	3.0	0.4	0.2	0.6	1.7	1.0	1.8	4.9	0.3	100.0
52.1	0.5	2.2	0.4	1.0	1.2	1.1	0.6	1.8	3.5	0.1	100.0
41.7	1.0	4.8	0.4	0.1	0.9	1.6	0.9	3.8	6.7	0.3	100.0
		1.4	0.3	0.1	0.6	1.5	6.1	4.0	11.0	0.1	100.0
					1.3					14.9	100.0
4.1		2.2	0.3		0.6	1.7	0.5	0.0	1.8	0.1	100.0
											100.0
2.1		9.8	0.3		0.0	0.7	0.1		3.7	0.1	100.0
4.5	0.0	6.2	0.4	0.1	0.4	2.9	1.8	1.4	5.7	0.2	100.0
32.1	0.3	6.1	0.5	0.1	1.0	3.3	0.7	0.7	2.8	0.3	100.0

	0	1	2	3	4	5	6
EC members							
Belgium	6758.3	885.9	5579.3	6258.2	314.0	10211.9	20477.4
Denmark	2335.4	251.4	963.0	1584.8	122.5	2489.7	4456.5
France	13794.4	1547.5	7210.3	13898.8	549.1	16950.3	28338.6
West Germany	19187.7	2064.9	14641.3	16818.7	758.8	20915.8	41494.0
Greece	1453.1	120.7	591.8	476.5	45.4	1129.1	2071.3
Ireland	1348.8	155.2	401.2	786.9	57.2	1780.8	2172.9
Italy	13859.8	1305.2	11042.4	12074.4	707.1	14154.8	21696.4
Luxembourg							
Netherlands	9969.6	1077.4	5508.5	10217.4	552.8	10132.1	15748.6
Portugal	1397.8	149.8	1017.5	1655.5	70.8	1445.9	3015.2
Spain	4560.0	672.6	4378.5	6487.9	197.0	5724.5	7422.7
United Kingdom	13143.6	2247.3	7928.3	8052.6	509.2	12976.6	29126.4
EFTA members							
Austria	1742	137	1690	2365	76	3366	6263
Finland	1097	91	1392	2188	25	2367	3482
Iceland	107	25	71	101	4	123	284
Norway	1125	144	1704	850	59	1900	4320
Sweden	2538	351	2084	3128	87	4588	7696
Switzerland	2960	652	1484	2252	56	5721	10994
CMEA members							
Bulgaria	34.9	6.0	12.1	2.0	0.3	58.1	101.4
Czechoslovakia	863.3	129.4	1160.9	4723.1	45.1	1045.2	1411.3
East Germany	3449.6	182.9	1280.5	91.5	91.7	1712.4	2979.2
Hungary	609	81	667	1675	5	1482	1617
Poland	1005	123	948	1873	60	1238	1444
Romania	20190.5	912.3	24282.3	28682.6	912.3	38784.5	59216.5
USSR	9.2	0.1	1.4	0.3	0.1	6.2	1.5
Others							
Albania							
Cyprus	105.6	29.3	19.1	121.8	16.1	86.5	262.6
Gibraltar							
Liechtenstein							
Malta							
Monaco							
Turkey	369	192	1322	3172	146	215	2341
Yugoslavia	559	29	160	2201	18	1921	2097

Source: OECD/UN

SITC Classification:

0 Food and live animals
1 Beverages and tobaccco
2 Crude materials excluding fuels
3 Mineral fuels etc
4 Oils and fats

5 Chemicals
6 Basic manufactures
7 Machinery and transport equipment
8 Miscellaneous manufactured goods
9 Others

Title: Imports by Commodity: SITC Classification 1989

Unit: US $ (millions)

	7	8	9	Total	Notes
EC members					
Belgium	20922.2	8177.9	4833.2	84418.4	a
Denmark	6789.2	2778.3	580.9	22351.7	
France	61325.2	21675.5	600.9	165890.6	
West Germany	67685.1	32151.6	6364.4	222082.2	
Greece	2872.7	729.7	30.9	9521.2	
Ireland	5307.9	1814.4	413.0	14238.3	
Italy	36021.8	9420.5	5847.1	126129.4	
Luxembourg					
Netherlands	26882.7	11533.5	549.1	92171.6	
Portugal	5692.8	1094.6	21.8	15561.6	
Spain	21885.2	5442.3	110.7	56881.3	
United Kingdom	60372.1	23225.8	4563.6	162145.7	
EFTA members					
Austria	11351.1	5640.4	6.7	32637.6	b
Finland	8611	2761	8.0	22022.1	
Iceland	589	289	3.7	1597.7	
Norway	9186	3873	15.3	23175.0	
Sweden	18090	6929	220.0	45709.7	
Switzerland	15974.6	10414.9	49.7	50557.2	b
CMEA members					
Bulgaria	4380.0	855.0	165.0	15000.0	b,c
Czechoslovakia	40286.0	5936.0	3346.0	125449.0	b,c
East Germany	18550.0	3620.0	543.0	90500.0	b,c
Hungary	3026.1	629.3	64.1	9855.6	
Poland	3494.5	621.0	37.2	10843.7	b,c
Romania	32680.0	8210.0	1190.0	171100.0	b,d
USSR	19620.0	3900.0	650.0	72400.0	b,d
Others					
Albania					
Cyprus	160.0	53.0	10.0	659.0	c,d
Gibraltar			49.8	113.2	c,d
Liechtenstein					
Malta					
Monaco					
Turkey	4054.3	420.6	1.1	12230.9	b
Yugoslavia	770.5	843.9	3.8	8602.9	b

Source: OECD/UN
Notes:
a BLEU
b 1987
c Estimates based on trade with industrialised West
d 1986

Database name: External Trade by Destination and Commodity
Sector name: External Trade by Commodity

Table No: 0508

Title: Imports by Commodity: SITC Classification 1989

Unit: %

	0	1	2	3	4	5	6
EC members							
Belgium	8.0	1.0	6.6	7.4	0.4	12.1	24.3
Denmark	10.4	1.1	4.3	7.1	0.5	11.1	19.9
France	8.3	0.9	4.3	8.4	0.3	10.2	17.1
West Germany	8.6	0.9	6.6	7.6	0.3	9.4	18.7
Greece	15.3	1.3	6.2	5.0	0.5	11.9	21.8
Ireland	9.5	1.1	2.8	5.5	0.4	12.5	15.3
Italy	11.0	1.0	8.8	9.6	0.6	11.2	17.2
Luxembourg							
Netherlands	10.8	1.2	6.0	11.1	0.6	11.0	17.1
Portugal	9.0	1.0	6.5	10.6	0.5	9.3	19.4
Spain	8.0	1.2	7.7	11.4	0.3	10.1	13.0
United Kingdom	8.1	1.4	4.9	5.0	0.3	8.0	18.0
EFTA members							
Austria	5.3	0.4	5.2	7.2	0.2	10.3	19.2
Finland	5.0	0.4	6.3	9.9	0.1	10.7	15.8
Iceland	6.7	1.5	4.5	6.3	0.3	7.7	17.8
Norway	4.9	0.6	7.4	3.7	0.3	8.2	18.6
Sweden	5.6	0.8	4.6	6.8	0.2	10.0	16.8
Switzerland	5.9	1.3	2.9	4.5	0.1	11.3	21.7
CMEA members							
Bulgaria	0.2	0.0	0.1	0.0	0.0	0.4	0.7
Czechoslovakia	0.7	0.1	0.9	3.8	0.0	0.8	1.1
East Germany	3.8	0.2	1.4	0.1	0.1	1.9	3.3
Hungary	6.2	0.8	6.8	17.0	0.0	15.0	16.4
Poland	9.3	1.1	8.7	17.3	0.6	11.4	13.3
Romania	11.8	0.5	14.2	16.8	0.5	22.7	34.6
USSR	0.0	0.0	0.0	0.0	0.0	0.0	0.0
Others							
Albania							
Cyprus	16.0	4.5	2.9	18.5	2.4	13.1	39.8
Gibraltar							
Liechtenstein							
Malta							
Monaco							
Turkey	3.0	1.6	10.8	25.9	1.2	1.8	19.1
Yugoslavia	6.5	0.3	1.9	25.6	0.2	22.3	24.4

Source: OECD/UN
SITC Classification:
0 Food and live animals
1 Beverages and tobaccco
2 Crude materials excluding fuels
3 Mineral fuels etc
4 Oils and fats

5 Chemicals
6 Basic manufactures
7 Machinery and transport equipment
8 Miscellaneous manufactured goods
9 Others

Database name: External Trade by Destination and Commodity
Sector name: External Trade by Commodity

Title: Imports by Commodity: SITC Classification 1989

Unit: %

Table No: 0508

	7	8	9	Total	Notes
EC members					
Belgium	24.8	9.7	5.7	100.0	a
Denmark	30.4	12.4	2.6	100.0	
France	37.0	13.1	0.4	100.0	
West Germany	30.5	14.5	2.9	100.0	
Greece	30.2	7.7	0.3	100.0	
Ireland	37.3	12.7	2.9	100.0	
Italy	28.6	7.5	4.6	100.0	
Luxembourg					
Netherlands	29.2	12.5	0.6	100.0	
Portugal	36.6	7.0	0.1	100.0	
Spain	38.5	9.6	0.2	100.0	
United Kingdom	37.2	14.3	2.8	100.0	
EFTA members					
Austria	34.8	17.3	0.0	100.0	b
Finland	39.1	12.5	0.0	100.0	
Iceland	36.8	18.1	0.2	100.0	
Norway	39.6	16.7	0.1	100.0	
Sweden	39.6	15.2	0.5	100.0	
Switzerland	31.6	20.6	0.1	100.0	b
CMEA members					
Bulgaria	29.2	5.7	1.1	100.0	b,c
Czechoslovakia	32.1	4.7	2.7	100.0	b,c
East Germany	20.5	4.0	0.6	100.0	b,c
Hungary	30.7	6.4	0.7	100.0	
Poland	32.2	5.7	0.3	100.0	b,c
Romania	19.1	4.8	0.7	100.0	b,d
USSR	27.1	5.4	0.9	100.0	b,d
Others					
Albania					
Cyprus	24.3	8.0	1.5	100.0	c,d
Gibraltar			44.0	100.0	c,e,f
Liechtenstein					
Malta					
Monaco					
Turkey	33.1	3.4	0.0	100.0	b
Yugoslavia	9.0	9.8	0.0	100.0	b

Source: OECD/UN
Notes: a BLEU
           b 1987
           c Estimates based on trade with industrialised West
           d 1986
           e 1985
           f Section 9 includes Sections 2,4,5,6,7,8

Database name: External Trade by Destination and Commodity
Sector name: External Trade by Commodity

Table No: 0509

Title: Exports by Commodity: SITC Classification 1989

Unit: US$ (millions)

	0	1	2	3	4	5	6
EC members							
Belgium	6993.4	567.3	2302.7	2837.3	388.5	11311.1	27117.8
Denmark	5932.4	237.8	1246.2	695.3	105.3	2033.1	2557.7
France	16806.9	4898.6	5755.4	3101.4	384.8	19610.6	25968.7
West Germany	11312.9	1612.0	5216.2	3465.4	796.9	36358.5	51310.2
Greece	745.2	230.5	256.9	217.8	59.0	164.3	1179.0
Ireland	3749.5	345.8	704.3	79.9	15.4	2421.6	1342.4
Italy	5607.4	1305.2	1633.8	2212.8	401.2	8240.5	26075.8
Luxembourg							
Netherlands	16996.6	1753.6	5988.7	9146.4	720.7	15091.4	13272.5
Portugal	419.3	320.4	1083.7	354.9	45.4	535.5	2396.2
Spain	4917.6	622.6	1483.1	1730.0	347.6	3541.6	8169.7
United Kingdom	5668.3	3095.1	2687.5	7606.1	112.5	13893.4	19303.8
EFTA members							
Austria	845.9	74.5	1445.8	492.5	12.1	2440.9	8958.3
Finland	371.1	44.8	2726.6	383.6	24.3	1283.6	9339.9
Iceland	1038.5	0.8	25.2	0.0	31.8	0.6	237.4
Norway	1799.8	16.4	981.9	8147.4	67.6	1852.6	5374.3
Sweden	787.9	60.6	4594.9	1083.4	91.9	3559.0	13256.3
Switzerland	1153.5	227.5	525.8	62.1	18.9	9975.5	8732.4
CMEA members							
Bulgaria	1959.7	1170.6	730.9	4269.1	15.9	1169.5	1477.8
Czechoslovakia	468.5	84.5	639.8	718.3	8.8	1215.7	3460.3
East Germany	926.3	41.9	2232.3	11751.6	212.0	6865.4	8928.6
Hungary	1529.2	150.8	410.8	401.7	800.1	1111.6	1311.5
Poland	1213.8	62.4	743.1	1373.7	20.4	875.9	2234.1
Romania	827.7	74.9	501.5	4740.9	37.1	425.9	2094.3
USSR	859.4	106.5	11931.8	72258.5	99.4	5795.5	11278.4
Others							
Albania							
Cyprus	129.7	42.6	15.5	29.0	13.5	25.2	34.8
Gibraltar	0.1	7.0	0.4	55.2		1.5	
Liechtenstein							
Malta							
Monaco							
Turkey	2163.4	324.0	516.7	238.4	83.2	675.1	2668.6
Yugoslavia	498.8	113.6	563.1	239.9	10.8	1246.2	2030.6

Source: National Trade Statistics/Euromonitor
Notes: SITC Classification:
0   Food and live animals
1   Beverages and tobacco
2   Crude materials excluding fuels
3   Mineral fuels etc
4   Oils and fats

5   Chemicals
6   Basic manufactures
7   Machinery and transport equipment
8   Miscellaneous manufactured goods
9   Others

	7	8	9	Total	Notes
EC members					
Belgium	20894.0	6158.4	3888.4	82458.8	a
Denmark	5985.9	3368.3	1307.0	23469.0	
France	60441.1	14778.3	724.3	152470.2	
West Germany	136374.9	30217.4	3509.9	280174.3	
Greece	135.2	1104.6	112.5	4205.1	
Ireland	5408.7	2297.3	659.0	17023.8	
Italy	42754.7	26495.1	1269.8	115996.4	
Luxembourg					
Netherlands	20987.5	7733.2	3694.1	95384.6	
Portugal	1985.0	3282.1	13.6	10436.1	
Spain	13823.5	4097.1	184.3	38917.2	
United Kingdom	48751.5	16465.6	7227.6	124811.4	
EFTA members					
Austria	9087.1	3796.3	7.9	27161.3	b
Finland	6186.8	1828.4	20.2	22209.3	
Iceland	69.3	23.0	7.0	1433.6	
Norway	3362.5	805.4	10.1	22418.0	
Sweden	21320.1	4695.8	300.8	49750.7	
Switzerland	15045.2	9548.1	71.8	45360.6	b
CMEA members					
Bulgaria	1721.4	1395.1	211.9	14089.0	c,d
Czechoslovakia	11005.7	2373.7	320.8	2029.5	d
East Germany	5433.6	5517.5	207.4	42119.8	c,d
Hungary	3248.6	1151.5	175.6	10291.4	b
Poland	4096.3	960.7	624.5	12204.8	c,d
Romania	814.7	2972.2	50.1	12542.6	c,d
USSR	2471.6	644.9	2144.9	107528.4	c,d
Others					
Albania					
Cyprus	63.9	145.2	3.9	503.2	b
Gibraltar	3.4	3.4		70.9	b
Liechtenstein					
Malta					
Monaco					
Turkey	1085.4	2411.1	24.1	10190.0	b
Yugoslavia	3437.6	2263.1	31.8	10435.5	b

Source: National Trade Statistics/Euromonitor
Notes:
a BLEU
b 1987
c 1986
d Estimates based on trade with Industrialised West

Database name: External Trade by Destination and Commodity
Sector name: External Trade by Commodity

Table No: 0510

Title: Exports by Commodity: SITC Classification 1989

Unit: %

	0	1	2	3	4	5	6
EC members							
Belgium	8.5	0.7	2.8	3.4	0.5	13.7	32.9
Denmark	25.3	1.0	5.3	3.0	0.4	8.7	10.9
France	11.0	3.2	3.8	2.0	0.3	12.9	17.0
West Germany	4.0	0.6	1.9	1.2	0.3	13.0	18.3
Greece	17.7	5.5	6.1	5.2	1.4	3.9	28.0
Ireland	22.0	2.0	4.1	0.5	0.1	14.2	7.9
Italy	4.8	1.1	1.4	1.9	0.3	7.1	22.5
Luxembourg							
Netherlands	17.8	1.8	6.3	9.6	0.8	15.8	13.9
Portugal	4.0	3.1	10.4	3.4	0.4	5.1	23.0
Spain	12.6	1.6	3.8	4.4	0.9	9.1	21.0
United Kingdom	4.5	2.5	2.2	6.1	0.1	11.1	15.5
EFTA members							
Austria	3.1	0.3	5.3	1.8	0.0	9.0	33.0
Finland	1.7	0.2	12.3	1.7	0.1	5.8	42.1
Iceland	72.4	0.1	1.8		2.2	0.0	16.6
Norway	8.0	0.1	4.4	36.3	0.3	8.3	24.0
Sweden	1.6	0.1	9.2	2.2	0.2	7.2	26.6
Switzerland	2.5	0.5	1.2	0.1	0.0	22.0	19.3
CMEA members							
Bulgaria	13.9	8.3	5.2	30.3	0.1	8.3	10.5
Czechoslovakia	23.1	4.2	31.5	35.4	0.4	59.9	170.5
East Germany	2.2	0.1	5.3	27.9	0.5	16.3	21.2
Hungary	14.9	1.5	4.0	3.9	7.8	10.8	12.7
Poland	9.9	0.5	6.1	11.3	0.2	7.2	18.3
Romania	6.6	0.6	4.0	37.8	0.3	3.4	16.7
USSR	0.8	0.1	11.1	67.2	0.1	5.4	10.5
Others							
Albania							
Cyprus	25.8	8.5	3.1	5.8	2.7	5.0	6.9
Gibraltar	0.2	9.9	0.6	77.8		2.1	
Liechtenstein							
Malta							
Monaco							
Turkey	21.2	3.2	5.1	2.3	0.8	6.6	26.2
Yugoslavia	4.8	1.1	5.4	2.3	0.1	11.9	19.5

Source: National Trade Statistics/Euromonitor
Notes: SITC Classification:

0 Food and live animals
1 Beverages and tobacco
2 Crude materials excluding fuels
3 Mineral fuels etc
4 Oils and fats

5 Chemicals
6 Basic manufactures
7 Machinery and transport equipment
8 Miscellaneous manufactured goods
9 Others

	7	8	9	Total	Notes
EC members					
Belgium	25.3	7.5	4.7	100.0	a
Denmark	25.5	14.4	5.6	100.0	
France	39.6	9.7	0.5	100.0	
West Germany	48.7	10.8	1.3	100.0	
Greece	3.2	26.3	2.7	100.0	
Ireland	31.8	13.5	3.9	100.0	
Italy	36.9	22.8	1.1	100.0	
Luxembourg					
Netherlands	22.0	8.1	3.9	100.0	
Portugal	19.0	31.4	0.1	100.0	
Spain	35.5	10.5	0.5	100.0	
United Kingdom	39.1	13.2	5.8	100.0	
EFTA members					
Austria	33.5	14.0	0.0	100.0	b
Finland	27.9	8.2	0.1	100.0	
Iceland	4.8	1.6	0.5	100.0	
Norway	15.0	3.6	0.0	100.0	
Sweden	42.9	9.4	0.6	100.0	
Switzerland	33.2	21.0	0.2	100.0	b
CMEA members					
Bulgaria	12.2	9.9	1.5	100.0	c,d
Czechoslovakia	542.3	117.0	15.8	100.0	d
East Germany	12.9	13.1	0.5	100.0	c,d
Hungary	31.6	11.2	1.7	100.0	b
Poland	33.6	7.9	5.1	100.0	c,d
Romania	6.5	23.7	0.4	100.0	c,d
USSR	2.3	0.6	2.0	100.0	c,d
Others					
Albania					
Cyprus	12.7	28.8	0.8	100.0	b
Gibraltar	4.8	4.8		100.0	b
Liechtenstein					
Malta					
Monaco					
Turkey	10.7	23.7	0.2	100.0	b
Yugoslavia	32.9	21.7	0.3	100.0	b

Source: National Trade Statistics/Euromonitor
Notes: a   BLEU
         b   1987
         c   1986
         d   Estimates based on trade with Industrialised West

TABLE 0502: EXPORTS
Billion US dollars

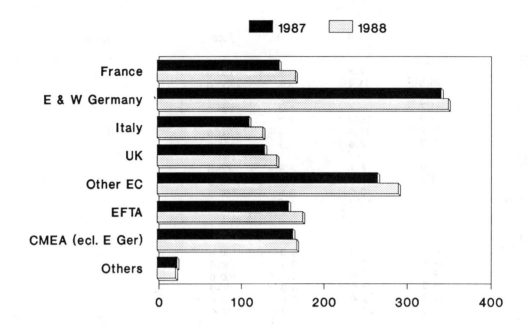

1987   1988

France
E & W Germany
Italy
UK
Other EC
EFTA
CMEA (ecl. E Ger)
Others

0   100   200   300   400

TABLE 0503: EC IMPORTS
According to Source 1988

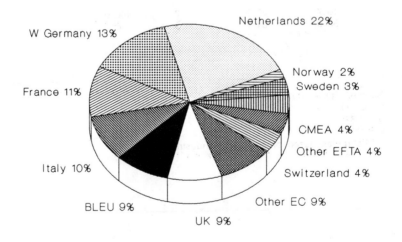

Netherlands 22%
W Germany 13%
Norway 2%
Sweden 3%
France 11%
CMEA 4%
Other EFTA 4%
Switzerland 4%
Italy 10%
Other EC 9%
BLEU 9%
UK 9%

Database name: Labour Force Indicators
Sector name: Employment

Table No: 0601

Title: General Level of Employment 1977-1988

Unit: 000s

	1977	1980	1982	1983	1984	1985	1986	1987	1988	% growth 1977-87	Notes
EC members											
Belgium	3752	3797	3672	3634	3635	3662	3734	3751		0.0	a
Denmark	2414	2400	2375	2389	2488	2553	2662	2643		9.5	
France	21493	21638	21554	21481	21287	21219	21268	21280	21179	-1.0	a
West Germany	25041	25797	25177	24793	24835	25004	25257	25456		1.7	
Greece		3500	3502	3540	3553	3589	3601	3597			a
Ireland	1068	1141	1133	1108	1090	1056	1062	1087	1112	1.8	
Italy	20145	20674	20668	20725	20809	20894	20856	20836	21103	3.4	a
Luxembourg	157	158	158	158	159	161	165	170		8.3	a
Netherlands	4701	4970	5010	4950	4980	5076	5153	5251		11.7	
Portugal	3764	3924	3959	4353	4293	4279	4084	4191	4299	11.3	a
Spain	12252	11502	11061	10984	10668	10571	10821	11369		-7.2	a
United Kingdom	24538	25004	23584	23208	23734	24120	24221	25379	26212	3.4	
EC total	119325	124505	121853	121323	121531	122184	122884	125010		42.9	
EFTA members											
Austria	2737	2789	2766	2735	2745	2760	2780	2785	2810	1.8	b
Finland	2266	2359	2407	2419	2442	2466	2431	2423	2431	6.9	a
Iceland	99	106	113	115	116	121	122	117		18.2	c
Norway	1824	1908	1943	1945	1970	2014	2086	2126	2114	16.6	a
Sweden	4099	4232	4219	4224	4255	4299	4269	4337	4399	5.8	a
Switzerland	3036	3170	3190	3149	3142	3171	3219				
EFTA total	14061	14564	14638	14587	14670	14831	14907	11788		49.2	
CMEA members											
Bulgaria	3870	4025	4100	4114	4098	4095	4077	4084		5.5	d,e
Czechoslovakia	7149	7358	7435	7466	7534	7606	6992	7028	7048	-1.7	
East Germany	7574	7758	7845	7886	7917	7935	7929	7932		4.7	e
Hungary	5075	5044	4986	4955	4927	4902	4879	4865		-4.1	
Poland	11910	12000	11574	11583	11608	11674	11769	11756	11631	-1.3	d,e
Romania	6740	7340	7553	7600	7585	7661	7712				d,e
USSR	120588	125626	127896	128766	129474	130303	130883	130800	129500	8.5	e
CMEA total	162906	169151	171389	172370	173143	174176	174241	166465		11.6	
Others											
Albania											
Cyprus	169	193	202	207	214	222	224	226	233	33.7	
Gibraltar		12	12	11	11	12	13	13			
Liechtenstein											
Malta	114	118	110	111	111	113	117	122		7.0	
Monaco											
Turkey	2191	15031	15302	15412	15611	15790	16092	16450		650.8	
Yugoslavia	5148	5798	6104	6222	6355	6516	6716	6866	6884	33.4	
Total	7622	21152	21730	21963	22302	22653	23162	23677		724.9	
European total	303914	329372	329610	330243	331646	333844	335194	326940		828.6	

Source: International Labour Office
Notes: Notes:
    a Including armed forces
    b Insured persons only
    c Number of 'work years'
    d Social sector only
    e Employees only

Database name: Labour Force Indicators
Sector name: Unemployment

Table No: 0602

Title: Trends in Total Unemployed 1977-1988

Unit: 000s

	1977	1980	1982	1983	1984	1985	1986	1987	1988	% growth 1977-88
EC members										
Belgium	300.7	368.8	535.0	589.5	595.8	558.3	516.8	500.8	459.4	52.78
Denmark	163.7	183.8	262.8	283.0	276.3	251.8	217.3	221.9	242.4	48.08
France	1121.8	1470.5	1919.6	1960.8	2311.8	2425.9	2516.6	2621.7	2562.9	128.46
West Germany	1030.0	888.9	1883.2	2258.2	2265.6	2304.0	2228.0	2228.8	2236.6	117.15
Greece	27.7	37.2	50.6	61.6	71.2	89.0	110.5	110.0	109.0	293.50
Ireland	106.4	101.5	156.6	192.7	214.2	230.6	236.4	247.3	241.4	126.88
Italy	1538.0	1684.0	2052.0	2264.0	2303.0	2382.0	2611.0	2832.0	2885.0	87.58
Luxembourg	0.8	1.1	2.0	2.5	2.7	2.6	2.3	2.7	2.5	212.50
Netherlands	203.5	248.0	541.7	800.6	822.4	761.0	710.7	685.5	682.0	235.14
Portugal	308.5	330.0	315.7	365.7	393.9	397.0	381.6	319.6	262.2	-15.01
Spain	539.6	1277.3	1872.6	2198.9	2475.2	2642.0	2758.7	2924.1	2858.3	429.71
United Kingdom	1402.7	1664.9	2916.9	3104.7	3159.8	3271.2	3289.1	2953.4	2370.4	68.99
EC total		8256.0	12508.7	14082.2	14891.9	15315.4	15579.0	15647.8		
EFTA members										
Austria	51.2	53.2	105.4	127.4	130.5	139.5	152.0	164.5	158.6	209.77
Finland	140.0	114.0	135.0	138.0	133.0	129.0	138.0	130.0	116.0	-17.14
Iceland	0.4	0.5	0.8	1.2	1.5	1.1	0.8	0.6		
Norway	16.1	22.3	41.4	63.5	66.6	51.4	36.2	32.4	49.3	206.21
Sweden	34.2	43.6	80.4	91.7	91.9	84.9	84.2	78.1	61.1	78.65
Switzerland	12.0	6.3	13.2	26.3	35.2	30.3	25.7	24.7	22.2	85.00
EFTA total		239.9	376.2	448.1	458.7	436.2	436.9	430.3		
CMEA members										
Bulgaria										
Czechoslovakia										
East Germany										
Hungary										
Poland										
Romania										
USSR										
CMEA total										
Others										
Albania										
Cyprus	6.1	4.3	6.4	7.8	8.0	8.3	9.2	8.7	7.4	21.31
Gibraltar	0.2	0.2	0.4	0.4	0.5	0.6	0.5	0.3		
Liechtenstein										
Malta	4.6	4.0	10.4	10.3	10.4	10.1	9.4	5.8		
Monaco										
Turkey	142.7	256.3	425.7	549.1	760.9	934.6	1054.6	1124.0	1156.1	710.16
Yugoslavia	700.4	785.5	862.5	910.3	974.8	1039.6	1086.7	1080.6	1131.8	61.59
Total		1050.3	1305.4	1477.9	1754.6	1993.2	2160.4	2219.4		
European total		9546.2	14190.3	16008.2	17105.2	17744.8	18176.3	18297.5		

Source: International Labour Office

Database name: Labour Force Indicators
Sector name: Employment

Table No: 0603

Title: Level of Employment in Manufacturing 1977-1988

Unit: 000s

	1977	1980	1982	1983	1984	1985	1986	1987	1988	% growth 1977-88	Notes
EC members											
Belgium	952	870	792	773	765	753	741	740			a
Denmark	378	355	354	353	371	398	407	397	385	1.9	
France	5449	5235	4991	4882	4743	4589	4550	4393	4325	-20.6	a
West Germany	8341	8427	7916	7599	7526	7606	7716	7717	7684	-7.9	a
Greece	650	675	674	679	679	679	717	716	669	2.9	a
Ireland	214	227	215	203	197	189	185	183	183	-14.5	b
Italy	4771	4745	4535	4404	4205	4101	4038	3986	4049	-15.1	a
Luxembourg	45	41	39	38	37	37	38	37			a
Netherlands	1056	1028	996	928	948	955	963	983	965	-8.6	a
Portugal	792	921	924	960	901	926	927	968			a
Spain	2839	2620	2351	2272	2191	2116	2163	2251			a,e
United Kingdom	7316	6936	5854	5511	5396	5368	5243	5149	5244	-28.3	a
EC total	32803	32080	29641	28602	27959	27717	27688	27520			
EFTA members											
Austria	922	921	874	845	843	843	842	823			
Finland	579	608	599	582	577	578	570	546	527	-9.0	a,c
Iceland	25	25	25	25	26	26	26	27			d
Norway	393	372	351	324	326	327	347	340			a
Sweden	634	602	548	529	533	535	535	548	551	-13.1	
Switzerland	906	924	892	865	861	872	883	890	883	-2.5	
EFTA total	3459	3452	3289	3170	3166	3181	3203	3174			
CMEA members											
Bulgaria	1180	1217	1244	1254	1251	1256	1273				a,d
Czechoslovakia	2323	2370	2390	2399	2411	2420	2435	2434	2428	4.5	
East Germany	3445	3496	3525	3539	3558	3569	3552	3534			a,d
Hungary	1444	1384	1319	1269	1261	1278	1269	1240	1202	-16.8	a,d
Poland	4129	4145	3839	3780	3747	3712	3579	3538			a,d,f
Romania	3027	3109	3235	3288	3288	3340					a,d
USSR	35417	36391	37610	37830	37957	38103	38223	38300	37550	6.0	a,d
CMEA total	50965	52112	53162	53359	53473	53678	50331	49046			
Others											
Albania											
Cyprus	32	40	42	43	44	45	46	45	47	46.9	
Gibraltar	3	3	3	3	3	3	3	3			a
Liechtenstein											
Malta	42	40	35	34	34	34	34	36			
Monaco											
Turkey	1010	1024	1029	1056	1150	1161	1170	1180			a
Yugoslavia	1862	2068	2211	2269	2334	2413	2508	2588			d
Total	2949	3175	3320	3405	3565	3656	3761	3852			
European total	90176	90819	89412	88536	88163	88232	84983	83592			

Source: International Labour Office
Notes:
a Employees only
b Employment in establishments with more than 10 workers
c Includes mining, quarrying, electricity, gas, water
d Social sector only
e Revised methodology in 1987
f Changes in classification 1980, 1986

Database name: Labour Force Indicators
Sector name: Hours of Work   Table No: 0604

Title: Average Working Week in Non-Agricultural Activities 1977-1988

Unit: Hours

	1977	1980	1982	1983	1984	1985	1986	1987	1988	% growth 1977-87	Notes
EC members											
Belgium	35.4	33.8	33.6	33.6	33.7	33.3	33.2	33.2	33.6	-6.2	
Denmark											
France	41.4	40.8	39.5	39.2	39.0	38.9	38.9	39.0	39.0	-5.8	
West Germany	41.7	41.6	40.7	40.5	40.9	40.7	40.5	40.2	40.2	-3.6	a
Greece											
Ireland											
Italy	7.7	7.8	7.7	7.7	7.8	7.8	7.7	7.7	7.8	0.0	b
Luxembourg	39.5	40.2	41.3	41.2	40.1	40.6	41.0	41.2		4.3	a
Netherlands	40.7	40.6	40.4	40.4	40.4	40.3	40.3	40.2		-1.2	a
Portugal	38.5	38.4	38.4	38.9	38.2	37.7	38.8				
Spain	42.3	40.1	39.5	38.8	37.9	37.5	37.6	36.1		-14.7	
United Kingdom			42.1	42.4	42.5	42.8	42.7	43.1	43.5		
EFTA members											
Austria											
Finland											
Iceland	49.5	49.3	49.4	48.7	48.9	48.6	48.5	49.2		-0.6	a
Norway	36.8	36.3	36.0	35.6	35.9	36.2	36.6	35.9		-2.4	
Sweden	35.7	35.4	35.3	35.4	35.8	36.0	36.5	37.1	37.3	3.9	
Switzerland	44.8	44.3	44.1	43.7	43.5	43.4	43.0	42.8	42.4	-4.5	a
CMEA members											
Bulgaria											
Czechoslovakia											
East Germany											
Hungary											
Poland		150.0	155.0	158.0	159.0	159.0	159.0	159.0			c
Romania											
USSR											
Others											
Albania											
Cyprus	44.0	42.0	42.0	41.0	41.0	41.0	41.0	41.0	40.0	-6.8	a
Gibraltar	47.5	43.2	44.7	44.3	45.1	44.5	44.0	42.7		-10.1	a
Liechtenstein											
Malta											
Monaco											
Turkey											
Yugoslavia	185.0			182.0		185.0					a,c

EPR
EPR

Source: International Labour Office
Notes: a Hours paid for
         b Hours per day; estimates for 1985 and 1986
         c Hours per month

Database name: Labour Force Indicators
Sector name: Hours of Work   Table No: 0605

Title: Average Working Week in Manufacturing 1977-1988

Unit: Hours

	1977	1980	1982	1983	1984	1985	1986	1987	1988	% growth 1977-87	Notes
EC members											
Belgium	35.1	33.4	33.6	33.5	33.7	33.1	33.0	33.0	33.4	-6.0	
Denmark	32.7	32.6	32.5	33.0	33.0	32.1	33.0	32.5		-0.6	
France	41.1	40.6	39.4	38.9	38.7	38.6	38.6	38.7	38.7	-5.8	
West Germany	41.7	41.6	40.7	40.5	41.0	40.7	40.4	40.1	40.0	-3.8	a
Greece	41.0	40.7	38.6	38.5	38.2	39.3	39.1	39.2	41.1	-4.4	
Ireland	42.6	41.1	40.5	40.8	41.1	41.1	41.2	41.1	41.9	-3.5	
Italy	7.7	7.7	7.7	7.7	7.8	7.8	7.7	7.7	7.8	0.0	b
Luxembourg	38.9	40.0	41.2	41.0	39.7	40.2	40.5	40.8		4.9	a
Netherlands	40.9	40.8	40.6	40.5	40.3	40.3	40.1	39.9		-2.4	a
Portugal	39.8	39.0	38.8	38.6	38.6	38.1	38.9				
Spain	41.1	38.8	38.2	37.7	36.7	36.5	36.9	35.4		-13.9	
United Kingdom			41.0	41.5	41.7	41.8	41.6	42.2	42.4		
EFTA members											
Austria	146.9	146.0	145.5	144.3	145.2	144.9	142.1	139.9	141.0	-4.8	c
Finland	32.8	33.2	32.5	32.4	32.3	32.3	31.9	32.2		-1.8	
Iceland											
Norway	38.2	38.3	37.9	37.9	38.0	38.4	38.4	37.2		-2.6	
Sweden	37.9	37.6	37.6	37.7	38.1	38.3	38.3	38.4		1.3	
Switzerland	44.6	43.8	43.7	43.2	43.0	42.9	42.6	42.4		-4.9	a
CMEA members											
Bulgaria											
Czechoslovakia	43.7	43.5	43.1	43.1	43.0	43.1	43.1	43.1	43.0	-1.4	
East Germany											
Hungary	163.5	160.8	153.9	152.4	147.1	145.2	144.7	148.0	147.9	-9.5	c
Poland	163.0	159.0	149.0	152.0	152.0	153.0	151.0	151.0		-7.4	c
Romania											
USSR	40.6	40.5	40.4	40.3							
Others											
Albania											
Cyprus	44.0	41.0	41.0	41.0	41.0	41.0	41.0	41.0	40.0	-6.8	a
Gibraltar	44.9	45.8	47.7	47.6	50.4	48.7	47.3	43.9		-2.2	a
Liechtenstein											
Malta											
Monaco											
Turkey											
Yugoslavia	185.0			181.0		184.0					a,c

Source: International Labour Office
Notes: Data refer to hours actually worked
a Hours paid for; estimates for 1985-1988
b Hours per day
c Hours per month

Database name: Labour Force Indicators
Sector name: Economically Active Population

Table No: 0606

Title: Structure of the Economically Active Population: Latest Official Estimates

Unit: As stated

	Year	Total '000	% Total Population	Males '000	% Total EAP	Females '000	% Total EAP	% Unem- ployed	Notes
EC members									
Belgium	1987	4211	42.7	2513	59.7	1698	40.3	12.2	
Denmark	1987	2816	55.6	1526	54.2	1290	45.8	7.6	
France	1987	23972	44.3	13596	56.7	10377	43.3	11.2	
West Germany	1987	29230	47.9	17692	60.5	11539	39.5	8.1	
Greece	1987	4069	40.7	2674	65.7	1394	34.3	6.4	
Ireland	1987	1319	37.2	912	69.1	408	30.9	19.2	
Italy	1987	23819	41.7	15150	63.6	8670	36.4	14.2	
Luxembourg	1987	158	42.8	102	64.6	56	35.4	1.7	
Netherlands	1987	6559	35.2	4104	62.6	2455	37.4	11.9	
Portugal	1987	4732	46.0	2744	58.0	1988	42.0	7.1	
Spain	1987	14307	28.0	9590	67.0	4717	33.0	21.2	
United Kingdom	1987	27387	48.2	15887	58.0	11500	42.0	10.9	
EC total		142579		86490	60.7	56092	39.3		
EFTA members									
Austria	1987	3430	45.3	2054	59.9	1376	40.1	5.6	
Finland	1987	2372	49.8	1219	51.4	1153	48.6	5.1	
Iceland	1986	118	48.4	65	55.1	53	44.9	0.5	
Norway	1987	2171	49.6	1209	55.7	962	44.3	2.1	
Sweden	1987	4421	51.0	2300	52.0	2122	48.0	1.9	
Switzerland	1987	3244	49.4	2038	62.8	1206	37.2	0.8	
EFTA total		15756		8885	56.4	6872	43.6		
CMEA members									
Bulgaria	1987	5004	55.7	2650	53.0	2355	47.0		a
Czechoslovakia	1986	7705	49.7	4091	53.1	3614	46.9		
East Germany	1987	10825	65.0	5608	51.8	5217	48.2		a
Hungary	1988	4845	45.7	2624	54.2	2221	54.8		
Poland	1987	21857	57.9	11290	51.7	10567	48.3		a
Romania	1985	7660	33.7	4260	55.6	3400	44.4		
USSR	1985	117700	42.2	58967	50.1	58732	49.9		
CMEA total		175596		89490	51.0	86106	49.0		
Others									
Albania	1984	1289	44.4	730	56.6	559	43.4		
Cyprus	1988	262	53.0	166	63.4	96	36.6	2.8	
Gibraltar	1987	13	45.0	9	69.2	4	30.8		
Liechtenstein	1986	13	47.9	8	61.5	5	38.5		
Malta	1987	128	36.9	96	75.0	32	25.0	4.4	
Monaco									
Turkey	1985	18423	36.2	12879	69.9	5544	30.1	11.9	
Yugoslavia	1985	6493	28.1	4039	62.2	2454	37.8	13.6	
Total		26621		17927	67.3	8694	32.7		
European total		360552		202792	56.2	157764	43.8		

Source: National Statistical Offices/Eurostat/ILO/Euromonitor
Notes: EAP = economically active population
a Population of working age only

	Year	A	B	C	D	E	F
EC members							
Belgium	1986	2.5	0.5	19.0	0.7	4.9	16.9
Denmark	1986	5.7	0.1	19.9	0.7	7.0	14.3
France	1987	6.7	0.4	19.4	0.8	6.6	14.4
West Germany	1987	4.8	1.2	30.5	0.9	6.3	14.9
Greece	1986	26.5	0.6	19.3	0.9	6.5	15.0
Ireland	1987	12.7	0.7	17.9	1.1	7.4	16.1
Italy	1987	9.1	1.0	19.4		7.8	18.7
Luxembourg	1987	3.2	0.1	18.7	0.6	8.8	20.7
Netherlands	1987	4.5	0.2	16.8	0.8	5.8	16.4
Portugal	1987	20.6	0.6	22.8	0.8	7.9	13.0
Spain	1987	14.5	0.9	24.4	0.7	9.9	16.1
United Kingdom	1987	2.1	0.8	19.3	1.0	5.6	18.2
EFTA members							
Austria	1987	8.4	0.4	28.1	1.2	8.2	17.7
Finland	1987	10.2	0.3	21.6	1.2	7.9	14.1
Iceland							
Norway	1987	6.5	1.1	16.5	1.1	7.7	17.6
Sweden	1987	3.9	0.2	21.8	0.9	6.2	13.8
Switzerland	1986	6.4	0.2	29.6	0.7	6.9	18.6
CMEA members							
Bulgaria	1985	17.0	37.0			7.8	8.3
Czechoslovakia							
East Germany	1986	10.8	40.8			6.7	10.3
Hungary	1987	20.9	31.3			7.0	10.5
Poland							
Romania							
USSR							
Others							
Albania							
Cyprus	1986	16.0	0.5	19.7	0.7	9.9	22.7
Gibraltar							
Liechtenstein							
Malta	1987	2.5	0.7	28.1	1.5	4.6	9.4
Monaco							
Turkey	1985	39.5	0.7	12.7	0.1	4.0	10.1
Yugoslavia	1981	30.6	25.2			7.9	9.4

Source: United Nations/ILO/National Statistical Offices
Notes:
A Agriculture/forestry/fishing
B Mining and quarrying
C Manufacturing
D Electricity, gas and water
E Construction

F Wholesale/retail trade, restaurants and hotels
G Transport, storage and communications
H Financing, insurance, real estate and business services
I Community, social and personal services
J Not adequately defined

Database name: Labour Force Indicators
Sector name: Economically Active Population

Table No: 0607

Title: Economically Active Population by Industry: Latest Year

Unit: % of the total

	Year	G	H	I	J	Total	Notes
EC members							
Belgium	1986	6.2	7.1	30.0	12.2	100.0	a
Denmark	1986	6.9	8.1	35.7	1.6	100.0	
France	1987	5.4	7.3	27.9	11.1	100.0	a
West Germany	1987	5.6	6.4	27.6	1.8	100.0	b
Greece	1986	6.5	3.7	16.4	4.6	100.0	a
Ireland	1987	5.4	6.5	22.6	9.6	100.0	a
Italy	1987	4.9	3.3	23.9	11.9	100.0	a,f
Luxembourg	1987	6.7	10.1	26.7	4.4	100.0	
Netherlands	1987	5.4	8.5	30.8	10.8	100.0	a
Portugal	1987	4.0	7.2	23.1	0.0	100.0	b
Spain	1987	5.6	3.9	16.0	8.0	100.0	b
United Kingdom	1987	5.4	9.3	26.7	11.6	100.0	a
EFTA members							
Austria	1987	6.5	5.7	22.7	1.2	100.0	b
Finland	1987	7.2	7.0	29.6	0.9	100.0	b
Iceland							
Norway	1987	8.3	7.2	33.1	0.9	100.0	b
Sweden	1987	7.0	7.4	36.8	2.0	100.0	b
Switzerland	1986	6.2	9.3	21.3	0.8	100.0	
CMEA members							
Bulgaria	1985	6.8	21.6		1.5	100.0	c,d
Czechoslovakia							
East Germany	1986	7.3	24.1			100.0	c,e
Hungary	1987	8.3	22.0		0.0	100.0	c,d
Poland							
Romania							
USSR							
Others							
Albania							
Cyprus	1986	5.8	5.4	19.3		100.0	b
Gibraltar							
Liechtenstein							
Malta	1987	7.0	38.5		7.7	100.0	a,d
Monaco							
Turkey	1985	4.4	2.2	14.0	12.3	100.0	a
Yugoslavia	1981	5.1	2.3	18.1	1.5	100.0	c

Source: United Nations/ILO/National Statistical Offices
Notes:
a Column J includes unemployed
b National figures differ significantly from external estimates in Table 0606
c Division B includes divisions C and D
d Division H includes division I
e Division H includes divisions I and J
f Division C includes division

Table No: 0608

Title: Economically Active Population by Age Group: Latest Year

Unit: Percentage of the total

	Year	Under 15	15-19	20-24	25-29	30-34	35-39	40-44	45-49
EC members									
Belgium	1981		5.3	14.7	15.8	14.7	11.1	10.2	9.9
Denmark	1986		9.2	11.7	11.6	12.0	12.8	11.7	9.1
France	1987		2.3	11.3	14.6	14.6	15.2	12.6	9.5
West Germany	1986		7.1	14.0	12.4	11.3	11.2	10.6	13.0
Greece	1985	0.3	4.6	9.0	11.9	12.2	12.6	10.4	11.8
Ireland	1987		7.8	17.0	15.0	12.8	11.1	9.6	7.6
Italy	1987		5.7	12.4	12.8	12.8	13.1	11.2	10.8
Luxembourg	1987		5.1	14.1	15.7	14.6	13.4	10.9	9.8
Netherlands	1988		7.5	14.9	14.9	13.7	14.0	11.7	8.8
Portugal	1987	1.4	10.0	11.4	11.0	11.4	11.6	10.2	9.6
Spain	1987		7.3	15.2	13.6	11.5	10.5	10.2	8.2
United Kingdom	1981		8.5	12.5	10.9	12.0	10.7	10.1	9.7
EFTA members									
Austria	1987		9.0	14.7	14.1	12.2	12.0	11.0	12.0
Finland	1987		5.0	11.0	12.9	14.2	15.5	13.1	10.4
Iceland									
Norway	1987		6.6	11.6	11.6	12.6	12.5	12.9	9.1
Sweden	1987		4.7	11.3	11.4	12.1	13.1	14.1	10.7
Switzerland									
CMEA members									
Bulgaria									
Czechoslovakia									
East Germany									
Hungary									
Poland									
Romania									
USSR									
Others									
Albania									
Cyprus									
Gibraltar									
Liechtenstein									
Malta									
Monaco									
Turkey	1985	4.3	15.9	14.3	12.8	12.3	8.7	8.8	7.8
Yugoslavia	1981		4.3	13.1	15.5	13.6	9.8	11.3	11.2

Source: National trade statistics/Euromonitor

	Year	50-54	55-59	60-64	65+	Total
members						
Belgium	1981	9.1	6.6	1.9	0.7	100.0
Denmark	1986	7.5	7.0	4.1	3.4	100.0
France	1987	9.2	7.1	2.6	0.9	100.0
West Germany	1986	9.8	7.7	2.4	0.6	100.0
Greece	1985	10.9	8.5	4.5	3.2	100.0
Ireland	1987	6.8	5.5	4.2	2.7	100.0
Italy	1987	9.0	6.6	3.2	2.3	100.0
Luxembourg	1987	8.5	5.5	1.8	0.6	100.0
Netherlands	1987	7.1	4.6	1.9	1.0	100.0
Portugal	1987	9.3	6.9	4.8	2.4	100.0
Spain	1987	9.6	8.1	4.7	1.1	100.0
United Kingdom	1981	9.6	8.9	5.2	2.0	100.0
TA members						
Austria	1987	7.8	5.5	1.1	0.4	100.0
Finland	1987	8.4	6.0	2.6	0.9	100.0
Iceland						
Norway	1987	7.1	6.7	5.6	3.7	100.0
Sweden	1987	8.8	8.1	5.8		100.0
Switzerland						
EA members						
Bulgaria						
Czechoslovakia						
East Germany						
Hungary						
Poland						
Romania						
USSR						
ers						
Albania						
Cyprus						
Gibraltar						
Liechtenstein						
Malta						
Monaco						
Turkey	1985	6.7	4.7	2.3	1.4	100.0
Yugoslavia	1981	8.8	5.1	2.3	5.0	100.0

	Year	AB	C	D	E	F	G	HIJ	K	Total
EC members										
Belgium	1981	623.2	75.2	701.2	309.2	327.1	117.8	1331.9	33.5	3519.1
Denmark	1986	603.0	99.7	500.1	195.0	327.3	130.0	887.5	35.5	2778.1
France	1982	3359.1	58.3	4062.5	1866.7	2544.1	1803.4	7346.8	166.0	21206.9
West Germany	1985	4014.0	1001.0	5173.0	2412.0	3058.0	1280.0	9077.0	611.0	26626.0
Greece	1986	420.4	62.7	348.5	372.5	336.4	1032.6	1114.4	52.5	3740.0
Ireland	1987	194.6	35.0	173.2	126.0	129.3	171.6	350.3	86.9	1266.9
Italy	1981	2600.8	3609.7	2164.6	2501.1	2610.1	2097.3	4662.9		20246.5
Luxembourg	1981	18.3	1.6	31.1	13.5	19.9	8.1	55.8	1.7	150.0
Netherlands	1987	1344.9	240.1	1026.4	634.3	729.4	306.4	1428.1	127.0	5836.6
Portugal	1987	316.5	60.4	547.4	401.0	493.7	968.0	1486.0	108.1	4381.1
Spain	1987	1164.3	195.2	1407.5	1382.5	1812.2	1957.2	4817.1	373.2	13109.2
United Kingdom	1981	4137.8	2311.7	3945.3	1404.1	3062.7	353.3	8004.7	220.8	23440.4
EFTA members										
Austria	1987	452.6	179.5	543.4	307.9	364.1	290.6	1242.2	10.5	3390.8
Finland	1987	543.0	114.0	358.0	197.0	320.0	266.0	719.0	6.0	2523.0
Iceland										
Norway	1987	467.0	137.0	232.0	220.0	288.0	139.0	631.0	13.0	2127.0
Sweden	1987	1375.0	700.0		383.0	421.0	174.0	1282.0	3.0	4338.0
Switzerland										
CMEA members										
Bulgaria	1985	1218.1	138.0	47.6	283.3	188.7	594.0	2216.0	0.5	4686.2
Czechoslovakia										
East Germany										
Hungary										
Poland										
Romania										
USSR										
Others										
Albania										
Cyprus	1985	21.1	3.0	29.1	21.9	26.7	1.0	77.5	56.3	236.6
Gibraltar	1987	1.5	0.7	3.0	0.9	2.3		4.8		13.2
Liechtenstein										
Malta										
Monaco										
Turkey	1985	1031.8	189.6	899.0	1155.6	1128.8	7382.3	4697.7	142.0	16626.8
Yugoslavia	1981	922.1	153.7	890.7	476.9	529.4	2518.0	2947.9	341.0	8779.7

Source: United Nations/ILO/National Statistical Offices
Notes: AB Professional, technical and related workers   HIJ Production/related workers, transport equipment
          C Administrative and managerial workers   operators and labourers
          D Clerical and related workers   K   Workers not classifiable by occupation
          E Sales workers
          F Service workers
          G Agricultural, animal husbandry and forestry workers, fishermen and hunters

TABLE 0602: UNEMPLOYMENT
Thousands

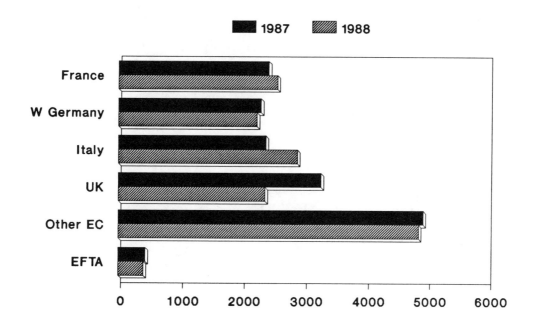

TABLE 0603: EMPLOYMENT IN MANUFACTURING
Millions

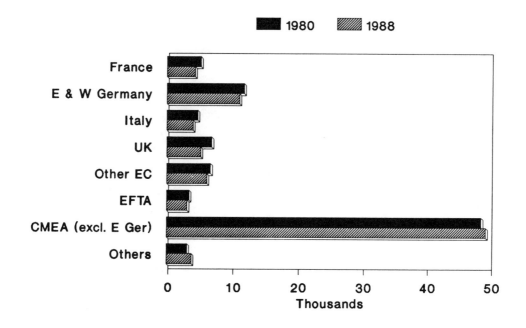

Database name: Industrial Resources and Output
Sector name: Industrial Output   Table No: 0701

Title: Indices of General Industrial Production 1977-1988

Unit: 1980 = 100

	1977	1978	1979	1980	1981	1982	1983	1984	1985	1986	1987	1988
EC members												
Belgium	95	97	101	100	97	98	99	102	104	105	107	113
Denmark	94	97	100	100	100	102	106	116	121	129	125	127
France	93	96	100	100	98	97	98	99	98	101	104	108
West Germany	92	95	100	100	98	95	96	99	104	107	107	111
Greece	87	93	99	100	101	102	101	104	107	107	106	111
Ireland	88	95	101	100	105	104	111	125	128	132	146	162
Italy	87	88	95	100	98	95	92	95	97	99	103	108
Luxembourg	96	100	103	100	94	90	99	113	121	124	125	130
Netherlands	97	98	101	100	98	94	97	102	106	106	107	107
Portugal	83	88	95	100	100	105	107	106	118	123	128	136
Spain	96	98	99	100	99	98	101	101	103	107	112	115
United Kingdom	100	103	107	100	96	98	102	103	108	110	114	119
EFTA members												
Austria	88	91	97	100	99	98	99	104	109	110	111	116
Finland	80	84	92	100	103	104	107	112	116	118	123	128
Iceland												
Norway	81	89	96	100	99	99	108	118	121	126	135	142
Sweden	96	94	100	100	98	97	101	107	110	110	113	116
Switzerland	93	93	95	100	99	96	95	97	103	108	108	115
CMEA members												
Bulgaria	85	91	96	100	105	110	115	120	124	129	134	143
Czechoslovakia	89	93	97	100	102	104	107	111	115	118	122	124
East Germany	87	91	95	100	105	108	112	117	122	127	131	135
Hungary	95	99	102	100	103	105	106	109	110	112	116	115
Poland	96	99	101	100	86	85	90	95	99	103	106	111
Romania				100							147	
USSR	90	94	97	100	103	106	111	115	119	125	129	136
Others												
Albania												
Cyprus												
Gibraltar												
Liechtenstein												
Malta												
Monaco												
Turkey				100							172	
Yugoslavia	82	89	96	100	102	104	105	111	114	119	120	122

Source: United Nations/OECD/Comecon

Database name: Industrial Resources and Output
Sector name: Industrial Output

Table No: 0702

Title: Indices of Mining Production 1977-1988

Unit: 1980 = 100

	1977	1978	1979	1980	1981	1982	1983	1984	1985	1986	1987	1988
EC members												
Belgium	115	105	97	100	94	95	89	90	84	75	65	56
Denmark	102	101	106	100	80	84	89	100	110	138	122	124
France	101	100	101	100	96	89	92	91	88	85	84	82
West Germany	96	95	99	100	99	96	92	92	93	91	87	85
Greece	97	95	102	100	101	148	161	178	183	184	181	189
Ireland	79	92	99	100	91	88	92	108	73	80	84	70
Italy	97	97	104	100	104	98	97	99	100	101	108	117
Luxembourg	183	124	106	100	77	46	37	32	29	27	72	30
Netherlands	108	100	106	100	91	78	84	86	93	87	88	78
Portugal	75	76	92	100	88	87	81	97	109	100	84	96
Spain	73	77	82	100	114	120	129	131	130	124	107	102
United Kingdom	62	78	99	100	107	117	124	118	129	133	130	120
EFTA members												
Austria	90	87	100	100	104	109	107	113	110	108	112	84
Finland	85	89	96	100	103	115	115	119	123	127	125	147
Iceland												
Norway	42	68	81	100	96	97	114	131	138	147	164	181
Sweden	93	83	101	100	86	74	87	98	103	102	103	91
Switzerland												
CMEA members												
Bulgaria												
Czechoslovakia	95	98	101	100	99	99	101	102	101	101	102	107
East Germany												
Hungary	101	104	106	100	97	100	97	97	99	99	99	95
Poland	101	102	106	100	85	97	99	102	104	104	106	105
Romania												
USSR	96	98	99	100	101	102	104	105	107	111	113	116
Others												
Albania												
Cyprus	103	103	99	100	85	79	75	65	71	64	68	66
Gibraltar												
Liechtenstein												
Malta												
Monaco												
Turkey												
Yugoslavia	91	93	97	100	102	105	107	109	115	116	121	123

Source: United Nations/OECD/Comecon

Database name: Industrial Resources and Output
Sector name: Industrial Output   Table No: 0703

Title: Indices of Manufacturing Production 1977-1988

Unit: 1980 = 100

	1977	1978	1979	1980	1981	1982	1983	1984	1985	1986	1987	1988
EC members												
Belgium	94	97	102	100	98	98	100	102	104	106	109	114
Denmark	93	96	100	100	100	102	106	117	122	131	127	129
France	95	96	100	100	98	97	97	97	98	98	100	105
West Germany	92	95	100	100	98	95	96	99	104	107	107	112
Greece	87	93	99	100	101	99	97	98	101	100	98	103
Ireland	88	96	102	100	106	105	114	125	131	134	150	169
Italy	87	88	94	100	98	95	92	95	96	99	103	108
Luxembourg	95	99	102	100	93	90	99	114	122	125	125	126
Netherlands	94	96	99	100	100	99	101	106	109	112	112	128
Portugal	82	88	93	100	101	105	106	105	117	122	128	136
Spain	98	100	100	100	98	96	99	99	101	105	111	114
United Kingdom	109	110	110	100	92	95	97	101	104	105	111	119
EFTA members												
Austria	88	91	97	100	98	97	99	104	109	110	109	115
Finland	79	83	92	100	103	104	107	112	116	118	123	128
Iceland												
Norway	101	99	102	100	99	99	98	104	106	108	110	109
Sweden	96	95	100	100	98	97	102	107	110	110	113	117
Switzerland	93	94	95	100	107	108	94	97	103	107	107	115
CMEA members												
Bulgaria												
Czechoslovakia	89	93	97	100	102	104	107	111	116	119	122	124
East Germany												
Hungary	95	99	102	100	103	106	107	110	110	112	117	117
Poland	96	99	101	100	86	84	89	94	97	102	105	111
Romania												
USSR	88	92	96	100	104	107	112	116	120	126	131	136
Others												
Albania												
Cyprus												
Gibraltar												
Liechtenstein												
Malta												
Monaco												
Turkey												
Yugoslavia	81	88	96	100	101	103	105	112	114	117	116	115

Source: United Nations/OECD/Comecon

Database name: Industrial Resources and Output
Sector name: Industrial Output   Table No: 0704

Title: Indices of Construction Output 1977-1988

Unit: 1980 = 100

	1977	1978	1979	1980	1981	1982	1983	1984	1985	1986	1987	1988	Notes
EC members													
Belgium	126	118	95	100	83	80	64	57	54	54	54	60	
Denmark				100	81	72	71	80	85	97	*		
France	103	99	98	100	100	95	89	84	83	87	92	98	
West Germany	95	94	102	100	93	88	90	91	84	89	89	92	
Greece													
Ireland													
Italy													
Luxembourg	91	92	99	100	98	95	91	81	74	80	86	92	
Netherlands	106	105	99	100	92	87	85	87	87	88			
Portugal													
Spain													
United Kingdom	100	105	106	100	90	92	98	83	100	114	118		
EFTA members													
Austria													
Finland													
Iceland													
Norway													
Sweden													
Switzerland													
CMEA members													
Bulgaria	81	90	96	100	104	107	111	111	107				a
Czechoslovakia	89	94	96	100	102	100	100	102	104				
East Germany	97	101	100	100	99	97	99	104	104				
Hungary	91	97	100	100	99	98	99	100	93				
Poland	104	106	101	100	82	84	88	92	90				
Romania	73	84	95	100	100	102	104	109	108				
USSR	97	99	99	100	102	104	109	112	115				
Others													
Albania													
Cyprus													
Gibraltar													
Liechtenstein													
Malta													
Monaco													
Turkey													
Yugoslavia													

Source: United Nations/OECD/Comecon
Notes: a   output of construction materials industry

Database name: Industrial Resources and Output
Sector name: Mineral Production

Table No: 0705

Title: Production of Selected Minerals 1988

Unit: 000 metric tonnes unless otherwise stated

	Iron Ore	Bauxite	Copper Ore	Lead Ore	Tin	Zinc	Silver (tonnes)	Gold (metric tonnes)
EC members								
Belgium					0.2			
Denmark				19.4				
France	9756	978	0.2	2.0		31.3	22.1	2.7
West Germany	69		0.7	17.9	0.2	75.6	20.0	0.1
Greece	1896	2533		25.9	0.2	21.2	61.3	
Ireland				32.5		176.5	5.5	
Italy		17		16.5		37.9	91.6	
Luxembourg								
Netherlands					4.0			
Portugal	23		8221.0		0.1		0.9	0.3
Spain	4300	3	18.1	74.9	0.1	266.0	530.0	a
United Kingdom	224		0.7	1.2	3.4	5.5	2.1	
EFTA members								
Austria	2300			3.3		19.1		
Finland	556		18.4	1.9		63.9	28.4	0.6
Iceland								
Norway	2644		15.9	2.8	0.1	34.4		
Sweden	20441		74.5	85.3		193.1	225.0	3.9
Switzerland								
CMEA members								
Bulgaria	1850		80.0	90.0		65.0	24.5	
Czechoslovakia	1773		10.0	2.8	0.6	7.0	35.0	
East Germany			10.0		2.8		40.0	
Hungary		2906						0.6
Poland	6		441.0	49.5		183.4	1063.0	
Romania	2400	500	26.0	32.8		37.0	21.5	2.0
USSR	250000	5900	990.0	520.0	15.0	960.0	1580.0	280.0
Others								
Albania			17.0					
Cyprus			0.1					
Gibraltar								
Liechtenstein								
Malta								
Monaco								
Turkey	5713	269	36.2	10.1		41.0	16.0	
Yugoslavia	5545	3034	103.5	103.3		71.2	140.0	4.6

Source: British Geological Survey: World Mineral Statistics 1984-1988

Title: Production of Selected Metals 1988

Unit: 000 metric tonnes

	Pig Iron	Crude Steel	Aluminium	Smelted Copper	Refined Copper	Refined Lead	Refined Tin	Slab Zinc
EC members								
Belgium	9147	11220		0.2	504.3	126.6	4.1	323.8
Denmark		649				0.4		
France	14784	19046	327.7		43.2	255.7		274.1
West Germany	31890	41022	752.9	162.5	596.2	345.1	1.1	352.4
Greece	160	959	126.8			15.1		
Ireland		271				11.7		
Italy	11385	23760	226.3		75.4	168.4		242.1
Luxembourg	2519	3661						
Netherlands	4994	5518	278.2			39.5	4.0	211.0
Portugal	444	811			5.4	7.0		5.5
Spain	4691	11640	293.9	115.0	158.8	110.8	1.3	245.4
United Kingdom	13055	18950	300.2		124.0	373.8	9.5	76.0
EFTA members								
Austria	3665	4650	95.5	36.1	38.4	25.0		26.3
Finland	2064	2664		95.7	53.9			149.8
Iceland			80.0					
Norway	367	840	864.2	31.7	31.7		0.7	121.2
Sweden	2492	4779	98.6	95.7	90.3	85.4		
Switzerland	70	988	71.8			1.5		
CMEA members								
Bulgaria	1437	2880		80.0	78.0	113.0		105.0
Czechoslovakia	9706	15319	31.4	34.8	27.1	26.0	0.8	
East Germany	2786	8131	61.0	25.0	80.0	55.0	3.5	21.0
Hungary	2093	3583	74.7	3.6	15.6			
Poland	10264	16873	47.7	358.0	400.6	90.7		173.6
Romania	9500	14500	250.0	26.0	33.0	44.0		50.0
USSR	115000	163000	2440.0	1120.0	1380.0	795.0	19.0	1035.0
Others								
Albania				16.5	16.0			
Cyprus								
Gibraltar								
Liechtenstein								
Malta								
Monaco								
Turkey	4461	8009	56.5	12.9	68.4	11.0		22.4
Yugoslavia	2916	4487	312.6	106.5	145.4	109.9		127.5

Source: British Geographical Survey: World Mineral Statistics 1984-1988

Database name: Industrial Resources and Output
Sector name: Metal Production

Table No: 0706

Title: Production of Selected Metals 1987

Unit: 000 metric tonnes

	Pig Iron	Crude Steel	Aluminium	Smelter Copper	Refined Copper	Refined Lead	Refined Tin	Slab Zinc	Notes
EEC members									
Belgium	8067	9792		108.0	476.4	108.0	3.9	308.6	e
Denmark		600						248.3	
France	12984	17724	322.8		49.2	165.6			
West Germany	28620	36252	738.0	207.7	422.4	357.6	1.0	588.0	a
Greece			132.0			16.7			a
Ireland									
Italy	12096	22740	261.6			126.4		249.6	
Luxembourg	2304	3300							
Netherlands	4572	5088	409.2				3.7	196.6	
Portugal	432	420			4.8	38.4			
Spain	4956	11760	355.2	138.7	154.8	124.8	1.5	208.3	d,f,g
United Kingdom	12204	17424	294.0		122.4	336.0	9.2	76.2	
EFTA members									
Austria	3432	4476	93.6	36.1	43.2	19.2		19.4	f,h
Finland	2064	2664		83.4	60.0			151.4	
Iceland			80.0						d
Norway	1128	840	758.4	29.8	30.0		0.6	90.4	a
Sweden	2304	4596	76.8	105.6	81.6	76.8			d,f
Switzerland		1010	80.6						c,d
CMEA members									
Bulgaria	1656	3048			75.9	120.6		90.0	f,g
Czechoslovakia	9888	15420	33.6	26.2	29.0	23.1	0.6		a,e,f,g
East Germany	2760	8244	65.7				3.3		a
Hungary	2112	3624	73.2	0.4	13.2				
Poland	10476	17148	47.9	400.1	391.2	90.0		176.6	d
Romania									
USSR	113640	161868	2392.8	1180.1	1421.8	801.0	18.0	1022.0	a,b,d,f,g
Others									
Albania									
Cyprus									
Gibraltar									
Liechtenstein									
Malta									
Monaco									
Turkey	3480	3816	62.0	19.5	75.6			25.2	b,d,f
Yugoslavia	2952	1872	280.8	139.0	140.4	112.8		116.8	b,c,f

Source: Statistisches Jahrbuch der Eisen- und Stahlindustrie/World Metal Bureau
Notes:
a   Refined tin: 1986
b   Pig iron: 1986
c   Steel: 1986
d   Aluminium: 1986
e   Smelter copper: 1986
f   Refined copper: 1986
g   Refined lead: 1986
h   Slab zinc: 1986
K   Workers not classifiable by occupation

Database name: Industrial Resources and Output
Sector name: Production of Soap and Detergent   Table No: 0707

Title: Production of Selected Soaps and Detergents 1988

Unit: Tonnes

	A	B	C	D	E	F	G	H	I	J	K	L	M	Notes
EC members														
Belgium	939	522	9378	100	117758	18033		1700	7968	65661	77722	39485	11642	
Denmark	2481	241	7100	900	70542	2385		3039		19912	32877	62596	47	
France	61190	7500	42600	23305	569056	60126	1939	4771	68372	133483	108265	165768	13067	
West Germany	62338	2930	74417	2792	707225	80253	1000	2838	150303	181740	283548	98931	37125	
Greece	4600	2300	8900	2600	70000	1900			1500	28000	12500	66500	3000	
Ireland														
Italy														
Luxembourg														a
Netherlands	10986			923	157752	1974		506	15590	38853	40301	19363	28286	
Portugal	9627	691	8361	42953	66650	1909		2926	4972	47188	4223	29137	3562	
Spain	12000	3300	38000	10250	532243	11548			39552	277861	225108	106827	20679	
United Kingdom	120500	4300	13300	33000	527400	40200		36000	90000	187000	186400	286000	57500	
EFTA members														
Austria	682	184	3181	450	71902	8327		678	12929	10385	17647	4936	6593	
Finland	679	342	2591		28778	7563		1370		7322	6806	11334	404	
Iceland														
Norway	3200	41		212	15386	1875				5823	5007	8406	1765	
Sweden	2511		10000		70442				69250				190	
Switzerland	4398			322	65742	14016	13904	6534	10507		21181	8209	6071	

CMEA members
Bulgaria
Czechoslovakia
East Germany
Hungary
Poland
Romania
USSR

Others
Albania
Cyprus
Gibraltar
Liechtenstein
Malta
Monaco
Turkey
Yugoslavia

Source: Association Internationale de la Savonnerie et de la Detergence
           A Toilet soap   G D/washing powders (hand)   M Liquid scourers
           B Shaving products   H Powdered surface cleaners
           C Shampoos   I Fabric washing liquids
           D Household soap   J Dishwashing liquids
           E Fabric washing powders   K Liquid fabric conditioners
           F D/washing powders (automatic) L Liquid surface cleaners

Notes: a Included with Belgium

Database name: Industrial Resources and Output
Sector name: Textile Production

Table No: 0708

Title: Production of Selected Textiles 1988

Unit: 000 metric tonnes

	Cotton Yarn	Woven Cotton Fabric	Wool Yarn	Woven Wool Fabric	Rayon and Acetate	Rayon & Acetate Fabrics	Notes
EC members							
Belgium	45.6	48.0	89.6	35.9	4.6	124.2	
Denmark							
France	192.0	135.6	86.6	65.8	15.2	19.2	
West Germany	194.4	182.4	49.0	33.0	178.8	65.8	g,h
Greece	142.8				7.2		
Ireland			5.0				
Italy	191.3	222.0			30.0		
Luxembourg							
Netherlands	8.4		4.9				i
Portugal	123.6	72.0	2.8	10.4	0.8	1.4	
Spain							
United Kingdom	43.2	218.4	146.5	90.1	102.2	15.4	a,b,c
EFTA members							
Austria	16.8	16.8	8.2	3.8		2.9	
Finland	3.6	4.8					
Iceland							
Norway	4.0	2.4	2.3	0.6			
Sweden	4.5	6.0	1.0			8.6	
Switzerland	48.3	25.4					
CMEA members							
Bulgaria	84.0	361.2	33.4	45.0		40.1	a,c,d
Czechoslovakia	147.6	651.6	1.3	58.9	56.0		a,b,g,h,j
East Germany	146.4	288.0	36.1	41.0	120.0	49.8	b,e,f,g,k
Hungary	62.4	294.0	8.3	15.6	4.2	29.6	b,f
Poland	204.0	781.2	83.9	100.9	74.3	51.5	a,c,d,h
Romania	168.0	684.0					e
USSR	1754.0	8113.2		708.5		1050.0	f
Others							
Albania							
Cyprus							
Gibraltar							
Liechtenstein							
Malta							
Monaco							
Turkey	50.4	492.0	49.8				a
Yugoslavia	134.4	358.8	48.6	104.4		51.2	b,e,f,i

Source: OECD/UN

Notes:
a Woven cotton fabric in million metres
b Woven wool fabric in million square metres
c Woven rayon/acetate fabric in million metres
d Woven wool fabric in million metres
e Woven cotton fabric in million square metres
f Woven rayon/acetate fabric in million square metres
g Woven wool fabric: 1987
h Woven rayon/acetate fabric: 1987
i Wool yard: 1987
j Woven cotton fabric: 1987
k Cotton yarn: 1987

TABLE 0701: INDUSTRIAL PRODUCTION INDEX
1980 ▪ 100

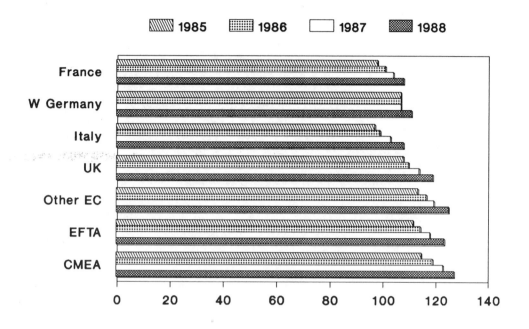

| | 1985 | 1986 | 1987 | 1988 |

TABLE 0706: EC STEEL PRODUCTION
By volume: 1988

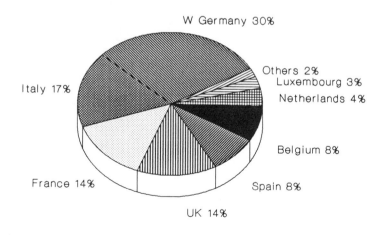

Database name: Energy Resources and Output put
Sector name: Energy Consumption

Table No: 0801

Title: Primary Energy Consumption: Selected Materials, 1989
Unit: Million tonnes of oil equivalent

	Solid Fuels	Crude Oil	Natural Gas	Hydro-Electricity	Nuclear Electricity	Total Primary Energy	Notes
EC members							a
Belgium	9.4	23.1	9.3	0.1	9.1	51.0	
Denmark	5.6	9.1	1.7			16.4	
France	18.7	88.4	24.4	10.0	59.9	201.4	
West Germany	73.2	107.4	44.9	3.7	33.1	262.3	
Greece	7.9	13.6	0.1	0.5		22.1	
Ireland	3.5	4.0	1.4	0.2		9.1	
Italy	14.3	94.3	37.0	9.4		155.0	
Luxembourg							
Netherlands	8.2	34.3	30.8		1.0	74.3	
Portugal	2.9	9.3		1.0		13.2	
Spain	19.2	46.6	4.5	3.8	12.5	86.6	
United Kingdom	61.4	81.2	44.9	1.4	15.0	203.9	
EFTA members							
Austria	3.1	10.4	4.6	8.5		26.6	
Finland	3.2	11.0	1.9	3.2	4.5	23.8	
Iceland	0.1	0.7		0.9		1.7	
Norway	0.5	8.9		23.4		32.8	
Sweden	2.3	15.4	0.4	19.8	17.5	55.4	
Switzerland	0.3	11.9	1.3	7.9	5.6	27.0	
CMEA members							b
Bulgaria	17.3	13.0	5.2				b
Czechoslovakia	44.1	12.8	9.2				b
East Germany	68.2	14.7	7.6				b
Hungary	8.4	8.6	9.5				b
Poland	103.8	13.0	9.8				b
Romania	19.6	14.3	39.0				
USSR	288.6	434.7	563.3	57.4	45.4	1389.4	
Others							b
Albania	1.0	1.2	0.4				b
Cyprus	0.1	1.1					
Gibraltar							
Liechtenstein							b
Malta	0.1	0.3					
Monaco							
Turkey	24.6	22.1	0.3	4.5		51.5	b
Yugoslavia	18.2	12.9	5.7				

Source: UN Energy Statistics Yearbook/OECD/National Accounts/BP
Notes: MTOE: the energy content of the fuel in question in terms of oil
Hydro-electricity production includes other sources
(wind generation, geo-thermal, etc)
a Includes Luxembourg
b Data for 1987

Title: Primary Energy Production: Hydrocarbons, 1989

Unit: Million tonnes of oil equivalent

	Solid Fuels	Crude Oil	Natural Gas
EC members			
Belgium	2.1		
Denmark		5.5	
France	8.2	3.6	2.6
West Germany	73.2	3.8	13.6
Greece	6.3		
Ireland			
Italy	0.2	4.5	15.3
Luxembourg			
Netherlands			52.9
Portugal			
Spain	17.9		
United Kingdom	60.8	91.9	37.9
EFTA members			
Austria	0.8	1.3	
Finland			
Iceland			
Norway		74.9	28.8
Sweden			
Switzerland			
CMEA members			
Bulgaria	15.4		
Czechoslovakia	41.0		
East Germany	65.3		
Hungary	5.7		
Poland	111.8		
Romania	12.2		
USSR	309.7	607.5	644.5
Others			
Albania			
Cyprus			
Gibraltar			
Liechtenstein			
Malta			
Monaco			
Turkey	22.7	2.6	
Yugoslavia	20.9		

Source: BP Statistical Review of World Energy 1989
Note: Luxembourg included under Belgium

Database name: Energy Resources and Output
Sector name: Energy Production

Table No: 0803

Title: Refinery Capacities, Latest Year

Unit: Million tonnes of oil per year

	Year	
EC members		
Belgium	1989	35.0
Denmark	1987	8.7
France	1989	84.4
West Germany	1989	77.9
Greece	1987	18.2
Ireland	1987	2.8
Italy	1989	114.4
Luxembourg		
Netherlands	1989	69.2
Portugal	1987	14.4
Spain	1989	70.5
United Kingdom	1989	89.6
EFTA members		
Austria	1987	9.7
Finland	1987	12.0
Iceland		
Norway	1987	12.1
Sweden	1987	20.6
Switzerland	1987	6.9
CMEA members		
Bulgaria	1987	15.0
Czechoslovakia	1987	22.7
East Germany	1987	26.6
Hungary	1987	11.0
Poland	1987	19.5
Romania	1987	30.9
USSR	1987	610.6
Others		
Albania	1987	3.7
Cyprus	1987	0.8
Gibraltar		
Liechtenstein		
Malta		
Monaco		
Turkey	1987	28.5
Yugoslavia	1987	15.0

Source: OECD/UN Energy Statistics/BP Statistical Review of World Energy
Notes: Luxembourg included under Belgium
Monaco included under France
Liechtenstein included under Switzerland

Database name: Energy Resources and Output
Sector name: Energy Consumption

Table No: 0804

Title: Consumption of Refined Products 1988

Unit: 000 tonnes

	Motor Gasoline	Diesel/ Gasoil	Aviation Fuels	Liquefied Gases	Lubricating Oils (c)	Notes
EC members						
Belgium	2936	8415	657	476	205	
Denmark	1582	4666	661	134	79	
France	17107	34830	3349	3415	873	
West Germany	26798	53313	4020	2424	1019	
Greece	2288	4347	1096	211	112	
Ireland	848	1411	246	130	46	
Italy	12477	27218	1875	2792	665	
Luxembourg	330	588	105	23	10	
Netherlands	3372	5305	1476	2472	147	
Portugal	1193	2313	478	668	103	
Spain	7197	12327	2283	3557	470	
United Kingdom	23277	17826	6201	3070	827	
EFTA members						
Austria	2552	2912	264	125	205	
Finland	1819	3832	348	167	117	
Iceland	124	293	78		7	
Norway	1779	3072	497	918	100	
Sweden	4455	5793	555	584	222	
Switzerland	3471	6381	1021	175	77	
CMEA members						
Bulgaria	1750	4000	220	73		a
Czechoslovakia	1500	1091	415	135		a
East Germany	4680	5765	13	220		a
Hungary	1290	3468	224	314		a
Poland	3534	6189	270	171		a
Romania	1700	4090	470	250		a
USSR	71950	78600	34750	8940		a
Others						
Albania	210	325	70		25	a
Cyprus	140	239	9	46	6	a
Gibraltar	8					a
Liechtenstein						b
Malta	40	40	5	15		a
Monaco						d
Turkey	2675	7038	381	1325	252	
Yugoslavia	1954	4113	369	417	490	a

Source: OECD Quarterly Oil and Gas Statistics/CMEA Handbook
Notes:
a 1987
b Included in Switzerland
c Except for France, West Germany, Netherlands, UK and Finland, data refer to domestic output.
d Included in France

Database name: **Energy Resources and Output**
Sector name: **Motor Gasoline** Table No: 0805

Title: Consumption of Motor Gasoline 1978-1989

Unit: 000 tonnes

	1978	1980	1981	1982	1983	1984	1985	1986	1987	1988	1989	Note
EC members												
Belgium	3148	2940	2623	2675	2605	2603	2576	2785	2890	2936	2817	
Denmark	1756	1523	1479	1413	1456	1507	1544	1550	1594	1582	1526	
France	17210	16321	17421	17765	18051	18090	16525	16591	16914	17107	16618	
West Germany	23035	22897	22087	24605	25462	25725	24236	25265	26051	26798	26705	
Greece	1360	1377	1447	1513	1569	1672	2055	2102	2222	2288	2363	
Ireland	943	1032	1041	997	969	907	874	867	833	848	881	
Italy	11213	13948	13996	12169	11283	10978	12104	12180	12309	12477	12946	
Luxembourg	247	286	311	312	297	293	308	308	327	330	379	
Netherlands	4325	3849	3687	3691	3614	4183	3635	4266	4125	3372	3413	
Portugal	794	752	778	838	821	802	855	939	1081	1193	1259	
Spain	5476	5758	5303	5569	5536	5579	6015	6264	6778	7197	7695	
United Kingdom	17436	18553	18174	18417	18658	19615	20409	21501	22210	23277.0		
EFTA members												
Austria	2322	2523	2395	2333	2544	2709	2425	2471	2517	2552	2610	
Finland	1392	1370	1460	1437	1550	1574	1527	1648	1740	1819	1950	
Iceland	91	89	92	97	91	98	98	120	118	124	108	
Norway	1402	1446	1423	1425	1495	1494	1687	1793	1762	1779	1783	
Sweden	3660	3516	3462	3487	3578	3718	3961	4189	4303	4455	4588	
Switzerland	2608	2751	2860	2889	3010	3086	3066	3204	3343	3471	3529	
CMEA members												
Bulgaria	1720	1850	1800	1800	1800	1800	1800	1800	1750			
Czechoslovakia	1710	1639	1785	1706	1763	1902	1900	1900	1500			
East Germany	2852	3109	3242	3156	2673	3438	3575	3644	4680			
Hungary	1376	1401	1351	1281	1211	1219	1240	1327	1290			
Poland	3553	3988	3868	2974	3019	2956	2909	3519	3534			
Romania	2303	1847	1590	2725	1729	1656	1405	1500	1700			
USSR	62090	65900	67500	68500	69000	71000	71080	71500	71950			
Others												
Albania	140	160	155	250	225	200	200	200	210			
Cyprus	100	100	99	101	111	118	124	130	140			
Gibraltar	3	4	4	4	4	4	5	4	8			
Liechtenstein												b
Malta	41	39	40	40	45	41	20	46	40			
Monaco												a
Turkey	2214	1862	1932	1819	1784	1770	1940	2171	2408	2675	2729	
Yugoslavia	2028	2176	2069	2426	2192	3300	2978	2190	1954			

Source: UN Energy Statistics Yearbook, OECD Quarterly oil statistics and energy balances
Notes:
a included in France
b included in Switzerland

Data for some East European countries are estimates based on
assumed refinery output and trade with Western Europe.

Database name: Energy Resources and Output
Sector name: Electrical Energy   Table No: 0806

Title: Electrical Energy: Supply, Production 1988

Unit: GWh

	Public Supply	Self-Producer Supply	Net Total Production	% Conventional Thermal	% Nuclear	% Hydro Electric/ Geo-Thermal/ Wind Power	Per capita Consumption Kwh per annum	Notes
EC members								
Belgium	62625	2723	61913	32.1	66.0	1.9	5592	
Denmark	27302	690	26176	98.7		1.3	5522	
France	346948	31336	359900	10.3	69.8	19.9	5447	a
West Germany	367314	63850	402754	60.9	34.1	5.0	6307	
Greece	32730	664	30618	91.6		8.4	2796	
Ireland	13008	220	12434	90.4		9.6	3058	
Italy	178622	24939	193176	76.2		23.8	3525	
Luxembourg	862	471	1289	37.5		62.5	11035	
Netherlands	58476	11135	67144	94.8	5.2		4757	
Portugal	21142	1347	21679	44.2		55.8	2032	
Spain	134129	4382	132348	36.5	36.5	27.0	2950	
United Kingdom	288543	19687	288031	78.3	19.3	2.4	2826	
EFTA members								
Austria	42436	6588	47594	24.4		75.6	5377	
Finland	53304	447	51291	10.6	36.0	53.6	11158	
Iceland	4202	5	4157	0.1		99.9	15200	a
Norway	86439	17844	109018	0.4		99.6	22143	b
Sweden	130767	7884	143066	4.4	46.4	49.2	15075	c, d
Switzerland	56090	4691	58964	1.7	36.5	61.8	6665	d
CMEA members								
Bulgaria	40682	4338	43240	59.2	34.8	6.0	4767	
Czechoslovakia	77091	10283	81299	67.9	26.7	5.4	4891	d
East Germany	110538	7790	106388	88.1	10.3	1.6	5782	
Hungary	28228	988	26642	52.0	47.4	0.6	3180	
Poland	135933	8407	134345	96.9		3.1	3205	
Romania	70150	3929	69060	84.9		15.1	3060	a
USSR	1625000	73400	1580293	72.9	12.7	14.4	4949	
Others								
Albania								
Cyprus	1647	22	1591	100.0			1987	d
Gibraltar								
Liechtenstein								
Malta	1030		946	100.0				
Monaco								
Turkey	44872	3177	45649	30.6		69.4	707	d
Yugoslavia			78452	59.7	5.0	35.3	2959	

Source: UN ECE Annual Bulletin of Electrical Energy Statistics for Europe
Notes:
a 1987
b Gross supply data 1987
c Gross supply data 1986
d Per capita consumption 1987

Database name: Energy Resources and Output (1986: below)
Sector name: Electrical Energy
Table No: 0806

Title: Electrical Energy: Supply, Production 1987

Unit: GWh

	Public Supply	Self-Producer Supply	Net Total Production	% Conventional Thermal	% Nuclear	Hydro Electric/ Geo-Thermal Wind Power	Per capita Consumption Kwh per annum	Notes
EEC members								
Belgium	60484	2883	59999	31.3	66.3	2.4	5376	
Denmark	38903	495	27528	99.2		0.8	5438	
France	346948	31336	359900	10.3	69.8	19.9	5447	
West Germany	355048	63214	392665	63.3	31.5	5.2	6220	
Greece	29737	535	27856	89.4		10.6	2599	
Ireland	12866	198	12236	91.0		9.0	3020	
Italy	167427	24903	182606	69.9	4.6	25.5	3192	a
Luxembourg	633	385	983	41.5		58.5	10605	
Netherlands	58692	8466	64589	93.9	6.1		4364	a
Portugal	19139	1216	19502	57.0		43.0	1853	a
Spain	129002	4166	126787	47.0	31.2	21.8	2884	
United Kingdom	282695	19759	282453	80.8	17.1	2.1	4716	
EFTA members								
Austria	44314	6204	49184	27.3		72.7	5220	
Finland	53042	423	50906	36.8	36.4	26.8	10824	
Iceland	4202	5	4157	0.1		99.9	15200	
Norway	82586	14698	103319	0.5		99.5	22228	b
Sweden	130767	7884	142776	4.6	45.1	50.3	15075	b
Switzerland	55455	4435	58161	1.8	37.3	60.9	6665	
CMEA members								
Bulgaria	39038	4426	43464	65.6	28.6	5.8	4841	d
Czechoslovakia	75512	10313	79722	67.9	25.9	6.1	4891	
East Germany	105947	8233	102366	88.1	10.2	1.7	5787	
Hungary	28754	995	27215	61.5	37.9	0.6	3181	
Poland	137412	8420	135804	97.0		3.0	3155	
Romania	67993	3602	66677	84.2		15.8	2883	c
USSR	1305686	112413	1664924	75.6	11.2	13.2	5008	b,d,e
Others								
Albania								
Cyprus	1501	11	1441	100.0			1987	
Gibraltar								
Liechtenstein								
Malta	944		870	100.0				
Monaco								
Turkey	41271	3082	41684	49.9		50.1	707	
Yugoslavia	63852	2719	75933	55.9	10.1	34.0	2885	b

Source: UN ECE Annual Bulletin of Electrical Energy Statistics for Europe
Notes:
a 1986
b Gross supply data 1986
c 1984
d All production data gross
e Per capita consumption 1985

Database name: Energy Resources and Output
Sector name: Electrical Energy

Title: Electrical Energy : Supply, Production 1986

Table No: 0806

Unit: GWh

	Public Supply	Self-Producer Supply	Net Total Production	% Conventional Thermal	% Nuclear	Hydro Electric/ Geo-Thermal	Per capita Consumption Kwh per annum	Note
EEC members								
Belgium	55828	2848	55505	30.3	67.2	2.5	5116	
Denmark	30286	434	28760	99.4		0.6	5249	
France	331685	30195	345800	11.7	69.8	18.5	5297	
West Germany	346597	61669	383419	65.7	29.5	4.8	6364	
Greece	27697	540	26127	87.2		12.8	2495	
Ireland	12466	186	11897	89.5		10.5	2910	
Italy	161868	23872	176254	69.7	3.8	26.5	3107	
Luxembourg	568	454	975	47.3		52.7	12051	a
Netherlands	55151	7627	64571	93.9	6.1		4596	
Portugal	19139	1216	19502	57.0		43.0	1838	b
Spain	124989	3697	122352	48.7	29.3	22.0	2795	
United Kingdom	282272	18816	281492	79.2	18.4	2.4	5049	
EFTA members								
Austria	39073	5580	43194	29.1		70.9	5038	
Finland	48829	376	46915	35.5	38.4	26.1	10182	
Iceland	4029	15	3852	0.1		99.9	14675	a
Norway	87311	15981	102350	0.3		99.7	22158	a
Sweden	128749	8391	133183	5.0	41.9	53.1	14140	a
Switzerland	53351	4293	55880	1.8	38.1	60.1	6515	
CMEA members								
Bulgaria	37442	4414	41856	65.6	28.8	5.6	5090	
Czechoslovakia	74443	10331	78717	73.9	21.1	5.0	4733	
East Germany	106926	8365	103519	88.5	9.8	1.7	5687	
Hungary	27039	1005	25704	72.1	27.2	0.6	2983	
Poland	131588	8706	130541	97.1		2.9	3035	
Romania	67993	3602	66677	84.2		15.8	2883	b
USSR	1305686	112413	1598890	76.4	10.0	13.5	5009	
Others								
Albania								
Cyprus	1423		1355	100.0			2022	
Gibraltar								
Liechtenstein								
Malta	850		796	100.0				
Monaco								
Turkey	36921	2771	37189	65.1		34.9	667	
Yugoslavia	63852	2719	73590	57.7	5.2	37.1	2805	

Source: UN ECE Annual Bulletin of Electrical Energy Statistics for Europe

Notes:
a 1985
b 1984
c 1983

Database name: Energy Resources and Output
Sector name: Electrical Energy

Table No: 0807

Title: Electricity: Supplies to Households 1977-1988

Unit: 000 GWh

	1977	1978	1979	1980	1981	1982	1983	1984	1985	1986	1987	1988	Notes
EC members													
Belgium	14.8			13.8	14.1	14.4	14.9	15.3	16.2	16.6	17.6	16.8	
Denmark	6.9	7.4	7.7	7.4	7.4	7.4	7.4	7.8	8.4	8.7	9.2	8.9	
France		53.3	58.0	60.2	64.3	67.1	74.0	79.9	83.7	89.6	94.7		
West Germany		80.7	83.2		86.8	88.0	90.2	94.1	97.1	97.6	100.7	97.7	
Greece	4.2	4.8	8.6	9.2	9.7	10.1	6.8	7.2	7.7	7.8	8.5	8.8	c
Ireland	3.0	3.3	3.7	3.6	3.6	3.6	3.7	3.8	4.0	4.1	4.2	4.2	a
Italy	31.9	34.4	36.4	37.8	38.9	41.1	41.0	43.4	44.5	45.7	48.1	49.3	
Luxembourg	0.6	0.6	1.0	1.0	1.1	1.1	1.2	1.2	1.3	1.3	0.6		a
Netherlands	13.6	14.1	15.0	15.6	15.4	15.7	15.3	15.9	16.6	16.2	16.6	15.5	
Portugal	2.6	2.8	3.0	3.3	3.5	3.5	4.2	4.3	4.5	4.7	4.9	5.1	
Spain	14.4	16.0	17.7	19.6	20.4	20.3	21.8	23.5	23.3	24.9	26.6	27.5	
United Kingdom	85.9	85.8	89.7	86.1	84.4	82.8	83.0	83.9	88.2	91.7	93.3		
EFTA members													
Austria	7.7	8.2		8.8	8.9	9.1	9.4	9.7	10.2	10.4	10.8		
Finland	6.4	6.9	7.9	8.2	8.7	9.1	9.4	10.4	12.2	12.5	13.8	14.2	
Iceland	0.5	0.6	0.7	0.6	0.7	0.7	0.8	0.8	0.7	0.8			a
Norway	21.3	21.9	23.5	23.6	25.1	25.1	25.8	28.2	28.9	30.2	30.2	29.9	
Sweden	20.0	21.1	22.7	22.8	23.9	26.2	27.6	30.2	34.6	35.1			
Switzerland	8.2	8.6	9.4	9.7	9.8	9.6	10.1	10.9	11.8	12.1	12.5	12.7	
CMEA members													
Bulgaria	5.5	5.8	6.5	6.8									
Czechoslovakia	7.4	8.1	8.2	8.6	8.8	9.0	9.7	10.3	11.0	11.5	11.9	12.2	
East Germany	10.1	10.9	11.3	12.0	12.2	12.6	13.2	14.5	15.3	16.2	17.5	17.4	
Hungary	4.0	4.6	5.0	5.0	5.4	5.9	6.4	7.0	7.4	7.5	8.1	8.2	
Poland	8.5	9.2	9.9	10.7	12.2	12.6	11.9	14.1	16.2	16.9	18.5	19.3	
Romania	4.8		5.4	4.9	5.1	5.1	5.0	4.8		5.0	4.8		
USSR							199.7	208.0	219.0	231.0	240.0		b
Others													
Albania													
Cyprus	0.2	0.2	0.2	0.2	0.2	0.2	0.2	0.2	0.3	0.3	0.3	0.4	
Gibraltar													
Liechtenstein													
Malta													
Monaco													
Turkey	2.6	2.8	2.8	3.0	3.2	3.5	4.1	4.6	5.0	5.2	5.9	7.2	
Yugoslavia	12.1	13.1	14.2	15.6	16.1	17.2		17.2	17.8	18.6	20.3	21.1	

Source: UN ECE Annual Bulletin of Electrical Energy Statistics for Europe
Notes:
a   Includes power supplied to agriculture, forestry and fishing industries
b   Includes commercial, agricultural etc, and public use
c   Change in methodology between 1979 and 1982

Database name: Energy Resources and Output
Sector name: Solid Fuel

Table No: 0808

Title: Solid Fuels: Production, Gross Consumption, Conversions 1987/8

Unit: 000 tonnes

	Production	Gross Consumption	Converted by Energy Producers	Notes
EC members				
Belgium	8045	653	460	
Denmark		9956	8900	
France	22036	37876	26211	b
West Germany	212638	215539	190645	
Greece	48454	51132	48353	
Ireland	42	3293	1754	
Italy	8298	28647	22793	b
Luxembourg		1615	460	
Netherlands	2920	15495	12783	
Portugal	515	3537	2301	a,b
Spain	34975	41058	35016	
United Kingdom	110737	121160	99309	
EFTA members				
Austria	3865	7553	4896	
Finland	470	7213	5200	
Iceland		86		
Norway	400	1595	290	a
Sweden	937	5202	3452	
Switzerland		594	16	b
CMEA members				
Bulgaria	36708	43309	33401	b
Czechoslovakia	135326	137091	78772	b
East Germany	404615	59232	22018	
Hungary	23823	28676	20262	
Poland	285446	248832	196372	
Romania	49350			
USSR	864853			c
Others				
Albania				
Cyprus		90700		
Gibraltar				
Liechtenstein				
Malta				
Monaco				
Turkey	42608	45130	24052	
Yugoslavia	74101	78193	73646	

Source: United Nations Annual Bulletin of Coal Statistics for Europe 1987   1988
Notes:
a Consumption figures: 1986 1987
b Conversion figures: 1987
c Production figure: 1985

Database name: Energy Resources and Output
Sector name: Solid Fuels

Table No: 0809

Title: Solid Fuels: Household Consumption 1977-1988

Unit: Million tonnes

	1977	1980	1981	1982	1983	1984	1985	1986	1987	1988	Notes
EC members											
Belgium	1.7	1.5	1.4	1.5	1.4	1.4	1.7	1.6	0.2	0.1	a
Denmark	0.1	0.0	0.0	0.1	0.1	0.1	0.1	0.1	0.5		
France	5.8	5.0	4.4	4.1	4.2	4.1	4.2	4.0	3.3	2.9	
West Germany	8.0	7.7					5.0	4.5	3.9	2.9	
Greece	0.1	0.1	0.1	0.1	0.1	0.1	0.1	0.1	0.1	0.1	
Ireland	0.7	1.0					1.2	1.3	1.2	1.1	b
Italy		0.6			0.2	0.3	0.3	0.2	0.2	0.5	
Luxembourg	0.0	0.0	0.1	0.1	0.1	0.0	0.0	0.0	0.0	0.0	
Netherlands	0.1	0.1	0.1	0.1	0.1	0.1	0.1	0.1	0.1	0.1	
Portugal		0.0	0.0	0.0	0.0						
Spain	0.5	0.4	0.6	0.8	0.6	0.7	0.7	0.6	0.4	0.5	
United Kingdom	14.8	11.7	10.9	10.8	10.1	8.0	10.7	10.5	9.2	8.6	
EFTA members											
Austria	1.4	1.8	1.4	1.5	1.3	1.9	1.6	1.5	1.5	1.4	b
Finland	0.1	0.1	0.1	0.1	0.1	0.1	0.0	0.0	0.0		
Iceland											
Norway	0.1	0.0	0.1	0.0	0.0	0.0	0.0	0.0	0.0	0.0	
Sweden								0.0			
Switzerland	0.2	0.1	0.1	0.1	0.1	0.1	0.1	0.1	0.1	0.1	
CMEA members											
Bulgaria	1.0	1.4	1.4	1.4	1.4	1.2			2.4		
Czechoslovakia	10.3	11.0	10.4								
East Germany	14.3	17.0	17.0	17.1	15.4	16.0	18.2	18.3	19.1	17.1	
Hungary	4.5	5.1	5.1	4.4	5.2	5.4	6.5	5.8	5.9	5.8	
Poland	34.4								35.6	27.7	
Romania											
USSR											
Others											
Albania											
Cyprus											
Gibraltar											
Liechtenstein											
Malta											
Monaco											
Turkey	3.1	5.5			6.2	6.0	7.4	10.4	11.4	11.4	
Yugoslavia	6.1							7.3	6.8		b

Source: UN ECE Annual Bulletin of Coal Statistics for Europe
Notes: a New series from 1987
         b Includes commercial, retailing, catering, agricultural and public sectors

Entries of 0.0 signify consumption of less than 50,000 tonnes

	Production	Gross Consumption	Gas Used in Electricity Production	Notes
EC members				
Belgium	137592	437923	59416	
Denmark	108387	72427	4005	a
France	437476	1335529	42659	
West Germany	1026264	2406369	198195	
Greece	35128	29351	2773	
Ireland	59150	64434	22451	a
Italy	885768	1802025	316716	
Luxembourg	15350	32796	5254	
Netherlands	2262412	1508458	424396	
Portugal	33039	52487	574	
Spain	225792	372921	18269	
United Kingdom	1983306	2339853	38336	
EFTA members				
Austria	121334	266577	50274	
Finland	31027	94321	21254	
Iceland				
Norway	1162909	154617		
Sweden	29943	61520	7840	
Switzerland	12332	71217	1872	
CMEA members				
Bulgaria	19119	209990	23363	b
Czechoslovakia	246553	597978		
East Germany	287755	516744	129811	
Hungary	250002	423860	79010	
Poland	368561	618183	7127	
Romania	1509996			
USSR	26753332	23099254	7967403	b
Others				
Albania				
Cyprus	2334	3258		
Gibraltar				
Liechtenstein				
Malta	0	728	0	a
Monaco				
Turkey	105216	146412	36864	a
Yugoslavia	172658	323062	24585	

Database name: Energy Resources and Output
Sector name: Gas

Table No: 0810

Title: Gas: Production, Gross Consumption 1988

Unit: TJ (Terajoules, Gross Calorific Value)

Source: United Nations Annual Bulletin of Gas Statistics for Europe 1990/BP
Production includes natural gas, gaswork output, LPG, other petroleum gases and coke-oven/blast furnace gases

Notes: a 1987
b 1986

				Gas Supplies to Households 1977-1988						
Database name: Energy Resources and Output
Sector name: Gas

Table No: 0811

Title: Gas Supplies to Households 1977-1988

Unit: 000 terajoules

	1977	1980	1981	1982	1983	1984	1985	1986	1987	198
EC members										
Belgium	105.7	132.4	129.9	122.1	122.9	123.4	133.8	117.1	117.6	108.
Denmark		5.5		6.0	5.8		17.0	30.5	34.2	
France	291.4	430.8	443.6	440.0	463.1	490.8	517.8	494.8	482.6	448.
West Germany	341.1	472.7	498.8	489.2	530.4	593.2	638.4	582.4	642.4	574.
Greece	5.9	7.3	6.4	5.3	5.7	5.1	5.1	4.5	4.5	4.
Ireland					5.9	5.6	5.7	6.2	6.4	
Italy	398.1	461.5	471.4	500.8	506.6	543.1	594.1	574.5	607.2	636.
Luxembourg	4.1	5.6	6.1	6.2	6.5	6.8	7.5	6.4	7.7	
Netherlands	463.2	536.9	496.8	454.2	445.1	427.3	474.0	402.3	391.6	334.
Portugal	4.2	3.9	6.1	5.4	8.1	12.0	17.5	17.4	18.0	19.
Spain	93.2	107.8	101.1	102.3	96.1	106.2	109.8	101.1	103.6	107.
United Kingdom	701.6	901.8	936.0	931.3	945.8	957.9	1038.1	1017.2	1031.2	1009.
EFTA members										
Austria	40.7	53.2	48.8	43.0	42.7	46.5	55.8	49.8	50.3	51.
Finland	1.8	1.5	1.6	1.4	1.4	1.6	1.5	1.2	1.6	2.
Iceland										
Norway		0.5	0.5	0.2	0.2	0.1	0.1	0.1	0.1	0.
Sweden		2.4		2.5	2.0	1.9	3.0	3.6		
Switzerland		16.1	18.1	16.1	17.6	19.2	21.9	19.2	21.1	22.
CMEA members										
Bulgaria							3.3	4.0		
Czechoslovakia	42.3	54.2		53.0		59.0	63.8	65.5	71.4	70.
East Germany	32.2	38.8	39.1	40.5	40.4	43.9	46.4	46.2	49.6	45.
Hungary	31.0	38.5	38.8	42.4	42.4	48.5	54.8	60.3	69.5	69
Poland		75.6	79.2	91.5	84.6	85.6	105.9	112.0	124.9	131.
Romania										
USSR	644.3	1674.0								1316
Others										
Albania										
Cyprus	1.5	1.7	1.7	1.9	2.0	2.0	2.1	2.0	2.1	2
Gibraltar										
Liechtenstein										
Malta	1.0	0.5		0.6	0.7	0.7			0.7	
Monaco										
Turkey	31.1	27.7		40.7	45.7	46.7	48.4	51.6	53.6	62
Yugoslavia	16.7	16.3	17.3	18.0	16.7	17.7				

Source: UN ECE Annual Bulletin of Gas Statistics for Europe 1990

Database name: Energy Resources and Output
Sector name: Nuclear Energy   Table No: 0812

Title: Nuclear Energy Capacity 1986/2000

Unit: As stated

	Nuclear Stations (MW, end 1986)	Installed capacity (MW, net):	
		1986	2000 forecast
EC members			
Belgium	8	5480	6900
Denmark			
France	49	44968	65800
West Germany	21	18927	22600
Greece			
Ireland			
Italy	3	1300	4800
Luxembourg			
Netherlands	2	516	500
Portugal			
Spain	8	5577	9400
United Kingdom	38	11824	11300
EFTA members			
Austria			
Finland	4	2310	2310
Iceland			
Norway			
Sweden	12	9681	9681
Switzerland	5	2951	2600
CMEA members			
Bulgaria	4	1632	6400
Czechoslovakia	7	2756	8400
East Germany	5	1702	6900
Hungary	3	1224	3500
Poland			
Romania			
USSR	54	31976	127000
Others			
Albania			
Cyprus			
Gibraltar			
Liechtenstein			
Malta			
Monaco			
Turkey			
Yugoslavia	1	632	1600

Source: Comité Professional du Pétrole

Database name: Energy Resources and Output
Sector name: Nuclear Energy

Table No: 0813

Title: Nuclear Energy Consumption 1983-1989

Unit: Million tonnes of oil equivalent (MTOE)

	1983	1984	1985	1986	1987	1988	1989	Notes
EC members								
Belgium	5.3	6.4	7.9	9.1	9.7	9.9	9.1	a
Denmark								
France	30.1	38.5	45.1	31.9	53.8	54.7	59.9	
West Germany	14.9	21.3	28.8	26.6	29.0	32.4	33.1	
Greece								
Ireland								
Italy	2.1	1.7	1.8	2.2				
Luxembourg								
Netherlands	0.9	0.9	1.0	1.2	0.8	0.9	1.0	
Portugal								
Spain	2.5	5.2	6.3	8.4	9.1	11.3	12.5	
United Kingdom	10.7	11.5	13.0	12.6	11.7	13.5	15.0	
EFTA members								
Austria								
Finland	4.2	4.4	4.5	4.5	4.6	4.6	4.5	
Iceland								
Norway								
Sweden	10.7	12.7	14.5	16.8	16.2	18.5	17.5	
Switzerland	3.8	4.5	3.5	3.5	5.6	5.5	5.6	
CMEA members								
Bulgaria								
Czechoslovakia								
East Germany								
Hungary								
Poland								
Romania								
USSR	23.4	30.2	35.5	34.2	39.7	42.5	45.4	
Others								
Albania								
Cyprus								
Gibraltar								
Liechtenstein								
Malta								
Monaco								
Turkey					1.7			
Yugoslavia								

Source: BP Statistical Review of World Energy 1990
Notes: MTOE: the amount of oil required to fuel an oil fired plant in order to generate the same amount of electricity
a Belgium and Luxembourg combined

TABLE 0805: GASOLINE CONSUMPTION
1988

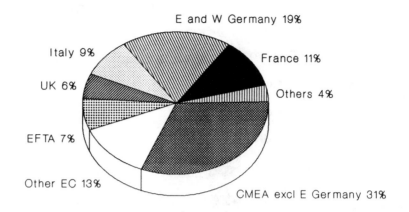

E and W Germany 19%
Italy 9%
France 11%
UK 6%
Others 4%
EFTA 7%
Other EC 13%
CMEA excl E Germany 31%

TABLE 0806: ELECTRICITY
Total Generation 1988

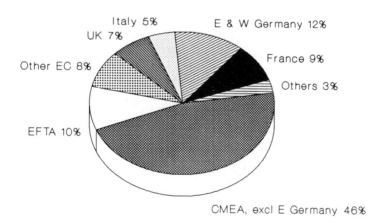

Italy 5%
UK 7%
E & W Germany 12%
Other EC 8%
France 9%
Others 3%
EFTA 10%
CMEA, excl E Germany 46%

TABLE 0812: NUCLEAR CAPACITY FORECASTS
Installed capacity (megawatts)

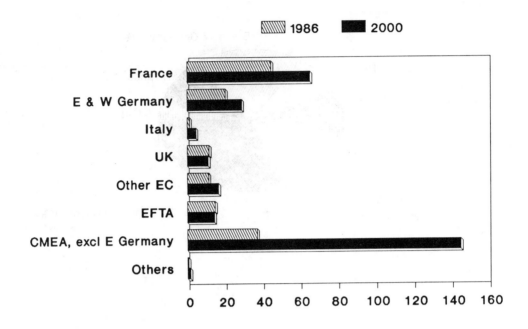

**09
DEFENCE**

Database name: Defence
Sector name: Defence Spending and Personnel   Table No: 0901

Title: Defence Expenditure 1988 and Personnel 1989

Unit: $ US millions/persons

	Defence Spending	% of GDP	Regular Forces	Reserve Forces	Army Personnel	Naval Personnel	Air Force Personnel	Conscripts as % of Regular Forces	Note
EC members									
Belgium	2800	1.8	92400	145000	67800	4700	19900	41	
Denmark	2010	1.9	31600	74700	17000	7700	6900	29	
France	30700	3.2	451600	356000	292000	65500	94100	51	
West Germany	29170	2.4	482700	850000	340700	36000	106000	45	
Greece	2490	4.8	208500	404000	160000	20500	28000	69	
Ireland	386	1.2	13000	16300	11200	1000	800	0	
Italy	16130	2.0	390000	769000	265000	52000	73000	70	
Luxembourg	74	1.2	800	0	800	0	0	0	
Netherlands	7050	3.1	98800	170300	63700	16900	18200	48	
Portugal	1270	3.4	75300	190000	44000	16100	15200	63	
Spain	6540	1.9	285000	1030000	210000	39000	36000	74	
United Kingdom	33760	5.5	311600	319800	155500	64650	91450	0	
EFTA members									
Austria	1430	1.1	42500	242000	38000		4500	48	
Finland	1520	1.5	31000	700000	27800	1400	1800	76	
Iceland									a
Norway	2934	3.2	33400	200000	19000	5300	9100	64	
Sweden	4780	2.7	64500	609000	44500	12000	8000	76	
Switzerland	3260	1.8	3500	601000	3500			91	b
CMEA members									
Bulgaria	2465	3.6	182000	216500	81900	8800	26800	77	
Czechoslovakia	5360	3.7	199700	280000	148600	0	51100	59	
East Germany	12750	6.8	173100	390000	120000	16000	37100	53	
Hungary	932	3.8	91000	127000	68000	0	23000	53	
Poland	1270	2.0	347000	491000	217000	25000	105000	56	
Romania	812	1.2	171000	556000	128000	9000	34000	60	
USSR	120000	4.8	2481000	6217000	1596000	437000	448000	63	
Others									
Albania	196	4.7	38000	155000	31500	2000	4500	55	
Cyprus	121	2.9	13000	60000	13000			100	
Gibraltar									
Liechtenstein									
Malta	22	1.2		0				0	
Monaco									
Turkey	2040	3.4	650400	951000	528000	55000	67400	94	
Yugoslavia	2080	2.7	180000	440000	138000	10000	32000	56	

Source: International Institute for Strategic Studies

Notes: a Iceland has no armed forces
               b Army includes Air Corps
               c Army consists of National Guard

Database name: Defence
Sector name: Defence Equipment   Table No: 0902

Title: Defence Equipment 1989

Unit: Numbers

	Combat Aircraft	Tanks	Submarines	Aircraft Carriers	Other Combat Vessels	Notes
EC members						
Belgium	126	467	0	0	4	
Denmark	89	262	3	0	59	
France	535	1570	21	2	42	
West Germany	507	5005	24	0	14	
Greece	330	1941	10	0	21	
Ireland	14	14	0	0	7	
Italy	337	1720	10	1	29	
Luxembourg	0	0	0	0	0	
Netherlands	189	913	6	0	15	
Portugal	99	86	3	0	35	
Spain	217	838	8	1	77	
United Kingdom	570	1561	31	2	93	
EFTA members						
Austria	24	56	0	0	0	
Finland	75	100	0	0	21	
Iceland						
Norway	83	150	12	0	43	
Sweden	417	540	11	0	45	
Switzerland	272	820	0	0	0	
CMEA members						
Bulgaria	258	2200	4	0	24	
Czechoslovakia	377	4585	0	0	0	
East Germany	335	3140	0	0	57	
Hungary	101	1435	0	0	0	
Poland	565	3300	4	0	27	
Romania	295	3200	1	0	88	
USSR	4595	53350	368	4	660	
Others						
Albania	95	190	2	0	40	
Cyprus	1	24	0	0	0	
Gibraltar						
Liechtenstein						
Malta	0	0	0	0	0	
Monaco						
Turkey	366	3727	15	0	70	
Yugoslavia	421	1635	5	0	75	

Source: International Institute for Strategic Studies

Database name: Defence
Sector name: Defence Equipment   Table No: 0902

Title: Defence Equipment 1988

Unit: Numbers

	Combat Aircraft	Tanks	Submarines	Aircraft Carriers	Other Combat Vessels	Notes
EEC members						
Belgium	122	467	0	0	4	
Denmark	95	262	4	0	52	
France	580	1570	24	2	41	
West Germany	459	4937	24	0	16	
Greece	329	2160	10	0	21	
Ireland	14	14	0	0	5	
Italy	399	1720	10	1	29	
Luxembourg	0	0	0	0	0	
Netherlands	227	913	5	0	16	
Portugal	89	66	3	0	35	
Spain	209	965	8	2	21	
United Kingdom	553	1517	32	3	47	
EFTA members						
Austria	23	50	0	0	0	
Finland	74	115	0	0	23	
Iceland						
Norway	88	150	12	0	45	
Sweden	446	985	14	0	51	
Switzerland	272	850	0	0	0	
CMEA members						
Bulgaria	255	4250	4	0	28	
Czechoslovakia	450	3400	0	0	0	
East Germany	330	2850	0	0	56	
Hungary	135	1400	0	0	0	
Poland	625	4050	4	0	26	
Romania	350	1860	1	0	110	
USSR	4400	54500	372	4	674	
Others						
Albania	95	190	2	0	40	
Cyprus	0	24	0	0	0	
Gibraltar						
Liechtenstein						
Malta	0	0	0	0	0	
Monaco						
Turkey	409	3600	17	0	65	
Yugoslavia	431	1583	5	0	74	

Source: International Institute for Strategic Studies

TABLE 0901: DEFENCE EXPENDITURE
In US dollars 1988

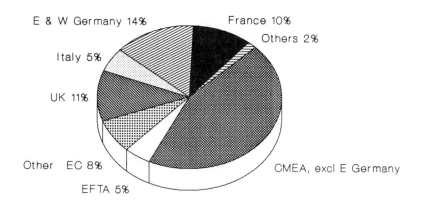

E & W Germany 14%

France 10%

Others 2%

Italy 5%

UK 11%

CMEA, excl E Germany

Other EC 8%

EFTA 5%

TABLE 0901: REGULAR TROOPS
Manpower 1989

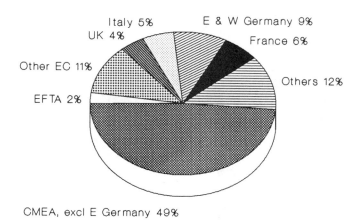

Italy 5%

E & W Germany 9%

UK 4%

France 6%

Other EC 11%

Others 12%

EFTA 2%

CMEA, excl E Germany 49%

10
ENVIRONMENTAL DATA

Database name: Environmental Data
Sector name: Air Pollution

Table No: 1001

Title: Total Emissions of Air Pollutants: Latest Year

Unit: 000 tonnes

	Year	SOx	NOx	CO	HC	Particulate Matter	Notes
EC members							
Belgium	1983	610	271		339		a
Denmark	1987	248	266				
France	1987	1517	1652	6198	1972	373	a
West Germany	1986	2223	2969	8926	2426	562	
Greece	1980	546			130		
Ireland	1985	138	68	456	64	117	
Italy	1986	2075	1570	5571	767	413	b
Luxembourg	1985	13	22		11		a
Netherlands	1986	274	560	1229	470	153	
Portugal	1985	286	303	267	61	93	c
Spain	1980	543	937	3780	843		d
United Kingdom	1987	3867	2303	5264	2355	230	
EFTA members							
Austria	1986	145	206	1084	250	51	e
Finland	1987	323	260		155		f
Iceland							
Norway	1987	93	232	649	183	25	g
Sweden	1982	220	300	1754	446	170	
Switzerland	1984	95	214	621	339	22	h
CMEA members							
Bulgaria							
Czechoslovakia							
East Germany							
Hungary							
Poland							
Romania							
USSR							
Others							
Albania							
Cyprus							
Gibraltar							
Liechtenstein							
Malta							
Monaco							
Turkey							
Yugoslavia	1984	1450					

Source: OECD
Notes: SOx Oxides of sulphur (SO2 equivalent weight)
           NOx Oxides of nitrogen (NO2 equivalent weight)
           CO Carbon monoxide
           HC Hydrocarbons (excluding methane)

a HC 1980
b Excluding industrial processes
c CO and particulates 1983
d Excluding CO emissions from power stations
e HC 1985
f SOx 1986, HC 1985
g Particulates exclude industrial processes
h HC 1985, particulates 1980

	Year	pH Value	SO4 (mg/l)	NO3 (mg/l)	Notes
EC members					
Belgium	1987	2.84	3.12	2.25	
Denmark	1985	4.50	1.98	1.75	
France	1987	4.54	4.59	4.47	
West Germany	1987	4.50	6.30		a
Greece					
Ireland	1982	5.14	0.95		
Italy					
Luxembourg					
Netherlands	1986	4.90	12.00	5.80	a
Portugal	1985	6.02	2.91	1.33	
Spain					
United Kingdom	1987	5.10	0.91	0.50	b
EFTA members					
Austria	1982	4.44	5.04	2.26	
Finland	1987	4.54	3.30	2.04	
Iceland	1982	5.34	0.86		
Norway	1987	4.38	2.22	1.90	
Sweden	1987	4.10	3.90	2.52	
Switzerland					
CMEA members					
Bulgaria					
Czechoslovakia					
East Germany					
Hungary					
Poland					
Romania					
USSR					
Others					
Albania					
Cyprus					
Gibraltar					
Liechtenstein					
Malta					
Monaco					
Turkey					
Yugoslavia	1985	5.33	4.45	1.77	

Source: OECD
Notes: SOx Oxides of sulphur (SO2 equivalent weight)   a HC 1980
               NOx Oxides of nitrogen (NO2 equivalent weight)   b Excluding industrial processes
               CO Carbon monoxide   c CO and particulates 1983
               HC Hydrocarbons (excluding methane)   d Excluding CO emissions from power stat
                                                                     e HC 1985
                                                                     f SOx 1986, HC 1985
                                                                     g Particulates exclude industrial proces
                                                                     h HC 1985, particulates 1980

	Fresh Water	Sea Water	Notes
EC members			
Belgium	75.5	44.4	
Denmark	86.0	79.2	
France	75.6	83.3	
West Germany	80.0		a
Greece		77.7	
Ireland		100.0	
Italy	60.7	84.1	b
Luxembourg	85.0		
Netherlands	80.5		a
Portugal		28.0	c
Spain	81.1		a
United Kingdom		59.0	
EFTA members			
Austria			
Finland		100.0	d
Iceland			
Norway		0.0	c
Sweden			
Switzerland			
CMEA members			
Bulgaria			
Czechoslovakia			
East Germany			
Hungary			
Poland			
Romania			
USSR			
Others			
Albania			
Cyprus			
Gibraltar			
Liechtenstein			
Malta			
Monaco			
Turkey			
Yugoslavia		82.0	c

Source: European Commission/OECD
Notes: Data represent percentage of sampling points conforming to EC Directive 76/160/EEC
          (or equivalent)
          a Fresh and sea water combined
          b Fresh water refers to lakes only
          c 1980 figures
          d 1985 figures

Database name: Environmental Data
Sector name: Waste

Title: Municipal Waste 1980/1985

Unit: 000 tonnes and kg per capita

Table No: 1004

	Amount of Waste(a)		Amount per Capita		Increase per	
	1980	1985	1980	1985	Capita %	Notes
EC members						
Belgium	3082		313			
Denmark	2046	2161	399	423	6.02	
France	14000	15000	260	272	4.62	
West Germany	21417	19387	348	318	-8.62	b
Greece	2500		259			
Ireland	640	1100	188	311	65.43	b
Italy	14041	15000	252	263	4.37	
Luxembourg	128	131	351	357	1.71	
Netherlands	6565	6510	464	449	-3.23	c
Portugal	1984	2246	213	221	3.76	
Spain	8028	10600	215	275	27.91	d
United Kingdom	15816	17737	319	355	11.29	e
EFTA members						
Austria	1673	1727	222	228	2.70	f
Finland		2000		408		
Iceland						
Norway	1700	1970	416	474	13.94	
Sweden	2510	2650	302	317	4.97	
Switzerland	2240	2500	351	383	9.12	
CMEA members						
Bulgaria						
Czechoslovakia						
East Germany						
Hungary						
Poland						
Romania						
USSR						
Others						
Albania						
Cyprus						
Gibraltar						
Liechtenstein						
Malta						
Monaco						
Turkey						
Yugoslavia						

Source: OECD

Notes:
a Household, commercial etc waste collected by municipal agency
b Data for 1980 and 1984
c Data for 1981 and 1985; figures are not fully comparable due to differences in investigation methods
d Data for 1978 and 1985
e Data for 1980 and 1987; England and Wales only
f Data for 1979 and 1983; household waste only

Database name: Environmental Data
Sector name: Waste

Title: Paper and Cardboard Waste Recycling 1980-1985

Unit: %

Table No: 1005

	1980	1985	Notes
EC members			
Belgium	14.7		
Denmark	26.2	31.0	
France		33.0	
West Germany	33.9	41.2	
Greece			
Ireland	15.0		
Italy			
Luxembourg			
Netherlands	45.5	50.3	a
Portugal	38.0		
Spain	38.1	4.1	
United Kingdom	29.0	27.0	
EFTA members			
Austria	30.0	36.8	
Finland		30.0	
Iceland			
Norway	21.9	21.1	
Sweden	34.0	40.0	
Switzerland	38.0		b
CMEA members			
Bulgaria			
Czechoslovakia			
East Germany			
Hungary			
Poland			
Romania			
USSR			
Others			
Albania			
Cyprus			
Gibraltar			
Liechtenstein			
Malta			
Monaco			
Turkey			
Yugoslavia			

Source: OECD
Notes: a Reutilisation in the paper industry only
b 1979

	000 tonnes 1988	% of total consumption: 1981	1985	1988	Notes
EC members					
Belgium	166	33	42	50	
Denmark	46	8	19	27	
France	676	20	26	34	
West Germany	1176	24	39	39	
Greece	14			16	
Ireland	9	8	7	10	
Italy	610	20	25	40	
Luxembourg					
Netherlands	261	41	53	53	
Portugal	31		10	13	
Spain	278		13	23	
United Kingdom	264	5	12	15	
EFTA members					
Austria	98	20	38	50	
Finland	2	20		3	
Iceland					
Norway	3			6	
Sweden	31		20	22	
Switzerland	156	36	46	55	a
CMEA members					
Bulgaria					
Czechoslovakia					
East Germany					
Hungary					
Poland					
Romania					
USSR					
Others					
Albania					
Cyprus					
Gibraltar					
Liechtenstein					
Malta					
Monaco					
Turkey	40			33	
Yugoslavia					

Source: OECD
Notes: a Excluding returnable empties

Database name:	Environmental Data					
Sector name:	Land Use				Table No:	1007

Title: Wetlands 1950-1985

Unit: Square kilometres

	1950	1970	1980	1985	% change 1950-85	Notes
EC members						
Belgium						
Denmark			3400			a
France			2781	2695		
West Germany	2471	1697	1174	1072	-57	b
Greece						
Ireland						
Italy						
Luxembourg						
Netherlands	1450	1100	737	659	-54.6	c
Portugal						
Spain			10853	10830		
United Kingdom						
EFTA members						
Austria			93	73		d
Finland	27150	23000	20900	20951	-22.8	
Iceland						
Norway		20300	20300			e
Sweden	26100	24240	24400	23837	-9	a
Switzerland						
CMEA members						
Bulgaria						
Czechoslovakia						
East Germany						
Hungary						
Poland						
Romania						
USSR						
Others						
Albania						
Cyprus						
Gibraltar						
Liechtenstein						
Malta						
Monaco						
Turkey		485				f
Yugoslavia						

Source: OECD
Notes:
a Bogs and fens only
b Excludes marshes; 1985 column actually refers to 1984
c 1980 refers to 1979
d Data refer to 1983 and 1986 and include uncultivated marshes only
e 1980 refers to 1983
f 1970 refers to 1971

TABLE 1004: MUNICIPAL WASTE
Kilos per capita 1985

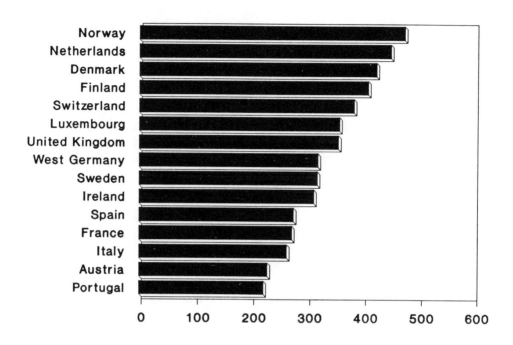

TABLE 1006: GLASS RECYCLING
Percentage recycled 1988

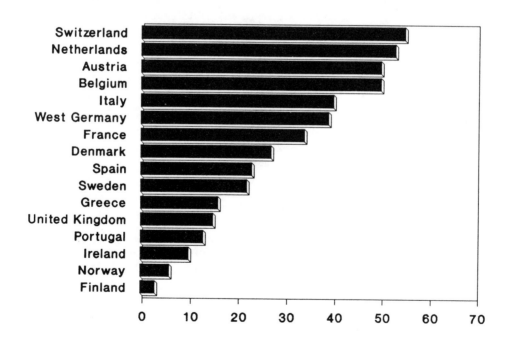

Database name: Consumer Expenditure Patterns
Sector name: Total Expenditure

Table No: 1101

Title: Total Consumer Expenditure 1977-1989

Unit: National currencies (millions)

	1977	1978	1979	1980	1981	1982	1983	1984	1985
EC members									
Belgium	1764125	1887455	2047950	2212366	2396200	2622204	2762708	2961397	3199155
Denmark	158900	174890	195814	208814	228566	255639	279963	307889	337215
France	1162000	1308400	1511478	1735974	2000445	2294757	2531030	2730381	2871425
West Germany	669560	713910	779250	834030	879200	910280	947320	1003570	1038340
Greece	643102	747508	904947	1094389	1362300	1694750	2023350	2623899	2998500
Ireland	3661	4309	5170	6158	7490	8001	8814	9590	10415
Italy	121303	141026	170741	212488	254661	299470	343981	389136	497350
Luxembourg	60877	65064	71326	79242	86969	96544	109600	117575	125834
Netherlands	165470	179170	192430	205780	213230	221830	229860	234730	247720
Portugal	450400	535327	667713	820725	1019300	1399273	1584000	1986600	2387700
Spain	6990726	7325600	8679300	10080400	11457900	13143300	14808100	16313200	17985300
United Kingdom	86679	99873	119426	137234	152544	167362	182877	195711	217023
EC total									
EFTA members									
Austria	456860	468860	509060	550900	594800	640200	694840	733180	775050
Finland	71268	76420	87011	99320	112035	134200	149600	160503	175330
Iceland	2345	3659	5514	8842	14393	23088	39674	54551	75830
Norway	103915	110670	120104	135242	155205	175310	192979	210921	245439
Sweden	197806	218410	240810	270049	298681	333897	362697	397911	437795
Switzerland	92480	95540	100720	108040	115685	122060	127340	133610	140555
EFTA total									
CMEA members									
Bulgaria	11000	11600	12000	14000	15800	16500	17100	18300	19100
Czechoslovakia	230812	239016	247520	257325	262627	271232	279736	287339	401595
East Germany	103891	107387	111465	115154	126806	153118	164284	173120	178557
Hungary	327600	360300	399600	441200	477700	515100	551200	600500	649300
Poland	1230200	1340000	1540000	1658000	2041000	3476700	4486900	5427600	6397000
Romania	250000	288000	310000	354200	381300	442500	439800	456100	490700
USSR	290000	300000	320000	340000	360000	380000	400000	430000	450000
CMEA total									
Others									
Albania	8200	9200	10600	12000	15300	17100	19400	22900	25200
Cyprus	305	454	481	508	566	669	739	815	895
Gibraltar	38	40	42	45	46	48	50	53	55
Liechtenstein	332	350	385	402	431	443	452	518	540
Malta	170	186	206	254	279	306	307	318	333
Monaco	571	640	743	852	982	1127	1243	1341	1410
Turkey	1300000	1650000	2100000	2993900	4494500	6067600	8449000	14369000	19035000
Yugoslavia	510000	530000	700000	818800	1143300	1510600	2087700	3207200	5659400
Total									
European total									

Source: National Accounts/Euromonitor estimates
Notes: a Billions

250

Title: Total Consumer Expenditure 1977-1989

Unit: National currencies (millions)

	1986	1987	1988	1989	% growth 1977-1989	% share 1989	Total $ million 1989	$ per capita 1989	Notes
EC members									
Belgium	3300349	3347040	3587783	3924600	122.47	2.23	99599	10034	
Denmark	363131	374610	388672	403400	153.87	1.23	55185	10730	
France	3042800	3222200	3401300	3570500	207.27	12.52	559631	9970	
West Germany	1068610	1112680	1156810	1213360	81.22	14.44	645404	10477	
Greece	3693000	4319400	5104500	6060700	842.42	0.84	37315	3704	
Ireland	11102	11686	12250	13600	271.50	0.43	19299	5469	
Italy	549448	601848	657394	718000	491.91	11.71	523285	9062	a
Luxembourg	131348	140000	143000	155100	154.78	0.09	3936	10581	
Netherlands	256150	263180	268280	279600	68.97	2.95	131843	8901	
Portugal	2900800	3414000	3871900	4546900	909.52	0.65	28877	2798	
Spain	20341000	22714000	24928000	28470000	307.25	5.38	240497	6141	
United Kingdom	239535	264120	296165	324348	274.19	11.90	531892	9292	
EC total						64.38	2876763	8823	
EFTA members									
Austria	803170	835090	874780	927000	102.91	1.57	70063	9226	
Finland	188430	206245	235100	257000	260.61	1.34	59890	12067	
Iceland	97970	130100	162230						b
Norway	278909	297641	308777	316700	204.77	1.03	45869	10823	
Sweden	478200	526280	590900	634000	220.52	2.20	98342	11620	
Switzerland	144925	150210	157015	165600	79.07	2.27	101229	15342	
EFTA total						8.40	375392	11692	
CMEA members									
Bulgaria	19900	20497	21094			0.28	12408	1374	b
Czechoslovakia	415702	427900	440098			1.05	46819	2996	b
East Germany	183897	195100	206303			2.47	110322	6627	b
Hungary	695500	805336	962650			0.43	19100	1795	b
Poland	7916800	10066200	16916000			0.88	39294	1041	b
Romania	510000	520000	530000			0.83	37123	1624	b
USSR	480000	510000	540000			19.75	882353	3108	b
CMEA total						25.68	1147419	2894	
Others									
Albania	28200	30500	32800			0.12	5467	1721	
Cyprus	950	1015	1210			0.06	2595	3604	
Gibraltar	57	59	61			0.00	108	3615	
Liechtenstein	580	582	584			0.01	400	13333	
Malta	357	382	392			0.03	1186	3390	
Monaco	1484	1578	1672			0.01	281	10024	
Turkey	26400000	36600000	64280000			1.01	45194	851	
Yugoslavia	11063787	24424272	71815000			0.31	13782	583	
total						1.54	69014	851	
European total						100.00	4468588	5347	

Source: National Accounts/Euromonitor estimates
Notes: a Billions
b Dollar total based on 1988 figures

Database name: Consumer Expenditure Patterns
Sector name: Total Expenditure

Table No: 1102

Title: Consumer Expenditure by Object 1988

Unit: US dollars (millions)

	Food	Alcoholic Drinks	Non-Alcoholic Drinks	Tobacco	Clothing	Footwear	Housing	Household Fuels
EC members								
Belgium	16645	2883	997	1515	5070	1065	11851	4289
Denmark	8831	1879	357	1729	2754	394	11766	3755
France	91584	11380	3061	6379	38695	7689	63754	34912
West Germany	113452	14509	3502	11361	44857	10733	103513	28305
Greece	14125	786	321	982	2270	234	4079	1133
Ireland	3979	2025	250	859	902	233	967	957
Italy	111853	6241	1938	6920	38443	10685	54206	18612
Luxembourg	543	58	23	207	230	25	503	278
Netherlands	19151	1927	639	1809	7087	2271	16612	8097
Portugal	10191	459	51	403	1490	459	2650	
Spain	57316	2359	948	2976	12786	3549	29628	7716
United Kingdom	60016	32997	5345	14155	29590	5979	61254	18528
EFTA members								
Austria	12026	1624	471	1397	6200	1701	12942	4470
Finland	9467	2110	271	1032	2207	412	7796	1802
Iceland	1017			79	306		405	
Norway	9042	1682	544	1020	2789	621	4961	3174
Sweden	15235	2900	432	1881	5545	1058	18876	4370
Switzerland	21209	5231	926	1879	4234	1076	14580	4627
CMEA members								
Bulgaria	2361	1327	128	331	933	328	269	272
Czechoslovakia	11516	3688	705	2328	2749	501	1066	987
East Germany	28066	11007	1654	4157	11231	2538	1689	921
Hungary	5010	1817	473	393	1311	220	723	502
Poland	10712	4005		674	2780	867	5567	706
Romania	8425	2370	668	836	2931	784	751	350
USSR	242087	106716	7368	21176	134594	31849	28711	33932
Others								
Albania	1350	274	98	124	682	81	263	220
Cyprus	495	37	33	32	389	28	170	52
Gibraltar	33	1	0	1	11	2	15	
Liechtenstein	49	25	5	8	25	4	78	15
Malta	309	53	46	41	99	26	53	29
Monaco	51	6	2	4	20	4	35	19
Turkey	18078	542	1198	4068	2038	822	3752	2395
Yugoslavia	5828	830	178	257	565	486	582	716

Source: Euromonitor
Notes: Entries of 0 signify less than $0.5 million
a Communications included in Transport
b Leisure included among Others
c Non-alcoholic drinks included under Alcoholic drnks
d Household fuels included under Housing

Database name: Consumer Expenditure Patterns
Sector name: Total Expenditure

Table No: 1102

Title: Consumer Expenditure by Object 1988

Unit: US dollars (millions)

	Household Goods & Services	Health	Transport	Communications	Leisure	Others	Total	Notes
EC members								
Belgium	12560	11146	11521	962	9845	7228	97579	
Denmark	3931	1038	8232	787	5559	6724	57735	
France	65860	62649	51258	7973	32463	93329	570985	
West Germany	60825	32308	91043	10819	64759	68713	658701	
Greece	3395	1171	3701	604	1624	1559	35983	
Ireland	1294	260	1851	246	1827	1876	17529	
Italy	44454	28131	60465	5582	47486	70049	505066	
Luxembourg	357	283	665		150	565	3886	a
Netherlands	10832	16726	11016	1819	12891	24852	135728	
Portugal	1733	892	3312	764	892	3603	26898	
Spain	15674	8818	29760	2315	16974	23174	213993	
United Kingdom	31178	6414	69482	8373	47212	137119	527641	
EFTA members								
Austria	5101	3755	10164	1377	3967	5650	70844	
Finland	3534	2065	8423		4716	12371	56206	a
Iceland	428				316	1221	3772	a,c
Norway	3614	1857	5436	836	4207	7594	47380	
Sweden	6571	1567	16532		8955	12514	96439	a
Switzerland	5412	12157	11724		10545	13702	107302	a
CMEA members								
Bulgaria	2045	494	1140			2782	12408	a,b
Czechoslovakia	6050	2819	2859			11551	46819	a,b
East Germany	13335	4368	2253			29102	110322	a,b
Hungary	1299	1174	1608			4570	19100	a,b
Poland	2453	2260	3525	117		5630	39294	b,c
Romania	2031	1499	1498			14979	37123	a,b
USSR	70865	23438	25867			155749	882353	a,b,c
Others								
Albania	539	199	378			1260	5467	a,b
Cyprus	297	62	432			568	2595	a,b
Gibraltar	10	9	10			16	108	a,b,d
Liechtenstein	25	52	51			81	417	a,b
Malta	120	46	203			162	1186	a,b
Monaco	40	42	30			27	281	a,b
Turkey	4612	4927	2768			-6	45194	a,b
Yugoslavia	1104	468	1268			1500	13782	a,b

Database name: Consumer Expenditure Patterns
Sector name: Total Expenditure

Table No: 1103

Title: Consumer Expenditure by Object 1988

Unit: Percentage of total expenditure

	Food	Alcoholic Drinks	Non-Alcoholic Drinks	Tobacco	Clothing	Footwear	Housing	Household Fuels
EEC members								
Belgium	17.1	3.0	1.0	1.6	5.2	1.1	12.1	4.4
Denmark	15.3	3.3	0.6	3.0	4.8	0.7	20.4	6.5
France	16.0	2.0	0.5	1.1	6.8	1.3	11.2	6.1
West Germany	17.2	2.2	0.5	1.7	6.8	1.6	15.7	4.3
Greece	39.3	2.2	0.9	2.7	6.3	0.7	11.3	3.1
Ireland	22.7	11.6	1.4	4.9	5.1	1.3	5.5	5.5
Italy	22.1	1.2	0.4	1.4	7.6	2.1	10.7	3.7
Luxembourg	14.0	1.5	0.6	5.3	5.9	0.6	12.9	7.2
Netherlands	14.1	1.4	0.5	1.3	5.2	1.7	12.2	6.0
Portugal	37.9	1.7	0.2	1.5	5.5	1.7	9.9	
Spain	26.8	1.1	0.4	1.4	6.0	1.7	13.8	3.6
United Kingdom	11.4	6.3	1.0	2.7	5.6	1.1	11.6	3.5
EFTA members								
Austria	17.0	2.3	0.7	2.0	8.8	2.4	18.3	6.3
Finland	16.8	3.8	0.5	1.8	3.9	0.7	13.9	3.2
Iceland	27.0			2.1	8.1		10.7	
Norway	19.1	3.6	1.1	2.2	5.9	1.3	10.5	6.7
Sweden	15.8	3.0	0.4	2.0	5.7	1.1	19.6	4.5
Switzerland	19.8	4.9	0.9	1.8	3.9	1.0	13.6	4.3
CMEA members								
Bulgaria	19.0	10.7	1.0	2.7	7.5	2.6	2.2	2.2
Czechoslovakia	24.6	7.9	1.5	5.0	5.9	1.1	2.3	2.1
East Germany	25.4	10.0	1.5	3.8	10.2	2.3	1.5	0.8
Hungary	26.2	9.5	2.5	2.1	6.9	1.2	3.8	2.6
Poland	27.3	10.2		1.7	7.1	2.2	14.2	1.8
Romania	22.7	6.4	1.8	2.3	7.9	2.1	2.0	0.9
USSR	27.4	12.1	0.8	2.4	15.3	3.6	3.3	3.8
Others								
Albania	24.7	5.0	1.8	2.3	12.5	1.5	4.8	4.0
Cyprus	19.1	1.4	1.3	1.2	15.0	1.1	6.6	2.0
Gibraltar	30.5	1.1	0.4	1.0	9.9	2.1	13.7	
Liechtenstein	11.8	6.1	1.1	2.0	6.0	1.0	18.6	3.5
Malta	26.0	4.5	3.9	3.4	8.4	2.2	4.4	2.4
Monaco	18.1	2.3	0.5	1.3	7.2	1.6	12.5	6.9
Turkey	40.0	1.2	2.7	9.0	4.5	1.8	8.3	5.3
Yugoslavia	42.3	6.0	1.3	1.9	4.1	3.5	4.2	5.2

Source: Euromonitor
Notes: Entries of 0 signify less than $0.5 million
a Communications included in Transport
b Leisure included among Others
c Non-alcoholic drinks included under Alcoholic drnks
d Household fuels included under Housing

Database name: Consumer Expenditure Patterns
Sector name: Total Expenditure

Table No: 1103

Title: Consumer Expenditure by Object 1988

Unit: Percentage of total expenditure

	Household Goods & Services	Health	Transport	Communi-cations	Leisure	Others	Total	Notes
EC members								
Belgium	12.9	11.4	11.8	1.0	10.1	7.4	100.0	
Denmark	6.8	1.8	14.3	1.4	9.6	11.6	100.0	
France	11.5	11.0	9.0	1.4	5.7	16.3	100.0	
West Germany	9.2	4.9	13.8	1.6	9.8	10.4	100.0	
Greece	9.4	3.3	10.3	1.7	4.5	4.3	100.0	
Ireland	7.4	1.5	10.6	1.4	10.4	10.7	100.0	
Italy	8.8	5.6	12.0	1.1	9.4	13.9	100.0	
Luxembourg	9.2	7.3	17.1		3.9	14.5	100.0	a
Netherlands	8.0	12.3	8.1	1.3	9.5	18.3	100.0	
Portugal	6.4	3.3	12.3	2.8	3.3	13.4	100.0	
Spain	7.3	4.1	13.9	1.1	7.9	10.8	100.0	
United Kingdom	5.9	1.2	13.2	1.6	8.9	26.0	100.0	
EFTA members								
Austria	7.2	5.3	14.3	1.9	5.6	8.0	100.0	
Finland	6.3	3.7	15.0		8.4	22.0	100.0	a
Iceland	11.4				8.4	32.4	100.0	a,c
Norway	7.6	3.9	11.5	1.8	8.9	16.0	100.0	
Sweden	6.8	1.6	17.1		9.3	13.0	100.0	a
Switzerland	5.0	11.3	10.9		9.8	12.8	100.0	a
CMEA members								
Bulgaria	16.5	4.0	9.2			22.4	100.0	a,b
Czechoslovakia	12.9	6.0	6.1			24.7	100.0	a,b
East Germany	12.1	4.0	2.0			26.4	100.0	a,b
Hungary	6.8	6.1	8.4			23.9	100.0	a,b
Poland	6.2	5.8	9.0	0.3		14.3	100.0	b,c
Romania	5.5	4.0	4.0			40.4	100.0	a,b
USSR	8.0	2.7	2.9			17.7	100.0	a,b,c
Others								
Albania	9.9	3.6	6.9			23.1	100.0	a,b
Cyprus	11.4	2.4	16.6			21.9	100.0	a,b
Gibraltar	8.8	8.4	9.4			14.7	100.0	a,b,d
Liechtenstein	5.9	12.4	12.2			19.4	100.0	a,b
Malta	10.1	3.9	17.1			13.6	100.0	a,b
Monaco	14.1	15.1	10.6			9.8	100.0	a,b
Turkey	10.2	10.9	6.1			0.0	100.0	a,b
Yugoslavia	8.0	3.4	9.2			10.9	100.0	a,b

Database name: Consumer Expenditure Patterns
Sector name: Expenditure on Food

Table No: 1104

Title: Consumer Expenditure on Food 1977-1989

Unit: National currencies (millions)

	1977	1978	1979	1980	1981	1982	1983	1984	1985
EC members									
Belgium	349354	365284	379755	403876	415188	471420	519822	560649	590649
Denmark	28760	31555	33149	35894	40265	44526	47182	52049	53872
France	230513	255661	281427	291393	332360	377700	416615	457389	484970
West Germany	138820	143524	150905	163088	173552	182464	186632	191216	193984
Greece	219713	260236	321724	405359	528343	621245	755050	886235	1109000
Ireland	986	1084	1351	1548	1819	2024	2217	2383	2409
Italy	35216	40767	47778	56787	66260	77437	87949	105274	110065
Luxembourg	12064	12250	12592	13103	14202	15681	16832	18014	18697
Netherlands	26990	27730	28700	30630	32390	33910	33630	35310	36110
Portugal	165180	188310	228613	250400	300000	437865	541800	753000	980000
Spain	1930800	2149000	2450000	2620600	2936800	3404900	3788100	4219900	4732000
United Kingdom	16047	17927	20364	22876	24207	25649	26379	27591	28642
EC total									
EFTA members									
Austria	88130	97390	104320	110740	118460	123620	131700	137170	140680
Finland	16286	17688	19993	22131	27108	27370	29406	31829	33776
Iceland	801	1125	1605	2522	3972	6237	11805	15097	23208
Norway	21480	23115	24280	27285	31381	35744	38758	41858	46706
Sweden	41996	45448	44806	49699	57205	60719	66643	74112	79506
Switzerland	18880	19445	20140	21750	23290	24470	25530	26985	28250
EFTA total									
CMEA members									
Bulgaria	1949	2239	2384	2409	2772	3123	3147	3256	3570
Czechoslovakia	59374	69558	76807	77843	81985	82503	83884	87163	90960
East Germany	38052	39205	40230	41127	42024	42792	43305	44586	45483
Hungary	80111	84794	96334	107456	113979	120251	129951	141742	169589
Poland	353900	383600	457300	516900	661400	1314800	1489200	1548400	1916000
Romania	57120	58920	71400	67080	75300	80100	90660	96670	98880
USSR	92100	94000	95500	85770	98910	107730	117630	128700	133650
CMEA total									
Others									
Albania	1312	1608	1796	2259	3074	3538	4018	5770	6259
Cyprus	76	112	108	121	130	145	161	180	187
Gibraltar	12	12	13	14	14	15	16	16	17
Liechtenstein	58	54	61	64	67	66	58	67	68
Malta	49	56	61	75	84	92	94	101	98
Monaco	119	132	144	145	175	198	226	247	263
Turkey	572000	709500	934500	1197560	1887690	2305688	3295110	5747600	7652070
Yugoslavia	240108	235426	317100	315238	449317	602125	842178	1402509	2346387
Total									
European total									

Source: National Accounts/Euromonitor estimates
Notes:
a Billions
b Euromonitor estimates
c Dollar values based on 1988 results

| Database name: | Consumer Expenditure Patterns |
| Sector name: | Expenditure on Food |

Table No: 1104

| Title: | Consumer Expenditure on Food 1977-1989 |

| Unit: | National currencies (millions) |

	1986	1987	1988	1989	% growth 1977-1989	% share 1989	Total $ million 1989	$ per capita 1989	Notes
EC members									
Belgium	607503	609965	611996	614027	75.76	1.70	15583	1570	
Denmark	56468	58300	59449	60546	110.52	0.90	8283	1610	
France	506727	521311	545555	601583	160.98	10.27	94291	1680	
West Germany	197920	201202	199245	210439	51.59	12.19	111935	1817	
Greece	1360000	1695529	2003711	2536000	1054.23	1.70	15614	1550	
Ireland	2536	2653	2781	3000	204.32	0.46	4257	1206	
Italy	116770	123540	145588	159010	351.53	12.62	115888	2006928	a
Luxembourg	19121	19545	19969	22587	87.23	0.06	573	1541	
Netherlands	37045	37423	37854	38285	41.85	1.97	18053	1219	
Portugal	1200000	1293550	1467047	1640543	893.19	1.13	10419	1010	
Spain	5320000	6083740	6676740	7446065	285.65	6.85	62900	1606	
United Kingdom	30064	34400	33687	36020	124.47	6.43	59069	1032	
EC total						56.28	516864	1585	
EFTA members									
Austria	145554	149987	148500	155577	76.53	1.28	11759	1548	
Finland	35370	37575	39599	46832	187.56	1.19	10914	2199	
Iceland	26519	35127	43735	52343	6434.71	0.10	918	3656	b
Norway	51597	55681	58927	59255	175.86	0.93	8582	2025	
Sweden	85386	90451	93350	94925	126.03	1.60	14724	1740	
Switzerland	29360	29945	31035	33015	74.87	2.20	20182	3059	
EFTA total						7.30	67078	2089	
CMEA members									
Bulgaria	3776	3894	4013			0.26	2361	261	c
Czechoslovakia	97346	102696	108252			1.25	11516	737	c
East Germany	46636	49555	52484			3.06	28066	1686	c
Hungary	184808	212609	252494			0.55	5010	471	c
Poland	2394307	2890382	4611550			1.17	10712	284	c
Romania	99100	109200	120285			0.92	8425	368	c
USSR	137160	142800	148157			26.36	242087	853	c
CMEA total						33.56	308177	777	
Others									
Albania	6578	7320	8099			0.15	1350	425	c
Cyprus	189	198	231			0.05	495	687	c
Gibraltar	18	18	19			0.00	33	1103	c
Liechtenstein	71	70	69			0.01	47	1567	c
Malta	100	103	102			0.03	309	882	c
Monaco	272	287	302			0.01	51	1812	c
Turkey	10560000	14640000	25712000			1.97	18078	340	c
Yugoslavia	4696578	10348564	30370672			0.63	5828	246	c
Total						2.85	26190	323	
European total						100.00	918309	1099	

	1977	1978	1979	1980	1981	1982	1983	1984	1985
EC members									
Belgium	62692	66543	70480	77032	81222	89331	95364	96062	100239
Denmark	6478	6944	7396	7953	8819	9785	11112	11489	12037
France	30181	33050	35961	39430	44305	49751	54129	56026	58920
West Germany	16500	18956	19195	20978	22323	23470	24010	24240	24830
Greece	17850	20955	21591	26673	32337	41008	45923	54451	68013
Ireland	423	486	575	695	844	1010	1041	1155	1234
Italy	2548	2864	3347	4097	4700	5322	6097	6687	6624
Luxembourg	1058	1075	1232	1423	1620	1750	1784	1787	1885
Netherlands	3930	4070	4120	4060	4250	4620	4578	4580	4650
Portugal	12056	17481	23909	20167	26461	31110	33350	35500	43700
Spain	85890	103000	116900	131200	143900	159400	174100	193900	217500
United Kingdom	6545	7283	8665	9955	11152	12003	13370	14430	15783
EC total									
EFTA members									
Austria	14300	14680	14520	15440	16191	17360	18470	18130	18610
Finland	2916	3331	3912	4330	4860	5563	6229	6683	7020
Iceland	79	112	171	265	400	694	1130	1682	2201
Norway	3848	3782	4368	4826	5309	5393	6144	6629	7522
Sweden	8456	9050	8995	9977	11007	12189	13182	14068	14982
Switzerland	4789	4927	5248	5307	5727	6167	6398	6673	7007
EFTA total									
CMEA members									
Bulgaria	1610	1791	1755	1924	1864	1924	1961	2009	2033
Czechoslovakia	26408	26926	27443	28306	29515	30205	30723	30895	31586
East Germany	13196	13709	14221	14990	15631	16015	16399	17040	17681
Hungary	30439	31861	36878	39554	41059	46662	49003	51178	62885
Poland	151000	160000	172600	184700	189800	396700	558900	616300	762300
Romania	23340	24060	25200	26340	28140	28680	29700	30600	32400
USSR	34100	35800	37400	35100	41490	43200	45540	51030	54180
CMEA total									
Others									
Albania	413	576	618	667	820	888	1127	1192	1276
Cyprus	8	10	9	11	12	12	14	14	15
Gibraltar	1	1	1	1	1	1	1	1	1
Liechtenstein	20	21	23	24	25	27	28	32	34
Malta	10	13	19	22	23	17	16	15	15
Monaco	16	17	18	21	23	26	29	30	32
Turkey	13000	19800	27300	35927	53934	72811	101388	172428	228420
Yugoslavia	27795	29786	37170	49619	71571	96074	129855	213920	362202
Total									
European total									

Source: National Accounts/Euromonitor estimates
Notes:
a Billions
b Including non-alcoholic beverages
c Dollar values based on 1988 figures

Database name: Consumer Expenditure Patterns
Sector name: Expenditure on Alcoholic Drinks

Table No: 1105

Title: Consumer Expenditure on Alcoholic Drinks 1977-1989

Unit: National currencies (millions)

	1986	1987	1988	1989	% growth 1977-1989	% share 1989	Total $ million 1989	$ per capita 1989	Notes
EC members									
Belgium	100157	104679	106008	107337	71.21	1.22	2724	274	
Denmark	12562	12600	12648	12881	98.84	0.79	1762	343	
France	63253	66530	67788	72300	139.55	5.07	11332	202	
West Germany	25312	25421	25481	27855	68.82	6.63	14816	241	
Greece	79387	94297	111436	131495	636.67	0.36	810	80	
Ireland	1321	1350	1415	1625	284.34	1.03	2306	653	
Italy	7199	7522	8123	8872	248.19	2.89	6466	112	a
Luxembourg	1963	2041	2119	2319	119.17	0.03	59	158	
Netherlands	4760	4811	3808	2805	-28.62	0.59	1323	89	
Portugal	51680	58210	66017	68829	470.91	0.20	437	42	
Spain	230500	250369	274774	322616	275.62	1.22	2725	70	
United Kingdom	16474	17250	18521	20065	206.57	14.72	32904	575	
EC total						34.75	77665	238	
EFTA members									
Austria	19237	19778	20050	21006	46.89	0.71	1588	209	
Finland	7885	8377	8828	9523	226.58	0.99	2219	447	
Iceland	2697	3903							
Norway	8200	9582	10964	10197	164.99	0.66	1477	348	
Sweden	15836	17573	17770	18266	116.01	1.27	2833	335	
Switzerland	7382	7400	7655	8159	70.36	2.23	4987	756	
EFTA total						5.86	13104	408	
CMEA members									
Bulgaria	2130	2193	2256			0.59	1327	147	c
Czechoslovakia	32104	33376	34671			1.65	3688	236	c
East Germany	18065	19315	20583			4.93	11007	661	c
Hungary	65979	76507	91581			0.81	1817	171	c
Poland	995600	1139600	1723996			1.79	4005	106	b,c
Romania	34800	34320	33834			1.06	2370	104	c
USSR	57150	61200	65310			47.75	106716	376	c
CMEA total						58.59	130930	330	
Others									
Albania	1409	1525	1641			0.12	274	86	c
Cyprus	15	15	17			0.02	37	52	c
Gibraltar	1	1	1			0.00	1	40	c
Liechtenstein	34	35	35			0.01	24	810	c
Malta	16	17	17			0.02	53	151	c
Monaco	34	36	39			0.00	6	232	c
Turkey	316800	439200	771360			0.24	542	10	c
Yugoslavia	722465	1531402	4323516			0.37	830	35	c
Total						0.79	1768	22	
European total						100.00	223467	267	

Source: National Accounts/Euromonitor estimates
Notes: a Billions
b Including non-alcoholic beverages
c Dollar values based on 1988 figures

Database name: Consumer Expenditure Patterns
Sector name: Expenditure on Non-Alcoholic Drinks   Table No: 1106

Title: Consumer Expenditure on Non-Alcoholic Drinks 1977-1989

Unit: National currencies (millions)

	1977	1978	1979	1980	1981	1982	1983	1984	1985
EC members									
Belgium	16760	17792	18844	20561	21814	24619	27626	29361	29361
Denmark	1046	1207	1228	1262	1313	1453	1628	1751	1932
France	3000	3506	5158	7338	8583	10317	11760	12784	13847
West Germany	3890	4150	4400	4950	5150	5460	5620	5770	5950
Greece	7098	8673	9261	10836	12351	16335	19345	22938	28651
Ireland	44	59	65	79	109	110	129	131	151
Italy	360	399	567	606	723	863	1002	1246	1523
Luxembourg	281	298	332	355	426	511	560	567	685
Netherlands	900	990	1050	1090	1140	1310	1360	1360	1480
Portugal	1094	1374	1712	1724	2143	2921	2700	3000	4000
Spain	15000	21000	31000	44600	50100	56300	62800	75000	81000
United Kingdom	1161	1307	1459	1602	1568	1595	1896	2107	2339
EC total									
EFTA members									
Austria	3100	3220	3410	4100	4303	4615	5210	5110	5240
Finland	379	401	578	640	675	688	771	864	917
Iceland	13	19	27	40	55	90	170	250	330
Norway	1045	1158	1246	1327	1377	1726	1824	2008	2309
Sweden	1024	1105	1271	1410	1460	1530	1633	1752	2009
Switzerland	799	810	852	956	1031	1110	1152	1202	1262
EFTA total									
CMEA members									
Bulgaria	133	157	145	157	194	194	194	194	182
Czechoslovakia	4315	4833	5178	5351	5178	3797	5351	5523	5868
East Germany	1922	2050	2178	2306	2306	2434	2434	2562	2691
Hungary	5937	7526	9199	9868	10202	11624	12209	12794	16056
Poland									
Romania	5160	5520	5940	5940	7020	7080	7860	8280	8940
USSR	2800	2800	2900	2790	3420	3330	3420	3600	3780
CMEA total									
Others									
Albania	83	119	137	154	179	203	236	260	296
Cyprus	6	7	7	8	9	9	9	11	11
Gibraltar	0	0	0	0	0	0	0	0	0
Liechtenstein	3	3	4	4	5	5	5	6	6
Malta	4	3	4	5	7	10	10	11	13
Monaco	2	2	3	4	5	10	6	7	8
Turkey	12675	35080	69563	68860	121352	182028	253470	445439	571050
Yugoslavia	7089	8321	11130	14411	17950	24019	32359	53560	94512
Total									
European total									

Source: National Accounts/Euromonitor estimates
Notes: a   Billions
             b   Dollar values based on 1988 figures

Database name: Consumer Expenditure Patterns
Sector name: Expenditure on Non-Alcoholic Drinks   Table No: 1106

Title: Consumer Expenditure on Non-Alcoholic Drinks 1977-1989

Unit: National currencies (millions)

	1986	1987	1988	1989	% growth 1977-1989	% share 1989	Total $ million 1989	$ per capita 1989	Notes
EC members									
Belgium	32973	34419	36643	38867	131.90	3.01	986	99	
Denmark	2100	2108	2400	2444	133.68	1.02	334	65	
France	14794	16070	18233	20106	570.18	9.60	3151	56	
West Germany	6110	6135	6151	6893	77.20	11.17	3666	60	
Greece	33210	38535	45539	62000	773.49	1.16	382	38	
Ireland	154	167	175	197	344.70	0.85	280	79	
Italy	1813	2090	2522	2754	665.00	6.12	2007	35	a
Luxembourg	771	810	830	911	224.11	0.07	23	62	
Netherlands	1580	1600	1264	928	3.12	1.33	438	30	
Portugal	5000	6468	7335	8203	649.79	0.16	52	5	
Spain	92000	100616	110423	128767	758.44	3.31	1088	28	
United Kingdom	2586	2800	3000	3200	175.62	15.99	5248	92	
EC total						53.79	17655	54	
EFTA members									
Austria	5405	5769	5810	6087	96.35	1.40	460	61	
Finland	1012	1075	1133	1340	253.55	0.95	312	63	
Iceland	499	585							
Norway	2841	3194	3547	3399	225.26	1.50	492	116	
Sweden	2183	2378	2650	2963	189.38	1.40	460	54	
Switzerland	1314	1320	1355	1455	82.15	2.71	890	135	
EFTA total						7.96	2614	81	
CMEA members									
Bulgaria	194	205	217			0.39	128	14	b
Czechoslovakia	6214	6419	6625			2.15	705	45	b
East Germany	2947	3024	3093			5.04	1654	99	b
Hungary	17143	19892	23827			1.44	473	44	b
Poland									
Romania	9180	9360	9540			2.04	668	29	b
USSR	3960	4233	4509			22.45	7368	26	b
CMEA total						33.50	10995	28	
Others									
Albania	403	488	588			0.30	98	31	b
Cyprus	12	13	15			0.10	33	45	b
Gibraltar	0	0	0			0.00	0	16	b
Liechtenstein	6	6	6			0.01	4	145	b
Malta	14	15	15			0.14	46	131	b
Monaco	8	9	9			0.00	2	55	b
Turkey	726000	988200	1704004			3.65	1198	23	b
Yugoslavia	180340	354152	926325			0.54	178	8	b
Total						4.75	1559	19	
European total						100.00	32823	39	

	Database name:	Consumer Expenditure Patterns				Table No: 1107			

Database name: Consumer Expenditure Patterns
Sector name: Expenditure on Tobacco

Table No: 1107

Title: Consumer Expenditure on Tobacco 1977-1989

Unit: National currencies (millions)

	1977	1978	1979	1980	1981	1982	1983	1984	1985
EC members									
Belgium	32057	31931	34375	35400	37616	45147	49159	53441	54422
Denmark	5832	6299	6941	7130	7554	8425	9292	10174	10653
France	12384	13533	15621	18029	20950	25030	28125	31034	32410
West Germany	14310	15040	15770	16309	17355	18246	18663	19122	19398
Greece	17090	20035	23168	27433	34817	46766	58889	69825	87216
Ireland	151	170	194	239	297	368	422	478	507
Italy	2484	2851	3417	4013	4996	6595	7776	8334	9319
Luxembourg	1800	2000	3500	4500	6000	6250	7000	7414	8028
Netherlands	3280	3600	3670	3830	3970	4020	4230	4510	4460
Portugal	7825	9894	12322	17488	22551	31768	28500	31000	38000
Spain	62700	77000	91000	122300	165600	183600	206900	230500	258500
United Kingdom	3628	3885	4234	4821	5515	5881	6209	6622	7006
EC total									
EFTA members									
Austria	11750	11930	12500	13620	14090	14420	15540	15500	16210
Finland	1532	1714	2074	2296	2240	2739	3189	3562	3462
Iceland	85	130	205	270	346	563	990	1456	1967
Norway	2191	2423	2570	2764	3190	3557	4017	4436	5064
Sweden	4475	4861	4999	5585	6114	6731	7420	8250	8667
Switzerland	1952	1788	1720	1887	2036	2192	2274	2372	2490
EFTA total									
CMEA members									
Bulgaria	242	339	278	327	375	412	448	472	484
Czechoslovakia	14153	16224	17433	17605	17778	17605	17778	17605	18296
East Germany	4997	5253	5381	5765	5894	6150	6278	6534	6790
Hungary	5854	6272	8195	8697	9115	10537	11038	11540	13380
Poland	33100	34200	36800	41300	60900	77200	98400	100400	120000
Romania	6480	6720	7140	8100	8640	9060	10500	10800	11160
USSR	7600	7800	8200	7740	8640	9090	9630	10440	10980
CMEA total									
Others									
Albania	165	248	324	349	448	483	545	596	615
Cyprus	8	14	13	14	14	13	14	14	13
Gibraltar	0	0	0	0	0	1	1	1	1
Liechtenstein	8	8	8	8	9	10	10	11	12
Malta	8	9	10	14	14	14	13	13	13
Monaco	6	7	8	10	11	13	15	17	18
Turkey	18052	33000	52500	89817	139330	188096	261919	494329	988978
Yugoslavia	4488	14300	17500	22600	30800	40900	60000	87100	159000
Total									
European total									

Source: National Accounts/Euromonitor estimates
Notes: a Billions
b Dollar values based on 1988 figures

Database name: Consumer Expenditure Patterns
Sector name: Expenditure on Tobacco

Table No: 1107

Title: Consumer Expenditure on Tobacco 1977-1989

Unit: National currencies (millions)

	1986	1987	1988	1989	% growth 1977-1989	% share 1989	Total $ million 1989	$ per capita 1989	Notes
EC members									
Belgium	55635	54629	55709	56789	77.15	1.59	1441	145	
Denmark	11560	11600	11639	11971	105.26	1.81	1638	318	
France	33998	35997	37998	39998	222.98	6.94	6269	112	
West Germany	19820	19100	19953	20555	43.64	12.10	10934	177	
Greece	96410	117871	139295	152500	792.33	1.04	939	93	
Ireland	515	573	601	659	336.28	1.03	935	265	
Italy	9994	10249	9007	9838	296.05	7.93	7170	124	a
Luxembourg	7757	7486	7633	7780	332.22	0.22	197	531	
Netherlands	4470	4542	3576	4620	40.85	2.41	2179	147	
Portugal	44000	51095	57948	58601	648.89	0.41	372	36	
Spain	278000	315887	346677	389099	520.57	3.64	3287	84	
United Kingdom	7471	7653	7945	8169	125.17	14.82	13396	234	
EC total						53.95	48757	150	
EFTA members									
Austria	17000	17200	17250	17316	47.37	1.45	1309	172	
Finland	3854	4094	4315	5103	233.09	1.32	1189	240	
Iceland	2646	2987							
Norway	5906	6456	6650	6870	213.57	1.10	995	235	
Sweden	9200	10000	11523	12464	178.53	2.14	1933	228	
Switzerland	2610	2615	2750	2883	47.70	1.95	1762	267	
EFTA total						7.95	7189	224	
CMEA members									
Bulgaria	545	553	562			0.37	331	37	b
Czechoslovakia	18468	20111	21883			2.58	2328	149	b
East Germany	7047	7414	7774			4.60	4157	250	b
Hungary	14216	16509	19792			0.43	393	37	b
Poland	157500	185918	290054			0.75	674	18	b
Romania	11460	11700	11941			0.93	836	37	b
USSR	11520	12240	12960			23.43	21176	75	b
CMEA total						33.08	29895	75	
Others									
Albania	604	671	741			0.14	124	39	b
Cyprus	14	14	15			0.04	32	45	b
Gibraltar	1	1	1			0.00	1	36	b
Liechtenstein	12	12	11			0.01	8	262	b
Malta	13	13	13			0.04	41	116	b
Monaco	18	20	21			0.00	4	125	b
Turkey	1574492	2681785	5786623			4.50	4068	77	b
Yugoslavia	300500	550000	1340777			0.28	257	11	b
total						5.02	4535	56	
European total						100.00	90375	108	

Database name: Consumer Expenditure Patterns
Sector name: Expenditure on Clothing

Table No: 1108

Title: Consumer Expenditure on Clothing 1977-1989

Unit: National currencies (millions)

	1977	1978	1979	1980	1981	1982	1983	1984	1985
EC members									
Belgium	95903	100631	116555	124316	131942	150088	153049	157713	167515
Denmark	8605	8984	9811	10183	9533	12208	13562	14986	16904
France	101059	108401	116539	112016	129561	143144	157436	169638	183385
West Germany	55200	58290	60200	61853	63498	63022	64974	66789	69726
Greece	64518	76288	94964	100245	117550	139049	145001	186157	208051
Ireland	225	302	356	370	390	406	472	538	627
Italy	9202	10206	12222	16119	18468	20940	22537	25605	37616
Luxembourg	4384	4733	5006	5278	5750	6060	6624	6703	7303
Netherlands	9140	12030	11690	12240	12600	12440	12446	11380	12230
Portugal	31649	37604	54185	75752	94424	102000	116480	130000	159000
Spain	400800	479400	533000	639300	725600	800400	895600	946700	1066300
United Kingdom	5520	6482	7549	8103	8506	8856	9860	10735	12298
EC total									
EFTA members									
Austria	41309	41796	45686	50050	53115	57120	61370	64900	66840
Finland	3062	3146	3735	4517	5436	5845	6510	7134	8158
Iceland	278	400	617	972	1549	2432	4002	6211	8503
Norway	7088	7456	7995	9001	9773	11671	11914	13179	15866
Sweden	13488	14246	15663	16530	17843	19375	21141	23515	26664
Switzerland	3850	3965	4210	4743	5030	5100	5293	5408	5679
EFTA total									
CMEA members									
Bulgaria	992	1198	1283	1307	1356	1416	1404	1440	1464
Czechoslovakia	17778	17778	17778	18296	19331	20539	21057	22438	23301
East Germany	15118	15631	16271	17040	16912	16271	16271	16912	17681
Hungary	23164	24669	27178	28850	31275	32028	35206	37213	44571
Poland	128000	131200	141600	156000	185600	209800	284700	357200	494517
Romania	31140	31260	32700	34200	36300	37320	37680	38400	39600
USSR	45000	46000	47500	45000	47790	52920	62100	66600	71370
CMEA total									
Others									
Albania	825	1151	1129	1242	1588	1948	2273	3002	3371
Cyprus	25	40	40	46	56	67	75	104	126
Gibraltar	4	4	4	4	4	4	5	5	5
Liechtenstein	21	19	21	24	25	25	27	31	32
Malta	16	16	21	24	24	21	21	23	28
Monaco	52	56	60	59	68	75	85	92	100
Turkey	66300	85800	109200	149695	256187	364056	515389	790295	970785
Yugoslavia	23001	25016	34020	40039	52020	90032	100001	144324	235997
Total									
European total									

Source: National Accounts/Euromonitor estimates
Notes:
a Billions
b Including footwear
c Dollar values based on 1988 figures

Database name:	Consumer Expenditure Patterns
Sector name:	Expenditure on Clothing

Table No: 1108

Title: Consumer Expenditure on Clothing 1977-1989

Unit: National currencies (millions)

	1986	1987	1988	1989	% growth 1977-1989	% share 1989	Total $ million 1989	$ per capita 1989	Notes
EC members									
Belgium	178501	182022	186419	190816	98.97	1.31	4843	488	
Denmark	18236	19100	18540	19069	121.60	0.71	2609	507	
France	199677	216302	230500	244698	142.13	10.38	38353	683	
West Germany	73379	76136	78777	90815	64.52	13.07	48306	784	
Greece	230111	272463	321987	389050	503.01	0.65	2395	238	
Ireland	645	602	631	692	207.41	0.27	982	278	
Italy	40601	46355	50038	54541	492.71	10.76	39750	688	a
Luxembourg	7869	8158	8447	8736	99.28	0.06	222	596	
Netherlands	12562	13499	14008	14072	53.96	1.80	6636	448	
Portugal	168000	189182	214556	223749	606.97	0.38	1421	138	
Spain	1180500	1357142	1489427	1621711	304.62	3.71	13699	350	
United Kingdom	13644	15082	16609	17238	212.28	7.65	28268	494	
EC total						50.73	187483	575	
EFTA members									
Austria	73184	74169	76555	81196	96.56	1.66	6137	808	
Finland	8015	8366	9233	10427	240.53	0.66	2430	490	
Iceland	9089	11709	13158						b,c
Norway	17946	18062	18178	19221	171.18	0.75	2784	657	
Sweden	28682	31012	33976	40461	199.98	1.70	6276	742	
Switzerland	5980	6050	6195	6670	73.25	1.10	4077	618	
EFTA total						5.87	21704	676	
CMEA members									
Bulgaria	1489	1537	1586			0.25	933	103	c
Czechoslovakia	23819	24818	25839			0.74	2749	176	c
East Germany	18065	19510	21001			3.04	11231	675	c
Hungary	46294	54441	66090			0.35	1311	123	c
Poland	696914	794344	1196615			0.75	2780	74	c
Romania	41340	41600	41846			0.79	2931	128	c
USSR	75600	79050	82371			36.42	134594	474	c
CMEA total						42.36	156528	395	
Others									
Albania	3422	3752	4090			0.18	682	215	c
Cyprus	141	151	181			0.11	389	541	c
Gibraltar	5	5	6			0.00	11	357	c
Liechtenstein	34	34	35			0.01	24	803	c
Malta	30	32	33			0.03	99	283	c
Monaco	107	114	120			0.01	20	720	c
Turkey	1185360	1647000	2899042			0.55	2038	38	c
Yugoslavia	451403	998953	2944433			0.15	565	24	c
Total						1.04	3828	47	
European total						100.00	369543	442	

Title: Consumer Expenditure on Footwear 1977-1989

Unit: National currencies (millions)

	1977	1978	1979	1980	1981	1982	1983	1984	1985
EC members									
Belgium	19976	20961	22734	26270	28550	31319	32034	35279	38343
Denmark	1581	1733	1943	2053	2010	2138	2157	2223	2335
France	16010	17799	20578	23532	26204	29842	32041	33681	36060
West Germany	9930	10680	11590	14862	15257	15143	15612	16048	16754
Greece	7288	8619	10728	11324	13278	16009	16396	21433	23953
Ireland	26	34	41	90	115	108	111	114	126
Italy	2100	2960	3850	4486	4875	6780	8020	9500	11131
Luxembourg	496	535	566	596	649	684	748	757	824
Netherlands	3240	3490	3650	3740	3560	3690	3790	3960	4140
Portugal	9827	12010	14800	18938	23606	33501	29100	34000	40100
Spain	126274	151024	170050	200500	217900	240400	258400	273100	307700
United Kingdom	1110	1348	1621	1761	1853	2068	2314	2525	2766
EC total									
EFTA members									
Austria	11261	11394	12454	14100	13400	15290	16310	17250	17770
Finland	645	657	687	799	861	1025	971	1062	1277
Iceland									
Norway	1507	1532	1704	2031	2207	2279	2438	2635	2972
Sweden	2010	2380	2601	2871	3099	3348	3657	4038	4915
Switzerland	1005	830	1420	1041	1104	1119	1161	1187	1246
EFTA total									
CMEA members									
Bulgaria	278	290	303	315	327	351	375	399	424
Czechoslovakia	2762	2934	3107	3279	3452	3538	3711	3797	3797
East Germany	3075	3203	3459	3459	3587	3587	3715	3844	4100
Hungary	4348	4767	4767	5017	5519	5603	6188	6774	8028
Poland	21700	23500	25100	31300	33500	49000	89600	101600	138553
Romania	5160	5520	5940	5940	6060	5520	6960	7860	8580
USSR	11200	12200	12300	11160	12780	12690	14130	15120	15480
CMEA total									
Others									
Albania	124	228	245	236	243	265	309	362	410
Cyprus	6	10	9	8	7	7	8	8	9
Gibraltar	1	1	1	1	1	1	1	1	1
Liechtenstein	4	4	6	5	5	5	5	6	6
Malta	2	3	3	5	5	5	5	4	5
Monaco	8	9	11	12	14	16	17	18	20
Turkey	16900	33000	44100	65866	98879	133487	185878	344856	437805
Yugoslavia	10700	12300	15500	19800	26400	35600	51800	95994	226559
Total									
European total									

Source: National Accounts/Euromonitor estimates
Notes: a Billions
b Included in "Clothing"
c Dollar values based on 1988 figures

Database name: Consumer Expenditure Patterns
Sector name: Expenditure on Footwear

Table No: 1109

Title: Consumer Expenditure on Footwear 1977-1989

Unit: National currencies (millions)

	1986	1987	1988	1989	% growth 1977-1989	% share 1989	Total $ million 1989	$ per capita 1989	Notes
EC members									
Belgium	38989	39362	39155	38948	94.97	1.14	988	100	
Denmark	2547	2600	2650	2726	72.42	0.43	373	73	
France	39501	43389	45801	50504	215.46	9.15	7916	141	
West Germany	17380	17914	18849	19185	93.20	11.80	10205	166	
Greece	25317	28108	33217	50222	589.11	0.36	309	31	
Ireland	143	155	163	179	600.65	0.29	254	72	
Italy	12122	13383	13908	14880	608.57	12.54	10845	188	a
Luxembourg	847	879	911	938	89.11	0.03	24	64	
Netherlands	4210	4380	4488	4578	41.30	2.50	2159	146	
Portugal	53230	58210	66017	70894	621.42	0.52	450	44	
Spain	335000	376724	413444	468878	271.32	4.58	3961	101	
United Kingdom	2994	3220	3356	3503	215.59	6.64	5745	100	
EC total						49.97	43228	133	
EFTA members									
Austria	19450	20026	21000	21487	90.81	1.88	1624	214	
Finland	1355	1448	1725	1805	179.83	0.49	421	85	
Iceland									b
Norway	3406	3897	4050	4147	175.17	0.69	601	142	
Sweden	5475	5841	6485	7279	262.16	1.31	1129	133	
Switzerland	1520	1565	1575	1584	57.66	1.12	969	147	
EFTA total						5.48	4743	148	
CMEA members									
Bulgaria	508	533	558			0.38	328	36	c
Czechoslovakia	3884	4279	4711			0.58	501	32	c
East Germany	4228	4487	4747			2.93	2538	152	c
Hungary	8272	9422	11080			0.25	220	21	c
Poland	182355	226955	373317			1.00	867	23	c
Romania	9660	10400	11193			0.91	784	34	c
USSR	16290	17850	19492			36.81	31849	112	c
CMEA total						42.87	37088	94	
Others									
Albania	430	458	484			0.09	81	25	c
Cyprus	10	11	13			0.03	28	39	c
Gibraltar	1	1	1			0.00	2	75	c
Liechtenstein	6	6	6			0.00	4	134	c
Malta	6	8	9			0.03	26	75	c
Monaco	21	24	26			0.01	4	158	c
Turkey	580800	732000	1168727			0.95	822	15	c
Yugoslavia	501698	976971	2533944			0.56	486	21	c
Total						1.68	1454	18	
European total						100.00	86512	104	

Title: Consumer Expenditure on Housing 1977-1989

Unit: National currencies (millions)

	1977	1978	1979	1980	1981	1982	1983	1984	1985
EC members									
Belgium	167755	187187	205350	228050	258752	285313	313481	341095	365970
Denmark	27858	31781	35478	39359	43447	48761	54234	59061	63281
France	112550	127277	147114	172780	203612	232297	263750	292864	322202
West Germany	81590	85990	97170	104430	111420	119270	135000	150090	159340
Greece	61469	76010	93203	114624	140414	173505	192990	242237	347132
Ireland	210	204	275	327	387	462	505	546	614
Italy	14600	17018	19050	24018	28381	33426	40213	49557	54857
Luxembourg	7805	8318	8857	9549	10405	11452	12960	14385	15600
Netherlands	15010	16590	19970	22100	24500	26900	30740	32150	32150
Portugal	31807	49614	68985	94690	118030	167503	210000	230000	250000
Spain	756875	900681	1101100	1469900	1649200	1890000	2094100	2295200	2469800
United Kingdom	9978	11358	13353	16048	19445	22236	23525	25012	26922
EC total									
EFTA members									
Austria	48000	60000	73760	87340	97466	112987	125215	139920	144257
Finland	10979	12150	13392	14992	17740	20142	22799	22294	23324
Iceland	406	612	856	1391	2224	3493	7654	9469	12754
Norway	10071	11379	12320	13864	16036	18484	21138	23623	25766
Sweden	35948	41577	46292	51394	66857	74332	81073	88050	92510
Switzerland	12505	12705	12970	13360	14175	15750	16885	17580	18425
EFTA total									
CMEA members									
Bulgaria	278	290	290	303	327	351	375	399	412
Czechoslovakia	7249	7077	7249	7594	8630	8630	9148	9148	9148
East Germany	1000	1153	1409	1537	2050	2050	2178	2434	2691
Hungary	11540	12293	13296	14216	15721	16223	18397	20070	22746
Poland	36600	40100	48100	66700	76900	101700	300500	561007	731628
Romania	7980	8220	8400	8640	8880	9060	9240	9660	9840
USSR	9200	9600	9900	9180	10710	11070	13410	13950	14670
CMEA total									
Others									
Albania	330	437	442	493	525	857	982	1107	1253
Cyprus	18	28	28	33	36	50	53	56	60
Gibraltar	5	5	6	6	7	7	7	7	8
Liechtenstein	51	54	57	59	63	72	80	93	98
Malta	8	9	14	17	17	15	15	14	15
Monaco	58	66	75	92	107	122	143	158	175
Turkey	42403	142296	275153	209573	328099	473273	684369	1178258	1617975
Yugoslavia	8313	8586	13090	18587	22752	30061	41754	73445	191288
Total									
European total									

Source: National Accounts/Euromonitor estimates
Notes: a Billions
b Partly estimated by Euromonitor
c Dollar values based on 1988 figures

Database name: Consumer Expenditure Patterns
Sector name: Expenditure on Housing

Table No: 1110

Title: Consumer Expenditure on Housing 1977-1989

Unit: National currencies (millions)

	1986	1987	1988	1989	% growth 1977-1989	% share 1989	Total $ million 1989	$ per capita 1989	Notes
EC members									
Belgium	387100	412713	435750	458787	173.49	2.53	11643	1173	
Denmark	67495	73016	79212	80673	189.59	2.40	11036	2146	
France	338986	368003	379777	391551	247.89	13.33	61371	1093	
West Germany	166240	173340	181790	192240	135.62	22.20	102255	1660	
Greece	390611	489618	578612	623000	913.52	0.83	3836	381	b
Ireland	652	645	676	707	236.95	0.22	1004	284	
Italy	61242	66616	70555	74494	410.23	11.79	54292	940	a
Luxembourg	16569	17538	18507	19572	150.77	0.11	497	1335	
Netherlands	32834	33012	32835	32855	118.89	3.36	15493	1046	
Portugal	300000	336323	381432	426541	1241.03	0.59	2709	263	b
Spain	2750000	3144826	3451361	3849000	408.54	7.06	32514	830	b
United Kingdom	29047	31202	34382	37140	272.22	13.22	60905	1064	
EC total						77.64	357554	1097	
EFTA members									
Austria	151000	155050	159813	164576	242.87	2.70	12439	1638	
Finland	24500	28554	32608	35589	224.15	1.80	8293	1671	
Iceland	13984	19515	17406						c
Norway	29270	31555	32333	33580	233.43	1.06	4864	1148	
Sweden	101048	110091	115660	128660	257.90	4.33	19957	2358	
Switzerland	19440	20375	21335	22464	79.64	2.98	13732	2081	
EFTA total						12.87	59284	1846	
CMEA members									
Bulgaria	436	447	458			0.06	269	30	c
Czechoslovakia	9493	9756	10018			0.23	1066	68	c
East Germany	3075	3122	3159			0.37	1689	101	c
Hungary	25171	29797	36414			0.16	723	68	c
Poland	902333	1279100	2396395			1.21	5567	147	c
Romania	10080	10400	10726			0.16	751	33	c
USSR	15390	16473	17571			6.23	28711	101	c
CMEA total						8.42	38776	98	
Others									
Albania	1350	1464	1579			0.06	263	83	c
Cyprus	62	66	79			0.04	170	236	c
Gibraltar	8	8	8			0.00	15	495	c
Liechtenstein	100	104	109			0.02	74	2478	c
Malta	16	17	17			0.01	53	150	c
Monaco	185	197	210			0.01	35	1256	c
Turkey	2138400	3001200	5336034			0.81	3752	71	c
Yugoslavia	419318	976971	3031768			0.13	582	25	c
Total						1.07	4944	61	
European total						100.00	460557	551	

Title: Consumer Expenditure on Fuel 1977-1989

Unit: National currencies (millions)

	1977	1978	1979	1980	1981	1982	1983	1984	1985
EC members									
Belgium	91497	100353	118230	138347	161400	179304	184544	202797	229089
Denmark	8366	9214	13854	16473	18878	20459	19243	19655	21508
France	52562	61608	73028	93994	108964	125469	144501	159389	177287
West Germany	29050	32060	38040	40300	45550	52910	54490	59740	64340
Greece	15900	18746	20153	28976	41554	51789	66146	83025	94789
Ireland	197	212	267	350	442	503	528	562	628
Italy	2987	5238	7134	9286	11733	14176	17425	20227	23732
Luxembourg	3554	3788	4638	6711	8048	8578	9108	9979	10803
Netherlands	6500	7260	9200	10530	11500	12770	13305	13840	15670
Portugal									
Spain	185500	195000	221000	246600	344000	400100	459700	503100	541400
United Kingdom	4219	4613	5292	6355	7728	8696	9399	9575	10657
EC total									
EFTA members									
Austria	18850	32050	35450	39895	41300	47020	51730	54250	56799
Finland	2362	2546	2825	3210	3722	4078	6059	6698	7567
Iceland									
Norway	4205	5165	6173	7406	8846	10285	11570	13086	15927
Sweden	8518	10000	12055	15484	10576	12247	13762	22142	24285
Switzerland	3400	4423	7500	8050	8095	8105	8235	8890	9380
EFTA total									
CMEA members									
Bulgaria	133	157	169	182	230	242	206	218	278
Czechoslovakia	2934	3107	3625	3797	4315	4660	4660	5868	6559
East Germany	769	384	769	1153	1537	1666	1666	1666	1666
Hungary	8362	9115	9366	10704	13547	13965	15805	17895	18230
Poland	12500	14100	16700	21700	21300	75900	72700	89900	105200
Romania	3060	3360	3540	4200	5160	6180	6480	7500	4680
USSR	7600	8000	8000	9450	11700	13680	16380	16560	17370
CMEA total									
Others									
Albania	206	238	255	287	512	701	764	873	1048
Cyprus	4	7	7	9	10	12	14	16	18
Gibraltar									
Liechtenstein	14	17	20	15	16	17	17	18	19
Malta	5	5	6	6	7	7	7	8	8
Monaco	27	32	38	50	58	66	79	87	97
Turkey	52000	66000	105000	164665	269670	333718	506940	862140	1027890
Yugoslavia	22287	24221	32270	43069	63567	82177	112318	147210	283536
Total									
European total									

Source: National Accounts/Euromonitor estimates
Notes: a Billions
b Included under "Housing"
c Dollar values based on 1988 figures

	1986	1987	1988	1989	% growth 1977-1989	% share 1989	Total $ million 1989	$ per capita 1989	Notes
EC members									
Belgium	190381	173997	157715	165000	80.33	2.27	4187	422	
Denmark	23294	25460	25279	25745	207.74	1.91	3522	685	
France	186522	197018	207969	218920	316.50	18.64	34313	611	
West Germany	55900	51010	49710	52250	79.86	15.10	27793	451	
Greece	101838	136005	160725	193000	1113.84	0.65	1188	118	
Ireland	641	638	669	734	272.72	0.57	1041	295	
Italy	22214	23618	24226	26439	785.14	10.47	19269	334	a
Luxembourg	9771	10000	10229	11542	224.76	0.16	293	787	
Netherlands	16004	16004	16005	16222	149.57	4.16	7649	516	
Portugal									b
Spain	572000	818965	898792	935555	404.34	4.29	7903	202	
United Kingdom	10061	10250	10400	10888	158.07	9.70	17855	312	
EC total						67.91	125013	383	
EFTA members									
Austria	59200	60984	55200	54083	186.91	2.22	4088	538	
Finland	6657	6620	7539	8251	249.32	1.04	1923	387	
Iceland									c
Norway	18093	18555	20687	19746	369.58	1.55	2860	675	
Sweden	23446	24809	26777	30921	263.01	2.61	4796	567	
Switzerland	7625	7225	6770	7000	105.88	2.32	4279	649	
EFTA total						9.75	17946	559	
CMEA members									
Bulgaria	363	410	462			0.15	272	30	c
Czechoslovakia	6386	7702	9282			0.54	987	63	c
East Germany	1409	1561	1723			0.50	921	55	c
Hungary	17895	20939	25291			0.27	502	47	c
Poland	135000	176200	303944			0.38	706	19	c
Romania	4680	4836	4995			0.19	350	15	c
USSR	18405	19584	20766			18.43	33932	120	c
CMEA total						20.46	37671	95	
Others									
Albania	1120	1220	1321			0.12	220	69	c
Cyprus	19	20	24			0.03	52	73	c
Gibraltar									c
Liechtenstein	20	20	21			0.01	14	473	c
Malta	9	9	9			0.02	29	82	c
Monaco	105	110	116			0.01	19	694	c
Turkey	1399200	1939800	3406840			1.30	2395	45	c
Yugoslavia	632849	1331123	3729170			0.39	716	30	c
Total						1.87	3446	42	
European total						100.00	184075	220	

Database name: Consumer Expenditure Patterns
Sector name: Expenditure on Household Goods and Services   Table No: 1112

Title: Consumer Expenditure on Household Goods and Services 1977-1989

Unit: National currencies (millions)

	1977	1978	1979	1980	1981	1982	1983	1984	1985
EC members									
Belgium	260754	268821	280392	310803	318564	335029	341451	364200	385500
Denmark	13316	14050	15147	15333	16049	17563	19112	20808	23097
France	123078	141050	166987	171292	200891	234609	265197	293760	325170
West Germany	76760	80250	88290	96640	97560	97700	82090	91200	92170
Greece	54231	66784	74094	89740	111604	135334	172267	216884	275470
Ireland	270	320	395	449	470	498	589	597	708
Italy	11560	14381	18500	24766	29338	32132	34730	38193	42868
Luxembourg	6212	6621	6620	7000	8191	8741	9412	10581	11565
Netherlands	17000	16886	17720	18590	17570	17190	15223	17511	17920
Portugal	46685	51519	64384	84510	95000	121000	152000	162000	177000
Spain	555684	690008	794300	810500	888200	989500	1123900	1209300	1325100
United Kingdom	6340	7547	9036	9956	10553	11217	12172	12999	14067
EC total									
EFTA members									
Austria	43130	40730	41840	43230	46100	48760	51790	54250	55680
Finland	4594	5052	6022	9931	10880	12488	13304	12312	12310
Iceland	180	300	471	610	781	1261	2000	5579	7455
Norway	9672	10069	10721	11878	13215	14099	15086	16507	19060
Sweden	15381	16212	17488	19051	19987	21779	23521	27570	33490
Switzerland	4940	5730	5910	6315	6550	6625	6735	6925	7125
EFTA total									
CMEA members									
Bulgaria	1331	1610	1682	1912	2663	3195	2856	3038	3147
Czechoslovakia	23474	23991	29342	34002	40388	45221	48328	50572	51607
East Germany	9609	10122	9865	10506	13709	14478	17553	18834	20756
Hungary	23164	24836	28516	29603	33031	34286	37296	35122	44571
Poland	129600	141500	163100	179100	199400	283200	357100	365500	477100
Romania	20760	21900	23040	22200	22020	22200	24180	25080	25800
USSR	28000	29200	30400	29160	34560	35100	36000	34290	35910
CMEA total									
Others									
Albania	797	1092	1129	1335	1627	1964	2509	2300	2506
Cyprus	36	54	53	61	69	82	90	96	104
Gibraltar	4	4	4	4	4	4	5	5	5
Liechtenstein	20	25	26	28	29	29	29	30	32
Malta	24	25	31	38	36	36	35	36	34
Monaco	65	74	87	93	108	125	147	162	180
Turkey	130000	181500	199500	299390	539340	679571	887145	1580590	1922535
Yugoslavia	43809	47276	60410	77622	102783	135048	178498	304043	503687
Total									
European total									

Source: National Accounts/Euromonitor estimates
Notes: a   Billions
            b   Consumer durables only
            c   Dollar values based on 1988 figures

Database name: Consumer Expenditure Patterns
Sector name: Expenditure on Household Goods and Services   Table No: 1112

Title: Consumer Expenditure on Household Goods and Services 1977-1989

Unit:

	1986	1987	1988	1989	% growth 1977-1989	% share 1989	Total $ million 1989	$ per capita 1989	Notes
EC members									
Belgium	422400	443200	461814	480428	84.25	3.15	12192	1228	
Denmark	24520	24584	26465	27500	106.52	0.97	3762	731	
France	342109	369610	392322	432613	251.50	17.54	67807	1208	
West Germany	95610	101480	106820	115233	50.12	15.86	61294	995	
Greece	334810	407562	481641	505000	831.20	0.80	3109	309	
Ireland	791	863	905	955	253.57	0.35	1355	384	
Italy	48088	52011	57861	63068	445.57	11.89	45965	796	a
Luxembourg	12203	12670	13138	13605	119.01	0.09	345	928	
Netherlands	19050	20300	21410	22520	32.47	2.75	10619	717	
Portugal	200560	219904	249398	278892	497.39	0.46	1771	172	
Spain	1480000	1663669	1825832	2071462	272.78	4.53	17498	447	
United Kingdom	14085	16250	17500	18750	195.74	7.95	30748	537	
EC total						66.35	256466	787	
EFTA members									
Austria	58678	60984	62984	69270	60.61	1.35	5235	689	
Finland	12801	14005	14780	16357	256.05	0.99	3812	768	
Iceland	9674	14049	18424			0.11	428	1706	c
Norway	21633	22955	23552	24428	152.57	0.92	3538	835	
Sweden	37346	37346	40264	46547	202.62	1.87	7220	853	
Switzerland	7435	7630	7920	8210	66.19	1.30	5019	761	
EFTA total						6.53	25252	787	
CMEA members									
Bulgaria	3268	3372	3476			0.53	2045	226	c
Czechoslovakia	54369	55627	56868			1.57	6050	387	c
East Germany	21909	23412	24936			3.45	13335	801	c
Hungary	50091	56374	65495			0.34	1299	122	c
Poland	530000	650713	1055892			0.63	2453	65	c
Romania	28200	28600	28995			0.53	2031	89	c
USSR	38250	40800	43369			18.33	70865	250	c
CMEA total						25.37	98077	247	
Others									
Albania	2858	3050	3236			0.14	539	170	c
Cyprus	112	118	138			0.08	297	412	c
Gibraltar	5	5	5			0.00	10	320	c
Liechtenstein	34	34	35			0.01	24	792	c
Malta	35	38	40			0.03	120	343	c
Monaco	200	218	236			0.01	40	1417	c
Turkey	2587200	3660000	6559184			1.19	4612	87	c
Yugoslavia	903911	1975924	5752944			0.29	1104	47	c
Total						1.74	6745	83	
European total						100.00	386541	463	

Title: Consumer Expenditure on Health Goods and Medical Services 1977-1989

Unit: National currencies (millions)

	1977	1978	1979	1980	1981	1982	1983	1984	1985
EC members									
Belgium	183474	202695	215614	229713	252048	278363	304962	324787	347233
Denmark	2805	3126	3366	3760	4176	4632	5100	5572	6001
France	105147	124478	147044	171292	200891	234609	265197	293760	325170
West Germany	29268	31356	32890	36020	38700	40340	42550	47460	49310
Greece	21096	25042	37243	43216	50269	58883	78012	97919	111793
Ireland	69	85	98	122	116	128	147	159	165
Italy	5906	6937	8264	10685	13802	17830	20681	23110	27900
Luxembourg	4361	4883	5243	5863	6362	7043	7287	7941	8390
Netherlands	17430	19290	22750	24830	26580	28410	29220	29790	30640
Portugal	17856	23644	29251	37057	45556	63536	68200	81000	85000
Spain	293207	320300	360500	394400	447700	528900	591500	662400	706200
United Kingdom	732	828	999	1261	1489	1752	2064	2284	2604
EC total									
EFTA members									
Austria	17730	20850	22820	24870	26890	28840	33300	37200	39680
Finland	1844	2068	2196	2404	4176	4063	4832	5499	6087
Iceland	90	160	304	545	861	1372	2000	2947	3891
Norway	4400	4906	5249	5676	6387	7407	8180	8586	9298
Sweden	2953	3243	3516	3973	4432	5034	5786	6539	7244
Switzerland	9140	9485	9990	10660	11475	12410	13255	13960	14840
EFTA total									
CMEA members									
Bulgaria	352	401	432	469	526	596	548	581	671
Czechoslovakia	10287	11064	11461	11927	13394	14550	16725	18589	19055
East Germany	3459	3203	3075	3331	4100	5509	6022	6662	6662
Hungary	18648	21073	22244	24920	27429	29436	32111	28516	40139
Poland	93500	101700	119000	134300	158900	190000	215050	241000	357100
Romania	9240	9840	10380	10500	10980	11520	13920	16080	16800
USSR	10100	10400	10700	9630	10890	11160	11790	12060	12420
CMEA total									
Others									
Albania	248	318	334	411	538	779	745	809	934
Cyprus	5	7	8	10	12	16	19	20	21
Gibraltar	2	3	3	4	4	4	4	4	4
Liechtenstein	41	44	49	52	55	59	63	71	75
Malta	8	11	11	11	10	12	13	13	13
Monaco	54	64	75	91	106	123	144	159	177
Turkey	8219	14822	22465	91564	119664	164442	263563	937749	2541496
Yugoslavia	10710	11978	14490	30787	41273	51058	71399	121553	235997
Total									
European total									

Source: National Accounts/Euromonitor estimates
Notes: a Billions
b Dollar values based on 1988 figures

Database name: Consumer Expenditure Patterns
Sector name: Expenditure on Health

Table No: 1113

Title: Consumer Expenditure on Health Goods and Medical Services 1977-1989

Unit: National currencies (millions)

	1986	1987	1988	1989	% growth 1977-1989	% share 1989	Total $ million 1989	$ per capita 1989	Notes
EC members									
Belgium	368164	387438	409833	432228	135.58	4.71	10969	1105	
Denmark	6569	6569	6986	7115	153.65	0.42	973	189	
France	336678	353540	373191	411517	291.37	27.67	64500	1149	
West Germany	51000	53160	56740	60320	106.10	13.76	32085	521	
Greece	120410	140539	166083	186700	785.00	0.49	1149	114	
Ireland	170	173	182	199	190.21	0.12	283	80	
Italy	31037	36081	36615	37322	531.93	11.67	27201	471	a
Luxembourg	9070	9750	10430	11110	154.76	0.12	282	758	
Netherlands	31610	32330	33060	33790	93.86	6.84	15933	1076	
Portugal	88000	113186	128367	143548	703.92	0.39	912	88	
Spain	840500	935960	1027191	1176394	301.22	4.26	9937	254	
United Kingdom	2916	3375	3600	3825	422.54	2.69	6273	110	
EC total						73.14	170497	523	
EFTA members									
Austria	40891	43424	46363	48450	173.27	1.57	3662	482	
Finland	6713	7526	8636	9380	408.68	0.94	2186	440	
Iceland	6093	8326	9000.0			0.09	209	834	b
Norway	10301	11203	12105	11922	170.95	0.74	1727	407	
Sweden	7878	8571	9603	10683	261.75	0.71	1657	196	
Switzerland	15810	16780	17790	18500	102.41	4.85	11309	1714	
EFTA total						8.90	20750	646	
CMEA members									
Bulgaria	800	820	840			0.21	494	55	b
Czechoslovakia	20885	23535	26499			1.21	2819	180	b
East Germany	7431	7804	8169			1.87	4368	262	b
Hungary	40725	48320	59185			0.50	1174	110	b
Poland	478100	593200	972747			0.97	2260	60	b
Romania	19020	20176	21394			0.64	1499	66	b
USSR	12690	13515	14344			10.05	23438	83	b
CMEA total						15.47	36051	91	
Others									
Albania	1006	1098	1191			0.09	199	62	b
Cyprus	22	24	29			0.03	62	85	b
Gibraltar	5	5	5			0.00	9	303	b
Liechtenstein	73	73	72			0.02	50	1653	b
Malta	15	15	15			0.02	46	132	b
Monaco	193	221	252			0.02	42	1511	b
Turkey	5448807	5490000	7007464			2.11	4927	93	b
Yugoslavia	431488	889044	2439795			0.20	468	20	b
Total						2.49	5802	72	
European total						100.00	233101	279	

Source:
Notes:

Database name: Consumer Expenditure Patterns
Sector name: Expenditure on Transport

Table No: 1114

Title: Consumer Expenditure on Transport 1977-1989

Unit: National currencies (millions)

	1977	1978	1979	1980	1981	1982	1983	1984	1985
EC members									
Belgium	194686	212107	233408	256125	275821	302172	328447	351596	372493
Denmark	22872	24868	28049	27515	30103	34376	40598	46059	48666
France	120302	137589	152599	158567	182509	218936	237538	245300	272452
West Germany	90088	97962	110500	114808	120263	123851	131862	135513	139776
Greece	75759	90544	109178	126099	160818	207700	240560	301840	340265
Ireland	482	602	662	782	945	1011	1057	1169	1249
Italy	12948	14624	18731	25538	31761	37511	47966	54958	59035
Luxembourg	8740	9800	11271	13359	15454	17878	18916	20028	21282
Netherlands	15870	17190	19360	16700	18670	20990	22718	24130	22900
Portugal	55981	70722	89341	115802	153549	219482	243300	299200	368800
Spain	734400	891600	1028400	1320900	1505100	1701400	2016600	2256700	2447500
United Kingdom	11455	13890	17594	20300	22765	24538	27577	28966	31866
EC total									
EFTA members									
Austria	66560	63504	72160	83450	91378	95030	103656	108577	113680
Finland	11114	12412	14750	17628	20384	23715	25501	28806	30918
Iceland	480	673	872	1095	1446	2414	4100	6919	6725
Norway	14328	13581	15672	18389	20799	23619	25711	36356	37037
Sweden	20485	23542	35907	39325	44413	51616	55792	61039	68835
Switzerland	10540	11120	11835	12755	13925	14240	14400	14770	15310
EFTA total									
CMEA members									
Bulgaria	944	1198	1295	1380	1501	1501	1501	1513	1586
Czechoslovakia	11737	12600	13290	15534	19849	21748	21748	21230	21575
East Germany	2370	2562	2691	2819	3075	3203	3459	3587	3715
Hungary	20906	23080	24251	28014	30857	33031	36794	40139	55275
Poland	87800	100000	113800	131100	166600	240900	370800	399900	420000
Romania	10380	12000	14280	14400	14520	15000	15780	17100	18120
USSR	9900	10300	10800	10170	10800	11250	12060	12690	13230
CMEA total									
Others									
Albania	413	546	599	698	768	935	1091	1384	1822
Cyprus	68	98	97	106	111	119	132	137	146
Gibraltar	4	4	4	5	5	5	5	5	6
Liechtenstein	42	46	50	54	59	60	60	66	68
Malta	28	31	38	51	51	51	51	51	58
Monaco	61	70	77	83	95	113	127	130	145
Turkey	156000	214500	231000	353280	539340	740247	1013880	1436900	1713150
Yugoslavia	47685	54590	73290	100303	138797	177042	243843	355037	629891
Total									
European total									

Source: National Accounts/Euromonitor estimates
Notes:
a Billions
b Including communications
c Dollar values based on 1988 figures

Database name: Consumer Expenditure Patterns
Sector name: Expenditure on Transport   Table No: 1114

Title: Consumer Expenditure on Transport 1977-1989

Unit: National currencies (millions)

	1986	1987	1988	1989	% growth 1977-1989	% share 1989	Total $ million 1989	$ per capita 1989	Notes
EC members									
Belgium	364571	393077	423619	454161	133.28	2.54	11526	1161	
Denmark	51233	54333	55420	56507	147.06	1.70	7730	1503	
France	286645	289260	305338	345050	186.82	11.92	54082	964	
West Germany	145035	152300	159890	172444	91.42	20.22	91726	1489	
Greece	379451	444283	525036	600000	691.99	0.81	3694	367	
Ireland	1219	1234	1294	1353	180.96	0.42	1920	544	
Italy	64134	70668	78701	85957	563.86	13.81	62646	1085	a
Luxembourg	22065	23272	24479	26065	198.22	0.15	661	1778	b
Netherlands	23388	24825	21774	25370	59.86	2.64	11963	808	
Portugal	372542	420404	476790	496166	786.31	0.69	3151	305	
Spain	2760000	3158865	3466769	3774673	413.98	7.03	31886	814	
United Kingdom	34826	37000	39000	45672	298.71	16.51	74896	1308	
EC total						78.44	355882	1091	
EFTA members									
Austria	120500	123615	125500	133967	101.27	2.23	10125	1333	
Finland	32134	34299	35233	40518	264.57	2.08	9442	1902	b
Iceland	8390	11059							c
Norway	42758	40006	35429	40455	182.35	1.29	5859	1383	
Sweden	77379	90534	101294	112838	450.83	3.86	17503	2068	b
Switzerland	15800	16355	17155	18032	71.08	2.43	11023	1671	b
EFTA total						11.89	53952	1680	
CMEA members									
Bulgaria	1755	1845	1937			0.25	1140	126	b,c
Czechoslovakia	24509	25674	26872			0.63	2859	183	b,c
East Germany	3972	4097	4212			0.50	2253	135	b,c
Hungary	66899	72480	81065			0.35	1608	151	b,c
Poland	590600	823500	1517574			0.78	3525	93	c
Romania	20220	20800	21389			0.33	1498	66	b,c
USSR	13770	14790	15831			5.70	25867	91	b,c
CMEA total						8.54	38750	98	
Others									
Albania	2000	2135	2266			0.08	378	119	b,c
Cyprus	155	167	201			0.10	432	600	b,c
Gibraltar	6	6	6			0.00	10	341	b,c
Liechtenstein	72	72	71			0.01	49	1625	b,c
Malta	60	65	67			0.04	203	581	b,c
Monaco	154	166	178			0.01	30	1065	b,c
Turkey	2112000	2562000	3937150			0.61	2768	52	b,c
Yugoslavia	993528	2220166	6607948			0.28	1268	54	b,c
Total						1.13	5138	63	
European total						100.00	453722	543	

Database name: Consumer Expenditure Patterns
Sector name: Expenditure on Communications

Table No: 1115

Title: Consumer Expenditure on Communications 1977-1989

Unit: National currencies (millions)

	1977	1978	1979	1980	1981	1982	1983	1984	198
EC members									
Belgium	14499	16237	17499	19568	20913	23177	25143	27271	2915
Denmark	1962	2237	2487	2714	3353	3830	4099	4200	431
France	9726	11763	14312	18391	21576	25409	28526	32596	3687
West Germany	10363	11269	12710	13172	13798	14209	15128	15547	1603
Greece	9364	11191	13960	16124	20563	28880	31030	39055	4893
Ireland	21	27	31	42	63	66	86	106	13
Italy	967	1180	1650	1947	2564	3196	3355	3550	435
Luxembourg									
Netherlands	1980	2130	2260	2450	2610	2750	2892	3080	319
Portugal	19168	24529	31156	39028	54030	70000	80000	88000	9900
Spain	48600	57100	65800	88100	106700	123300	141600	160500	18560
United Kingdom	1244	1470	1688	2247	2793	3101	3182	3527	394
EC total									
EFTA members									
Austria	9000	9980	11500	13670	14281	16909	16203	16427	1814
Finland									
Iceland									
Norway	1307	1509	1681	1831	2287	2883	3477	3908	430
Sweden									
Switzerland									
EFTA total									
CMEA members									
Bulgaria									
Czechoslovakia									
East Germany									
Hungary									
Poland	5000	6000	7200	8600	9100	11800	16600	19900	2900
Romania									
USSR									
CMEA total									
Others									
Albania									
Cyprus									
Gibraltar									
Liechtenstein									
Malta									
Monaco									
Turkey									
Yugoslavia									
Total									
European total									

Source: National Accounts/Euromonitor estimates
Notes: a Billions
b Included under "Transport"

Title: Consumer Expenditure on Communications 1977-1989

Unit: National currencies (millions)

	1986	1987	1988	1989	% growth 1977-1989	% share 1989	Total $ million 1989	$ per capita 1989	Notes
EC members									
Belgium	30544	32333	35366	38400	164.84	2.31	975	98	
Denmark	4677	5091	5300	5509	180.79	1.79	754	147	
France	39797	44996	47497	49998	414.07	18.59	7837	140	
West Germany	16645	17914	19000	20086	93.82	25.34	10684	173	
Greece	58592	72536	85720	105000	1021.32	1.53	646	64	
Ireland	153	164	172	180	752.28	0.61	255	72	
Italy	5893	6604	7266	7845	711.27	13.56	5718	99	a
Luxembourg									b
Netherlands	3260	3486	3596	3680	85.86	4.12	1735	117	
Portugal	105000	97016	110029	139843	629.57	2.11	888	86	
Spain	201500	245690	269638	293586	504.09	5.88	2480	63	
United Kingdom	4256	4575	4700	4886	292.77	19.01	8012	140	
EC total						94.85	39984	123	
EFTA members									
Austria	16169	16482	17000	17810	97.89	3.19	1346	177	
Finland									b
Iceland									b
Norway	4378	5110	5450	5700	336.11	1.96	826	195	
Sweden									b
Switzerland									b
EFTA total						5.15	2172	68	
CMEA members									
Bulgaria									b
Czechoslovakia									b
East Germany									b
Hungary									b
Poland	39300	41832	50300						
Romania									b
USSR									b
CMEA total									
Others									
Albania									b
Cyprus									b
Gibraltar									b
Liechtenstein									b
Malta									b
Monaco									b
Turkey									b
Yugoslavia									b
Total									
European total						100.00	42155	50	

Database name: Consumer Expenditure Patterns
Sector name: Expenditure on Leisure and Education 1977-1989   Table No: 1116

Title: Consumer Expenditure on Leisure and Education 1977-1989

Unit: National currencies (millions)

	1977	1978	1979	1980	1981	1982	1983	1984	1985
EC members									
Belgium	155756	167333	177107	194417	214000	237200	257400	279300	298700
Denmark	15321	16655	17993	18992	21407	23936	26383	29608	32440
France	72000	76882	88686	100853	114710	130100	145666	158111	165234
West Germany	70000	74500	79500	84090	87523	89900	92300	95810	98980
Greece	29189	36187	43231	52917	59906	67830	89271	112051	127928
Ireland	351	444	502	619	780	750	830	886	991
Italy	9010	10551	12416	15343	19000	22495	30212	35499	41433
Luxembourg	2410	2501	2530	2707	2930	3457	3833	4193	4336
Netherlands	14490	15520	18700	20050	20300	20500	20830	21950	22590
Portugal	21773	25349	31809	39671	49546	50000	60000	75000	82000
Spain	562000	604000	642000	708400	813600	943800	1076100	1194800	1292000
United Kingdom	8073	9393	10965	12727	14031	15412	16651	18013	19593
EC total									
EFTA members									
Austria	30120	31850	33140	34940	37780	38460	41430	37390	39560
Finland	5314	6207	7179	8158	9925	10750	12576	16841	16908
Iceland								4214	6184
Norway	9048	9612	10361	11626	13403	14488	15882	17572	20196
Sweden	19978	21630	23929	26469	29626	32201	34871	38430	41058
Switzerland	8395	8575	9075	9925	10700	11315	11870	12345	13325
EFTA total									
CMEA members									
Bulgaria	944	980	1113	1162	1283	1331	1452	1513	1634
Czechoslovakia	10183	11219	11392	12082	12945	13118	13635	13808	14326
East Germany	4228	4740	4869	6022	8072	8840	9225	11018	11146
Hungary	32530	37213	40808	45491	51679	56195	59875	65226	79861
Poland	45000	47823	50500	55662	60422	99200	110000	135493	134273
Romania	23340	24600	25440	26040	26940	26460	26460	27720	28260
USSR	19700	20300	20700	19170	22680	22860	25470	34110	35910
CMEA total									
Others									
Albania	413	576	618	657	832	1013	1164	1171	1367
Cyprus	16	25	28	37	46	52	52	50	53
Gibraltar	4	4	4	4	4	4	5	5	5
Liechtenstein	35	37	40	44	47	50	52	58	70
Malta	14	15	17	22	23	23	21	23	21
Monaco	42	45	52	61	69	78	90	97	102
Turkey	37794	66000	84000	149695	179780	242704	236988	259560	331320
Yugoslavia	17901	19981	25970	33407	45275	59367	82464	127738	170025
Total									
European total									

Source: National Accounts/Euromonitor estimates
Notes: a Billions

Database name: Consumer Expenditure Patterns
Sector name: Expenditure on Leisure and Education 1977-1989   Table No: 1116

Title: Consumer Expenditure on Leisure and Education 1977-1989

Unit: National currencies (millions)

	1986	1987	1988	1989	% growth 1977-1989	% share 1989	Total $ million 1989	$ per capita 1989	Notes
EC members									
Belgium	312900	333200	361980	390760	150.88	2.70	9917	999	
Denmark	35353	35636	37421	38111	148.75	1.42	5214	1014	
France	173841	183198	193381	213241	196.17	9.10	33423	595	
West Germany	103950	108866	113730	118452	69.22	17.15	63006	1023	
Greece	160430	194941	230373	240500	723.94	0.40	1481	147	
Ireland	1063	1218	1277	1336	281.05	0.52	1895	537	
Italy	47591	51695	61808	71921	698.24	14.27	52417	908	a
Luxembourg	4729	5122	5515	5908	145.15	0.04	150	403	
Netherlands	23510	24370	25480	26590	83.51	3.41	12538	846	
Portugal	90000	113186	128367	143548	559.29	0.25	912	88	
Spain	1545000	1801723	1977342	2152961	283.09	4.95	18187	464	
United Kingdom	24262	25000	26500	28000	246.84	12.50	45917	802	
EC total						66.71	245056	752	
EFTA members									
Austria	40962	43424	48988	54552	81.12	1.12	4123	543	
Finland	17872	18800	19728	20656	288.71	1.31	4814	970	
Iceland	8021	10798	13575	16352		0.08	287	1142	b
Norway	23861	25730	27415	29100	221.62	1.15	4215	994	
Sweden	46076	50622	54870	59118	195.92	2.50	9170	1084	
Switzerland	14020	14695	15430	16202	92.99	2.70	9904	1501	
EFTA total						8.85	32512	1013	
CMEA members									
Bulgaria	1694	1742	1793			0.29	1055	117	b
Czechoslovakia	14671	14977	15403			0.45	1639	105	b
East Germany	11531	12291	12997			1.89	6950	417	b
Hungary	83624	96640	115518			0.62	2292	215	b
Poland	200250	226400	380460			0.24	884	23	b
Romania	29700	30160	30740			0.59	2153	94	b
USSR	39600	42330	44820			19.94	73235	258	b
CMEA total						24.01	88208	222	
Others									
Albania	1500	1617	1738			0.08	290	91	b
Cyprus	54	54	64			0.04	138	191	b
Gibraltar	5	5	6			0.00	10	333	b
Liechtenstein	79	80	80			0.01	55	1827	b
Malta	25	27	27			0.02	83	237	b
Monaco	109	116	123			0.01	21	737	b
Turkey	420000	555000	974738			0.19	685	13	b
Yugoslavia	279768	500500	1471627			0.08	282	12	b
Total						0.43	1563	19	
European total						100.00	367339	440	

Database name:	Consumer Expenditure Patterns								
Sector name:	Expenditure on Hotels and Restaurants					Table No: 1117			

Title: Consumer Expenditure on Hotels and Restaurants 1977-1989

Unit: National currencies (millions)

	1977	1978	1979	1980	1981	1982	1983	1984	1985
EC members									
Belgium			85963	95759	70190	74330	79380	82070	90060
Denmark	7719	8327	9336	9738	10788	12486	13509	14923	16210
France	77554	87126	100294	117956	136379	156880	177288	192472	207273
West Germany									
Greece	34810	40932	51634	61481	78437	89201	113414	142355	165525
Ireland									
Italy	9058	10461	12959	15899	19647	24263	27773	31502	36000
Luxembourg									
Netherlands	4230	4620	5080	9660	10050	10560	10880	11610	11980
Portugal	37689	49232	66142	77288	92917	123409	140000	154400	151000
Spain	746086	891573	1062200	1178800	1422900	1755800	2052500	2300500	2670700
United Kingdom	4955	5605	6765	7970	8239	8837	10278	11215	12339
EFTA members									
Austria	49550	53190	57970	63630	70190	74330	79380	82070	90060
Finland	4107	4782	5600	6495	7458	8477			
Iceland									
Norway	3958	4240	4560	5150	6042	6960	8009	9148	10865
Sweden	6521	6830	7406	8253	8591	12683	18770	20272	22907
Switzerland									
CMEA members									
Bulgaria									
Czechoslovakia									
East Germany									
Hungary				30500	30700	44600			
Poland									
Romania									
USSR									
Others									
Albania						70	89	112	
Cyprus									
Gibraltar									
Liechtenstein									
Malta									
Monaco									
Turkey									
Yugoslavia									

Source: National Accounts/WTO/OECD
Notes: a Billions

Database name: Consumer Expenditure Patterns
Sector name: Expenditure on Hotels and Restaurants

Table No: 1117

Title: Consumer Expenditure on Hotels and Restaurants 1977-1989

Unit: National currencies (millions)

	1986	1987	1988	1989	% growth 1977-1989	% share 1989	Total $ million 1989	$ per capita 1989
EC members								
Belgium	94442	93772	101872	109971		1.61	2791	281
Denmark	18993	19189	20150	20521	165.86	1.62	2807	546
France	229801	233015	245967	271227	249.73	24.57	42511	757
West Germany								
Greece	249343	247076	291985	304820	775.67	1.08	1877	186
Ireland								
Italy	50568	51772	61900	72028	695.19	30.34	52495	909
Luxembourg								
Netherlands	12676	12624	13199	13774	225.62	3.75	6495	438
Portugal	194033	187565	212722	237879	531.16	0.87	1511	146
Spain	3275860	3509850	3851965	4194081	462.14	20.48	35429	905
United Kingdom	14625	14750	15635	16520	233.40	15.66	27091	473
EFTA members								
Austria								
Finland								
Iceland								
Norway								
Sweden								
Switzerland								
CMEA members								
Bulgaria								
Czechoslovakia								
East Germany								
Hungary								
Poland								
Romania								
USSR								
Others								
Albania								
Cyprus								
Gibraltar								
Liechtenstein								
Malta								
Monaco								
Turkey								
Yugoslavia								

Notes: a   Billions

TABLE 1101: ALL CONSUMER SPENDING
In US Dollars 1989

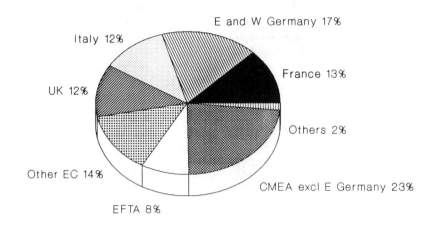

Italy 12%

E and W Germany 17%

France 13%

UK 12%

Others 2%

Other EC 14%

CMEA excl E Germany 23%

EFTA 8%

TABLE 1104: FOOD SPENDING
In US Dollars 1989

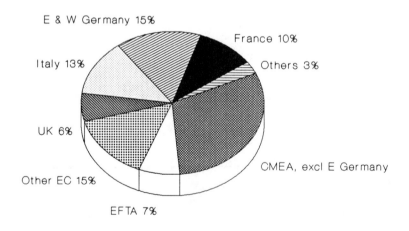

E & W Germany 15%

France 10%

Italy 13%

Others 3%

UK 6%

CMEA, excl E Germany

Other EC 15%

EFTA 7%

12
RETAILING AND RETAIL DISTRIBUTION

Database name: Retailing and Retail Distribution
Sector name: Retail Sales

Table No: 1201

Title: Trends in Retail Sales 1977-1989

Unit: National currencies (billions)

	1977	1978	1979	1980	1981	1982	1983	1984	1985
EC members									
Belgium	850	920	1005	1055	1110	1252	1318	1388	147
Denmark	72	73	76	82	90	104	119	131	13
France	560	625	795	810	890	977	1073	1160	124
West Germany	310	330	343	355	368	385	403	418	43
Greece	415	490	580	690	835	975	1250	1500	185
Ireland	2	3	3	3	4	4	4	5	
Italy	93	85	103	123	136	164	189	192	28
Luxembourg	34	36	38	42	48	52	55	58	6
Netherlands	85	88	89	93	95	98	99	101	10
Portugal	344	425	495	577	693	869	975	1125	145
Spain	4300	4500	4900	5291	6189	7147	8295	8806	1010
United Kingdom	39	42	51	60	64	70	76	82	9
EFTA members									
Austria	175	170	200	220	235	250	263	266	28
Finland	40	43	50	57	63	69	74	77	8
Iceland						9	16	22	3
Norway	40	47	54	58	64	71	76	83	9
Sweden	96	103	109	126	154	162	177	193	20
Switzerland	44	44	44	48	50	51	53	56	6
CMEA members									
Bulgaria	10	10	10	12	13	13	14	14	1
Czechoslovakia	227	241	250	255	261	269	277	285	29
East Germany	89	92	96	100	102	104	104	109	11
Hungary	256	281	313	342	381	411	441	480	52
Poland	1049	1131	1235	1334	1511	2690	2979	4370	515
Romania	138	155	165	219	230	257	265	278	27
USSR	231	241	247	255	304	304	314	324	33
Others									
Albania		6							
Cyprus	0	1	1	1	1	1	1	1	
Gibraltar									
Liechtenstein									
Malta	0	0	0	0	0	0	0	0	
Monaco									
Turkey	240	302	661	1044	1490	1490	2256	4500	750
Yugoslavia						612	804	1236	210

Source: Euromonitor Retail Database
Notes: Retail sales exclude vehicle and petrol sectors
0 = less than 500 million
a 000 billions
b Dollar values based on 1988 figures

| Database name: | Retailing and Retail Distribution | | | | | | | | |
| Sector name: | Retail Sales | | | | Table No: | 1201 | | | |

Title: Trends in Retail Sales 1977-1989

Unit: National currencies (billions)

	1986	1987	1988	1989	% growth 1977-1989	% share 1989	Total $ million 1989	$ per capita 1989	Notes
EC members									
Belgium	1471	1496	1525	1650	94.12	2.12	41874	4219	
Denmark	140	142	146	150	108.33	1.04	20520	3990	
France	1333	1395	1455						
West Germany	449	466	483	504	62.58	13.57	268085	4352	
Greece	2280	2785	3670	4180	907.23	1.30	25736	2555	
Ireland	5	5	5	5	127.27	0.36	7095	2011	
Italy	305	332	354			13.77	271973	4710	a,b
Luxembourg	63	65	67	69	102.94	0.09	1751	4707	
Netherlands	108	110	111	112	31.76	2.67	52813	3566	
Portugal	1630	1860	2140	2460	615.12	0.79	15623	1514	
Spain	10700	11900	13000	14500	237.21	6.20	122487	3128	
United Kingdom	97	105	115	123	214.58	10.21	201705	3524	
						52.12	1029662	3158	
EFTA members									
Austria	282	291	303	316	80.57	1.21	23883	3145	
Finland	91	98	104	111	177.50	1.31	25867	5212	
Iceland	38	45	55	62		0.06	1087	4330	
Norway	108	110	108	110	175.00	0.81	15932	3759	
Sweden	222	239	257	295	207.29	2.32	45758	5407	
Switzerland	62	63	64	66	50.00	2.04	40345	6115	
						7.74	152872	4761	
CMEA members									
Bulgaria	15	16	17			0.51	10000	1107	b
Czechoslovakia	304	314	329			1.77	35000	2240	b
East Germany	118	122	127			3.44	67914	4079	b
Hungary	564	640	697			0.70	13829	1300	b
Poland	6315	9000	13534			1.59	31438	833	b
Romania	280	290							
USSR	341	351	376			31.10	614379	2164	
						39.11	772561	1949	
Others									
Albania	18								
Cyprus	1	1							
Gibraltar									
Liechtenstein									
Malta									
Monaco		2							
Turkey	9800	12000	20000	35000	14483.33	0.84	16496	310	
Yugoslavia	4496	9887	26784	300000		0.20	3865	163	b
						1.03	20361	251	
						100.00	1975456	2364	

Database name: Retailing and Retail Distribution
Sector name: Retail Sales

Table No: 1202

Title: Index of Retail Sales Volume 1982-1989

Unit: 1982 = 100

	1982	1983	1984	1985	1986	1987	1988	1989
EC members								
Belgium	100	98	99	100	98	99	101	105
Denmark	100	99	100	106	109	107	107	106
France	100	100	101	102	106	108	111	
West Germany	100	102	105	106	110	113	116	119
Greece	100	106	108	112	112	115	120	115
Ireland	100	98	96	97	98	98	98	99
Italy	100	100	100	101	104	108	110	
Luxembourg	100	100	100	101	103	104	106	108
Netherlands	100	97	96	94	97	99	99	99
Portugal	100	99	98	99	101	104	109	115
Spain	100	99	99	103	101	108	113	118
United Kingdom	100	104	108	110	116	121	129	133
EFTA members								
Austria	100	102	97	99	99	100	101	
Finland	100	103	104	107	108	112	117	121
Iceland	100	96	100	104	105	106	103	100
Norway	100	99	102	111	115	109	102	100
Sweden	100	100	101	97	104	108	110	113
Switzerland	100	101	102	103	106	106	108	109
CMEA members								
Bulgaria	100	103	106	110	114	118	121	
Czechoslovakia	100	102	104	105	109	113	118	
East Germany	100	100	98	104	109	114	118	
Hungary	100	100	101	103	107	113	106	
Poland	100	91	96	99	106	112	116	118
Romania	100	98	101	104	103	104		
USSR	100	103	103	106	110	112	118	
Others								
Albania								
Cyprus								
Gibraltar								
Liechtenstein								
Malta								
Monaco								
Turkey								
Yugoslavia	100	101	106	105	106	105	105	105

Source: Euromonitor Retail Database

Database name: Retailing and Retail Distribution
Sector name: Total Retail Trade   Table No: 1203

Title: Numbers of Retail Outlets, Employees: Latest Year

Unit: 000s

	Year	Total Outlets	Foods Outlets	Non-foods Outlets	Employment	Notes
EC members						
Belgium	1987	113.7	36.0	77.7	245.0	
Denmark	1985	48.7	13.3	35.4	200.0	
France	1989	518.7	167.4	351.3	1158.4	a
West Germany	1985	382.3	124.9	257.4	2478.0	
Greece	1984	184.9	63.6	121.3	301.3	
Ireland	1977	23.0				
Italy	1987	849.6	316.0	533.5		b
Luxembourg	1984	3.7	1.2	2.5	16.5	c
Netherlands	1989	160.9	47.1	113.8		
Portugal	1987	89.0	45.0	44.0	231.5	
Spain	1988	728.7	289.9	438.8		g
United Kingdom	1987	345.5	157.8	187.7	2319.0	
EFTA members						
Austria	1983	38.1	9.0	29.1	227.0	
Finland	1986	36.6	12.4	24.2	147.7	
Iceland	1987	1.9	0.8	1.1	9.4	
Norway	1987	38.6	12.0	26.6	133.9	
Sweden	1988	48.0	18.0	30.0	284.9	d
Switzerland	1985	52.3	14.9	37.4	256.1	
CMEA members						
Bulgaria	1988	41.2	15.1	26.1		
Czechoslovakia	1988	62.8	23.1	39.7		
East Germany	1988	85.0	50.0	35.0		
Hungary	1988	63.7	22.5	41.2	341.4	e
Poland	1985	219.8	52.8	167.0		
Romania	1985	53.1	17.9	35.2	283.1	f
USSR	1986	709.9	212.6	497.3		
Others						
Albania	1978	12.6				
Cyprus	1987				19.6	
Gibraltar	1986				1.1	
Liechtenstein	1986	0.3			0.9	
Malta	1986	2.5			11.0	
Monaco						
Turkey	1985	369.1	170.5	198.6	697.0	
Yugoslavia	1989	94.7			530.0	e

Source: Euromonitor Retail Database
Notes: a Employment refers to 1986   d Employment refers to 1985
           b Fixed outlets only   e Employment refers to 1987
           c Businesses, not outlets;   f Outlets exclude kiosks
              employment figures refer to 1981   g Including vehicle and fuel outlets

Database name: Retailing and Retail Distribution
Sector name: Total Retail Trade   Table No: 1204

Title: Retail Trade by Form of Organisation 1988

Unit: % total retail trade

	Co-op	DVS	Mult	Affi	Inde	Total	Notes
EC members							
Belgium	0	6	13	12	69	100	
Denmark	18	6	18	33	25	100	
France	2	7	30	19	42	100	
West Germany	4	11	24	40	21	100	
Greece							
Ireland	1	6	38	7	48	100	
Italy	2	5	10	83		100	a
Luxembourg	0	6	10	20	64	100	
Netherlands	0	5	28	33	34	100	
Portugal	4	3	32	8	53	100	
Spain	1	4	14	4	77	100	
United Kingdom	5	16	51	5	23	100	
EFTA members							
Austria	8	7	31	25	29	100	
Finland	20	3	17	32	28	100	
Iceland							
Norway	14	6	4	24	22	100	b
Sweden	15	7	20	37	22	100	
Switzerland	28	11	21	10	30	100	
CMEA members							
Bulgaria							
Czechoslovakia							
East Germany							
Hungary							
Poland							
Romania							
USSR							
Others							
Albania							
Cyprus							
Gibraltar							
Liechtenstein							
Malta							
Monaco							
Turkey							
Yugoslavia							

Source: Euromonitor Retail Database
Notes: a   Affiliated includes independents   DVS   Department and variety stores, mail order
          b   Merchants' department stores included with independents   Mult Multiples, including hypermarkets
                                                                         Affi Voluntary associations and buying groups
                                                                         Inde Non-affiliated independents

Database name: Retailing and Retail Distribution
Sector name: Total Retail Trade

Table No: 1205

Title: Retail Sales by Form of Outlet 1988

Unit: % of all sales

	Mail order	Depart. Store	Variety Store	Hyper-market	Super-market	Other self service	Other	Total	Notes
EC members									
Belgium	1		7		18	74		100	a
Denmark	2		8	6	19	10	55	100	
France	3	2	2	20	12		61	100	
West Germany	6	5		13	15	15	46	100	
Greece									
Ireland									
Italy			11				89	100	b
Luxembourg									
Netherlands	2		6	2	15	10	65	100	c
Portugal									
Spain									
United Kingdom									
EFTA members									
Austria	3	2		5	9	5	76	100	
Finland	1	8		3	14	15	59	100	
Iceland									
Norway	3			1	21	20	55	100	
Sweden	4	11		5	27	6	47	100	
Switzerland	3	9		8	15	15	50	100	
CMEA members									
Bulgaria									
Czechoslovakia									
East Germany									
Hungary									
Poland									
Romania									
USSR									
Others									
Albania									
Cyprus									
Gibraltar									
Liechtenstein									
Malta									
Monaco									
Turkey									
Yugoslavia									

Source: Euromonitor Retail Database

a Variety Stores include Department Stores and Hypermarkets
b Variety Stores include All Large Stores and All Large Self-Service Stores
c Variety Stores include Department Stores

Database name: Retailing and Retail Distribution
Sector name: Food Retailing

Table No: 1206

Title: Numbers of Food Outlets by Type: Latest Year

Unit: Number of outlets

	Year	General	Fruit/Veg	Dairy	Meat	Fish	Bakery
EC members							
Belgium	1987	14209	2359	2367	8165	1431	2198
Denmark	1985	6735	1401		1755	544	
France	1989	57021	17033	4880	49138	7717	
West Germany	1985	59592					
Greece	1978	37734	5193	2097	11558	1227	81!
Ireland	1988	6575	501		1954	149	50(
Italy	1986	197709	43545		66542	9965	5668!
Luxembourg							
Netherlands	1989	8349	6154	4637	6109	1837	549'
Portugal	1976				4818	1368	
Spain							
United Kingdom	1986	41815	16805	9700	20721	3158	755!
EC average							
EFTA members							
Austria	1983						
Finland	1982	5647		528			
Iceland							
Norway	1986	7323			281	318	42
Sweden	1987						
Switzerland	1985				3083	4103	
CMEA members							
Bulgaria	1988	7569	3134	202	1208		280!
Czechoslovakia							
East Germany							
Hungary							
Poland							
Romania	1983		2998		1499		267!
USSR							
Others							
Albania							
Cyprus	1983	1912			576		
Gibraltar							
Liechtenstein							
Malta							
Monaco							
Turkey							
Yugoslavia	1986						

Source: Euromonitor Retail Database
Notes: a   Tobacco includes confectionery and newsagents

Database name: Retailing and Retail Distribution
Sector name: Food Retailing

Table No: 1206

Title: Numbers of Food Outlets by Type, Latest Year

Unit: Number of outlets

	Year	Confect	Drinks	Tobacco
EC members				
Belgium	1987	1190	1686	664
Denmark	1985	1383		
France	1989	21370	5383	4887
West Germany	1985		7895	10469
Greece	1978	3125	1590	
Ireland	1988	2882	1405	
Italy	1986		13765	
Luxembourg				
Netherlands	1989	1557	3361	3312
Portugal	1976		395	
Spain				
United Kingdom	1986		8736	47774
EFTA members				
Austria				3983
Finland	1982		210	
Iceland				
Norway	1986		108	
Sweden			333	1800
Switzerland	1985			
CMEA members				
Bulgaria	1988			
Czechoslovakia				
East Germany				
Hungary				
Poland				
Romania	1983			
USSR				
Others				
Albania				
Cyprus	1983			
Gibraltar				
Liechtenstein				
Malta				
Monaco				
Turkey				
Yugoslavia	1986		1591	

Source: Euromonitor Retail Database

Database name: Retailing and Retail Distribution
Sector name: Non-Food Retailing

Table No: 1207

Title: Number of Non-Food Specialists by Type: Latest Year

Unit: Number of outlets

	Year	Chemists Drugstores	Perfumeries	Opticians	Photo	Bookshops	Stationers	Newsagents	Fashion
EC members									
Belgium	1987	5796	1901	1230	965	2249	1149	2825	8997
Denmark	1985	410	756		510	894		675	2728
France	1989	22159			7640	28674			92955
West Germany	1985	22889			3460	5161	5253	2701	49000
Greece	1984	6594						14041	20276
Ireland	1988	1269							
Italy	1986			16571		28332		19354	150978
Luxembourg	1984	143				213			637
Netherlands	1989	2697	1082	1573	1715	3015	960		19902
Portugal	1976	1806	230		658	1895			8874
Spain									
United Kingdom	1986	12538			980	7483			23942
EFTA members									
Austria	1983	2375		486			792	626	5400
Finland	1984	1486							3414
Iceland									
Norway	1986	407	780		359	690			2693
Sweden	1986	857			703	1173		2583	7374
Switzerland	1985	2642			1157		4381		
CMEA members									
Bulgaria	1988					1816			3495
Czechoslovakia									
East Germany									
Hungary	1988	1470							3546
Poland									
Romania	1983	1353	358			2120			7737
USSR									
Others									
Albania									
Cyprus	1980	285				168			1411
Gibraltar									
Liechtenstein									
Malta									
Monaco									
Turkey	1985	11612							66876
Yugoslavia	1986	109	303		143	686	821		7899

Source: Euromonitor Retail Database
Notes:
a Newsagents includes bookshops
b Clocks/jewellery includes opticians; TV/radio includes records; housewares/hardware includes appliances
c Chemists includes perfumeries; furniture includes furnishings
d Bookshops includes stationers; opticians included with clocks/jewellery
e Fashion includes furnishings; opticians includes photographic

Database name: Retailing and Retail Distribution
Sector name: Non-Food Retailing   Table No: 1207

Title: Number of Non-Food Specialists by Type: Latest Year

Unit: Number of outlets

	Year	Footwear	Houseware Hardware	Furnishings	Furniture	Appliances	TV/Audio	Records	DIY
EC members									
Belgium	1987	2828	3275	1670	2533	2473	1730	733	
Denmark	1985	947	1458		3848		2224		
France	1989	15776	9456	7872	12014	17701			
West Germany	1985	13494			10528	6229	11951		
Greece	1984	9783	11708	3321	15298				
Ireland	1988	671	2072			1242			
Italy	1986	38823	54493		33931	36401			
Luxembourg	1984			34	574				
Netherlands	1989	3898	2935		4584	3123	3748		3041
Portugal	1976	1908	4091	180	2385	2561			1793
Spain									
United Kingdom	1986	11447	8000	5199	14639	16304			8331
EFTA members									
Austria	1983	1408	1435	1290		1581			
Finland	1984	677			1267	1369			
Iceland									
Norway	1986	802	718		873	1316		600	
Sweden	1986	1484	6242		2337	1404	2221		1500
Switzerland	1985	1514	2204		1247	698			
CMEA members									
Bulgaria	1988	463			388	383			
Czechoslovakia									
East Germany									
Hungary	1988		2263						
Poland									
Romania	1983		4061		854				
USSR									
Others									
Albania									
Cyprus	1980	292	336			379			
Gibraltar									
Liechtenstein									
Malta									
Monaco									
Turkey	1988				3884				
Yugoslavia	1986					344			

Source: Euromonitor Retail Database

Notes:
f   Fashion includes footwear; books includes stat/news
g   Photo includes opticians
h   Bookshops includes stat/news
j   Appliances includes TV/audio
k   Chemists/drugstores includes cosmetics
l   Chemists/drugstores includes perfumeries; newsagents include books, cigarettes; footwear includes leat appliances includes TV/audio; toys/sports includes guns
m   Fashion includes textiles; appliances include TV/Audio
n   State and co-operative outlets only; Chemists/drugstores: pharmacists only; houseware/hardware include techinical goods and glassware
r   Furniture includes furnishings

Database name: Retailing and Retail Distribution
Sector name: Non-Food Retailing

Table No: 1207

Title: Number of Non-Food Specialists by Type: Latest Year

Unit: Number of outlets

	Year	Clocks/Jewellery	Pets	Toys/Sports	Florists	Total	Notes
EC members							
Belgium	1987	1930	916	2089	3887	49176	
Denmark	1985	1419			1077	14218	b,d
France	1989	10404			20122	247963	d,g,j,s
West Germany	1985	9598	4298	8309	14158	167029	
Greece	1984			2946		83967	l
Ireland	1977	360		410			
Italy	1984	18931		12709	18913		e
Luxembourg	1984						f
Netherlands	1989	2467	1985	3284	8468	68471	d,r
Portugal	1976	1321			462		
Spain							
United Kingdom	1986	8096		9403	6645	133007	h
EFTA members							
Austria	1983	1310		1167	1051	18921	a
Finland	1984						c,k
Iceland							
Norway	1986	1230		1224	973		d,j
Sweden	1986	2400		5957	2106		d
Switzerland	1985	1566	272	1400	1232	18313	
CMEA members							
Bulgaria	1988					6545	m
Czechoslovakia							
East Germany							
Hungary	1988					7279	n
Poland							
Romania	1983						
USSR							
Others							
Albania							
Cyprus	1980						
Gibraltar							
Liechtenstein							
Malta							
Monaco							
Turkey	1985					82372	c
Yugoslavia	1986						j

Database name: Retailing and Retail Distribution
Sector name: Hypermarkets and Superstores   Table No: 1208

Title: Food Distribution by Form of Organisation 1987

Unit: % value share

	Co-op	Multi	Affi	Inde	Other	Total	Notes
EEC members							
Belgium		48	30	18	5	100	
Denmark	38	21	37	4		100	
France	3	30	25		42	100	a
West Germany	11	24	59		6	100	
Greece							
Ireland							
Italy	13	10	22	55		100	
Luxembourg							
Netherlands	1	50	24		25	100	
Portugal	1	10		86	3	100	b
Spain		15	1	80	4	100	
United Kingdom	12	58			30	100	
EFTA members							
Austria	15	44	36		5	100	a
Finland	31	3	63		3	100	a
Iceland							
Norway	23	23			54	100	
Sweden	21	8	44		27	100	
Switzerland	40	12			48	100	a

CMEA members
Bulgaria
Czechoslovakia
East Germany
Hungary
Poland
Romania
USSR

Others
Albania
Cyprus
Gibraltar
Liechtenstein
Malta
Monaco
Turkey
Yugoslavia

Source: Euromonitor Retail Database
Notes: a Independents included with affiliated
            b Affiliated included with independents
            Co-op   Co-operated
            Multi   Food multiples
            Affi   Voluntary associations and buying groups
            Inde   Non-affiliated independents
            Other   Department and variety stores, specialists

Database name: Retailing and Retail Distribution
Sector name: Hypermarkets and Superstores   Table No: 1209

Title: Numbers of Hypermarkets and Superstores 1980-1989

Unit: Number of stores

	1980	1981	1982	1983	1984	1985	1986	1987	1988	1989	Notes
EC members											
Belgium	79	80	81	82	86	88	91				
Denmark	29	30	36	38	38	42	45				a
France	421	447	482	515	553	585	629	670	712	768	
West Germany	813	840	860	880	910	930	952	980	1013	996	b
Greece			1	2	2	4	6				
Ireland							35				c
Italy	14	17	17	20	20	20	22				
Luxembourg	3	3	3	4	4	5	5				
Netherlands	37	39	37	35	34	34	34				
Portugal										20	c
Spain	34	38	48	58	62	80	89	100	108		
United Kingdom	201	232	260	287	316	346	416				
EFTA members											
Austria	51	53	54	53	56	58	60				
Finland	27	28	28	30	32	33	35	40	44	50	
Iceland											
Norway	67	70	72	73	75	78	80				
Sweden	65	68	70	73	73	74	75				
Switzerland	81	82	82	82	83	84	85				
CMEA members											
Bulgaria											
Czechoslovakia											
East Germany											
Hungary											
Poland											
Romania											
USSR											
Others											
Albania											
Cyprus											
Gibraltar											
Liechtenstein											
Malta											
Monaco											
Turkey											
Yugoslavia											

Source: Retail trade associations/National Statistical Offices/Euromonitor Retail Database
Notes:
a Estimates, except 1980
b 1981-1984 estimated
c Estimates

Database name: Retailing and Retail Distribution
Sector name: Hypermarkets and Superstores

Table No: 1210

Title: Hypermarkets and Superstores : Market Shares, Selling Space, Latest Year

	Year	Market Share Total %	Market Share Food %	Density 000/store	Sales Area 000m2	Notes
EC members						
Belgium	1986	15	20	113	540	
Denmark	1988	6	15	116	235	
France	1988	19	22	78	3881	
West Germany	1988	7		64	5800	a
Greece	1985	0	1			
Ireland	1986	5	13			
Italy	1988		1	1300	149	
Luxembourg	1983	11	18			
Netherlands	1988	3	4	416	160	a
Portugal	1985	3	5			
Spain	1989	9	17		750	
United Kingdom	1988	9	37	119	1600	a
EFTA members						
Austria	1988	4	11	108	350	
Finland	1988	6	5	133	170	
Iceland						
Norway	1988	1	2	278	42	
Sweden	1988	5	6	45		
Switzerland	1986	8	15	73	457	
CMEA members						
Bulgaria						
Czechoslovakia						
East Germany						
Hungary						
Poland						
Romania						
USSR						
Others						
Albania						
Cyprus						
Gibraltar						
Liechtenstein						
Malta						
Monaco						
Turkey						
Yugoslavia						

Source: Retail trade associations/National Statistical Offices/Euromonitor retail database
Notes: a Estimated sales area

Database name: Retailing and Retail Distribution
Sector name: Large Mixed Retailers

Table No: 1211

Title: Retail Sales Through Department and Variety Stores 1981-1989

Unit: National currencies (billions)

	1981	1982	1983	1984	1985	1986	1987	1988	1989	Market Value 1988 $ million	Note
EC members											
Belgium	41.0	44.0	45.0	46.0	47.0	49.0	50.1	51.0	51.7	1387.1	
Denmark	11.0	12.0	13.3	14.5	16.1	18.2	20.3	21.0	21.0	3119.4	
France	45.5	49.0	52.0	54.0	55.0	55.5	56.0	56.5		9484.8	
West Germany	29.0	28.1	28.4	27.5	27.8	27.6	28.1	28.7		16342.1	
Greece											
Ireland	0.2	0.3	0.3	0.3	0.3	0.3	0.3	0.4		572.4	
Italy	1.5	2.0	2.4	2.5	3.2	3.6	3.9	4.0		3073.1	a
Luxembourg											
Netherlands	4.6	4.7	4.8	4.9	5.2	5.4	5.7	5.9		2984.9	
Portugal											
Spain	270.0	300.0	335.0	380.0	425.0	450.0	490.0	530.0		4549.7	
United Kingdom	9.9	11.2	12.4	13.5	14.7	15.6	16.7				
EFTA members											
Austria	14.0	14.0	14.0	13.6	13.4	13.0	12.5	12.5		1012.3	
Finland	10.1	10.9	12.2	12.8	13.7	14.6	15.0	16.0	17.5	3825.2	
Iceland											b
Norway	4.5	4.8	5.3	5.8	6.3	6.8	6.9				
Sweden	14.5	15.0	15.5	15.8	16.1	16.5	17.4	17.8	18.4	2905.1	b
Switzerland	4.9	5.0	5.2	5.5	5.7	5.8	6.0				
CMEA members											
Bulgaria											
Czechoslovakia											
East Germany											
Hungary											
Poland											
Romania											
USSR											
Others											
Albania											
Cyprus											
Gibraltar											
Liechenstein											
Malta											
Monaco											
Turkey											
Yugoslavia											

Source: Euromonitor Retail Database
Notes: a 000 billion
b Excluding merchants' department stores

Database name: Retailing and Retail Distribution
Sector name: Large Mixed Retailers   Table No: 1212

Title: Numbers of Department and Variety Stores, Market Shares 1988

	Department Stores 1988	Variety Stores 1988	Market Share 1980 %	Market Share 1987 %	Market Share 1988 %	Notes
EC members						
Belgium			3.7	3.3	3.3	a
Denmark	13	100	13.4	13.2	13.0	
France	128	600	5.0	4.0	3.9	
West Germany	480	275	7.9	6.0	5.9	
Greece	20	20	0.3	0.5		
Ireland	20	30	6.8	6.2		
Italy	830		0.8	1.4		b
Luxembourg						
Netherlands	80	225	4.8	5.2	5.3	
Portugal	30		0.8	1.2		
Spain	140		4.7	4.2		b
United Kingdom	639	1300	15.0	16.2	16.4	
EFTA members						
Austria			6.8	5.5	5.3	
Finland	160		14.0	12.0	11.5	
Iceland						
Norway	215		6.9	6.4	6.2	
Sweden	185		9.5	7.5	7.6	
Switzerland	200	75	8.3	9.0	9.0	
CMEA members						
Bulgaria						
Czechoslovakia						
East Germany	29	232				
Hungary		196				
Poland						
Romania						
USSR						
Others						
Albania						
Cyprus						
Gibraltar						
Liechtenstein						
Malta						
Monaco						
Turkey	748					b
Yugoslavia						

Source: Euromonitor Retail Database
Notes: a   Change of classification between 1980 and 1988
            b   First column is Department and Variety stores combined

Database name: Retailing and Retail Distribution
Sector name: Co-operatives

Table No: 1213

Title: Co-operatives: Numbers, Members, Market Shares: Latest Available Year

Unit: As stated

	Year	Number Major Co-ops	Member Outlets	Market Share Total %	Market Share Grocery %	Notes
EC members						
Belgium	1989	1		0	0	
Denmark	1989	740	1511	18	37	b
France	1984		5900	2	8	
West Germany	1988		1300	4	2	a
Greece						
Ireland	1984			1	3	
Italy	1986			2	13	
Luxembourg	1987	1		0		
Netherlands	1987	1	50	0	1	
Portugal				4		
Spain	1987			1	3	
United Kingdom	1986	100	3500	5	13	
EFTA members						
Austria	1989	1	1025	8	15	
Finland	1989	3	2600	20	30	
Iceland						
Norway	1989	464	1350	14	23	d
Sweden	1989	135	1687	15	20	e
Switzerland	1989	2	2000	27	38	
CMEA members						
Bulgaria	1988		27051	30		
Czechoslovakia	1983		18988	26		
East Germany	1988		30362	25		
Hungary	1988		15091	30		
Poland	1988		33183	30		
Romania	1983		39011	23		
USSR	1983		366304	28		
Others						
Albania						
Cyprus						
Gibraltar						
Liechtenstein						
Malta						
Monaco						
Turkey						
Yugoslavia						

Source: Euromonitor Retail Database
Notes: Market shares of 0 refer to levels of less than 0.5 per cent
a Outlets refer to Co-op AG only
b 824 regional co-ops, all members of one federation
c Outlets: food and drink only
d 464 regional co-ops, all members of one federation
e 135 regional coops, all members of one federation

Database name: Retailing and Retail Distribution
Sector name: Mail Order   Table No: 1214

Title: Sales Through Mail Order Groups 1981-1988

Unit: National currencies (billion)

	1981	1982	1983	1984	1985	1986	1987	1988	Value 1988 $ million	Notes
EC members										
Belgium	15.0	15.5	16.2	18.6	19.7	20.6	21.8	22.9	581	
Denmark	1.5	1.7	1.9	2.1	2.3	2.6	2.9	2.8	383	
France	20.1	23.3	25.5	28.4	30.5	34.1	36.5	37.6	5893	
West Germany	23.5	22.2	21.7	22.4	22.5	24.0	26.4	25.3	13457	
Greece				0.1	0.2	0.2	0.2	0.2	1231	a
Ireland										
Italy	0.7	0.8	0.9	1.0	1.2	1.3	1.5	1.7	1239	a
Luxembourg										
Netherlands	1.3	1.3	1.4	1.6	1.7	1.7	1.8	1.9	896	
Portugal							0.5			
Spain							20.0			
United Kingdom	2.2	2.4	2.6	2.7	3.0	3.3	3.5	3.8	6232	
EFTA members										
Austria	6.4	6.8	7.4	7.6	8.0	8.5	8.8	9.0	680	
Finland	0.4	0.5	0.7	0.7	0.8	0.9	1.2	1.7	396	
Iceland										
Norway	1.1	1.2	1.5	1.9	2.4	2.8	3.2	3.1	449	
Sweden	1.7	2.3	3.3	3.9	4.5	5.9	6.9	6.7	1039	
Switzerland	1.0	1.1	1.2	1.3	1.4	1.5	1.6	1.6	978	

CMEA members
 Bulgaria
 Czechoslovakia
 East Germany
 Hungary
 Poland
 Romania
 USSR

Others
 Albania
 Cyprus
 Gibraltar
 Liechtenstein
 Malta
 Monaco
 Turkey
 Yugoslavia

Source: Euromonitor Retail Database/Mail order trade associations
Notes: a 000 billion

	Database name:	Retailing and Retail Distribution			Table No: 1215

Database name: Retailing and Retail Distribution
Sector name: Mail Order

Table No: 1215

Title: Mail Order Market Shares 1987-1988

Unit: Percentage of total retail sales

	Total Sales 1987	Total Sales 1988	Non-food Sales 1987	Non-food Sales 1988
EC members				
Belgium	1.4	1.5	2.3	2.4
Denmark	2.0	1.9	4.0	4.0
France	2.7	2.6	5.4	5.3
West Germany	5.7	5.2	8.0	8.1
Greece				
Ireland	0.3		0.7	
Italy	0.4	0.5	0.8	0.9
Luxembourg	1.2		2.0	
Netherlands	1.7	1.7	3.5	3.5
Portugal				
Spain	0.1	0.1	0.2	0.2
United Kingdom	3.4	3.3	5.5	5.3
EFTA members				
Austria	3.1	3.0	5.5	5.3
Finland	1.2	1.7	2.2	3.0
Iceland				
Norway	2.9	2.9	5.6	5.7
Sweden	2.9	3.1	5.5	5.7
Switzerland	2.5	2.6	4.5	4.7
CMEA members				
Bulgaria				
Czechoslovakia				
East Germany				
Hungary				
Poland				
Romania				
USSR				
Others				
Albania				
Cyprus				
Gibraltar				
Liechtenstein				
Malta				
Monaco				
Turkey				
Yugoslavia				

Source: Euromonitor Retail Database/Mail order trade associations

Database name: Retailing and Retail Distribution
Sector name: Retail Technology

Table No: 1216

Title: Scanning Stores, Bar-coding 1988/1989

	Number Scanning Stores 1989	of which: Self-service Grocery 1989	Est. Number Scanning Lanes 1988	Number Bar-coding Manufacturers 19 1989	% of All Food Lines Coded 1988/89	Notes
EC members						
Belgium	863	779	3000	1273	98	
Denmark	1061	883	1500	1700	97	a
France	4648	2975	25000	10900	97	
West Germany	3434	2200	12500	9474	99	d
Greece	0	0	0	210		
Ireland	30	29		498		c
Italy	3600	1678	9000	9359	95	b
Luxembourg	18			35		c
Netherlands	800	600	3000	831	99	
Portugal	220	15		681	80	
Spain	1603		5000	4948	97	
United Kingdom	3999	1128	25000	6468	99	
EFTA members						
Austria	552		1400	1778	100	
Finland	1310	1115	4000	1082	92	a
Iceland	20	18		120	60	
Norway	1136	716	4000	1507	98	a
Sweden	1725	1400	4000	1777	96	a
Switzerland	575	175	1100	809	97	
CMEA members						
Bulgaria						
Czechoslovakia	1	0		151	3	
East Germany	3	0		1298		a
Hungary	18	9		490	20	
Poland						
Romania						
USSR	2	0		3862		
Others						
Albania						
Cyprus	5	5		144		
Gibraltar						
Liechtenstein						
Malta						
Monaco						
Turkey	0	0	0	21		
Yugoslavia	62	15		837	70	

Source: European Article Numbering Association/National numbering associations/Euromonitor estimates

Notes:
a Number bar-coding manufacturers = Number of allocated identification numbers
b Estimates
c 1988
d Grocery stores estimated

Database name: Retailing and Retail Distribution
Sector name: Retail Technology

Table No: 1217

Title: Number of Scanning Stores 1980-1989

Unit: Number of stores

	1980	1981	1982	1983	1984	1985	1986	1987	1988	1989	Notes
EC members											
Belgium	6	35	47	67	125	201	278	344	648	863	
Denmark							97	193	530	1061	
France			35	162	480	1023	1626	1945	3471	4648	
West Germany	19	43	76	175	429	719	966	1246	2252	3600	
Greece									0	0	
Ireland							7		30		
Italy							450	618	1250	3434	a
Luxembourg									18		
Netherlands		5	34	90	131	163	300	488	740	800	
Portugal									83	220	
Spain							123	281	912	1603	
United Kingdom		10	41	83	185	520	793	843	2792	3999	
EFTA members											
Austria							150	275	354	552	
Finland							73	186	838	1310	
Iceland									14	20	
Norway							225	449	998	1136	
Sweden							425	650	1050	1725	
Switzerland							45	75	344	575	
CMEA members											
Bulgaria										0	
Czechoslovakia							1	1	1	1	
East Germany									2	3	
Hungary							1		10	18	
Poland										0	
Romania										0	
USSR									2	2	
Others											
Albania											
Cyprus							3		5	5	
Gibraltar											
Liechtenstein											
Malta											
Monaco											
Turkey									0		
Yugoslavia							44		49	62	

Source: International Article Numbering Association (EAN)/National numbering associations
Notes: a 1988 estimated

Title: Sales Through Direct Selling Companies, Direct Salespersons 1988

Unit: National currencies (millions), rest as stated

	Number Companies	Sales Staff 000s	Sales Value	Market Share %	Notes
EC members					
Belgium	11	12	2288	0.15	
Denmark					
France	70	220	5550	0.38	
West Germany	17	136	2419	0.50	
Greece	5	15	3634	0.10	
Ireland	10	2	8	0.16	
Italy	25	143	1130	0.32	a
Luxembourg					
Netherlands	7	11	170	0.15	
Portugal	11	50	14500	0.68	
Spain	13	86	54772	0.42	
United Kingdom	36	376	438	0.38	
EFTA members					
Austria					
Finland	8	12	222	0.21	
Iceland					
Norway	10	4	393	0.36	
Sweden	37	22	750	0.29	
Switzerland	32	6	235	0.37	
CMEA members					
Bulgaria					
Czechoslovakia					
East Germany					
Hungary					
Poland					
Romania					
USSR					
Others					
Albania					
Cyprus					
Gibraltar					
Liechtenstein					
Malta					
Monaco					
Turkey					
Yugoslavia					

Source: Fédération Européenne pour la Vente et le Service à Domicile (FEVSD)/Euromonitor retail database
Notes: a Sales value billions

Database name: Retailing and Retail Distribution
Sector name: Service Stations

Title: Outlets, Fuel Sales 1987/88

Table No: 1219

	1988 Outlets 000s	% Major group Owned	Self-service Outlets 000s	Average Fuel Sales 1987 (a)	Notes
EC members					
Belgium	6.0	65		750	b,c
Denmark	3.5		3.0	808	b,c
France	29.0	68	8.5	820	
West Germany	19.0	60	16.9	1670	
Greece					
Ireland					
Italy	34.5	70		610	b
Luxembourg					
Netherlands	7.3	50		770	b
Portugal					
Spain	4.7			1950	b,c
United Kingdom	20.0	35	9.1	1400	
EFTA members					
Austria	4.0		1.2	715	b,c
Finland	2.0		1.7	1100	c
Iceland					
Norway	2.5		2.6	800	
Sweden	4.0		2.0	1300	
Switzerland	4.0		3.4	920	
CMEA members					
Bulgaria					
Czechoslovakia					
East Germany					
Hungary	1.2				
Poland					
Romania					
USSR					
Others					
Albania					
Cyprus					
Gibraltar					
Liechtenstein					
Malta					
Monaco					
Turkey					
Yugoslavia					

Source: National petrol federations/Comité Professional du Pétrole/Statistical offices
Notes:
a Tonnes per station
b Average fuel sales 1986
c Total outlets 1987

Database name: Retailing and Retail Distribution
Sector name: Own Brands

Table No: 1220

Title: Retailers' Own Brand Shares 1981-1988

Unit: % of all food sales

	1981	1985	1987	1988	Notes
EC members					
Belgium	16	21	23	24	
Denmark					
France	19	23	25	26	
West Germany	5	10	14	14	a
Greece					
Ireland					
Italy	5	7	8	8	
Luxembourg					
Netherlands	13	21			
Portugal					
Spain					
United Kingdom	17	25	30	32	
EFTA members					
Austria	13	17	20		
Finland					
Iceland					
Norway	11	14	16		
Sweden	21	24	28	29	
Switzerland					
CMEA members					
Bulgaria					
Czechoslovakia					
East Germany					
Hungary					
Poland					
Romania					
USSR					
Others					
Albania					
Cyprus					
Gibraltar					
Liechtenstein					
Malta					
Monaco					
Turkey					
Yugoslavia					

Source: Euromonitor Retail Database; many figures estimates
Notes: a Excludes Aldi

| | | | | Sales | |
	Year	Franchisors	Franchisees	ECU million	Notes
EC members					
Belgium	1989	82	3102	2400	
Denmark	1988	80	2500		
France	1989	740	32500	16000	
West Germany	1988	180	9000	4800	
Greece	1983	25	1800		
Ireland					
Italy	1988	197	11500	4500	a
Luxembourg					
Netherlands	1989	271	8432	5600	
Portugal	1983	37	680	220	
Spain	1989	117	14500		
United Kingdom	1989	295	16600	3500	
EFTA members					
Austria	1983	53	1583		
Finland					
Iceland					
Norway	1988	120	850	500	
Sweden	1988	44	752	400	
Switzerland	1988	200			
CMEA members					
Bulgaria					
Czechoslovakia					
East Germany					
Hungary					
Poland					
Romania					
USSR					
Others					
Albania					
Cyprus					
Gibraltar					
Liechtenstein					
Malta					
Monaco					
Turkey					
Yugoslavia					

Source: European Franchise Association
Notes: NB figures exclude vehicles, petrol, soft drinks bottling and hotels
a   Sales in billion lire

TABLE 1201: RETAIL SALES
In US Dollars 1989

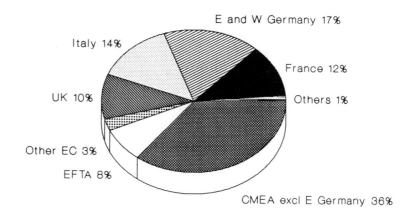

E and W Germany 17%

Italy 14%

France 12%

Others 1%

UK 10%

Other EC 3%

EFTA 8%

CMEA excl E Germany 36%

TABLE 1211: VARIETY STORE SALES
In US Dollars 1989

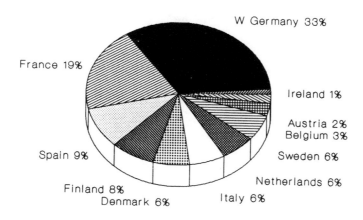

W Germany 33%

France 19%

Ireland 1%

Austria 2%
Belgium 3%

Spain 9%

Sweden 6%

Netherlands 6%

Finland 8%

Denmark 6%

Italy 6%

13
ADVERTISING PATTERNS AND MEDIA ACCESS

Database name: Advertising Patterns and Media Access
Sector name: Advertising Expenditure

Table No: 1301

Title: Trends in Advertising Expenditure 1982-1989

Unit: National currencies (millions)

	1982	1983	1984	1985	1986	1987	1988	1989	Notes
EC members									
Belgium	18057	21113	23449	25534	27730	32209	35296	39171	
Denmark	3350	3626	4000	4350	4715	4690	5340	5430	
France	17955	21655	23945	26945	30865	35775	41320	46390	
West Germany	11957	12598	13828	14425	15105	15790	16756	17534	
Greece	9210	10845	13846	16651	23603	30581	42681	58654	
Ireland	72	72	82	98	116	141	154	175	
Italy	2096	2729	3306	3981	4742	5805	6594	7341	a
Luxembourg									
Netherlands	2892	2938	3146	3310	3532	3795	4120	4211	
Portugal	5922	7376	9283	12580	18275	29771	42654	54614	
Spain	140400	164400	197100	240000	317000	413000	520100	654625	
United Kingdom	3115	3564	4039	4418	5088	5781	6779	7311	
EFTA members									
Austria	5020	5752	6419	7003	7529	8230	9221	10303	
Finland	2931	3551	4158	4649	5063	5511	6322	7209	
Iceland									
Norway	2835	2970	3520	3978	4690	5125	5032	5024	
Sweden	4063	4628	5858	6431	6855	7863	9877	10251	
Switzerland	1831	1957	2063	2294	2478	2737	2887	3095	
CMEA members									
Bulgaria									
Czechoslovakia									
East Germany									
Hungary									
Poland									
Romania									
USSR									
Others									
Albania									
Cyprus									
Gibraltar									
Liechtenstein									
Malta									
Monaco									
Turkey	26500	28836	44594	76285	89725	151054	315084	490900	
Yugoslavia									

Source: National advertising associations
Note: a Billions

Database name: Advertising Patterns and Media Access
Sector name: Advertising Expenditure

Table No: 1302

Title: Advertising Expenditure by Medium 1989

Unit: National currencies (millions)

	TV	News-papers	Magazines	Radio	Cinema	Outdoor	Total	Notes
EC members								
Belgium	10004	13119	9221	560	640	5627	39171	
Denmark	420	3420	1278	100	51	161	5430	
France	11680	13122	12608	3170	370	5440	46390	
West Germany	2415	7486	5937	891	189	616	17534	
Greece	25160	8634	15560	4050	400	4850	58654	
Ireland	54	78	12	19	na	12	175	
Italy	3455	1745	1503	266	24	348	7341	a
Luxembourg								
Netherlands	575	2200	900	75	11	450	4211	
Portugal	23584	13813		5217	8900	3100	54614	b
Spain	209500	240000	107500	71000	4625	22000	654625	
United Kingdom	2275	3131	1451	153	30	271	7311	
EFTA members								
Austria	2849	3117	2234	1298	62	743	10303	
Finland	800	5432	683	155	4	135	7209	
Iceland								
Norway	75	3928	808	40	56	117	5024	
Sweden	0	8324	1491			376	10191	
Switzerland	215	1850	610	43	32	345	3095	
CMEA members								
Bulgaria								
Czechoslovakia								
East Germany								
Hungary								
Poland								
Romania								
USSR								
Others								
Albania								
Cyprus								
Gibraltar								
Liechtenstein								
Malta								
Monaco								
Turkey	240020	220500		5880		24500	490900	b
Yugoslavia								

Source: National advertising associations
Notes: a Billions
        b Newspapers includes magazines

Database name: Advertising Patterns and Media Access
Sector name: Press   Table No: 1303

Title: Number of National Newspapers 1989

Unit: Number

	Nationals	Sundays	Total
EC members			
Belgium	5		5
Denmark	7	5	12
France	9		9
West Germany	6	2	8
Greece	8	7	15
Ireland	7	4	11
Italy	15		15
Luxembourg			
Netherlands	5		5
Portugal	12		12
Spain	10	3	13
United Kingdom	11	11	22
EFTA members			
Austria	5		5
Finland	6		6
Iceland			
Norway	4		4
Sweden	2		2
Switzerland	17		17
CMEA members			
Bulgaria	2		2
Czechoslovakia	13.0		13
East Germany	9.0		9
Hungary	8.0		8
Poland	7.0		7
Romania	4.0		4
USSR	11.0		11
Others			
Albania			2
Cyprus			10
Gibraltar			1
Liechtenstein			2
Malta			4
Monaco			2
Turkey	12		12
Yugoslavia			

Source: Press/media associations/UNESCO

	Daily	Sunday	Total	Notes
EC members				
Belgium	1058		1058	a
Denmark	990	1056	2046	
France	2230		2230	a
West Germany	5784	2811	8595	
Greece	1504		1504	a
Ireland	641	893	1534	
Italy	7575		7575	a
Luxembourg				
Netherlands	1767		1767	a
Portugal	1025		1025	a
Spain	1145	1515	2660	
United Kingdom	14462	17518	31980	
EFTA members				
Austria	1656		1656	a
Finland	1112		1112	a
Iceland				
Norway	971		971	a
Sweden	1610		1610	a
Switzerland	1725		1725	a
CMEA members				
Bulgaria	1100		1100	a
Czechoslovakia	4573		4573	a
East Germany	4435		4435	a
Hungary	1333		1333	a
Poland	1559		1559	a
Romania				
USSR	104000		104000	a
Others				
Albania				
Cyprus				
Gibraltar				
Liechtenstein				
Malta				
Monaco				
Turkey	3322		3322	a
Yugoslavia	866.0		866	a

Source: Press/media associations
Notes: a No Sunday newspapers

Database name: Advertising Patterns and Media Access
Sector name: Press

Table No: 1305

Title: Mainstream Consumer Publications 1989

	Consumer Publications (Number)	Combined Circulation (000s)	Total Audited Publications (Number)
EC members			
Belgium	39	5489	125
Denmark	20	3345	38
France	84	37573	855
West Germany	62	61482	2500
Greece	23	1966	325
Ireland	14	446	65
Italy	53	17778	255
Luxembourg			
Netherlands	51	14353	102
Portugal	13	1430	195
Spain	23	4853	900
United Kingdom	63	25960	1600
EFTA members			
Austria	29	8771	200
Finland	24	3643	65
Iceland			
Norway	32	4312	50
Sweden	33	7743	150
Switzerland	36	7300	2500
CMEA members			
Bulgaria	7	500	
Czechoslovakia	12	2835	
East Germany	20	9000	
Hungary	10	5055	
Poland	20	7496	
Romania			
USSR	13	76800	
Others			
Albania			
Cyprus			
Gibraltar			
Liechtenstein			
Malta			
Monaco			
Turkey	13	345	
Yugoslavia			

Source: Press/media organisations/Euromonitor
Notes: "Mainstream" includes TV guides, business, men's and women's, motoring, home and general interest

Database name: Advertising Patterns and Media Access
Sector name: TV and Radio

Table No: 1306

Title: Number of TV and Radio Stations 1989

Unit: Number

EC members	Radio Stations:			National TV Stations:		Notes
	National Commercial	National Non-Commercial	Local Commercial	Commercial	Non-Commercial	
EEC members						
Belgium	5	2	c700	4	2	
Denmark		1	150	2	1	
France	5		1758	6		
West Germany		1	127	4	2	a
Greece	2		c600	8		
Ireland	2		27	2		
Italy	4		c1000	14		
Luxembourg						
Netherlands	3	2	3	4		
Portugal	5	1	300+	2		
Spain	4		600+	12		b
United Kingdom		4	60	4	2	
EFTA members						
Austria	2	1	11	2		
Finland	1		49	4		
Iceland						
Norway		2	462	2	1	
Sweden		3	0	0	2	
Switzerland		1	33	4	1	
CMEA members						
Bulgaria					2	
Czechoslovakia	1			2		
East Germany	6			2		
Hungary	3	2		2		
Poland		1		2		
Romania						
USSR		14			2	
Others						
Albania						
Cyprus						
Gibraltar						
Liechtenstein						
Malta						
Monaco						
Turkey	1			4		
Yugoslavia						

Source: Industry
Notes: a Regional commercial radio stations are state-owned; also numerous private stations
b There are six important regional commercial TV stations

Database name: Advertising Patterns and Media Access
Sector name: Cinema

Table No: 1307

Title: Cinema Screens, Attendances: Latest Year

Unit: As stated

	Year	Screens (number)	Attendances (000s)	Notes
EC members				
Belgium	1988	395	16500	
Denmark	1989	397	11000	a
France	1989	4753	122000	
West Germany	1989	3132	110000	
Greece	1989	600	17500	b
Ireland	1989	146	10000	
Italy	1989	3500	100000 ٥٦٧	
Luxembourg				
Netherlands	1989	436	15600	
Portugal	1989	290	16900	
Spain	1989	1882	116000	
United Kingdom	1989	1509	88000	
EFTA members				
Austria	1989	378	11200	
Finland	1989	344	7200	
Iceland	1982	na	2200	
Norway	1989	274	12700	
Sweden	1989	458	19200	
Switzerland	1989	328	15000	
CMEA members				
Bulgaria	1987	3028	84200	c
Czechoslovakia	1987	2634	73800	c
East Germany	1987	2064	58000	c
Hungary	1987	1057	55900	c
Poland	1987	1704	88800	c
Romania	1987	625	161400	c
USSR	1985	142400	188200	
Others				
Albania	1983	103		c
Cyprus				
Gibraltar	1981	4	170	
Liechtenstein				
Malta	1987	16	600	c
Monaco	1981	3	100	c
Turkey	1988	250	38000	
Yugoslavia	1987	1174	69900	c

Source: Cinema associations and film companies, various countries/UNESCO
Notes: a Estimated
b Summer months, 343 in winter
c Number of cinemas, not screens

Database name: Advertising Patterns and Media Access
Sector name: Outdoor Advertising   Table No: 1308

Title: Number of Sites 1987-1989

Unit: Number

	1987	1989
EC members		
Belgium	95000	105000
Denmark	17670	17672
France	173333	50000
West Germany	257527	260175
Greece	23300	24450
Ireland	6668	7000
Italy	88124	108100
Luxembourg		
Netherlands	69250	75000
Portugal	6148	2420
Spain		45000
United Kingdom	120319	122363
EFTA members		
Austria	110000	75000
Finland	60851	55000
Iceland		
Norway	19225	19140
Sweden	12966	25860
Switzerland	153900	150000
CMEA members		
Bulgaria		
Czechoslovakia		
East Germany		
Hungary		
Poland		
Romania		
USSR		
Others		
Albania		
Cyprus		
Gibraltar		
Liechtenstein		
Malta		
Monaco		
Turkey	4590	4590
Yugoslavia		

Source: Local industry

Database name: Advertising Patterns and Media Access
Sector name: Direct Marketing

Table No: 1309

Title: Volume of Addressed Direct Mail 1983-1987

Unit: Million items

	1983	1984	1985	1986	1987
EC members					
Belgium	409	449	474	506	533
Denmark	140	150	165	190	225
France	1603	1737	1973	2000	2376
West Germany	3004	3113	3078	3261	3357
Greece					
Ireland	7	9	13	19	20
Italy					
Luxembourg					
Netherlands	451	512	541	558	588
Portugal	58	58	61	66	85
Spain					
United Kingdom	1084	1261	1303	1401	1626
EFTA members					
Austria					
Finland	171	199	213	220	240
Iceland	121	135	177	204	215
Norway	404	434	457	481	511
Sweden	534	542	565	582	615
Switzerland					
CMEA members					
Bulgaria					
Czechoslovakia					
East Germany					
Hungary					
Poland					
Romania					
USSR					
Others					
Albania					
Cyprus					
Gibraltar					
Liechtenstein					
Malta					
Monaco					
Turkey					
Yugoslavia					

Source: Services Postaux Européens

Database name: Advertising Patterns and Media Access
Sector name: Media Access

Table No: 1310

Title: Home Ownership of Media Equipment 1989

Unit: % homes equipped

	Radio	TV	VCR	Cable	Viewdata	Satellite Dish	Notes
EC members							
Belgium	95	93	35	92	neg		
Denmark	99	94	40	34	na	1	
France	98	96	30	2	5	neg	
West Germany	98	93	41	28	9	neg	
Greece	100	90	38				
Ireland	95	94	40	37	21	2	
Italy	93	99	20		1		
Luxembourg							
Netherlands	99	98	46	80	20	1	
Portugal	94	94	23		neg		
Spain	93	98	34	9	neg		
United Kingdom	97	97	56	2	18	3	
EFTA members							
Austria	99	97	37	22	7	1	
Finland	99	97	37	22	22	1	
Iceland							
Norway	98	95	48	34	na	4	
Sweden	96	97	46	31	13	1	
Switzerland	98	94	40	68	na	neg	
CMEA members							
Bulgaria	95	76	5				
Czechoslovakia	96	82	3	4			
East Germany	99	96	na			neg	
Hungary	97	73	9	11			
Poland	95	70	11				
Romania	95	52					
USSR	97	60	1				
Others							
Albania	500	250					b
Cyprus	195	90					b
Gibraltar	36						b
Liechtenstein	18	9					b
Malta	155	128					a
Monaco	27	20					b
Turkey	75	67	14				b
Yugoslavia	8000						b

Source: Industry sources/Euromonitor
Notes: a '000 licences issued
b '000 receivers in use, 1986

Database name: Advertising Patterns and Media Access
Sector name: Media Access

Table No: 1311

Title: Cable Television Penetration in Selected Countries 1989

Unit: As stated

	TV Households ('000s)	Homes Connected ('000s)	% TV Households
EC members			
Belgium	3600	3286	92.0
Denmark	2200	750	34.0
France	20000	240	1.2
West Germany	24346	6800	28.0
Greece	3000		
Ireland	983	360	36.6
Italy	2100		
Luxembourg			
Netherlands	5547	4410	79.5
Portugal	2670		
Spain	10693	967	9.0
United Kingdom	21135	93	0.5
EC total			
EFTA members			
Austria	2780	600	21.6
Finland	1900	580	30.5
Iceland			
Norway	1550	600	38.7
Sweden	3090	970	31.4
Switzerland	2355	1600	67.9
EFTA total			
CMEA members			
Bulgaria			
Czechoslovakia			
East Germany			
Hungary			
Poland			
Romania			
USSR			
CMEA total			
Others			
Albania			
Cyprus			
Gibraltar			
Liechtenstein			
Malta			
Monaco			
Turkey			
Yugoslavia			
Total			
European total			

Source: Saatchi & Saatchi

TABLE 1301: ADVERTISING
Total spending in US dollars 1989

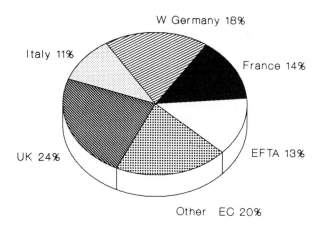

W Germany 18%

Italy 11%

France 14%

EFTA 13%

UK 24%

Other EC 20%

TABLE 1305: CONSUMER PUBLICATIONS
Titles, 1989

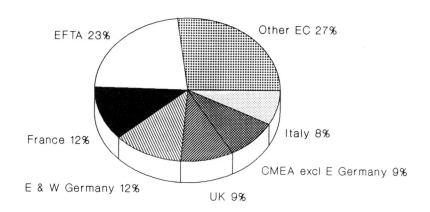

EFTA 23%

Other EC 27%

Italy 8%

France 12%

CMEA excl E Germany 9%

E & W Germany 12%

UK 9%

Database name: Consumer Market Sizes
Sector name: Meat and Fish Consumption

Table No: 1401

Title: Per Capita Consumption of Meat and Fish 1989

Unit: Kg per capita

	Total Meat	Beef and Veal	Pork	Mutton Lamb Goat	Poultry	Fresh Fish	Dried Fish	Shell Fish	Notes
EC members									
Belgium	103.2	22.0	49.0	1.8	17.2	4.8	0.7	4.7	
Denmark	108.9	17.9	68.6	0.8	12.4	39.1	2.3	1.6	
France	109.9	30.1	37.6	4.8	20.2	5.3	0.4	1.9	
West Germany	104.9	23.6	62.7	0.9	11.3	6.8	0.5	0.2	
Greece	76.4	18.7	21.9	14.0	15.6	3.6	1.3	2.4	
Ireland	87.3	18.7	34.6	6.5	19.6	12.5	0.3		
Italy	87.5	26.7	30.5	1.6	19.5	6.1	0.9	3.3	
Luxembourg					16.1				
Netherlands	88.8	19.3	47.2	0.7	17.4	3.9	1.9	4.1	
Portugal	68.4	13.5	25.8	3.2	18.0	13.1	8.8	1.9	
Spain	95.0	11.4	47.0	6.1	21.4	10.5	1.0	6.3	
United Kingdom	77.3	21.6	24.8	6.6	18.2	0.9	0.3	2.3	
EFTA members									
Austria	92.8	21.9	47.8	0.5	13.7	1.8	0.1	0.1	
Finland	68.5	20.1	31.4	0.2	6.2	5.4	1.2		
Iceland									
Norway	53.6	17.7	19.1	5.0	4.2	13.0	1.9	9.0	
Sweden	58.5	16.1	31.9	0.7	5.3	9.2	1.1	1.3	
Switzerland	87.6	26.1	43.2	1.7	10.9	3.3	0.3	0.8	
CMEA members									
Bulgaria	77.8					7.7			
Czechoslovakia	89.0					5.4			a
East Germany	99.4					7.9			a
Hungary	79					2			a
Poland	74					7			a
Romania	59								a
USSR	64.1					18.0			a
Others									
Albania		9.0	2.9	8.7	4.8	4.0			a,b
Cyprus									
Gibraltar									
Liechtenstein									
Malta									
Monaco									
Turkey									
Yugoslavia	59.7					3.7			c

Source: OECD/GATT/US Department of Agriculture/Euromonitor database
Notes; a 1987
b Based on production figures
c 1988

328

	Cereals Total	Rice	Vegetables	Potatoes	Fruit	Citrus Fruit	Non-Citrus Fruit	Dried Fruit	Notes
EC members									
Belgium	97.3	5.4	97.2	99.1	74.8	20.8	54.0	1.3	
Denmark	93.1	2.3	82.2	63.6	65.9	16.5	49.4	2.1	
France	100.4	4.0	120.2	74.5	78.0	22.4	55.5	1.3	
West Germany	97.7	3.0	77.7	70.6	116.8	34.2	82.7	1.5	
Greece	144.1	6.3	205.6	87.7	44.4	40.0	4.4	3.0	
Ireland	142.0	2.6	98.3	140.8	49.0	16.7	32.3	2.6	
Italy	157.7	5.2	173.4	38.2	102.0	33.5	68.5	0.6	
Luxembourg									
Netherlands	73.7	5.3	98.8	88.1	141.4	78.6	62.7	3.0	
Portugal	125.2	15.7	132.2	111.5	37.2	12.4	24.8	1.0	
Spain	97.1	90.0	164.1	107.0	91.5	37.9	53.6	0.4	
United Kingdom	119.1	3.8	67.8	108.3	62.4	26.2	36.2	2.8	
EFTA members									
Austria	92.2	4.0	72.2	61.5	92.8	18.6	74.3	1.6	
Finland	92.3	4.8	51.2	64.1	60.6	17.1	43.5	1.8	
Iceland									
Norway	84.9	1.9	41.3	63.5	59.5	15.1	44.4	1.7	
Sweden	78.9	3.9	38.3	62.6	65.3	13.7	51.6	1.7	
Switzerland	77.4	5.9	80.3	50.2	78.7	18.9	59.7	1.4	
CMEA members									
Bulgaria			140.0	28.1	110.3	1.2	109.1		
Czechoslovakia			77.0	73.0					
East Germany			102.0	155.0		73.0			
Hungary			145.0	50.0					
Poland			116.0	143.0					
Romania			192.0						
USSR			100.0	105.0					
Others									
Albania				44.0					
Cyprus									
Gibraltar									
Liechtenstein									
Malta									
Monaco									
Turkey	192.2	4.9	189.3	67.6	91.4	13.3	78.1	3.9	a
Yugoslavia	151.4		79.1	44.7	47.9	3.7	44.2	0.2	b

Source: OECD/Euromonitor database
Notes: a Non-citrus fruit 1987; others 1985
b 1988

Database name: Consumer Market Sizes
Sector name: Dairy Products Consumption

Table No: 1403

Title: Per Capita Consumption of Dairy Products 1989

Unit: Kg per capita except milk (litres)

	Eggs	Butter	Cheese	Cream	Yoghurt	Milk	Notes
EC members							
Belgium	13.1	8.5	12.6	3.8	7.3	62.0	
Denmark	13.8	11.3	12.8	9.7	8.2	62.0	
France	15.1	8.4	22.4	3.2	15.7	50.1	
West Germany	15.4	8.5	17.9	7.8	11.1	54.6	
Greece	12.1	1.0	22.1	0.6	6.7	60.3	
Ireland	10.2	4.0	5.4	2.0	3.4	171.7	
Italy	11.3	2.4	17.6	1.2	2.7	67.9	
Luxembourg				13.4	8.1	94.1	
Netherlands	11.1	3.9	15.1	2.6	19.8	60.6	
Portugal	7.0	0.9	5.2	1.3	6.5	46.8	
Spain	15.7	0.5	5.5	1.4	8.1	95.2	
United Kingdom	11.6	5.2	8.6	2.3	4.2	119.7	
EFTA members							
Austria	14.0	4.2	4.9	4.7	9.5	101.4	
Finland	12.3	6.9	11.9	6.4	8.1	88.7	
Iceland							
Norway	12.3	2.8	13.7	8.0	2.6	91.3	
Sweden	11.6	5.7	14.1	8.7	5.2	100.4	
Switzerland	12.4	5.3	13.2	6.8	16.4	96.2	
CMEA members							
Bulgaria	12.5	15.4				196.0	a
Czechoslovakia	16.3	8.1					a
East Germany	14.5	1.9					a
Hungary	17.0	2.5				194.0	b
Poland	9.3	3.0					a
Romania	14.3						a
USSR	13.0	10.0					a
Others							
Albania	4.5						a
Cyprus							
Gibraltar							
Liechtenstein							
Malta							
Monaco							
Turkey	4.7	2.1				14.9	a
Yugoslavia	8.7	17.1				98.8	b

Source: OECD/US Department of Agriculture/Euromonitor database
Notes: a   1987
          b   1988

Database name: Consumer Market Sizes
Sector name: Bakery Products Consumption

Table No: 1404

Title: Per Capita Consumption of Bakery Products 1989

Unit: Kg per capita

	Bread	Breakfast Cereals	Pasta	Flour	Biscuits	Notes
EC members						
Belgium	84.6	0.6	1.6	62.0	5.2	
Denmark	29.7	3.5	1.6	76.4	5.3	
France	64.8	0.6	6.3	66.4	6.4	
West Germany	60.8	0.7	5.0	65.0	3.1	
Greece	25.9		6.5		7.9	
Ireland	58.1	6.8	2.3	62.3	11.9	
Italy	132.6	0.1	21.3		6.8	
Luxembourg	48.4					
Netherlands	60.2	0.7	1.4	51.7	2.7	
Portugal	8.7		5.8		3.0	
Spain	52.8	0.2	3.3		5.8	
United Kingdom	44.4	7.0	3.5	5.4	10.6	
EFTA members						
Austria	51.1	0.8	3.6	63.5	5.1	
Finland	37.7	4.6	2.2	77.8	3.8	
Iceland						
Norway	46.0	1.7	0.2		3.8	
Sweden	38.3	2.7	3.8	21.6	5.7	
Switzerland	22.9	4.2	6.1	6.2	6.1	
CMEA members						
Bulgaria	144.0			50.0		a
Czechoslovakia	112.0					a
East Germany	99.0					a
Hungary	112.0			108.0		b
Poland	118.0					a
Romania	142.0					a
USSR	132.0					a
Others						
Albania						
Cyprus						
Gibraltar						
Liechtenstein						
Malta						
Monaco						
Turkey						
Yugoslavia	170.0					a

Source: Euromonitor database/Comecon/National sources
Notes: a 1987
b 1988

Database name: Consumer Market Sizes
Sector name: Consumption of Convenience and Miscellaneous Foods   Table No: 1405

Title: Per Capita Consumption of Convenience and Miscellaneous Foods 1989

Unit: Kg per capita, except soup (litres)

	Frozen Foods	Canned Foods	Baby Foods	Pet Foods	Soups	Sugar	Jams	Notes
EC members								
Belgium	16.0	34.6		8.5		43.5	3.6	b
Denmark	36.2	15.2		9.9		46.7	2.1	
France	21.1	37.7	1.9	16.7	5.3	38.0	3.8	
West Germany	22.8	35.0	1.3	8.3	13.1	34.9	3.3	
Greece	5.9	26.6		1.1		33.9	1.1	
Ireland	23.2	23.8		7.7		52.4	1.7	
Italy	6.1	12.4	1.0	3.6	7.0	30.7	1.0	
Luxembourg								
Netherlands	16.3	16.9		16.3		53.4	1.1	
Portugal	5.9	6.7		1.2		35.4	1.0	
Spain	12.1	11.7	0.7	1.3		29.4	1.0	
United Kingdom	22.4	26.8	1.4	23.1		43.3	1.7	
EFTA members								
Austria	12.9	12.2	0.7	1.8		50.0	1.4	
Finland	13.3	19.7			1.0	47.4	2.4	a
Iceland								
Norway	20.1	13.9		2.6		38.2	2.4	
Sweden	27.9	18.9		5.7	1.0	45.8	3.1	
Switzerland	22.1	15.2	0.4	7.6		42.4	1.2	
CMEA members								
Bulgaria						35.7		a
Czechoslovakia						37.3		a
East Germany						40.8		a
Hungary						34.0		c
Poland						46.1		a
Romania						26.0		a
USSR						46.6		a
Others								
Albania								a
Cyprus						33.0		a
Gibraltar								
Liechtenstein								
Malta						45.0		c
Monaco								
Turkey						30.0		c
Yugoslavia						38.9		c

Source: Euromonitor database/ISO
Notes: a   1987
                b   Including Luxembourg
                c   1988

Database name: Consumer Market Sizes
Sector name: Consumption of Snack Foods and Hot Beverages

Table No: 1406

Title: Per Capita Consumption of Snack Foods and Hot Beverages 1989

Unit: Kg per capita

	Confectionery:		Ice Cream	Savoury Snacks	Tea	Coffee	Notes
	Chocolate	Sugar					
EC members							
Belgium	7.0	5.3	9.8	3.2	0.1	6.7	a
Denmark	7.2	6.6	8.9	1.7	0.4	10.7	
France	5.2	2.8	4.7	1.7	0.2	5.6	
West Germany	5.8	8.8	7.7	2.9	0.2	8.4	
Greece	2.4	2.7	5.3		0.0	3.1	
Ireland	8.2	7.4	7.9		3.0	1.7	
Italy	1.3	2.9	6.1	0.7	0.1	4.5	
Luxembourg			10.8				
Netherlands	5.9	5.5	4.5	3.9	0.6	9.1	
Portugal	0.5	2.3	1.8		0.0	2.6	
Spain	2.3	2.4	3.7	1.4	0.0	4.0	
United Kingdom	8.2	5.0	7.0	4.3	2.7	2.3	
EFTA members							
Austria	7.5	2.5	4.5		0.2	10.5	
Finland	3.2	4.0	11.3	0.4	0.2	12.7	
Iceland							
Norway	7.8	4.5	12.3	4.2	0.2	10.1	
Sweden	6.0	4.6	13.6	2.2	0.3	11.0	
Switzerland	10.5	3.0	7.3		0.2	8.5	
CMEA members							
Bulgaria					0.1		
Czechoslovakia					0.2		
East Germany					0.2		
Hungary					0.2	2.7	
Poland					0.9	2.7	
Romania					0.1		
USSR					0.5		
Others							
Albania							
Cyprus							
Gibraltar							
Liechtenstein							
Malta							
Monaco							
Turkey					2.5		
Yugoslavia					0.2		

Source: Euromonitor database/International Tea Committee
Notes: Entries of 0.0 denote consumption levels below 50 grammes per capita
a Including Luxembourg, except ice cream

Database name: Consumer Market Sizes
Sector name: Drinks Consumption   Table No: 1407
Subsector name:
Title: Per Capita Consumption of Drinks 1989

Unit: Litres per capita

	Carbonated Drinks	Mineral Water	Fruit Juices	Beer	Wine	Spirits	Notes
EC members							
Belgium	73.9	74.3	16.0	125.4	24.3	3.2	a
Denmark	44.5	10.5	18.7	127.0	22.6	3.9	
France	34.5	61.4	6.3	39.4	90.0	5.7	
West Germany	86.5	68.5	36.4	145.0	26.6	6.2	
Greece	32.3	12.0	4.4	24.8	31.1	14.9	
Ireland	55.3	2.0	10.2	91.0	10.8	4.0	
Italy	31.6	54.7	5.9	21.4	74.5	3.4	
Luxembourg							
Netherlands	56.1	14.6	16.3	87.8	16.2	6.9	
Portugal	30.8	23.3	3.4	45.6	57.2	2.6	
Spain	42.2	28.3	9.4	72.6	38.0	6.6	
United Kingdom	123.2	3.5	17.9	108.8	13.1	4.4	
EFTA members							
Austria	59.3	62.7		116.4	40.8	3.4	
Finland	37.3	7.9	31.0	71.2	5.2	11.3	
Iceland							
Norway	81.2	6.2	8.3	51.4	6.6	2.6	
Sweden	40.5	11.4	15.2	58.7	12.6	4.6	
Switzerland	92.1	61.0	14.7	70.4	50.3	33.5	
CMEA members							
Bulgaria	63.2			60.0	22.0	3.4	b
Czechoslovakia				133.4	12.3	3.4	b
East Germany				141.3	11.7	5.1	b
Hungary				101.0	22.0	4.5	d
Poland				29.7	8.2	4.7	b
Romania							
USSR				18.1	15.5	3.3	b
Others							
Albania				7.0			c
Cyprus				43.0	11.0	2.1	d
Gibraltar							
Liechtenstein							
Malta				50.0	29.0	4.5	d
Monaco							
Turkey				6.4	0.2	1.1	
Yugoslavia				50.1	27.5	5.6	b

Source: Euromonitor
Notes: a   Including Luxembourg
               b   1987
               c   1988
               d   1985

Database name: Consumer Market Sizes
Sector name: Tobacco Consumption

Table No: 1408

Title: Per Capita Consumption of Tobacco Products 1989

Unit: Units/grammes per capita

	Cigarettes (Millions)	Cigars/Cigarillos Per capita	OMT grammes	Cigarettes per capita	Notes
EC members					
Belgium	17000	66.5	604.5	1712.7	
Denmark	6780	71.2	543.1	1318.3	
France	92500	25.7	100.7	1648.0	
West Germany	116000	24.4	267.9	1883.1	
Greece	33400	0.5	3.4	3315.5	
Ireland	5200	5.1	72.8	1473.5	
Italy	95000	2.9	13.6	1645.2	
Luxembourg					
Netherlands	16750	36.5	1201.1	1131.4	
Portugal	13750	2.4	18.9	1332.5	
Spain	77000	18.3	81.7	1966.3	
United Kingdom	96000	25.7	125.7	1677.0	
EFTA members					
Austria	14000	4.2	36.1	1843.6	
Finland	7500	13.1	326.4	1511.2	
Iceland					
Norway	2650	3.5	836.7	625.3	
Sweden	10948	10.3	713.2	1293.6	
Switzerland	12900	40.0	266.7	1955.1	
		20.5			
CMEA members					
Bulgaria	9030			1003.2	a
Czechoslovakia	25400			1628.2	a
East Germany	27600	27.0	21.0	1657.7	a
Hungary	26500			2495.3	a
Poland	98700			2607.7	a
Romania	33000			1441.0	a
USSR	378000			1333.3	a
Others					
Albania	2300			734.0	a
Cyprus	2500			3571.4	a
Gibraltar					
Liechtenstein					
Malta	1000			2857.1	a
Monaco					
Turkey	67240		11.1	1293.1	b
Yugoslavia	55800			2364.4	b

Source: Euromonitor database/World Tobacco
Notes: a 1987
b 1988

335

Database name: Consumer Market Sizes
Sector name: Consumption of Household Cleaning Products

Table No: 1409

Title: Per Capita Consumption of Household Cleaning Products 1989

Unit: Kg per capita

	Textile Washing Powders	Textile Washing Liquids	Fabric Conditioners	Dishwashing Liquids	Automatic Dishwashing Powders	Toilet Soaps	Surface Cleaners
EC members							
Belgium	10.1	1.1	5.3	5.3	1.6	0.8	3.5
Denmark	8.9	1.9	4.5	1.4	1.9	1.0	10.1
France	9.8	3.5	3.0	1.7	0.9	0.6	2.9
West Germany	10.6	1.9	4.8	2.6	1.1	0.6	3.2
Greece	5.7	4.0	0.7	3.1	0.2	0.8	2.5
Ireland	4.8	1.4	1.1	2.6	0.6	0.6	2.0
Italy	6.9	2.1	2.2	4.7	0.4	0.7	4.5
Luxembourg							
Netherlands	10.1	1.7	2.8	2.9	0.4	0.7	2.2
Portugal	5.3	1.0	0.3	5.2	0.2	0.7	2.9
Spain	13.3	1.1	0.6	6.6	0.3	0.3	3.2
United Kingdom	6.1	2.6	2.7	2.4	1.2	1.2	6.9
EFTA members							
Austria	7.9	1.7	2.4	1.4	1.1	0.7	1.7
Finland	5.0	1.0	1.4	1.8	0.8	0.4	2.8
Iceland							
Norway	4.7	1.7	2.4	1.9	0.9	1.2	7.8
Sweden	11.5			8.3	0.7	0.6	8.3
Switzerland	9.2	1.7	2.4	1.7	2.3	0.9	4.8
CMEA members							
Bulgaria							
Czechoslovakia							
East Germany							
Hungary							
Poland							
Romania							
USSR							
Others							
Albania							
Cyprus							
Gibraltar							
Liechtenstein							
Malta							
Monaco							
Turkey							
Yugoslavia							

Source: Euromonitor database/AIS

	Toilet Tissues	Boxed Facial Tissues	Sanitary Products	Disposable Nappies
EC members				
Belgium	118.0	7.8	41.9	21.2
Denmark	52.0	4.3	19.8	22.6
France	559.6	42.3	219.4	627.0
West Germany	542.6	281.9	332.4	462.8
Greece	67.7	10.8	59.1	10.5
Ireland	29.8	7.8	14.9	24.1
Italy	298.8	72.9	266.0	338.9
Luxembourg	3.6	0.3	1.3	0.7
Netherlands	148.5	39.1	240.5	82.5
Portugal	38.7	4.1	12.4	14.3
Spain	236.5	32.1	211.2	67.6
United Kingdom	763.9	213.1	232.8	582.0
EC total	2859.7	716.6	1651.7	2254.2
EFTA members				
Austria	77.1	29.5	122.8	31.6
Finland	52.4	6.1	14.4	42.9
Iceland				
Norway	65.9	3.5	5.2	33.3
Sweden	182.3	7.5	115.6	73.7
Switzerland	62.4	25.7	101.5	45.2
EFTA total	440.0	72.2	359.5	226.7
CMEA members				
Bulgaria				
Czechoslovakia				
East Germany				
Hungary				
Poland				
Romania				
USSR				
Others				
Albania				
Cyprus				
Gibraltar				
Liechtenstein				
Malta				
Monaco				
Turkey				
Yugoslavia				

Source: Euromonitor database

Title: Retail Sales of Cosmetics and Toiletries 1989

Unit: $ million

	Women's Fragrances	Men's Fragrances	Colour Cosmetics	Skincare	Suncare	Haircare
EC members						
Belgium	71.8	32.2	81.1	126.5	10.8	165.0
Denmark	35.6	27.9	36.9	62.9	7.9	97.1
France	827.6	385.0	794.7	1100.3	141.1	1144.2
West Germany	516.0	351.1	563.8	1074.5	159.6	1159.6
Greece	41.9	3.8	17.2	50.5	12.9	110.5
Ireland	22.7	9.9	35.5	28.4	4.3	45.4
Italy	433.6	420.5	627.5	932.9	139.9	792.2
Luxembourg						
Netherlands	93.4	22.2	102.8	125.0	17.0	216.9
Portugal	43.5	18.8	21.3	33.0	5.0	36.5
Spain	169.8	83.2	235.7	236.5	50.7	371.7
United Kingdom	655.7	295.1	598.4	606.6	123.0	954.1
EC total	2911.5	1649.6	3114.8	4377.0	672.0	5093.2
EFTA members						
Austria	63.5	44.1	90.7	188.2	31.7	216.2
Finland	35.7	19.8	64.8	57.1	6.1	86.0
Iceland						
Norway	11.2	9.3	40.7	53.2	9.1	109.9
Sweden	28.7	22.0	102.4	95.4	17.4	199.3
Switzerland	33.6	28.7	63.6	122.3	33.0	130.2
EFTA total	172.6	124.0	362.1	516.1	97.3	741.6

CMEA members
Bulgaria
Czechoslovakia
East Germany
Hungary
Poland
Romania
USSR

Others
Albania
Cyprus
Gibraltar
Liechtenstein
Malta
Monaco
Turkey
Yugoslavia

Source: Euromonitor database

Title: Retail Sales of Cosmetics and Toiletries 1989

Unit: $ million

	Bath and Shower	Deodorant	Oral Hygiene	Shaving Products	Baby Care
EC members					
Belgium	35.5	68.5	52.3	36.0	14.7
Denmark	17.8	29.5	56.1	11.5	3.3
France	276.6	327.6	435.0	308.8	93.3
West Germany	361.7	311.2	659.6	628.7	194.1
Greece	7.7	12.0	27.7	8.6	2.0
Ireland	12.8	15.6	29.8	21.3	7.1
Italy	364.4	245.6	437.3	604.9	53.9
Luxembourg					
Netherlands	56.6	53.8	95.3	46.2	24.5
Portugal	10.7	12.1	12.7	13.4	5.6
Spain	135.2	95.5	126.7	119.1	33.8
United Kingdom	196.7	245.9	418.0	409.8	216.4
EC total	1475.7	1417.2	2350.4	2208.4	648.7
EFTA members					
Austria	64.2	64.6	75.6	64.7	13.2
Finland	6.1	32.6	29.8	8.6	2.1
Iceland					
Norway	15.4	36.5	39.8	5.6	4.6
Sweden	31.0	45.8	58.2	36.1	12.4
Switzerland	55.0	52.6	81.3	54.4	14.1
EFTA total	171.7	232.1	284.7	169.5	46.4
CMEA members					
Bulgaria					
Czechoslovakia					
East Germany					
Hungary					
Poland					
Romania					
USSR					
Others					
Albania					
Cyprus					
Gibraltar					
Liechtenstein					
Malta					
Monaco					
Turkey					
Yugoslavia					

Source: Euromonitor database

Database name: Consumer Market Sizes
Sector name: Market Sizes : OTC Healthcare

Title: Retail Sales of OTC Healthcare Products 1989

Unit: $ million

Table No: 1412

	Total	Analgesics	Cough/Cold Remedies	Digestive Remedies	Medicated Skincare	Vitamins/ Tonics
EC members						
Belgium	233.5	63.4	28.6	32.4	20.2	41.9
Denmark	128.0	31.2	13.1	25.3	7.9	18.3
France	753.6	67.7	228.8	55.8	116.3	153.6
West Germany	2597.9	292.6	346.8	308.5	352.1	454.8
Greece	49.3	7.4	11.7	5.5	6.8	5.5
Ireland	86.5	9.9	15.6	8.5	9.9	24.1
Italy	1455.4	145.0	164.7	178.6	147.2	38.6
Luxembourg	7.6	1.9	0.9	1.0	0.6	1.3
Netherlands	224.5	43.9	24.5	22.2	22.6	34.0
Portugal	50.5	7.1	11.9	3.5	7.6	7.6
Spain	297.8	35.5	74.3	40.1	42.2	38.0
United Kingdom	1109.8	211.5	193.4	124.6	173.8	270.5
EC total	6994.4	917.1	1114.4	805.9	907.3	1088.2
EFTA members						
Austria	209.6	25.1	33.3	22.7	16.2	64.2
Finland	139.1	23.8	28.0	16.3	13.0	6.1
Iceland						
Norway	56.2	13.9	11.2	6.5	5.9	10.9
Sweden	129.7	21.7	24.8	14.3	12.4	6.8
Switzerland	257.4	30.6	37.3	24.5	18.3	85.6
	791.9	115.0	134.5	84.2	66.0	173.6
CMEA members						
Bulgaria						
Czechoslovakia						
East Germany						
Hungary						
Poland						
Romania						
USSR						
Others						
Albania						
Cyprus						
Gibraltar						
Liechtenstein						
Malta						
Monaco						
Turkey						
Yugoslavia						

Source: Euromonitor database

Database name: Consumer Market Sizes
Sector name: Market Sizes: Clothing and Footwear

Table No: 1413

Title: Retail Sales of Clothing and Footwear 1989

Unit: $ million except footwear (million pairs)

	Men's Outerwear	Women's Outerwear	Underwear Nightwear	Knitwear	Socks, Stockings and Tights	Clothing Accessories	Footwear	Notes
EC members								
Belgium	1307.0	2197.2	835.7	597.7	326.5	275.7	37.0	
Denmark	557.5	921.3	314.6	246.9	98.5	109.4	22.0	
France	6452.8	6907.7	3840.1	4013.8	1863.2	2228.8	320.0	
West Germany	11209.6	17038.8	5207.4	5267.6	2759.6	2025.5	281.0	
Greece	444.0	765.9	313.7	327.9	99.7	85.6	22.0	
Ireland	177.3	251.1	68.1	106.4	31.2	38.3	14.0	
Italy	8760.3	10706.9	5028.8	4769.3	1655.1	1524.7	290.0	
Luxembourg	41.2	80.6	30.0	34.3	13.5	10.0		
Netherlands	1590.5	2101.2	706.8	1538.2	183.9	425.3	61.0	
Portugal	393.8	708.8	276.3	290.9	93.7	75.6	22.0	
Spain	2238.6	4316.6	1512.1	1689.5	489.9	380.1	146.0	
United Kingdom	6482.0	11509.8	4182.0	3396.7	1065.6	1403.3	259.0	
EC total	39654.5	57506.0	22315.6	22279.1	8680.4	8582.4	1474.0	
EFTA members								
Austria	1538.7	2332.8	986.5	825.2	272.9	248.2	35.0	
Finland	582.6	939.6	335.6	426.5	96.7	167.8	20.0	
Iceland								
Norway	666.2	1006.4	153.8	273.7	118.0	182.5	24.0	
Sweden	1536.4	2216.9	494.8	592.8	216.4	97.7	29.0	
Switzerland	874.1	1326.5	556.3	482.9	162.0	165.0	39.0	
EFTA total	5198.0	7822.2	2526.9	2601.1	866.0	861.2	147.0	
CMEA members								
Bulgaria				368.0	152.0		30.7	b
Czechoslovakia				1320.0	425.0		88.0	b
East Germany				1475.0	495.0		90.0	a,b
Hungary			111.5	207.0	58.0		38.6	a,b
Poland				543.0	182.0		151.6	a,b
Romania				490.0	95.0		121.4	c
USSR				20740.0	4603.0		800.7	b
CMEA total				25143.0	6010.0		1321.0	
Others								
Albania								
Cyprus							3.0	d
Gibraltar								
Liechtenstein								
Malta							2.0	a
Monaco								
Turkey								
Yugoslavia							91.0	d

Source: Euromonitor database/Shoe & Allied Trades Research Association
Notes:
a Estimated
b 1985, except for footwear (1987)
c Knitwear, socks, stockings: 1980; Footwear: 1987
d 1985

Database name: Consumer Market Sizes
Sector name: Market Sizes: Home Furnishings and Housewares

Table No: 1414

Title: Retail Sales of Home Furnishings and Housewares 1989

Unit: $ million

	Furniture	Floor Coverings	Household Textiles	Glassware	China and Porcelain	Ceramic Housewares	Cutlery
EC members							
Belgium	2282.8	987.2	1197.8	167.2	61.7	50.5	60.1
Denmark	1593.7	313.3	450.1	28.7	37.3	17.2	14.5
France	8996.9	782.1	3558.0	627.0	317.4	179.5	501.6
West Germany	17127.7	3010.6	3148.9	1497.3	803.2	614.4	404.3
Greece	538.7			23.7	23.6	35.1	36.9
Ireland	255.3	126.2	146.1	29.8	9.9	19.9	7.1
Italy	12171.1	1494.1	4795.6	940.2	375.3	236.9	236.9
Luxembourg							2.4
Netherlands	2305.8	693.2	1207.1	174.5	77.8	34.4	66.0
Portugal	539.8			231.8	44.5	65.4	28.6
Spain	5617.5	692.7	2213.2	625.1	152.1	152.1	163.9
United Kingdom	6180.3	2901.6	3904.9	631.1	231.1	450.8	172.1
EC total	57609.7	11001.0	20621.8	4976.5	2134.0	1856.1	1694.3
EFTA members							
Austria	2040.7	650.0	1133.7	36.3	45.3	30.2	42.3
Finland	1251.4	137.5	375.2	86.2	20.0	69.9	52.4
Iceland							
Norway	1209.4	195.5	533.0	44.9	29.5	24.6	40.1
Sweden	1768.3	316.4	983.4	149.7	90.0	36.5	31.0
Switzerland	1659.6	501.3	865.0	97.2	29.3	20.2	17.7
EFTA total	7929.3	1800.7	3890.3	414.3	214.2	181.4	183.6

CMEA members
Bulgaria
Czechoslovakia
East Germany
Hungary
Poland
Romania
USSR

Others
Albania
Cyprus
Gibraltar
Liechtenstein
Malta
Monaco
Turkey
Yugoslavia

Source: Euromonitor database

Database name: Consumer Market Sizes
Sector name: Market Sizes: White Goods

Table No: 1415

Title: Retail Sales of White Goods 1989

Unit: 000s

	Refrigerators	Fridge-Freezers	Freezers	Cookers	Microwave Ovens	Washing Machines	Dryers	Dishwashers	Notes
EC members									
Belgium	225	136	160	225	217	290	116	65	
Denmark	150	139	82	150	58	120	40	50	
France	1450	535	741	1970	1600	1900	650	750	
West Germany	1735	345	880	2510	2700	1720	700	700	
Greece	350	340	374	310	26	62	20	12	
Ireland	40	19	56	100	37	117	25	14	
Italy	800	767	365	970	237	1510	26	290	
Luxembourg	10	10	12	19	19	13	11	9	
Netherlands	360	118	200	355	190	424	180	97	
Portugal	466	469	86		45	219	12	77	
Spain	1836	1987	330		290	1570	115	136	
United Kingdom	900	860	555	1100	2360	1910	870	487	
EC total	8322	5725	3841	7709	7779	9855	2765	2687	
EFTA members									
Austria	217	220	119	180	137	195	28	105	
Finland	123	38	74	120	340	138	23	87	
Iceland									
Norway	112	23	170	100	164	100	50	63	
Sweden	63	147		244	420	180	74	100	
Switzerland	297	278	100	125			50	115	
EFTA total	812	706	463	769	1061	613	225	470	
CMEA members									
Bulgaria	122					220			a,b
Czechoslovakia	571					370			a,b
East Germany	649					374			a
Hungary	551					400			a,b
Poland	830					1186			a,b
Romania									
USSR	5224					6034			a,b
CMEA total	7947					8584			

Others
Albania
Cyprus
Gibraltar
Liechtenstein
Malta
Monaco
Turkey
Yugoslavia

Source: Euromonitor database/Comecon
Notes: a Data for 1987. Freezers includes fridge/freezers and freezers
b Washing machines include dryers

	Colour TVs	Video Recorders	Video Cameras	Home Computers	Audio Separates	CD Players	Notes
EC members							
Belgium	370	320	3	125	220	60	
Denmark	200	95	1	45	315	38	
France	4100	1900	200	1170	2320	1100	
West Germany	4400	2670	410	1780	5700	1570	
Greece	190	185	2	30	76	10	
Ireland	130	65	1	35	90	9	
Italy	2600	1370	163	900	1550	385	
Luxembourg	83				80	6	
Netherlands	642	415	4	185	860	125	
Portugal	260	150		20	280	16	
Spain	2600	820		372	660	57	
United Kingdom	4100	2100	167	1390	3150	475	
EC total	19675	10090	951	6052	15301	3851	
EFTA members							
Austria	325	275		90	400	42	
Finland	245	155	7	38	200	40	
Iceland							
Norway	166	120	4	40	300	10	
Sweden	455	300	9	90	500	92	
Switzerland	400	260	1	100	600	210	
EFTA total	1591	1110	21	358	2000	394	
CMEA members							
Bulgaria	199						a
Czechoslovakia	507						a
East Germany	723						a
Hungary	414						a
Poland	647						a
Romania	484						a
USSR	9081						a
CMEA total	12055						
Others							
Albania							
Cyprus							
Gibraltar							
Liechtenstein							
Malta							
Monaco							
Turkey							
Yugoslavia	591						a

Source: Euromonitor database/Comecon
Notes: a Apparent consumption 1987: Colour and black/white TVs

Database name: Consumer Market Sizes
Sector name: Market Sizes: Consumer Electronics

Table No: 1416

Title: Retail Sales of Consumer Electronics 1989

Unit: 000s

	Personal Stereos	Portable Cassettes	Radio Recorders	Portable Radios	In-Car Entertainment
EC members					
Belgium	280	80	280	100	525
Denmark	100	100	270	90	265
France	2760	570	2200	1000	3100
West Germany	4110	830	4100	1370	5600
Greece	300	140	110	319	119
Ireland	140	90	120	30	220
Italy	1700	390	1100	800	1700
Luxembourg		8		10	117
Netherlands	800	240	425	260	680
Portugal	185	170	165		190
Spain	820	385	1370		837
United Kingdom	4350	280	2500	1870	3870
EC total	15545	3283	12640	5849	17223
EFTA members					
Austria	250	40	340	120	345
Finland	215	90	280	57	227
Iceland					
Norway	90	65	190	80	275
Sweden	360	115	540	177	815
Switzerland	360	75	280	465	335
EFTA total	1275	385	1630	899	1997

CMEA members
Bulgaria
Czechoslovakia
East Germany
Hungary
Poland
Romania
USSR

Others
Albania
Cyprus
Gibraltar
Liechtenstein
Malta
Monaco
Turkey
Yugoslavia

Source: Euromonitor database/Comecon

	Watches $ mn	Clocks 000s	Toys/Games $ mn	Cameras 000s	Films mns	Pre-recorded Cassettes mns	Blank Audio Cassettes mns
EC members							
Belgium	133	1540	279	375	21	3	29
Denmark	87	976	144	93	14	2	11
France	878	10000	3009	1871	85	40	51
West Germany	529	11200	1941	3480	115	58	115
Greece	82	1080	91	70	10	3	7
Ireland	27	565	68	165	6	2	3
Italy	510	6200	1458	1040	73	24	55
Luxembourg	5	63					
Netherlands	130	2380	340	775	29	3	42
Portugal	191	1180	83	50	5	2	6
Spain	452	4455	655	585	28	27	39
United Kingdom	377	9000	1654	3900	90	83	108
EC total	3401	48639	9722	12404	476	247	466
EFTA members							
Austria	133	1312	162	115	13	2	18
Finland	43	1007	219	145	19	5	14
Iceland							
Norway	68	740	156	97	13	4	15
Sweden	85	980	419	180	27	5	20
Switzerland	60	1200	241	230	23	7	12
EFTA total	389	5239	1197	767	95	23	79
CMEA members							
Bulgaria							
Czechoslovakia							
East Germany							
Hungary	358						
Poland							
Romania							
USSR							
CMEA total	358						
Others							
Albania							
Cyprus							
Gibraltar							
Liechtenstein							
Malta							
Monaco							
Turkey							
Yugoslavia							
Total							
European total	4148	53878	10919	13171	571	270	545

Source: Euromonitor database

346

Database name: Consumer Market Sizes
Sector name: Market Sizes: Personal and Leisure Goods

Table No: 1417

Title: Retail Sales of Personal and Leisure Goods 1989

	Compact Discs mns	Singles EPs mns	LPs Records mns	Blank Video Cassettes mns	Gardening Goods $mn	Bicycles 000	Books $mn
EC members							
Belgium	6.3	6	2	15	705.5	430	748.7
Denmark	2.8	1	4	9		400	429.5
France	40.0	35	16	54	4341.7	2300	2032.1
West Germany	56.0	32	48	83		3300	5212.8
Greece	0.3	1	5	4		155	114.5
Ireland	0.3	1	1	7		105	79.4
Italy	10.0	3	16	41	112.2	1800	838.1
Luxembourg	0.7						7.2
Netherlands	23.2	4	4	22	488.0	1250	288.6
Portugal	0.5	1	2	2		185	52.1
Spain	4.8	2	20	35		1120	794.1
United Kingdom	41.0	36	37	48	3336.1	2300	1785.2
EC total	185.9	122	155	320	8983.6	13345	12382.4
EFTA members							
Austria	3.1	2	3	12	377.9	370	279.6
Finland	1.5	1	3	6		690	563.9
Iceland							
Norway	2.8	1	2	8		280	506.9
Sweden	4.6	5	10	18		560	496.4
Switzerland	10.9	2	3	13	299.5	210	379.0
EFTA total	22.9	11	21	57	677.4	2110	2225.9
CMEA members							
Bulgaria							
Czechoslovakia							
East Germany							
Hungary							
Poland							
Romania							
USSR							
Others							
Albania							
Cyprus							
Gibraltar							
Liechtenstein							
Malta							
Monaco							
Turkey							
Yugoslavia							

Database name: Consumer Market Sizes
Sector name: Market Sizes: Small Electrical Appliances   Table No: 1418

Title: Retail Sales of Small Electrical Appliances 1989

Unit: 000s

	Electric Blankets	Drinks Makers	Food Processors	Hair Dryers	Irons	Shavers	Space Heaters	Vacuum Cleaners	Toasters	Notes
EC members										
Belgium	55	470	1050	560	635	410	255	700	240	
Denmark	22	380	320	230	160	180	325	190	80	
France	305	2560	4300	2330	3470	1100	3800	2750	1049	a
West Germany	1400	5970	2500	4400	3900	3000	2100	3500	1780	a
Greece	15	39	20	170	260	67	310	140	5	
Ireland	115	10	180	190	140	100	76	190	167	
Italy	270	300	1580	1600	3010	880	980	950	230	a
Luxembourg	19	20	50	30	28	25	12	33		
Netherlands	85	1135	670	880	755	800	410	400	455	
Portugal	15	100	240	250	335	115	155	200		
Spain		515	1160	2790	970	730	1500	267		
United Kingdom	1380	2000	1430	2580	3920	2900	2100	3410	1950	a
EC total	3681	13499	13500	16010	17583	10307	12023	12730	5956	
EFTA members										
Austria	135	450	430	540	480	190	240	290	100	
Finland	70	420	250	140	190	230	615	215		
Iceland										
Norway	90	317	135	250	210	210	820	325		
Sweden	110	500	520	366	400	310	740	327	240	
Switzerland	227	342	365	590	360		100	360	135	
EFTA total	632	2029	1700	1886	1640	940	2515	1517	475	
CMEA members										
Bulgaria								96		b
Czechoslovakia										
East Germany								463		c
Hungary								204		c
Poland								746		c
Romania								133		d
USSR								3418		c
								5060		
Others										
Albania										
Cyprus										
Gibraltar										
Liechtenstein										
Malta										
Monaco										
Turkey										
Yugoslavia										

Source: Euromonitor database/Comecon
Notes:
a   Hair dryers: 1988
b   1986
c   1985
d   1980

348

TABLE 1417: COLOUR TV SALES
1989

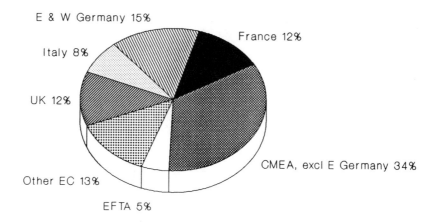

E & W Germany 15%

France 12%

Italy 8%

UK 12%

CMEA, excl E Germany 34%

Other EC 13%

EFTA 5%

CMEA figures include black/white sets

TABLE 1417: VIDEO RECORDER SALES
1989

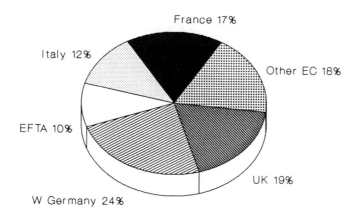

France 17%

Italy 12%

Other EC 18%

EFTA 10%

UK 19%

W Germany 24%

15
CONSUMER PRICES AND COSTS

Database name: Consumer Prices and Costs
Sector name: Consumer Prices

Table No: 1501

Title: Trends in Consumer Prices 1980-1989

Unit: 1980 = 100

	1980	1981	1982	1983	1984	1985	1986	1987	1988	1989	Notes
EC members											
Belgium	100.0	107.6	117.0	126.0	134.0	140.5	142.3	144.5	146.2	150.8	
Denmark	100.0	111.7	123.0	131.5	139.8	146.4	151.7	157.8	165.0	172.9	
France	100.0	113.4	126.8	139.0	149.3	157.9	161.9	167.3	171.8	177.5	
West Germany	100.0	106.3	111.9	115.6	118.4	121.0	120.9	121.1	122.7	126.1	a
Greece	100.0	124.5	150.5	181.4	214.3	255.7	314.8	366.4	416.0	473.0	
Ireland	100.0	120.4	141.1	155.8	169.3	178.4	185.2	191.0	195.2	203.0	
Italy	100.0	119.5	139.2	159.5	176.8	193.0	204.3	214.0	221.7	233.4	
Luxembourg	100.0	108.1	118.2	128.4	135.7	141.2	141.6	141.3	142.2	147.0	
Netherlands	100.0	106.7	113.0	116.2	120.0	122.7	122.8	121.9	123.1	124.5	
Portugal	100.0	120.0	147.3	184.3	237.6	284.2	317.6	347.7	380.9	425.2	
Spain	100.0	114.5	131.0	147.0	163.6	178.0	193.6	203.9	213.7	227.0	
United Kingdom	100.0	111.9	121.5	127.1	133.4	141.5	146.4	152.4	159.9	172.3	
EFTA members											
Austria	100.0	106.8	112.6	116.3	122.9	126.9	129.0	130.9	133.4	136.8	
Finland	100.0	112.0	122.7	133.0	142.2	150.7	155.9	161.6	169.5	180.7	
Iceland	100.0	150.9	227.8	419.8	542.2	717.7	871.0	1050.0	1291.0	1551.0	
Norway	100.0	113.7	126.5	137.3	145.9	154.2	165.1	179.5	191.5	200.2	
Sweden	100.0	112.1	121.7	132.6	143.2	153.8	160.3	167.0	176.7	188.1	
Switzerland	100.0	106.5	112.5	115.9	119.3	123.4	124.3	126.0	128.4	132.5	
CMEA members											
Bulgaria	100.0	100.5	100.8	102.2	102.9	104.6	108.3	108.3	109.0		
Czechoslovakia	100.0	101.5	106.2	107.2	108.1	109.9	110.9	111.0	111.3		
East Germany	100.0	100.2	100.2	100.2	100.2	100.1	100.1	100.1	100.2		
Hungary	100.0	104.6	111.8	120.0	130.0	139.1	146.4	159.2	184.2	214.3	
Poland	100.0	121.2	243.4	297.2	341.8	393.4	463.0	579.7	928.7	1925.9	b
Romania	100.0	102.2	119.5	125.7	127.1	126.6	126.5	127.0			
USSR	100.0	101.3	104.6	105.2	104.2	104.6	106.5	107.0			
Others											
Albania											
Cyprus	100.0	110.6	117.7	123.6	131.1	137.6	139.5	143.4	147.7	152.1	
Gibraltar	100.0	100.0	109.3	114.9	122.5	129.9	134.6	141.0	146.1	152.5	
Liechtenstein	100.0	106.5	112.5	115.9	119.3	123.4	124.3	125.1			
Malta	100.0	111.5	118.0	117.0	117.5	118.1	118.5	119.1	120.3	120.7	c
Monaco											
Turkey	100.0	136.6	178.7	237.5	352.4	510.9	687.7	1327.3	2322.2	3553.0	
Yugoslavia	100.0	139.8	183.9	257.9	399.0	687.3	1312.0	2891.0	8518.0	83585.0	d

Source: IMF/ILO/Statistical Offices
Notes: Bulgaria, Czechoslovakia: State retail price index
East Germany: Index of retail prices, service charges and fares
a Derived from a series rebased from 1985
b 1989: average first three quarters of year
 of daily quotations
c Derived from a series rebased from 1983
d 1989 average to end of November only

		Database name:	Consumer Prices and Costs									

Database name: Consumer Prices and Costs
Sector name: Food Prices

Table No: 1502

Title: Trends in Food Prices 1980-1989

Unit: 1980 = 100

	1980	1981	1982	1983	1984	1985	1986	1987	1988	1989	Notes
EC members											
Belgium	100.0	106.0	116.2	126.0	135.9	140.6	143.3	142.7	142.7	147.2	
Denmark	100.0	112.0	124.0	130.0	142.0	148.0	151.0	152.0	158.0	164.0	
France	100.0	114.0	128.4	140.3	151.4	158.9	164.4	167.3	169.9	176.1	
West Germany	100.0	104.8	111.3	114.3	116.0	116.9	117.6	117.0	117.3	119.8	a
Greece	100.0	130.1	157.5	185.8	219.8	262.7	315.9	355.7	395.4	467.4	
Ireland	100.0	114.9	130.1	140.6	154.3	160.2	167.2	171.8	176.7	185.0	
Italy	100.0	116.3	135.4	152.0	165.9	180.3	190.2	198.3	206.1	216.4	
Luxembourg	100.0	108.4	119.8	129.4	138.1	143.2	147.4	145.3	146.9	151.6	b
Netherlands	100.0	105.5	111.7	112.3	116.9	117.8	116.7	115.1	115.4	116.4	
Portugal	100.0	119.5	148.3	185.5	242.6	285.5	311.6	338.9	371.4	420.9	
Spain	100.0	113.6	130.7	144.6	162.8	178.3	197.2	207.2	214.5	229.6	
United Kingdom	100.0	108.4	117.0	120.7	127.4	131.4	135.7	139.9	144.7	152.9	
EFTA members											
Austria	100.0	105.9	110.6	113.4	119.8	122.5	125.4	126.3	127.3	129.0	
Finland	100.0	113.1	126.8	135.9	146.0	157.3	163.0	166.4	170.1	176.2	
Iceland	100.0	155.3	226.1	437.6	572.7	788.5	968.0	1119.0	1524.0	1816.0	
Norway	100.0	117.4	133.6	144.7	154.2	164.2	178.9	194.1	205.2	210.8	
Sweden	100.0	115.0	129.2	144.2	161.0	172.9	185.3	191.1	201.6	213.2	
Switzerland	100.0	110.5	118.0	120.6	125.1	128.9	130.6	132.1	135.3	137.6	
CMEA members											
Bulgaria	100.0	100.2	100.9	103.9	105.4	107.8	112.4	115.2			
Czechoslovakia	100.0	100.0	109.4	110.0	110.8	113.7	114.1	114.3	114.0	113.9	
East Germany	100.0	100.0	100.1	100.1	100.1	100.1	100.1	100.1	100.2		
Hungary	100.0	103.4	108.4	113.9	127.7	135.7	138.7	151.4	175.5	206.9	
Poland	100.0	130.1	294.4	353.0	400.7	448.4	517.0	638.0	985.7	2248.4	
Romania	100.0	101.7	117.8	124.2	126.6	125.9	126.2	127.0			
USSR	100.0	102.3	106.2	106.5	106.6	108.5	114.2				
Others											
Albania											
Cyprus	100.0	111.5	120.5	125.7	136.3	142.6	146.7	151.4	156.2	160.9	
Gibraltar	100.0	100.0	109.1	113.2	118.6	124.0	128.4	134.0	138.6	144.1	
Liechtenstein											
Malta	100.0 `	113.0	121.5	119.0	117.5	116.4	119.1	121.3	120.7		c
Monaco											
Turkey	100.0	140.7	181.5	235.2	198.0	278.5	363.3	507.8	869.0	1337.5	
Yugoslavia	100.0	143.0	198.0	288.0	423.0	721.0	1370.0	2889.0	8894.0	85656.1	d

Source: ILO/UN
Notes:
a Derived from a series rebased to 1985
b Derived from a series rebased to 1984
c Derived from a series rebased to 1983
d 1989: year to end November only

| Database name: | Consumer Prices and Costs | |
| Sector name: | Food Costs | Table No: 1503 |

Title: Costs of Selected Food and Drink 1989

Unit: National currencies

	White Bread 500 g	Milk 1 ltr	Chicken 1 kg	Butter 250 g	Pota- toes 1 kg	Apples 1 kg	Sugar 1 kg	Instant Coffee 250 g	Tea 100 g	Red Table Wine 1 litre	Beer 1/3 l	Scotch Whisky Bottle	20 Cigar- ettes	Notes
EC members														
Belgium	22.3	25.1	135.8	50.7	8.4	29.5	47.0	263.3		79.4	15.5	450.0	77.0	
Denmark	9.1	5.9		10.1	4.3	9.7	14.4		11.1		5.0	300.0	27.0	
France	5.0	4.9	20.0	8.7	2.6	8.0	6.2	37.7		6.8	2.8	90.0	10.3	
West Germany	2.2	1.2		2.2	0.9	2.6	1.9	18.3	7.2	3.8	0.6	21.0	4.2	
Greece	43.0	115.0	376.0	157.0	51.0	100.0	122.0	1095.0			59.0	2000.0	240.0	
Ireland	0.4	0.5		0.7	0.3	0.6	0.7		0.5			12.5	2.0	
Italy	1587.0	1200.0	4780.0	2611.0	644.0	1811.0	1376.0		5992.0	1463.0	596.0	10000.0	3000.0	
Luxembourg	34.0	28.5	144.0	49.0	8.6	49.0	49.0	368.8	110.0	47.0	13.2		56.0	
Netherlands	1.4	1.4	6.9	2.4	0.6	1.9	2.3	12.6	1.7	5.7	0.7	30.0	3.8	
Portugal	57.7	60.0	294.6	210.8	34.5	117.0	131.8	1423.2	166.2	105.4	32.8	2000.0	250.0	
Spain	189.0	81.0	284.0	274.0	41.0	98.0	123.0	876.0	480.0	88.0	34.0	1500.0	180.0	
United Kingdom	0.4	0.5	1.9	0.6	0.2	0.7	0.5	3.3	0.4		0.5	8.5	1.8	
EFTA members														
Austria	22.4	11.5	42.0	23.0	6.3	17.3	16.7		38.0	55.7	5.0	315.0	38.0	
Finland	10.0	3.6	21.7	9.8	2.9	7.5	7.1		18.2	26.0		160.0	14.0	
Iceland	87.2	55.4	536.7	94.5	115.6	116.0	35.0	511.6	164.0	1040.0		275.0	26.8	
Norway	12.4	6.3	62.7	7.6	3.9	17.7	9.7	87.2	35.7	57.1	8.2	250.0	19.9	
Sweden	12.4	5.1	25.9	9.5	3.9	12.1	7.4	56.1	12.7	34.7	8.1			
Switzerland	1.8	1.8	8.7	4.6	1.0	2.7	1.4	15.3	3.0	13.0	1.1	41.0	3.1	
CMEA members														
Bulgaria	0.2	0.4	3.2	1.4	0.3	0.6	1.2	30.0	1.7	1.2	0.3			
Czechoslovakia	2.0	3.1	30.0	10.0	1.6	6.0	7.3	140.0	19.0	34.0	2.6		0.7	
East Germany	0.5	0.7	8.4	2.4	0.2	1.3	1.6		2.4	11.2	0.5		0.2	
Hungary		5.2	75.1	23.4	8.9	12.3	26.2	490.0	14.4		8.0		51.0	
Poland	28.8	36.5	340.0	222.3	46.3	176.1	165.0		220.0	1175.0	93.3		4500.0	
Romania														
USSR			2.5	0.9	0.2	5.0	0.9						1.6	
Others														
Albania														
Cyprus														
Gibraltar														
Liechtenstein														
Malta														
Monaco														
Turkey	242.0	939.0	2836.0	2063.0	207.0	501.0	524.0	2250.0	350.0	2800.0	377.0		3100.0	
Yugoslavia	1046.0	1387.0	7445.0	3771.0	1502.0	1597.0	2934.0		3371.0	2391.0	685.0			a

Source: Confederation of British Industry/ILO/Euromonitor
Notes: a New dinars at 1990 rates after currency reform (1 new dinar = 1,000 dinars)

Figure for instant coffee is an average from the supermarket and small shop prices

le: Costs of Miscellaneous Consumer Goods 1987 and 1989

it: National currencies

	Colour 22" TV	Fridge	Gas Cooker	Vacuum Cleaner	Men's Suit	Women's Dress	Men's Shoes	Women's Shoes	Notes
members									
Belgium	32000	16000	14500	6500	25000	15000	6000	5000	
Denmark	8500	6500	6000	2500	3000	1000	800	600	
France	5500	4000	3500	1400	1800	850	750	550	
West Germany	1600	1150	800	300	500	300	180	150	
Greece	200000	95000	90000	32000	65000	30000	12500	11000	a
Ireland	575	325	550	130	225	190	55	70	
Italy	1290000	600000	460000	350000	250000	90000	90000	50000	
Luxembourg									
Netherlands	1850	1075	800	350	675	500	217	152	
Portugal	80000	100000	40000	15000	35000	14500	8750	6350	
Spain	110000	65000	33000	16000	45000	23000	10000	9500	
United Kingdom	340	130	360	88	175	60	55	30	
TA members									
Austria	13000	5500	8490	2990	5000	3500	750	1500	
Finland	2800	2050	2350	900	1250	500	330	385	
Iceland									
Norway	7250	4085	4100	1575	3000	2000	900	750	a
Sweden	4500	5300	3700	1850	3000	750	800	500	
Switzerland	1500	850	550	500	550	150	160	150	
MEA members									
Bulgaria									
Czechoslovakia					2500	900	490	450	
East Germany									
Hungary					7000	4000	5500	4500	
Poland					250000	250000	60000	80000	
Romania									
USSR	771				150	70	40	40	
hers									
Albania									
Cyprus									
Gibraltar									
Liechtenstein									
Malta									
Monaco									
Turkey									
Yugoslavia									

urce: Confederation of British Industry/Euromonitor
tes: Electrical goods 1987, clothing and footwear 1989
Data for consumer durables are for 1987; for clothing and footwear 1989
a   Refers to electric cookers, not gas

Database name: Consumer Prices and Costs
Sector name: Costs of Services

Table No: 1505

Title: Costs of Miscellaneous Services 1989

Unit: National currencies

	Telephone Rental (a)	Local Call 1 min	Telex Rent	Inland Letter	Electricit (b)	Gas (b)	Water (b)	Heating Oil (c)	Car Hire (d)	Notes
EC members										
Belgium	400.0	6.0	45500.0	13.00	3000.0	650.0	575.0	700.0	30000.0	
Denmark	96.0	0.8	9600.0	2.80	500.0	365.0	180.0	398.0	5000.0	
France	45.0	0.4	1764.0	2.20	500.0	125.0	200.0	300.0	4000.0	
West Germany	27.0	0.2	3406.0	0.80	105.0	150.0	85.0	38.5	550.0	
Greece		6.0	54000.0	18.00	7500.0	1100.0	1250.0	3583.0	75000.0	
Ireland	11.1	0.1	1300.0	0.26	50.0	70.0	15.0	25.0	250.0	
Italy	7000.0	360.0	2000000.0	5500.00	90000.0	70000.0	35000.0	90000.0	1000000.0	
Luxembourg	250.0	5.0			2500.0	2000.0	500.0	800.0	15000.0	
Netherlands	25.2	0.5	3700.0	0.70	110.0	225.0	100.0		700.0	
Portugal	1365.0	7.8	133800.0	22.50	12500.0	7000.0	6000.0	4800.0	80000.0	
Spain	1260.0	20.0		17.00	35000.0	5500.0	4250.0	3500.0	150000.0	
United Kingdom	6.0	0.2	1875.0	0.20	60.0	70.0	20.0	35.0	275.0	
EFTA members										
Austria	190.0	4.0	15000.0	5.00	2000.0	1500.0	200.0	450.0	7000.0	
Finland	57.0	0.5	11160.0	1.60	80.0	30.0	150.0	115.0	4000.0	
Iceland										
Norway	129.0	1.0	13000.0	2.50	1250.0			170.0	5500.0	
Sweden	60.0	0.2	8000.0	2.10	350.0		225.0	381.0	2500.0	
Switzerland	48.0	0.2	2700.0	0.50	150.0	75.0	80.0	30.0	1500.0	
CMEA members										
Bulgaria										
Czechoslovakia	50.0	1.0			60.0	45.0		175.0	8500.0	
East Germany										
Hungary		2.0			600.0	1750.0	140.0	920.0	23000.0	
Poland	4960.0	90.0			90000.0	100000.0	30000.0	190000.0	6000000.0	
Romania										
USSR	2.7	0.0			6.0	4.0	5.0		215.0	
Others										
Albania										
Cyprus										
Gibraltar										
Liechtenstein										
Malta										
Monaco										
Turkey		150.0			50000.0	20000.0	50000.0	67000.0	1500000.0	
Yugoslavia	31.4	0.2			1013.0	132.4	200.0	260.0	5000.0	e

Source: Confederation of British Industry/Euromonitor
Notes:
a Average monthly cost
b Monthly average cost for family of four
c Cost for 100 litres
d Weekly cost
e New dinars, expressed in 1990 values (1 new dinar = 1,000 old dinars)

Database name: Housing and Household Facilities
Sector name: Housing Stock

Table No: 1601

Title: Total Housing Stock 1977-1988

Unit: 000s

	1977	1980	1981	1982	1983	1984	1985	1986	1987	1988	Not
EC members											
Belgium	3686	3811	3948	3939	3959	3979	3997	4020	4060	4085	
Denmark	2033	2118	2162	2181	2188	2208	2228	2260	2282	2307	
France	17310	21573	22618	23716	24264	24528	24758	24988	25219	25464	
West Germany	24369	25406	25748	26076	26399	26782	27081	27317	27524	27670	
Greece	2210	2425	2577	2616	2716	2890	2930	3000	3133	3208	
Ireland	841	901	923	944	951	969	985	991	999	1005	
Italy	18719	20995	21937	22800	23150	23190	24051	24903	25110	25219	
Luxembourg	131	138	140	141	143	144	144	145	145	146	
Netherlands	4577	4850	4957	5072	5178	5289	5384	5483	5589	5669	
Portugal	3301	3319	3323	3342	3356	3386	3403	3459	3505	3534	
Spain	12714	14580	14841	14958	15205	15253	15300	15317	15475	15631	
United Kingdom	20378	21031	21182	21338	21520	21711	21891	22655	22829	22987	
EC total	110269	121147	124356	127123	129029	130329	132152	134538	135870	136925	
EFTA members											
Austria	2694	3042	3037	3100	3115	3128	3140	3151	3249	3275	
Finland	1687	1838	1870	1901	1923	1945	1975	2000	2044	2077	
Iceland	67	73	75	76	78	79	81	82	85	86	
Norway	1480	1524	1540	1593	1635	1670	1694	1720	1748	1778	
Sweden	3505	3599	3651	3670	3705	3797	3863	3897	3930	3958	
Switzerland	2590	2701	2744	2789	2793	2833	2878	2969	3011	3054	
EFTA total	12023	12777	12917	13129	13249	13452	13631	13819	14067	14228	
CMEA members											
Bulgaria	2643	2839	2906	2970	3035	3100	3162	3205	3266	3326	
Czechoslovakia	5154	5441	5524	5370	5526	5600	5867	5747	5807	5869	a
East Germany	6423	6540	6563	6610	6695	6763	6831	6911	6964	7002	
Hungary	3699	3647	3710	3725	3737	3786	3846	3891	3923	3962	
Poland	9090	9326	9962	10731	10310	10253	10666	10834	11003	10789	
Romania	7010	7220	7250	7330	7420	7550	7600	7700	7700	7773	
USSR	66995	72460	74212	76013	77902	79050	79900	80050	82300	83861	
CMEA total	101014	107473	110127	112749	114625	116102	117872	118338	120963	122582	
Others											
Albania	608	660	675	688	700	714	730	745	745	745	
Cyprus	121	151	155	164	172	174	180	187	200	205	
Gibraltar	7	7	8	8	8	8	8	8	8	8	
Liechtenstein	10	10	10	11	11	11	11	12	12	12	
Malta	100	104	109	110	112	112	113	114	116	116	
Monaco	11	11	11	11	12	12	12	12	12	12	
Turkey	10980	11441	11450	11456	11685	11740	11821	11950	12150	12234	
Yugoslavia	5932	6322	6388	6405	6539	6665	6787	6910	7025	7052	
Total	17770	18707	18805	18853	19238	19436	19662	19937	20268	20383	
European total	241076	260104	266205	271854	276141	279319	283317	286632	291168	294118	

Source: National Statistical Offices/UN/Eurostat
Notes: a State sector only

Database name: Housing and Households
Sector name: Housing Stock
Subsector name:
Title: New Dwellings Completed 1977-1989

Table No: 1602

Unit: Units

	1977	1980	1981	1982	1983	1984	1985	1986	1987	1988	1989
EC members											
Belgium	71382	46839	32751	28552	28027	24400	28919	24444	29340	35429	
Denmark	36276	30345	21925	20768	22152	26863	22613	28489	26912	25500	
France	450900	502600	488500	425100	371800	343500	349800	356200	380600	414800	
West Germany	409012	363094	337968	315336	312217	366816	252248	251940	217343	208344	
Greece	158269	136044	108174	102173	113944	72852	88477	109643	108432	107000	
Ireland	24548	27785	28917	26798	26138	24944	23948	22680	18292	15700	
Italy	227475	222000	211823	233763	200595	192386	173605	154400	151500	155500	
Luxembourg	1583	2469	1954	1601	1609	1363	1348	1417	1500	1450	
Netherlands	111047	113756	121582	114394	117387	103355	98131	108900	115700	123500	
Portugal	37220	38231	38597	39791	38127	41250	35983	36061	37901	41900	
Spain	126101	130485	149317	168212	170147	176333	178190	193410	202600	222300	
United Kingdom	313500	251814	240943	205744	180065	203172	212172	208555	212448	225400	
EC total	1967313	1865462	1782451	1682232	1582208	1577234	1465434	1496139	1502568	1576823	
EFTA members											
Austria	43500	73300	47477	40100	35900	37600	37300	38838	38494	39300	
Finland	56966	49648	46988	47997	50500	50337	50306	41910	43635	46500	
Iceland	2300	2200	2100	1900	1700	1650	1700	1500	1600	1500	
Norway	38597	38092	34672	36700	31400	29500	26200	25700	28200	30100	
Sweden	54800	51438	51597	45108	43374	34988	32932	28791	30884	40600	
Switzerland	32297	40070	45348	43465	41605	45449	44228	42570	40230	44900	
EFTA total	228460	254748	228182	215270	204479	199524	192666	179309	183043	202900	
CMEA members											
Bulgaria	73157	73300	70400	67200	68500	67800	63600	64870	63640	62926	38800
Czechoslovakia	137693	128876	105729	100000	95701	91863	104524	78700	79600	82900	88200
East Germany	106826	120209	125731	122417	122636	121657	99000	101000	91000	93500	83400
Hungary	86333	89100	76975	75356	74214	70432	72507	69428	57200	50600	51500
Poland	267000	217100	187000	186100	195800	195900	217900	185700	191400	189600	149800
Romania	161500	197800	161400	161200	146600	131900	105600	108100	110400	104200	
USSR	1060000	2004000	1997000	2002000	2030000	2035000	2100000	2100000	2265000	2230000	2200000
CMEA total	1892509	2830385	2724235	2714273	2733451	2714552	2763131	2707798	2858240	2813726	2611700
Others											
Albania											
Cyprus		9200	8900	9100	9000	6300	7500	6586	6727	6915	
Gibraltar											
Liechtenstein											
Malta											
Monaco											
Turkey		139200	118800	116000	113500	115600	118200	168600	191000	119332	
Yugoslavia											
Total		148400	127700	125100	122500	121900	125700	175186	197727	126247	
European total	4088282	5098995	4862568	4736875	4642638	4613210	4546931	4558432	4741578	4719696	2611700

Source: National Statistical Offices/UN/OECD

| | Database name: | Housing and Households |
| Sector name: | Housing Stock |

Table No: 1603

Title: Dwellings by Number of Rooms : Latest Year

Unit: 000s

	Year	1 room	2 rooms	3 rooms	4 rooms	5 or more rooms	Total	Notes
EC members								
Belgium	1985	1.0	18.0	21.4	24.0	35.6	100.0	
Denmark	1989	5.1	17.1	23.2	27.0	27.6	100.0	
France	1983	9.1	11.9	16.6	26.5	35.9	100.0	a
West Germany	1985	2.4	8.3	23.3	29.7	36.4	100.0	
Greece	1985	9.3	15.3	26.4	28.2	20.8	100.0	
Ireland	1981	2.4	4.9	11.7	23.1	57.9	100.0	b
Italy	1981	1.7	10.2	21.4	32.0	34.6	100.0	
Luxembourg	1981	2.3	3.1	9.9	19.8	64.9	100.0	b
Netherlands	1985	5.9	8.9	20.7	56.3	8.2	100.0	a
Portugal	1986	15.0	25.0	30.0	26.0	4.0	100.0	
Spain	1986	11.5	20.0	26.0	19.0	23.5	100.0	
United Kingdom	1986	9.1	12.0	23.5	30.3	25.1	100.0	
EC average		6.3	12.9	21.2	28.5	31.2	100.0	
EFTA members								
Austria	1986	7.0	15.0	30.0	26.0	22.0	100.0	
Finland	1985	17.3	29.8	22.8	18.0	12.1	100.0	
Iceland	1986	10.0	20.4	34.2	25.9	9.5	100.0	d
Norway	1980	5.0	14.0	19.0	26.0	36.0	100.0	
Sweden	1985	13.0	22.5	24.3	18.8	21.4	100.0	
Switzerland	1980	8.5	12.8	21.9	32.8	24.0	100.0	c
EFTA average		10.1	19.1	25.4	24.6	20.8	100.0	
CMEA members								
Bulgaria	1985	4.0	21.0	35.0	27.2	12.8	100.0	
Czechoslovakia	1986	25.0	41.2	28.9	3.2	1.7	100.0	
East Germany	1981	8.0	33.0	37.0	15.1	6.9	100.0	
Hungary	1988	18.9	48.1	18.7	10.3	4.1	100.0	
Poland	1986	1.3	6.3	25.7	46.0	20.7	100.0	a
Romania	1970	12.0	35.0	34.8	13.9	4.3	100.0	
USSR	1986	15.0	39.0	30.0	12.0	4.0	100.0	
CMEA average		12.0	31.9	30.0	18.2	7.8	100.0	
Others								
Albania	1986	29.0	30.0	32.0	4.5	4.5	100.0	
Cyprus	1986	0.5	3.0	6.5	15.0	75.0	100.0	a
Gibraltar	1981	8.2	19.0	37.6	24.6	10.6	100.0	
Liechtenstein	1980	8.2	9.0	12.7	20.9	49.3	100.0	
Malta	1986	10.0	20.0	30.0	24.0	16.0	100.0	
Monaco	1986	8.0	12.2	20.6	26.8	32.4	100.0	
Turkey	1987	0.7	9.9	37.5	32.8	19.1	100.0	a
Yugoslavia	1984	23.9	40.5	24.2	7.7	3.7	100.0	
Average		11.1	18.0	25.1	19.5	26.3	100.0	
European average		9.9	20.5	25.4	22.8	21.4	100.0	

Source: National Statistical Offices/UN/Eurostat/Euromonitor estimates
Notes: a   New dwellings only
              b   Based on households
              c   Occupied dwellings only
              d   Including holiday homes

Database name:
Sector name:

Housing and Households
Housing Stock

Table No: 1604

Title:

Housing amenities: Latest Available Year

Unit:

% with specific amenities

	Year	Water supply	Bath or shower	Central heating	Own toilet	Notes
EC members						
Belgium	1985	99.2	99.3	94.2	96.2	
Denmark	1989	99.5	88.0	88.1	95.7	
France	1984	99.6	84.7	69.7	97.2	
West Germany	1981	98.0	84.0	51.0	87.0	
Greece	1981	80.0	69.0	30.0	78.0	
Ireland	1981	90.0	82.0	39.0	89.8	
Italy	1984	92.3	87.6	39.7	96.0	
Luxembourg	1981	99.9	86.1	73.9	97.2	
Netherlands	1985	100.0	96.0	72.3	100.0	
Portugal	1983	58.2	46.8	10.0	63.4	
Spain	1981	90.5	70.0	21.0	91.0	
United Kingdom	1984	90.5	97.0	66.0	97.0	
EC average		93.3	84.9	52.2	92.6	
EFTA members						
Austria	1989	98.5	89.2	59.0	95.0	
Finland	1985	93.9	84.8	87.2	91.1	
Iceland	1986	99.6	99.6	75.1	95.0	a
Norway	1980	98.2	82.2	91.0	78.5	
Sweden	1985	99.0	99.0	96.0	98.0	
Switzerland	1986	99.5	97.0	78.0	100.0	
EFTA average		98.1	91.9	81.3	94.1	
CMEA members						
Bulgaria	1986	80.2	75.0	20.0	65.0	
Czechoslovakia	1980	89.5	75.0	35.0	77.2	
East Germany	1985	99.2	74.0	50.0	68.0	
Hungary	1987	77.9	73.7	15.4	66.5	
Poland	1987	93.1	78.4	69.3	82.8	b
Romania	1986	82.4	68.2	20.0	70.0	
USSR	1983	90.8	81.7	77.9	90.0	b
CMEA average		90.2	79.6	67.5	85.4	
Others						
Albania	1986	72.0	67.0	40.0	60.0	
Cyprus	1986	100.0	100.0	8.7	100.0	a
Gibraltar	1981	96.6	87.8	24.0	87.6	
Liechtenstein	1980	99.0	92.1	88.4	86.4	
Malta	1986	85.0	80.0	15.0	90.0	
Monaco	1986	100.0	99.2	82.0	100.0	
Turkey	1987	99.0	85.0	13.4	90.0	a
Yugoslavia	1984	45.2	53.5	15.9	70.0	
Average		80.6	74.4	15.2	82.7	
European average		91.0	81.7	57.3	88.4	

Source: National Statistical Offices/UN/Eurostat/Euromonitor estimates
Notes: a   New dwellings only
                b   Urban households only

Database name: Housing and Household Facilities
Sector name: Household Composition
Subsector name:
Title: Number of Households 1977-1989

Table No: 1605

Unit: 000s

	1977	1980	1981	1982	1983	1984	1985	1986	1987	1988	1989	Notes
EC members												
Belgium	3305	3336	3348	3380	3307	3590	3615	3620	3628	3650		
Denmark	2013	2062	2080	2094	2114	2136	2160	2182	2205	2224	2246	
France	18274	19136	19343	19590	20100	20222	20413	20623	21100	21305		
West Germany	23631	24229	24544	24835	25131	25345	26553	26785	26939	26282		
Greece	2678	2755	2974	3061	3151	3290	3387	3444	3455	3538		
Ireland	800	850	850	852	856	857	859	863	870	875		
Italy	17190	17509	17520	17614	17767	17823	17891	17967	18003	18081		
Luxembourg	123	127	128	128	129	129	130	131	132	132		
Netherlands	4680	5006	5111	5215	5318	5420	5522	5643	5655	5736		
Portugal	2750	2900	3075	3105	3150	3203	3289	3300	3330	3360		
Spain	12522	13016	13202	13450	13603	13881	14015	14329	14389	14534		a
United Kingdom	19580	19995	19943	19990	20270	20560	20879	21005	21025	21050		b
EC total	107546	110921	112118	113314	114896	116456	118713	119892	120730	120767		
EFTA members												
Austria	2649	2860	2764	2766	2752	2771	2810	2863	2869	2912	2940	
Finland	1695	1728	1745	1820	1839	1850	1888	1943	1948	1979		a
Iceland	93	96	97	98	99	100	101	102	103	104		c
Norway	1378	1410	1524	1536	1557	1570	1592	1620	1624	1651		
Sweden	3443	3595	3610	3615	3610	3690	3670	3680	3688	3714		
Switzerland	2280	2459	2500	2575	2646	2666	2687	2701	2707	2745		
EFTA total	11538	12148	12240	12410	12503	12647	12748	12909	12938	13106		
CMEA members												
Bulgaria	2603	2680	2695	2708	2800	2873	2912	2949	2955	3010		
Czechoslovakia	5061	5274	5308	5319	5380	5411	5450	5470	5481	5540		
East Germany	6409	6485	6510	6510	6510	6525	6540	6572	6586	6621		
Hungary	3692	3719	3740	3786	3798	3831	3852	3877	3885	3924		
Poland	10718	11175	11230	11290	11330	11660	11923	12213	12238	12000		
Romania	6855	7115	7160	7196	7250	7310	7372	7423	7438	7509		
USSR	63274	65600	65580	65800	66010	66300	66750	67000	67134	68408		
CMEA total	98612	102048	102223	102609	103078	103910	104799	105504	105717	107011		
Others												
Albania	675	720	740	775	800	840	900	912	914	914		c
Cyprus	187	192	194	197	201	204	212	216	217	222		c
Gibraltar	7	7	7	7	7	7	7	7	7	7		
Liechtenstein	9	9	10	10	10	10	10	11	11	11		
Malta	96	101	102	102	103	105	107	109	110	110		c
Monaco	10	11	11	11	12	12	12	12	12	12		c
Turkey	7510	8603	8670	8900	8950	8995	9043	9090	9108	9171		
Yugoslavia	6187	6780	6945	7100	7189	7234	7256	7289	7304	7332		
Total	14681	16423	16679	17102	17271	17407	17547	17646	17683	17779		
European total	232377	241540	243260	245435	247748	250420	253807	255951	257069	258663		

Source: Euromonitor from National Statistical Offices
Notes: a Partly estimated
b 1985 and 1986 estimated
c Estimated

	Database name:	Housing and Households						

Database name: Housing and Households
Sector name: Household Composition   Table No: 1606

Title: Household Size by Number of Persons: Latest Year

Unit: % analysis

	Year	1 person	2 persons	3 persons	4 persons	5+ persons	Un-specified	Notes
EC members								
Belgium	1981	23.2	29.7	20.0	15.7	11.4		
Denmark	1989	33.6	32.6	15.0	13.6	5.1	0.1	
France	1984	24.2	29.2	18.5	16.8	11.3		
West Germany	1988	34.6	30.3	16.9	12.7	5.5		
Greece	1989	18.5	26.0	19.5	22.5	13.5		a
Ireland	1981	17.1	20.2	15.0	15.4	32.3		
Italy	1982	12.9	22.0	22.4	21.2	17.6	3.9	
Luxembourg	1988	21.8	29.0	21.0	16.5	11.7		
Netherlands	1985	27.5	29.9	15.6	20.7	6.3		
Portugal	1988	15.0	23.0	27.0	20.0	15.0		a
Spain	1986	12.0	24.0	27.0	18.5	18.5		a
United Kingdom	1988	25.5	31.5	17.1	13.1	6.0	6.8	
EC average		22.8	27.6	19.8	16.7	11.3	1.8	
EFTA members								
Austria	1988	28.3	28.9	18.4	15.9	8.5		
Finland	1987	29.4	28.3	17.6	16.4	8.2	0.1	
Iceland	1986	14.0	31.3	22.7	16.9	15.1		a
Norway	1982	40.7	26.8	11.7	13.9	6.8	0.1	
Sweden	1985	36.1	31.4	13.6	13.4	5.5		
Switzerland	1983	13.4	15.9	20.2	33.1	17.4		
EFTA average		29.0	26.6	16.5	18.6	9.3		
CMEA members								
Bulgaria	1975	17.0	20.7	21.6	21.1	19.6		
Czechoslovakia	1970	17.9	23.5	20.8	20.9	16.9		
East Germany	1983	27.1	29.2	20.9	15.0	7.8		
Hungary	1970	13.1	25.4	23.1	20.5	17.9		
Poland	1980	19.6	21.7	22.8	21.6	14.3		
Romania	1970	14.2	23.4	23.3	19.9	19.2		
USSR	1970		25.4	26.2	24.1	24.3		b
CMEA average								
Others								
Albania	1986	8.0	30.0	26.0	26.0	10.0		a
Cyprus	1986	12	30	23	21	13.7		a
Gibraltar	1981	12.5	24.2	18.2	21.3	23.8		
Liechtenstein	1980	23.9	23.9	16.8	18.9	16.5		
Malta	1986	10.0	24.6	26.2	20.9	18.3		a
Monaco	1986	24.0	31.2	26.7	15.0	3.1		a
Turkey	1980	6.5	11.3	12.7	16.2	53.3		
Yugoslavia	1981	14.0	24.0	22.0	20.0	20.0		
Average		9.1	16.3	16.3	17.8	40.7		
European average (non-CMEA)		20.5	25.3	21.8	19.8	18.8	4.8	

Source: European Commission/United Nations
Notes: a Estimate based on current trends
            b Households of 2 or more members only

Database name: Housing and Households
Sector name: Household Composition

Table No: 1607

Title: Average Household Size 1977-1988

Unit: Persons per average household unit

	1977	1978	1979	1980	1981	1982	1983	1984	1985	1986	1987	1988
EC members												
Belgium	2.82	2.82	2.83	2.80	2.80	2.77	2.83	2.61	2.60	2.60	2.60	2.57
Denmark	2.40	2.38	2.41	2.36	2.34	2.32	2.30	2.27	2.25	2.23	2.21	2.19
France	2.76	2.74	2.79	2.67	2.66	2.64	2.59	2.58	2.54	2.55	2.50	2.49
West Germany	2.41	2.40	2.47	2.41	2.39	2.36	2.32	2.29	2.18	2.17	2.16	2.22
Greece	3.29	3.29	3.35	3.33	3.11	3.04	2.97	2.86	2.79	2.75	2.75	2.69
Ireland	3.89	3.87	4.00	3.80	3.84	3.88	3.89	3.92	3.93	3.89	3.87	3.84
Italy	3.09	3.07	3.11	3.06	3.06	3.05	3.04	3.04	3.03	3.03	3.03	3.02
Luxembourg	2.79	2.77	2.80	2.72	2.71	2.72	2.70	2.70	2.67	2.63	2.65	2.67
Netherlands	2.81	2.78	2.85	2.68	2.65	2.61	2.57	2.53	2.49	2.45	2.46	2.44
Portugal	3.36	3.32	3.40	3.24	3.04	3.04	3.02	3.01	2.95	2.96	2.95	2.91
Spain	2.76	2.72	2.82	2.73	2.71	2.68	2.67	2.62	2.62	2.56	2.56	2.55
United Kingdom	2.73	2.72	2.73	2.68	2.69	2.68	2.64	2.61	2.55	2.57	2.57	2.58
EC average	2.79	2.77	2.82	2.75	2.73	2.71	2.68	2.65	2.60	2.59	2.58	2.58
EFTA members												
Austria	2.71	2.71	2.71	2.51	2.60	2.60	2.61	2.59	2.55	2.51	2.51	2.47
Finland	2.66	2.63	2.67	2.63	2.61	2.52	2.51	2.51	2.47	2.40	2.41	2.38
Iceland	2.27	2.26	2.31	2.26	2.26	2.27	2.27	2.27	2.27	2.26	2.28	2.27
Norway	2.79	2.78	2.81	2.75	2.56	2.55	2.52	2.51	2.48	2.44	2.45	2.41
Sweden	2.28	2.26	2.29	2.20	2.19	2.19	2.19	2.15	2.16	2.16	2.16	2.15
Switzerland	2.64	2.56	2.65	2.47	2.44	2.39	2.34	2.30	2.25	2.29	2.29	2.27
EFTA average	2.58	2.55	2.59	2.47	2.45	2.43	2.41	2.39	2.36	2.35	2.35	2.32
CMEA members												
Bulgaria	3.21	3.17	3.22	3.14	3.13	3.13	3.03	2.96	2.92	2.89	2.88	2.84
Czechoslovakia	2.82	2.80	2.86	2.76	2.74	2.74	2.72	2.71	2.70	2.70	2.70	2.68
East Germany	2.49	2.48	2.48	2.45	2.44	2.44	2.44	2.43	2.42	2.40	2.40	2.39
Hungary	2.74	2.70	2.75	2.74	2.72	2.69	2.67	2.65	2.63	2.60	2.60	2.57
Poland	3.08	3.04	3.13	3.02	3.04	3.05	3.07	3.01	2.96	2.91	2.92	2.98
Romania	3.00	2.98	3.06	2.96	2.97	2.97	2.96	2.94	2.97	2.97	2.93	2.90
USSR	3.89	3.88	3.96	3.85	3.88	3.90	3.92	3.94	3.97	3.97	4.01	3.94
CMEA average	3.60	3.59	3.66	3.56	3.58	3.60	3.61	3.62	3.63	3.63	3.66	3.61
Others												
Albania	3.53	3.54	3.68	3.52	3.50	3.41	3.37	3.28	3.13	3.15	3.20	3.25
Cyprus	3.11	3.11	3.15	3.10	3.10	3.09	3.07	3.06	2.98	2.96	2.98	3.00
Gibraltar	4.07	3.94	4.07	4.07	4.07	3.94	3.94	3.94	4.07	4.07	3.94	3.94
Liechtenstein	2.68	2.73	2.91	2.66	2.60	2.55	2.49	2.63	2.58	2.42	2.42	2.50
Malta	3.29	3.30	3.43	3.42	3.39	3.35	3.48	3.44	3.40	3.36	2.98	3.01
Monaco	2.38	2.38	2.38	2.25	2.25	2.25	2.23	2.14	2.14	2.14	2.06	2.13
Turkey	5.28	5.24	5.51	4.91	4.97	4.94	4.91	5.10	5.18	5.26	5.36	5.41
Yugoslavia	3.34	3.31	3.40	3.14	3.07	3.03	3.01	3.02	3.03	3.03	3.05	3.05
Average	4.56	4.52	4.73	4.27	4.29	4.26	4.23	4.36	4.42	4.48	4.55	4.60
European average	3.32	3.30	3.38	3.26	3.27	3.26	3.25	3.26	3.25	3.26	3.27	3.26

Source: Euromonitor calculations

Database name: Households and Households
Sector name: Household Ownership

Table name: 1608

Title: Ownership of Consumer Electronics 1988

Unit: % of households

	Colour/ mono TV	Radio	Video recorder	Cassette recorder	Record player	Music centre
EC members						
Belgium	95	90	13	53	30	
Denmark	96	98	15	72	60	30
France	98	98	10	66	65	39
West Germany	93	84	30	86	72	54
Greece	97	92	5	35	46	
Ireland	94		18	38	61	
Italy	94	92	9	52	60	16
Luxembourg						
Netherlands	97	97	32	77	81	
Portugal	85	60		22	40	
Spain	98	95	19	38	49	27
United Kingdom	98	90	49	80	29	32
EFTA members						
Austria	96	95	6	64	27	30
Finland	72	96	5	75	62	34
Iceland						
Norway	99	98	22	70	64	
Sweden	90	93	10	68	64	48
Switzerland	88	99	14	86	65	42
CMEA members						
Bulgaria	93	95		46		
Czechoslovakia	95	75		52		
East Germany	43	99		64	50	
Hungary	21	40		53	36	21
Poland	70	79			33	32
Romania	77	45			20	
USSR	45	96		39		
Others						
Albania						
Cyprus	56					
Gibraltar						
Liechtenstein						
Malta						
Monaco						
Turkey		75				
Yugoslavia	61	85		59	40	

Source: Euromonitor estimates

Database name: Households and Households
Sector name: Household Ownership

Table No: 1609

Title: Ownership of Major Appliances 1988

Unit: % of households

	Micro-wave Oven	Tumble Dryer	Spin Dryer	Washing Machine	Dish-washer	Fridge	Deep Freezer	Food Processor	Toaster	Drinks Maker	Vacuum Cleaner	Hair Dryer
EC members												
Belgium	8	21	28	86	27	94	58	91	56	79	91	
Denmark	9			67	27	84	63	83	76	80	75	
France	17			87	27	97	37	83	59	78	88	7
West Germany	20		15	91	34	91	78	92	53	88	97	2
Greece				42		74	25	24			39	
Ireland	20	12	21	77	10	92	21	41	53	51		
Italy	10	10		91	24	88	42	48	37	81	90	8
Luxembourg				91			70	90				4
Netherlands	22	13	41	89	9	98	47	84	66	65	99	6
Portugal	4			31		74	18	37	34		45	4
Spain	2	2		94	13	94	18	50	85	22	47	4
United Kingdom	35	31	17	83	9	93	39	80	57	59	97	8
EFTA members												
Austria	12	8	23	87	27	97	61	82	41	75	97	8
Finland	28	5	23	82	15	97	52	72	69	45	76	9
Iceland												
Norway	18	28	27	85	24	85	80	74	80		98	7
Sweden	25	25	24	60	30	96	70	77	80	65	99	8
Switzerland	15	14	26	68	32	96	68	91	81	57	98	9
CMEA members												
Bulgaria				96		96	12				30	
Czechoslovakia				57		90					49	
East Germany				94		99	35					
Hungary			80	99		90	10				85	
Poland				25		91					15	
Romania						30					49	
USSR												
Others												
Albania												
Cyprus												
Gibraltar												
Liechtenstein												
Malta												
Monaco												
Turkey												
Yugoslavia												

Source: Euromonitor estimates
Notes:

Title: Sanitary Facilities, Immunisation: Latest Year

Unit: % population provided

	Year	Safe Water	Adequate Sanitary Facilities	Immunisation of infants:			Notes
				DPT	Measles	Polio	
EC members							
Belgium	1984	95.0	99.0	95.0	90.0	99.0	a
Denmark	1982	100.0	100.0	97.2	20.0	100.0	b
France	1983	98.0	85.0	95.0	30.0	95.0	c
West Germany	1984	100.0	88.0	50.0	35.0	80.0	c,d
Greece	1981			31.0		95.0	
Ireland	1984	96.6	94.0	81.0	60.0	76.0	b
Italy	1981	98.8	98.7	99.0	5.0	99.0	e
Luxembourg	1984	100.0	100.0	90.0		90.0	
Netherlands	1982	99.8	100.0	96.9	92.5	96.9	b
Portugal	1980	57.0	41.0	90.0	70.0	85.0	f
Spain	1983	95.0	90.0	97.0	61.0	87.0	e
United Kingdom	1985	100.0	100.0	84.0	60.0	84.0	e
EFTA members							
Austria	1980	100.0	85.0	90.0	90.0	90.0	d
Finland	1984	79.0	72.0	93.9	80.0	82.2	b
Iceland	1984	100.0	100.0	92.0	90.0	91.3	f
Norway	1983	99.0	85.3	90.0	80.0	90.0	
Sweden	1983	100.0	85.0	93.9	46.7	96.8	c
Switzerland	1984	99.1	85.0				c
CMEA members							
Bulgaria	1980	96.0		97.0	98.0	98.0	d
Czechoslovakia	1983	74.5	60.5	97.0	99.0	98.0	
East Germany	1985	90.0	70.0	94.1	97.1	96.9	f
Hungary	1984	84.0	60.0	99.9	99.6	99.1	b
Poland	1980	67.0	50.0	94.7	89.3	89.7	f
Romania	1980	77.0	50.0	100.0	100.0	100.0	b
USSR	1983	100.0	50.0	95.0	95.0	95.0	c,d
Others							
Albania	1981	92.0		94.0	90.0	92.0	
Cyprus							
Gibraltar							
Liechtenstein							
Malta	1983	100.0	100.0	89.1		89.1	
Monaco							
Turkey	1980	67.0	10.0	58.0	45.0	62.0	a,b
Yugoslavia	1981	67.8	58.4	91.0	89.0	89.0	b

Source: WHO World Health Statistics
Notes: a   Sanitary facilities: 1982   d   DPT: 1981
           b   DPT: 1983   e   DPT: 1984
           c   Sanitary facilities: 1982   f   DPT: 1982

Database name: Health and Living Standards
Sector name: Medical Services

Table No: 1702

Title: Provision of Medical Services: Latest Year

Unit: Numbers

	Year	In-Patient Beds	Practising Doctors	Practising Dentists	Nurses	Active Pharmacists	Notes
EC members							
Belgium	1987	88321	30942	6241	9599	11027	
Denmark	1987	35606	13144	4795	30749	1476	
France	1987	573635	143323	34946	233313	49606	
West Germany	1988	672384	171487	38826	267423	33903	
Greece	1986	52864	30491	9131	24364	6261	
Ireland	1987	15225	5180	1131	25261		a
Italy	1987	440187	245116	3697	227000		
Luxembourg	1987		666	175	112	274	
Netherlands	1988	176900	37144	7585	1046	2103	
Portugal	1987	49200	26381	681		4728	
Spain	1987	202969	138506	7304	148723	32307	
United Kingdom	1988	372823	31203	17851	488995	17589	
EFTA members							
Austria	1988	78648	23907	2553	42754	1954	
Finland	1987	16351	9272	3609	46388	580	
Iceland	1986	2835	654	205	1846	160	
Norway	1986	66373	9443	3702	35552	3041	b
Sweden	1987	106885	25379	9200	70917	1246	
Switzerland	1987	54470	10491	3147	51101	1417	c
CMEA members							
Bulgaria	1984	84300	24718	5623	57500	4235	
Czechoslovakia	1985	158300	55871		106968	7261	
East Germany	1988	165950	41639	12932	116600	4310	
Hungary	1988	109832	36188	3988	67985	4501	
Poland	1988	263300	77496	17679	191800	16004	
Romania	1985	203200	40050	7300		6558	
USSR	1986	3663000	1170000			91000	b
Others							
Albania	1977	11087	4957		6968	532	
Cyprus	1987	3360	998	374	2279	92	
Gibraltar							
Liechtenstein	1986		26	9		2	
Malta	1982		413	57	3187	396	
Monaco	1982		59	32	214	56	
Turkey	1988	113010	42502	9639	38923	14567	
Yugoslavia	1988	142957	55140		91253	6321	d

Source: Measuring Health Care 1960-1983 (OECD)/WHO/Statistical Yearbook (Comecon)/
national sources
Notes: Nurses includes professionals, auxiliary nurses and midwives
a Personnel 1984
b Personnel 1985
c Nurses 1983
d Doctors includes dentists

Database name:	Health and Living Standards								
Sector name:	Illness			Table No: 1703					

Title: Incidence of Major Illnesses

Unit: Death rate per 100,000 population

	A	B	C	D	E	F	G	H	Notes
EC members									
Belgium	6.6	224.4	341.5	70.6	32.7	64.3	19.6	21.0	c
Denmark	5.1	231.9	374.2	54.2	31.5	68.9	12.4	26.8	b
France	9.0	205.9	236.3	40.8	42.3	73.0	20.9	22.1	b
West Germany	5.8	210.6	381.7	43.3	40.5	45.0	11.6	15.5	a
Greece	5.0	159.6	379.8	42.2	25.7	43.6	18.7	3.7	c
Ireland	5.7	218.3	462.5	119.5	24.5	44.2	12.7	7.9	b
Italy	4.0	205.6	356.4	56.2	47.0	45.0	15.2	7.6	c
Luxembourg	2.1	227.5	411.2	51.7	42.6	72.8	23.3	17.3	a
Netherlands	4.2	224.7	305.6	50.2	25.7	34.9	10.8	10.9	b
Portugal	8.4	157.9	386.9	61.3	46.1	67.6	26.9	7.9	a
Spain	8.4	166.7	341.9	70.1	45.7	40.6	14.5	6.6	d
United Kingdom	4.0	223.7	388.6	82.7	25.8	32.7	8.6	7.3	a
EFTA members									
Austria	3.8	199.9	412.9	35.2	43.5	68.9	17.6	22.6	a
Finland	7.2	175.9	444.8	57.2	29.3	82.9	10.3	26.7	b
Iceland	5.5	195.8	324.1	100.2	17.2	51.6	12.5	16.1	a
Norway	5.6	180.2	365.7	61.9	25.5	55.3	8.8	15.4	b
Sweden	4.0	166.1	372.5	50.1	23.6	51.7	8.4	17.3	b
Switzerland	7.3	195.9	296.3	40.3	23.5	65.9	13.3	20.7	a
CMEA members									
Bulgaria	7.6	156.2	714.3	78.7	33.8	60.7	12.2	16.0	b
Czechoslovakia	3.5	245.1	595.8	64.1	47.7	76.0	10.6	18.1	a
East Germany	4.2	185.6	577.4	60.2			10.5		a
Hungary	9.2	255.1	620.6	50.9	69.6	110.6	16.6	39.9	a
Poland	9.5	212.0	580.4	47.2	35.3	71.2	14.9	13.0	a
Romania	8.8	141.7	762.4	139.2	55.1	69.6			e
USSR									
Others									
Albania									
Cyprus									
Gibraltar									
Liechtenstein									
Malta	10.5	161.5	489.6	86.0	26.1	22.8	3.9	2.3	a
Monaco									
Turkey									
Yugoslavia	13.5	166.1	570.2	63.5	41.3	61.0	17.5	17.0	b

Source: World Health Statistics

Notes:
A	Infectious and parasitic diseases	E	Diseases of the digestive system	a	1988
B	Malignant neo-plasms	F	Injury and poisoning	b	1987
C	Diseases of the circulatory system	G	Motor traffic accidents	c	1986
D	Diseases of the respiratory system	H	Suicide	d	1985
				e	1984

Database name: Health and Living Standards
Sector name: Health Expenditure

Title: Health Expenditure 1986

Unit: National currencies (millions)

Table No: 1704

	Total Expenditure	Pharmaceutical Goods	Notes
EC members			
Belgium	351188	37975	a
Denmark	41010	2723	a
France	424148	73834	d
West Germany	230867	15400	a,c
Greece	295051	45900	a
Ireland	1255	93	a,b
Italy	55452	7368	a
Luxembourg	14000	1670	a
Netherlands	35700	1493	
Portugal	167977	59723	
Spain	1153152	222135	a,b
United Kingdom	22362	2428	a
EFTA members			
Austria	56773	8706	a
Finland	23809	2680	e
Iceland	2500	6843	f,g
Norway	32796	1500	a,b
Sweden	80500	8580	h
Switzerland	18000	1420	a
CMEA members			
Bulgaria			
Czechoslovakia			
East Germany			
Hungary			
Poland			
Romania			
USSR			
Others			
Albania			
Cyprus	71		d
Gibraltar			
Liechtenstein			
Malta			
Monaco			
Turkey	71220		f
Yugoslavia			

Source: Measuring Health Care 1960-1983 (OECD)/national sources/EFPIA
Notes: Italy: billion units
a Pharmaceuticals at ex-factory prices
b Public expenditure only
c Total expenditure 1985
d 1987 data
e Pharmaceuticals 1985
f Total expenditure 1983
g Pharmaceuticals 1979
h Pharmaceuticals 1987

Title: Utilisation of Medical Services (1983/Latest Available Year)

	Hospital Admissions (a)	Length of Stay (b)	Doctors' Consultations	Dental Visits (c)	Pharmaceutical Consumption (d)	Notes
EC members						
Belgium	13.9	13.5	7.1	1.1	9.9	
Denmark	19.2	11.9	8.4	3.3	6.3	
France	11.8	14.1	4.7	1.4	28.9	e
West Germany	18.1	18.7				
Greece	11.9	13.0	5.3	0.5	7.4	
Ireland	17.6	9.0	6.0		9.5	
Italy	15.4	12.0	8.3			
Luxembourg	18.1	21.0				
Netherlands	11.8	34.1	3.2	2.1		f
Portugal	9.6	14.4	3.8		15.5	
Spain	9.2	14.6	4.7		11.9	f
United Kingdom	12.7	18.6	4.2	0.6	6.8	
EFTA members						
Austria	20.7	16.3		1.3	14.9	
Finland	20.9	22.2	3.4	1.8	4.9	
Iceland	20.2	18.0	4.9		4.8	g
Norway	14.9	13.0	4.5			
Sweden	19.2	22.7	2.7	0.4	4.6	
Switzerland	12.8	25.4	5.6			
CMEA members						
Bulgaria						
Czechoslovakia						
East Germany						
Hungary						
Poland						
Romania						
USSR						
Others						
Albania						
Cyprus						
Gibraltar						
Liechtenstein						
Malta						
Monaco						
Turkey	4.0	8.8	1.2			
Yugoslavia						

Source: Measuring Health Care 1960-1983 (OECD)
Notes:
a Persons admitted as percentage of total population
b Patient days per admission to in-patient care
c Average number of dental procedures per year per person
d Average number of medicines per person per year

e Dental visits: 1980
f Consultations: 1980
g Pharmaceuticals: 1980

18
LITERACY AND EDUCATION

Database name: Literacy and Education
Sector name: Basic Education Indicators

Table No: 1801

Title: Adult Literacy Rates, School Leaving Age: Latest Year

	Year	Adult Literacy Rate(%)	School Leaving Age
EC members			
Belgium	1983	98	18
Denmark	1981	99	15
France	1984	99	16
West Germany	1985	99	18
Greece	1981	91	15
Ireland	1984	99	15
Italy	1985	97	13
Luxembourg	1982	100	15
Netherlands	1984	98	16
Portugal	1985	84	14
Spain	1985	97	15
United Kingdom	1984	99	16
EFTA members			
Austria	1983	98	15
Finland	1982	99	16
Iceland	1984	100	15
Norway	1984	100	15
Sweden	1982	99	16
Switzerland	1984	100	16
CMEA members			
Bulgaria	1983	95	14
Czechoslovakia	1981	99	15
East Germany	1985	99	16
Hungary	1983	98	16
Poland	1983	98	14
Romania	1983	98	16
USSR	1981	99	17
Others			
Albania	1983	75	13
Cyprus	1984	99	15
Gibraltar	1985	98	15
Liechtenstein	1985	100	14
Malta	1985	84	16
Monaco	1983	99	16
Turkey	1985	70	14
Yugoslavia	1983	90	15

Source: UNESCO/National statistics

Database name: Literacy and Education
Sector name: Pre-Primary Education   Table No: 1802

Title: Pre-Primary Schools, Pupils, Staff: Latest Year

	Year	Pre-Primary Schools	Pupils ('000)	Staff ('000)	Notes
EC members					
Belgium	1987	4060	371.5	19.8	a
Denmark	1986		56.1	3.7	
France	1987	18285	2518.6	70.4	
West Germany	1986	27229	1685.8		
Greece	1985	5203	160.1	7.6	
Ireland	1985		147.9	5.2	
Italy	1987	28406	1586.9	108.2	b
Luxembourg	1986		7.8	0.4	
Netherlands	1984	7951	399.4	22.5	
Portugal	1985	2547	128.1	6.4	
Spain	1986	16254	1084.8	39.2	
United Kingdom	1988	1298	57.6	2.7	
EFTA members					
Austria	1987	3790	192.6	8.8	
Finland	1986	2086	99.4	8.6	
Iceland	1986		4.5		
Norway	1986	3487	104.3	21.8	a
Sweden	1986	9425	267.9		c
Switzerland	1987		132.9		
CMEA members					
Bulgaria	1987	4840	344.4	28.7	
Czechoslovakia	1987	11395	660.0	50.4	
East Germany	1987	13334	770.3	71.4	
Hungary	1987	4786	398.3	33.9	
Poland	1987	26150	1409.0	82.5	
Romania	1987	12291	828.1	31.3	
USSR	1987	137000	12253.0	1499.0	
Others					
Albania	1987	3170	118.3	5.2	
Cyprus	1987	480	19.6	0.8	
Gibraltar	1984	2	0.2		d
Liechtenstein	1987		0.8		
Malta	1987	50	8.3	0.4	
Monaco	1982	9		0.7	
Turkey	1987	3237	103.2	6.2	
Yugoslavia	1987	4047	396.9	40.3	

Source: UNESCO/National Statistical Offices
Notes: a   1985 staff figure
          b   1984 staff figure
          c   1983 schools figure
          d   Pupils 0.15, staff 0.005

Database name: Literacy and Education
Sector name: Primary Education

Table No: 1803

Title: Primary Schools, Pupils, Staff: Latest Year

	Year	Primary Schools	Pupils ('000)	Staff ('000)	Notes
EC members					
Belgium	1987	4263	728.7	71.1	
Denmark	1986	2536	391.9	34.4	
France	1987	46384	4151.7	202.3	
West Germany	1986	19594	2287.6	131.4	
Greece	1985	8675	887.7	38.0	
Ireland	1985	3334	420.2	15.7	
Italy	1987	26643	3370.7	276.6	a
Luxembourg	1986		22.0	1.8	
Netherlands	1986	8465	1447.8	85.0	
Portugal	1985	12741	1235.3	73.3	
Spain	1986	18772	3412.9	133.8	
United Kingdom	1988	24482	4560.0	210.1	
EFTA members					
Austria	1987	3394	350.7	33.3	
Finland	1987	4230	390.5	25.1	b
Iceland	1986	183	24.6	1.4	c
Norway	1986	3509	325.6	50.3	
Sweden	1987	4770	593.3	92.7	d
Switzerland	1987		375.3		
CMEA members					
Bulgaria	1987	2938	1093.5	62.1	
Czechoslovakia	1987	6236	2062.2	97.7	
East Germany	1987	5683	945.7	57.2	
Hungary	1987	3540	1277.3	90.9	
Poland	1987	17365	5036.1	321.6	
Romania	1987	13895	3027.2	141.6	
USSR	1987	127000	24423.0	2807.0	
Others					
Albania	1987	1668	543.1	27.3	
Cyprus	1987	379	56.5	2.6	
Gibraltar	1984	13	2.8	0.2	
Liechtenstein	1987		1.7	0.1	
Malta	1987	106	36.6	1.7	
Monaco	1982	6	1.4		
Turkey	1987	50457	6880.3	220.9	
Yugoslavia	1987	11978	1432.5	62.5	

Source: UNESCO/National Statistical Offices
Notes:
a 1984 staff figure
b 1983 schools and staff figures
c 1975 schools and staff figures
d 1984 schools and 1983 staff figures

Database name: Literacy and Education
Sector name: Secondary Education   Table No: 1804

Title: Secondary Schools, Pupils, Staff: Latest Year

	Year	Secondary Schools	Total Pupils ('000)	Staff ('000)	in Training Colleges ('000)	at Tech. Colleges ('000)	Notes
EC members							
Belgium	1987	2314	805.6	114.6		372.4	
Denmark	1986	164	488.8			156.5	
France	1987	11181	5383.9	313.4		1242.1	b
West Germany	1986	5416	6777.6	412.1		2473.4	
Greece	1985	3134	813.5	50.4		109.4	
Ireland	1985	815	338.3	21.2		22.7	
Italy	1987	17615	5338.0	547.1	189.7	1858.1	a
Luxembourg	1986		27.7	2.3	0.1	17.1	a
Netherlands	1986	3316	1393.6	98.7	2.1	617.7	
Portugal	1985	1511	552.1	40.3		7.5	a
Spain	1986	4861	4660.8	220.2		1220.0	
United Kingdom	1988	5020	3701.5	244.9		418.0	
EFTA members							
Austria	1987	2069	626.8	70.5	8.5	163.5	
Finland	1987	1082	398.9	37.4	1.0	110.4	b
Iceland	1986	115	28.2	2.3	0.3	7.5	c,d
Norway	1986	937	378.9		0.7	104.3	
Sweden	1987	534	619.9	51.5	0.1	220.0	b,e
Switzerland	1987		388.3		8.1	27.6	
CMEA members							
Bulgaria	1987	526	389.4	27.9		221.6	
Czechoslovakia	1987	2269	351.2	34.3	8.0	207.0	
East Germany	1987	1429	1425.4	159.1		364.4	
Hungary	1987	587	426.9	22.8	5.0	315.9	c
Poland	1987	10544	1689.0	160.1	26.6	1290.0	d,f
Romania	1987	1728	1529.4	46.3	4.9	1422.0	c
USSR	1987	48600	21139.0		221.0	3356.0	
Others							
Albania	1987	397	188.5	8.4	2.3	132.8	
Cyprus	1987	92	42.2	3.4		3.5	
Gibraltar	1986		1.7	0.1		0.1	
Liechtenstein	1987	10	3.9	0.2			
Malta	1987	87	28.8	2.5		6.5	
Monaco	1982		3.1			1.2	
Turkey	1987	7809	3288.3	144.5	11.8	670.2	
Yugoslavia	1987	1490	2358.1	135.9	25.3	678.8	

Source: UNESCO/National Statistical Offices
Notes: a   1984 staff figure
            b   1983 staff figure
            c   1975 staff figure
            d   1985 figures for pupils at training and tech. colleges
            e   1984 figures for pupils at training and tech. colleges
            f   1985 staff figure

	Year	Establish-ments	Teaching Staff ('000)	Students ('000)	University Teachers ('000)	University Students ('000)	% Students at University	Notes
EC members								
Belgium	1987	190	19.5	252.2	5.3	103.5	41.0	
Denmark	1986	50	22.7	118.6		93.8	79.1	
France	1987		45.8	1327.8	45.8	997.5	75.1	a
West Germany	1986	238	183.5	1579.1	139.0	1366.1	86.5	
Greece	1986	107	12.4	197.8	7.1	116.0	58.6	
Ireland	1985	25	6.0	70.3	3.3	39.1	55.6	
Italy	1986	796	51.7	1141.1	51.1	1132.4	99.2	
Luxembourg	1985		0.4	0.8				
Netherlands	1986	451	12.4	399.8	12.3	172.3	43.1	
Portugal	1985	126	12.5	103.6	7.6	70.2	67.8	
Spain	1986	254	49.0	954.0	48.4	900.4	94.4	
United Kingdom	1988	719	125.0	906.7	31.2	320.9	35.4	
EFTA members								
Austria	1987	44	12.5	188.2	10.5	175.5	93.3	
Finland	1986	571		139.4	7.5	99.2	71.2	
Iceland	1987	3	0.3	4.7	0.5	2.8	59.6	a
Norway	1986	198	8.9	104.2	4.3	44.3	42.5	
Sweden	1987			184.3		113.3	61.5	
Switzerland	1987	12	6.2	121.7	6.2	78.5	64.5	a,b,c
CMEA members								
Bulgaria	1987	30	16.9	135.9	15.9	120.2	88.4	
Czechoslovakia	1987	36	26.5	170.6	26.5	170.6	100.0	
East Germany	1987	54	42.3	437.9	30.4	155.7	35.6	c
Hungary	1987	54	15.3	99.0	11.8	64.2	64.8	
Poland	1987	92	58.4	458.6	58.4	363.6	79.3	a,c
Romania	1987	44	12.0	157.0	12.0	157.0	100.0	
USSR	1987	5301	382.0	5025.7				b,d
Others								
Albania	1987	8	1.6	23.8	1.6	23.8	100.0	
Cyprus	1987	16	0.4	4.2				
Gibraltar								
Liechtenstein								
Malta	1987	1	0.1	1.5	0.1	1.5	100.0	
Monaco								
Turkey	1987	310	24.4	534.5	25.5	341.9	64.0	
Yugoslavia	1987	340	25.9	348.1	23.0	297.0	85.3	

Source: UNESCO/National Statistical Offices
Notes:
a University teachers only
b 1985 staff figure
c Establishments refers to universities only
d Includes evening and correspondence courses

19
AGRICULTURAL RESOURCES

Database name: Agricultural Resources
Sector name: Agricultural Output   Table No: 1901

Title: Indices of Agricultural Output 1977-1988

Unit: 1979-1981 = 100

Calendar year	1977	1980	1981	1982	1983	1984	1985	1986	1987	1988
EC members										
Belgium	91.6	97.2	103.3	99.8	96.1	106.0	106.3	112.5	112.4	115.7
Denmark	97.3	99.3	100.8	110.6	103.1	125.8	122.6	119.8	118.6	119.7
France	86.1	101.0	98.7	104.4	100.3	109.6	108.4	107.0	104.9	103.7
West Germany	95.3	101.0	100.4	109.2	105.9	113.0	108.4	115.2	109.2	112.0
Greece	89.4	103.8	105.1	107.9	102.6	104.2	113.8	107.2	98.8	108.2
Ireland	98.1	109.0	92.0	97.7	100.0	111.4	111.2	106.9	111.2	104.6
Italy	92.1	102.3	101.6	99.4	108.3	100.0	102.0	100.1	105.5	100.1
Luxembourg										
Netherlands	88.9	96.4	107.7	109.6	107.7	110.5	108.6	115.8	115.9	115.4
Portugal	91.7	98.0	88.1	106.1	92.6	102.3	107.5	103.6	113.4	107.0
Spain	86.6	107.4	95.1	104.6	97.5	114.0	110.4	116.4	121.8	114.9
United Kingdom	92.2	102.5	100.8	103.0	105.1	115.4	110.0	110.3	108.9	106.4
EFTA members										
Austria	93.8	103.5	98.6	111.8	106.5	111.2	109.0	109.9	104.3	104.7
Finland	97.0	103.5	93.0	106.8	116.9	115.8	112.7	112.3	102.4	102.6
Iceland	95.6	99.7	100.4	103.0	103.1	105.5	108.2	107.6	97.4	105.4
Norway	93.5	100.2	103.0	108.3	103.2	110.7	107.2	111.2	110.7	112.1
Sweden	97.1	99.3	102.9	105.3	104.3	114.4	107.7	105.4	95.4	93.0
Switzerland	95.4	100.2	98.7	108.9	104.7	107.9	107.7	110.0	107.3	111.4
CMEA members										
Bulgaria	89.1	95.7	102.3	109.6	99.2	107.8	95.3	104.2	100.2	100.3
Czechoslovakia	100.7	102.6	102.1	108.9	113.2	120.1	120.4	124.7	119.1	124.6
East Germany	91.3	98.2	102.6	97.4	97.8	105.7	112.3	115.6	118.0	116.5
Hungary	95.6	102.4	101.4	111.7	108.8	115.2	107.6	108.0	108.6	104.6
Poland	98.1	95.3	96.1	99.3	103.3	106.5	108.9	116.2	111.0	108.5
Romania	96.8	100.0	98.1	105.3	101.8	115.2	109.2	125.0	122.7	114.4
USSR	101.5	100.0	98.0	104.4	109.0	109.1	109.9	117.1	116.1	116.6
Others										
Albania	92.3	100.0	99.0	102.0	108.4	108.3	108.7	108.7	108.3	113.2
Cyprus	97.9	104.4	99.2	107.3	91.8	102.8	95.9	95.9		
Gibraltar										
Liechtenstein										
Malta	99.1	105.5	100.3	114.3	115.7	109.1	115.0	118.7	102.4	111.1
Monaco										
Turkey	94.3	99.8	102.1	106.4	105.3	105.4	108.8	113.4	102.9	102.8
Yugoslavia	100.1	99.5	100.8	110.0	104.6	108.4	100.5	113.6	102.4	

Source: FAO Production Yearbook
Notes: Belgium and Luxembourg are combined
          Figures for Cyprus are based on year ending mid-1981 = 100

Database name:	Agricultural Resources										
Sector name:	Agricultural Output				Table No: 1902						

Title: Indices of Food Output 1977-1988

Unit: 1979-1981 = 100

Calendar year	1977	1980	1981	1982	1983	1984	1985	1986	1987	1988
EC members										
Belgium	91.5	97.2	103.4	99.8	96.1	105.9	106.2	112.5	112.5	115.8
Denmark	97.3	99.3	100.8	100.6	103.1	125.8	122.6	119.8	118.6	119.7
France	86.0	101.0	96.7	104.5	100.4	109.7	108.5	107.1	104.9	103.8
West Germany	95.3	101.0	100.4	109.2	105.9	113.0	108.4	115.2	109.2	112.0
Greece	88.6	104.2	105.0	108.5	102.3	103.2	112.5	104.3	95.3	104.4
Ireland	98.1	109.1	92.0	97.7	100.0	111.4	111.3	106.9	111.3	104.6
Italy	92.2	102.4	101.6	99.2	108.1	99.7	101.6	99.9	105.3	99.8
Luxembourg										
Netherlands	88.9	96.4	107.7	109.6	107.7	110.5	108.6	115.8	115.9	115.4
Portugal	91.3	98.0	88.1	106.3	92.5	102.3	107.6	103.8	113.8	107.3
Spain	86.8	107.4	94.7	104.6	97.6	114.2	110.3	116.2	121.8	114.1
United Kingdom	92.2	102.5	100.8	103.0	105.1	115.5	110.0	110.3	108.8	106.2
EFTA members										
Austria	93.7	103.5	98.6	111.8	106.5	111.8	109.0	109.9	104.3	104.7
Finland	97.0	103.5	93.0	106.8	116.9	115.8	112.7	112.3	102.4	102.6
Iceland	97.0	103.5	93.0	106.8	116.9	115.8	112.7	112.3	97.5	105.7
Norway	93.5	100.2	103.1	108.3	103.0	110.7	107.1	111.2	110.6	112.1
Sweden	97.1	99.3	102.9	105.3	104.7	107.9	107.7	110.0	95.4	93.0
Switzerland	95.4	100.2	98.6	109.0	104.7	107.9	107.7	110.0	107.4	111.5
CMEA members										
Bulgaria	98.2	96.5	103.2	110.3	101.4	108.9	95.8	106.5	101.3	103.3
Czechoslovakia	100.8	102.5	102.1	108.9	113.2	120.1	120.3	124.8	119.1	124.7
East Germany	91.3	98.2	102.5	97.3	97.7	105.3	112.0	115.3	117.6	116.0
Hungary	95.4	102.6	101.4	111.7	108.9	115.4	107.8	108.2	108.9	104.7
Poland	98.0	95.4	96.1	99.6	103.5	106.7	108.8	116.2	111.2	109.0
Romania	96.5	99.8	98.3	105.5	102.0	115.2	109.1	125.3	122.9	114.4
USSR	101.3	99.9	97.5	104.4	109.5	110.2	110.4	118.6	117.9	117.9
Others										
Albania	93.6	100.2	100.2	99.0	102.3	109.5	108.9	109.4	108.9	111.1
Cyprus	98.1	98.8	102.1	111.2	120.1	102.9	95.9	96.0		
Gibraltar										
Liechtenstein										
Malta	99.1	105.5	100.3	114.4	115.7	109.2	115.1	118.8	102.4	111.1
Monaco										
Turkey	93.1	99.6	102.5	106.9	105.1	105.4	109.3	114.3		
Yugoslavia	99.9	99.7	100.7	109.9	104.6	108.2	100.0	112.9	102.6	103.2

Source: FAO Production Yearbook
Notes: Belgium and Luxembourg are combined
Cyprus figures are year ending mid-1981 = 100

Database name: Agricultural Resources
Sector name: Land Use

Table No: 1903

Title: Land Use and Irrigation 1987

Unit: 000 hectares

	Total Area	Land Area	Arable Land	Permanent Crops	Permanent Pasture	Forest and Woodland	Other Land	Irrigated Land	% of Land Area
EC members									
Belgium	3310	3282	802	16	695	699	1070	1	0.03
Denmark	4307	4237	2596	4	206	493	938	419	9.9
France	55150	55010	18166	1293	11894	14688	8969	1190	2.2
West Germany	24858	24428	7270	206	4480	7328	5144	325	1.3
Greece	13199	13085	2891	1049	5255	2620	1270	1156	8.8
Ireland	7028	6889	980	3	4686	337	883		
Italy	30127	29406	9120	3047	4942	6735	5562	3050	10.4
Luxembourg									
Netherlands	3733	3392	895	29	1090	300	1078	540	15.9
Portugal	9239	9195	2045	710	530	3641	2269	632	6.9
Spain	50478	49944	15567	4858	10324	15725	3470	3270	6.5
United Kingdom	24488	24160	6930	58	11570	2324	3278	155	0.6
EFTA members									
Austria	8385	8273	1436	74	1982	3200	1581	4	0.05
Finland	33813	30461	2411		127	23222	4701	62	0.2
Iceland	10300	10025	8		2274	120	7623		
Norway	32390	30683	856		100	8330	21397	93	0.3
Sweden	44996	41162	2953		565	28020	9624	108	0.3
Switzerland	4129	3977	391	21	1609	1052	904	25	0.6
CMEA members									
Bulgaria	11091	11055	3825	306	2035	3868	1021	1257	11.4
Czechoslovakia	12787	12538	5000	134	1644	4603	1157	227	1.8
East Germany	10833	10524	4694	240	1254	2980	1356	150	1.4
Hungary	9303	9234	5048	241	1222	1669	1054	143	1.5
Poland	31268	30446	14480	259	4052	8730	2925	100	0.3
Romania	23750	23034	10080	606	4407	6340	1601	3366	14.6
USSR	2240220	2227200	228200	4370	371600	944000	679030	20485	0.9
Others									
Albania	2875	2740	590	124	397	1047	582	409	14.9
Cyprus	925	924	103	54	5	123	639	31	3.4
Gibraltar	1	1					1		
Liechtenstein	16	16	4		6	3	3		
Malta	32	32	12	1			19	1	3.1
Monaco									
Turkey	77945	76963	24964	2963	8700	20199	20137	2170	2.8
Yugoslavia	25580	25540	7039	727	6357	9340	2077	150	0.6

Source: FAO Production Yearbook
Notes: Belgium and Luxembourg are combined

Database name: Agricultural Resources   rces
Sector name: Livestock

Table No: 1904

Title: Circulation of Livestock 1988

Unit: 000 head

	Horses	Cattle	Pigs	Sheep	Goats
EC members					
Belgium	23	2950	5881	184	8
Denmark	29	2266	9214	128	
France	292	21100	12577	10360	1150
West Germany	350	14887	23670	1414	46
Greece	60	800	1190	10816	3488
Ireland	55	5580	960	4301	3
Italy	250	8794	9383	11457	1206
Luxembourg					
Netherlands	64	4546	14226	1100	34
Portugal	29	1387	2800	5220	745
Spain	250	4980	16941	17894	2900
United Kingdom	180	11849	7915	27820	58
EC total	1582	79139	104757	90694	9644
EFTA members					
Austria	45	2590	3947	24	34
Finland	36	1434	1291	63	3
Iceland	57	72	14	770	
Norway	17	945	788	2306	94
Sweden	58	1667	2217	402	
Switzerland	49	1837	1941	367	72
EFTA total	262	8545	10198	3932	203
CMEA members					
Bulgaria	123	1649	4034	8886	428
Czechoslovakia	33	5044	7235	1075	50
East Germany	104	5721	12503	2656	19
Hungary	88	1664	8216	2333	16
Poland	1051	10322	19605	4377	10
Romania	693	7120	15224	18793	990
USSR	5885	120593	77403	140783	6400
CMEA total	7977	152113	144220	178903	7913
Others					
Albania	42	672	214	1432	979
Cyprus	1	45	266	310	220
Gibraltar					
Liechtenstein		9	10	3	
Malta	1	14	95	5	5
Monaco					
Turkey	620	12000	10	40000	13100
Yugoslavia	362	4881	8323	7824	126
Total	1026	17621	8918	49574	14430
European total	10847	257418	268093	323103	32190

Source: FAO Production Yearbook
Notes: Belgium and Luxembourg are combined

| Database name: | Agricultural Resources |
| Sector name: | Food Production |

Table No: 1905

Title: Production of Dairy Products 1988

Unit: 000 metric tonnes

	Cow Milk Fresh	Cow Milk Dried	Evaporated Milk	Cheese	Butter and Ghee	Hen Eggs	Honey
EC members							
Belgium	3900	53	14	100	80	160	1
Denmark	4728	97	12	265	91	75	
France	27510	209	164	1351	516	912	24
West Germany	23978	155	473	1030	412	726	16
Greece	630			206	5	124	12
Ireland	5463	42		85	130	34	
Italy	10869	3	3	690	75	706	9
Luxembourg							
Netherlands	11315	175	452	563	170	600	1
Portugal	909		2	46	5	74	3
Spain	6620	10	107	184	23	758	17
United Kingdom	14981	106	153	291	140	790	2
EFTA members							
Austria	3630	18	20	100	36	103	2
Finland	2753	14		88	54	77	2
Iceland	114	0.3		5	2	4	
Norway	1953	1	10	75	23	57	1
Sweden	3429	6	11	123	68	117	3
Switzerland	3790	13	3	129	35	44	3
CMEA members							
Bulgaria	2177			195	27	161	10
Czechoslovakia	6963		166	223	148	280	12
East Germany	9204		134	267	322	335	7
Hungary	2825	7	5	84	35	200	16
Poland	15420	48	20	448	267	445	15
Romania	4300			108	44	400	17
USSR	105950	320	600	2030	1794	4656	192
Others							
Albania	347			14	4	14	1
Cyprus	76			8		7	1
Gibraltar							
Liechtenstein	20						
Malta	29					7	
Monaco							
Turkey	3000			140	118	306	35
Yugoslavia	4700	14		140	10	242	6

Source: FAO Production Yearbook
Notes: Belgium and Luxembourg are combined

Database name:	Agricultural Resources						
Sector name:	Food Production				Table No:	1906	

Title: Production of Meat 1988

Unit: 000 metric tonnes

	Beef and Veal	Mutton and Lamb	Pig Meat	Horse Meat	Goat Meat	Poultry	Total (incl. others)
EC members							
Belgium	324	7	811	5		179	1347
Denmark	220	1	1125	1		114	1464
France	1832	152	1740	22	8	1429	5477
West Germany	1608	29	3342	4		407	5428
Greece	82	85	160	3	40	149	524
Ireland	460	51	140	2		61	714
Italy	1144	64	1287	56	4	1047	3822
Luxembourg							
Netherlands	525	11	1540	2	1	442	2520
Portugal	97	22	190	1	3	135	459
Spain	447	218	1680	6	18	826	3287
United Kingdom	964	321	1016	10		1079	3396
EFTA members							
Austria	222	4	392			87	711
Finland	112	1	169	1		28	322
Iceland	3	13	2	1		2	23
Norway	82	24	98	1		12	226
Sweden	129	5	293	2		42	495
Switzerland	157	4	285	1	1	29	481
CMEA members							
Bulgaria	130	89	381		7	178	788
Czechoslovakia	405	11	914	1		241	1616
East Germany	432	22	1400	2		161	2038
Hungary	109	4	985			482	1607
Poland	700	29	1748	19		380	2894
Romania	230	60	850	6	7	390	1559
USSR	8600	850	6324		25	3127	19213
Others							
Albania	28	19	9		8	15	79
Cyprus	4	5	26		4	13	54
Gibraltar							
Liechtenstein							
Malta	2		7			4	13
Monaco							
Turkey	245	305	1	4	75	290	941
Yugoslavia	310	63	850			336	1567

Source: FAO Production Yearbook
Notes: Belgium and Luxembourg are combined

Database name: Agricultural Resources
Sector name: Food Production

Table No: 1907

Title: Production of Cereals 1988

Unit: 000 metric tonnes

	Wheat	Barley	Maize	Oats	Rye	Rice	Total (incl. others)
EC members							
Belgium	1327	802	40	95	14		2298
Denmark	2080	5419		202	366		8092
France	29677	10086	13996	1074	276	65	56178
West Germany	12044	9609	1435	2036	1558		27131
Greece	2550	695	2116	74	31	116	5584
Ireland	418	1538		117	1		2074
Italy	7945	1561	6318	383	18	1094	17423
Luxembourg							
Netherlands	816	311	5	63	27		1222
Portugal	401	48	663	76	73	151	1422
Spain	6514	12070	3577	537	357	499	23660
United Kingdom	11605	8765	1	557	33		20983
EFTA members							
Austria	1430	1135	1640	250	280		4833
Finland	285	1612		857	49		2826
Iceland							
Norway	200	600		480	3		1285
Sweden	1357	1942		1402	140		4952
Switzerland	553	299	237	48	19		1159
CMEA members							
Bulgaria	4713	1306	1625	52	58	60	7858
Czechoslovakia	6547	3411	996	366	534		11861
East Germany	3697	3798	1	508	1783		9816
Hungary	6962	1161	6027	134	245	52	14635
Poland	7582	3804	204	2222	5501		24504
Romania	9000	2200	19500	160	60	150	31090
USSR	84500	47000	16000	16500	16000	2900	187060
Others							
Albania	589	40	306	30	11	11	1024
Cyprus	13	130		1			144
Gibraltar							
Liechtenstein							
Malta	5	5					10
Monaco							
Turkey	20500	7500	2100	276	293	263	30985
Yugoslavia	6303	616	7697	253	76	36	14996

Source: FAO Production Yearbook
Notes: Belgium and Luxembourg are combined

Database name: Agricultural Resources
Sector name: Food Production

Table No: 1908

Title: Production of Selected Crops 1988

Unit: 000 metric tonnes

	Sugar Beet	Hops	Rapeseed	Potatoes	Tomatoes	Apples	Grapes
EC members							
Belgium	6156	1.0	14	2000	180	255	25
Denmark	2708		528	942	16	45	
France	28606	1.0	2469	6344	743	2357	7419
West Germany	19602	30.0	1181	7353	19	2467	1450
Greece	1900			850	1929	295	1565
Ireland	1404		10	680	13	10	
Italy	13428		56	2330	4643	2326	9831
Luxembourg							
Netherlands	6737		24	6742	550	398	1
Portugal	10	0.2		795	865	74	1400
Spain	9056	3.0	13	4578	2596	852	3700
United Kingdom	8500	5.0	1039	6812	132	241	
EFTA members							
Austria	2030	0.2	81	901	20	268	310
Finland	944		121	855	28	13	
Iceland				11	1		
Norway			12	414	9	50	
Sweden	2353		305	1241	12	84	
Switzerland	923		50	748	19	540	152
CMEA members							
Bulgaria	677	0.7		359	809	314	929
Czechoslovakia	5483	15.0	380	3659	124	468	229
East Germany	4619	4.0	424	11473	70	697	
Hungary	4200	1.0	80	1128	450	900	450
Poland	14069	2.0	1199	34707	527	1393	
Romania	6500	0.3	40	8000	2300	800	2245
USSR	87800	10.0	425	62700	7200	5700	5600
Others							
Albania	360			137	48	20	88
Cyprus				195	28	7	175
Gibraltar							
Liechtenstein				12			
Malta				13	17	1	3
Monaco							
Turkey	11000			4350	5250	1954	3350
Yugoslavia	4558	4.7	68	1935	402	518	1186

Source: FAO Production Yearbook
Notes: Belgium and Luxembourg are combined

Database name: Agricultural Resources
Sector name: Forestry Products   Table No: 1909

Title: Production of Forestry/Paper Products 1988

Unit: As stated

	A	B	C	D	E	F	G	H
EC members								
Belgium	4018	538	1009	304	848	414	85	114
Denmark	2082	481	861	70	326	130	18	
France	42643	10436	10334	2201	6313	2374	298	373
West Germany	34954	3656	10395	2358	10576	4398	746	897
Greece	3303	2320	410	18	282	62	85	10
Ireland	1282	46	300		29			
Italy	9733	4423	2078	651	5513	2208	264	265
Luxembourg								
Netherlands	1141	106	390	182	2462	691	171	304
Portugal	10151	648	2060	1408	627	168	45	
Spain	16095	2320	2643	1604	3418	826	219	175
United Kingdom	6400	155	1919	421	4296	1159	439	530
EFTA members								
Austria	14830	1413	6478	1493	2650	1204	93	252
Finland	48620	3111	7823	9001	8652	4373	165	1400
Iceland								
Norway	10984	926	2387	1974	1670	339	32	882
Sweden	52751	4424	11267	10074	8161	1660	289	2064
Switzerland	4521	884	1668	335	1216	348	141	263
CMEA members								
Bulgaria	4471	1810	1342	235	476	81		
Czechoslovakia	18435	1610	5126	1324	1266	147	47	74
East Germany	10874	710	2489	662	1348	193		124
Hungary	6589	2949	1217	56	554	155	27	
Poland	22848	3123	6013	829	1448	359	160	22
Romania	20369	4575	2758	672	819	139	23	108
USSR	391800	86800	10300	10374	10216	1310		1750
Others								
Albania	2330	1608	200	16	8			
Cyprus	76	22	57					4
Gibraltar								
Liechtenstein								
Malta								
Monaco								
Turkey	16809	10500	4923	375	400	75	19	21
Yugoslavia	15186	3861	4587	838	1381	320		36

Source: FAO Yearbook of Forestry Products
Notes: Belgium and Luxembourg are combined
            A Roundwood '000m3   E Paper and paperboard '000 MT
            B Fuelwood and charcoal '000m3   F Printing and writing paper '000 MT
            C Sawnwood and sleepers '000m3   G Household and sanitary paper '000 MT
            D Wood pulp '000 MT   H Newsprint '000 MT

Database name: Agricultural Resources
Sector name: Fishery Products

Table No: 1910

Title: Production of Fishery Products 1987

Unit: 000 metric tonnes

	A	B	C	D	E	F	Notes
EC members							
Belgium	40.4	10.0	3.9	12.2		1.2	a
Denmark	1695.7	205.4	28.7	71.4	85.0	264.5	
France	843.7	112.6	14.4	104.6	3.7	20.3	
West Germany	201.8	147.4	13.3	115.7	8.1	27.0	
Greece	135.1	8.0	7.6	1.8			
Ireland	247.4	112.1	1.9	1.3	4.4	3.7	
Italy	554.5	60.0	3.9	109.1		4.5	
Luxembourg							
Netherlands	435.2	235.0	33.3	16.9			
Portugal	395.3	58.2	5.0	42.4	2.1	7.1	
Spain	1393.4	291.4	27.5	117.6	8.5	78.9	
United Kingdom	962.9	129.8	21.4	6.4	6.9	51.0	
EFTA members							
Austria	4.6		0.1				
Finland	159.3	11.8	3.8	1.9		1.6	
Iceland	1633.1	165.4	95.1	2.3	82.1	159.3	
Norway	1929.3	263.8	84.8	55.6	77.8	183.1	
Sweden	214.5	29.2	3.0	37.4	2.7	10.0	
Switzerland	4.8	0.1	0.1	1.5			
CMEA members							
Bulgaria	110.5	76.6	3.9	14.5		7.3	
Czechoslovakia	20.7		7.1	20.6			
East Germany	193.6	26.0	28.0	55.6			
Hungary	36.8	4.5		1.2			
Poland	670.9	170.5	58.5	62.4	1.0	74.4	
Romania	264.4	124.9	39.5	20.2	0.6	12.5	
USSR	11159.6	3272.0	841.2	1348.5	111.3	766.6	
Others							
Albania	12.5						
Cyprus	2.6						
Gibraltar							
Liechtenstein							
Malta	1.0						
Monaco	1.5						
Turkey	625.7	24.0	4.0	2.1	9.1	45.0	
Yugoslavia	81.3	0.9	0.1	30.7	0.4	2.9	

Source: FAO Yearbook of Fishery Statistics
Notes:
A   Fish, crustaceans, molluscs (nominal catch)
B   Fresh, chilled or frozen fish
C   Dried, salted or smoked fish
D   Fish products and preparations
E   Oils and fats of aquatic animal origin

F   Meals, solubles etc of aquatic animal
a   Belgium and Luxembourg

TABLE 1901: AGRICULTURAL OUTPUT
Base: 1980 ▪ 100

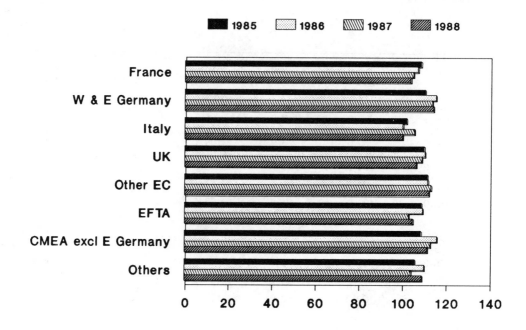

Database name: Communications
Sector name: Telephones   Table No: 2001
Subsector name:
Title: Trends in Number of Telephones in Use 1977-1987

Unit: 000s

	1977	1980	1981	1982	1983	1984	1985	1986	1987
EC members									
Belgium	3100	3636	3819	3959	4111	4243	4346	4560	
Denmark	2718	3283	3448	3595	3675	3828	4005	4195	4434
France	17635	24859	27136	29595	31483	33002	34346		
West Germany	22932	28554	30122	31370	35137	36582	37899	39128	
Greece	2320	2796	2957	3113	3313	3529	3721	3920	
Ireland	519	650	720	779	824	894	942		
Italy	16125	19277	20453	21680	22992	24331	25615	26874	38053
Luxembourg	186	207	215	220	226	234	241	250	257
Netherlands	5845	7357	7769	8023	8272	8535	8785	9080	9388
Portugal	1199	1372	1456	1567	1685	1764	1835	1936	2121
Spain	9528	11845	12386	12820	13345	13825	14259	14748	15377
United Kingdom	21672	26651	27784	28632	29062	29518			
EFTA members									
Austria	2443	3010	3178	3330	3469	3594	3720	3840	3979
Finland	2032	2374	2511	2644	2777	2899	3028	3423	3622
Iceland	95	109	111	117	125	130	138	149	153
Norway	1571	1881	2025	2204	2395	2579	2950	3130	3230
Sweden	5930	6621	6889	7132	7410	7669	7270	8000	8151
Switzerland	4145	4612	4781	4955	5113	5270	5436	5623	
CMEA members									
Bulgaria	946	1255	1513	1514	1790	1930	1980	2000	2010
Czechoslovakia	2863	3150	3226	3306	3402	3499	3591	3707	4468
East Germany	2860	3156	3252	3344	3441	3527	3630	3755	3875
Hungary	1104	1261	1297	1338	1383	1433	1485	1541	1614
Poland	2925	3387	3506	3648	3846	4028	4215	4418	
Romania									
USSR	19600	23707	25069	26667					
Others									
Albania									
Cyprus	83		129	143	164	196	220	241	
Gibraltar	9	10	10	10	11	11	11	11	13
Liechtenstein	9	11	11	11	11	12	13	13	
Malta	55	79	91	98	113	115	122	140	
Monaco	27	30	31	32	35	35	37		
Turkey	1379			2368	2665	3091	3455	4222	
Yugoslavia	1556	2139	2303	2541	2795	3031		3598	

Source: UIT/Statistical Offices
Notes:

Database name:	Communications										
Sector name:	Telephones				Table No: 2002						
Subsector name:											
Title:	Trends in Total Telephone Traffic 1977-1988										

Unit: Million calls

	1977	1980	1981	1982	1983	1984	1985	1986	1987	1988	Notes
EC members											
Belgium	1621	1917	2005	2375	2570	2728	2891				
Denmark	2791	3140	3246	3404	3528	3556	3955	4141	4343		
France	37590	56486	63008	68070	74489	78894	82897	87606	94237	96686	a
West Germany	16267	21193	22779	24164	25408	26432	27616	28989	30326		
Greece	2571	3763	3987	3583	4784	5437	6921	8437			
Ireland	772	1130	1451	1615	1977	2207	2298	2569	2799		a
Italy	11378	13924	14554	15012	15902	17395	18078	18937			
Luxembourg	97	139		127		150	166	173	174		a,b
Netherlands	3946	4935	5122	5329	5538	5785	6007	6240	6401	6609	
Portugal	2822	3521	3747	4288	4444	4646	5038	7061	8073		a,b
Spain	1496	2072	2169	2321	2415	2566	2819	2998	3094		b
United Kingdom	16011	19963	20291	20937	21551	22976	28842				
EFTA members											
Austria	19620	25755	23664	24873	26847	25085	26371	27015			c
Finland		1641	1688	1807	1957	2185	2349	2487			
Iceland	394	446	469	442	491	523	552	579	637	826	a,b
Norway	2979	3856	4262	4622	4977	5400	6138	6745	7607		a,b
Sweden	20191	23010	24395	23353	26195	27696	30194	33031	35854	37122	a
Switzerland	8319	9451	9680	10381	10919	11175	11650	12243			
CMEA members											
Bulgaria	44	41		31	33	35	37	38			
Czechoslovakia	4154	3459	3819	4101	2070	4916	5472	6074			
East Germany	1849	1960	1981	2015	2230	2151	2082	2141	2400		
Hungary	1015	1644	1836	2006	1084	2574	2950	3199			a
Poland	787	1011	999	894		1142	1239				
Romania											
USSR	963	1267	1364	1457			1824	1994	2218	2396	b,f
Others											
Albania											
Cyprus	7	12	14	18	22	24	26	28	32		c,d
Gibraltar	0	0	1	2	2	2	3				c,d
Liechtenstein	8	10	10	11	11	11	12	13			
Malta	35	43	51	62	65	125	140	189			
Monaco	86	139	151	163	179	191	222				a
Turkey	1204	1926	2424	3150	4535	5332	6957	8946	12665		a,b
Yugoslavia	8761	14369	15606	17842	20788	22000		33463	25045		a

Source: UIT/Statistical Offices
Notes:
a Million pulses
b National traffic only
c Million minutes
d International traffic only
e Included with Switzerland
f Long-distance calls only

Database name: Communications
Sector name: Telex
Subsector name:
Title: Trends in Number of Telex Lines 1977-1988

Table No: 2003

Unit: Number

	1977	1980	1981	1982	1983	1984	1985	1986	1987	1988	Notes
EC members											
Belgium	17500	20700	21500	22835	23970	25379	26464	27570	27620	25027	
Denmark	8007	9456	10107	11342	11414	12700	13307	13367	13042		
France	65884	83211	89060	96706	104986	114008	124515	134293	141792	147255	
West Germany	114000	137000	143500	148405	152826	157093	161482	164952	167697	158279	
Greece	8000	12200	13780	14829	15178	18232	20202	21643			
Ireland	3900	5300	6051	6500	7000	7255	7269	7143	6637	5634	
Italy	27800	40900	45500	50091	55746	61222	65416	69363	73133	72769	
Luxembourg	1205	1672	1790	1952	2089	2257	2391	2576	2731		
Netherlands	27270	33178	34458	35654	36616	38114	39600	40200	39000		
Portugal	3957	7581	9678	11687	14412	16528	18427	20898	24339		
Spain	20946	30571	32532	33818	37879	43334	46822	51884	52496	55751	
United Kingdom	64800	85800	89900	92400	92600	95115	98975				
EFTA members											
Austria	16000	19000	21000	21858	22928	24016	25015	25774	25954		
Finland	5400	6400	6800	7200	7500	7700	8400	7681	7179		
Iceland	250	320	343	371	320	340	442	520	576		
Norway	6200	7300	7990	8607	9195	10197	10817	11026	10145		
Sweden	11895	15526	16231	16906	17393	18513	19361	19583	19660	18318	
Switzerland	27960	32912	34865	36958	38478	40021	41896	42797			
CMEA members											
Bulgaria	4399	5356	5814	5900	6030	6060	6120	6140			
Czechoslovakia	8010	9340	9740	10030	10170	10499	10818	11119			
East Germany	12000	15000	15330	15695	15957	16200	16476	16724	17020		
Hungary	6699	8132	8659	9222	9761	10289	10782	11345	11960		
Poland	17300	25000	27000	27099	27858	28737	29606	30733			
Romania			6750								
USSR	930	1226	1317	1446	1512	1611	1704				
Others											
Albania											
Cyprus	1038		1889	2249	2581	3013	3344	3479			
Gibraltar	76	135	153	153	155	163	188				
Liechtenstein		366	392	409	426	438	447	468			a
Malta	312	537	585	628	747	787	832	928			
Monaco	310	450	502	555	597	630	672				
Turkey	3835	6344	7520	7625	8048	8262	14775	17550			
Yugoslavia	7000	9000	10000	11000	12000	11462	12262	12999			

Source: UIT/Statistical Offices
Notes: a included with Switzerland

Database name:	Communications	
Sector name:	Telex	Table No: 2004
Subsector name:		
Title:	Trends in Total Telex Traffic 1977-1988	

Unit: 000 minutes

	1977	1980	1981	1982	1983	1984	1985	1986	1987	1988	Notes
EC members											
Belgium	81308	11581	114354	118103	116971	128274	129455	140974	136762	119955	a
Denmark	31425	37984	42033	43451	45463	48694	55673	59611	70013		
France	246004	328253	358106	374856	413153	474550	519886	541612			
West Germany			515385	532114	557205	565883	572856	561961	567530	565203	
Greece	30725	40806	47668	47531	48540	52964	55354	54923			
Ireland	10250	18552	19208	18867	18305	20902	32234	34319	34269	27076	
Italy	162597	222197	204702	257431	278338	306272	325794	336146	334407	309829	
Luxembourg	9403	13809	14898	16335	17604	18610	19474	20564	21779		
Netherlands	53626	71782	76612	78586	82957	86009	88080	88064	82600	71900	a
Portugal	15095	31665	38718	49044	57024	64360	70927	77070	84806		
Spain	49142	70600	79407	86450	94823	102802	109622	115928	122108		
United Kingdom	124729	168264	179647	186220	202007	218746					b
EFTA members											
Austria	101341	115840	105166	102579	105324	110514	113344	124700	127900		
Finland		22074	24484	25018	25808	25988	26099	25150	22413	18164	
Iceland	671	905	957	996	1048	1276	1441	1414	1525		a
Norway	24404	27008	30650	33343	36034	37755	40217	40009	37012	30601	
Sweden	22690	27926	30989	31311	32770	31759	32308	31759	28470	23056	a
Switzerland	94889	111558	120019	128082	139426	147414	157425	159146			
CMEA members											
Bulgaria	30659	35917	36442	30145	30732						
Czechoslovakia	6137	5881	6034	5865	5997	6174	6309	6481			a
East Germany		228816	237395	225956	262088	279428	297248	299336			c
Hungary	143278	172017	161944	160819	200391	213097	226573	211885			c
Poland	9308	10475	9318	7040	9050	9574	10098	9236			a
Romania		3683									a
USSR	6896	8157	8003	8458	9581						a
Others											
Albania											
Cyprus	701	1282	1505	1807	2123	2436	2687	2752	2812		b
Gibraltar	184	294	319	292	333	363	436				
Liechtenstein	450	645	651	687	719	753	787	835			
Malta	788	1649	1749	1573	2038	2135	2440	2692			
Monaco	911	1409	1970	4415	4254						a
Turkey	5233	5818	6812	8078	10945	10434	14022	18204	17684		a
Yugoslavia	14054	13110	13237	13380	13500	15004	18052	17344			a

Source:	UIT/Statistical Offices
Notes:	a International traffic only
	b '000 calls
	c '000 pulses

TABLE 2001: TELEPHONES IN USE
1987 including Euromonitor estimates

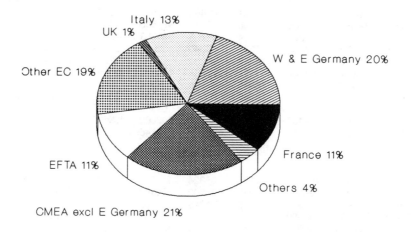

Italy 13%
UK 1%
Other EC 19%
W & E Germany 20%
EFTA 11%
France 11%
Others 4%
CMEA excl E Germany 21%

TABLE 2002: TELEPHONE TRAFFIC
1988: including Euromonitor estimates

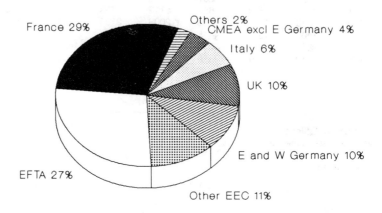

France 29%
Others 2%
CMEA excl E Germany 4%
Italy 6%
UK 10%
E and W Germany 10%
Other EEC 11%
EFTA 27%

Database name: Automotives
Sector name: Registrations

Table No: 2101

Title: New Registrations of Passenger Cars 1977-1989

Unit: 000s

	1977	1980	1982	1983	1984	1985	1986	1987	1988	1989	Note
EC members											
Belgium	428.8	407.2	362.2	356.5	370.0	378.2	395.0	406.3	427.2	461.0	b
Denmark	141.2	73.8	85.4	116.2	134.3	157.5	169.4	129.4	88.6	78.0	b
France	1907.0	1873.2	2056.5	2017.6	1757.7	1766.3	1911.5	2105.2	2217.1	2274.0	b
West Germany	2561.3	2426.2	2155.5	2426.8	2393.9	2379.3	2829.4	2915.7	2807.9	2832.0	b
Greece			80.0	75.2	85.9	109.4	65.2	50.5	57.6	50.0	
Ireland	82.3	91.7	73.3	61.1	55.9	60.4	59.8	55.7	60.8	78.0	a
Italy	1291.2	1530.5	1851.2	1581.0	1634.9	1745.9	1825.4	1976.5	2184.3	2362.0	b
Luxembourg			25.2	26.1	26.4	26.9	29.1	29.8	30.7	30.0	
Netherlands	551.9	450.1	407.0	459.4	461.4	495.7	560.5	555.7	482.6	496.0	b
Portugal	76.5	58.4	85.2	92.3	85.6	104.2	114.2	129.2	227.1	193.0	b
Spain	662.9	574.1	535.7	550.4	522.2	575.1	689.1	796.0	998.0	1121.0	a,c
United Kingdom	1323.5	1513.8	1555.0	1791.7	1749.6	1832.0	1882.5	2013.7	2215.6	2301.0	b
EFTA members											
Austria	295.9	227.5	201.2	256.7	215.6	242.7	262.2	243.2	253.1	276.0	a
Finland	90.1	103.2	128.0	119.4	127.0	138.3	143.2	152.3	173.5	177.0	b
Iceland			8.6	4.7	7.1	5.7	13.4	18.1	12.2		d
Norway	145.2	95.6	115.6	109.7	107.2	159.1	167.4	115.1	67.8	55.0	b
Sweden	241.4	192.6	218.4	217.1	231.1	263.0	271.1	316.0	344.0	314.0	b
Switzerland	234.2	280.5	290.9	273.9	267.5	265.5	300.2	303.3	319.4	320.0	a
CMEA members											
Bulgaria						48.0		61.7	57.2		
Czechoslovakia											
East Germany											
Hungary				89.1	92.0	101.3	121.1	147.1	128.3		d
Poland				292.2	274.1	259.9	263.7	260.7	268.7		
Romania											
USSR											
Others											
Albania											
Cyprus			11.4	12.0	10.8	12.2	10.2	8.5	11.8		
Gibraltar						2.0	2.3	2.2			
Liechtenstein											
Malta			4.4	3.1	2.3	4.1	4.0	5.6	9.2		
Monaco											
Turkey						63.9	103.8	105.8	116.3		
Yugoslavia			175.3	190.8	207.6	151.4	138.9	159.5	190.1		e

Source: Society of Motor Manufacturers & Traders Ltd (SMMT)
World Automotive Statistics/Motor trades organisations

Notes:
a From national statistics
b From trade association
c Includes Canary Is., Ceuta, Melilla
d Figures refer to new imports
e Sales of domestic production/assembly only

	1977	1980	1981	1982	1983	1984	1985	1986	1987	1988	Notes
EC members											
Belgium	28.4	32.5	28.1	26.7	27.3	26.8	31.9	36.4	41.0	42.0	b
Denmark	34.9	19.5	16.3	18.3	22.2	32.2	38.5	44.7	38.0	23.0	b
France	298.4	323.3	334.5	362.7	346.3	316.1	342.2	390.6	418.0	429.0	b
West Germany	138.0	175.5	148.6	123.6	144.1	130.5	134.6	143.3	153.0	161.0	b
Greece				46.0	32.0	23.2	19.0	14.8	16.0	20.0	
Ireland	9.5	12.2	12.2	10.7	12.0	13.7	16.2	14.8	13.0	16.0	a
Italy	110.1	122.3	140.0	144.8	101.9	97.6	100.7	105.4	124.0	144.0	b
Luxembourg			1.6	1.5	1.3	3.0	3.4	3.9	5.0	5.0	
Netherlands	43.3	48.0	42.7	39.0	38.8	48.9	63.1	80.2	85.0	60.0	b
Portugal	32.8	47.0	53.3	52.2	27.2	21.5	23.1	32.1	50.0	57.0	b
Spain	101.3	104.5	91.0	100.9	111.4	98.0	122.0	147.0	205.0	246.0	a,c
United Kingdom	230.9	272.0	217.8	231.0	267.8	269.0	286.7	291.2	315.0	357.0	b
EFTA members											
Austria	18.7	21.8	19.9	18.2	20.3	21.1	22.3	23.4	26.0	30.0	a
Finland	13.2	17.7	18.2	18.4	18.7	18.1	19.0	20.1	23.0	28.0	b
Iceland			1.4	1.2	0.8	0.8	0.8	0.5	1.0	1.0	d
Norway	17.2	15.1	19.2	22.2	25.2	28.0	42.5	43.1	32.0	23.0	b
Sweden	19.9	19.7	18.8	18.8	18.1	20.3	22.9	24.6	31.0	37.0	b
Switzerland	10.8	22.4	22.3	20.3	18.6	19.5	20.5	23.6	25.0	28.0	a
CMEA members											
Bulgaria											
Czechoslovakia											
East Germany											
Hungary					23.0	25.0	27.0	25.0	25.0	17.0	d
Poland					47.0	58.0	39.0	50.0	51.0	54.0	
Romania											
USSR											
Others											
Albania											
Cyprus			3.7	5.8	8.0	5.2	5.4	4.3	5.0	6.0	
Gibraltar											
Liechtenstein											
Malta			1.5	1.7	0.6	0.6	0.6	0.3	0.5	0.5	
Monaco											
Turkey							25.2	25.4	16.8	15.0	
Yugoslavia			22.1	21.3	24.6	22.4	23.8	24.4	24.0	23.0	e

Source: Society of Motor Manufacturers & Traders Ltd (SMMT)
World Automotive Statistics/Motor trades organisations

Notes:
a From national statistics
b From trade association
c Includes Canary Is., Ceuta, Melilla
d Figures refer to new imports
e Sales of domestic production/assembly only

Database name: Automotives
Sector name: Vehicle Production

Table No: 2103

Title: Production of Passenger Cars 1977-1988

Unit: 000s

	1977	1980	1981	1982	1983	1984	1985	1986	1987	1988	Not
EC members											
Belgium	1053.6	882.0	852.0	950.4	972.3	865.3	986.2	1021.6	1123.4		
Denmark											
France	3092.4	2938.6	2611.9	2777.1	2960.8	2713.3	2632.4	2773.1	3051.8	3234.0	
West Germany	3790.5	3520.9	3577.8	3761.4	3877.6	3790.2	4166.7	4310.8	4373.6	4346.3	
Greece											
Ireland	49.9	44.6	35.7	26.5	23.0						
Italy	1440.5	1445.2	1257.3	1297.4	1395.5	1439.3	1389.2	1652.5	1713.3	1884.3	
Luxembourg											
Netherlands	53.4	80.8	77.9	90.6	105.6	108.6	108.1	119.0	125.2	119.8	
Portugal	72.6	45.5	60.9	64.8	65.9	61.2	61.0	62.1	70.8	71.1	
Spain	989.0	1028.8	855.3	927.5	1141.6	1176.9	1230.1	1281.9	1402.6	1498.0	
United Kingdom	1327.8	923.7	954.7	887.7	1044.6	908.9	1048.0	1019.0	1143.0	1226.8	
EFTA members											
Austria		7.5	7.1	7.1	6.1	5.6	7.1	6.8	7.0	7.3	
Finland	23.0	21.5	22.8	30.0	33.6	33.3	38.7	43.0	45.9	42.5	
Iceland											
Norway											
Sweden	235.4	235.3	258.3	294.8	344.7	352.6	400.7	421.3	431.8	407.1	
Switzerland											
CMEA members											
Bulgaria							15.0	20.0	20.0	14.7	
Czechoslovakia	159.0	185.0	182.0	175.5	177.5	173.7	177.1	184.7	172.4	159.2	
East Germany	167.0	176.8	180.2	182.9	188.3	202.0	210.4	217.9	217.1		
Hungary											
Poland	296.2	364.5	240.3	228.3	270.2	279.1	283.0	295.3	296.8	296.3	
Romania	68.1	79.3	90.9	103.7	90.2	107.2	114.4	105.4	129.3		
USSR	1280.0	1327.0	1324.0	1307.0	1317.7	1300.0	1305.0	1300.0	1306.5	1318.9	
Others											
Albania											
Cyprus											
Gibraltar											
Liechtenstein											
Malta											
Monaco											
Turkey		31.5	25.3	31.2	42.5	54.8	60.4	82.0	107.2	120.8	
Yugoslavia	231.1	255.2	239.6	211.4	210.1	236.0	217.8	239.8	288.1	294.1	

Source: SMMT/Motor trades organisations
Notes: Includes vehicles assembled in each country

Database name: Automotives
Sector name: Vehicle Production

Table No: 2104

Title: Production of Commercial Vehicles 1977-1988

Unit: 000s

	1977	1980	1981	1982	1983	1984	1985	1986	1987	1988	Notes
EC members											
Belgium	80.1	47.0	42.1	47.3	36.5	52.1	48.7	73.2	72.3	90.5	
Denmark											
France	415.4	439.9	407.5	371.7	375.0	348.9	383.7	421.5	441.4	474.5	
West Germany	313.7	357.6	319.2	301.2	276.8	255.3	279.2	286.1	260.4	279.0	
Greece											
Ireland	2.5	2.6									
Italy	144.1	165.1	176.4	155.7	179.6	161.9	183.8	179.2	199.3	226.7	
Luxembourg											
Netherlands	34.5	32.1	12.2	13.6	11.8	13.6	14.3	15.4	17.6	29.1	a
Portugal	33.5	58.4	57.9	54.1	29.1	23.1	26.5	33.9	48.5	60.5	
Spain	140.7	152.8	132.1	142.0	147.1	131.9	187.5	250.7	301.9	368.5	
United Kingdom	386.4	389.2	229.6	268.8	244.5	224.8	266.0	228.7	246.7	318.0	
EFTA members											
Austria	8.2	8.5	7.8	8.1	6.1	5.4	11.2	11.9	10.3	10.6	
Finland		1.1	1.0	0.7	0.7	0.7	0.8	0.7	0.8	0.8	
Iceland											
Norway											
Sweden	51.5	63.1	55.5	54.3	52.0	59.0	60.3	65.9	70.0	76.5	
Switzerland	1.3	1.2	1.0	0.8							
CMEA members											
Bulgaria					2.5	2.5	2.7	2.6	2.7	2.4	
Czechoslovakia	44.9	53.0	46.0	50.6	52.7	55.5	57.7	50.2	51.3	55.2	
East Germany	37.2	39.8	42.4	41.2	41.2	44.8	47.3	46.5	43.7		
Hungary	14.0	15.2	12.0	12.7	13.3	15.2	14.0	16.1	14.6	14.5	
Poland	113.5	116.0	98.7	47.9	51.4	55.1	57.1	59.4	60.8	61.8	b
Romania	46.4	49.1	19.5	22.8	18.2	17.9	19.8	19.0	17.1		
USSR	808.0	872.0	873.5	865.7	860.4	600.0	610.0	600.0	610.0	600.0	
Others											
Albania											
Cyprus											
Gibraltar											
Liechtenstein											
Malta											
Monaco											
Turkey		19.4	21.9	27.3	34.4	36.8	37.3	30.9	31.7	28.9	
Yugoslavia	26.6	28.5	26.9	29.9	37.9	36.4	40.5	41.9	36.4	36.3	

Source: SMMT/Motor trades organisations
Notes: a New series from 1981
b Includes agricultural tractors

Database name: Automotives
Sector name: Circulation

Table No: 2105

Title: Passenger Cars in Use 1977-1989

Unit: 000s

	1977	1978	1979	1980	1981	1982	1983	1984	19
EC members									
Belgium	2871.3	2973.4	3076.4	3158.7	3206.5	3231.0	3262.7	3300.2	3342
Denmark	1374.9	1407.7	1423.4	1389.5	1366.9	1358.2	1390.3	1440.0	1500
France	16990.0	17720.0	18440.0	19150.0	19750.0	20300.0	20600.0	20800.0	20940
West Germany	20377.2	21619.7	22613.5	23236.1	23680.9	24035.9	24688.8	25377.6	26099
Greece	618.8	650.0	839.3	879.8	900.0	999.3	1073.4	1100.0	1188
Ireland	572.7	638.7	683.0	734.4	774.6	709.0	718.6	711.1	709
Italy	16466.2	16240.9	17073.2	17686.2	18603.4	19616.1	20388.6	21000.0	21500
Luxembourg	141.4	153.1	164.0	147.4	173.1	159.6	145.8	151.6	152
Netherlands	3851.0	4016.0	4313.0	4515.0	4595.0	4630.0	4728.0	4818.0	4901
Portugal	862.0	888.0	912.0	941.0	990.0	1040.0	1092.0	1136.0	1185
Spain	5944.9	6530.4	7057.5	7556.5	7943.3	8354.1	8714.1	8874.4	9273
United Kingdom	14372.8	14417.0	14926.6	15437.7	15632.7	16074.7	16611.5	17313.4	19458
EC total	84443.2	87254.9	91521.9	94832.3	97616.4	100507.9	103413.8	106022.3	110250
EFTA members									
Austria	1965.3	2040.3	2138.7	2247.0	2312.9	2361.1	2414.5	2468.5	2530
Finland	1075.4	1115.3	1169.5	1225.9	1279.2	1352.1	1410.4	1464.4	1546
Iceland	67.0	73.0	80.0	80.0	82.0	94.7	96.0	96.0	100
Norway	1106.6	1146.9	1189.8	1233.6	1278.8	1337.9	1383.4	1429.7	1514
Sweden	2857.1	2856.2	2868.3	2883.0	2893.2	2936.0	3006.8	3081.0	3151
Switzerland	1932.8	2055.0	2154.3	2246.8	2394.5	2473.3	2520.6	2552.1	2617
EFTA total	9004.2	9286.7	9600.6	9916.3	10240.6	10555.1	10831.7	11091.7	11459
CMEA members									
Bulgaria	480.0	480.0	480.0	500.0	500.0	600.0	600.0	600.0	600
Czechoslovakia	1560.0	1700.0	1900.0	1950.0	2000.0	2487.8	2551.2	2575.0	2575
East Germany	2236.7	2392.3	2500.0	2532.9	2677.7	2812.0	2850.0	3157.1	3306
Hungary	738.0	834.0	839.1	925.0	1105.5	1105.0	1258.5	1344.1	1435
Poland	1290.1	1300.0	2002.4	2269.9	2534.0	2634.0	2900.0	3425.8	3450
Romania	200.0	220.0	235.0	250.0	250.0	250.0	250.0	250.0	250
USSR	3000.0	5000.0	7000.0	7000.0	8250.0	9500.0	10500.0	10500.0	11000
CMEA total	9504.8	11926.3	14956.5	15427.8	17317.2	19388.8	20909.7	21852.0	22617
Others									
Albania									
Cyprus	71.5	78.8	86.2	92.0	109.1	104.5	110.6	118.1	120
Gibraltar	5.6	6.0	6.5	6.5	6.6	7.9	8.7	8.7	8
Liechtenstein									
Malta	56.0	64.3	66.5	66.2	67.0	70.0	79.8	80.0	75
Monaco									
Turkey	471.5	602.0	658.7	700.0	700.0	760.0	825.0	825.0	983
Yugoslavia	1923.9	2142.5	2284.7	2416.9	2562.7	2698.6	2770.7	2872.6	2849
Total	2528.5	2893.6	3102.6	3281.6	3445.4	3641.0	3794.8	3904.4	4036
European total	105480.7	111361.5	119181.6	123458.0	128619.6	134092.8	138950.0	142870.4	148363

Source: SMMT/Motor trades organisations
Notes: a Estimated (SMMT) - may refer only to some years in each country
b Included with Switzerland

Database name: Automotives
Sector name: Circulation

Table No: 2105

Title: Passenger Cars in Use 1977-1989

Unit: 000s

	1986	1987	1988	1989	% growth 1977-88	% share 1977	% share 1988	Notes
EC members								
Belgium	3360.3	3497.8	3573.3	3697.0	24.4	2.7	2.2	
Denmark	1557.9	1587.6	1596.1	1606.0	16.1	1.3	1.0	
France	21250.0	21970.0	22520.0	23100.0	32.5	16.1	13.6	
West Germany	27223.8	28304.2	29190.3	29950.0	43.2	19.3	17.6	
Greece	1301.1	1378.5	1437.7	1450.0	132.3	0.6	0.9	a
Ireland	711.1	736.6	749.5	760.0	30.9	0.5	0.5	
Italy	22000.0	22500.0	23500.0	24500.0	42.7	15.6	14.2	
Luxembourg	156.0	162.5	162.5	165.0	14.9	0.1	0.1	
Netherlands	4950.0	5117.7	5250.6	5385.0	36.3	3.7	3.2	
Portugal	1236.0	1290.0	1427.0	1474.0	65.5	0.8	0.9	
Spain	9643.4	9750.0	10500.0	11250.0	76.6	5.6	6.3	
United Kingdom	19390.2	20605.5	21347.7	22100.0	48.5	13.6	12.9	a
EC total	112779.8	116900.4	121254.7	125437.0	43.6	80.1	73.3	
EFTA members								
Austria	2609.4	2684.8	2784.8	2903.0	41.7	1.9	1.7	
Finland	1619.8	1698.7	1795.9	1900.0	67.0	1.0	1.1	
Iceland	104.4	105.0	133.7		99.6	0.1	0.1	a
Norway	1592.2	1623.1	1622.0	1620.0	46.6	1.0	1.0	
Sweden	3253.6	3366.6	3482.7	3578.0	21.9	2.7	2.1	
Switzerland	2678.9	2732.7	2745.5	2760.0	42.0	1.8	1.7	
EFTA total	11858.3	12210.9	12564.6	12761.0	39.5	8.5	7.6	
CMEA members								
Bulgaria	750.1	775.0	1000.0		108.3	0.5	0.6	a
Czechoslovakia	2700.0	2700.0	2750.0		76.3	1.5	1.7	a
East Germany	3722.0	3462.2	3743.6		67.4	2.1	2.3	
Hungary	1510.0	1660.3	1789.6		142.5	0.7	1.1	
Poland	3600.0	3650.0	4519.0		250.3	1.2	2.7	a
Romania	260.0	850.0	850.0		325.0	0.2	0.5	a
USSR	11500.0	11750.0	12500.0		316.7	2.8	7.6	
CMEA total	24042.1	24847.5	27152.2		185.7	9.0	16.4	
Others								
Albania								
Cyprus	125.0	130.0	164.7		130.3	0.1	0.1	a
Gibraltar	9.0	9.5	11.0		96.4	0.0	0.0	a
Liechtenstein								b
Malta	80.0	80.0	89.5		59.8	0.1	0.1	a
Monaco								
Turkey	1052.0	1087.8	1175.0		149.2	0.4	0.7	
Yugoslavia	2935.3	2972.8	3023.7		57.2	1.8	1.8	
Total	4201.3	4280.1	4463.9		76.5	2.4	2.7	
European total	152881.5	158238.9	165435.4		56.8	100.0	100.0	

Database name: Automotives
Sector name: Circulation

Table No: 2106

Title: Commercial Vehicles in Use 1977-1988

Unit: 000s

	1977	1978	1979	1980	1981	1982	1983	1984	198
EC members									
Belgium	330.1	332.8	344.6	354.5	339.7	340.1	344.0	347.5	356.
Denmark	268.8	271.9	271.1	260.1	250.4	244.1	244.4	252.7	267.
France	2340.0	2440.0	2550.0	2570.0	2716.0	2890.0	3230.0	3310.0	3426.
West Germany	1412.7	1477.6	1548.3	1616.7	1646.2	1647.8	1673.7	1693.3	1722.
Greece	276.1	316.0	367.2	418.7	430.0	532.4	555.7	560.0	565.
Ireland	59.5	65.1	66.9	70.2	72.2	74.5	76.9	91.5	101.
Italy	1283.3	1285.0	1286.6	1428.8	1547.4	1641.7	1764.4	1833.0	1824.
Luxembourg	15.3	15.0	15.0	15.5	15.9	14.9	14.5	14.3	14.
Netherlands	337.0	337.0	361.0	376.0	386.0	388.0	390.0	405.0	428.
Portugal	198.5	214.5	233.0	264.0	298.0	331.0	341.0	346.0	356.
Spain	1157.7	1231.6	1303.3	1380.9	1440.1	1504.9	1572.8	1486.0	1570.
United Kingdom	1911.7	1854.7	1932.8	1912.8	1880.2	1849.5	1697.0	1595.3	1650.
EC total	9590.7	9841.2	10279.8	10668.2	11022.1	11458.9	11904.4	11934.6	12281.
EFTA members									
Austria	176.6	183.9	195.4	208.2	215.9	219.6	224.6	232.5	232.
Finland	152.2	155.5	160.1	166.9	173.4	180.6	182.5	192.2	200.
Iceland	8.5	8.5	9.0	9.0	9.0	12.0	12.0	12.0	12.
Norway	153.2	156.6	163.1	164.5	171.7	180.6	194.6	214.1	249.
Sweden	181.9	185.5	190.5	194.4	199.3	206.7	215.3	223.6	231.
Switzerland	151.7	163.5	171.5	180.5	179.0	189.7	201.2	203.6	211.
EFTA total	824.1	853.5	889.6	923.5	948.3	989.2	1030.2	1078.0	1137.
CMEA members									
Bulgaria	110.0	110.0	130.0	130.0	130.0	150.0	150.0	150.0	150.
Czechoslovakia	290.0	320.0	350.0	370.0	375.0	395.0	402.7	405.0	405.
East Germany	570.0	600.7	645.0	613.2	400.0	410.0	425.0	408.9	416.
Hungary	146.0	160.0	180.4	190.0	147.3	152.0	197.5	213.4	216.
Poland	524.2	540.0	565.0	650.0	725.0	740.0	750.0	811.9	815.
Romania	100.0	110.0	125.0	130.0	130.0	150.0	150.0	150.0	150.
USSR	4500.0	5500.0	6500.0	6500.0	7300.0	8000.0	8500.0	8750.0	9000.
CMEA total	6240.2	7340.7	8495.4	8583.2	9207.3	9997.0	10575.2	10889.2	11152.
Others									
Albania									
Cyprus	17.4	18.7	21.3	25.2	33.9	35.0	38.9	43.9	45.
Gibraltar	0.6	0.7	0.7	0.7	0.7	1.3	1.0	1.0	1.
Liechtenstein									
Malta	15.5	14.9	15.6	14.2	15.0	15.0	18.8	19.0	17.
Monaco									
Turkey	307.7	407.0	401.3	400.0	442.3	450.0	475.0	475.0	500.
Yugoslavia	276.6	300.8	317.2	237.6	253.1	265.3	261.5	269.8	299.
Total	617.8	742.1	756.1	677.7	745.0	766.6	795.2	808.7	862.
European total	17272.8	18777.5	20420.9	20852.6	21922.7	23211.7	24305.0	24710.5	25434.

Source: SMMT/Motor trades organisations
Notes:
a Estimated (not necessarily for each year)
b Included with Switzerland

Database name: Automotives
Sector name: Circulation

Table No: 2106

Title: Commercial Vehicles in Use 1977-1988

Unit: 000s

	1986	1987	1988	% growth 1977-88	% share 1977	% share 1986	Notes
EC members							
Belgium	353.1	382.7	363.2	10.0	1.9	1.2	
Denmark	283.1	294.6	301.7	12.2	1.6	1.0	
France	3546.0	4223.0	4570.0	95.3	13.5	15.1	
West Germany	1759.9	1813.8	1858.9	31.6	8.2	6.1	
Greece	600.0	627.2	675.0	144.5	1.6	2.2	a
Ireland	109.6	119.4	127.4	114.1	0.3	0.4	
Italy	1856.0	1897.0	1990.0	55.1	7.4	6.6	
Luxembourg	14.1	14.9	15.0	-2.0	0.1	0.0	
Netherlands	464.0	506.5	538.2	59.7	2.0	1.8	
Portugal	369.0	393.5	422.0	112.6	1.1	1.4	
Spain	1720.4	1750.0	1975.0	70.6	6.7	6.5	
United Kingdom	1700.0	2915.0	3151.9	64.9	11.1	10.4	a
EC total	12775.2	14937.6	15988.3	55.2	55.5	52.7	
EFTA members							
Austria	244.6	255.4	271.8	53.9	1.0	0.9	
Finland	209.1	221.0	238.3	56.6	0.9	0.8	
Iceland	13.5	13.0	16.8	97.6	0.0	0.1	
Norway	282.8	303.2	313.9	104.9	0.9	1.0	
Sweden	243.7	259.6	281.4	54.7	1.1	0.9	
Switzerland	217.8	228.8	250.8	65.3	0.9	0.8	
EFTA total	1211.5	1281.0	1373.0	66.6	4.8	4.5	
CMEA members							
Bulgaria	150.0	150.0	150.0	36.4	0.6	0.5	a
Czechoslovakia	425.0	425.0	425.0	46.6	1.7	1.4	a
East Germany	420.0	449.1	510.2	-10.5	3.3	1.7	
Hungary	220.0	175.0	179.2	22.7	0.8	0.6	
Poland	825.0	850.0	1012.0	93.1	3.0	3.3	a
Romania	155.0	250.0	250.0	150.0	0.6	0.8	a
USSR	9500.0	9500.0	9000.0	100.0	26.1	29.7	a
CMEA total	11695.0	11799.1	11526.4	84.7	36.1	38.0	
Others							
Albania							
Cyprus	45.0	47.0	65.0	273.6	0.1	0.2	a
Gibraltar	1.1	1.0	1.3	116.7	0.0	0.0	a
Liechtenstein							b
Malta	19.0	19.0	17.2	11.0	0.1	0.1	a
Monaco							
Turkey	525.0	590.6	550.0	78.7	1.8	1.8	
Yugoslavia	301.2	789.4	831.5	200.6	1.6	2.7	
Total	891.3	1447.0	1465.0	137.1	3.6	4.8	
European total	26573.0	29464.7	30352.7	69.4	100.0	100.0	

Database name: Automotives
Sector name: Registrations

Table No: 2107

Title: New Registrations of Diesel Cars 1981-1988

Unit: 000s

	1981	1982	1983	1984	1985	1986	1987	1988	Notes
EC members									
Belgium	63.3	63.5	83.5	103.6	95.0	104.0	109.3	132.3	b
Denmark	2.5	4.1	7.4	10.3	10.4	9.6	6.4	4.1	
France	215.3	221.3	192.8	240.4	264.8	299.4	384.1	522.4	
West Germany	335.0	326.2	270.5	321.8	530.7	775.6	567.5	382.5	
Greece									
Ireland				7.1	8.6	8.6	7.2	7.6	a
Italy	260.8	327.9	295.2	425.9	438.7	449.0	483.5	404.8	b
Luxembourg	2.8	3.0	3.5	3.6	3.5	3.6	3.4	4.2	
Netherlands	36.9	37.2	43.7	60.9	71.3	73.6	72.2	66.6	
Portugal	6.9	5.5	2.2	1.5	2.3	2.4	3.9	8.1	b
Spain	44.9	63.6	102.7	123.5	125.2	95.1	118.2		
United Kingdom	9.7	14.5	24.5	45.4	66.2	77.5	93.2	101.1	
EFTA members									
Austria	8.0	10.9	11.5	13.8	32.2	40.9	50.2	58.1	
Finland	11.2	13.4	15.0	14.1	14.4	12.7	11.4	10.1	
Iceland	0.3	0.3	0.3	0.4	0.4	0.4	0.5		c
Norway	7.4	6.1	4.7	2.7	1.7	1.4	1.0	0.8	
Sweden	12.6	13.5	11.7	9.5	5.7	3.4	4.0	3.0	
Switzerland	3.9	4.8	4.6	7.1	9.3	12.0	17.6	12.1	

CMEA members
Bulgaria
Czechoslovakia
East Germany
Hungary
Poland
Romania
USSR

Others
Albania
Cyprus
Gibraltar
Liechtenstein
Malta
Monaco
Turkey
Yugoslavia

Source: SMMT/Motor trades organisations
Notes:
a Not collated separately prior to 1984
b Sales figures
c Imports

	1982	1983	1984	1985	1986	1987	1988
Database name:	Automotives						
Sector name:	Two-Wheeler Production				Table No:	2108	
Title:	Production of Two-Wheelers 1982-1988						
Unit:	000s						

	1982	1983	1984	1985	1986	1987	1988
EC members							
Belgium		53.2	55.8	58.3	47.0	48.7	
Denmark							
France	503.5	578.5	449.3	448.4	291.2	280.0	311.6
West Germany	70.2	136.8	115.3	84.9	63.6	59.8	49.1
Greece							
Ireland							
Italy	596.5	529.0					
Luxembourg							
Netherlands	6.1	8.0	6.5	7.4	28.9	28.9	28.9
Portugal							
Spain	166.5	179.2	177.2	173.5	182.6	255.4	265.7
United Kingdom							
EFTA members							
Austria	123.4	124.8	134.4	148.7	98.7	55.7	23.0
Finland	16.3	15.4	15.0	14.8			
Iceland							
Norway							
Sweden							
Switzerland							
CMEA members							
Bulgaria	130.6	103.8	94.4				
Czechoslovakia				218.9	201.1		
East Germany							
Hungary							
Poland	150.0	162.0	155.0	142.5	113.0	117.0	106.0
Romania							
USSR							
Others							
Albania							
Cyprus							
Gibraltar							
Liechtenstein							
Malta							
Monaco							
Turkey							
Yugoslavia				76.0	78.0		

Source: International Road Federation

Database name: Automotives
Sector name: Circulation

Table No: 2109

Title: Two-Wheelers Use in 1982-1988

Unit: 000s in use at 31 December

	1982	1983	1984	1985	1986	1987	1988	Notes
EC members								
Belgium	401.6	183.1	124.8	124.3	134.5	133.5		a
Denmark	207.8	209.4	199.2	186.4	191.3			
France	5250.0	5150.0	5065.0	4030.0	3675.0	3370.0		
West Germany	2882.2	2949.8	2894.7	2868.3	2688.7	2519.9	2429.9	
Greece	164.7	163.7	153.5	169.0				
Ireland	25.7	25.2	26.3	26.0	25.7	25.8	24.9	
Italy	4523.2	5231.5	5464.0	5673.0	5727.8	6285.0		
Luxembourg	2.0	2.2	2.5	2.6	2.8	2.8	2.8	
Netherlands			784.0	662.0	691.0	695.0	635.0	
Portugal	97.9	100.1	101.8	103.1	106.9			
Spain	1282.9	1310.0		1389.1	2339.1	2621.3	2656.2	
United Kingdom	1370.0	1290.0	1225.0	1048.0	1065.0	978.0	912.0	
EFTA members								
Austria	634.8	638.5	645.7	648.3	629.1	610.1	601.3	
Finland	208.9	205.2	200.8	196.0	182.0	181.0	177.0	
Iceland	0.8	0.8	0.8	0.9	0.9	0.9	1.0	b
Norway	164.1	167.6	176.1	186.6	199.0	199.1	202.9	
Sweden	16.8	19.0	22.0	26.3	29.0	31.0	32.5	
Switzerland	834.5	861.8	846.7	862.1	853.2	853.2	834.1	
CMEA members								
Bulgaria	423.0	422.8	420.0	469.0	406.0	478.2	490.2	
Czechoslovakia								
East Germany								
Hungary	630.1	422.0		395.6				
Poland	1616.2	1624.2	1664.0	1546.5	1515.2	1470.1	1464.1	
Romania								
USSR								
Others								
Albania								
Cyprus	39.5	40.8	43.3	40.0	41.4	43.4		
Gibraltar	1.2	1.3	1.4	1.5	1.8			
Liechtenstein								
Malta								
Monaco	4.0	4.1	4.1	4.0	4.2			
Turkey						354.1	411.1	
Yugoslavia	167.1	158.3	157.8	112.7	102.2			

Source: International Road Federation
Notes:
a New series from 1983
b Excluding mopeds

Database name: Automotives
Sector name: Two-Wheeler Registrations

Table No: 2110

Title: New Registrations of Two-Wheelers 1982-1988

Unit: 000s

	1982	1983	1984	1985	1986	1987	1988	Notes
EC members								
Belgium	11.0	10.6	8.5	7.5	6.6	6.5		
Denmark	2.8	3.8	3.2	2.6	2.0	2.0		
France	116.9	98.3	78.6	71.6	84.7	91.8	102.4	a
West Germany		128.5	104.0	84.4	81.3	86.9	85.5	
Greece	19.0	18.5	14.9	14.6				
Ireland	4.2	4.0	4.1	4.1	3.5	3.2	2.7	
Italy	762.0	635.1						
Luxembourg				0.5				
Netherlands	54.6	51.3	58.1	54.0	65.3	71.3		
Portugal			1.8	1.4	3.8	6.1	6.7	
Spain					45.2	60.2	63.2	a
United Kingdom					126.0	91.0	90.0	
EFTA members								
Austria	56.1	56.5	42.9	38.2	37.2	29.6	26.9	
Finland	4.0	4.9	4.5	4.4	3.6	3.3	3.7	a
Iceland								
Norway	16.8	11.6	14.3	23.6	26.5	19.9	14.7	
Sweden	31.5	28.1	22.2	11.3	8.1	7.3	7.3	a
Switzerland	31.2	29.9	31.2	31.2	33.0	29.8	28.6	
CMEA members								
Bulgaria				16.0		17.5	8.6	
Czechoslovakia								
East Germany								
Hungary								
Poland	78.7	104.6	76.9	50.0	48.0	47.4	42.6	
Romania								
USSR								
Others								
Albania								
Cyprus	5.0	4.8	4.8	4.3	3.2	4.1	5.6	
Gibraltar								
Liechtenstein								
Malta								
Monaco								
Turkey	22.2	12.4					57.0	
Yugoslavia			14.3	12.3	7.0	7.6		

Source: International Road Federation
Notes: a Excludes mopeds

409

TABLE 2103: CAR PRODUCTION
1988

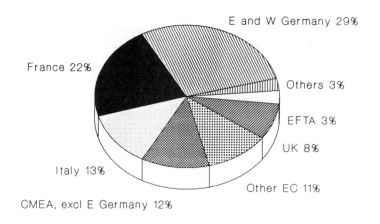

E and W Germany 29%

France 22%

Others 3%

EFTA 3%

UK 8%

Italy 13%

Other EC 11%

CMEA, excl E Germany 12%

TABLE 2101: NEW CAR REGISTRATIONS
1989: EC and EFTA only

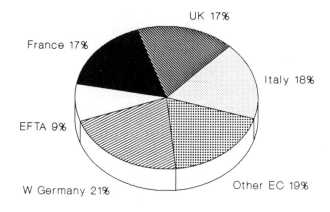

UK 17%

France 17%

Italy 18%

EFTA 9%

W Germany 21%

Other EC 19%

			Highway	Secondary	Others		Density	
	Total	Motorway	(National)	(Regional)	(Local)	% Paved	(Km per Km2)	Notes

Database name: Transport Infrastructure
Sector name: Road Transport

Table No: 2201

Title: Road Network 1988 (End of Year)

Unit: Kilometres

	Total	Motorway	Highway (National)	Secondary (Regional)	Others (Local)	% Paved	Density (Km per Km2)	Notes
EC members								
Belgium	128319	1567	12902	13850	100000	96.00	4.20	f
Denmark	70666	599	3958	7085	59024	100.00	1.63	
France	805070	6570	28500	350000	420000	100.00	1.46	a
West Germany	493590	8618	31196	63393	390383	99.00	1.97	f
Greece	106306	92	8700	28700	68814	83.40	0.80	d,e
Ireland	92303	8	5255	10566	76474	94.00	1.31	
Italy	301846	5997	45779	108404	141666	100.00	1.00	e
Luxembourg	5085	75	866	1828	2316	99.00	2.00	
Netherlands	115305	2060	2058	8692	102495	88.00	2.76	
Portugal	19052	238	18814					f
Spain	318022	2142	18421	130274	167185	56.00	0.63	
United Kingdom	352296	2981	12425	34900	301990	100.00	1.52	
EFTA members								
Austria	107099	1405	10270	25424	70000	100.00	1.30	
Finland	77509	214	11214	29703	36378	59.00	0.22	
Iceland	11394	0	3812	4460	3122	17.40	0.11	
Norway	87137	74	26031	26859	34173	67.00	0.27	
Sweden	132047	999	14176	84372	32500	70.80	0.40	
Switzerland	71090	1486	18407	51197			1.70	b
CMEA members								
Bulgaria	36897	258	2934	3799	29906	95.30	0.34	
Czechoslovakia	73022	518	9612	17956	44936	100.00	0.57	
East Germany	124610	1855	11330	34025	77400	100.00	1.15	f
Hungary	95234	324	6373	23014	65523	53.50	0.97	
Poland	360629	220	45257	128775	186377	61.00	0.96	
Romania	72816	113	14570	58133		49.00	0.31	f
USSR	1586416		99740	175872	1310804	73.90	0.10	e
Others								
Albania								
Cyprus	12173		3192		8981	48.00	1.29	c,f
Gibraltar								
Liechtenstein								
Malta						92.00	4.64	
Monaco	50		50			100.00	25.26	
Turkey	320611	138	31062	27853	261558	14.20	0.40	d
Yugoslavia	119401	646	16507	31640	70608	58.00	0.47	e

Source: International Road Federation/National Statistical Offices
Notes:
a Total and others exclude 700,000 km rural roads
b Others included in secondary
c Highways includes motorways and secondary
d National roads
e 1986
f 1987

Database name: Transport Infrastructure
Sector name: Road Transport   Table No: 2202

Title: Trends in Car Traffic Volume 1978-1988

Unit: Million car kilometres

	1978	1979	1980	1981	1982	1983	1984	1985	1986	1987	1988
EC members											
Belgium	38400	39741	40861	41594	41581	41632	41745	42101	42562		
Denmark	23800	23100	21800	21500	21200	22000	23100	24200	25300	26800	28100
France	235800	239000	240000	246000	253000	255000	256000	262000	275000	292000	305000
West Germany	279300	291000	297400	282700	294400	304400	314000	313400	338300	356900	376500
Greece	10300	10000									
Ireland	13350	14055	14798								
Italy	182700	189000	190608	197524	208544	199280	205336	213543	219097	230920	
Luxembourg			1382	1417	1618	1539	1999	2191	2438	2500	2613
Netherlands	55500	60600	61400	61000	60300	63100	65300	65000	68100	71230	75931
Portugal				18040	19050	20300	21200	22500			
Spain	48525	51200	52780	53874	55550	55750	56582	56300	61930	64407	69599
United Kingdom	220300	221000	201100	201390	208770	213170	221790	228000	236000	257000	270000
EFTA members											
Austria	25095	25664	25840	21000	26000	26200	27150	27500		41900	
Finland	21400	21900	22200	22600	23400	24200	24900	25970	26840	28640	30730
Iceland	988	962	986	1014							
Norway	14221	14753									
Sweden		36000						52900			53000
Switzerland											
CMEA members											
Bulgaria											10302
Czechoslovakia											
East Germany											
Hungary	12431										
Poland	16519	19053	20494	18440	15849	17484	18842	20193	21790	23274	27115
Romania											
USSR											
Others											
Albania											
Cyprus											
Gibraltar											
Liechtenstein											
Malta											
Monaco											
Turkey	11300		7444	8044	8415	8800			7961	9415	10254
Yugoslavia								24000	25135		

Source: International Road Federation
Notes: UK refers to Great Britain only

Database name: Transport Infrastructure
Sector name: Road Transport   Table No: 2203

Title: Trends in Average Annual Distance Travelled (Cars) 1978-1988

Unit: Kilometres

	1978	1979	1980	1981	1982	1983	1984	1985	1986	1987	1988
EC members											
Belgium	12914	12917	12743	12874	12873	12760	12649	12595	12486		
Denmark	15700	14800	14000	13900	14100	14700	15100	15200	15700	16290	16990
France	13305		13000			12400	12300	12500	13000	13600	13500
West Germany	14700	14400	14300	13300	13600	13800	14000	13600	14100	14300	14600
Greece	13700	11900						16500			
Ireland											
Italy	12600	12000	11400	11300	11200	10000	9900	9900	9900	10000	
Luxembourg			10744	10628	11730	10880					
Netherlands	13700	14360	13800	13565	13860	14220	14460	14680	14830	14980	15430
Portugal					15000						
Spain	7431	7255	6985	6782	6649	9500	9100	9100	9100	9100	9100
United Kingdom	15400	15200	13200	13000	13000	13000	13000	14000	14000	14800	14648
EFTA members											
Austria	12300	12000	11500*	11000	11000	11000	11000	11000		15600	
Finland	19500	19100	18500	18000	17800	17500	17300	17200	17000	17300	17600
Iceland	13600	12300	11800	11500							
Norway	12400	12400			12900	12900	13200	13500	13900	14000	14100
Sweden	12800	12000	12000	12000	12000	12000	12000	12000	12000	12500	12500
Switzerland											
CMEA members											
Bulgaria											8700
Czechoslovakia											
East Germany											
Hungary	15800										
Poland	9000	9000	8600	7000	5500	5500	5500	5500	5500	5500	6000
Romania											
USSR											
Others											
Albania											
Cyprus											
Gibraltar											
Liechtenstein											
Malta											
Monaco											
Turkey											
Yugoslavia	15000	15000	15000	15000	12500	12500	12500	8500	8500		

Source: International Road Federation
Notes: Spain: national roads only
UK: Great Britain only

Database name: Transport Infrastructure
Sector name: Road Transport

Table No: 2204

Title: Trends in Total Goods Transported 1978-1987

Unit: Million tonne-kilometres

	1978	1980	1981	1982	1983	1984	1985	1986	1987
EEC members									
Belgium	15645	16738	17056	17236	17324	19046	19124		
Denmark	12100	9600	8100	8000	8300	8800	9500	10050	
France	105100	115500	111000	108000	103000	105000	106000	110000	119000
West Germany	116300	124400	121700	119800	125300	128400	132200	138500	142500
Greece									
Ireland									
Italy	88022	119629	129136	137071	143441	140494	144129		150648
Luxembourg	259	278		263	198			239	
Netherlands	16614	17663	17871	17375		18366	18431	19249	20225
Portugal		11800			7220				
Spain	88800	94800	95400	91480	92400	111500	108100	116800	118891
United Kingdom	99100	95900	97100	100000	100400	106900	102100	104100	
EFTA members									
Austria	6632	7931	8398	6831	7264	8685			
Finland		17900	17700	19300	21000	20700	22000	20100	21900
Iceland	464								
Norway	4930	5252	5115	5424	5695	6022	6418	7069	
Sweden	20320	21362	20950	21135	21105	22986	21177		22611
Switzerland		5689	6030	6331	6140	6337	6646		
CMEA members									
Bulgaria	9932	10078	11226	10577	7193	7262	7082	7495	7556
Czechoslovakia	18743	21335	21715	20962	20646	20919	11729	12201	12533
East Germany	21225	21020	19920	16236	15378	14491	15056	15293	
Hungary	10350	10258	11759	11883	11951		9716		
Poland	42601	44546	36847	34024	35472	36577	36593	37029	37183
Romania		11756	11792	11150	8260	7300	5957		
USSR		131000	140000	143000	142000	138000	142000		
Others									
Albania									
Cyprus									
Gibraltar									
Liechtenstein									
Malta									
Monaco									
Turkey	39042	37507	39233	40802	42678			54018	58831
Yugoslavia	16873	18997	19673	19267	20528	21540	21814	22340	

Source: International Road Federation
Notes: Spain: On national road network only
UK: Great Britain only
Czechoslovakia, East Germany: public and works goods transport only

Database name:	Transport Infrastructure									
Sector name:	Rail Transport				Table No: 2205					

Title: Length of Public Railway Network Operated (End of Year) 1977-1987

Unit: Kilometres

	1977	1978	1979	1980	1981	1982	1983	1984	1985	1986	1987
EC members											
Belgium	4003	4046	3978	3971	3930	3920	3842	3741	3667	3618	3568
Denmark	2498	2450	2461	2461	2461	2461	2448	2448	2471	2471	2476
France	34150	34096	34032	33886	34107	34108	34193	34688	34676	34663	34646
West Germany	31721	28539	28565	28497	28375	28270	28039	27993	27628	27484	27421
Greece	2479	2479	2479	2479	2479	2479	2479	2479	2479	2461	2461
Ireland	2004	2007	1988	1987	1987	1987	1944	1944	1944	1944	1944
Italy	19890	16391	16439	16480	16503	16473	16404	16349	16114	16068	15983
Luxembourg	274	270	270	270	270	270	270	270	270	270	270
Netherlands	2850	2876	2880	2880	2850	2850	2852	2852	2824	2817	2809
Portugal	3592	3588	3588	3588	3611	3616	3614	3614	3603	3603	3608
Spain	15799	13418	13420	13431	13432	13461	13464	13466	12710	12721	12686
United Kingdom	17973	17901	17735	17645	17431	17229	16964	16816	16752	16670	16630
EFTA members											
Austria	5857	5857	5851	5847	5815	5759	5753	5756	5766	5745	5747
Finland	6089	6079	6101	6096	6089	6090	6090	5998	5900	5899	5884
Iceland											
Norway	4241	4241	4239	4242	4242	4242	4242	4242	4242	4216	4217
Sweden	12077	12074	12006	12006	11952	12362	12323	12063	11745	11715	11194
Switzerland	4995	2921	2921	2926	2934	2941	2960	2969	2969	2969	2990
CMEA members											
Bulgaria	4295	4341	4341	4267	4267	4273	4278	4279	4297	4297	4297
Czechoslovakia	13190	13166	13142	13131	13130	13142	13141	13114	13130	13116	13102
East Germany	14215	14199	14164	14248	14233	14231	14226	14226	14054	14005	14008
Hungary	8063	8001	7950	7826	7829	7823	7824	7830	7837	7836	7628
Poland	23953	23975	24415	24356	24360	24348	24329	24353	24361	24333	24241
Romania	11127	11119	11110	11110	11093	11125	11106	11169			
USSR	228800	228100	234200	239400	240400	242600	244200	246400	247200		
Others											
Albania	330	330	330	330	330	330	330	330	330	330	330
Cyprus											
Gibraltar											
Liechtenstein											
Malta											
Monaco											
Turkey	8139	8139	8132	8193	8193	8156	8169	8169	8169	8170	8169
Yugoslavia	9967	9762	9381	9465	9393	9389	9409	9279	9283	9246	9270

Source: UN/Union Internationale des Chemins de Fer (UIC)

| Database name: | Transport Infrastructure | | | | | | | | | | |
| Sector name: | Rail Transport | | | | Table No: 2206 | | | | | | |

Title: Trends in Railway Passenger-Kilometres 1977-1987

Unit: Million passenger-kilometres

	1977	1978	1979	1980	1981	1982	1983	1984	1985	1986	1987
EC members											
Belgium	7668	7136	6955	6963	7080	6924	6624	6456	6552	6096	6270
Denmark		3484	3315	4456	4482	4496	4391	4421	4508	4536	4782
France	51828	53508	53592	54492	55656	56856	58428	60276	60780	59904	59732
West Germany	36540	38256	40668	41352	41556	36828	39336	38616	41208	41724	39174
Greece	1620	1572	1536	1392	1512	1500	1560	1536	1500	1668	1973
Ireland	876	960	1008	1032	996	828	756	816	948	1008	1196
Italy	38364	39096	39600	39492	39972	39540	36132	39048	37404	40500	41395
Luxembourg	300	300	300	300	312	312	300	288	288	273	216
Netherlands	8016	8148	8520	8916	9240	9372	9048	8940	9228	8916	9396
Portugal	5232	5508	5628	6072	5856	5412	5196	5448	5724	5808	5907
Spain	13104	12792	12672	13524	14526	14642	15096	15567	15972	15600	15394
United Kingdom	29304	30744	32004	31704	30696	27780	30156	30084	29688	30780	33140
EFTA members											
Austria		8351	8454	8643	8333	8541					7363
Finland	2976	2988	3024	3216	3276	3324	3336	3276	3228	2676	3106
Iceland											
Norway	2004	2064	2268	2400	2424	2244	2172	2184	2232	2220	2187
Sweden	5586	5524	6198	7019	7108	6612	6688	6690	6803	6363	6013
Switzerland	9240	8094	8294	9179	9100	9279	9313	9554	9703	9653	10050
CMEA members											
Bulgaria	7344	7140	6852	7056	6960	7092	7260	7536	7788	8040	
Czechoslovakia	19176	18636	18156	18048	17904	19044	18792	19320	19836	19836	20029
East Germany	22356	22320	22284	23136	23028	22704	22608	22920	22452	22356	22522
Hungary	13020	12612	12492	12372	12372	11868	10392	10512	10464	10452	9621
Poland	44316	46716	45468	46320	48240	49272	50148	53184	51984	48528	48285
Romania											
USSR	322200	332124	335304	332064	344580	347856					
Others											
Albania											
Cyprus											
Gibraltar											
Liechtenstein											
Malta											
Monaco											
Turkey	5088	5616	6804	6012	6108	5436	5760	6276	6492	6060	6174
Yugoslavia	10464	10440	10776	10272	10416	10824	11592	11736	12216	12384	11827

Source: UN/Union Internationale des Chemins de Fer (UIC)
Notes: UK: Great Britain only

Database name: Transport Infrastructure
Sector name: Rail Transport

Table No: 2207

Title: Trends in Railway Freight Carried 1977-1987

Unit: Million net tonne-kilometres

	1977	1978	1979	1980	1981	1982	1983	1984	1985	1986	1987
EC members											
Belgium	6492	7116	8532	8004	7536	6792	6864	7884	8256	7416	8564
Denmark		1162	1701	1619	1477	1652	1627	1715	1649	1791	1748
France	66216	67320	70680	69468	64392	61200	59376	60120	58488	52800	52521
West Germany	55752	57264	66156	65292	62040	57264	55920	59844	63876	60468	59331
Greece	852	852	840	816	696	588	672	768	732	708	610
Ireland	600	636	564	576	648	624	540	552	552	528	563
Italy	17580	16644	17736	18384	17112	16908	16752	17868	17964	17472	19490
Luxembourg	564	648	720	660	588	552	504	588	648	600	588
Netherlands	2808	2880	3372	3468	3312	2844	2784	3120	3276	3048	3103
Portugal	888	936	888	996	1008	1056	1044	1236	1308	1452	1648
Spain	11424	10377	10262	10528	10267	10193	10210	11645	14546	13994	14114
United Kingdom	20112	19980	19896	17640	17508	15876	17148	12456	15732	15936	
EFTA members											
Austria		9498	10698	11002	10318	10103	10230	11247	11903	11599	11387
Finland	6408	6336	7368	8340	8388	8004	8088	7980	8064	6948	7481
Iceland											
Norway	2628	2712	3084	3084	2880	2544	2460	2652	2928	3036	2822
Sweden	14782	14764	17347	16648	15410	14331	15445	17776	18420	18553	17761
Switzerland	6324	6516	7308	7752	7152	6504	6408	6888	7044	6972	6812
CMEA members											
Bulgaria	17076	17148	17652	17676	18048	18276	18060	18132	18168	18324	
Czechoslovakia	71544	72360	73044	72636	72264	71580	73068	73992	73596	75156	67985
East Germany	58224	53016	54372	56400	55764	54012	54888	56652	58668	58884	58841
Hungary	23556	23916	24072	23868	23856	22728	22560	22308	21816	22092	21387
Poland	135408	138096	135360	134736	109836	112692	118032	123504	120648	121776	121425
Romania											
USSR	3330900	3429372	3349248	3439860	3503208	3464484	3600000				
Others											
Albania											
Cyprus											
Gibraltar											
Liechtenstein											
Malta											
Monaco											
Turkey	6348	5676	5616	5028	5940	6012	6120	7680	7752	7224	7404
Yugoslavia	22224	23376	26928	24996	25440	25812	27564	28476	28320	27564	26071

Source: UN/UIC
Notes: UK: National railway (Great Britain only)
Sweden: National railway only
Switzerland: National railway only

Database name: Transport Infrastructure
Sector name: Rail Transport
                                            Table No: 2208

Title: Railway Statistics of Major National Carriers 1987

	No. of Locomotives (Units)	Rail Motor Vehicles (Units)	Passengers Carried (Million)	Average Length of Journey (Km)	Total Goods Carried (Million MT)	
EC members						
Belgium	1038	688	142.2	44.1	78.2	
Denmark	391	540	145.8	32.8	7.5	
France	5768	1639	773.0	77.3	149.0	
West Germany	6226	2101	994.2	39.4	278.0	
Greece	214	119	11.7	167.5	3.9	
Ireland	126	80	24.9	48.0	3.0	
Italy	3235	1656	394.2	105.0	54.5	
Luxembourg	85	16	10.5	20.7	14.8	
Netherlands	544	699	222.0	42.3	19.9	
Portugal	319	227	228.0	25.9	6.6	
Spain	1362	719	190.3	80.9	36.2	
United Kingdom	2469	3337	727.2	45.6	144.5	a
EFTA members						
Austria	1225	299	158.9	46.3	56.8	
Finland	691	169	41.3	75.1	30.8	
Iceland						
Norway	384	179	36.7	59.6	19.9	
Sweden	1225	300	70.5	85.3	52.1	
Switzerland	1495	230	276.1	41.5	46.6	
CMEA members						
Bulgaria						
Czechoslovakia	4705	1414	415.8	48.2	291.4	
East Germany	6048	709	603.2	37.4	338.1	
Hungary			198.2	48.0	114.8	
Poland			977.0	49.4	429.0	
Romania						
USSR						
Others						
Albania						
Cyprus						
Gibraltar						
Liechtenstein						
Malta						
Monaco						
Turkey	990	108	129.9	47.5	14.4	
Yugoslavia	1417	443	119.7	98.8	84.2	

Source: Union Internationale des Chemins de Fer (UIC)
Notes: a   Great Britain only, excludes parcels

Title: Trends in Total Distance Flown (Scheduled) 1977-1988

Unit: Million kilometres

	1977	1980	1981	1982	1983	1984	1985	1986	1987	1988
EC members										
Belgium	48.2	54.8	51.2	49.8	48.6	49.6	52.5	52.8	57.3	60.7
Denmark	38.4	33.0	30.6	34.8	32.0	35.9	39.4	42.2	45.0	47.8
France	270.0	276.3	270.5	274.6	275.2	270.8	275.8	288.1	318.3	342.0
West Germany	181.5	196.2	195.4	198.7	208.1	215.3	228.5	253.5	289.6	315.7
Greece	39.2	40.1	40.0	40.4	41.7	47.5	52.8	48.6	51.3	52.0
Ireland	20.0	21.9	20.0	19.7	19.1	20.5	21.1	20.9	23.0	34.5
Italy	137.9	139.2	126.1	129.4	128.9	132.6	142.8	139.3	145.6	145.3
Luxembourg	3.8	2.7	2.0	2.8	2.5	2.6	2.9	3.5	4.0	4.3
Netherlands	99.4	108.8	107.2	113.4	115.6	118.4	121.8	128.6	141.8	152.3
Portugal	34.6	39.2	39.3	39.0	38.0	37.2	37.8	39.7	41.8	48.5
Spain	139.8	164.3	154.7	160.5	158.0	156.5	157.2	154.9	158.1	175.8
United Kingdom	335.7	426.3	396.4	366.8	355.5	387.3	414.5	444.3	474.0	516.8
EC total	1348.5	1502.8	1433.4	1429.9	1423.2	1474.2	1547.1	1616.4	1749.8	1895.7
EFTA members										
Austria	17.7	22.0	23.3	25.6	23.2	23.0	23.1	23.2	27.1	29.3
Finland	28.3	35.5	37.0	37.1	36.6	37.0	38.4	38.1	43.4	48.6
Iceland	14.3	11.1	10.1	12.1	13.6	16.5	17.0	16.9	20.3	20.1
Norway	53.9	58.1	55.3	56.1	59.6	59.0	63.7	70.7	75.4	78.4
Sweden	62.6	66.2	66.5	69.1	74.2	78.8	80.0	90.7	95.1	103.8
Switzerland	89.3	97.8	96.6	102.4	106.0	103.6	106.4	113.4	117.9	129.3
EFTA total	266.1	290.7	288.8	302.4	313.2	317.9	328.6	353.0	379.2	409.5
CMEA members										
Bulgaria	10.6	12.7	12.7	19.5	24.1	25.8	28.4	28.5	30.4	32.4
Czechoslovakia	26.8	24.7	22.8	19.5	20.7	21.6	23.4	23.5	24.3	25.7
East Germany										
Hungary	12.4	16.2	17.6	17.6	16.6	17.6	18.5	18.2	18.2	17.8
Poland	29.4	35.1	30.6	11.8	19.0	22.8	26.2	27.7	27.4	30.1
Romania	19.4	19.7	19.3	17.1	17.7	19.5	20.3	21.0	21.3	21.9
USSR				125.1	122.9	125.0	114.0	113.0	125.0	155.2
CMEA total	98.6	108.4	103.0	210.6	221.0	232.3	230.8	231.9	246.6	283.1
Others										
Albania										
Cyprus	7.0	9.5	8.7	8.8	9.3	10.2	10.3	11.0	11.6	11.8
Gibraltar										
Liechtenstein										
Malta	3.6	6.0	5.9	6.3	5.7	5.1	5.4	6.4	6.5	7.3
Monaco				0.2	0.2	0.3	0.3	0.4	0.4	0.4
Turkey	23.1	14.5	19.7	19.7	21.6	25.1	27.1	29.0	31.6	35.9
Yugoslavia	31.9	34.8	30.5	28.5	27.5	29.8	36.0	39.3	43.5	46.4
Total	65.6	64.8	64.8	63.5	64.3	70.5	79.1	86.1	93.6	101.8
European total	1778.8	1966.7	1890.0	2006.4	2021.7	2094.9	2185.6	2287.4	2469.2	2690.1

Source: International Civil Aviation Organisation (ICAO)

Database name: Transport Infrastructure
Sector name: Civil Aviation

Table No: 2210

Title: Trends in Passenger-kilometres 1979-1988

Unit: Million passenger-kilometres

	1979	1980	1981	1982	1983	1984	1985	1986	1987	1988
EC members										
Belgium	4824	4848	5196	5280	5292	5652	5664	5556	5973	6528
Denmark	3060	3048	2976	2940	3000	3072	3120	3204	3748	3935
France	32784	34128	36504	37608	38316	38472	39252	39240	44443	47799
West Germany	19848	21048	21636	21624	22704	24276	24432	26640	31810	34097
Greece	5136	5064	5196	4920	5328	6300	7464	6384	7122	7531
Ireland	2220	2052	2184	2340	2124	2196	2460	2496	2737	3567
Italy	11508	12396	12072	12576	12612	13644	14580	13992	18647	19168
Luxembourg					100	108	111	115	128	151
Netherlands	14016	14196	15324	15912	16068	17004	18240	19236	22605	24144
Portugal	3924	3432	4008	4140	3960	4236	4236	4476	5014	5673
Spain	15180	15516	15996	16452	16332	17460	18816	19152	20409	22272
United Kingdom	47004	50160	50616	43956	44448	45048	51228	51012	77161	83042
EFTA members										
Austria	1092	1116	1236	1236	1296	1404	1428	1380	1691	2031
Finland	1980	2136	2496	2580	2616	2676	2928	2916	3587	4034
Iceland	1992	1296	1140	1380	1680	2400	2400	2268	2586	2342
Norway	3912	4068	4080	4116	3552	3744	3864	3960	5389	5632
Sweden	5298	5342	5451	5573	5877	6230	6365	6810	7275	7830
Switzerland	10332	10836	11628	11772	12204	12060	12612	12876	13834	14525
CMEA members										
Bulgaria									2100	2279
Czechoslovakia	1740	1536	1464	1596	1632	1692	1860	1872	2063	2242
East Germany										
Hungary	960	1020	1188	1212	1140	1200	1284	1092	1181	1178
Poland	2316	2352	2136	804	1308	1776	2232	2196	2301	2701
Romania	1179	1209	1252	1145	1223	1372	1462	1427	1544	1669
USSR	150708	160296	171324	172212	176484	183276	187608	194352	200123	
Others										
Albania										
Cyprus	684	792	852	852	924	1128	1320	1404	1586	1629
Gibraltar										
Liechtenstein										
Malta	588	600	612	648	564	564	660	744	633	698
Monaco										
Turkey									3269	3497
Yugoslavia							3845	4284	5229	5667

Source: International Civil Aviation Organisation (ICAO)

Database name: Transport Infrastructure
Sector name: Civil Aviation

Table No: 2211

Title: Trends in Freight - Tonne-Kilometres 1979-1988

Unit: Million tonne-kilometres

	1979	1980	1981	1982	1983	1984	1985	1986	1987	1988
EC members										
Belgium	411.1	405.8	444.5	492.2	503.0	541.7	583.4	594.0	535.5	650.5
Denmark	131.7	128.5	132.6	128.6	123.1	127.4	127.7	129.3	108.0	114.4
France	2031.3	2092.9	2239.9	2297.8	2596.6	2893.9	2980.5	3195.5	3385.6	3681.6
West Germany	1585.7	1584.5	1583.7	1687.6	2041.6	2345.3	2498.5	2958.9	3247.7	3470.0
Greece	68.0	68.1	75.1	66.4	74.1	79.1	114.9	101.4	104.3	101.9
Ireland	99.3	91.9	86.4	79.4	91.3	104.4	86.7	79.0	80.8	102.5
Italy	496.2	542.1	492.5	582.0	633.4	710.1	780.0	859.9	911.6	1029.2
Luxembourg									0.4	0.5
Netherlands	912.9	995.5	1100.1	1086.2	1244.9	1455.9	1484.8	1595.8	1734.3	1881.8
Portugal	122.6	111.8	108.6	106.7	105.3	125.6	142.9	133.0	124.6	141.4
Spain	404.8	417.6	454.8	482.2	477.1	517.2	556.8	568.5	564.2	597.9
United Kingdom	1247.6	1369.6	1519.3	1225.5	1355.4	1648.0	1757.6	1878.8	2362.5	3142.3
EFTA members										
Austria	14.5	14.6	17.3	20.3	21.3	23.5	23.4	23.5	23.4	22.9
Finland	46.0	52.8	56.8	66.9	77.2	79.4	84.3	92.9	97.8	100.1
Iceland		23.6	21.4	23.7	27.0	28.6	22.4	25.0	25.8	34.3
Norway	141.1	132.6	143.8	139.1	129.9	134.1	135.1	137.3	115.9	120.8
Sweden	201.5	195.8	201.8	194.9	188.2	195.7	193.4	195.7	169.2	175.0
Switzerland	434.3	453.2	489.9	500.7	565.8	680.2	685.9	722.3	784.5	813.7
CMEA members										
Bulgaria									9.6	9.0
Czechoslovakia	18.0	14.6	14.3	17.1	17.4	16.9	21.2	21.0	20.7	17.2
East Germany										
Hungary	7.8	9.2	9.6	9.2	8.8	8.6	10.3	9.4	7.3	5.8
Poland	18.4	18.8	18.6	6.4	8.0	9.3	10.8	12.0	10.3	13.5
Romania	11.9	10.0	9.3	9.0	6.1	11.2	9.7	10.1	11.6	12.8
USSR	2099.0	2151.8	2240.2	2185.7	2648.2	2744.9	2688.3	2650.4	2827.2	2720.8
Others										
Albania										
Cyprus	26.7	19.8	18.1	19.9	19.1	26.6	25.8	28.1	30.4	26.6
Gibraltar										
Liechtenstein										
Malta	5.4	4.5	4.8	3.8	3.6	3.9	4.8	4.5	4.7	4.7
Monaco										
Turkey									46.9	52.7
Yugoslavia				53.6	58.1	81.4	81.9	100.2	99.1	124.4

Source: International Civil Aviation Organisation (ICAO)

Database name: Transport Infrastructure
Sector name: Civil Aviation

Table No: 2212

Title: National Airlines: Kilometres Flown, Passengers, Goods Carried 1987

	Aircraft Kilometres ('000)	Aircraft Departures (Units)	Aircraft Hours (Units)	Passengers Carried ('000)	Freight Carried ('000 Tonnes)	Passenger Load Factor (%)	Weight Load Factor (%)
EEC members							
Belgium	57300	45914	93833	2362	102	68	71
Denmark	42000	48599	64397	3100	25	69	66
France	219832	163680	348935	13421	470	70	68
West Germany	283400	255291	500569	16889	584	66	67
Greece	51300	81576	104916	6685	63	66	50
Ireland	22500	36659	50510	2279	33	72	68
Italy	108684	103212	193099	9149	179	65	67
Luxembourg	3800						
Netherlands	129500	73106	185099	5909	300	69	70
Portugal	42100	26955	62112	2571	45	71	62
Spain	158100	148965	239832	14102	175	71	66
United Kingdom	263645	204426	420800	19032	263	72	69
EFTA members							
Austria	24800	29282	47863	1732	19	53	48
Finland	43400	65049	75867	3444	32	65	56
Iceland	20300	17539	31446	873	9	76	70
Norway	46299	73945	87795	4218	33	69	66
Sweden	59048	76492	107209	5315	38	70	66
Switzerland	117800	96362	175965	6808	190	64	64
CMEA members							
Bulgaria							
Czechoslovakia	24300	21796	33458	1070	5	71	67
East Germany							
Hungary	18200	17339	25269	1231	8	65	53
Poland	27400	30220	50398	1570	5	74	64
Romania	21300	23652	36927	1281	9	62	41
USSR	125000	52000	159000	118302	3023	87	87
Others							
Albania							
Cyprus	11600	6430	18178	684	10	74	66
Gibraltar							
Liechtenstein							
Malta	6500	4666	10883	429	3	67	61
Monaco							
Turkey	30000						
Yugoslavia	43500	51081	72708	3977	42	69	66

Source: International Civil Aviation Organisation

Database name: Transport Infrastructure
Sector name: Merchant Shipping

Table No: 2213

Title: Size of Fleet 1977-1989

Unit: 000 gross tons

	1977	1980	1981	1982	1983	1984	1985	1986	1987	1988	198
EC members											
Belgium	1595.5	1809.8	1916.8	2271.1	2273.5	2406.7	2400.3	2419.7	2268.4	2118.4	2043.
Denmark	5331.2	5390.4	5047.7	5214.1	5115.1	5211.3	4942.2	4651.2	4873.5	4501.7	4962.
France	11613.9	11924.6	11450.0	10770.9	9868.1	8945.0	8237.4	5936.3	5371.3	4506.2	4413.
West Germany	9592.3	8355.6	7708.2	7706.7	6897.0	6242.5	6177.0	5565.2	4317.6	3917.3	3966.
Greece	29517.1	39471.7	42005.0	40035.2	37477.6	35058.6	31031.5	28390.8	23559.9	21978.8	21324.
Ireland	211.9	209.0	267.5	239.1	222.8	221.4	194.0	149.3	153.6	172.8	167.
Italy	11111.2	11095.7	10641.2	10375.0	10015.2	9157.9	8843.2	7896.6	7817.4	7794.2	7602.
Luxembourg										1.7	3.
Netherlands	5290.4	5723.8	5467.5	5393.1	4939.8	4586.0	4301.3	4324.1	3908.2	3726.5	3655.
Portugal	1281.4	1356.0	1376.5	1401.6	1357.7	15710.0	1436.9	1114.4	1048.2	988.8	762.
Spain	7186.1	8112.2	8133.7	8130.7	7504.7	7004.9	6256.2	5422.0	4949.4	4415.1	3961.
United Kingdom	31646.4	27135.2	25419.4	22505.3	19121.5	15874.1	14343.5	11567.1	8405.6	8206.4	7645.
EFTA members											
Austria	53.3	88.8	62.2	101.0	113.7	129.2	134.2	124.8	193.5	201.3	204.
Finland	2262.1	2530.1	2444.5	2377.0	2358.1	2168.5	1974.0	1469.9	1122.2	838.0	944.
Iceland	166.7	88.2	183.1	181.4	179.4	178.6	180.3	176.4	173.6	174.6	183.
Norway	27801.5	22007.5	21674.9	21861.6	19230.0	17662.9	15338.6	9294.6	6359.3	9350.3	15596.
Sweden	7429.4	4234.0	4033.9	3787.6	3432.7	3520.4	3161.9	2516.6	2269.5	2116.1	2166.
Switzerland	252.7	310.8	315.3	315.2	321.3	319.3	342.0	346.2	354.6	259.4	220.
CMEA members											
Bulgaria	964.2	1233.3	1193.9	1248.2	1293.3	1283.0	1322.2	1385.0	1551.2	1392.4	1375.
Czechoslovakia	148.7	155.3	185.2	184.8	184.3	184.3	184.3	197.9	157.0	157.9	190.
East Germany	1486.8	1532.2	1570.2	1438.6	1420.8	1421.7	1434.4	1518.9	1494.0	1442.8	1499.
Hungary	63.0	75.0	83.5	81.5	81.5	80.0	77.2	86.4	77.3	76.1	76.
Poland	3447.5	3639.1	3579.1	3650.6	3686.1	3267.3	3315.3	3457.2	3469.7	3849.4	3416.
Romania	1218.2	1856.3	2031.5	2203.3	2390.8	2666.8	3023.8	3233.9	3263.8	3560.7	3783.
USSR	21438.3	23443.5	23492.9	23788.7	24549.4	24492.5	24745.4	24960.9	25232.0	25784.0	25853.
Others											
Albania	55.9	56.1	56.1	56.1	56.1	56.1	56.1	56.1	56.1	56.1	56.
Cyprus	2787.9	2091.1	1819.0	2149.9	3450.2	6727.9	8196.1	10616.8	15650.2	18390.6	18134.
Gibraltar	10.5	2.3	40.1	15.7	231.1	247.5	583.3	1612.9	2827.1	3041.8	2611.
Liechtenstein											
Malta	100.4	132.9	231.4	425.6	906.7	1366.1	1855.8	2014.9	2140.4	2148.5	3239.
Monaco											
Turkey	1288.3	1454.8	1663.7	2127.9	2524.4	3124.8	3684.4	3423.7	3336.1	3281.2	3239.
Yugoslavia	2284.5	2466.6	2540.6	2531.5	2546.6	2681.9	2699.3	2872.6	3164.9	3476.4	3680.

Source: Lloyd's Register of Shipping, Statistical Tables
Notes: Ships of 100 gross tons or more
Gross tonnage (gt) is a measure of the total volume within the hull, and above deck, available for cargo, passengers, crew, fuel, stores etc.
1 gt = 100 ft3

Database name: Transport Infrastructure
Sector name: Shipping
Table No: 2214

Title: Goods Loaded in International Seaborne Trade 1977-1989

Unit: Million tonnes

	1977	1980	1981	1982	1983	1984	1985	1986	1987	1988	1989
EC members											
Belgium	38.7	42.8	42.7	40.2	39.0	47.1	49.5	45.8	45.5	45.7	
Denmark	7.2	7.8	7.1	8.0	8.9	11.8	11.0	11.2	12.0	13.5	
France	58.7	54.1	59.4	49.3	52.2	52.3	55.0	56.0	57.1	55.6	
West Germany	32.4	35.1	40.3	43.0	40.8	43.6	44.5	40.1	42.6	44.0	
Greece	14.6	21.4	23.3	20.2	19.7	20.2	21.4	22.9	23.9		
Ireland	8.7	3.5	3.3	3.7	3.6	5.2					
Italy	36.4	35.0	39.4	36.0	34.5	35.0	35.3	38.8	36.9	38.5	
Luxembourg											
Netherlands	77.0	78.0	74.9	75.7	75.0	80.7	78.7	79.5	82.7	87.9	
Portugal	2.9	4.5	5.4	4.9		5.8					
Spain	26.1	33.2	48.7	40.7	44.0	44.7	46.8	45.1	40.3	41.3	
United Kingdom	77.6	100.8	122.0	127.2	129.7	136.1	143.8	153.7		129.1	
EFTA members											
Austria											
Finland	14.1	17.9	18.4	16.0	17.8	20.7	20.3	20.2	22.4	23.4	22.4
Iceland	0.5	0.7	0.6	0.5		0.7	0.8				
Norway	29.8	37.1	35.7	33.4	39.6	47.1	63.5	58.4	57.4	63.7	
Sweden	30.8	34.9	33.4	34.9	40.7	42.9	42.4	41.8	43.5	44.6	
Switzerland											
CMEA members											
Bulgaria	3.1	3.6	3.2	4.5	5.6	3.8	5.5				
Czechoslovakia											
East Germany	3.5	5.6	5.1	7.3	9.0						
Hungary											
Poland	37.8	28.1	20.6	22.4	30.6	39.4	33.0	29.9	31.6	32.0	
Romania											
USSR											
Others											
Albania		1.0	2.1	1.2	1.2						
Cyprus	1.8	1.9	1.6	1.7	1.5	1.8	1.3	1.9	2.3	2.0	2.4
Gibraltar											
Liechtenstein											
Malta	0.2	0.3	0.3	0.2	0.4	0.2	0.3	0.4	0.2		
Monaco											
Turkey	4.8	22.2	26.6	32.5	33.8	45.1	54.7	58.5	77.0	85.2	
Yugoslavia	4.7	5.2	6.1	5.4	6.3	6.5	6.7	7.5	9.9	8.5	8.1

Source: United Nations Monthly Bulletin of Statistics

Database name: Transport Infrastructure
Sector name: Shipping

Table No: 2215

Title: Total Goods Unloaded in International Seaborne Trade 1977-1989

Unit: Million tonnes

	1977	1980	1981	1982	1983	1984	1985	1986	1987	1988	1989
EC members											
Belgium	57.8	69.5	66.0	72.6	65.9	72.1	73.7	76.2	81.5	86.8	
Denmark	33.4	35.6	31.9	29.5	29.8	31.0	33.3	33.0	32.3	30.5	
France	231.4	219.6	196.2	177.2	167.9	172.3	170.9	177.3	172.0	177.0	
West Germany	104.2	114.0	96.6	89.2	80.8	85.0	91.9	93.2	89.7	94.2	
Greece	24.1	33.3	31.6	28.0	27.1	27.7	26.3	29.5			
Ireland	16.9	12.5	12.0	11.2	12.4	12.8					
Italy	217.6	225.4	214.3	202.0	187.6	194.7	193.4	208.8	199.2		
Luxembourg											
Netherlands	248.1	268.6	245.2	241.7	229.0	244.1	249.7	257.5	249.6	266.5	
Portugal	14.1	24.0	24.5		23.9	18.3					
Spain	84.0	94.3	104.5	95.0	92.6	88.8	91.5	97.4	97.0	105.6	
United Kingdom	158.2	132.5	120.6	121.6	117.2	136.1	139.9	147.5		159.7	
EFTA members											
Austria											
Finland	25.6	31.5	30.2	30.3	30.9	29.4	31.6	30.0	31.3	31.9	33.6
Iceland	1.3	1.4	1.4	1.4		1.4	1.6				
Norway	21.8	22.4	18.3	18.1	16.4	17.6	18.1	17.6	20.5	18.9	
Sweden	52.8	55.0	49.0	47.7	48.2	48.8	52.3	55.8	59.5	55.2	
Switzerland											
CMEA members											
Bulgaria	24.8	28.1	27.6	24.6	24.7	25.3	27.5				
Czechoslovakia											
East Germany		14.8	14.4	9.6	12.7						
Hungary											
Poland	24.0	22.8	14.8	15.8	14.9	15.9	15.9	14.8	17.4	18.2	
Romania											
USSR											
Others											
Albania		0.5	0.6	0.6	0.6						
Cyprus	1.8	2.2	2.4	2.5	2.6	3.2	2.8	3.2	3.6	4.0	3.9
Gibraltar											
Liechtenstein											
Malta	1.1	1.4	1.6	1.5	1.5	1.4	1.5	1.9	1.7		
Monaco											
Turkey	21.4	21.1	20.2	24.3	35.5	36.3	36.9	37.7	52.3	48.5	
Yugoslavia	16.5	23.1	24.0	21.5	22.1	22.3	24.0	24.9	25.4	25.5	25.3

Source: United Nations Monthly Bulletin of Statistics

Database name: Transport Infrastructure
Sector name: Merchant Shipping

Table No: 2216

Title: Shipping Fleets by Principal Types of Vessel 1989

Unit: 000 gross tonnes

	Oil Tankers	Oil/ Chemical Tankers	Chemical Tankers	Liquid Gas Carriers	Ore & Bulk Carriers	General Cargo Single Deck	General Cargo Multi-Deck	Container Ships
EC members								
Belgium	112.0	161.2	5.8	171.0	798.0	3.2	47.8	200.1
Denmark	1522.1	518.9	11.4	105.2	325.7	50.7	168.1	1164.0
France	1929.8	13.9	6.2	218.1	698.4	22.6	132.1	560.0
West Germany	130.5	153.0	37.5	132.0	150.1	63.1	788.3	1628.5
Greece	7925.9	303.1	65.9	66.3	9077.4	418.3	1105.7	179.1
Ireland	6.9	12.2	0.0	0.0	0.0	45.5	10.6	17.1
Italy	2399.3	61.4	131.9	178.3	1557.2	160.5	166.0	320.1
Luxembourg	1.7	0.0	0.0	0.0	0.0	0.0	0.0	0.0
Netherlands	365.4	209.7	62.7	31.7	327.6	256.3	568.7	520.4
Portugal	322.8	0.0	4.3	0.0	178.0	29.9	29.6	7.0
Spain	1470.2	15.7	88.4	64.0	897.4	192.4	123.6	81.6
United Kingdom	2583.9	19.9	37.8	138.2	1007.1	112.9	122.7	1367.7
EFTA members								
Austria	0.0	0.0	0.0	0.0	136.3	45.9	21.9	0.0
Finland	115.6	39.4	4.4	20.8	71.5	41.9	52.9	0.0
Iceland	1.0	1.2	0.0	0.0	12.4	1.0	23.7	0.0
Norway	6575.8	498.5	671.3	1263.9	2818.6	135.5	376.9	68.7
Sweden	173.2	38.0	87.8	80.9	85.4	57.1	41.1	87.9
Switzerland	0.0	0.0	10.9	0.0	183.0	14.0	1.6	0.0
CMEA members								
Bulgaria	285.3	0.0	0.0	0.0	611.6	78.6	197.4	19.1
Czechoslovakia	0.0	0.0	0.0	0.0	96.5	10.0	84.2	0.0
East Germany	35.9	0.0	2.7	14.3	323.9	103.5	645.2	114.3
Hungary	0.0	0.0	0.0	0.0	0.0	9.0	67.2	0.0
Poland	126.3	27.8	0.0	0.0	1609.8	86.9	823.0	50.5
Romania	595.6	0.0	0.0	0.0	1758.4	165.7	873.2	15.2
USSR	3991.2	136.4	42.6	183.1	3156.7	2023.1	3538.1	617.6
Others								
Albania	0.0	0.0	0.0	0.0	0.0	16.1	38.8	0.0
Cyprus	5461.7	177.0	41.9	6.1	6966.5	787.6	2033.6	335.6
Gibraltar	2027.5	32.9	4.3	4.2	190.7	8.1	99.9	0.0
Liechtenstein								
Malta	1347.3	57.4	1.0	0.0	1108.4	192.3	432.6	5.1
Monaco								
Turkey	783.4	9.5	21.0	4.9	1082.2	429.5	384.0	0.0
Yugoslavia	311.6	0.0	8.1	0.0	1653.0	268.3	906.5	103.5

Source: Lloyd's Register of Shipping, Statistical Tables 1989

TABLE 2202: TOTAL ROAD TRAFFIC
Billion passenger-kilometres 1988

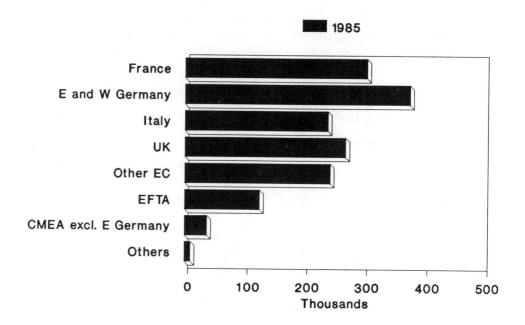

TABLE 2204: TOTAL ROAD FREIGHT
Billion tonne-kilometres 1988

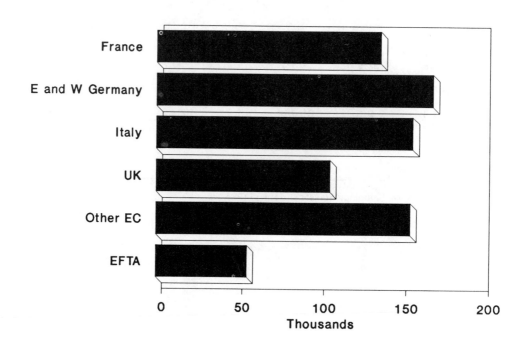

23
TOURISM AND TRAVEL

Database name: Tourism and Travel
Sector name: Tourism Receipts and Expenditure

Table No: 2301

Title: Trends in Tourism Receipts 1977-1988

Unit: Million current US Dollars

	1977	1978	1979	1980	1981	1982	1983	1984
EC members								
Belgium	1107	1300	1629	1810	1585	1330	1450	1664
Denmark	940	1125	1312	1337	1239	1305	1308	1292
France	4384	5903	6826	8197	7193	6991	7226	7598
West Germany	3972	4847	5741	6565	6279	5392	5453	5506
Greece	981	1326	1668	1734	1881	1527	1176	1313
Ireland	322	414	527	574	537	477	409	461
Italy	4762	6285	8218	8213	7554	8339	9034	8595
Luxembourg						248	263	254
Netherlands	1110	1254	1325	1662	1571	1545	1470	1694
Portugal	405	592	942	1147	1023	859	819	960
Spain	4003	5488	6484	6968	6716	7126	6836	7717
United Kingdom	4104	4796	5996	6922	5931	5531	6083	6119
EC total	26090	33330	40668	45129	41509	40670	41527	43173
EFTA members								
Austria	3748	4721	5610	6442	5690	5695	5255	5049
Finland	377	441	533	677	690	579	497	489
Iceland	15	19	22	23	22	25	27	34
Norway	485	558	635	751	758	733	673	660
Sweden	648	753	890	962	963	1005	1080	1128
Switzerland	1943	2446	2568	3149	3035	3015	3147	3163
EFTA total	7216	8938	10258	12004	11158	11052	10679	10523
CMEA members								
Bulgaria	235	240	250	260	269	265	271	288
Czechoslovakia	184	352	385	338	252	268	299	328
East Germany	120	120	150	150	150	245	250	260
Hungary	320	415	452	504	452	411	426	452
Poland	170	224	261	282	116	65	85	101
Romania	118	121	125	136	303	203	202	209
USSR	250	275	300	325	325	330	160	160
CMEA total	1397	1747	1923	1995	1867	1787	1693	1798
Others								
Albania	5	6	7	8	9	10	10	10
Cyprus	58	89	141	203	244	292	332	361
Gibraltar	5	5	5	6	7	9	10	10
Liechtenstein	13	14	15	16	17	18	19	19
Malta	81	127	206	329	265	185	152	130
Monaco	230	240	250	260	270	280	280	290
Turkey	205	230	281	327	381	600	800	1100
Yugoslavia	841	985	825	1115	1350	844	929	1054
Total	1438	1696	1730	2264	2543	2238	2532	2974
European total	36141	45711	54579	61392	57077	55747	56431	58468

Database name: Tourism and Travel
Sector name: Tourism Receipts and Expenditure

Table No: 2301

Title: Trends in Tourism Receipts 1977-1988

Unit: Million current US Dollars

	1985	1986	1987	1988	% growth 1977-88	% share 1977	% share 1988
EC members							
Belgium	1663	2271	2980	3438	210.6	3.1	3.3
Denmark	1326	1759	2219	2423	157.8	2.6	2.3
France	7942	9724	11870	13783	214.4	12.1	13.2
West Germany	4748	6294	7678	8449	112.7	11.0	8.1
Greece	1428	1834	2268	2396	144.2	2.7	2.3
Ireland	531	639	839	999	210.2	0.9	1.0
Italy	8758	9855	12174	12399	160.4	13.2	11.8
Luxembourg	147	193	201	238			0.2
Netherlands	1661	2229	2695	2857	157.4	3.1	2.7
Portugal	1137	1533	2145	2404	493.6	1.1	2.3
Spain	8151	12058	14760	16686	316.8	11.1	15.9
United Kingdom	7120	8163	10225	11023	168.6	11.4	10.5
EC total	44612	56552	70054	77095	195.5	72.2	73.6
EFTA members							
Austria	5084	6954	8863	8520	127.3	10.4	8.1
Finland	501	598	823	877	132.6	1.0	0.8
Iceland	41	60	86	108	620.0	0.0	0.1
Norway	755	1059	1261	1443	197.5	1.3	1.4
Sweden	1190	1552	2033	2347	262.2	1.8	2.2
Switzerland	3145	4227	5345	5618	189.1	5.4	5.4
EFTA total	10716	14450	18411	18913	162.1	20.0	18.0
CMEA members							
Bulgaria	343	356	357	359	52.8	0.7	0.3
Czechoslovakia	307	336	386	436	137.0	0.5	0.4
East Germany	270	350	420	470	291.7	0.3	0.4
Hungary	512	611	827	759	137.2	0.9	0.7
Poland	118	136	184	193	13.5	0.5	0.2
Romania	182	178	165	176	49.2	0.3	0.2
USSR	163	163	198	216	-13.6	0.7	0.2
CMEA total	1895	2130	2537	2609	86.8	3.9	2.5
Others							
Albania	10	13	16	17	240.0	0.0	0.0
Cyprus	380	497	666	782	1248.3	0.2	0.7
Gibraltar	15	18	15	15	200.0	0.0	0.0
Liechtenstein	20	26	31	35	169.2	0.0	0.0
Malta	149	203	327	382	371.6	0.2	0.4
Monaco	300	380	470	560	143.5	0.6	0.5
Turkey	1482	1215	1721	2355	1048.8	0.6	2.2
Yugoslavia	1061	1337	1668	2024	140.7	2.3	1.9
Total	3417	3689	4914	6170	329.1	4.0	5.9
European total	60640	76821	95916	104787	189.9	100.0	100.0

Source: WTO Yearbook of Tourism Statistics/OECD/National reports/Euromonitor estimates/
International Passenger Survey/Euromonitor Travel and Tourism Data
a New series from 1983

Database name: Tourism and Travel
Sector name: Tourism Receipts and Expenditure

Table No: 2302

Title: Trends in Tourism Expenditure 1977-1988

Unit: Million current US Dollars

	1977	1978	1979	1980	1981	1982	1983	1984
EC members								
Belgium	1583	2380	2969	3272	2644	2190	2095	1953
Denmark	942	1147	1542	1560	1269	1330	1212	1227
France	3923	4276	5193	6027	5752	5157	4281	4271
West Germany	10984	14316	17754	20599	17853	16223	13274	12430
Greece	89	142	202	190	249	231	362	339
Ireland	237	353	518	535	513	454	453	411
Italy	894	1206	1507	1907	1664	1731	1822	2098
Luxembourg								
Netherlands	2454	3402	4804	4664	3648	3406	3289	3277
Portugal	135	161	247	290	247	247	229	222
Spain	533	567	922	1229	1008	1008	894	835
United Kingdom	1909	2974	4497	6410	6478	6237	6223	6197
EC total	23683	30924	40155	46683	41325	38214	34134	33260
EFTA members								
Austria	2098	2453	2966	2847	2788	2744	2898	2624
Finland	377	399	505	544	536	630	622	681
Iceland	27	33	38	42	53	54	66	85
Norway	861	1078	1189	1310	1433	1641	1587	1488
Sweden	1412	1642	2022	2235	2239	1895	1619	1713
Switzerland	1114	1668	2030	2357	2122	2216	2296	2282
EFTA total	5889	7273	8750	9335	9171	9180	9088	8873
CMEA members								
Bulgaria	33	37	38	40	40			
Czechoslovakia	271	346	276	266	190	193	229	229
East Germany	200	225	250	270	270			
Hungary	167	190	190	196	164	142	152	157
Poland	256	319	352	380	289	111	195	225
Romania						84	92	85
USSR						140	140	140
CMEA total	927	1117	1106	1152	953	670	808	836
Others								
Albania	3	3	4	4	3			
Cyprus	29	37	45	56	57	66	68	71
Gibraltar								
Liechtenstein	3	3	3	3	3			
Malta	23	26	21	41	50	57	53	50
Monaco	6	6	6	6	6			
Turkey	268	102	95	115	103	109	127	277
Yugoslavia	98	128	155	130	143	107	86	85
Total	430	305	329	355	365	339	334	483
European total	30929	39619	50340	57525	51814	48403	44364	43452

Source: WTO/OECD/International Passenger Survey/Euromonitor
Notes: a Luxembourg included with Belgium

Database name: Tourism and Travel
Sector name: Tourism Receipts and Expenditure

Table No: 2302

Title: Trends in Tourism Expenditure 1977-1988

Unit: Million current US Dollars

	1986	1987	1988	% growth 1977-88	% share 1977	% share 1988	Notes
EC members							
Belgium	2889	3881	4428	179.7	5.1	4.6	
Denmark	2119	2860	3087	227.7	3.0	3.2	
France	6513	8493	9712	147.6	12.7	10.1	
West Germany	18000	23341	25036	127.9	35.5	26.0	
Greece	494	508	735	725.8	0.3	0.8	
Ireland	685	839	999	321.5	0.8	1.0	
Italy	2758	4536	6053	577.1	2.9	6.3	
Luxembourg							a
Netherlands	4901	6592	6888	180.7	7.9	7.2	
Portugal	329	421	533	294.8	0.4	0.6	
Spain	1513	1938	2440	357.8	1.7	2.5	
United Kingdom	8942	11939	14650	667.4	6.2	15.2	
EC total	49143	65348	74561	214.8	76.6	77.5	
EFTA members							
Austria	4016	5592	4842	130.8	6.8	5.0	
Finland	1060	1512	1651	337.9	1.2	1.7	
Iceland	129	213	200	640.7	0.1	0.2	
Norway	2511	3073	3405	295.5	2.8	3.5	
Sweden	2819	3784	4572	223.8	4.6	4.8	
Switzerland	3368	4339	5019	350.5	3.6	5.2	
EFTA total	13903	18513	19689	234.3	19.0	20.5	
CMEA members							
Bulgaria					0.1		
Czechoslovakia	31	30	32	-88.2	0.9	0.0	
East Germany					0.6		
Hungary	241	276	725	334.1	0.5	0.8	
Poland	186	203	205	-19.9	0.8	0.2	
Romania	57	57	56			0.1	
USSR	175	175	175			0.2	
CMEA total	690	741	1193	28.7	3.0	1.2	
Others							
Albania					0.0		
Cyprus	99	118	136	369.0	0.1	0.1	
Gibraltar							
Liechtenstein					0.0		
Malta	69	102	121	426.1	0.1	0.1	
Monaco					0.0		
Turkey	314	448	358	33.6	0.9	0.4	
Yugoslavia	132	91	91	-7.1	0.3	0.1	
Total	614	759	706	64.2	1.4	0.7	
European total	64350	85361	96149	210.9	100.0	100.0	

Source:
Notes: a   Luxembourg included with Belgium

Database name: Tourism and Travel
Sector name: Tourist Arrivals

Table No: 2303

Title: Foreign Tourist Arrivals at Frontiers 1977-1988

Unit: 000s

	1977	1980	1981	1982	1983	1984	1985	1986	1987	1988	Note
EC members											
Belgium						2237	2460	2454	2516	2700	
Denmark						1300	1281	1216	1171	1150	
France	26265	30100	31340	33467	34018	35429	36748	36080	36974	38288	
West Germany						11942	12686	12217	12780	13113	
Greece	3961	4796	5094	5033	4778	5523	6574	7025	7564	7778	
Ireland	1963	2258	2223	2250	2257	2514	2529	2464	2664	3007	
Italy	17549	22087	20036	22297	22140	23043	25047	24762	25749	26155	a
Luxembourg						594	622	616	645	760	
Netherlands						3218	3329	3134	3353	3322	
Portugal	1347	2730	3021	3164	3714	4119	4989	5409	6102	6624	a
Spain	21000	22500		26106	25583	27176	27477	29910	32900	35000	
United Kingdom	12281	12421	11452	11636	12464	13644	14449	13897	15566	15798	b
EFTA members											
Austria						15110	15168	15092	15761	16571	
Finland	259	365	380	418	451	489	543	598	823	877	
Iceland	73	66	72	73	78	85	97	114	129	129	a
Norway						1745	1933	1637	1782	1704	
Sweden						839	853	824	814	830	
Switzerland	8341	8872	9383	11450	11490	11900	11900	11400	11600	11700	
CMEA members											
Bulgaria	4570	5486	6046	5647	5771	6138	7295	7567	7594	8295	b,c,d
Czechoslovakia	6821	5055	4787	3990	5007	5208	4869	5330	6126	14028	a,c,d
East Germany	2000	2100	2200	2500	2500	1508	1555	1950	2102	2231	
Hungary	7194	9413	10450	6473	6764	8731	9724	10613	11826	10562	a,c,d
Poland	4700	5664	1737	1123	1920	2398	2749	2500	2484	2495	
Romania	3685	6742	7002	5940	5802	6584	4772	4535	5142	5514	b
USSR	4400	5900	5870	3680	3930	4203	4340	4309	5246	6007	
Others											
Albania	30	32	32	35	40	45	50	55	60	60	
Cyprus	178	353	429	548	600	666	770	828	949	1112	
Gibraltar	54	75	66	66	63	65	86	101	86	86	a
Liechtenstein	80	73	80	90	90	88	91	76	75	72	
Malta	362	729	706	511	491	480	518	574	746	784	a
Monaco	450			260	260	240	242	211	214	232	
Turkey	1268	902	1405	1012	1288	1727	2230	2079	2468	3715	
Yugoslavia	5621					7224	8436	8464	8907	9018	

Source: WTO Yearbook of Tourism Statistics/National reports/International Passenger Survey/Euromonitor estimates
Notes:
a From 1982, data are for foreign tourist nights
b Includes day-trippers
c 1988 excludes residents of Eastern Europe
d New series from 1988

Database name: Tourism and Travel
Sector name: Tourist Arrivals   Table No: 2304

Title: Foreign Tourist Arrivals at Registered Accommodation Units 1977-1988

Unit: 000s

	1977	1980	1981	1982	1983	1984	1985	1986	1987	1988	Notes
EC members											
Belgium	1500	1900	2000	2200	2234	2237	2460	2454	2516	2430	
Denmark	3406	3500	3570	3690	1218	1300	1281	1216	1171	1142	e
France		5664	6080	6086	6120	6523	6928	5829	5962	7421	b,f
West Germany	9793	10356	11122	11075	11328	11942	12686	12217	12780	13113	
Greece	5049	5850						6415	6490		
Ireland	1470	1650			1715		2450	2367	2095	2436	
Italy	14836	18137	16580	18459	18483	19279	19789	19096	21349	21851	
Luxembourg					608	594	622	616	645	760	c,g
Netherlands	2693	2784	2846	3083	3150	3218	3329	3134	3353	3322	
Portugal	1479	2283	2347	2394	2554	2805	3294	3551	3829	3988	
Spain	11785	9228	10586	11184	11728	12908	12442	13587	14886	14302	a
United Kingdom	10118										
EFTA members											
Austria	11748	13879	14241	14253	14482	15110	15168	15092	15752	16563	
Finland							2487	2294	2486	2583	d
Iceland	66	68									
Norway	1238	1252	1280	1212	1272	1745	1933	1637	1782	1704	a,h
Sweden			673	683	807	839	853	824	814	800	
Switzerland	8341	8872	9383	9186	9200	9482	9528	9157	9324	9359	
CMEA members											
Bulgaria					2767	2790	2833	2659	3052	3082	
Czechoslovakia	2696	4236	4270	2222	2276	3139	3204	3543	3822	4167	
East Germany	1101	1067	1038	1500	1500	1500	1500				
Hungary	2357	2448	2867	2835	3115	3549	3656	3571	4052	3628	
Poland	1865	1843	676	296	615	755	896				e
Romania	1737	1997	1967	1386	1291	1434	1598	1358	1460	1344	
USSR											
Others											
Albania	10	10									
Cyprus	126	254			395	437	517	567	586	731	950	
Gibraltar	105	33	26								
Liechtenstein					85	84	88	91	81	75		
Malta	356	675						567	586		783	c,i
Monaco	225	240			200	200	200	242	211	214	232	
Turkey	531	413	628	786	1094	1582	1733	2011	2662	3412	
Yugoslavia	6116	6410	6616	5955	5947	7224	8436	8464	8907	9018	

Source: WTO Yearbook of Tourism Statistics/OECD/National Passenger Survey/Euromonitor estimates
Notes:
a Arrivals at hotels
b Arrivals at hotels; Ile de France (Paris) region only   g New series from 1984 and 1988
c 1988 hotels only   h New series from 1984
d Tourist nights   i New series from 1988
e New series from 1983
f New series from 1985 and 1988

Database name: Tourism and Travel
Sector name: Tourist Arrivals

Table No: 2305

Title: Method of Arrival 1988

Unit: 000s

	Air	Road	Rail	Sea	Total	% by Air	Notes
EEC members							
EC members							
Denmark							
France							
West Germany							
Greece							
Ireland							
Italy	5091	44855	4537	1207	55690	9.1	b
Luxembourg							
Netherlands							
Portugal	2463	13270	145	199	16077	15.3	b
Spain	17140	32802	2548	1688	54178	31.6	b
United Kingdom	10967			4831	15798	69.4	c
EFTA members							
Austria	1422	147556	7759		156737	0.9	b
Finland							
Iceland							
Norway							
Sweden							
Switzerland							
CMEA members							
Bulgaria	1011	6558	649	78	8295	12.2	
Czechoslovakia	417	18213	5911	53	24593	1.7	b
East Germany	407	9134	3897	107	13545	3.0	b
Hungary	641	13542	3682	100	17965	3.6	b
Poland							
Romania	303	3083	2001	127	5514	5.5	
USSR							
Others							
Albania							
Cyprus	1102			136	1238	89.0	b
Gibraltar							
Liechtenstein							
Malta							
Monaco							
Turkey	2113	1284	67	709	4173	50.6	a,b
Yugoslavia	1571	26161	1241	662	29635	5.3	b

Source: WTO Yearbook of Tourism Statistics/National Reports/Euromonitor estimates
Notes:
a Includes arrivals for employment and transit
b Includes all arrivals regardless of purpose of visit

| Database name: | Tourism and Travel |
| Sector name: | Accommodation |

Table No: 2306

Title: Use of Tourist Accommodation 1988

	Stay in Accommodation ('000 nights):		Hotel Bed Occupancy Rate %	Average Stay (nights):		Notes
	International	Domestic		In an Accommodation Establishment	In the Country	
EC members						
Belgium	10573	21829	18.6	3.2	4.5	a,g
Denmark	8011	12322	37.0	2.5	4.1	a,g
France	47108	13328		2.8	9.0	a,f
West Germany	34475	16166	38.2	2.0	4.0	g
Greece	34492	11385		5.0	14.0	c,g
Ireland	3743		39.0	4.5	10.0	a,j
Italy	107030	250836	40.9	4.9	7.0	g
Luxembourg	2428	288		2.0	3.0	
Netherlands	13989	469	35.2	4.0	4.5	c,g,j
Portugal	17787	11996	47.5	4.0	7.0	j
Spain	92685	55087	54.5	6.0	10.0	j
United Kingdom	172900	505000	60.0		10.0	
EFTA members						
Austria	87575	28137	34.2	5.3	7.0	g
Finland	2611	9506	53.9	2.0	5.0	h,g
Iceland					8.0	g
Norway	3560	8631	38.0	1.0	5.0	g
Sweden	7113	27825	35.0	8.0	6.0	c
Switzerland	34496	38926	40.8	3.6	4.5	g
CMEA members						
Bulgaria	19909	24733	72.8	6.0	5.0	j
Czechoslovakia	11532	27833	59.4	2.0	3.0	
East Germany	9020	67796		2.6	2.0	d
Hungary	15897	11938	59.1	4.0	6.0	
Poland	3435			3.0		d
Romania	5137			3.0		
USSR			57.6		6.0	b,e
Others						
Albania						
Cyprus	8181	243	63.3	11.0	13.0	h
Gibraltar	279		52.3		4.0	g,j
Liechtenstein	243		30.7		2.0	b,j
Malta	9849		68.5		12.0	j
Monaco	695		58.0	3.0	4.0	h,j
Turkey	11655	5578	50.8	3.4	9.0	
Yugoslavia	52351	55148	46.4	5.8	7.0	g

Source: WTO Yearbook of Tourism Statistics/OECD/National reports

Notes:
a Accommodation average stay 1983
b Average stay in the country 1986
c Accommodation average stay 1986
d Accommodation average stay 1984
e Hotel bed occupancy rate 1986
f Nights registered in Ile de France region (Domestic)
g Average stay in the country 1987
h Accommodation average stay 1987
j Hotel bed occupancy rate 1987

Database name: Tourism and Travel
Sector name: Tourist Arrivals

Table No: 2307

Title: Principal Countries of Origin of Foreign Tourists 1988

Unit: % of tourist arrivals

	No. 1	%	No. 2	%	No. 3	%	No. 4	%	Note
EC members									
Belgium	Netherlands	38.5	W.Germany	16.0	France	9.2	UK	9.2	
Denmark	W.Germany	35.2	Sweden	20.7	Norway	12.3	Netherland	6.4	
France	W.Germany	23.8	UK	17.4	Netherlands	10.6	Italy	9.0	a
West Germany	USA	14.3	Netherlands	14.3	UK	9.0	Sweden	6.2	
Greece	UK	23.0	W.Germany	17.8	Italy	7.0	France	6.0	
Ireland	UK	69.5	Canada	12.8	W. Germany	3.8	France	3.7	
Italy	Switzerland	21.1	W.Germany	18.8	France	16.1	Austria	11.1	
Luxembourg	Belgium	27.2	W.Germany	14.6	Netherlands	13.7	France	9.8	
Netherlands	W.Germany	20.0	UK	18.2	USA	11.5	France	7.8	
Portugal	Spain	45.1	UK	16.1	France	8.5	W.Germany	8.0	
Spain	France	20.8	Portugal	17.4	UK	13.2	W.Germany	11.9	
United Kingdom	USA	16.6	France	12.5	W.Germany	11.6	Ireland	7.9	
EFTA members									
Austria	W.Germany	54.3	Netherlands	8.0	Italy	5.2	UK	4.5	
Finland	Sweden	24.3	W.Germany	14.0	USSR	19.3	USA	8.8	
Iceland	USA	22.3	Sweden	13.4	Denmark	12.7	W.Germany	12.3	
Norway	Denmark	19.2	Sweden	17.2	W.Germany	16.1	USA	10.4	
Sweden	Norway	32.1	W.Germany	19.4	Denmark	9.1	Finland	8.3	
Switzerland	W.Germany	33.4	USA	10.7	France	7.7	UK	7.1	
CMEA members									
Bulgaria	Turkey	38.9	Yugoslavia	17.5	Poland	11.1	USSR	5.7	
Czechoslovakia	E.Germany	38.2	Hungary	26.0	Poland	19.4	Yugoslavia	3.3	
East Germany	Czechoslovakia	11.7	USSR	10.8	Poland	4.7	Bulgaria	1.7	c
Hungary	Czechoslovakia	21.2	Poland	18.0	E.Germany	12.9	W.Germany	10.7	
Poland	USSR	28.1	Czechoslovakia	22.9	E.Germany	17.5	Hungary	9.2	
Romania	Yugoslavia	24.2	Poland	14.9	Bulgaria	12.7	Hungary	11.8	
USSR	Finland	11.6	W.Germany	4.0	USA	2.5	Italy	1.9	
Others									
Albania									
Cyprus	UK	36.5	Sweden	10.5	W.Germany	9.5	Finland	5.2	
Gibraltar									
Liechtenstein	W.Germany	27.9	Switz	21.5	USA	14.4	Italy	4.8	b
Malta	UK	60.8	W.Germany	9.9	Italy	6.5	France	3.1	a
Monaco	Italy	25.4	France	22.2	USA	14.1	UK	9.1	
Turkey	W.Germany	18.4	UK	11.1	Greece	10.3	Yugoslavia	6.1	d
Yugoslavia	W.Germany	30.5	Italy	13.7	Austria	8.9	UK	7.5	

Source: WTO Yearbook of Tourism Statistics/OECD Tourism Policy and International Tourism
a UK includes Ireland
b 1987
c Tourists by the GDR Travel Agency
d Includes travellers for employment

Database name: Tourism an Travel
Sector name: Accommodation
Subsector name:
Title: Hotels and Similar Establishments: Available Capacity by Type 1987

Table No: 2308

Unit: 000 beds/places

	Hotels	Apartment Hotels	Motels	Inns	Guest and Boarding Houses	Holiday Villages	Other	Total	Notes
EC members									
Belgium	87							87	
Denmark	84							84	
France	1037					242		1279	
West Germany	528	226		229	125	123		1131	
Greece	342	23	3	1	21		6	396	
Ireland	41						4	45	
Italy	1670							1670	
Luxembourg	16							16	i
Netherlands	100				5			105	
Portugal	63	15	1	3	43	15	9	159	
Spain	683				173		225	1081	
United Kingdom	748				103			851	a,g,h
EFTA members									
Austria	654							654	
Finland	69				9	3	2	84	b
Iceland	5							5	c
Norway	106							106	
Sweden	106				47	47		200	
Switzerland	236		6	30				272	e
CMEA members									
Bulgaria	111							111	d
Czechoslovakia	103		3	18		29	42	196	
East Germany	218							218	
Hungary	52			14	10		12	87	
Poland	52		2	32	7	483		577	
Romania	167			8				175	
USSR	64							64	f
Others									
Albania									
Cyprus	24	18						42	
Gibraltar	2							2	f
Israel	52	1				8	5	66	
Liechtenstein	1							1	
Malta	16				1	13		30	
Monaco									
Turkey	85		4	2	4	16	1	112	
Yugoslavia	333		11	2	6		6	358	

Source: WTO/OECD
Notes:
a England only (1989)
b Licensed hotels only; include motels
c 1984
d Hotels include motels
e Hotels include boardinghouses
f 1986
g Hotels include motels, inns and guest
h Other includes bed and breakfast
i 1987

Database name: Tourism and Travel
Sector name: Accommodation

Table No: 2309

Title: Bed Capacity for Tourists in Supplementary Accommodation Licensed/Reporting 1988

Unit: 000 beds/places

	Youth Hostels	Caravan/ Camp Site Places	Recreation/ Holiday Centres(a)	Rented Accomm.	Health Estab.	Other	Total	Notes
EC members								
Belgium		349	87		3		439	
Denmark	10						10	
France		2452				178	2629	f
West Germany	89		142	174	120		525	
Greece		75		219		31	326	
Ireland								
Italy	8	1173	58	2218		125	3582	f
Luxembourg		51			0	4	55	
Netherlands	6		540			2	549	b
Portugal		248	11				259	
Spain		457		10921		8	11387	c,f
United Kingdom		355	37			20	411	f
EFTA members								
Austria	10			428	45	31	515	
Finland	3	23					26	
Iceland								
Norway	6						6	
Sweden	15	364					379	
Switzerland	8	272		360	7	235	882	e
CMEA members								
Bulgaria		18		186	134	28	365	
Czechoslovakia		229		52			282	
East Germany	24	385			553		963	
Hungary		88		146			234	
Poland	41	418		66	22	19	266	
Romania		47		21	46	12	126	
USSR								
Others								
Albania								
Cyprus	0	1		6			7	
Gibraltar								
Liechtenstein								
Malta				8			8	
Monaco								
Turkey		10					10	
Yugoslavia	60	372	118	475	18	24	1067	

Source: WTO Yearbook of Tourism Statistics/OECD

Notes:
a Some holiday villages are classified by WTO as hotels and similar establishments, but by OECD as supplementary
b 1986
c Including 10,593,000 second homes (declared as non-commercial)
d England only (1988)
e Collective accommodation (includes recreation centres)
f "Other" includes farms

TABLE 2302: TOURISM EXPENDITURE
Million US dollars 1988

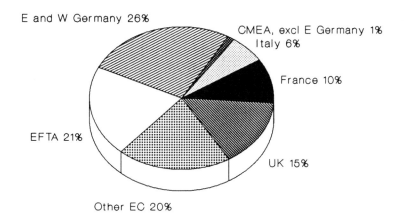

E and W Germany 26%

CMEA, excl E Germany 1%

Italy 6%

France 10%

EFTA 21%

UK 15%

Other EC 20%

TABLE 2306: HOTEL USE
Bed-nights by foreign visitors 1988

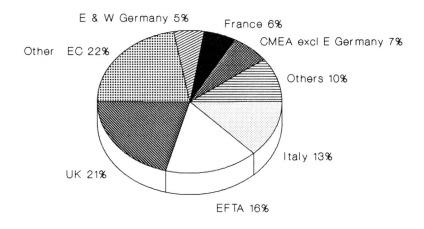

E & W Germany 5%

France 6%

Other   EC 22%

CMEA excl E Germany 7%

Others 10%

Italy 13%

UK 21%

EFTA 16%

Title: Selected Data on Libraries : Latest Year

	Year	Public Libraries	Service Points	Book Stocks (million volumes)	Borrowers ('000)	National Libraries	Higher Education Libraries	School Libraries	Special Libraries	Non-Specialised Libraries
EC members										
Belgium	1985	2351		24.1	1731.3	1			717	
Denmark	1986	250		35.6	1990.0	1	18		23	
France	1983	1141	2422	64.4	6094.0	1	61			
West Germany	1985	11529	13945	88.1	6600.0	7	3347		2100	86
Greece	1986	615	615	8.3	1395.0	1			100	
Ireland	1986	31	387	10.9	668.0	1	8		21	
Italy	1985	47		16.1	3400.2	2			700	6
Luxembourg	1986					1	1			
Netherlands	1986	473	988	39.6	4182.0	1	690			
Portugal	1983	178	454	7.5	2303.8	3	138	677	126	9
Spain	1983	1677	1787	14.0	1621.7	2	408	626	435	
United Kingdom	1982	160	16244	131.3		3	554			
EFTA members										
Austria	1987	2081	2313	7.4	802.3	1	796		1434	9
Finland	1986	461	1776	31.7	2084.0	1	28	5200	19	
Iceland	1985	234		1.6		1	1		52	
Norway	1986	448	1377	17.6	1100.0	1	123	3658	149	20
Sweden	1987	382	2096	45.7		1	15	5387	38	51
Switzerland	1986			24.2		1	13			33
CMEA members										
Bulgaria	1986	5591		56.0	2286.3	1	50	3446	673	27
Czechoslovakia	1986	9453	12095	52.8	2765.6	15	1743			
East Germany	1986	8919	18868	52.0	4863.1	2	29			3
Hungary	1986	4765	9383	49.7	2268.3	1	221	3908		1
Poland	1987	10129	23286	129.7	7795.1	1	992	19868	4254	128
Romania	1987	7181		69.6	5094.0	2	43	10984	3158	
USSR	1987	11822	296454	1523.1	106980.0	1		154000		450
Others										
Albania	1980	45	3633	5.7	515.5	1	2	1847		40
Cyprus	1981		103	0.2					68	
Gibraltar	1983	1	1	0.0						
Liechtenstein	1986	3	3	0.0	1.4		1			
Malta	1986	1	56	0.3	73.0	1	1	45	9	
Monaco	1986					1		4		
Turkey	1986	206	836	6.6	645.7	1				
Yugoslavia	1986	892	2012	29.0	18893.0	8	426	8263	1038	19

Source: UNESCO/National Statistics
Notes: Gibraltar book stocks: 0.02 million

| Database name: | Cultural Indicators | | | | | | | | | | |
| Sector name: | Book Publishing | | | | | Table No: | 2402 | | | | |

Title: Book Titles Published 1977-1987

Unit: Number of titles

	1977	1978	1979	1980	1981	1982	1983	1984	1985	1986	1987
EC members											
Belgium	5964	9012	10040	9009	9736	7207	8065	6527	8327		
Denmark	8021	8642	9415	9256	8563	10189	9460	10660	9554	10957	11129
France	31673	21225	25019	32318	37308	42186	37576	37189	37860	43505	
West Germany	48736	50950	59666	64761	56568	58592	58489	48836	54442	63724	65670
Greece	4981		4664	4048					4651		
Ireland	500	632	623	696	715	706	672	799	2679		
Italy	10116	10679	11162	12029	13457	12926	13718	14312	15545	16297	17109
Luxembourg	250		270	297	380	305	359	341	297	367	355
Netherlands	13111	13393	13429	14591	13939	13324		13209	12629	13368	13329
Portugal	6122	6274	5726	6085	6714		8647	9041	10293	10782	7733
Spain	24896	23231	24569	28195	29180	32138	32457	30764	34684	38405	38302
United Kingdom	36196	38641	41864	48069	42972	48029	50981	51411	52861		
EFTA members											
Austria	6800	6439	6783	7098	6214	6736	9374	9059	8440	9560	8910
Finland	3679	3367	4834	6511	8227	7436	8594	8563	8930	8694	9106
Iceland	801	1045	1035	1193	1179	1329	1121				
Norway	4823	4407	5405	5578	5042	5175	5540	2653	3559	3284	5481
Sweden	6009	5256	5396	7598	8582	8509	8036	10373	9532	10587	11516
Switzerland	9894	10077	10765	10362	10544	11405	11355	11806	11822	11626	12046
CMEA members											
Bulgaria	4088	4234	4600	4681	5036	5070	4924	5367	5171	4924	4583
Czechoslovakia	9568	9588	10089	11647	10493	10519	9574	9911	9844	10020	10565
East Germany	5844	5680	5816	5915	5979	5938	6175	6175	6218	6486	6515
Hungary	9048	9579	9120	9254	8810		8469	10421	9389	9857	9111
Poland	11552	11849	11191	11919	10435	9814	8789	9195	9649	9881	10416
Romania	7218	7562	7288	7350	7242	6702	5771	5632	5276		
USSR	85395	84727	80560	80676	83007	80674	82589	82790	83976	83472	83011
Others											
Albania				948	1043	1149	997	1130	939	959	
Cyprus	570	1054	1335	1137							
Gibraltar											
Liechtenstein							278				
Malta	120	154	125	110	132	247		313	357	346	421
Monaco	86	52	137	109	76	105					
Turkey	6830		5071	4318	5610	6190	7180	7224	6685		
Yugoslavia	10418	10509	12061	11301	11088	10535	10931	10918	11175	10374	10619

Source: UNESCO/National Statistical Offices

Database name: Cultural Indicators
Sector name: Book Publishing

Table No: 2403

Title: Books Published by Subject 1987

Unit: Number of titles

	General	Philosophy	Religion	Social Sciences	Philology	Pure Sciences
EC members						
Belgium	169	240	480	1235	291	343
Denmark	216	407	299	872	291	524
France	718	1431	1391	1886	767	1245
West Germany	5819	2710	3727	4530	2548	1808
Greece	70	128	170	1061	226	267
Ireland	3		47	270	11	36
Italy	411	882	1218	1116	397	374
Luxembourg	18	16	8	35	2	22
Netherlands	67	505	658	477	246	322
Portugal	935	192	415	860		
Spain	1507	1195	2099	1536	2690	1633
United Kingdom	2178	1497	2179	9420	1234	4442
EFTA members						
Austria	181	344	318	906	268	957
Finland	384	188	342	1022	319	744
Iceland	27	22	11	102	26	
Norway	219	119	249	715	113	387
Sweden	297	228	393	412	279	504
Switzerland	211	501	787	1069	179	901
CMEA members						
Bulgaria	205	48	13	965	159	181
Czechoslovakia	761	162	56	815	386	689
East Germany	95	113	276	608	335	360
Hungary	241	83	88	1001	429	571
Poland	175	185	444	860	392	721
Romania	105	61	47	503	162	756
USSR	2471	1540	330	10827	1820	5844
Others						
Albania	5	8		115		134
Cyprus				11	23	30
Gibraltar						
Liechtenstein						
Malta	7	2	125	55	11	0
Monaco						
Turkey	86	96	522	1670	152	184
Yugoslavia	183	181	363	1064	215	256

Database name: Cultural Indicators
Sector name: Book Publishing

Table No: 2403

Title: Books Published by Subject 1987

Unit: Number of titles

	Applied Sciences	Arts	Literature	Geography/ History	Total Including Others	Notes
EC members						
Belgium	1153	890	2807	719	8327	b
Denmark	1858	382	2566	934	11129	
France	2227	1455	13844	4550	43505	c
West Germany	6030	2522	13068	7560	65670	
Greece	468	257	1569	435	4651	b
Ireland	51	44	141	214	2679	b
Italy	1949	1097	4029	1606	17109	
Luxembourg	20	24	47	48	355	
Netherlands	1223	35	2832	1036	13329	
Portugal	939	na	1960	692	7733	
Spain	2790	2239	12248	2942	38302	
United Kingdom	6695	2836	11917	5651	52861	b
EFTA members						
Austria	943	549	985	704	8910	
Finland	1858	382	2566	934	9106	
Iceland		45	318	113	1121	a
Norway	521	352	1875	317	5481	
Sweden	872	400	2595	1019	11516	
Switzerland	2333	905	1547	837	12046	
CMEA members						
Bulgaria	759	71	963	314	4583	
Czechoslovakia	2557	497	1693	356	10565	
East Germany	753	146	1517	370	6515	
Hungary	1630	420	1448	578	9111	
Poland	1589	422	1960	917	10416	
Romania	1881	250	1280	231	5276	b
USSR	21535	2875	11503	2199	83011	
Others						
Albania	281	8	254	36	959	c
Cyprus	3	2	6	7	82	b
Gibraltar						
Liechtenstein						
Malta	6	12	40	19	421	
Monaco						
Turkey	990	222	1294	326	6685	b
Yugoslavia	1093	704	2751	351	10619	

Source: UNESCO/National Statistics
Notes:
a 1983
b 1985
c 1986

Database name: Cultural Indicators
Sector name: Book Publishing

Title: Books Published by Subject 1987

Unit: % of all published titles

Table No: 2404

	General	Philosophy	Religion	Social Sciences	Philology	Pure Sciences
EC members						
Belgium	2.0	2.9	5.8	14.8	3.5	4.1
Denmark	1.9	3.7	2.7	7.8	2.6	4.7
France	1.7	3.3	3.2	4.3	1.8	2.9
West Germany	8.9	4.1	5.7	6.9	3.9	2.8
Greece	1.5	2.8	3.7	22.8	4.9	5.7
Ireland	0.1		1.8	10.1	0.4	1.3
Italy	2.4	5.2	7.1	6.5	2.3	2.2
Luxembourg	5.1	4.5	2.3	9.9	0.6	6.2
Netherlands	0.5	3.8	4.9	3.6	1.8	2.4
Portugal	12.1	2.5	5.4	11.1		
Spain	3.9	3.1	5.5	4.0	7.0	4.3
United Kingdom	4.1	2.8	4.1	17.8	2.3	8.4
EFTA members						
Austria	2.0	3.9	3.6	10.2	3.0	10.7
Finland	4.2	2.1	3.8	11.2	3.5	8.2
Iceland	2.4	2.0	1.0	9.1	2.3	
Norway	4.0	2.2	4.5	13.0	2.1	7.1
Sweden	2.6	2.0	3.4	3.6	2.4	4.4
Switzerland	1.8	4.2	6.5	8.9	1.5	7.5
CMEA members						
Bulgaria	4.5	1.0	0.3	21.1	3.5	3.9
Czechoslovakia	7.2	1.5	0.5	7.7	3.7	6.5
East Germany	1.5	1.7	4.2	9.3	5.1	5.5
Hungary	2.6	0.9	1.0	11.0	4.7	6.3
Poland	1.7	1.8	4.3	8.3	3.8	6.9
Romania	2.0	1.2	0.9	9.5	3.1	14.3
USSR	3.0	1.9	0.4	13.0	2.2	7.0
Others						
Albania	0.5	0.8		12.0		14.0
Cyprus				13.4	28.0	36.6
Gibraltar						
Liechtenstein						
Malta	1.7	0.5	29.7	13.1	2.6	
Monaco						
Turkey	1.3	1.4	7.8	25.0	2.3	2.8
Yugoslavia	1.7	1.7	3.4	10.0	2.0	2.4

Database name: Cultural Indicators
Sector name: Book Publishing

Table No: 2404

Title: Books Published by Subject 1987

Unit: % of all published titles

	Applied Sciences	Arts	Literature	Geography/ History	Total Including Others	Notes
EC members						b
Belgium	13.8	10.7	33.7	8.6	100.0	
Denmark	16.7	3.4	23.1	8.4	100.0	b
France	5.1	3.3	31.8	10.5	100.0	
West Germany	9.2	3.8	19.9	11.5	100.0	b
Greece	10.1	5.5	33.7	9.4	100.0	b
Ireland	1.9	1.6	5.3	8.0	100.0	
Italy	11.4	6.4	23.5	9.4	100.0	
Luxembourg	5.6	6.8	13.2	13.5	100.0	
Netherlands	9.2	0.3	21.2	7.8	100.0	
Portugal	12.1	0.0	25.3	8.9	100.0	
Spain	7.3	5.8	32.0	7.7	100.0	
United Kingdom	12.7	5.4	22.5	10.7	100.0	b
EFTA members						
Austria	10.6	6.2	11.1	7.9	100.0	
Finland	20.4	4.2	28.2	10.3	100.0	
Iceland		4.0	28.4	10.1	100.0	a
Norway	9.5	6.4	34.2	5.8	100.0	
Sweden	7.6	3.5	22.5	8.8	100.0	
Switzerland	19.4	7.5	12.8	6.9	100.0	
CMEA members						
Bulgaria	16.6	1.5	21.0	6.9	100.0	
Czechoslovakia	24.2	4.7	16.0	3.4	100.0	
East Germany	11.6	2.2	23.3	5.7	100.0	
Hungary	17.9	4.6	15.9	6.3	100.0	
Poland	15.3	4.1	18.8	8.8	100.0	
Romania	35.7	4.7	24.3	4.4	100.0	b
USSR	25.9	3.5	13.9	2.6	100.0	
Others						
Albania	29.3	0.8	26.5	3.8	100.0	
Cyprus	3.7	2.4	7.3	8.5	100.0	b
Gibraltar						
Liechtenstein						
Malta	1.4	2.9	9.5	4.5	100.0	
Monaco						
Turkey	14.8	3.3	19.4	4.9	100.0	b
Yugoslavia	10.3	6.6	25.9	3.3	100.0	

Source: UNESCO/National Statistics
Notes: a   1983
            b   1985

Database name: Cultural Indicators
Sector name: Museums

Table No: 2405

Title: Museums, Museum Visitors: Latest Year

	Year	National	Private	Other Public	Total Including Others	Visitors (millions)	Notes
EC members							
Belgium	1976	11	49	77	137	4.6	
Denmark	1985	39	26	215	280	8.5	
France	1979	37		1400	1437	12.9	a
West Germany	1985	14	808	1203	2025	60.8	
Greece	1985	171	4	69	244	3.2	
Ireland	1979				49	0.8	
Italy	1984	112		1094	1206	6.8	
Luxembourg	1979	1			1	0.1	
Netherlands	1985	45	4	69	118	16.0	
Portugal	1984	35	8	96	139	3.8	
Spain	1979	86	83	441	610	13.9	
United Kingdom	1985					18.0	
EFTA members							
Austria	1984	32		177	209	8.9	
Finland	1984	43	17	512	572	2.9	
Iceland	1982	3		11	14	0.1	
Norway	1978	17		178	195	4.6	
Sweden	1983	14	35	118	167	12.2	
Switzerland	1985				419	7.6	
CMEA members							
Bulgaria	1984	30		176	206	15.5	
Czechoslovakia	1984				348	17.7	
East Germany	1986	66		618	684	34.3	
Hungary	1986	30		564	594	19.2	
Poland	1984	468		57	525	19.6	
Romania	1981	5		407	412	17.1	
USSR	1984				1479	174.4	
Others							
Albania							
Cyprus	1979	23	1	2	26	0.1	
Gibraltar	1984				1	0.2	
Liechtenstein	1986					0.0	
Malta	1986	15	1	6	22	0.6	
Monaco	1979	1	1	2	4	1.6	
Turkey	1984	127			127	5.4	
Yugoslavia	1986			522	522	11.9	

Source: UNESCO/National Statistical Offices
Notes: a   National museum visitors

Database name: Cultural Indicators
Sector name: Cinemas

Title: Cinema Statistics 1987

Unit: As stated

Table No: 2406

	A	B	C	D	E	Notes
EC members		16	12	5		
Belgium	407	11	12	2		
Denmark	396	137	133	37	128	
France	5063	108	65	18	207	
West Germany	3252		22	0	260	
Greece		12	1	0	245	b
Ireland	125	109	116	30	161	d
Italy	4143				279	
Luxembourg						
Netherlands	445	16	18	0	332	e
Portugal	358	17	5	2	235	d
Spain	2234	86	69	7	344	d
United Kingdom	1226	75	51	0	265	f
EFTA members						
Austria	444	5	12	3	339	
Finland	328	7	15	3	195	
Iceland	47	3	1	0	231	a
Norway	426	12	7	0	240	
Sweden	1112	18	26	5	234	
Switzerland	431	16	32	11	421	
CMEA members						
Bulgaria	3028	84	35	1	300	
Czechoslovakia	2634	74	44	3	395	
East Germany	2064	58	16	1	126	
Hungary	1057	56	26	0	162	
Poland	1704	89	39	6	154	
Romania	625	161	26	0	95	b
USSR	142000	4100	156	7		
Others						
Albania	103		14		10	e
Cyprus					93	
Gibraltar	4	0				
Liechtenstein						
Malta	16	1				
Monaco	3	0				
Turkey	576	26	96		640	b
Yugoslavia	1174	70	30	3	166	

Source: UNESCO/National Statistics

Notes:
A Number of fixed cinemas (35mm +)
B Annual attendance (millions)
C Number of long films produced
D Of which co-productions
E Number of long films imported

a 1982
b 1985
c 1983
d Column E: data from 1985
e Column E: data from 1982
f Column E: data from 1983

TABLE 2402: BOOK PUBLISHING 1980-1987
Thousand titles

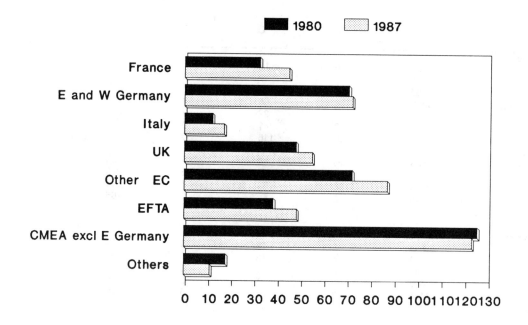

■ 1980   □ 1987

France
E and W Germany
Italy
UK
Other EC
EFTA
CMEA excl E Germany
Others

0 10 20 30 40 50 60 70 80 90 100110120130

TABLE 2402: BOOK PUBLICATION
Titles published 1988

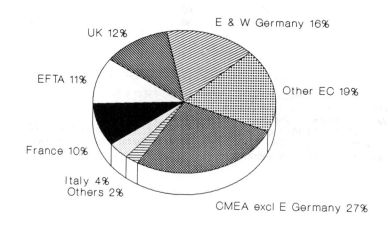

UK 12%
E & W Germany 16%
EFTA 11%
Other EC 19%
France 10%
Italy 4%
Others 2%
CMEA excl E Germany 27%

SUBJECT INDEX

2172

46)